ON THE FARM

ALSO BY STEVIE CAMERON

Ottawa Inside Out (1989)
On the Take (1994)
Blue Trust (1998)
The Last Amigo (2001)
The Pickton File (2007)

STEVIE CAMERON

ON THE FARM

ROBERT WILLIAM PICKTON AND THE TRAGIC STORY OF VANCOUVER'S MISSING WOMEN

ALFRED A. KNOPF CANADA

PUBLISHED BY ALFRED A. KNOPF CANADA

Copyright © 2010 Stevie Cameron

All photographs copyright © 2010 Stevie Cameron, unless otherwise noted

www.randomhouse.ca

Page 709 is a continuation of the copyright page.

Library and Archives Canada Cataloguing in Publication

Cameron, Stevie
On the farm : Robert William Pickton and the tragic story of Vancouver's missing
women / Stevie Cameron.

ISBN 978-0-676-97584-0 (bound).

1. Pickton, Robert William. 2. Serial murders—British Columbia. 3. Serial murder
investigation—British Columbia. 4. Serial murderers—British Columbia. 5. Murder
victims—British Columbia—Vancouver—Biography. 6. Murder victims—British
Columbia—Vancouver. 7. Port Coquitlam (B.C.)—Biography. I. Title.

HV6535.C33P64   2010 364.152'30971133   C2010–901918–0

Text design: CS Richardson

First Edition

Printed and bound in the United States of America

2 4 6 8 9 7 5 3 1

FOR ELAINE ALLAN

CONTENTS

PART TWO: THE MISSING WOMEN

PART THREE: ON THE FARM

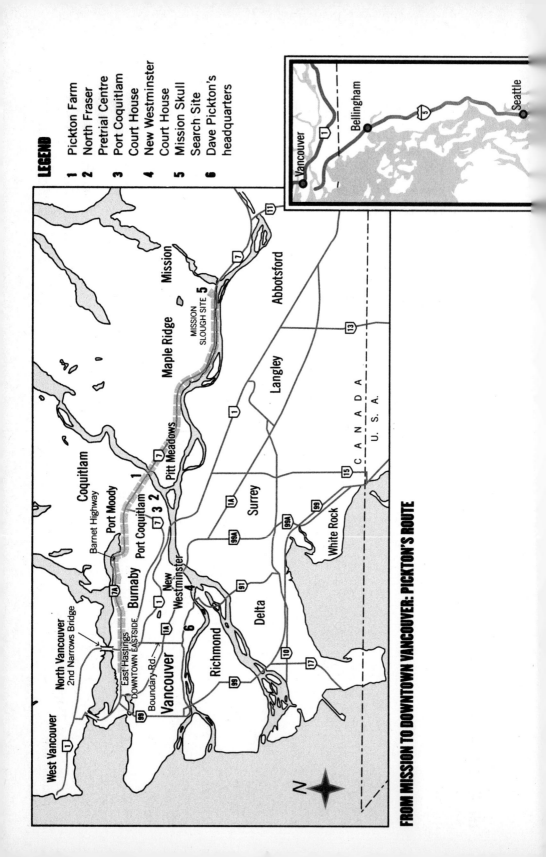

FROM MISSION TO DOWNTOWN VANCOUVER: PICKTON'S ROUTE

THE PIG FARM AND PORT COQUITLAM

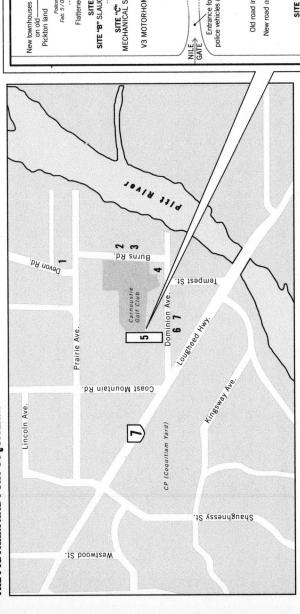

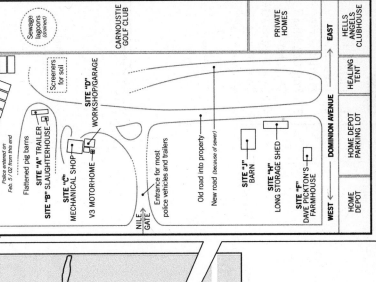

Sewage lagoons *(drained)*

CARNOUSTIE GOLF CLUB

PRIVATE HOMES

New townhouses on old Pickton land

Screeners for soil

Police entered on Feb. 5/02 from this end

Flattened pig barns

SITE "A" TRAILER

SITE "B" SLAUGHTERHOUSE

SITE "C" MECHANICAL SHOP

V3 MOTORHOME

SITE "D" WORKSHOP/GARAGE

Entrance for most police vehicles and trailers

Old road into property

New road *(because of sewer)*

NILE GATE

SITE "J" BARN

SITE "H" LONG STORAGE SHED

SITE "F" DAVE PICKTON'S FARMHOUSE

WEST → DOMINION AVENUE ← EAST

HOME DEPOT

HOME DEPOT PARKING LOT

HEALING TENT

HELLS ANGELS CLUBHOUSE

Devon Rd.

PITT RIVER

Burns Rd.

Carnoustie Golf Club

Tempest St.

Dominion Ave.

Lougheed Hwy.

Prairie Ave.

Coast Mountain Rd.

Lincoln Ave.

Kingsway Ave.

CP (Coquitlam Yard)

Shaughnessy St.

Westwood St.

LEGEND

1 Albert and Vera Harvey's blueberry farm, 3640 Devon Rd.

2 Dave Pickton's rancher house, 2600 Burns Rd.

3 Piggy's Palace, 2522 Burns Rd.

4 Bill Malone's house (former Barrett house)

5 Pig Farm, 963 Dominion Ave.

6 Healing Tent

7 Hells Angels Clubhouse

AUTHOR'S NOTE

Readers will find many conversations in this account of the Pickton murder case. Some of these come from transcripts of police interviews done during the investigation and made available to me by participants in these conversations. Other conversations, such as the one between a woman I am calling Sandra Gail Ringwald, a woman whose real name is still under a publication ban, and Robert Pickton in his trailer in 1997, were recounted in court; in this case, by Ms. Ringwald. (Her case is strange in Canadian law: Normally, all publication bans disappear when the Supreme Court upholds the verdict as they did in this case, but in an extraordinary ruling the trial Judge, James Williams, ordered the continuation of the ban on her real name and the matter is now before the courts.) To protect her identity, I am referring to the father of her children as Paul Campbell. Most of the conversations Pickton had with RCMP Constable Dana Lillies were recorded and played in court proceedings; so were the lengthy interviews with Pickton done by an undercover police officer in his cell, by Bill Fordy and by Don Adam. And some conversations were those Pickton had with women he picked up, women like Katrina Murphy, who shared them with me.

PART ONE

—

THE FAMILY

"And here I seen the calf hanging upside down there, they butchered my calf on me. Oh boy, I was mad. I couldn't talk to anybody for three or four days. I locked everybody out of my own mind, I didn't want to talk to anybody.

"That really upset me, but that happens. That's life. I mean we're only here for so long . . . When your time is over, your time is over."

—Robert William Pickton, writing about the loss of a calf he'd bought with his own money when he was about twelve.

JANE DOE

At first he thought it was an old brown bowl, just perched there on a bed of rocks, surrounded by reeds and bushes. But when he walked over to have a closer look, he could see it was a human skull—cut in half, yes, yet still recognizable as human. And Bill Wilson's first thought as he walked back to the road was that he should probably call the police. But this was a human skull and he had a serious police record. Maybe the first thing they'd do is start looking at him for it.

On this February 23, 1995, Wilson, who made his living as a woodcarver and handyman, had been on his way to get some water from a narrow slough that ran along the south side of the Lougheed Highway, close to the mouth of the Stave River, about forty kilometres east of Vancouver. He wanted to clean off his car, which was parked on the north side of the highway in a paved public lay-by where he kept a little roadside stand displaying his wooden bird feeders, birdhouses and whirligigs to drivers passing by. Wilson had just run across the road with a water bottle and clambered down the six-foot slope to the rocky edge of the slough when he spotted the skull about forty or fifty feet away. He walked over and, using the bottle, flipped it over; that was when he realized what he was looking at. He didn't do anything about his find immediately, Wilson told the police later; he had a doctor's appointment and some shopping to do that afternoon. But if he'd seen a police car coming along, he declared, he would have flagged it down. And as for why he didn't call them that night, well, he had bingo to go to, and anyway he didn't have a phone at home. Given his record—two convictions and jail time for indecent assault and sexual assault—he didn't want to get involved.

But twenty-four hours later on Friday afternoon, Wilson decided he'd better report what he had found. Just before five o'clock in the afternoon on February 24, 1995, he drove east into Mission, the nearest town with a police station. As soon as he saw a police car, he stopped it.

The police officer called the Mission RCMP station on Oliver Street, and almost right away the control officer called Constable Chris Annely, on duty in his cruiser, and asked him to meet Wilson, who would be waiting for him at the Stave River lay-by. Wilson, the dispatcher explained, would point out some human remains he'd found the day before.

Annely knew the location well. The Lougheed Highway, the old Number 7, once the main road between Vancouver and Hope, stitches together most of the small working-class towns along the north banks of the Fraser River. Running east from Vancouver, the Lougheed stretches through Burnaby, Coquitlam and Port Coquitlam—the Tri-Cities area, as it's called—to Maple Ridge, Mission and Agassiz before it reaches Hope. Most drivers choose the much faster Trans-Canada, the superhighway that runs along the south side of the Fraser, but the Lougheed is what you take if you're a local.

And this small stretch of the Lougheed, where Bill Wilson was waiting for Chris Annely, is one of the prettiest parts of the highway. Now, in early spring, leaves were just beginning to come out on the trees and the riverbanks were greening up.

Silvermere Lake is a popular resort area near the Stave River where many people have built new ranch-style houses back from the shoreline; their lawns are green and well-tended. A small Indian reserve is wedged into the few acres between the lake and the Stave River; across the highway is the Fraser River. In fact, the highway where Wilson was waiting is really just a bridge, not more than five hundred feet long and banked on each side by deep sloughs crammed with alders and dense brush. The south side beside the Fraser, crowded here with log booms, is where the main VIA Rail track runs on its way east to Toronto, perhaps a couple of hundred feet from the road. Local fishermen, most from the Stave River band, often make their way down the bank on this side to cast their lines into the river for salmon.

When Annely pulled his cruiser into the lay-by, he spotted Wilson waiting for him. Wilson led the policeman down the steep bank to an area about halfway between the highway and the train track. Three large rocks, left over from the highway construction, bumped up through the reeds and bracken. Water still pooled in the low spots, but Annely could see the small, dark object on the ground in front of the rocks. No question, he thought. Wilson's right. It's a human skull.

Annely hurried back to his car and grabbed his radio. "We need a camera here right now," he told Corporal Brad Zalys, the officer in charge at the detachment. The men didn't have long to wait; Zalys was there by 5:35 p.m., when there was still enough light left to get a few decent pictures of the skull on the ground. In fact, it was just half a skull—split in half vertically, cleanly, from the crown down through the back of the head and the jawbone in front. A small scrap of the first vertebra was attached to the neck, but there was no sign of the other half of the head. What they were almost certain of, however, was that this skull had not been there a long time; scraps of white flesh clung to the areas around the eye socket, and the nose was still attached.

For a minute the officers talked about whether or not the area was a crime scene, but on the whole they thought not. Annely and Zalys thought it had to be from a Native gravesite.

"We thought maybe it had floated down because . . . a few days earlier that slough had been flooded right up to the road and it obviously hadn't been there before," Annely said later. "An Indian burial that had been uncovered somewhere and just floated down." Still, that cut through the crown was odd.

The officers decided there was no need to seal off the area with yellow crime-scene tape. Zalys placed the skull in a box and drove it back to Mission. Annely followed in his own car, entered the skull in the exhibits record with the number 95–2409 and, because it was still damp, put it into a cardboard box and placed it on a shelf to dry.

Two days later, the file and the skull went to Corporal Tim Sleigh, a young detective in the RCMP's Investigative Section in Vancouver. Sleigh was intrigued; the skull was not just unusual, it was bizarre. It looked as if it had been cut in half with an electric saw. Sleigh wasn't in any doubt that this was a murder victim, and that was what Dr. James Ferris thought as well.

Ferris, a forensic pathologist who had performed several thousand autopsies by then, decided this was the skull of a young woman in her twenties. Although he believed the woman had died between twelve and twenty-four months earlier, he was sure it had been in the water for only a couple of weeks. That's because there was adipocere on it—a substance sometimes called grave wax or mortuary wax, formed when fats in the body break down and combine with water to form a waxy substance. Adipocere is more often found in cold damp or wet ground; it eventually turns into a hard coating over bone, almost like tartar on teeth. It is difficult to remove from bone and does not contain human DNA.

The adipocere on the woman's skull told Dr. Ferris that the skull had been in a damp place for at least a year or two. The fact that it had not yet been chewed on by animals in the slough also told him it hadn't been there for more than a few weeks.

"I was confident that we were dealing with a homicide case," he said later. "It made me fairly certain that other cases or bone fragments would show up eventually."

He thought the skull had been cut in half by someone who knew how to cut through bones, but it wouldn't have been a medical professional because the cut lines were uneven and didn't meet at the top. "I can't recall any cut through human bone that would have the errors in anatomical cutting that you see in this one."

The next step in trying to identify Jane Doe was to reconstruct her face. For this, the coroner's office called Tracy Rogers, a forensic anthropologist at the University of Toronto. Could she put together enough information for Corporal Cam Pye, an RCMP forensic artist, to reconstruct Jane Doe's face? Then they could give the drawing to the media and see if anyone recognized her and would come forward to identify her.

Rogers began by photographing the half-skull and then used the photographs to make mirror images of it to try to recreate the face. The pictures would provide the dimensions Pye would need—how far up the eyes would be, how high her cheeks would be. Rogers believed the person had been a young adult woman of European and Native American descent. Pye used Rogers's reconstruction to paint a face that was as close to the victim's as her age, race, bone structure and hair colour indicated.

But no one knew who she was. No one was reported missing who might be this victim. Even though a police dog and divers searched the swamp they found nothing. The woman remained "Jane Doe" and her skull would rest in a box in a police evidence locker for seven more years. Tim Sleigh moved to another detachment but never forgot her. In 1997 he and his family moved to a house beside this same marsh, and as he later told the *Vancouver Sun*'s Lori Culbert, he "continued to walk through the area and ponder who she was. He considered and then rejected multiple theories, such as the tides carrying the skull there or it being unearthed from a nearby burial spot. He never forgot Jane Doe."

What Sleigh couldn't know then, nor could Annely or Zalys, was that some of Jane Doe's bones were buried deep in a pit on a small farm just a few hundred feet north of the Lougheed Highway and about forty kilometres to the west of Mission Slough—a farm on the eastern edge of a small town called Port Coquitlam. A farm owned by two brothers, Robert and David Pickton, and their sister, Linda Pickton Wright.

CHAPTER ONE

THE FAMILY FARM

Calling the Pickton place a farm back in 1995 is probably a nice way of putting it. The property, at 963 Dominion Road, across the road from a new shopping centre, was nothing more than a junkyard of old cars, trucks and machinery and enormous mounds of dirt, many of which were covered with black plastic tarps. The Pickton brothers, among their many interests, were in the dirt-moving business. Their shabby white clapboard farmhouse needed painting and repair; the wooden outbuildings—a rickety mess of garages, workshops and sheds—always seemed on the verge of collapse. A shanty that had housed a pigpen had fallen down completely and no one had bothered to tidy up the mess. With no place to keep the pigs, Robert was now stuffing the live weanlings he bought every week at animal auctions into a small horse trailer until he got around to slaughtering them. Only an unpainted hip-roofed Dutch barn looked as if it could last a few more years.

Even though Port Coquitlam was a working-class town of fifty thousand people where few had money to spend fixing up their places, the Pickton farm was infamous, and not just because it was a mess. People knew that the Picktons, who were making a fortune selling off chunks of the land to real estate developers, could easily afford to keep the farm in good repair; it just never occurred to them. That was just how they'd been brought up, not to mind a little mess.

This property wasn't the family's original farm. Louise and Leonard Francis Pickton, the parents of David, Robert and Linda, had inherited a family homestead a few kilometres west, on the other side of town in the larger adjoining community of Coquitlam.

Louise and Leonard called it L. F. Pickton Ranch Poultry and Pigs. The address, in those days, was 2426 Pitt River Road but it later changed to 2426 Cape Horn.

Today much of this land is crammed with tract housing, but the area in those days was like a vast park blessed with woods, fields and streams, and bears that roamed through the forests around the new hospital. Although the communities here, east of Vancouver, were always mostly working-class, their situation in those days was as favoured as any in the area. The river brimmed with salmon, wild blackberry bushes competed with abundant harvests from the fields and gardens, and the climate was mild. The Coast Mountains to the north and the Cascade Mountains to the south, along the Canada–United States border, girdled the entire area except the western side, towards Point Grey, at the far end of Vancouver.

The Pickton children—Leonard, Harold, Clifford and Lillian—went to Millside Elementary School, which had been built in 1905, at 1432 Burnett Street in Coquitlam, and the family attended church services at St. Catherine's Anglican Church in Port Coquitlam.

Lillian married and left the farm, Clifford wound up running a nursing home called the Royal Crescent Convalescent Home and Harold became a night watchman at Flavelle Cedar, a local lumberyard. When Leonard finally inherited the property, he stayed on the farm, although his brothers built houses on lots carved out of the property.

During the 1940s, Leonard, who had been born in England on July 19, 1896, three years before his parents emigrated to Canada, was considered lazy and unambitious by most people who knew him. He seemed to be a confirmed bachelor, content just to work on the farm, but he astonished his relatives by announcing that he was engaged. And not just engaged: he'd snared a woman sixteen years younger than he was, someone he'd met in a coffee shop. It may have been one of his smarter moves; Helen Louise Pickton—born March 20, 1912, in Calgary, Alberta, but raised in a little place called Raymond's Creek, not far from Swift Current, Saskatchewan—became the driving force in the family.

Linda, their eldest, was born in 1948. Robert, who was called Robbie as a toddler and then almost always Willie, followed on October 24, 1949, and David arrived a year later, in 1950. Willie's birth was difficult; he was born with the umbilical cord wrapped around his neck and his family wondered afterwards if that had caused some kind of brain damage. But there was nothing wrong with his memory; it has always been remarkable. One of his earliest recollections, he always tells people, is of being only two, living in what had been a chicken coop, and having to lift a floorboard under his bed to get cold water from a spring that ran below. It was the only running water in the house for years.

He also likes to tell people about the time, when he was just three years old, that he crashed his father's truck, loaded with pigs, into a tree. He was sitting on the driver's side of his father's 1940 "Maple Leaf" truck, a Canadian-made General Motors vehicle beloved by farmers in the 1930s and '40s. Today a Maple Leaf truck is a collector's item; back then it was a just plain, solid workhorse. Years later, in 1991, Pickton described the incident in detail to a pen pal named Victoria when he sent her an audio letter he called "Bob's Memoirs."

"I turn around and the truck started rolling, the pigs all start jumping off and my dad's running behind the pigs trying to holler to stop the truck," he says on the tape. "I didn't know what to do so I smashed it right into a telephone pole. Totalled the truck right out. I sure got the hell beaten out of me. But that's what happens."

A year later his mother caught Willie smoking a cigarette and forced him to smoke a cigar to cure him for good. It worked. "That was the last cigarette I ever had," he said years later.

By anyone's standards, Louise Pickton was strange. She didn't just look weird; she behaved outside the norms of convention almost all the time, and as she got older her eccentricity became legendary. To start with, there is no getting past how she looked and how she talked. Like Leonard, she didn't pay attention to her teeth and eventually most of them rotted out. She lost most of her hair and covered the remaining wisps with a kerchief. Her chin sprouted so many hairs she developed a little goatee that neighbourhood children have never forgotten. "That would blow my mind as a little kid," remembers one man who occasionally visited the farm as a child. "I would just say to myself, Cut it off!"

And he remembers Louise's voice, a persistent high screech: "You kids git over here, now!" No one remembers seeing her in shoes, just a pair of men's thick rubber gumboots. "She waddled like a duck," another former neighbour says.

Stout and short, with a round face, Louise always wore a cotton housedress over a pair of men's jeans; when it rained she'd put on an old jacket of Leonard's. He dressed in much the same kind of costume as his wife: a grubby T-shirt hanging over dirty heavy blue jeans rolled over black rubber boots, and a beat-up old hat. Two of Louise's children, Linda and Dave, who are also round-faced and short, resemble her, while Willie, tall and narrow-faced with a long, pointed nose, looks like his father. "Rat-faced," people used to say.

The strongest memories that former neighbours have of Louise today are associated with the family house on Dawes Hill, and later on Dominion Avenue: the smell, the mess, the dirt. Louise didn't care if the farm animals—chickens, ducks, dogs, even the occasional pig or cow they raised—roamed in and out of the house. She didn't seem to notice the piles of manure they left behind; she was oblivious to the smell. It was basically a pig farm, after all, and anyone who has lived downwind of one knows what that smell of fresh pig manure is like: piercing and foul, clogging the back of your throat, sticking like scum to your hair and skin. Because the kids had to slop up to two hundred pigs and clean out their pens before and after school, they stank too. They also cleaned up after eight cows that the family milked by hand. In his taped letter to Victoria, Willie said his father delivered the milk to their neighbours.

"The old man also used to pick up garbage from Essondale for his pigs; he'd go up there with his truck to get a freebie," remembers a man who used to deliver a newspaper to the Picktons. "It seems to me they always had some old trucks around; they were scroungers. They were survivors, resourceful—they had their own ways of doing stuff.

"The farm . . . I can see it: ramshackle, a lot of buildings, went on for about half a block. There was a muddy path down the middle. It was just one shack after another, made up of scraps of lumber. I didn't go down there. It was so repulsive."

Once a week or so the kids might have a bath, but it was impossible to get rid of the smell. Neighbouring farmers called Leonard "Piggy" and he never seemed to mind. But the local kids called the boys the same thing, and it hurt. Their own memories of those years are not cozy and warm.

"Things are so modernized these days it's unbelievable—I had a hard life, I'm telling you, I had a hard life," Willie told his pen pal years later. He always told people about the homemade or hand-me-down clothes they wore, except for the time Louise bought him a crisp new outfit for Christmas. He was only about five years old, he said, but it was heavily starched and he hated it. "It hurts me, it hurts me," he complained to his mother, and then he remembers tearing it off and running away in his bare skin.

"These are the stupid things we kind of do," he told Victoria. "You're never used to new clothes . . . I was being brought up very, very poorly."

Even while she was oblivious to the squalor of their lives, Louise wanted her kids to go to Sunday school and birthday parties and ride the school bus like the other children.

"Linda and I went to elementary school together from grade one on and she used to come to the same birthday parties I went to," remembers one of her classmates. "She wore simple clothes [ordinarily] but her mother would get her party dresses."

As far as Sunday school went, the only child Louise could bully into going was Linda. Most of the local kids hated it. An elderly retired couple ran it from their small house, right next to the Pickton pig farm. "The Sunday school teacher would come to the foot of the driveway in her big old black Dodge, beep her horn and pick up all the kids," the classmate said.

Louise had some understanding that it was important for Linda to be like other kids, to have nice clothes, to be included. The same rules didn't apply to the boys. They didn't go to Sunday school; they rarely played with other kids. They hung out together, and when they weren't slopping pigs, they ran wild in the woods around the farm. Like their father, the children went to Millside Elementary on Burnett, where the salmon would come up from the Fraser Creek and spawn. The creeks ran through the farms, including the Picktons' place, so the boys fished, sometimes with a few neighbourhood children. The most exciting thing that could happen was the arrival of black bears that would amble around the hill looking for pigs to catch at the Pickton farm.

"When one showed up," remembers a former neighbour, "the Picktons would call the game warden, who'd track it down with dogs all over the farm. The kids would follow. Then they [the warden] would shoot the bear. And all this time the pigs were running free. There was no vegetation where the pigs were because they'd eaten everything and dug big mudholes under the roots of tree stumps. It was a zoo. We'd go there to try to make the pigs chase us."

As parents, it's clear that Louise and Leonard were appalling failures. Still, Louise tried in her own twisted way to do her best. She looked out for Willie in particular, knowing that he had a harder time than the others; he was shy and school was almost always an ordeal for him.

"Robert, he just adored Mom," his sister Linda told *Vancouver Sun* reporter Kim Bolan in 2002. "He and Mom were so close. Robert was never close to Dad. Robert was kind of Mom's boy."

Willie, who started grade one at Millside School in 1955, when he was one month away from his sixth birthday, remembered it later as a one-room school with four grades. "It was quite nice because we had four different blackboards," he told his pen pal. But a month after he started at Millside he was moved to Viscount Alexander, which was also in Coquitlam. His standard education test results were, according to school records, "very low."

Grade two was harder for him. His results were a bit better but still "low," and his teacher decided he needed to be held back and repeat the year. Like all the other kids, Willie had to take standard education tests; by the end of his second try at grade two he was performing at an "average" level. The tests in those years were a mix of standard elementary achievement tests not designed to take into account rural children who might not have access to the advantages of urban kids. In more recent years, with his rural background factored in, Pickton's test results might have shown him to be doing at least as well as his classmates. His parents certainly never read to him; they would not have encouraged his reading skills, and word recognition was an important factor in scoring higher on these tests.

By the time he was ready for grade three, in the fall of 1958, the school made a decision to place Willie in a class for slow students. He remained in "special education" for the rest of his years in school, even after transferring to a different public school, Mary Hill Elementary in Port Coquitlam. More tests showed that he was performing at the level of a grade-five student, but again the tests were, as teachers sometimes called them, "urbanized," or set for more sophisticated city kids.

The special ed classes, as they were known, usually had fewer students and more help from teachers. And his tests did show slight improvement year over year in both reading and arithmetic, from outright failure to bare passes in most courses. Robert's teachers at Mary Hill Elementary nudged him in the direction of occupational classes in high school—blue-collar jobs that wouldn't require a high level of education or training. So that's the stream he chose when he turned thirteen and moved on to grade eight at Mary Hill Secondary School in September 1963.

During these years Willie's attendance was as regular as any other student's; clearly his parents weren't putting up with any nonsense about skipping school. He must have wanted to, desperately. Free

time on the farm—what there was of it after the chores were done—
was basically unsupervised. School, on the other hand, was a nightmare, not just for Willie but for his brother and sister as well. Part
of the reason was that they were shunned by the children, most of
them doctors' kids, who lived closest to them.

For several years the Picktons' nearest neighbour was the
new Essondale Hospital, built on a thousand acres of cleared land at
the top of their hill to house mental patients. Essondale, named after
Dr. Henry Esson Young, the provincial politician responsible for it,
had been designed to replace B.C.'s first hospital for the mentally ill,
the Provincial Hospital for the Insane, which was built in 1878 in
New Westminster; five years later the government introduced work
therapy, putting the patients to work in the gardens. But soon there
were so many patients—more than three hundred by 1899 that
planning began to build a "Hospital for the Mind" in Coquitlam, to
care for psychiatric patients as well as physically and mentally handicapped children and adults. Construction started in 1905.

By the time the Pickton kids were climbing onto a school bus in
the 1950s, Essondale had become a sprawling hospital complex.
Five handsome houses on the hill were for the senior doctors who
worked there; others, known as "the mechanical homes," were for
the top engineers and administrators who kept the place running.
These were big houses, all with views over the hospital grounds and
the river; all with large living and dining rooms, floors laid of mahog-
any, plenty of bedrooms; all well landscaped on large lots. Most of
the kids on the school bus came from these houses; they walked
down the hill in nice clothes, through gardens and apple orchards,
to wait for the bus at the same roadside corner as the Pickton kids.

Along with the Picktons there were a few other students from
the bottom of the hill, poorer, from farm homes. These kids would
enter the bus with peashooters and pick fights. The problem for the
Pickton kids is that they didn't fit into this gang either.

"We were all terrible to the Picktons, especially to Robert," says
a doctor's daughter who now lives in Alberta. Part of the reason was

that the boys had speech problems. Dave talked too fast and high; he couldn't pronounce his R's, so he sounded like Elmer Fudd, especially when he was worked up about something. Willie was withdrawn and didn't talk much at all; when he did, he too would gabble in a high, fast voice. People remarked later on their strange voices, but to those who knew them in the old days they seemed perfectly normal—Leonard and his brothers had the same squeaky high voices.

"I remember all of us on the road taunting him," says the doctor's daughter. "We'd say to each other, 'Just let us at him now and we'll make him talk.' How were they different? Dirty and stinky. They always had their hair cut in a brush cut. Man, they stunk. Their house was a poor house with no yard and falling-down fences. There were no big trees, only some shrubs. I don't even remember them at school at all but I do remember them waiting for the school bus. Our bunch was mostly all doctors' kids. We were the best-dressed and had the nicest houses; almost everyone in the group is successful now."

What she and her pals share with the poor kids such as the Picktons—the kids they despised—is the memory that the area was a perfect place to grow up: "Essondale had orchards and they were ours for the picking. There was a lost lake called Mundy Lake, surrounded by trees and bushes, out in the middle of the forest. It was idyllic. We could do what we liked as long as we were home for supper. But the Pickton kids never played with us."

Paradise or not, it sounds more like *Lord of the Flies* than Tom Sawyer or Huckleberry Finn. Or perhaps even more like *One Flew over the Cuckoo's Nest*. That's because, along with Essondale, which served the entire province of British Columbia, the provincial government built even more institutions all around the farmland.

When the government first moved three hundred male patients from the overcrowded Provincial Hospital for the Insane, known as PHI, in New Westminster to the Coquitlam site near the Picktons, it changed the name of the New Westminster hospital to Woodlands and turned it into a residence mainly for mentally and physically disabled kids, including babies. As they grew up, Woodlands patients would be transferred to the rambling new thousand-acre hillside site now called Essondale. Several years later, the women from the New Westminster hospital were also moved to Essondale.

On the southwest side of the property, the building originally called the Male Building and then West Lawn held the men; the building on the east side was East Lawn, with room for 675 women. In the centre was the Acute Psychopathic Unit, where new patients were tested; it was later known as Centre Lawn. In those early years there were no corrections officers to handle the criminally insane, just nurses and a few supervisors and doctors. Patients slept in rows in large rooms; by day up to a hundred women, for example, could be in one large room in East Lawn, cared for by a handful of student nurses and two supervisors.

More units were added to the property. A veterans' building opened in 1934; two years later an old school for boys was renovated to become Valleyview Hospital Unit, an old-age home. Other buildings followed until the place was filled with one kind of patient after another. What they all had in common was that these were special-needs patients, and many of them were insane.

By 1951 Essondale, with 4,630 patients, was like a small town, with many of its inhabitants working on the various properties. Patients mowed the doctors' lawns and kept the gardens blooming and groomed. At the same time, many of them were allowed to wander all over the place; one day a sister and brother from one of the doctors' houses were playing in the water and found a dead patient floating there.

Patients who needed psychiatric assessment before being transferred to the appropriate centre at Essondale also worked in the dairy, fields and barns of Colony Farm. This was a working farm at the bottom of the hill below the Pickton property that provided food for all the patients and staff at Essondale and Woodlands. Government records show that farm supervisors used patient labour to clear and dike the original land there to prepare it for farming use. Doctors would take their children down to Colony Farm to see the prized Colony Clydesdales, which won awards at the Pacific National Exhibition every year. Government statistical records brag that it was regarded as "the best farm in Western Canada" and produced "over 700 tons of crops and 200,000 gallons of milk a year." The patient-labourers were the ones who made this possible. And some of those Colony Farm patients, like some from Essondale, often worked for the Picktons on their farm up on Dawes Hill.

There is a story you hear when local people get talking about the Picktons during the Dawes Hill years, that when he was little, Willie used to crawl into the carcasses of gutted hogs to hide from people who were angry with him. If this is true, the Picktons have never said so.

Willie himself has told another story, over and over again, to anyone who would listen, of an incident that devastated him when he was about twelve years old. He'd gone to a livestock auction with his parents and had enough money saved—thirty-five dollars—to buy a three-week-old black and white calf: "As really pretty as the day is long" is how he described it later to his pen pal Victoria. "It was a nice calf and I was going to keep the calf for the rest of my life." Every day after school he looked forward to coming home to feed it. Then one day when he returned, he couldn't find his calf; frantically he searched all around the property.

"I went everywheres looking for this here calf and I couldn't find it anywheres," he said years later. "They says, 'Oh, it must have got out.' I said, 'How can it get out the door? The door is locked.'"

Exasperated by his nagging, someone, probably his father, finally turned to him and suggested he look in the barn. Willie raced off and burst through the doors of the barn. "And here I seen the calf hanging upside down there, they butchered my calf on me. Oh boy, I was mad. I couldn't talk to anybody for three or four days. I locked everybody out of my own mind, I didn't want to talk to anybody."

Louise tried to appease him by giving him an extra twenty dollars for it. But he remained upset. "Like my mother says," he told a friend later, "'That was a good dollar for the calf. . . . You can go buy another.' And I says, 'No, I was going to keep that calf for the rest of my life and now it's gone.' That really upset me, but that happens. That's life. I mean we're only here for so long . . . When your time is over, your time is over."

And there is another story about him at that age, although he's not the one who tells it. A little girl who became his friend many years later remembers Willie today as "a sweet boy." At the time his parents were selling their meat from the small store the locals called "the meat locker," which they had opened on the north side of the Lougheed Highway at Shaughnessy Street in Port Coquitlam. Lisa Yelds, whose father was white and mother Chinese, and who was only five years old back in 1962, was being cared for by her grandparents after being abandoned by her parents. Her Chinese grandfather liked to take her fishing on the Stave River near Mission Slough, and on the way home to Coquitlam he'd often stop at the Picktons' store for meat. Lisa Yelds remembers seeing a young boy there, a boy the others called Willie.

"Willie was helping in the store, and I guess he was about nine or ten. What really struck me was his blond hair. He was working beside a stout and stocky older lady, his mother. One day he looked at me and smiled and then he gave me a bag of hot dogs. Like a present. I wasn't used to people being nice to me. I never forgot him."

It would be nearly another thirty years before Lisa Yelds and Willie Pickton met again, this time as neighbours on Dominion Avenue, where he would become her best friend. And she would become his.

CHAPTER TWO

DOMINION AVENUE

In 1963, when Willie was fourteen and Dave thirteen, their parents bought a new parcel of land on the far eastern side of Port Coquitlam. Coquitlam itself was expanding so quickly that the city had expropriated the original Pickton homestead on Cape Horn for a new highway and housing developments. Linda didn't go with them. She couldn't wait to get away from the family; in fact, she was so miserable at home that sometimes she would climb out a window in the farmhouse and disappear. By far the smartest one in the family, Linda finally made her escape. She left her grade eight class at public school in Port Coquitlam at Christmas and moved in with relatives in Vancouver, attending Lord Byng High School in the city's Dunbar area, a comfortable neighbourhood close to the University of British Columbia. After leaving she had as little to do with her family as possible. Who could blame her?

Louise and Leonard paid a family called Mernickle $18,000 for forty acres of low-lying property at 993 Dominion Avenue, on the eastern edge of Port Coquitlam about six kilometres from the Dawes Hill homestead. They had their old blue and white farmhouse pried off its foundations, lifted onto a flatbed and towed over to Dominion, where the neighbourhood was still rural. Later they hauled a Dutch-style hip-roofed barn from a property a few houses down on Dominion Avenue and resettled it behind the farmhouse.

Dominion Avenue ran east–west, roughly parallel to the Lougheed Highway, a few hundred feet to the south. It was only a few kilometres long, dead-ending at a dike that held back the wide, log-filled Pitt River, which is higher than the farmland beside it. At the time

Dominion was a rough dirt country road with deep, muddy sloughs on either side full of black water, weeds, frogs and thick blackberry stalks that clung to the banks, often reaching right across the slough. As Dominion petered out it met Burns Road, a north–south country lane about a mile long with small hobby farms on either side, most of them growing blueberries or raising a few chickens. Cam and Della Grant had a honey farm right at the corner where the two roads joined; their property ran back to the dike. Most of the houses were shabby fifties-style bungalows and split-level ranchers, although there were a few modest cottages that went back to the 1930s. On the eastern side of Burns Road, the hobby farms such as the Grants' were long and narrow, about two hundred feet wide and five hundred feet deep, and they ended at the dike. Anyone could walk along the raised dike road and look down at the properties.

Where Burns Road and Dominion Avenue met, high pools of water poured into the sloughs running along each side of Dominion and almost as far west as the Pickton farm. In those days, except for the Carnoustie Golf Club, which abutted their land at one end, the Pickton farm was one of the biggest pieces of property in the area.

No one thought much of the farm. Although it was well-treed and green, everyone knew that most of it was below the water table, which meant acres of brackish, swampy land as well as patches of dangerous quicksand on the eastern side. A foul lagoon took up space near the back, next to the Carnoustie land. Few crops would thrive on these acres, but the Picktons were not interested in crops; they planned to enlarge their pig and poultry business, continuing to raise and butcher the animals themselves. These were the days when few families had large freezers; it was common to order a side or quarter of beef, pork or lamb from a farmer and have him get it butchered and keep it in his freezer until needed. The Picktons bought several large commercial freezers and in 1965 registered a business as B&C Frosted Foods, with Louise as proprietor. She also registered their farm as a business, calling it B&C Frosted Food

Bank. Three years later she changed the name to B&C Lockers, a more appropriate description of the business. The Picktons bought a small wooden building at 2215 Coquitlam Avenue, the legal address of the Lougheed Highway and Shaughnessy Avenue intersection, a few kilometres east of their farm, to hold about a hundred frozen food lockers where their customers and other farmers stored their meat till they needed it. Customers called the place "the meat locker."

It didn't take long before the Picktons' new farm was just as slovenly as the one on Dawes Hill. The family kept about seven hundred pigs and hundreds of chickens; there were several sheds and barns on the place, and animals were allowed to run in and out of most of them—and in and out of the farmhouse. Willie and Dave were expected to get up very early each morning to slop the pigs. They came home from school at noon to slop them again, and did it again after school and before bed at night. Neighbours remember that the kids worked so hard on the farm they often missed school altogether; they also remember that the boys were always filthy and smelled terrible. There was no shower at the house—in fact, Willie grew up with an irrational fear of showers and particularly hated getting water on his face—and occasional baths never got rid of the stink of pigs. Years later Willie would claim that he had no sense of smell, which might go some way to explaining his indifference to basic hygiene, but it could also have been his standard defence. It was never one of Dave's excuses; he was as grubby and smelly as his brother, and it was now Dave, not his father, who was called Piggy to his face. He never seemed to mind.

"Money was no real problem," recalls a woman who, as a teenager, boarded her horse on the farm for $25 a month, "but the way they lived was something I'd never seen before in my life. They would wear the same clothes every day; the boys would do the pigs and come in with their boots on, with oil and grease everywhere. Their relationship with their mom seemed very strange to me; she seemed too old to be the mother of these kids. She was a woman who wore rubber boots, always had on a long shift dress over pants, always wore the same sweater, always wore a bandana over her head—I'd swear she had no hair and no teeth, but she had lots of hair on her chin and a thick moustache for a woman. She had little beady eyes. And she was a talker. Louise had a loud, shrill voice and would go on and on; because she had no teeth it was difficult to understand what she said.

"I only met Linda once. She seemed like she was cut from different cloth. She was clean, she had class. You wouldn't have believed she came from the same family.

"The place was an absolute pigsty. Walk into the kitchen and you couldn't see the counter for the dirt on it. The floor was covered with slop and dirt; there were papers, food everywhere; there was no proper furniture to speak of . . . I seem to remember the living room just had a mattress in it. I wouldn't go into any of the other rooms.

"But you know, the mom was very nice to me and she talked and talked and talked. The mom did the cooking and she always had her gumboots on. Later, Willie seemed to run the pig end of the business and Dave was always out doing construction jobs. It was all like something out of that movie *Deliverance*."

Another neighbour remembers Louise for only one thing: she kept all the kitchen cupboards locked and was the only one who had a key.

The missing person in this picture is Leonard Pickton. By the time he and Louise had bought the farm on Dominion he was seventy-seven years old. He was too old to run the place or do much of the hard work, so Louise managed it with help from her children and hired hands who sometimes lived with the family.

Every time he went there to do welding work on farm equipment or in the barns, Russ MacKay, a neighbour, was always shocked by the dirt, the smell and the mess. He worried about the kids—over the years he had heard many stories about them, especially Willie, suffering horrendous abuse at the hands of their father. The mother was no help, he figured; she was all business, all the time.

Linda Pickton has acknowledged that school was a nightmare for her brothers, especially for Willie. In an interview with the *Vancouver Sun*'s Kim Bolan she said that her little brother was marginalized by society and had few friends. "He dropped out about the age of fifteen." School records show that Willie was fourteen and in grade eight when he left his first year of high school in 1964. Many years later he told his friend Lisa Yelds, who had moved into a house nearby, his own version of why he finally quit school.

"What happened was that he was at the Cracker Jack, a local shop, and bought a pen with a flipping lady," Yelds says. "When the pen was turned upside down, it was rude underneath. The principal said he was going to beat him and Willie said, 'You do that and I quit.' The principal wasn't backing down, so Willie quit then and there."

Louise Pickton didn't care; it meant her son was available for farm chores full-time. One of the jobs she wanted him to learn was slaughtering the pigs, but he didn't want to do it. When Louise would send him to the barn to watch Bob Korac, a local butcher who worked on the Pickton hogs, he went unwillingly.

"He never much be interested in that. He go fishing," Korac remembered years later. But Willie agreed to begin an apprenticeship as a meat cutter. Contrary to popular belief, he wasn't stupid and he wasn't illiterate. He could read and write, but slowly, and he always used a ruler under the lines as he read. When he wrote, he would use a ruler to make straight lines to write on. His talk was full of his mother's aphorisms, which he used in place of real conversation. *There's always a reason for everything. Life goes on. I try to help. Quite a spell. Crock of shit. But that's what happens. That's life. That's not here nor there. We're here today; we're not here tomorrow. That's way above my head.*

Unlike his older brother, Dave Pickton stayed in school longer, dated girls and seemed to be able to function more or less normally. But he got into trouble more often than Willie, and it was always much more serious than anything his older brother did.

When he was sixteen, Dave got his driver's licence and would peel off in one of the family trucks as often as he could get out from under his mother's watchful eye. Early one evening, on October 17, 1967, he climbed into his father's 1960 GMC one-ton truck to take it for a drive. By seven thirty he had come down Burns Road from the north, turned the corner and was heading home, west along Dominion Avenue. No more than four hundred feet away on Dominion, fourteen-year-old Tim Barrett was leaving his best friend's house. It was a beautiful, mild evening and he'd dropped by to see if his pal was free—maybe to work on building model cars or airplanes, Tim's passion—but the other boy was busy.

Timothy Barrett, whose house was at 2475 Burns Road, just around the corner and two houses north of Dominion, had lived in the neighbourhood for only a year. His parents had moved there from Winnipeg, where his father worked for the Royal Canadian Air Force. Tim had lived with his family on the air force base there, a place a childhood friend of his describes as a wonderful playground for kids.

"I remember it as being a pretty grand time, not unlike the times Bill Bryson describes in his book about his childhood days, *The Life and Times of the Thunderbolt Kid*," remembers Bruce Adams, one of Tim's close friends in Winnipeg. "We all lived close to the barren prairie . . . From my house a half-block up the street, civilization stopped. It was a great playground that [we] explored at great lengths. The whole area was intertwined with paths. We would spend the summer re-exploring these 'monkey trails' on our bikes or playing war." When the Barrett family moved to British Columbia, their new neighbourhood on Dominion must have been very much like the wild playgrounds Tim had loved on the base.

Tim left his friend's house that October night at seven thirty and walked further west along the shoulder of Dominion Avenue, heading in the direction of the Pickton farm. He was wearing slacks and a dark brown jacket and he was walking with the traffic, not facing the oncoming cars.

At eleven o'clock that night Phillip Barrett phoned Tim's friend on Dominion but spoke to the father. "He wanted to know where Tim was," the father said later. "I said no, he wasn't there and I hadn't seen him since the beginning of the evening." Phillip Barrett, his wife, Lois, and these neighbours called each other several more times that night; they called the police, but there was no news. Early the next morning the two fathers met to search the road.

"We'd been out looking since early in the morning, as soon as it was light," explained the neighbour. "And we started to walk up Dominion together and that was when we found Tim. Mr. Barrett found Tim's shoe. It was lying on the grass and he picked it up and he said, 'Oh my God, that's Tim's shoe.' The ditch is perhaps ten feet off the actual road and we were walking along the pavement at the time. We walked over to the ditch and we could see him there, and Mr. Barrett practically collapsed."

By this time a police car was just up the road; the neighbour's sons, who were searching with the dads, raced over to ask the officer to come right away. Soon afterwards a doctor arrived, the neighbour said, and took Tim's father home.

What happened? Well, no one can say now whether Dave Pickton was speeding, but what is certain is that he slammed the truck into the younger boy from behind, stopped long enough to see Tim's body lying on the road, and then fled home in a panic. His parents didn't hesitate. They examined the truck and saw right away that the impact had dented the right front fender, making a deep dimple in it; Louise saw blood and other marks on the hood and fender and that the paint had flaked at the point of impact.

Take it to our garage right now, Leonard ordered Dave, and get the mechanic there to bang out that dent and paint over the scrapes and flaking paint. One of them took a cloth and tried to rub the blood off the truck's hood and fender. And then they noticed the turn signal was broken and wire was dangling from it. Get the mechanic to fix that too, they told Dave. Right now. Here's what you tell him.

While Dave drove the truck to the garage in Port Coquitlam, Louise hurried down Dominion to look for the person Dave said he had hit. She found Tim Barrett lying at the side of the road. Louise didn't hesitate. She hauled him ten feet to the edge of the slough and rolled him into it. Then she turned around and went home.

Dave, meanwhile, drove the truck over to the mechanic who fixed the family's vehicles. By now it was eight thirty and dark out, but the mechanic could see right away that there was damage to the fender and hood of the truck.

"Can you fix it?" Dave asked anxiously.

"He was quite excited," the mechanic said later. But because he'd dealt with Dave several times before now and, as he told authorities later, he knew the Picktons weren't "too fussy," he said he could—it would just be a matter of knocking the dent out and putting in a turn-signal bulb. Once he had a good look at the truck, however, he realized the accident had been more serious than he thought; the whole socket for the bulb had been knocked out.

Dave told him that a timber had fallen on the truck. We're building a tractor shed and one of the posts holding up the roof fell on the truck, he explained, ignoring the fact that the dent was bowl-shaped. The mechanic was surprised at the fuss over a new dent on an already banged-up truck. "Normally they let this kind of thing go unnoticed," he said afterwards. "I just picked up a large mechanic's hammer and pushed it out."

Then Dave wanted him to paint over it. Forget it, the mechanic told him. The truck was covered with scrapes and dents that were much worse than this one and they'd never done anything about them before. As far as paint went, the Picktons just used red house paint on it, applied with a brush over an original factory coat of brown, followed by a coat of black and finally by the red. What was the point of trying to paint this dent when all the others had been left alone? It took about ten minutes to make the repairs, and Dave drove off as soon as they were done. It wasn't until about ten o'clock the next morning, when the mechanic was listening to a radio news report, that he heard a boy had been killed by a hit-and-run driver on Dominion Avenue.

He thought immediately of Dave Pickton. "It struck me as funny, you know, not something in the sense of humorous, but something funny that he was in such a hurry to get that truck fixed. Rather than let it go unnoticed I would phone the RCMP and tell them what I done the previous night, and if it turned out to be nothing, okay; if it turned out to be fact I'd save them some work."

Dave's story about a post hitting the car did not work with the RCMP officer who came to see him, armed with a search warrant. "The damage on the hood looked to me as if it had been hit by a round object, something larger than a post," he told a coroner's jury later. "A post would have caused a crease; this was dished in as if by a sack of wheat."

The police seized the red truck and discovered that someone had rubbed mud on the outside of the passenger door. When they cleaned it off, they found fresh damage to the paint, damage identical to two other spots—one on the hood and one on the front. They took samples from each layer of paint on the truck and matched them against paint found on Tim Barrett's clothes; only the red paint matched. The truck, they found, was in good mechanical order; the brakes and tires were fine. Visibility on the road had been good; in fact, driving conditions were ideal.

The coroner's jury also heard from Dr. C. J. Coady, a pathologist at the Royal Columbian Hospital in New Westminster, who had performed the autopsy on Tim Barrett's body. His news was a shock: Tim hadn't been killed when the truck hit him. Although he had been badly injured—suffering a fractured and dislocated pelvis, deep bruises, hemorrhaging in the back of his head and body, and a fractured skull with a sub-cranial hemorrhage—these injuries wouldn't have killed him, the pathologist stated. Tim Barrett had drowned in the slough, in two feet of filthy brown water. They even had an idea of the time: his watch had stopped at 7:45 p.m. exactly.

Phillip and Lois Barrett buried their son on October 20, 1967, in the Port Coquitlam cemetery after a funeral service in the Garden Hill Funeral Chapel. Dave Pickton was charged in juvenile court with failing to remain at the scene of an accident and convicted on December 19, 1967. He was placed on indefinite probation and his driver's licence was suspended until he turned twenty-one, another four and a half years. His mother's role in the death of Tim Barrett was the stuff of neighbourhood gossip for years. She herself told one of her sons' friends what had happened, threatening him if he ever said a word to anyone else about it. And many years later Willie Pickton told his best friend, Lisa Yelds—the little girl he'd once been kind to at his parents' meat store—the whole story.

Louise Pickton was a tough, hard woman. Her eccentricities and penny-pinching were legendary. On a regular basis the Picktons would get cheap labour from New Westminster's Woodlands School for mentally and physically disabled kids. Willie would drive over to pick up the young people, and when it was time to return them to the hospital for the night, he would slip out around back and go though Woodlands' trash. He tried to time the return trip for just after the hospital's dinner hour, so that by the time Willie was going through the Dumpster, the half-eaten leftovers were still warm and reasonably fresh. Louise approved: all she had to do was cut off the dirty bits. What Willie remembers more about these foraging trips, though, is the sight of mentally ill or disabled teen-age girls flashing him at the hospital. It was disturbing. He didn't tell his mother but he would talk about it to a few of the women he befriended years later.

In spite of her bizarre appearance, miserly ways and brutal actions, some people actually liked Louise. One was Vera Harvey; she and her husband, Albert, ran a blueberry farm on Devon Road about three kilometres north of the Picktons. Albert, who has retired, comes across as a good-natured guy who was happy to talk with the pick-your-own folks who arrived at the farm for a few hours, or put the kettle on in his little weigh-and-pay shack for a cup of tea when an old friend dropped by. But Vera, who died in 2004 at seventy-eight after years of chain-smoking, had a saltier view of the world. A few weeks before she died, she sat propped up in bed, attached to an oxygen tank and with a large television blaring by her side, and stuck up for her friend Louise and her family.

"The Picktons would do anything for anybody," Vera gasped angrily, her hands twisting the coverlet. "They'd help a perfect stranger. The kids worked really hard but they were picked on their whole life." When Jack Campbell was the mayor of Port Coquitlam, contributed Albert, "he tried to scare her off the property. He was offering her about $700 an acre. Vera was mad. She called Louise and said, 'Don't you take that offer. The price is too cheap.' So she didn't. Think what it's worth now."

"That's how the kids got the place," Vera summed up with a triumphant grin. "As for Willie, he's smarter than people think. He's very intelligent. A workaholic."

By the early 1970s, the Pickton brothers' work patterns had become established. Willie was still working as an apprentice meat cutter while Dave worked on demolition and construction sites. They were still living at home, managing all the farm chores, while Willie spent any extra time he had tinkering with cars, trucks and farm machinery. He was also doing all the family's hog and cattle butchering—sometimes as many as two dozen animals a day.

The woman who, as a teenager, used to board her horse on the property remembers Willie well. "He always treated me like a gentleman. Not like Dave, who had the foulest mouth in town. Every other word was *fuck*. Dave was different from Willie—he never apologized."

Still, she says, they were nice guys. "Yeah, they'd do anything for you."

Willie was awkward with girls, but not Dave; by 1972 he had a steady girlfriend, Sandy Fehlauer, who lived just north of the Harveys' blueberry farm on Devon Road. Sandy was a beautiful girl with blue eyes, long pale blond hair and high cheekbones.

She had a gentle manner and was liked by everyone who knew her. No one really understood why she fell for Dave Pickton, who was only five feet five inches tall, sported a rough beard and was almost as unkempt in appearance as his older brother. Sandy's father, Ewald, who came from an immigrant German family, was a pipefitter in Port Moody, the town next to Port Coquitlam on the Burrard Inlet; he and his wife, Lilac, raised Sandy, five half-sisters from her mother's first marriage and two brothers in a two-storey suburban house on a large lot with a high cedar hedge in front and a driveway running down the side.

Sandy quit school after completing grade eight and went to work in a door factory. On April 14, 1973, when she was just seventeen and Dave was twenty-two, Sandy moved into the Pickton farmhouse with Dave. She found herself sharing it with Leonard, Louise, Willie and two hired hands, elderly men who managed the barns. Willie slept upstairs, Sandy later told people. And sometimes there were six or seven extra people staying in the house, which was larger than it looked. About forty-five feet across and forty-two feet deep—with a small room, about ten by twelve feet, added at the western end—it had a full basement and second floor. On the road side the main floor held a living room with a fireplace and a large kitchen that faced Dominion Avenue. Along the back of the house, facing the barn, were three bedrooms and a bathroom. There were two doors into the house, one at the front and one at the side. Upstairs were three more bedrooms, while the basement held one other bedroom, almost always used for the hired hands.

The Picktons made most of their money from selling the hogs that they raised and butchered and from doing the haying on local farms. Sometimes there was so much work there would be another half-dozen hired hands crammed into the house, grabbing a spare bed wherever they could find one. There was never any doubt about who was in charge—it was Louise, and she was the one who assigned the jobs to everyone each day.

By 1973 Leonard was eighty-six years old and too senile to recognize anyone. It had been many years since Leonard had had any influence with his family. Quiet and bullied by his wife, he kept out of everyone's way. Linda Pickton told a *Vancouver Sun* reporter that Willie would refer to his younger brother, Dave, as his father, pleading with people not to tell him things. "'I'll tell you, but don't go tell my Dad,' Linda quoted Willie as saying. 'Keep the secret from Daddy.'" Linda did not explain what kind of secrets Willie was trying to keep from his impatient brother.

It must have been difficult for a seventeen-year-old girl who soon became pregnant; on January 11, 1974, Sandy Fehlauer gave birth to a girl they called Tammy. A year and a half later Douglas John was born; everyone always called him DJ.

Even with two babies, Sandy started every morning at six and worked like every other farmhand on the property until about eleven at night. That meant hiring babysitters to keep an eye on the kids. Along with Willie, who had given up his meat-cutting job and was now driving a truck part-time for B.C. Electric, Sandy worked in the barns feeding and cleaning the animals, shipping them to the slaughterhouse and helping to collect animals from the auction. Having enough hogs and beef cattle on hand to meet the demand from their customers meant a trip to the livestock auctions every week, a family affair always led by Louise. In these years—from 1973 to 1977—there would be as many as 700 hogs on the farm and 120 head of cattle. "There was no time," Sandy explained later, "for movies or trips to the beach."

Still, Dave and Sandy knew that the farm couldn't generate enough income from the butcher hogs and haying to support everybody, which meant Dave would continue to work in construction and demolition. But he also saw an opportunity in the topsoil business: he realized he could simply remove it from the farm and sell it to farmers, gardeners and people building new homes in the developments that were springing up all around them in Port Coquitlam. He bought a ramp truck—a truck with a rear ramp that lowered, allowing other vehicles to be pulled up onto the back—so he could cart a bulldozer around to jobs to deliver the soil and spread it. He went into business with Sandy's brother, Sigmund, and they called their new operation D&S Bulldozing. To this day a major part of his business remains hauling soil and fill, and the name remains the same.

CHAPTER THREE

A MOTHER'S WILL

During these years Willie's life seemed to be Spartan at best. He didn't smoke or drink, he didn't hang out in bars, didn't date, never had a girlfriend. But by now he was more comfortable around his mother, and more assertive.

"His mother was always there," says a woman who visited the farm often at that time, "and she was a nuisance; she nagged him all the time. I remember her: 'Move that truck! Now!' and he'd just say, 'Aw, shut up, Ma.' Willie was cunning, sly and street-smart."

One of his favourite hobbies continued to be collecting pen pals, especially female ones, and writing to them. His favourite was a girl named Connie Anderson who lived in Pontiac, Michigan; in 1974, soon after he turned twenty-four in October, he made up his mind to take a trip to see her. It was the first holiday he had ever taken. Before he left, though, his brother and some friends took him out to celebrate and he got roaring, falling-down drunk, for the first and last time in his life. After he recovered, he bought a bus ticket and took off by himself in January on a six-week trip to Pontiac, working his way through the American Midwest with stops in Kansas City, St. Louis and Chicago. Chicago scared him, he told his pen pal Victoria, years later. He had to be careful about all the "black people" he saw. "You can't be out at nighttime or anything," he said in the audiotape he sent her. "It's really rough out there."

At some point during this odyssey, Willie was asked to be a male model—or so he told Victoria. "I had a good time. I met a lot of people and, believe it or not, once I had a chance for me. Believe it or not, me. I'm a plain old farm boy. They want me for a model.

A model? Me? Forget it. What's a model? What are they talking about? Modelling? Anyways, he says we want you in to change clothes, do this, do that."

Who knows what kind of modelling job this was, but according to Willie the pay would have been $40 an hour. He turned it down. "I don't think so. I don't know what I'm getting into here. I just want to know more about what the country's like."

Eventually Willie made his way to Pontiac and met Connie Anderson. By the time he left, he considered himself engaged to her. "I was engaged," he was to say later. "She was the love of my life. But she couldn't leave her job. I couldn't leave my job. I couldn't leave the farm."

Looming just as large in his memories of the trip as Connie's refusal was the holiday celebrating George Washington's birthday, always held on the third Monday of February. The hoary tradition is to bake a cherry pie to commemorate the president's determination to tell the truth, even as a child. His father, goes the story, had given the boy a hatchet and later noticed some cuts on a cherry tree in the garden. He asked young George what had happened. "I cannot tell a lie," George said, "I did it with my hatchet."

As many people will admit, we don't know if the story is true but we do know that Americans revere George Washington as the embodiment of honesty and celebrate his birthday with a madness of cherry pies. It irritated Willie beyond belief. "People kept trying to make me eat cherry pies," he'd say, adding that he never wanted any. In fact, he said, he was disgusted by the sight of all these crazy Americans with cherry pie all over their faces.

Willie returned to Port Coquitlam. The engagement to Connie, whatever form it took, fizzled out, and Willie stayed on the farm, working there full-time. Because the Picktons let local people keep and ride their horses on the property, Willie also became interested in horses and made up his mind to try the business for himself. He started with a mare that was being boarded on the farm and arranged to have her bred; the palomino colt that was born, named Goldie, became his pride and joy. "He was tickled pink with it," a friend remembers. "He took such pride in it—but I never saw him ride it."

This was about the same time he abandoned his meat-cutting apprenticeship, a move he said later that he regretted. If he'd stayed another six months he would have had the papers needed to work anywhere in Canada. "And then I turned around and threw it all out the door after six and a half years. I wanted to go back to the farm. I mean, I'm fed up with cutting the meat, doing this, doing that. I'm getting tired." But he still needed a job that would bring in a better income than he could make full-time on the farm, so he went to work as a truck driver for British Columbia Hydro.

By 1976 the routine at the Pickton farm had started to shift. Linda, who had married Byron Leigh Wright in Vancouver on November 25, 1977, was working in Vancouver. She was still emotionally distanced from her family and got involved only when there were business decisions to make about the property. In 1978, one calamity after another altered everything. Leonard became sick; it was cancer, and he died at ninety-one on January 1, 1978, not long after the diagnosis. And Sandy and Dave, who had never married, weren't getting along well, mostly because he had his eye on other women; Sandy finally moved out with the two children. This was a huge loss for Willie, who worshipped her; he told people afterwards that he had asked her to marry him but she turned him down. And then the piggery barns burned down, destroying at least six hundred pigs. Willie spent all his spare time trying to rebuild them but never finished the job.

The next year wasn't any easier. By now Louise was sick; again the diagnosis was cancer. As she became weaker and more in pain, it was Willie who fed, bathed, diapered and dressed her until she was moved to hospital for the last few weeks, where she died at sixty-seven, on April 1, 1979. He described her last days on the farm to a friend: "She was up and going and going and going and . . . you never keep her down even almost right to the end. We had to put her on a stretcher when she left here. She said, 'I want to have a look at this place one last time,' and so we sat her up and she had a look at the place . . . she looked all over the place. She never did come back."

Willie had loved his strange mother. When a policeman asked him years later what their relationship was like, his answer was characteristically terse: "Two peas in a pod."

For Dave's part, he didn't bat an eye about losing Sandy or his mother. Soon after Louise died, his new girlfriend, Vicky Evans, moved into the house. Within the year Sandy had married a man named John Humeny and moved with Tammy and DJ to their new home in Mission. Her parting with Dave was amicable, and she would bring the children to visit him once or twice a month.

Almost as soon as Vicky Evans moved into the farmhouse, her younger sisters, Alison and Samantha, began visiting the place regularly. For them it was a child's paradise. In those days parts of the property, especially at the back, north end, were still pretty, with trees, bushes and long grasses covering the hills and winding trails for horseback riding. Some of the fields were planted in grain and hay. And Willie was always good to the girls, letting them ride the horses and play with the baby pigs. Alison was only six when she began visiting the farm; many years later most of her memories were of good times. "A lot of space, a lot of fresh air and mud—a kid's dream." But she also recalled a "giant sludge pit" on the property used for dead piglets and pig waste, and what she called a "psycho" dog. Nor has she forgotten Willie's "scary, dark" basement bedroom, where he taught her how to make sausages with a meat grinder.

Her sister Samantha, who was fourteen, visited Vicky almost every day for two years, often babysitting her children, and frequently sleeping over. Her memories seem to be happier than Alison's. "I rode a lot of horses, met a lot of people, had a great time," she has said. And she was also old enough to lend a hand around the office, taking topsoil orders for Dave.

But as Dave took control of the place, the farm changed. His topsoil business was growing rapidly, and so was his work in demolition and construction. So two things happened: The arable soil was being steadily eroded as Dave scraped it off and trucked it away for his customers. And once-lush fields became muddy parking areas for the trucks, bulldozers and other heavy equipment he was using.

Willie added to the destruction of the land by hauling in old cars he had bought from various auctions, strewing them around wherever he could find a handy spot. He figured his mother's death had set him free. He and Dave and Linda now owned the farm, and it was worth a lot of money. But the best news was that there was no one to take care of anymore. No one to keep an eye on him.

The shock—one he never expected—was his mother's will. While Louise had left everything to her children, there were strict controls on Willie's inheritance that didn't apply to David or Linda. Except for an immediate lump-sum payment of $20,000, Willie wouldn't get any more money from the estate unless he stayed on the farm until he was forty years old. His shrewd old mother may have meant well, but now, at thirty, he was trapped for another ten years, forced to go cap in hand to his brother and sister for money, while they could live anywhere they wanted.

If only his mother had died first! Leonard's estate, made up of real estate holdings and a little cash, was worth $148,000. His will, signed on March 10, 1975, named Willie and David as his trustees, gave Linda a lump-sum payment of $20,000, and left everything else to be divided equally between his two sons. But that was only if Louise died before he did; if she lived, she got everything. After his death Louise paid no attention to what Leonard would have done; she had her own views about a fair division among her children.

The details of the wills and the probate documents tell us a great deal about the Pickton family, not just about the assets they had accumulated but also about how Leonard and Louise regarded their children.

Described as retired, Leonard left real estate holdings valued at $143,665.33 as well as two small life insurance policies worth $4,335.75. The real estate wasn't just the Dominion Avenue farm; it also included three other parcels of land. The first was a lot in Coquitlam in the New Westminster District, valued at $40,000; there was a mortgage on it of $22,069.39 held by the Caisse Populaire de Maillardville, a bank set up by the original French-Canadian settlers, leaving equity of $17,930.61. Then there were two small parcels of land in the northeastern corner of British Columbia, known as the Peace River Regional District; one was worth $2,245 and the other $460.

Last was the farm on Dominion. It was valued at $275,000, but because Leonard owned it jointly with Louise, his share was worth $137,500. There was a little debt left: two mortgages registered against the property, one for $7,000 with the Farm Credit Corporation, another with the Bank of Montreal for $21,940.56. What remained for Louise of his share was $123,029.72. But Leonard died first.

In her will, drawn up on March 18, 1977, Louise named all three children as her trustees and required them to pay Willie' (described as a farmer in the will) $20,000 in cash right away—sort of like his father's plan for Linda. The rest of the money, $88,517.61 each, was to be paid to Linda (an "accountant") and to Dave (a "truck driver") immediately, but Willie's share was to remain in trust, controlled by Dave and Linda. Although they were required to pay him the interest on his money on a regular basis, he would have to wait until he was forty to collect his share of the estate. The value of the farm in Port Coquitlam was still $275,000, but by the time Louise died the mortgages had shrunk to $9,954.61, so the equity now was $265,045.39. The land in the Peace River District remained at a value of $2,705 but there were two other small parcels there that Louise owned herself, valued at $200 each. So the total value of all the real estate after the mortgages were paid off was $287,029. Louise also had a bit of money in the Westminster Credit Union and the Caisse Populaire de Maillardville, adding up to $2,088.31.

Willie was devastated by his mother's will. It seemed so unfair. His sister certainly didn't need the money; Linda and her husband, Byron Wright, had good jobs. Dave had his demolition business and his soil business; contracts were pouring in and he was hiring truck drivers and construction workers all the time. The fact that he was going to receive $20,000 more than Linda and Dave was cold comfort to Willie, who felt trapped.

"Willie never spoke of what his family willed to him," says Lisa Yelds. "All he said was he wasn't allowed his share until he was forty. I had asked him why didn't he buy a place of his own, and for a while he did have realtors around talking to him. This was in the very early nineties. I guess it was around the time he was fighting with Dave all the time about his money."

The only bright note for him at this time was the 1977 Ford truck he bought for himself for $20,000—probably the same $20,000 Louise had left him as a consolation prize. But if Louise's thought was to protect him from himself, it backfired. Willie Pickton was angry—and frustrated by his mother's betrayal.

CHAPTER FOUR

THE PICKTON BROTHERS

The men around Willie Pickton had no trouble finding girlfriends. Even Dave had quickly replaced Sandy Fehlauer with Vicky Evans, and Dave was no prize—short, squat, dirty, bearded, smelly, foul-mouthed. But no one wanted to date Willie. The women who hung around the Pickton farm, and there were many, liked him well enough; they thought he was harmless and pleasant and, while he didn't have much to say, he liked being part of the gang. But no one would have dreamed of dating him. He stank and they all thought he was weird.

By now, in the early 1980s, Willie lived in his own small world. He had an aptitude for mechanics and a passion for cars and trucks. He could fix anything. He became a regular at used car auctions, and when he got the cars home, he would sell the usable parts and tear apart the rest for scrap, separating the copper, aluminum and brass. The auctioneers considered him a junk buyer, always looking for bargains.

And, as his parents had done for so many years, Willie continued to haunt the weekly livestock auctions, usually shopping on behalf of customers who ordered what they wanted a week or two in advance. Willie kept track of these clients in a Rolodex he kept on his desk; it had hundreds of names in it. Fraser Valley Auctions was a regular Saturday morning stop on his weekly rounds; here most of the locals called him Bob instead of Willie. Saturday mornings were set aside for everything from chickens, rabbits and geese to goats, sheep, llamas and cattle; if he had orders for calves, he would go on a Wednesday. Some of his customers wanted a lamb or a sheep, while others would order a goat or a pig, a calf, even horsemeat or an emu.

It was about this time that Willie began working with a Filipino butcher, a man named Patricio Casanova but always called Pat. He had been a gardener and a security guard with the Philippines Department of Agriculture and Natural Resources before emigrating to British Columbia in 1974 with his wife and four children. Casanova had been buying pigs from an elderly butcher who rented space from the Picktons in the late 1970s; his ambition was to provide barbecued pork to members of the Filipino community and to restaurants in Vancouver's Chinatown. He was trying out various methods of butchering and cooking the pigs to suit these customers when he met Willie. By the early 1980s, when Casanova was in his forties, the two men were working together at the farm about twice a month to get the pigs killed, cleaned and cut up, ready for barbecuing.

Along with the pigs he and Casanova bought, Willie would bring home the other animals he had bought at auction, then slaughter, butcher and package the meat for sale, using his parents' old freezers from the meat locker to store it all. If a cow or pig was too big to kill by slitting its throat with a knife—his favourite method— he would shoot it in the forehead, usually with a nail gun. Sometimes the emus that people ordered were too big to handle easily; these too he would shoot with his nail gun. Once the animal was dead he cut a deep slit in its ankle, thrust a large hook attached to a thick metal bar through the slit, and hoisted up the animal, foot first, on a chain. At other times he would simply hoist the live animal by its heel first and then slit its throat, catching its blood in a bucket as the failing heart pumped it out. Then he would gut it, skin it with a sharp filleting knife and finally dismember it with a hand saw.

Despite his six and a half years as an apprentice meat cutter, Willie wasn't a good butcher, so he usually got small local butchers to take the big hunks of meat he prepared and cut them into steaks, chops and roasts ready for sale. Sometimes Willie would buy baby goats and keep them until they were large enough to slaughter; these, like weanling piglets, were for spit-roasting whole.

As a buyer, Willie was well-known for picking out the worst-looking animals because the price was right. Once he brought home a blind cow to slaughter; other times he'd bring home piglets with sores. One auction house saved the culls for him to take home—the animals that they could not sell to anyone else because they were sick or dying. To get rid of all the bones and unwanted parts of the slaughtered animals, Willie used Dave's backhoes and bulldozers to dig deep holes around the property, especially at the northern and western edges of the farm. Some of the holes were thirty or forty feet deep. Willie would dump in bones, skin and meat until the hole was nearly full and then bulldoze dirt to fill it up.

One day an old friend, the woman who had boarded a horse there when she was a teenager and had been so appalled by the Pickton house and his mother, dropped by to say hello and found him busy digging a large hole in a far corner of the farm. She was surprised by his furtiveness. "Got a big old pig here," he told her, hustling to spread more dirt over the hole. "Just burying it." She thought the whole thing was odd, and frightening.

At this time Dave wanted nothing to do with farm life or animals—and certainly not with pigs. Dave's main business now was the demolition of buildings, everything from houses to high schools to country-and-western saloons. He had hired several men to drive his trucks and bulldozers for him.

But if he had been tough enough or brave enough, Dave Pickton would have chosen the life of a biker. The Hells Angels were his heroes. There were plenty of them in the community, some full-patch members and many more in the club's stratified layers of membership, including hang-arounds and wannabes and associates, all eager to help the outlaw bikers in their criminal activities—dealing drugs, stealing vehicles, running protection rackets and pimping prostitutes—and to join in on the loud, raucous parties.

The local police began sniffing around the Pickton property when stories reached them that the brothers were running a chop shop with the bikers. The stories turned out to be true. The farm was a great place to dump cars, trucks and other items that had been stolen and cannibalized for parts or claimed for insurance, a common scam with the provincial insurance company, the Insurance Corporation of British Columbia (ICBC). With the equipment available, the Picktons were able to dig deep holes to bury the stolen goods, even things as big as vehicles and parts. Or they would simply leave the vehicle where it was and let Dave's dump trucks pour tons of dirt over it.

Dave was busy with his demolition business, so it was left to Willie to oversee the work at the chop shop, something he could manage easily with his gift for vehicle scavenging. But Willie also had the pig farm to manage. In 1981 he hired three or four teenage boys to help him with the pigs, and in his lifelong effort to show that he liked to help people, even let a couple of them live there. They began by mucking out the pigpen, but to their dismay, helping went only so far: Willie refused to pay them. He liked to scare them by saying he could get rid of anyone. And then he tried to make friends with them again.

"One day he told me he had a ham for me and I should pick it up after my shift," remembers a man who was fifteen at the time. "Another kid told me not to take it. But at the end of my shift, I said, 'What about the ham you promised me?' And Willie returned with a mass of material. It wasn't brains but I don't know what it was. It was all stringy, and not ham. And it wasn't frozen."

The bikers prying apart the stolen vehicles and cutting them up started bullying and intimidating the teenagers. Before long they were sending the boys off to steal cars and bring them back to the farm. This time they were paid, so the boys didn't mind. One teenager, the son of a local Port Coquitlam politician, was arrested by the police, and that's when they discovered he was stealing cars for the Picktons. In the summer of 1981 two other boys were also hauled off by the police to be questioned about car thefts.

The Mounties sent two young officers, Tim Sleigh and Brian Brown, to investigate the activities at the farm; eventually they were involved in the excavation and recovery of stolen vehicles there. The relationship between the Pickton brothers seemed clear to the police at the time: Dave Pickton, Sleigh said later, had been giving parties for the Hells Angels, and when he was around Willie, he was condescending but protective. It was clear who was in charge. Willie, said Sleigh, was shy and cooperative—cooperative to the point where after Dave had been arrested he walked the officers around the property, showing them exactly where some of the stolen vehicles were. "He never blinked," Sleigh said later. "He seemed mentally diminished, submissive and very mechanical."

Everyone thought Dave was the one running the chop shop; no one thought his brother was capable of it. But boys who worked there said that Willie was the boss, the one who gave them their orders and paid them, and that his brother had nothing to do with it.

It's not surprising that the brothers argued and snapped at each other all the time. Dave was always his brother's toughest critic. Although his own hygiene was a subject of constant comment among the women in his crowd, Dave felt free to attack Willie on the same grounds. He would lose his temper over Willie's sheets and towels, which remained unwashed for months. He would yell at him when spring floods covered the basement floor, and most of Willie's possessions, in filth and mud and the house stank of it all.

Dave's girlfriend for eleven years, Vicky Evans, had had enough of the brothers and the farm shortly before the police began their investigation into the chop shop; she moved out. It didn't take Dave long to find a replacement for her: a bright and funny woman named Cathy Wayenberg, the single parent of two beautiful young girls, April and Tasha Wayenberg. Their first months on the farm were spent observing the police hassling Dave and Willie about the stolen vehicle scams.

Little came of this investigation. As far as the RCMP was concerned in those years, the activities at the farm between 1980 and 1982 were nothing more than run-of-the-mill thievery. The local

Mounties were far more preoccupied with catching a brutal serial killer who had been preying on children in the area. His name was Clifford Olson. A vicious con artist and psychopath, he lived in a housing complex in Coquitlam during a killing spree that lasted eighteen months, from December 1980 until July 1981. A teenage girl he stalked and assaulted during this time was named Janet Henry; on at least one occasion he and another man dragged her into a car, fed her drugs—probably chloral hydrate, a knockout drug he used on children—and assaulted her. She was one of the few he attacked who survived, but in the late nineties, Janet Henry, who found herself working the Low Track in the Downtown Eastside, may have met a different predator. She was reported missing on June 28, 1997, and is thought to have become another of Robert Pickton's victims, but he has not been formally charged with her murder.

In 1981 Olson was convicted of murdering eleven children; he cut a deal with the government of British Columbia to admit he killed them in exchange for $10,000 for each of the children's bodies he found for them. The uproar from the public scalded the police and the attorney general who agreed to Olson's demands. Olson pled guilty on January 14, 1982, and received a life sentence, but he continued to taunt the police with hints that he'd left many more bodies hidden in the woods. With eleven convictions, Olson was the country's worst serial killer ever.

As the Pickton brothers settled into their routines in Port Coquitlam in the early years after their parents' deaths, Linda continued to have as little to do with her brothers as possible. She had a baby boy, Brendan, on February 9, 1980, and Kevan Francis was born on June 11, 1982, but the children did not bring her closer to her brothers. At this time the connection was strictly business—they needed to decide how to deal with the farm property, and she began to turn this over in her mind.

One night in 1986, a young woman named Karen Kaufman, who was living out in Maple Ridge, was bored and looking for something to do. "I've got a gig tonight at a bar in Vancouver," her older sister said. "C'mon. You'll meet some of my friends. I've been telling you about this one guy, Dave Pickton—you'll like him. He's there a lot."

Her sister was a musician and she seemed to be having a good time, so Karen, who was twenty-four, said sure. Better than staying home alone. She'd heard a lot about the Picktons and was curious. The bar turned out to be the one in the American Hotel, a notorious biker hangout on Main Street in Vancouver, close to the Downtown Eastside. Right across the street is the Cobalt, another hotel with a wild reputation. Each has been infamous for its association with drug dealers and organized-crime gangs.

Dave was there, as Karen's sister had promised he would be, and he couldn't have been more affable. He introduced Karen to Cathy Wayenberg and, when he realized Karen was single, he made sure she met some of his pals. Karen, along with her sister, started hanging around at the Pickton farm. Because Cathy had the two little girls, she liked inviting her girlfriends to bring their kids to play. Like Sandy Fehlauer before her, Cathy was driving trucks as part of Dave's crew and had hired a babysitter who lived nearby.

Even though he still lived in the farmhouse, now in the basement bedroom the hired hands used to share, Willie was always in the background. "Willie was very much a loner," Karen says. "He was very unsociable. I thought he had the mentality of an eight-year-old." But he liked children and got a kick out of taking Cathy's girls to the auctions with him.

Ignoring Willie's weirdness, Karen enjoyed life on the farm. There were barbecues and there was lots of drinking, and despite the chop shop fiasco it remained a popular place for local bikers to hang out. One day when Cathy and Dave decided to go to a biker party in Port Coquitlam, being held to raise money for injured bikers, they made her come with them.

"We're gonna find you a shaggin' partner," Dave promised Karen. They did. Soon she was dancing with new man named Jim and was in no hurry to leave, but Cathy and Dave convinced them to go to a restaurant with them for a snack. Once there, Dave relaxed and began telling his friends about one of the stolen car scams they had been running at the farm. "Dave told us they were burying cars people claimed were stolen, but Willie squealed when the cops tricked him. They said they'd keep Dave in jail unless he showed them where the cars were." Still a little gullible, Willie had agreed.

Karen used to ask Cathy why Willie didn't have a girlfriend, and Cathy's answer was simple. Willie was shy, she told Karen. "He was never very sociable," Karen remembers. "He never partied with Dave. When the pig roasts were on, and he was responsible for cooking the pigs, he would socialize a bit, maybe for just an hour."

When Karen and Jim, a biker himself, decided to get married, everyone celebrated. Karen was under no illusions about the Pickton brothers, but she was young. "What the hell," she thought. But a few years later, after she had three children of her own, she usually left them at home with her mother when she went to the farm.

"Dave was rude and obnoxious," Karen says now. "If he thought a woman was overweight he would say, 'You fat cow.' He'd tell women quite openly, 'You're getting fat. You have a big ass.' He thought he was funny. But people used to laugh at him, making fun of him behind his back. He had a lisp and he said things like 'the twain went over the twacks.'

"You know, I considered him a good friend. He was a very good businessman, a workaholic. I stayed at the home overnight many times; Dave would get up at dawn and go out till dark. He worked with diesel machines and backhoes but he always showered when he got home. Not like Willie. And Dave paid for everything. He would supply us with booze but I never saw him drunk, I never saw him do drugs. He didn't like being out of control. His girlfriend would smoke pot but I never saw him do it."

Unlike Willie, Dave Pickton loved to have parties. People dropped in all the time. And by this time Dave had fully entered the biker world. At first he was not identified as a biker, just as a businessman who rode motorcycles. He began riding with independent bikers but then more and more often with the Hells Angels. He couldn't resist buying a Harley-Davidson and showing it off, and he began going to Angels functions.

One year Cathy decided to throw a big biker party at the farm for her birthday. As she and her friends sat around planning the menu, Cathy shuddered as she pointed out an old deep freezer in the house. "I will never eat meat from that freezer," she told them.

At the birthday party things got rough. One of the men tried to rape a close friend of Karen's; he forced the woman into a headlock and, when she fought back, kicking and clawing and punching, he told her he admired her spunk and, laughing, let her go. Dave and his new friends, most of them roaring drunk, ran their Harleys into the open fire pits. In those days it seemed to be a good place to have a good time.

Karen wasn't so sure. She was uneasy, especially about her three children. "One day we were going horseback riding," she remembers. "Cathy wanted to go. My son, Rory, was four and the girls eight and nine. I was uncomfortable; I went back and Rory was nowhere to be found. Ten minutes later Rory was back. He had been down at the pig farm and he was covered with soot . . . all I could see were his tiny blue eyes." Remembering this now, Karen shivers. She began to think about how to distance herself from the place, but the opportunity arrived more suddenly than she expected.

Describing the routine on the Pickton farm, Karen Kaufman remembers that Willie would come in at the end of the day and have his dinner. One afternoon before Willie came home, Dave showed her his brother's bedroom in the basement; to get to it they walked over a false floor, a necessity because the basement often flooded in winter. It led to Willie's bedroom door, which opened to reveal no bed, just a plain mattress on the floor with a black splotch down the middle. The next thing she saw was a horse's head on the wall. It was Goldie, the palomino colt he had bred many years before. It had injured its leg badly, so Willie had to put it down when it was about four years old; he had sawed off the head, taken it to a taxidermist and had it preserved. Another treasure was a set of three coats of arms he kept on his wall showing the distinguished Pickton antecedents. Then there was a book of local history with pictures and the history of the Pickton family. These were Willie's prized possessions.

Dave Pickton thought he was ridiculous. "Don't believe my brother or hang around him," he told one woman who had befriended Willie. "He is a few tiles short of a full load." But this was all precious stuff to Willie. Nothing enraged him more than having people nosing around his room. When anyone wanted to talk to him at night after he had gone to bed, most knew better than to go downstairs. They simply knocked on his bedroom window and he would come up.

Just as Dave was showing Cathy and Karen around his room that night, Willie appeared in the doorway. Seeing them there, he spat in Cathy's face. "If she ever comes into this room again," he hissed at his brother, "I will kill her."

One night over dinner, he threw a glass of milk in Karen's face. Karen had been hanging around the Pickton farm almost every day for three years, but now, like Cathy, she was afraid of Willie. It wasn't just that Willie gave her the creeps; she was starting to hear all kinds of rumours about him. "He was living in the basement," she said, and "he had this wild dog—the dog would tear your limbs off—he was crazy and wild and Willie would feed him raw meat. Willie was weird."

"I refused to eat any meat off the farm," Karen continued, "even though we had been out there every day." And, she added, "Back in 1988 Willie would never use his own pigs for a pig roast on the farm; his excuse would be 'Oh, the pigs are sick.' Cathy was so scared of him and the meat there. And I had friends who said those guys, the Picktons, were making snuff films." She stopped going to the farm.

As far as the police were concerned, the Pickton brothers were bad news. Their chop shop would have been enough to keep the police alert, but they also had an unsavoury reputation because, even after they'd been caught, the brothers continued to run with a gang of criminals. And there were lots of small things. David Pickton, for example, remained a careless driver, racking up plenty of traffic problems; in 1991 he was sued for damage resulting from traffic accidents, but he was able to settle the claims out of court.

The following year the trouble was more serious. Dave had a contract to excavate a site for construction and he kept a trailer on the property. One of the workers on the project was a woman who was working as a flag girl. Somehow Pickton got her in the trailer and sexually assaulted her.

"You could smell [Dave] before you saw him," the woman told a reporter at the Vancouver *Province*. "He had no respect for women at all."

She went to the police and filed a complaint, and Pickton was charged. But as they waited for the trial to begin, Dave's biker friends began to turn up at her home to intimidate her. Although Pickton was found guilty, the penalty was just a slap on the wrist: he was fined $1,000 and sent home on probation. His buddies remember the trial with cynical smiles.

"Dave is a little biker greaseball," says Scott Chubb, who worked for Dave Pickton for several years and remembers the incident with the flag girl well. "But he's smart. Part of his little edge is to play dumb. He stands up to the judge and says, 'Fuck, fuck, fuck.' The judge objects. Dave says, 'But that's the way I fucking talk.'" The terrified woman moved to a new city.

The conditions of Dave's conviction prohibited him from crossing the border into the United States, but red tape didn't worry him. He borrowed Willie's identification and driver's licence and made as many trips as he wanted, often to gamble at American casinos. Many of the brothers' associates were bikers, grifters, drug dealers and prostitutes, and they were all welcome at the Pickton farm.

Despite his reputation with women, Dave Pickton had no problem with hiring them to do traditional men's jobs, maybe because his mother had been the boss around the place for so long. Sandy (Fehlauer) Humeny, who had returned to work for him in 1986 because her relationship with John Humeny was not going well, drove a gravel truck for Dave from dawn to dusk, while Cathy Wayenberg, working the same long hours, drove a dump truck.

"I attended every morning at five or six a.m.," Sandy stated years later, "and worked every day—five, six, seven days. Willie would be here in the morning if I was picking the truck up and he would make sure everything was working fine. I would fuel up in the yard between the house and the cow barn. Willie was there every morning and every night."

Willie worshipped Sandy, but his relationship with his brother's girlfriend Cathy was cool. She thought he was a creep. During the years that she lived in the farmhouse with Dave and drove a dump truck, she had to hire a live-in babysitter, a woman in her forties, to look after Tasha and April, who were still very young. Karen Kaufman remembers that one year (she thinks it was about 1989 or 1990), she and her husband, Jim, went on a weekend holiday to Penticton with Cathy and Dave, taking the babysitter along to help with the kids. One day not long afterwards the babysitter just disappeared, Karen says. "She had a grown daughter, and when Dave and Cathy called her to ask where her mother was she said she had no idea. She said she hadn't heard from her mom."

Karen Kaufman says the woman was dismissed by the Picktons as a drifter, even though Cathy Wayenberg reported her disappearance to the police. "They did nothing," says Karen. She never heard whether the Picktons were interviewed and she has never heard if the woman was found.

Soon afterwards Cathy Wayenberg and her children left the farm for good. The girls grew up to become exotic dancers, performing across North America; they were also smart and saved their money. Eventually Tasha and April bought a horse farm in the Niagara region of Ontario, named it Blazing Colours and became successful horse breeders. Cathy Wayenberg moved to Ontario to be near them and tried to put the bad memories of the Pickton farm far behind her.

CHAPTER FIVE

GEOGRAPHY SPEAKS

Karen Kaufman was one of the few people in Port Coquitlam who, quite by accident, had seen Willie Pickton's vicious side. It was an unusual breach triggered by an unusual invasion of his privacy. Most of the time he kept his emotions under control. He wasn't looking for trouble at home, where he was content to watch his brother's rough pals and to play the quiet brother who just wanted to help. Instead he was starting to look for his own pleasure by cruising along the streets of Vancouver's Downtown Eastside, where so many of British Columbia's prostitutes, drug addicts, homeless and hopeless end up.

Pickton had started going there on a regular basis in the early 1980s to dump animal parts at West Coast Reduction, a massive rendering plant at 105 Commercial Drive North on Burrard Inlet, almost next door to the equally sprawling Rogers Sugar factory and just a block or so from where the prostitute stroll began. It wasn't long before he was so well-known at West Coast that he would just drive his truck up to the gate and he'd be waved in; no one bothered to inspect his containers. After all, who'd want to? And who could tell what was what in such a mess?

The area set aside for the collection vats stank. This didn't worry Willie a bit. Taking his turn in the stream of trucks lined up to dump their own barrels, he would back up to the loading dock, roll the barrels of muck to the end of the vehicle's flat deck and pour out their contents into a vast, deep pool.

When he couldn't get into town with his containers, Willie would arrange for someone to pick them up. At the time Jim Cress was a driver for West Coast Reduction; he would make regular trips out to Port Coquitlam to pick up barrels of trimmings from meat Willie collected. In a normal week, he said later, he would pick up two to five forty-five-gallon drums, and he did this for about four years, from 1992 to 1996. When he looked inside the drums, he noticed that the meat was black and in big chunks, and this surprised him. Most farmers whittled off every bit of meat they could find on an animal carcass, but Willie Pickton was just throwing it away. No one ever asked questions or inspected the barrels; regular customers like Willie could dump whatever they liked.

The rendering plant, which has two docking berths for container ships and large bulk tankers, ships its products all over the world. It has made its owner, Jack Diamond, one of the wealthiest men in British Columbia. A Polish immigrant who bought a small Vancouver pork-butcher shop in about 1930, Diamond quickly turned it into the largest meat-packing plant in western Canada. By 1964 he had created West Coast Reduction Ltd., where slaughterhouses, food companies and farmers could dispose of the carcasses, bone, meat, feathers and fur they couldn't process for food, and where dead animals—from household pets to horses, poultry, cows and raccoons—ended up. It was also where the kitchen grease from the city's restaurants got dumped. According to the company's website, they now pick up the discarded animal products in special vans:

> We receive and transport each type of raw material in custom-designed trucks which collect bones, fat, offal, feathers, fish, blood, and used restaurant grease. Each category of raw material is processed promptly and separately in fully-enclosed, computer controlled processing systems. Control over plant hygiene and control over product quality has earned West Coast Reduction the reputation it enjoys today. Achieving this control begins with prompt and hygienic collection from our suppliers.

His wealth allowed Jack Diamond to join the world of horse breeding and make a success of it, to become a member of the Sports

Hall of Fame and a philanthropist behind many good causes. He was Simon Fraser University's most generous donor. But what went on in the plant was something not widely discussed, just understood. Very few, if any, of the available articles about Jack Diamond tell you what his company actually did.

Willie Pickton was too small a player to enjoy hygienic collection in custom-designed trucks, but in the end the process was just the same. What he brought in was ground up by giant augers, moved into deep fat fryers and cooked until the grease could be separated. The grease moved through underground pipes into vast storage tanks that can hold 57,000 tonnes, waiting to be turned into—to name just a few things—cosmetics, soaps, paint, plastics, candles and textiles. Meat, fish, feathers and bone are processed into ground meal and, depending on the source, used as an ingredient in chicken feed, pet food, animal feed and bone meal. But the great spewing chimneys reaching into the sky tell the story better than any words can.

Willie relished his trips to West Coast. Every time he dropped off his cans of animal parts and entrails he would reward himself with a little drive around the neighbourhood, eyeing the women on the street. He'd heard all the talk back at the farm about the prostitutes in the Downtown Eastside; Dave's biker friends talked about them, and would often bring some of the women back to the biker bars, clubhouses and hangouts that were scattered throughout the New Westminster and Tri-Cities area.

Willie was fascinated.

People say there is no place on earth like Vancouver's Downtown Eastside, and that's the truth. Go there at night and you'll see the dark, skinny shapes of coyotes padding along the edges of railroad tracks, disappearing into the filthy puddled alleys between buildings, nosing through garbage in the parks, slinking past the junkies sleeping on benches or crouched in doorways.

The way most people picture it, the neighbourhood is only about eight blocks long and six blocks deep. In fact it is longer and deeper and more complex. When you think about this story in all its layers, you begin to understand that, along with poverty and neglect and drugs and disease and sex and murder, it is also, oddly enough, a story about geography.

The entire Fraser Valley, between the little town of Hope and Vancouver, is only 150 kilometres long; it takes only a couple of hours to drive from one end to the other. The Fraser River cuts right through the middle, and until you begin to enter the communities that make up the outskirts of Vancouver, the two biggest towns on the north side of the river are Mission and Maple Ridge; on the south side they are Abbotsford and Chilliwack.

So if you follow the Lougheed Highway west from Maple Ridge past Pitt Meadows, cross the little trestle bridge over the Pitt River and drive past Ottawa Street (the central road that leads through a vast shopping centre to Dominion Avenue and the Pickton farm) into the small town of Port Coquitlam, you'll pass on your right, at the intersection of Shaughnessy and the Lougheed, the building where Louise and Leonard Pickton ran their meat shop for many years. And if you stay on the Lougheed heading west until it connects to the Barnet Highway at the edge of Coquitlam and turns south, and keep going straight west on the Barnet Highway through Port Moody, you'll pass just a block north of the store where Willie bought all his butchering knives and where he had them sharpened.

By now you're running along the southern edge of Burrard Inlet. With the North Shore Mountains across the inlet, it's a beautiful drive until the Barnet runs into Burnaby and changes its name to Hastings Street. Within a few minutes you're into Vancouver proper and in a working-class neighbourhood where shabby industrial warehouses and small factories crowd the edges of a vast port area. Unless it's rush hour, from Port Coquitlam to this point the drive takes no more than thirty minutes.

It's when Hastings crosses Victoria Drive that you're really in the Downtown Eastside. Turn right on Victoria and drive north towards the inlet and you're in the heart of what people called, until very recently, the "kiddie stroll" because it was once the haunt of teenage prostitutes. Drive west along Hastings for two more blocks, turn north onto Commercial Drive, and you'll end up facing the bulky cement towers of Rogers Sugar and West Coast Reduction, squatting side by side on the water's edge.

Around West Coast Reduction and Rogers Sugar lies a sombre neighbourhood of low, old factories and bleak warehouses, some hiding small but very profitable pornographic film studios. A decayed little blue clapboard house, askew on its foundations, was an infamous crack den; one stucco-clad warehouse had rooms where sex-trade workers could bring their tricks. Few cars pass, there are almost no coffee shops or convenience stores, and the solitary pedestrians you do see, day or night, are almost all women, standing alone on a corner or huddled under an umbrella, pacing up and down the street. Today the kiddie stroll is called the Franklin stroll after Franklin Street, the heart of the prostitution business in this area. And sometimes it's called the tranny stroll, thanks to all the transsexuals who ply their wares along these streets. Late at night, if a woman or a tranny gets into trouble along these four or five blocks, will anyone pay attention to her screams or even hear them? Probably not.

But if you continue west along Hastings another six or seven blocks, things change. This is the Downtown Eastside you see on television news and in the movies. At Hastings and Vernon—1690 East Hastings, to be exact—is a rundown three-storey stucco and clapboard building that is closed now but was once home to women who had run right out of whatever luck they had left. Its real name was the Vernon Rooms but the women called it the "Ho Den." If you made it this far down you were probably so addicted, so infected with hep A, B or C and HIV, so scarred and scabbed, so thin and sick that the only tricks left were the nightmare men, especially the Vietnamese gang members, the ones the women whispered about to each other in the dark, the men suspected of making snuff films.

Doug Vickers, an associate of the Hells Angels, ran the place, and God help the women if they didn't buy their drugs from him or his managers in the hotel and if they didn't turn over ten or twenty bucks for every trick they took to their rooms; he would order a beating they never forgot. A hotel just as notorious as the Vernon Rooms was the Marr—another Hells Angel hotel famous for its bar and its brutality and now closed, thank God—which sits on the corner of Oppenheimer Park.

Further west the street is livelier, crowded, well lit, with small shops, diners and bars and low-rent hotels. At Hastings and Gore, where First United Church volunteers feed the poor, collect their mail, write their Christmas cards, fill out their tax forms, find them clothes, wash their feet and bury their dead, waves of people flood in and out all day long, sleep in the pews of the sanctuary and find a cup of coffee and some words of kindness from the people ministering to this desperate flock.

The church lends space to WISH, the Women's Information Safe House, an evening drop-in centre for sex-trade workers that runs Monday through Friday; they come for a hot meal, a shower, free clothes and companionship. And the reason so many come in every night—sometimes more than a hundred at a time—is that police and local politicians pushed the prostitutes out of safer residential and tourist areas in the 1970s and 1980s and kept them corralled in the far more dangerous streets of the Downtown Eastside.

Gordon Campbell, who was Vancouver's mayor in the late 1980s, was unapologetic about the strategy, telling reporters Neal Hall and Kim Pemberton it was unfortunate that prostitutes were being attacked and killed but citizens wanted them off the streets. "We do not want hookers around our high schools or our elementary schools," Campbell said. "We do not want them in our parks, we do not want them in our residential neighbourhoods." Then, as now, it was considered better to keep them in one neighbourhood, the poorest one in the city, than to let them set up shop where respectable people lived.

Prostitutes weren't the only ones who gravitated to the Downtown Eastside. So did thousands of psychiatric patients from hospitals such

as Coquitlam's Essondale and Riverview, who were deinstitutional-
ized by provincial governments in the 1970s. The Downtown Eastside
was the only place where they could afford to live and where they felt
welcome. Then, when cocaine became as widely available as heroin,
more drug users arrived, bringing with them more crime. .

It became easy to forget the area's historic origins as a place
where loggers and fishermen and sailors could come for a few days
of leave, find a cheap hotel, drink their fill in the local bar and find a
woman for sex. It had been a busy working-class community, with
plenty of banks, large department stores and decent hotels. When
Woodward's, the last remaining big department store in the area,
closed in 1992, it marked the end of the Downtown Eastside's fragile prosperity and respectability.

It doesn't take long to figure out that the worst hellholes in the area
are the single-room occupancy hotels (SROs) in which the prostitutes, addicts and crazy people live. North on the parallel streets
of Cordova, Powell and Alexander and around Oppenheimer Park
between Heatley and Columbia, the women and the dealers are busy
in their negotiations for sex or drugs. These are the streets where
many of the women live in tiny rooms in cramped, fetid SROs that
are just a step or two up from the Ho Den.

Here a dozen rooms can share one bathroom on each floor. The
occupants often fence stolen goods—whether it's a case of Ensure or
a carton of cigarettes or a bottle of shampoo—to the hotel manager
to pay for their drugs, which they just as often have to buy from the
same manager. These are the same managers who extort ten or twenty
dollars from every visitor who comes to see a woman living here.
Although the "guest fee" system is against the law and no landlord
anywhere else would get away with the practice, this is what happens here. Some of the busier hotels even have an informal fence for
each floor, someone who takes the goods the women steal and gives
them a fraction of their value to buy drugs. Most of the SROs have
problems with rats, cockroaches and bedbugs. Most are filthy. And

even the fixed-up Hazelwood on Hastings, which has private baths with the rooms, takes twenty-five dollars from anyone visiting a woman living there.

The most disgraceful scam is the way most of the hotels in the Downtown Eastside deal with welfare cheques. The monthly cost of a hotel room is $350, which is exactly the monthly shelter allotment that welfare gives its recipients. The hotel operators pay these recipients as little as forty or fifty dollars a month to buy their welfare allotment from them. But then they rent the same room to another addict, going through the same process of buying the shelter allotment from her. The operators will do this again and again for the same room, and in the meantime, the addict is homeless. Many of the hotels are run by organized crime—Hells Angels, the Russian mafia, Vietnamese gangs—and the addicts are too frightened to say no to them. Some of these places have only forty or fifty rooms but will sell three or four hundred rooms a month.

The Vancouver police used to go after the provincial welfare system, asking them to stop paying the corrupt hotel operators. "It created insurmountable homelessness problems," explained Elaine Allan, who is today the executive director of Shelternet BC, a provincial agency that helps organizations house homeless people. "It is blatant fraud that costs taxpayers millions of dollars a year. The police told me that each time they contacted the welfare office to report these frauds, the office would tell them that it was not the responsibility of the welfare system to police the hotels."

Many of the hotels along Hastings Street, including the Astoria, the Balmoral, the Savoy and the Patricia, to name a few, have bars on the ground floor. Men and women with nothing else to do hang out in these bars all day long, moving from one to the next, swapping gossip and sharing drugs and booze. There is less business on the streets south of Hastings, on Pender, Keefer and Georgia; this is Chinatown, and on the surface at least it is tidy, organized, under control, minding its own business.

Everything comes together a block west of First United, at the corner of Hastings and Main, the four corners of the Downtown Eastside. On the southwest corner is the Carnegie Centre, once one of Andrew Carnegie's most elegant public libraries, with swirling marble staircases and soaring stained glass windows. Today it is the community centre for what everyone now knows is the poorest postal code in Canada. It's a gathering place in times of crisis and grief, and its coffee shop, staffed by parolees and ex-cons trying to get work experience, offers good, cheap food. The building is crowded with the wretched and the mentally ill, who are all treated with tenderness and courtesy and cheerfulness by the people who work there, including four hundred volunteers.

Kitty-corner across the street and just north of Hastings is 212 Main, the police headquarters for the area; tucked up right beside it is the local courthouse, known as "222 Main." And across the street from the courthouse, at 223 Main, is DEYAS, the Downtown Eastside Youth Activities Society, better known as the needle exchange, the place that gives out hundreds of thousands of free needles to intravenous drug users every year and sends its vans around the neighbourhood to distribute free needles and pick up old ones. (Since 2003 there has also been a controversial safe injection site, called InSite, where as many as 700 people a day go to inject with clean needles in a trusting atmosphere and speak to a nurse or counsellor. For many of the most marginalized people in the neighbourhood, who tend to be older and with chronic addiction, this is where they receive primary health care.)

DEYAS is also part of this story. Run by former addict John Turvey until illness forced his retirement in 2004,* DEYAS was for years the real power centre in the Downtown Eastside. Turvey ran it with an iron fist, assisted by three others: his wife, Deb Mearns, who was in charge of the community policing office; Judy McGuire, Turvey's second-in-command at DEYAS; and a Vancouver Police

---

*John Turvey died on October 11, 2006, and DEYAS was shut down in 2009, mired in debt and facing serious questions of mismanagement.

Department cop, Dave Dickson, the local community police officer. Throughout the 1990s these four people effectively controlled the lives of most of the inhabitants of the Downtown Eastside.

Drifting back and forth along these few blocks of Hastings, day and night, is a muttering, aggressive crowd of drug dealers—dozens of them, selling heroin and cocaine at $10 a point, which is a tenth of a gram; an eight ball of powdered cocaine for about $350; rocks of crack (rocks cost about $10 each but dealers prefer to sell it in $20 chunks); and T&Rs—a mixture of Talwin, a painkiller, with Ritalin, a stimulant—known as the "poor man's speedball" because they cost only $2 (true speedballs are a $20 mix of heroin and cocaine packed in tiny envelopes called "flaps"). Some dealers stuff their cheeks with spitballs—drug hits wrapped in plastic; sometimes you see cops squeezing their jaws to force out the tiny packages.

Who's buying? Along with the neighbourhood's addicts, it's regular folks from better areas of town who drive along and stop their cars just long enough to get their drugs. If they have the money they'll often buy an eight ball—three and a half grams of powdered cocaine they can snort or mix with heroin if they prefer a speedball (crack cocaine is smoked in a pipe). It is, as people say, an open drug market, and the presence of police in cruisers or on foot does nothing to stop it. The small-time dealers moving up and down the street are just the public face of the drug trade here; what is harder to see is the major presence of Asian gangs, Colombian drug lords, the Russian mafia and, always, the Hells Angels.

The reeking alleys cutting through each block, the empty flaps and used condoms, the broken needles and junk-food wrappers, the devastated human beings hauled away in ambulances—the horror and sadness of the Downtown Eastside are not the whole story. Anyone can walk safely down Hastings Street. Anyone can drop into the Ovaltine, sit in a booth near cops and prosecutors and social workers and junkies and get a grilled cheese and a cup of coffee, and they'll be good. Anyone can move around the neighbourhood without being assaulted. At the corner of Hastings and Carroll is the Radio Station Café, a cheerful little joint with cheap, decent food, several free computers hooked up to the Internet and a laundromat. It was set up by Mark Townsend's Portland Hotel Society, which provides better accommodation, medical services and other assistance to the down-and-out in the community. They have even started a small bank kitty-corner from the café that will cash cheques and let high-risk poor customers open bank accounts—a necessity after the failure of the much larger Four Corners Bank at Hastings and Main, which had tried to do the same thing.

While no one can agree on the percentage of Aboriginal women living in the Downtown Eastside—estimates range from ten percent of the population to forty percent—the most reliable number appears to be between ten and fourteen percent. In the case of the community's missing women, nearly a third of them were of Aboriginal descent.

In spite of its difficulties, there is still a strong sense of community here. People know and look out for each other. The gossip, the good times, the shared meals and experiences make it a neighbourhood. The prostitutes make their rooms cozy with pictures of their children and coffee mugs and pillows and throws. Webbed dream catchers, often woven with bits of bone, glass, silver or feathers, hang in their windows to let the good dreams float through and catch the bad dreams that will die at dawn. The women, even those who are not Native, make them for each other and for their children, and they work tiny seed beads on looms to fashion bracelets and pins. But most precious, their lifeline, carefully stowed in secret corners of their spaces, is their identity—the Money Mart card needed to cash a cheque, the health card, the birth certificate, snapshots of their children.

You won't want to live on skid row, but spend some time here and you'll understand why people stay and why outsiders can't resist coming back. And you'll also see that there is a direct line from the Pickton farm in Port Coquitlam to the corner of Hastings and Main.

CHAPTER SIX

COPS UNDER FIRE

In the early 1980s, Kim Pemberton was a young but experienced police reporter at the *Vancouver Sun*. She'd turn up at the daily police briefings, and whenever a new female homicide was announced—and it happened often during these years—she never made it easy for the cops.

"Was she a prostitute?" she'd ask every time. The result was always the same: a certain rolling of eyes and exasperated sighs.

"The police were not interested in prostitute murders and they were loath to connect these murders to prostitutes," she says. "They were also loath to talk about serial killers."

Why? Simple. Serial killer investigations are almost always long, expensive and difficult. When the victims are throwaways, which is the way so many people saw these women, it's almost impossible to get the resources to manage the case. Yet in Vancouver in the 1980s, the police actually knew the identity of one serial killer who was still active: Gilbert Paul Jordan, an alcoholic barber with a long and serious criminal record of sexual assaults. Jordan would pick up destitute Native prostitutes, force them to drink a lethal amount of alcohol and then watch them die.

"The police would say, 'Oh, we have another Jordanesque,'" remembers Pemberton. "And what they meant by that comment was they'd found another dead Native woman poisoned by alcohol. Any body, in fact, found with high alcohol content was considered 'Jordanesque.' They knew who was doing it. But there was definitely a social hierarchy of those worth investigating—or not."

A team of *Sun* reporters that included Pemberton, Chris Rose and Bob Sarti decided to look at all the Jordanesque deaths, which had begun, as far as they could prove, in 1965 and would end in 1988. They enlisted the help of B.C.'s chief coroner at the time, Larry Campbell, a former RCMP drug squad officer who had worked on the Jordan case himself; he let them page through all his files.

"We looked for all the deaths with high alcohol readings," remembers Pemberton. The links they found between Jordan and the murdered women embarrassed the Vancouver Police Department (VPD) into a formal investigation; eventually they concluded that Jordan had killed at least ten women.

"Down the hatch, baby," Jordan is said to have coaxed one woman. "I'll give you ten dollars, twenty, fifty, whatever you want. Come on. I want to see you get it all down." But his murder charges were dropped to manslaughter. In 1988 he was finally convicted on one count of manslaughter, and he served six years in prison.*

Jordan wasn't the only one, of course. Throughout the 1980s Pemberton and another *Sun* reporter, Neal Hall, worked on other prostitute murders, but they were always fighting police apathy.

"We kept pressing. 'Aren't you going to do anything?'" Pemberton asked one senior homicide investigator. "You're not putting any resources on these murders."

He looked at her. "I'd rather solve one Aaron Kaplan over a dozen prostitutes." Aaron Kaplan was a two-year-old who'd been taken from his bed in Point Grey, a well-to-do district of Vancouver, and murdered.

So many women's bodies had been found by the mid-1980s that in 1987 the RCMP finally set up a special team. Twelve officers were assigned to investigate seventeen unsolved homicides going back to 1981. But they got stuck. It wasn't for a lack of suspects.

* *After Jordan's release in 1994 he was arrested again several times in western Canada, and public warnings were issued by the police. The last time was in Victoria, B.C., in 2005, but he has not been convicted of murder.*

There were plenty of those; what they didn't have was enough evidence to charge anyone. In 1989 the Mounties finally disbanded the unit, even though the killings and disappearances continued.

When the police gave up, Pemberton and Hall continued to write about the dead prostitutes. "We were trying to show they were human," said Pemberton. "We found their families and we tried to paint pictures of these women. They were somebody's mom, somebody's daughter . . . but the cops we were dealing with were racist and sexist and they all had grade twelve educations."

Larry Campbell was one of the few people with any authority who would help them. "I refuse to accept that anyone in our society is a throwaway," was what he said to reporter Ken McQueen, who was working for the *Sun* in those days.

On February 4, 1989, Pemberton and Hall wrote about three murdered prostitutes; one was found in a back alley, one in some bushes, one in an industrial lot. Since 1982, wrote Pemberton, fourteen women had been killed: eight strangled, five stabbed, one bound and tortured. All fourteen cases remained unsolved. "Is there," they asked, "a Ted Bundy or a Green River–style killer on the loose, preying on women?"

Staff Sergeant Bob Law of VPD Major Crime told them he didn't believe a serial killer was at work, although he conceded that the growing number of prostitute murders was alarming and that similarities in the way the women were killed might suggest one person was responsible. RCMP Inspector Bruce Terkelson said that the Mounties' special unit for unsolved female homicides had found no evidence to support the theory of a serial killer.

The group at risk—the prostitutes themselves—also tried to get the murders taken seriously. They gave the police descriptions of the men, or "tricks," as they are known, who attacked them, and they kept "bad trick" sheets with records of assaults, robberies and attacks by many of their customers. Most of the time they also had the licence plate numbers. By 1989 the reports from prostitutes to the police had grown to seventy—from forty in 1987.

Although the police said they reviewed the trick sheets carefully, nothing happened.

Along with all the unsolved homicides was the fact that from 1979 on, several other women had simply vanished altogether. Among the missing women Pemberton and Hall listed was Wendy Louise Allen, thirty-four, who had disappeared on March 30, 1979. Allen would become the earliest disappearance in the missing-women lists that appeared in the late 1990s.* She was followed by Rebecca Guno, twenty-three, who disappeared on June 22, 1983. Yvonne Marlene Abigosis, forty-four, who grew up in Brokenhead, Manitoba, was last seen on January 1, 1984. By the end of that same month, Sherry Rail, who was only eighteen and had long light brown hair, green eyes and a butterfly tattoo on her left shoulder blade, had also disappeared.

Was Robert "Willie" Pickton involved in any of these cases? Police officers don't rule him out but are cautious about stating anything definite about his activities during the early eighties. Other people disagree. In 2004, for example, one woman posted a note to an online newsmagazine stating that Pickton had assaulted a friend of hers twenty years earlier.

"I was speaking with a friend of mine about this who escaped from the clutches of Robert Pickton in his early years when she lived on the street in Vancouver," the woman wrote. "She was then a runaway from a molester adopted father and felt safer on the street than at home where social services had kept sending her back to. She actually did not remember the guy's name who had tried to kidnap her and who assaulted her. A couple of years ago, she decided to charge her father and had gotten all her records from Children and Families [Services]. When perusing them she found a police report with her statement of kidnapping and assault charges against Pickton.

---

*In 2006 Wendy Louise Allen was found alive in Ontario under an assumed name but did not want to contact her relatives or friends, nor did she want the news media told.

This was over twenty years ago now, and it has greatly disturbed her . . . they did nothing to Pickton back then about it, and the only thing done was that she was forced to go back home or go to a youth detention centre.

"Now she has had the case re-opened and wants heads to roll. She feels if something would have been done 20 years ago instead of punishing her for nothing, maybe dozens of women would still be alive.

"Today, I know she feels fortunate that she literally escaped, but is in anguish that her memory of it was lost in her struggles to get away from her family and to recover from them and living on the streets. She feels great anger towards the social workers and Vancouver Police. Because she had noted in her statement, in the early 80's, that the rumour was out he was beating, confining and maybe murdering prostitutes. In a sense, she feels she failed these murdered women by blocking that time out of her life so completely."

In October 1984, forty-nine-year-old Linda Louise Grant, a native of Port Moody, went missing. She had moved to the United States in 1983 after losing custody of her two daughters, Dawn and Briana. Her parents and friends had no idea where she had gone and reported her missing in 1984.*

Next was Laura Mah, a small aboriginal woman born on March 23, 1943. She was forty-two years old when she disappeared on August 1, 1985. She was followed that same year by Sheryl Donahue, thirty-nine, who came originally from Victoria. Donahue, a white woman with long blond hair, blue eyes and a sunny grin, was last seen on May 30, 1985, and reported missing on August 31. What is so tragic about Mah and Donahue is that so little is known about them. Yes, they vanished, but unlike most of the other missing women, they seem to have gone without leaving any sense of who

---

Linda Grant was also found alive, in June 2006; she came forward when she saw a reference to herself on the Internet.

they really were, whom they loved and who loved them, where they came from, what happened to them to put them in the Downtown Eastside.

Eight months later, on March 13, 1986, Elaine Allenbach, twenty-one, vanished. Allenbach, a lively young woman with long auburn hair, used a couple of names—Lisa Marie Morrison and Nancy Boyd. Most of her friends believed she was on her way to Seattle when she disappeared, because she often travelled between the two cities. Her friends also mentioned a diary she'd kept that could have incriminated various people, but say another prostitute broke into her apartment, found the diary and burned it. A friend explained it this way: "Maybe things have changed now that these women have seen so many of their friends disappear, but I know that fear rules most of their worlds . . . and they tend to keep their mouths shut and protect those that they fear most."

More than two years after Allenbach disappeared so did Taressa Ann Williams, who was just fifteen but the mother of two children. In her case the police had a few clues. A Native, Williams had run away from home with her best friend when they were only thirteen; she was on the streets of the Downtown Eastside almost right away, trying to survive. She was last seen on July 21, 1988, and when the police found her leg bone later the same year, in a park near West Coast Reduction, they had no way to identify it as hers until many years later.

In 1989 thirty-four-year-old Elaine Dumba, who had moved to Vancouver from Regina, disappeared; she was an addicted sex-trade worker who lived in the Downtown Eastside. She came from a large family in Saskatchewan and left behind a mother, two sisters and a brother, cousins, aunts and uncles and grandparents—all of whom worried about her and missed her. "She was dearly loved," said one cousin, "dearly loved. It was terrible for her family." The grief, even after all these years, is still sharp, and they don't want to talk about her.

There is more known about Ingrid Soet, from Burnaby, who was thirty and had been diagnosed with schizophrenia. Soet, who was blond, about five feet seven inches tall and about 111 pounds, was last seen on August 28, 1989. "She just disappeared," her mother, Mary, told a reporter. "She said 'see you later' and went to visit her boyfriend and never came back." After a psychic whom Mary Soet consulted in desperation told her that Ingrid was living on British Columbia's Sunshine Coast near Gibson's Landing, the Soets scoured the area. The exercise was futile but the Soets didn't give up hope, because Ingrid didn't fit the profile of the other missing women—she wasn't an addict and she wasn't a prostitute.

By this time, in 1989, a group made up mostly of aboriginal women living in the Downtown Eastside was just starting to come together to lobby the police for action on the missing and murdered women of Vancouver's Downtown Eastside. These were the victims' friends and families as well as advocates for sex-trade workers, a group that had been largely ignored or waved away as a nuisance. They tried to make sure that women working as prostitutes acted as spotters for each other, noting licence plates and descriptions of men as well as dates, times and locations. They nagged the police and tried to report women to the Vancouver Police Department's Missing Persons Unit, most of the time without any effect. In February 1991 the women established an annual Valentine's Day remembrance walk that started at the Carnegie Centre, a walk fuelled as much by rage against police indifference as it was by grief for the victims.

The Vancouver police may not have been interested in dead and missing prostitutes, but by 1991 the RCMP was willing to try again. Instead of setting up another lengthy investigation, they imported a team of highly trained criminal profilers to see if a fresh approach would help. At this time, profilers, who examine the behaviour of serial killers to find clues to their identities, were a new brand of cop viewed with disdain by most homicide detectives, especially those at the VPD, who believed knocking on doors, interviewing witnesses, matching fingerprints and examining motive and opportunity were the elements of the grind that solved heinous crimes. The profilers, known today as criminal investigative analysts, wouldn't disagree with the traditional methods of collecting evidence; in fact, they always insist they don't solve crimes and that the skills they offer are just another tool in the process. By studying the kind of victim chosen by a serial predator and by looking at the style and method of killing, they believe they help homicide detectives learn even more about the killer—his age, perhaps, or his education, income level, interests, family background, even what he might do for a living.

An agent named Howard Teten from the Federal Bureau of Investigation was probably the first criminal profiler. He helped to set up the FBI's Behavioral Science Unit in 1972; his successors, John Douglas and Robert Ressler, were pioneers in understanding serial killers, simply because they decided to start interviewing them to see what made them tick. Their subjects, most of whom were only too happy to relieve the tedium of a jail cell with some conversation about their past triumphs, included Ed Kemper, convicted of ten murders in California; Charles Manson, whose followers killed actress Sharon Tate; David Berkowitz, the Son of Sam killer in New York; and the Boston Strangler, Richard Speck. None of these men were executed, but Speck died of a heart attack in 1991. Kemper, Manson and Berkowitz are still serving life sentences in prison.

For years Douglas and Ressler talked to men like these on death row or serving life sentences in prisons across the United States to find out what motivated them, what had happened to them to turn them into such dangerous predators, and even how they planned and carried out their gruesome deeds. By 1984 the two had convinced their bosses to set up a centre within the FBI's Quantico Behavioral Science Unit to train profilers, not just to hunt serial killers but to help police forces in the United States and other countries find dangerous predators, whether they were stalkers, rapists, serial killers, arsonists, bombers, terrorists or kidnappers. Part of the help they offered was advice in interviewing suspects, advice gleaned from Douglas's and Ressler's interviews with serial killers themselves.

By the early 1980s, FBI profilers were welcomed by many police forces, but there were still plenty of skeptics around. This attitude changed dramatically in February 1991. Moviegoers were lining up for the new Jodie Foster hit, *The Silence of the Lambs,* which starred Anthony Hopkins as the terrifying serial killer Hannibal Lecter. The movie was based on the 1988 novel by Thomas Harris; its hero, played by John Gregg, was Jack Crawford, a character built around the real-life John Douglas. Foster played Clarice Starling, a young police officer training under Crawford's watchful eye. The book had been such a hit that the movie was under way by 1989 and finished in late 1990; as soon as it came out everyone knew what a profiler could do. To this day there are many police officers who don't believe in profiling, but it is now a standard part of difficult homicide investigations, especially cold cases—murder investigations that have gone stale and been dropped after months or years of work.

Thanks to the FBI, Canada had a few profilers too. RCMP inspector Ron MacKay, a highly regarded homicide investigator who worked in Vancouver for many years before moving to Ottawa, had been among the original scoffers, but in 1989, when the FBI offered to train foreign police officers in a program that lasted almost a year, MacKay agreed to go. A year later he emerged a believer, as the RCMP's first and only profiler, and quickly developed an international reputation for his skills. He became the model for Tony Hill, the hero of Scottish crime writer Val McDermid's successful series of novels that were eventually turned into a BBC series called *Wire in the Blood.*

MacKay was followed in 1990 by Kate Lines, a senior detective at the Ontario Provincial Police (OPP) headquarters in Orillia, but the next year, for budgetary reasons, the FBI decided to stop training foreign officers. It was a disappointment for Canadian hopefuls, but MacKay helped to train Keith Davidson, a young Mountie based in Vancouver. Before long Davidson and Lines helped to set up an international group of profilers to train people, an association that exists to this day.

The RCMP was disturbed by the Vancouver police's failure to find the persons responsible for the cold cases going back to the early 1980s, so the assignment they gave MacKay and Davidson was to analyze twenty-five unsolved murders of prostitutes. Like all RCMP projects in British Columbia, which is the force's E Division, this one was given a name that began with the letter E; it was called Project Eclipse. While they were trying to decide the best way to proceed, another woman vanished.

The last time anyone saw Nancy Clark, who worked under the street name of Nancy Greek, was on August 22, 1991, when she was spied about midnight, working the stroll on the corner of Broughton and Gordon streets in downtown Victoria. She was just twenty-five years old, had a tattoo of lilies and a butterfly on her left wrist and lived with her two little girls, one just an eight month-old baby and the other, Amber, eight years old. Clark disappeared on Amber's birthday, something that was completely out of character for a woman who was devoted to her children. Grant Smith, a former deputy police chief who knew Clark, described her as a caring and responsible woman. "It was out of the norm for her to be missing and not let her loved ones know where she was," he said later.

Clark's mother, Kathryn Derkson, brought the children to live with her after her daughter disappeared. She told people that Amber wouldn't let her out of her sight. "I don't want you to go missing like Mommy," she would tell her.

What the police didn't know was that just about this time, Willie Pickton made a rare trip to a Vancouver Island job site with some of the men who worked for his brother, Dave, on demolition projects. They took the ferry and Willie drove his own van.

MacKay and Davidson decided to hold a one-week brainstorming blitz from October 17 to 24, 1991, and brought in five other profilers to help. Kate Lines was one of them. She was so highly regarded that not long afterwards she was appointed chief superintendent of the

OPP's eighty-person Behavioural Sciences Unit, which routinely helps police forces across Canada on the most difficult unsolved cases.

John Edward (Eddie) Grant of the New York State Police also came; who is now retired and living in Tennessee, he was already well-known for working on two cases. The first was that of Arthur Shawcross, who murdered eleven women (and ate parts of their bodies) in upstate New York in the 1980s. The second was Long Island serial killer Joel Rifkin, who murdered seventeen women before his arrest in 1993.

Another participant was Dave Caldwell, a state police officer with the South Carolina Law Enforcement Division. He became famous in police circles three years later as the officer who interviewed Susan Smith before she confessed to murdering her young boys by deliberately letting her car slide down a boat ramp into a lake. The final two were Jim Wright and Gregg McCrary, both leaders with the FBI's Quantico unit. Today each is well-known in the United States, Wright for his commentaries on Court TV and McCrary most recently for his work in 2002 on the Washington sniper case.

Then there was the young Canadian officer from the Vancouver Police Department. Kim Rossmo, a constable with eight years' experience in the Downtown Eastside, was a gifted mathematician and computer analyst who had just started to develop a subspecialty he called geographic profiling, which involved linking a predator to his crime through geographical analysis. The idea, he explained to the senior detectives, was that serial offenders tended to work in areas they knew, where they felt comfortable, so if you looked at a list of suspects for a series of crimes your prime suspect would be the person who lived closest to where the crimes occurred. During the week Rossmo took his colleagues on a crime tour of Vancouver, impressing the Americans with his knowledge and insight.

By the end of the week the profilers had sorted the prostitute murders into different groups based on linkages among them. The largest cluster of murders they linked was four in Vancouver. There were several groups of two and one potential of three but the rest, they concluded, were not related to any of the other twenty-five cases they reviewed.

On October 23, near the end of Project Eclipse, the profilers gathered in the theatre of E Division headquarters, on West 37th Avenue in Vancouver, with the large group of investigators of all the unsolved female missing and homicide cases in the Lower Mainland. The room was full and the profilers were excited. They could hardly wait to share their analysis with the other officers. MacKay's results were stunning; as far as the team was concerned, with a cluster of four linked murders he had found a serial killer at work, and there could be two others out there as well. There was a discussion about the best way to put forward their results.

"Let's present our findings orally first," suggested MacKay to the team. "Then we can mail our written reports to the appropriate investigators."

That's what they did, and it was a complete flop. The presentations fell flat and none of the Vancouver Police Department investigators called MacKay back about the four linked cases he had written up. "I think the idea of using a profile to refocus a cold case was just too new in 1991," MacKay says today.

Kim Rossmo is less diplomatic. "Project Eclipse was telling the VPD, 'You have at least one serial killer here and maybe two or three.' But the VPD was not jumping up to take on serial murder cases when they were handed to them. Why? Laziness, lack of resources, the cost, the energy required—but most of all, no road map. The profile didn't say what to do next."

No road map. In other words, the VPD homicide officers needed a to-do list. But Rossmo points out that these cases require a lot of thought about how to proceed. "I really believe a lot of investigators don't really know how to do it. They're out of their depth."

Rossmo hit the nail on the head. The chilly reception of Project Eclipse was probably due to the simple fact that the Vancouver police did not have the first idea how to start and run an investigation into serial killings. Bluster, bravado and eye-rolling disguised ignorance.

If there was any comfort or good news to be had from Project Eclipse it was the fact that this was the first time a group of international profilers had brainstormed together, sharing information in such a creative manner. It opened the way for future collaboration that exists to this day.

Yet the project failed to change the way local police looked at the murders in the Downtown Eastside. Investigations went back to business as usual. Rossmo reflected with chagrin on something that had happened just as the Project Eclipse team was making its presentations to the homicide detectives. Something that showed Rossmo just what profilers were up against. Rossmo had been taking a class with Neil Boyd, a criminology professor at Simon Fraser University and an expert on violent crime. "I saw a thing on TV last night," he told Rossmo one day. "It was about a guy called David Milgaard. But it didn't fit."

The "thing" Boyd had seen was a CBC *Fifth Estate* documentary about a sixteen-year-old boy who had been convicted of the 1969 brutal rape and stabbing death of a young Winnipeg woman, Gail Miller. Milgaard was serving a life sentence in Manitoba's Stony Mountain Penitentiary, but the conclusion drawn by the program was that another man, Larry Fisher, was the more likely murderer. The story caused newspaper headlines, drew questions in the House of Commons and intrigued Boyd and Rossmo. They decided it was worth a look.

"So we go to Stony Mountain," remembers Rossmo, "and interview Milgaard, and then we interviewed all the witnesses, the cops and everyone else involved. When we got back, a couple of VPD detectives on Major Crime came in to discuss their cases and one of them said they noticed my involvement in the Milgaard case in the paper.

"And he asks, 'What are you doing with this?'

"I said there were lots of reasons to think Milgaard is innocent. And then he said to me, 'This isn't the sort of thing we do.'"

"'It's not what we do'?" Rossmo shot back. "Then you and I have a fundamental difference of opinion on what it is the police do."*

In the meantime, however, it was still 1991 and the Vancouver Police Department was floundering and defensive about the useless exercise they had just gone through with a bunch of smart-assed profilers who couldn't prove squat.

*A year after this conversation the Supreme Court of Canada set aside Milgaard's conviction and he was released from prison; five years later, DNA tests done in England proved he had not killed Gail Miller. The Saskatchewan government apologized and agreed to pay Milgaard $10 million for serving twenty-three years in prison for a crime he did not commit. And two years after that, Larry Fisher was convicted for Miller's murder.

CHAPTER SEVEN

A MOTLEY CREW

While the police in Vancouver were still insisting that any discussion of a serial killer in the Downtown Eastside was a waste of time, the Pickton brothers in Port Coquitlam continued their uneasy partnership on the family farm. The place became filthier and more chaotic every day. What had once been a pretty piece of property, with trees, green fields and borders of flowering shrubs shielding the family from the neighbours on three sides, now, in the early 1990s, looked like a municipal dump. Spills from the trucks and heavy equipment covered the old laneway, the one they called Piggery Road, that ran from the front entrance on Dominion Avenue through the property to the back. Old fill of crushed glass, pavement and dirt, along with odd bits of machinery and other junk, littered the road, infuriating Willie. He was always shoving it out of the way, but the last straw was the crushed glass, which cut the tires of his vehicles. Dave just laughed it off.

One truck driver, who now works in the Alberta oil fields but who worked for Dave in the early 1990s, remembers hauling in loads of contaminated soil from Vancouver's Pacific Park, the site of Expo 86. The park site was needed for residential development, but research done for the federal government's Canada Mortgage and Housing Corporation discovered that before Expo 86 the land had been used for an oil-gasification plant, landfill and rail yards. The soil contained benzene, toluene and heavy metals as well as polycyclic aromatic hydrocarbons (PAHs), a pollutant derived from burning fossil fuels such as coal. In the case of the Expo lands, any soil with coal tar contents was dug up; some, if not all, was hauled away by Dave Pickton's drivers. "We just mixed it in with other dirt on the Pickton land and took it back out to deliver for soil orders," the trucker said.

Contaminated soil was only part of the story. Dave arranged for his truck drivers to pick up fuel tanks at old gas stations—tanks filled with diesel oil—and bury them on the Dominion Avenue property. Even driving the trucks was hazardous. Scott Chubb, one of the men who used to drive for Dave, remembers it well. "When I first started with Dave, there was no real equipment. I drove the dump truck with only two brakes that worked; I'd go down a hill with the horn on. One time I couldn't slow it down and I just tore through the intersection."

Chubb, who worked with his old buddy Marty de Wolfe to get Dave's soil and fill business started, said that Dave also expected his employees to steal cars and trucks for him. "One time Dave sent me to a car dealership for a one-time drive," Chubb said. "He gave me ten dollars to get a key made. Three days later the car was on the property. And I have stolen U-Haul trailers for him, and other trailers."

Chubb was just one of a motley crew of truck drivers assembled by Dave Pickton to work for D&S Bulldozing and his newest company, P&B Used Building Materials. P&B was a demolition business started originally by Lilac Fehlauer, the mother of Dave's ex-girlfriend Sandy, the mother of his two children. Sandy had stopped working for him by 1989; a year later, when her relationship with her newest boyfriend, Brent Curry, wasn't going well, she began working with her mother at P&B. Not long afterwards Dave Pickton bought P&B from Mrs. Fehlauer and moved its headquarters to property the brothers owned a few kilometres away, on Tannery Road in Surrey. Dave continued to run D&S from the farmhouse on Dominion Avenue, so his employees moved back and forth between the two places.

Al Trautmann, a long-time resident of the area and close to the Picktons, was one of these workers. A heavy drinker and always looking for a fight, he once thrashed Scott Chubb after Chubb called him a goof. But there seemed to have been no hard feelings; Chubb later said that Trautmann once told him a strange story about Willie

Pickton. Willie, Trautmann recounted, had told him that he had helped get rid of two bodies on the farm.

Then there were the Palmer brothers, Tim and Clarence. Tim didn't have much to say, but was still a heavy drinker, a party animal, and someone Dave could count on to bring him a vehicle, no questions asked. On one occasion one of Willie's pigs—a huge one, much feared by many of the regulars on the property—trapped Tim Palmer in the garage-workshop at the back of the property near Willie's trailer. Palmer clambered up onto the workbench, where he waited until someone was able to call Willie to come and rescue him. Clarence Palmer was chunkier than Tim, also liked his booze and had, as they say, a mouth on him. He was a hotshot and a womanizer. Both brothers dealt a little dope from time to time.

The crew also included Marty de Wolfe and a machine operator called Pancho, whose real name was Myles Nord. The Picktons knew that many of their workers were stealing from them, and Pancho was one of them; he took tools, car and truck parts and welders' gear. His main claim to fame, however, was that he ran over Dave Pickton with his truck, crushing his foot. It was supposed to be an accident, and is the reason Dave now walks with a noticeable limp.

All of these men knew how to drive trucks as well as run a backhoe, a BobCat and all the other large machines on the property. But the work for Dave's drivers was seasonal. Once the winter rains starting pelting the Lower Mainland, jobs were fewer and farther apart.

When he was a child, Scott Chubb had moved with his family to British Columbia from Alberta. He grew up in a blue-collar, five-church mountain village called Sparwood, an old East Kootenays coal-mining community in the Elk Valley. It's just a speck on the map if you're headed for Alberta along the Crowsnest Highway, the kind of place that gives prizes to the best-decorated trailers and balconies at Christmas. The kind of place where everyone knows everyone else, and where Scott Chubb once knew a girl at school named Angela Jardine. Their stories would collide many years later at the Pickton farm.

Bright, loquacious and good-looking, with thick brown hair, a wicked grin and lazy eyes, Chubb is very much a ladies' man. He wanted to get straight into working when he finished high school, so he learned to drive large trucks. But early on, drugs became part of his life, and by 1986 he was snorting cocaine. After kicking around the East Kootenays for a while, Chubb moved to Vancouver in 1994. Desperate for a job, he went into a government employment office and found a notice for a truck driver's job in Port Coquitlam. It was a good day: he got the job and it lasted a full nine months, seven days a week, driving trucks for Dave Pickton for a large excavation project in Burnaby.

The crews would meet at the Pickton farm, leave most of their cars there and drive together to the excavation site, where all the trucks and machinery were parked. The team worked every day; on Sunday, when traffic was down, they hauled the dirt and fill back to the Pickton farm. Once the workday was over, the drivers hung out together at the farmhouse, drinking, smoking a little dope, talking about women and motorcycles and their badass days. Even when the project ended and the men were picking up smaller demolition and short-term excavation jobs from Dave, they stayed close. The Pickton farm was the place they all went to to relax.

Willie was usually there, hanging around, trying to be friendly. He would offer meat from his freezers to the guys, and the Palmer brothers and Al Trautmann often took some. Trautmann complained once to Chubb that a roast he took home was inedible—"It had a rancid smell," he said.

When Dave hired these men for the smaller jobs with less predictable work hours, he paid them under the table, but that wasn't good enough for Chubb, who was by now fed up with part-time work. He moved to a new job, moonlighting for Dave when he could. "I worked on the machines every once in a while, the Cats and whatever, and sometimes he'd call me and it would be a part of a foreman crew. So I'd go out and take care of, like, ten, maybe fifteen guys at a time."

Dave Pickton was a tough, foul-mouthed, demanding boss but he was extremely intelligent, says Scott Chubb. His bids on large demolition projects, including schools and hotels in the Port Coquitlam area, the Fraser Valley and cities such as Squamish and Richmond, were always well-prepared and professional. "Dave might act like he's stupid, but he's smart," Chubb has said. "I think it was one of his little edges . . . that he acts like a fuckin' idiot but in actual fact he's no idiot; he's pretty bright."

But Dave also liked a good time. He cruised the Downtown Eastside and would bring women back to the farm, Chubb remembers. Women from the Downtown Eastside remember him too; they remember that he would buy dope for them but that he never used it.

There was one man Dave Pickton trusted above the rest, the only man whose loyalty he could count on without a flicker of doubt. This was Bill Malone, who had moved to the neighbourhood in 1971. Malone was an odd man, a single loner who was so devoted to the Picktons, especially to Dave, that he wound up as more of a personal informant, surveillance man and caretaker than anything else. Short and obese, given to covering his round gut with oversized short-sleeved shirts that hang over his pants, Malone has a round baby face with a small, petulant mouth, high, fat pink cheeks and a thick head of white hair.

Malone lived (and still lives) in a bungalow on Burns Road that was once the home of Tim Barrett and his family, just near the corner where Dominion Avenue meets the Pitt River dike. Not a car goes up the road that Malone doesn't know about; if he isn't home to watch himself he can review the vehicles later, thanks to the surveillance camera he mounted on the front of his house. He was always so suspicious and so anxious to please Dave Pickton that Dave began paying him to keep an eye on the farm and let him know who was coming and going. Malone was commonly thought to be gay, but Dave's protection meant that his drivers left him alone. Anyone else would have been tormented mercilessly.

Scott Baker was another young man who worked as a driver for Dave Pickton. His father, Westley Baker, a New Westminster gun dealer, was a member of Dave's inner circle. After Dave and Cathy Wayenberg split up in 1991, Dave began dating a woman named Kathy Arcand, but before long she dumped him for Wes Baker. If she wanted someone who could intimidate Dave Pickton, she had picked the right man. And Wes had picked the right woman—not only could Kathy drive her own Harley-Davidson with as much confidence as Dave drove his, she became knowledgeable enough about the weapons in Wes's military surplus store to allow him to open a second shop. Even the toughest bikers hanging out with Dave treated Wes and Kathy with deference.

Westley's Military Surplus, at 653 Front Street in New Westminster, wedged into a row of second-hand shops at the foot of a steep hill beside the city's railroad yards, is an armoury. While blown-glass floats and fishing nets decorate the front windows, inside it is crammed with shotguns, rifles, pistols, revolvers and every type of knife, as well as rounds of ammunition, clips and cartridges. There is just as wide a selection of swords, tomahawks and knives, including Ka-Bar knives—fighting knives designed for trench warfare that the United States Army issued to its forces—as well as skinner knives, bowie knives, bayonet knives, survival knives, commando daggers (a famous British fighting knife) and Colt combat knives. Then there are surveillance cameras, camouflage gear and camping supplies, night-vision goggles, police radios, handguns, AK-47s, Uzis. Military goods are a specialty; Wes is famous for his Second World War paraphernalia and claymore mines. His customers have included police officers, bikers and other organized-crime gang members and plain folks.

"People all over Surrey knew to go to Wes for guns in the 1980s," said one Pickton farm regular. "And Wes came out a lot to see Dave. Wes was very good friends with Bill Malone. I also heard the police would buy some of their own stuff from Wes. In fact, people thought he might be a police informant."

Two other people who were at the farm all the time were Dave's children by Sandy Fehlauer, Tammy and DJ. The pair moved back and forth, but they would spend months at a time at the farm. And DJ, who soon learned how to drive trucks, started hanging around with his dad's friends.

During these years Dave and Willie had figured out a way to work together on the farm property. Willie operated at the edges of his brother's gang of friends, most of them drivers, who would come back to the farm after a day of shoving dirt or tearing buildings down to drink and horse around. For most of them Willie barely registered; if they thought about him at all it was as an amiable goof, a man who stank, who was, as Dave used to say, "two tiles short of a load," who kept to himself. Yet they also knew him as a genius with vehicles. He could fix anything, coax the worst wreck into sputtering life, and cheerfully help them when their cars needed repair. Willie was good for a tow, an oil change, a flat tire, whatever.

But Willie got on his brother's nerves. During the years they lived together in the farmhouse after their mother's death, what infuriated Dave most was his brother's choice of visitors who dropped by the farm to say hello, particularly the women whom Dave dismissed as gold-diggers or hookers. "Dave was extremely rude and mouthy towards them," remembers Lisa Yelds, who was living in her small house nearby on Dominion Avenue. "He never had anything nice to say about them—they were beneath him."

Dave was paranoid as well, always on the lookout for police officers poking around his business, and he never hesitated to chase people he didn't know off the property. One former neighbour, a diehard jogger, lived nearby on a street called Barbary and often ran along a narrow path through the woods north of the farm, an area that later was razed for townhouses. One day he found the path blocked, so he cut through the trees and found himself at the back of the Pickton property.

"I cut through this farm," he remembers, "and noticed a house and some outbuildings and some barns, and when I was almost at Dominion, I heard people yelling at me. There were about ten people out on this balcony, men and women both. They looked really rough. They were standing on a deck at the side of the house and they were truly pissed off that I was there. And then I heard dogs barking. I started to really run and I jumped over the fence on the edge of the property at the road and tried to jump over the ditch there too, but my foot got caught and I landed in the creek."

It was Bill Malone who decided to keep trespassers out with threatening signs, including the one he posted on the Picktons' Dominion gate entrance: "PIT BULL WITH AIDS. NO TRESPASSING." No one thought much of it, not even the police. They were used to the Picktons.

Dave Pickton's paranoia meant that he also kept a sharp eye on the call display feature of the phone. And if he felt like barging into Willie's room anytime to snoop around, he did. So did the others who hung around the place. Kids and adults didn't hesitate to go through Willie's room when he was out, pilfering cash from his wallet or taking credit cards and his chequebooks. Willie knew who was stealing from him but Dave wouldn't enforce any rules about staying out of his room.

The bathroom was another bone of contention: there was only one in the farmhouse, and when Willie did have a bath, usually at the urging of Yelds, who would tell him to his face that he reeked and it was time to scrub himself down, he would have to endure the continual intrusion of other people. There was no lock on the door and it didn't seem to occur to anyone to install one. Then Dave would yell at Willie for using too much hot water.

In turn, Willie was foul-tempered. On one occasion he went berserk. The thing he hated most was getting doused with water—and that meant people liked starting water fights around him, making sure he got splashed and drenched and enjoying the sight of him jumping up and down, yelling in rage.

One of Dave's girlfriends was a player in this domestic mess. She told Dave she didn't want Willie in the house. "He creeps me out," she said. For her the last straw was the coarse ground pork that Willie donated to the family groceries every so often. Dave's son, DJ, would complain that it looked like earthworms.

Finally, after one particularly violent argument, Dave told Willie to leave the farmhouse and find another place to stay. He didn't care where he went—just get out. Willie made up a bed on top of a freezer in a shed on the property and stayed there for months. But soon Dave had worked out a solution that suited them both. Because equipment was being stolen from job sites, it made sense to buy a couple of used motorhomes to park on the sites; someone could stay there while the work was under way to keep an eye on everything. Willie could have one on the farm until they worked out something more permanent. His choice was a small, boxy Dodge Fargo DeSoto motorhome. The only door opened into the driver's and passenger's seat area; behind these was a narrow corridor dividing two bench seats and a table from a counter with a stove, sink and refrigerator. A tiny shower, toilet and sink and a narrow closet were beyond the table area, opposite a larger closet. And at the end were a pair of narrow beds on either side of the corridor, with a cabinet between them.

The brothers agreed that this would be Willie's place and moved it closer to the back of the property so that they could stay out of each other's way. Dave was happy; he could party all he liked in the farmhouse without his brother creeping out the other people who hung around. Willie was happy; now he had some privacy. But he never minded sharing his place with others.

One was Tanya Carr, a friend of Dave's daughter, Tammy, who had been boarding her horse on the farm for several years. Carr moved into the motorhome with Willie early in 1994 and stayed about eighteen months, until the fall of 1995. Carr's late stepfather, Merle Armstrong, not only had been a good friend of Dave's but had kept his pigs with Willie; they had worked together in the slaughtering business, often with Tanya's help. After Merle died in 1992 and

Pat Casanova began working with Willie in the pig business, Tanya continued to help with the slaughtering. At the same time, though, she was having some troubles; she was working as a waitress and needed a place to stay because she was in a bad relationship with her boyfriend, Scott Baker, Wes Baker's son. Willie didn't like Scott and warned her against him. Finally, after she and Scott broke up, he invited her to stay with him till she sorted herself out.

Short, blond and chubby, Tanya wasn't a girlfriend. She was just the first of many women who would live with Willie for a while as someone to help do laundry, answer the phone for orders from Dave and from people who wanted meat, and sweep out the place from time to time—not that cleanliness was ever high on Willie's list of priorities. She also went with him to about four auctions on week-ends, a mix of sales of things that interested him, including general estate auctions for household goods, as well as auctions for horses, cattle and other livestock and car auctions. (Willie's interest in auctions is one of the few he shares with his sister, Linda Wright, who is well-known among collectors in Vancouver for pawing through tables at flea markets and yard sales.)

For Tanya Carr, this eighteen-month period was like living with an uncle. She has always said there was no sex, even though they slept in the same room: she was on the narrow bed on the driver's side while Willie slept in the passenger-side bed. She worked at Amigo's Pancake House from eight a.m. to two p.m. and often came back to help Willie afterwards. At night she sometimes went out to bars, and when she got home Willie wouldn't be there. She didn't know where he went; all she knew was that he had plenty of work off the farm at various job sites. She assumed he was working late.

After she finally moved out to live with a new boyfriend, Tanya would return to the farm every day to feed and groom her horse and to help Willie with the pigs. Willie was a pal, someone she liked and trusted, someone who had helped her out when she needed it most. She says she knew nothing about the other life he was living and the women he was meeting in the Downtown Eastside. An exception was Gina Houston, a woman who became a fixture on the Pickton farm and in Willie's life.

"I was downtown partying with a girlfriend of mine," recalled Gina Houston in later court testimony. "Her name was Vicky Black. And Vicky and I had went for a walk and we had ran into a gentleman who introduced himself to us as Willie. I told Willie my name was Alice, she told Willie her name was Vicky. We parked underneath—I believe it's called a Nuffy's Donuts downtown on Hastings there—and I had gotten out of the car. And I went and stood by a pole while Vicky and Willie talked. She was a street worker."

That was how Gina Houston and Willie Pickton met sometime in the 1990s—she can't quite remember the date; it was probably about 1994 or 1995. Houston was a sex-trade worker herself and that day she was "spotting" her friend, taking note of licence plate numbers and keeping an eye on her buddy. Willie was driving by when he spotted them.

That day Gina and Vicky were both high on crack cocaine, and even though they still had a little left, Vicky thought it would be prudent to have some money in her purse should they decide they wanted to buy some more. Vicky was working out of an apartment in the Downtown Eastside that served as a hangout for several prostitutes controlled by a notorious Jamaican pimp and drug dealer known all over town as Dr. Jay. His real name was Jeffrey Powell; he worked with another Jamaican known as Scorpio (whose nude murdered body later ended up on Wreck Beach, on the grounds of the University of British Columbia).

Gina didn't really consider herself a prostitute like the other girls. She preferred to think of herself as a professional con artist, and if selling sex to a man allowed her to con him into giving her money, then it was just part of the job.

So she wasn't a prostitute? She was asked once. "No, not really. I ripped a few johns off a few times when I was out with Vicky. We'd take him to a room and leave him naked and take his wallet and his keys and his vehicle. And his money and his credit cards."

Gina has her own views about what being a prostitute is exactly. "Well, I mean, there's different levels of prostitution. I mean, it's all about—I mean, door-to-door salesmen sell themselves. If you can sell yourself, you can sell your product, right? So I guess you could say there's different levels in every way people are prostituting themselves out to get what they want, right? In my life on the streets, I've always been a con artist. And if you can sell the person on yourself, you can pretty much get whatever you want out of him."

Gina was a con artist, a thief, a drug addict, a prostitute and, at various times, the madam of a busy brothel. At sixteen she was going to the Downtown Eastside with her boyfriend, Wade Sentes, with whom she had a baby girl. Sentes was a major drug dealer from Richmond and a friend of many women in the Downtown Eastside, because they were among his best customers. By the early 1990s Gina was leasing houses in the area; she ran a brisk business renting rooms to prostitutes as well as supplying their drugs. In effect, she was their pimp. And her customers, she bragged, were gentlemen: "We're not talking, like, just regular guys—but the gentlemen, the lawyers and some of the doctors would come for the evening, buy dinner, wine . . . they'd buy some dope . . . they wanted female companionship."

Gina became such an alcoholic during these early years that, as she admits, her daughter Felicia would have to make her a drink and bring it to her in bed just to encourage her to get up. She went to a treatment centre to dry out. As soon as she was out, Gina rented another house at 41st and Joyce, far away from the Downtown Eastside, and once again filled it with prostitutes, who lived in two suites upstairs. She hired a babysitter for the children and settled her into a basement bedroom, but because of the high demand for rooms, she started renting it out as well to prostitutes. "I went for it because when they were finished using the room, they wanted to buy dope, so I got their money for the room and money for the dope."

There was no one in the world of drugs and the sex trade whom Gina didn't know in those days, but her most notorious connections were the Dosanjh brothers. Ron and Jimmy Dosanjh, leaders of a dangerous Indo-Canadian gang of drug traffickers, were eventually murdered, Ron in 1994 and Jimmy in 1995. Gina was buying drugs from them, and on one occasion she took her car to Vancouver Island to retrieve a couple of duffle bags crammed with cocaine for them and take the bags back to Vancouver. (In an odd twist to this connection, Gina later testified about her friendship with Willie Pickton at the trial of Peter Gill, the man charged with the Dosanjh murders. The jury included a sexy blond bombshell named Gillian Guess. Peter Gill wound up having a torrid affair with Guess, and when people found out, she was charged with obstructing justice. The man who defended her in her sensational trial was Willie Pickton's lawyer, Peter Ritchie. He did not win.)

And Gina also did business with Jeffrey Powell, a.k.a. Dr. Jay, and his partner, the man who called himself Scorpio. They would rent rooms from her for prostitutes to give them, as she put it, "a little R and R" in her basement, away from "the mess of the lower Eastside." After several years of running brothels and working with many of British Columbia's most dangerous drug kingpins, Gina also knew most of the sex-trade workers in the Downtown Eastside.

The meeting with Willie that day in front of the donut shop was an accident. Gina wanted to go on smoking rock and Vicky wanted to get to work. "Willie was looking for some company, so when we parked [at] Nuffy's Donuts, I got out. The conversation—whatever, the exchange of money, the conversation—I didn't stay to really listen to. I just stood a few feet over in front of the vehicle with my back to the vehicle."

It wasn't long before Willie Pickton was on his way and Vicky was back with her money. The two women walked back to Dr. Jay's apartment with enough cash to continue their partying.

It would be years before Gina ran into Willie again. But back at that first meeting she remembers a man who was very comfortable picking up a prostitute on the street, getting a fast blow job in his car, paying up and driving away. A typical customer, a nice guy, in fact.

By this time the Downtown Eastside felt like home to Willie Pickton. He was working for Dave on a demolition project in North Vancouver that took nearly two years to complete, and every time he drove across the Second Narrows Bridge from Burnaby to North Vancouver he would pass right by the Hastings Street turn into the dark alleys and busy streets of Vancouver's Low Track. Buying sex there was always simple and cheap. After a few months of commuting thirty or forty minutes a day each way to work, Willie thought of a better plan. He took his new motorhome over to North Vancouver, parked it on a corner on the site and lived out of it. That way he could also guard the site against thieves coming to steal equipment. And he could drive around after work looking at the women on the street and picking out the ones he liked.

As he became more comfortable downtown, Willie started hanging out in the drinking rooms of welfare hotels. His favourite spot was the Astoria Hotel, on the north side of Hastings and about five blocks east of Hastings and Main. Like the Balmoral and the Savoy and the other infamous hotels along this strip, the Astoria has a warren of filthy rooms for the down-and-out, as well as a bar—a large, dark room with worn linoleum floors and small, round tables chipped at the edges. You go to the bar to get your own beer, and some people sit in here all day long. The Astoria even has its own liquor store, a small room by the entrance with cheap beer, wine and hard liquor on a few shelves. And since 1966 there has been a small boxing gym downstairs, reached by a staircase at the back of the saloon. The fights at the Astoria Boxing Club still draw men and women from many city neighbourhoods, from the richest ones to the streets of the Downtown Eastside.

Willie developed a coterie of drinking buddies, and the routine was always the same: he'd sip soft drinks and pay for the rounds of beer. Sometimes when he was with a woman he liked, he'd peel off a ten or a twenty from the thick wad of bills he carried, give it to her and tell her to get some dope. And sometimes he talked them into driving out to the country with him, out to his farm "where we can party."

Soon, despite his filthy clothes and gumboots, his scraggly hair and the persistent stink of pig shit that clung to him, the rolls of bills became thick and real and never-ending. The wet, messy chunk of poor farmland that Leonard and Louise Pickton bought in 1963, and that Louise had hung on to through difficult years and low-ball offers, had made the two brothers and their sister wealthier than they ever dreamed possible.

It was Linda, already a successful realtor, who had masterminded the process. Port Coquitlam, just thirty-five kilometres from Vancouver's downtown, had become a bedroom suburb where a young couple with a family could buy a decent house for less than half the price of something similar in the city. Townhouses, bungalows and backsplits rolled over Port Coquitlam's valleys and hills, gobbling up farmland, woods and mountainsides. The farm, just a few hundred feet from the Lougheed Highway, was close to the centre of town and near schools. It was perfect for developers.

In 1994 Linda Pickton negotiated the sale of the north end of the farm for $1.76 million to a company called Eternal Holdings, which quickly built a dense townhouse development called Parkside Place on curving streets that backed right onto the farm. And then, on July 12, 1995, came the sale of two more parcels. The City of Port Coquitlam bought one of these for $1.17 million; it would become Blakeburn Park. The second piece, sold for $2.3 million to the Coquitlam School District, was right beside it and was destined for the new Blakeburn Elementary School. Municipal assessors estimated that the remaining land was worth about $4.67 million, and developers lined up to talk about it. Linda Pickton has always said the family didn't really make any money from the land. Landfill, hydro, roads and other infrastructure expenses that added up to $196,000 an acre, she said, hacked away at their profits.

Whatever their costs might have been, the fact is that the Picktons ended up well off from the land sales. Willie always had enough money in his jeans to buy anything he wanted.

CHAPTER EIGHT

PRIME SUSPECT

On June 6, 1992, nine months after the Project Eclipse fiasco, thirty-nine-year-old Kathleen Wattley, wearing a yellow blouse and black miniskirt, simply vanished. Wattley, a vivacious black woman who was only five feet two inches tall and thin as a rail, had been arrested earlier that year and charged with soliciting after she approached a police officer on Quebec Street on Vancouver's Mount Pleasant stroll. Today, this working-class neighbourhood, south of the Downtown Eastside, is gentrifying quickly with the arrival of many artists, writers, television personalities and journalists such as Ian Hanomansing and David Beers, editor of *The Tyee,* but it has a well-known working girls' stroll around Main Street and Broadway, and that's where Kathleen Wattley was when she disappeared.

Four months later, on October 16, 1992, Elsie Sebastian, a forty-year-old aboriginal woman from the Pacheedaht First Nation on the west coast of Vancouver Island, also disappeared, leaving four grown children, Ann-Marie, Donalee, Neil and Willie. They were devastated by the news.

"Our hearts grieve for our mother and I often cry for her and wish she was still with me every day," Ann-Marie has written. "I feel guilty and remorseful that I did not treat her better and cherish the last moment that I spent with her, yet at the same time I was angry at her because she was in the throws of her addiction. Nevertheless, I love and miss my mother dearly and would give anything to hear my mom's laugh again and see her smile!"

Elsie's children remembered her sense of humour and the way she opened up to people, chatting easily to newcomers. "It feels as though my short time with my mother was a dream," Ann-Marie wrote on a website devoted to the missing women, "slowly fading from my memory. Please remember these women were mothers and sisters and friends, and they had children, husbands and grandchildren who love them dearly and miss them with all our hearts.

"I pray daily that God will send me a message and let me know when the time is right what happened to my mother. She was not a throwaway junkie and hooker, she was a respected and loving mother and joyous spirit who I will fight for until the day I die."

Once again it was almost impossible for family members to get the police to take these missing women seriously. A year after Elsie Sebastian disappeared, her sister-in-law, Ann Livingston, moved to Vancouver. Livingston, a community activist who was working with drug users, tried several times to have Elsie declared a missing person by the Vancouver police. Ann-Marie, who was only sixteen at the time, had been feeling helpless and ignored; maybe her aunt could make them pay attention. But Livingston later told reporter Greg Middleton of the Vancouver *Province* that trying to report a woman missing if she was a prostitute, especially if she was Native, was like trying to talk to a stone wall. "That is part of what went wrong here, part of the problem. We were told that forty-year-old Native women don't go missing."

Livingston tried many times. On one occasion the civilian clerk— the stone wall in the Missing Persons Unit—told her she wasn't a close enough relative to make a report; other efforts also ended in frustration. Only after making a constant nuisance of herself and finally resorting to threats could she get the police to make a report. "I'm an aggressive, white, middle-class woman and I couldn't make myself heard," Livingston told Greg Middleton. "It makes you wonder how many other women have gone missing and their relatives just gave up."

We know much less about the next woman to disappear, Teresa Louise Triff, who was thirty-one and vanished on April 15, 1993.

With blond curly hair and bright blue eyes, Teresa, who had grown up in Edmonton, was a tiny woman like Kathleen Wattley—just five feet two inches tall and weighing only 111 pounds.

Fifteen women vanished without a trace from the Downtown Eastside between 1979 and 1993. Other women, including several from the Downtown Eastside, had been murdered during the same period, but their bodies had been found, their families knew their fate and in some cases the killer had been caught and convicted. But the missing women? No one knew where they were or if they were ever coming back.

On December 17, 1993, the phone rang in Erin McGrath's kitchen and she rushed to answer it.

"Leigh! It's so good to hear from you! How are you doing?"

"Great, Erin. I'm fine, and guess what? I'm coming home for Christmas."

"Oh, Leigh, that is just great. Mom will be thrilled. Everyone will be. When will you be here?"

"I'm not sure yet. Soon. But look, Erin, I hate to ask, but I'm a little short these days. Do you think you can send me some money soon so I can get there?"

Erin's hand gripped the receiver tightly. She shut her eyes. "Sure. I'll get it off to you today."

"Thanks, Erin. Love you. See you soon."

"Great! Can't wait."

Erin hung up, her stomach in knots. As always these days, the conversation with Leigh had been brief. Her older sister would never change; she only called when she needed money. Leigh Miner was now thirty-five years old, living in squalor in the Downtown Eastside, working as a prostitute, and it was hard to remember when she hadn't been on drugs. Yet, infuriated as she was, Erin couldn't find it in her heart to blame her.

Leigh's life shouldn't have turned out this way. She had grown up in a well-to-do, close-knit family in the Santa Cruz Mountains in

California. The eldest child, Mark, was born in 1956; two years later, on March 24, 1958, twin girls Leigh and Leslie came along. Erin arrived in 1964. Beautiful, popular and strong-willed, the twins began experimenting with drugs in their teens after the family moved to San Francisco. That was the beginning of the bad time for the family. Their father died suddenly of a heart attack in 1975, when the four children were still young, and the loss was devastating.

A few years later Leigh was sure her life had turned around; she fell in love, married a caring and intelligent young man and was happy. Almost right away, though, Leigh discovered that her new husband suffered from depression. Nothing she could do made it better, and on one horrific day he shot himself in their apartment and died in her arms. Leigh couldn't cope. Nobody could blame her; nobody knew how to help her. Within a few years Leigh's solution was to turn to heroin. She tried to kick the habit, especially when she discovered she was pregnant in 1986, but she was just too addicted to manage. By the time her little girl was two, with Leigh's agreement, Erin and her mother realized they would have to raise the child themselves.

But they also knew they needed to get away from San Francisco. "We thought it would be wise, if we were to raise a child, to remove ourselves from what we thought was a drug-infested society," Erin wrote in a presentation she gave later to other families of missing women. "Where better to go than to British Columbia?"

Leigh's parents had originally been from Alberta, so moving back to Canada made sense. Both mother and daughter longed for a peaceful place near the ocean where they could build a new life. They chose Nanoose, a small, prosperous rural community on Vancouver Island stretched along a peninsula north of Victoria. Here the forests are dense with pine and spruce but there are also gentle areas of cleared land with neat farmhouses and well-cared-for crops. Summer cottages dot the shorelines, although most of the people live here year-round.

Leigh came to visit often and in the early 1990s decided to move to Vancouver to be closer to her daughter. Erin married a young

Newfoundland carpenter named John McGrath and they bought their own house, not far from her mother's, and soon had two girls of their own. A few years later her brother, Mark, moved to Nanoose to live with his mother and help raise Leigh's child.

The family felt settled and finally at peace, or at least a sort of peace. They worked constantly to persuade Leigh to enter a rehab clinic, but her drug use had taken over her life. Even the money the family could give her was never enough, and she had to move from a North Vancouver apartment to cheaper lodgings in the Downtown Eastside. It wasn't long before she turned to prostitution to support her habit. But she kept telling her family she was going to get her life together, go to school, kick drugs and raise her daughter.

"On Christmas Day we waited for Leigh to call and tell us she was on the ferry on her way over from Vancouver," Erin remembers. "We waited with unopened presents. We waited and we waited. My mom and my niece cried that night and for many nights after. I was consumed with anger. She ruined Christmas."

After New Year's the waiting continued, but there was still no word. Finally, on February 24, 1994, Erin's mother, Doreen Hanna, went to Vancouver to look for Leigh. She began hunting at the Regent Hotel at 160 East Hastings Street, where Leigh had been living, but the people there were unfriendly and she was frightened by the dirt, the smells and ugliness of the place. What could she do? All she could think of was going to the police and filing a missing-person report. She did it, but nothing happened. Leigh's picture, the one on the missing-person poster that eventually did appear, shows a happy, beautiful woman, her face not yet ravaged by disease and drugs. She's still a princess with the new car, the clothes, the well-cut hair, the even teeth, the good skin.

Erin remains bitter about the lack of interest the police showed in her sister's fate. "We had no idea at that time that if you went missing from a ten-block area known as the Downtown Eastside your disappearance did not get fully investigated—if, in fact, it got investigated at all." It's no surprise that Leigh Miner's disappearance was not a priority for the Vancouver police; that same year they began cutting staff for budget reasons. Over the next few years they cut forty-nine officers.

Ten months later Leigh's twin, Leslie, was killed in a car crash, leaving behind a young son. Ever since then Erin and John, along with her mother and brother, have been raising him with Leigh's daughter.

Leigh Miner was the sixteenth woman since 1979 to disappear from the Downtown Eastside. The next year, on August 19, 1994, Angela Arsenault, just seventeen years old, with thick black hair and a broad smile, had been shopping with her boyfriend in downtown Vancouver. After dinner she climbed on a bus to go home to Burnaby and was never seen again. Seventeen women between 1979 and 1994—slightly more than one a year. "Those numbers are unfortunate, but they're about normal for that district," says Kim Rossmo.*

It was the spike in the following year, 1995, that was the shocker. Although she was not technically missing, Jane Doe, the victim whose skull was found in Mission Slough in February 1995, is counted in this group because the flesh remaining on the skull indicated she had not been dead for long. If you include her, there were five in one year. The others were Catherine Gonzalez, who was twenty-seven years old when she disappeared in March; Catherine Knight, who was also twenty-seven, in April; Dorothy Spence, who was thirty-three, on July 30; and finally Diana Melnick, twenty, who was last seen on December 27 and was reported missing two days later.

Catherine Louise Gonzalez was a slight, blue-eyed blond who grew up in Timmins, Ontario. People say she knew Shania Twain's family there, and maybe she did; the ordinary folk in Timmins who loved her were shocked when she disappeared in March 1995. By this

---

*Arsenault is included in the numbers, but technically she was not a Downtown Eastside victim, because she didn't work or live there.

time her life had become sad and rocky. For a while Cathy had been in a loving relationship with a British Columbia man named Gordon Vieira and she had a daughter by him, but her alcoholism and drug addiction eventually drove them apart, leaving him with custody of their child. The police knew her well; her rap sheet shows arrests for stealing a wallet, for shoplifting from London Drugs and for using a stolen credit card. Another, odd charge was for stealing tools and motor oil. Cathy was homeless, according to police records, and lived on welfare; she had put "none" in the section of her records designating next of kin, even though Gordon and his family cared about her. Her last known effects consisted of a ring, some condoms, shoelaces, an earring and twenty dollars in cash.*

As always, the stories begin when the phone calls stop. The women who went missing from Vancouver's Downtown Eastside called their families all the time. They called their children to wish them happy birthday. They called their mothers on Mother's Day and their sisters just to gossip. They phoned on Christmas and at New Year's if their families wouldn't let them come to visit. They kept in touch.

Catherine Knight was like the rest; she phoned her family regularly, at least once a month. "Most of the time she was stoned," her sister, Geri Stewart, told Louise Dickson, a reporter with the Victoria *Times Colonist*. "She was right out of it. But she phoned to tell me she loved me, that everything was all right. She never really told me how she was, though."

*There is a horrific twist to the Cathy Gonzalez story. Although no one knows what happened to her, she is presumed dead. But Gordon Vieira, her former partner, is also dead, murdered in his home a year after she vanished. Vieira had been living with his little girl and his parents; one day his father heard shots from the garage and ran to see what had happened—he found his son with three bullet holes in his back. Soon afterwards Vieira's story unfolded, revealing a secret life as a drug dealer connected to the Hells Angels and Asian and Indo-Canadian gangs.

And Catherine always called before her birthday. But by May 5, 1995, when she turned thirty, her family still hadn't heard from her. "It was heart-wrenching," Geri Stewart told Dickson. "I've got these visions that her bones are in a bush somewhere. But I still don't know if her bones are there because of foul play or because she overdosed."

Catherine had been the youngest of nine children. The family was poor and rented a house that was so dilapidated it had been condemned. Their father was an alcoholic; their mother couldn't look after the children. "We all grew up in the same environment with physical, emotional and sexual abuse and we're all survivors of that. We were all sort of abandoned, left to fend for ourselves," Stewart told Dickson. "When I was really little I used to sleep in the Goodwill boxes they put out on the street corners. That was my safety net. Our Dad would come home drunk and you'd beat it out of there. I remember feeling sad when they got rid of [the boxes]. I wondered if there were other children out there who used to sleep in them."

The older kids left home as soon as they could, but there was little they could do to help Catherine. "She was just so lovable," Geri Stewart said. "Blue-eyed, blond hair, chubby-cheeked and searching for what we were all searching for—somebody to love us. But I think Cathy never felt loved. I think when you grow up with a lot of poverty, a lot of abuses, alcoholism, you don't know the meaning of love."

By the time she was fifteen Catherine was homeless, living on the street and prostituting herself to survive. She started taking drugs and drinking heavily, and by the time she was twenty there was no way back. Her arms where she injected her drugs were full of holes and abscesses. Geri would look for her, bring her home, clean her up and try to help, but her sister always stole from her; eventually Geri, like the rest of the family, gave up. Then, in 1993, Geri, now a nurse at the Victoria General Hospital, discovered her sister lying in a ward there, desperately sick, with injection sites in her arms that had become deeply infected.

"There were times I wished she'd hurry up and overdose, many times before she went missing," Geri admitted to Dickson. "I loved her so much, but the pain was unbearable. I'd secretly pray, 'Just give yourself enough to finish it,' not only for herself but for us too. It was just too painful to see this beautiful young lady turned into a drug-ridden form of a human being."

Coincidentally, like Catherine Knight, thirty-three-year-old Dorothy Anne Spence, who was the next woman to disappear, was also one of nine children. Her family was Native, with five boys and four girls. She disappeared on July 30, 1995. Her sister Rebecca, who was ten years younger but had been born on the same day as Dorothy, had been living with her for eight years in an apartment in Vancouver. The girls got along well, especially because Dorothy was a good cook and loved making meals that would please her little sister. But she had become an addict, and by now drugs controlled her life.

"When she was straight," Rebecca wrote in a note to an Internet site for the families of the missing women, "she had a heart of gold, very caring. She would call me up on the phone and if I wasn't home she would sing a little tune on my answering machine that would make me laugh. She had a great sense of humour. Dorothy, our other sister and I would always be making each other laugh with our little escapades.

"We all try to figure out what happened to her. She would have called or something. She is not the type to just leave and not tell anyone, we all love her a great deal and miss her."

When Rebecca first heard that Dorothy, who had moved to an apartment at 12th Street and Fraser in the East Broadway area, was missing, she herself was living in Ontario. She says that her heart sank at the news. "Something told me I would never see my sister again. I always have dreams of her. I had one funny dream that it was a cop doing these things to these girls."

Diana Melnick, another woman who vanished in 1995, is like Leigh Miner: an example of the reality that families with good incomes and few obvious problems can't protect their kids from stumbling into nightmare lives. The photograph on Diana Melnick's missing-person poster says it all; you see an impish kid in a private-school tunic, her collar askew, the shirt looking far too big, her tie loosely knotted.

"I went to school with Diana Melnick," a woman wrote in a posting to the website missingpeople.net for families of the missing women. "I remembered she loved horses, and would never wear her skirt for our uniform, always in jodhpurs, very happy, didn't like mornings, and always talking about boys, I contacted our school about her, they are praying and sending condolences as well, I don't remember the last time I saw her . . . we used to hang out in our mutual friends bedroom and listen to heavy metal, and gossip about boys, the dance coming up next, and her boyfriend in Vancouver, I hope someone finds her and brings her home."

Court records, as they so often do, tell part of Diana's story. She was only five feet two inches tall, weighed about a hundred pounds and usually wore her long brown hair in a ponytail. By the time she disappeared her face was gaunt. Her cheekbones had become two sharp points on her face and her mouth dragged down as if heroin had already started to destroy her teeth. Her hair was lank and her eyes were half-closed. The defiance, the energy, the life force you see in so many of the women on the Downtown Eastside, regardless of their years on the street, was missing in Diana Melnick.

By the time she vanished from skid row, Diana was trailing the usual sad list of charges and convictions that bedevilled so many of the women. There were four prostitution charges, one theft charge and one "failure to appear" in court, or FTA, as it is known. On June 2, 1995, for example, Diana and her boyfriend, Marc Maynard, were arrested for shoplifting at a downtown Shoppers Drug Mart. In October she was charged with defrauding a Money Mart when she tried to cash a cheque for fifty dollars that she had stolen from a friend. Another friend bailed her out the same day and she was ordered to appear in court on August 24; she didn't show up. An order went out on August 26 setting a new date to face the charges. Again, no show and another FTA on her record.

While the police were chasing Diana to face charges in court, one of her relatives was doing the same thing. This was her step-grandfather, Norman Szukala, who lived in West Vancouver; he was suing Diana; her mother, Julie Anne Melnick; her brother, Dan Melnick; and ten other family members for a larger share of his late wife's money. His wife, Patricia, who died in December 1994, had left most of her fortune to her children and grandchildren. Szukala's share included a legacy of $250,000, a Kawai grand piano and the right to take as much china, crystal, furniture and art as he wanted from their home, except for items his wife had reserved for the family.

Szukala claimed he had a taxable annual income of about $30,000, as well as about $330,000 of his own money; he wasn't going to be poor. But his wife's will enraged him. Not only did it state that he had to leave the matrimonial home within ninety days of her death, it also set aside jewellery, silver, a Sheraton sideboard, photographs, paintings by Group of Seven artists Lawren Harris and Arthur Lismer, and "articles of personal adornment" for her children and grandchildren. As Patricia's estate was worth nearly $6 million, the widower was mightily aggrieved, especially when he discovered that his stepdaughter Julie and her two children, Dan and Diana, were to receive the largest portions.

Like her brother, Diana was now a millionaire. Did she know how wealthy she had become? Probably not. She was supposed to show up in court on December 27; although people say they saw her that day, once again she failed to appear. Two days later her family reported her missing. No one ever saw her again.

The women who vanished from the Downtown Eastside in 1995 were not the community's only victims that year; they were just the ones whose fate was not known. The same year four other women— all prostitutes, all drug addicts—were murdered, but their bodies at least were found. Once again the *Vancouver Sun*'s Kim Pemberton put together lists of dead and missing women; this time it included at least thirty women from the Downtown Eastside who had been killed and whose bodies had been found, as well as another list of thirty-five prostitutes who had disappeared since 1989. One who went missing in 1995 was Mary Lidguerre, whose skeletal remains, found on Mount Seymour in 1997, showed she had been beaten without mercy.

People were finally talking about a serial killer hunting for victims in the Downtown Eastside when, in August 1995, the battered body of thirty-year-old Tracy Olajide was found in a wooded area near the Agassiz Mountains, about fifty kilometres east of Vancouver. Tammy Pipe's body was found three weeks later, on September 6, 1995, about nine kilometres from the site where Olajide's body had been dumped. The third victim in this group, found by a hunter near Mission, was Victoria Younker, thirty-five. Each was a prostitute from the Downtown Eastside, each was an addict, and all three had been living in the Vernon Rooms at Hastings and Vernon.

For a long time Ronald McCauley, a roofer from Mission, was the prime suspect in the Valley Murders, as these deaths were soon called by the newspapers. A violent offender, McCauley was out of prison on what is known as "jail release," or parole; it was quickly suspended when the police discovered McCauley had nearly killed a prostitute he'd picked up at the Astoria Hotel on East Hastings. McCauley had driven the woman west and north to the Hemlock Valley, a heavily wooded mountainous area near Mission, where he raped and beat her and then threw her out of his truck. Common sense made McCauley a good candidate for the Mission–Agassiz Mountain murders, but police cleared him after DNA tests proved he couldn't have killed the three women.

Next on the list of prime suspects for the Valley Murders was a man who had terrorized communities around Seattle, Washington, between 1982 and 1984 and who also left the bodies of his victims in remote woodland areas. He was known as the Green River Killer; while the police suspected a truck painter named Gary Leon Ridgway,

they didn't have enough evidence to arrest him. By 1985 they suspected he had killed at least forty-five prostitutes. In 1987 local police
searched his house and took saliva samples from him but still couldn't
put together a good case; the investigation ran out of steam.

Ridgway started coming to Vancouver and the Fraser Valley area
around this period. As far as the public knows, there is no firm evidence that he started killing women in Canada when he realized the
police were watching him closely in the United States, but there is a
case to be made for it. First of all, police had found maps of the Lower
Mainland in his van. One of the Canadian women he may have
assaulted at about the same time Tracy Olajide, Tammy Pipe and
Victoria Younker were killed was Renata Bond, a young prostitute
addicted to cocaine and heroin who worked around New Westminster
and Burnaby. Bond claims Ridgway attacked her one day in 1995,
when she was working along 12th Street in New Westminster.

"I had an occasion where he picked me up and I jumped out of
the car and he cut me," she testified later. "He had a knife. And I
jumped out of the car at a red light and I got six stitches in my finger
for my trouble." The man had glasses and was balding, she said,
although he still had a bit of brown hair. As for size and age, well,
"he wasn't fat, he was in his mid or late forties."

To add credence to her story, his neighbours confirmed that
Ridgway often drove his motorhome to British Columbia on holidays with his wife, Judith. And then there is the statement of a
Vancouver musician, Gary Bigg, who said his girlfriend, Heather
Chinnock, another prostitute and drug addict, used to party with
Ridgway in the motorhome. He was a trick, Bigg told a Vancouver
reporter years later, adding that Heather carried his phone number
in her wallet. "Heather said he was weird but she definitely saw him
a few times. I believe this was definitely Gary Leon Ridgway."

Gary Bigg and Renata Bond are not the only people who are
convinced Ridgway was attacking women in British Columbia; so is
Maggy Gisle. Then a prostitute and addict working out of the
Downtown Eastside, Gisle accepted a date in 1989 with a regular

trick, a man she liked and trusted; this time, however, when he picked her up, another man was in his car. The pair drove her to Mount Seymour, where they raped and beat her so savagely she nearly died; she escaped only by squeezing out a partly open back window of the car and running, naked and bleeding, out to the highway, where passersby picked her up and took her to the hospital. Maggy Gisle saw Ridgway's picture in 2001, when he was finally arrested, and was sure he had been the second man in the car.

The police knew that whoever was killing these women and dumping them in the Mission–Agassiz Mountain area was a serial killer. Once the DNA eliminated Ronald McCauley and the Green River Killer, they had one more suspect up their sleeve: Willie Pickton. The police knew Willie Pickton. As the expression goes, he was a "person of interest" to the Major Crimes Unit of the RCMP's Chilliwack division, and they kept an eye on his comings and goings in the area. And they weren't the only ones; so did the police in Coquitlam and Vancouver.

Don Adam served in the RCMP's Coquitlam office for ten years. "The Pickton brothers," he has said, "were well known to the police during those years." But he never explained why it was Robert, not Dave, who they thought might be a serial killer, and they finally obtained a sample of his DNA to run against the evidence found in the 1995 Mission–Agassiz Mountain murders. The DNA did not match. As Adam put it later, "He moved down in the suspect pool and then we eliminated him. There had been work done on him by Coquitlam RCMP that had basically gone nowhere."

But Willie Pickton knew the police were interested in him and his brother, and he knew they were keeping an eye on him, remembers Lisa Yelds. Even on his routine errands Pickton stayed alert. In 1995 he often drove out to the Fraser Valley to pick up scrap metal, bid on used cars or look for tractor parts. One trip took him to a large federal penitentiary, the Matsqui Institution in Abbotsford, about 110 kilometres east of Vancouver, where he wanted to bid on a vehicle being sold in an auction on the prison property. Another time he took two days to drive up into the mountains in the Fraser Valley, past a fish hatchery, to pick up three tons of scrap metal at another government auction. He often visited a used car lot near Matsqui, and sometimes he liked to drive across the Canada–United States border to buy groceries and look for tractor parts. And every time he took one of those trips, he would be glancing in his rear-view mirror for any sign that the police were following him.

Lisa Yelds was often with him on these outings. "I knew Willie was worried about cops and I knew Dave Pickton was too," she says. "But I didn't know why."

She was probably afraid enough for her own safety not to ask questions.

CHAPTER NINE

THE TRIALS OF KIM ROSSMO AND THE GROWING LIST OF MISSING WOMEN

It was October 16, 1995, when Kim Rossmo stepped into the elevator at police headquarters at 2120 Cambie Street on his first day as a senior officer. One of his colleagues joined him. There were no words of congratulation; he didn't even say good morning. Instead the other man turned his back on him and stared at the corner as the elevator ascended. Wordlessly the two men left the elevator on the sixth floor, where top management worked, and walked to their own offices.

"So that's the way it's going to be," thought Rossmo, his face flushed with humiliation and anger. He sat at his desk for a while, unable to concentrate, but finally turned on his computer and forced himself to think about work. The chilly reception was not a complete surprise. Even though his formal promotion had taken effect that same day and a press release went out the next day to announce his new rank and new job, the negative reaction within the officer corps of the VPD meant that it took several more months for the final contract details to be worked out. And though his chief, Ray Canuel, was his biggest supporter, the executive ranks (known behind their backs as the "Old Boys' Club") were so angry that Canuel felt he had no choice but to hold back the internal staff bulletin announcing the news.

Rossmo had left his years as a beat cop on skid row far behind. He believed his fortunes had improved: he had just become the first working policeman in Canada to obtain a doctorate in criminology, and his success with geographic profiling was attracting attention from police forces around the world.

Canuel, chief constable of the Vancouver police force, was one of the few top officers in the force who weren't jealous of Rossmo's star power or threatened by his abilities. To persuade him to stay with the force, Canuel had asked him just a few weeks earlier to put together a proposal for a new geographic profiling unit within the department. Rossmo had responded quickly with a report suggesting the VPD create a new plainclothes position at the detective-inspector level to offer geographic profiling services to the international police community as well as to Vancouver. Rossmo described an office that could produce, among other things, profiling preparation, criminal investigative analysis and research such as urban criminal patterns and statistics. And he suggested that the new job be a five-year contract, which would give him time to prove that geographic profiling worked and that he was just the person to do it.

What had seized everyone's interest, except that of the Old Boys' Club, was his invention as his doctoral thesis project of a computer program that he patented under the name Rigel. This software creates three-dimensional imaging that helps rank suspects in serial offender cases—not just killers but also bombers, arsonists, rapists and other predators. Other police forces were asking him to train their people to use the software but his own club was less than enthusiastic.

Rossmo's theory, that predators prefer to work in territory where they are most comfortable, would suggest that police look, for example, at all the sex offenders and rapists and violent men who prowl the Downtown Eastside. Find out who they are from bad-date sheets with licence plates noted or descriptions from victims or tips from snitches or police records. Find out where these men live. Look for a place where they can rape and torture and kill with maximum privacy. In his book, *Geographic Profiling*, Rossmo says most serial killers start with victims close to home but will expand their hunting areas as their confidence grows. He also says geographic profiling is recommended for cases where there are no bodies.

Finally, enter all the information into a computer loaded with the Rigel software and it will develop a three-dimensional image that looks like a volcanic mountain range, with a red hotspot at the top of the highest mountain, narrowing the police's target area by ninety-five percent. The prime suspect will be the one who lives closest to that hotspot. As Rossmo always insists, the software doesn't solve the crime, but it is an aid that can save time by directing police to the most likely area for the criminal. Like most profilers, he says that his job is not to solve the crime but to offer tools and advice to help investigators narrow a list of suspects.

Canuel agreed with Rossmo's proposal. He offered him a five-year contract during which he would hold the rank of detective inspector, a four-rank hike that incited the Old Boys to protest in every possible way. They were outraged that Rossmo's doctorate, in what they regarded as dubious science at best, should have vaulted him to such a high rank. He didn't deserve it and they weren't going to let him forget it. The snub on the elevator was just the beginning. The shunning was professional and it was personal. Classic stuff, really. One morning Deputy Chief John Unger changed the room of a meeting without letting Rossmo know; when he arrived, late and flustered, Unger stared at him and said, "Meetings are not going to work if people are coming in late all the time." The others smirked.

No insult was too petty. "I had a really small budget," Rossmo remembers. "Maybe $500 for office supplies. It was cut to $250 and I couldn't buy paper or ink cartridges. Another time someone wanted a bulletin board and he simply came in and took mine off the wall. He didn't talk to me about it. My colleagues would ignore my requests and refuse to share information with me."

Part of the problem was classic office politics; his large office on the sixth floor was a space normally deserved for a deputy chief. "People there got MOD," explained one senior officer responsible for assigning space. "You know, it's 'mad office disease'—your office is bigger than mine." Rossmo, he reasoned, needed it because he needed room for an assistant and for students who would be coming in from time to time. "He was teaching profiling to police officers from other forces and he had student interns helping him. I snagged this empty office on the sixth floor for him and Unger went crazy. 'You can't do that!' he yelled at me."

One floor above the management floor was the chief's office suite as well as the officers' mess, a small six-hundred-square-foot lounge with a bar, for anyone above the rank of inspector. Although Canuel told his senior staff that Rossmo's rank qualified him as a full member of the mess and that he expected them to invite him to mess functions, they wouldn't budge. They were blunt: the Old Boys told Rossmo he was just not welcome. "Some people went to bat for me so they reluctantly allowed me to be an associate member, but there was still bitter resistance," remembers Rossmo. "Literally there were people who never spoke to me again."

What was far more serious than this poisonous work atmosphere was the fact that for the next five years the detectives in Major Crime, the section responsible for murder cases, never asked him for his help. For Rossmo who was single and close to only a few people outside his immediate family, work had always been his solace and his inspiration—but work was now intolerable.

Rossmo had grown up in Saskatoon. His grandfather, Mike Roznavetz, a soldier who came from southern Galicia, in Ukraine, and believed Canada was the Promised Land, had emigrated to Saskatchewan and married a woman whose family was Norwegian and English. Roznavetz found work with the Canadian Pacific Railway and the young couple set up housekeeping in Sutherland, which is now part of Saskatoon. One of the first things they did was start a charge account at their local grocery store, but the storekeeper couldn't manage the name and shortened it to Rossmo. It suited everyone well—it was easy and sounded Canadian. Today Saskatoon's Rossmo Road is named after Mike Roznavetz.

Kim Rossmo's father, Bill, one of five children, also worked for the CPR for a while. During the Second World War he joined the Royal Canadian Navy, where he was put in charge of an anti-aircraft gun on a frigate on the North Atlantic run. Later he became a successful inventor with several patents, as well as a businessman, helped by his wife, Eunice. One of Bill Rossmo's most successful inventions was a self-aligning gate latch that is carried by Lee Valley Tools and other hardware store chains. Eunice and Bill had four children, two girls and two boys, all of whom seem to have inherited their parents' work ethic and fascination with ideas. Kim's brother, Kerry, runs the machinery at CSP Foods in Saskatoon, where they process grain coming in off the farms; Denise is a teacher-librarian; and Marla has a commerce degree and worked for a pharmaceutical company until she paused to raise her two children.

Like his brother and sisters, Kim did well at school. When he was a student at Evan Hardy Collegiate, he gained a certain notoriety for a perfect score on a final exam in algebra, although he had taken only one week of classes. He went on to study sociology at the University of Saskatchewan and worked for a short time after his 1978 graduation as a private detective. That gave him a taste for police work and he joined the Vancouver Police Department as a civilian staff member the same year. In 1980 he became a sworn member of the force; in 1983 he was promoted to first-class constable.

Although he is the one Rossmo child to leave Saskatchewan, Kim remains close to his family there. But he is not what you'd call a folksy prairie boy—far from it. Until he's comfortable with the company, Rossmo can be reserved and watchful, not advancing the conversation, gauging the group. His straight, dark hair is balding a bit on top and he's slightly stocky; his stare can be cool and unnerving. As soon as he trusts someone he's different: funny, eager, fast-talking, aggressive in his arguments, a careful listener. He's a manic late-night emailer; he lives on Starbucks coffee; he loves Asian food, good cognac, port and fine wine.

Sometimes people say that Rossmo's not a "real" cop, just a scientist. "That's just not true," snaps Toby Hinton, his former partner and a member of the legendary Downtown Eastside's Odd Squad, cops who work to educate kids on the dangers of drugs and prostitution in addition to policing the area. (Odd Squad Productions made a documentary that was released in 1999 called *Through a Blue Lens* to illustrate life for drug addicts on the Downtown Eastside. It was produced by the National Film Board and became their most requested film.)

"[Rossmo] is as tough as anyone I've ever worked with. I've seen him, alone, brace a bar full of drunken men and establish control. Kim was also ERT." Emergency response teams, more popularly known as SWAT teams, are called in to handle the most dangerous situations. Rossmo also served as a hostage negotiator, worked in VIP protection and even handled communications for a while.

But after years of working full time, studying full time and surviving on three hours' sleep a night, Rossmo completed his master's degree in criminology in 1987 and his PhD in 1995, both from Simon Fraser University in Burnaby.

His life should have been great, not the nightmare it was becoming at the VPD. The irony of his situation wasn't lost on him. The RCMP had wanted him so badly they'd offered him an inspector's job. He had received teaching offers from Northeastern University in the United States and Cambridge University in England. He was in demand as a consultant on serial killer cases across Canada and the United States. Yet now he was persona non grata among many of his senior colleagues.

In spite of the fact he had provoked a revolt among many of his most senior officers, Ray Canuel couldn't delay a formal announcement of Rossmo's appointment any longer. He finally sent out an internal announcement in late October 1995 that listed his credentials and described the position:

> In order to use Dr. Rossmo's expertise, the Chief Constable has announced the formation of a Geographical Profiling Unit, staffed by Dr. Rossmo, who will be hired under contract and assigned the title of Detective Inspector. The Unit will liaise with the international police community and assist other Departments

in solving serial murders, rapes and arsons. This capability will increase the [VPD's] stature in the policing community and provide an invaluable aid to investigations within the Department.

The contract also said he would work about a quarter of his time as a resource for Canuel and the rest of it on his geographic profiling work.

But it took until the following spring—May 6, 1996—for Rossmo to sign the contract. He was unhappy with some of the conditions in it and agreed to sign it only after the police board agreed that he would receive the same salary and benefits as other VPD inspectors and that he would remain a member of the VPD after his contract ended. During this long period of negotiation and waiting Rossmo was working hard, mostly with police forces in other regions, and helping to train other officers as geographic profilers. His own work environment remained poisonous. The Old Boys viewed his computers and his expertise with contempt.

It was classic "workplace mobbing," the expression University of Waterloo sociologist Kenneth Westhues describes as "an impassioned, collective movement by management and/or co-workers to exclude, punish and humiliate a targeted worker." Westhues, who has written several books on the subject, including *The Envy of Excellence*; *Winning, Losing, Moving On*; and *Workplace Mobbing in Academe*, explains it as a "desperate urge to crush and eliminate the target that spreads through the work unit, infecting one person after another like a contagious disease. The target comes to be seen as absolutely abhorrent, outside the circle of respectability, deserving of contempt." Vancouver journalist Allan Garr later summed it up well in the July 2, 2001, edition of the *Vancouver Courier*, where he wrote, "Rossmo was getting global accolades for his theory and was busy training other police forces in his techniques but on the Vancouver force some called geographic profiling 'voodoo.'"

But back in 1995, in his first year as a detective inspector and as the first geographic profiler in the world, could he have made a difference? What would he have wanted to know? His response is interesting and cautionary: "It wasn't the geographic profiling that was so much of value to the force then. It was my experience working with serial murder cases." And he understands why some of his colleagues didn't want to use his skills. "The main problem was that we just didn't know where the women went missing." They just knew where they came from.

To the fury of his colleagues Rossmo flourished without their support. Not only was he in demand as a speaker and conference participant all over the world, but major police forces in England, the United States and Europe lined up for his help on their most difficult murder cases. Important journals and magazines lauded his skill and inventiveness.

As a resentful Old Boys' Club continued to badmouth or ignore their star criminal profiler, Vancouver's women continued to disappear.

It was the end of March or early in April in 1996 and Shelley Morrison* was in the middle of her shift as a cosmetics salesperson at Shoppers Drug Mart on Fourth Avenue, in Vancouver's Kitsilano neighbourhood. She spied Frances Young, one of her favourite customers, browsing through an aisle of lipstick and nail polish.

"Hey, Franny! Great to see you," she said. "How's it going?"

"It's good, Shelley," Fran said. "Really good. I finished my chef's training a little while ago and I've got a job. I think I'm going to be able to get my act together. Finally."

Both women laughed. That was the thing about Fran, Shelley always thought—a good sense of humour mixed with realistic admission of her own failures. Shelley had pieced together Fran's tough, sad history. She'd been seeing her in the drugstore now for

*Not her real name.

the past five years and they'd got to know each other a bit. Sometimes it's easier to tell your story to a stranger than to a friend; over the years Shelley had learned that Fran, who was thirty-six, had been involved in drugs and prostitution for a while. But now that she had finished her program at the Vancouver Vocational Institute, where she specialized in pastry and desserts, she had a decent job and a new life.

Fran loved doing embroidery, she could paint and draw beautifully, she enjoyed her cats and dogs, and she got a kick out of life. Best of all, her family was behind her. She had a big, happy smile that disarmed everyone who met her. She was five feet four inches tall and 110 pounds, with curly light brown hair and blue eyes; she liked to look nice and enjoyed trying different makeup products. She was always interested in Shelley's kids and how work was going.

Her biggest problem was a criminal boyfriend, someone who had for far too long kept her in drugs and petty crime to feed their drug habit, so Shelley prayed that Fran was rid of him. To her Fran was a friend, not just a customer, and she loved her. Today Fran had filled her shopping cart by the time Shelley spotted her.

"Shelley," Fran asked, "I don't have enough cash on me for all this stuff. Would it be okay if I wrote a cheque?"

"Sure. I have to get my manager's approval, but it won't be a problem."

The drugstore manager was less enthusiastic about a personal cheque. It's okay, he warned Shelley, but you'll have to give your personal approval for it. If it bounces, it's your responsibility.

"It won't bounce."

Two days later the manager called Shelley into his office. "Your friend's cheque bounced and I'm holding you responsible."

When Shelley called Fran, she was mortified. "Oh no! Shelley, I am so sorry. Would it be okay to pay in cash? I expect to have some money immediately."

"Of course," Shelley said. "That would be fine."

Fran rushed in the next day, full of apologies, with a $100 bill in her hand. Shelley was trying to brush off her embarrassment, but the manager made things worse. The store had a policy of not accepting $100 bills, he told Fran. Now it was Shelley's turn to feel embarrassed.

"Listen, it's okay," Fran said. "I'll come back tomorrow with smaller bills." That was fine with everyone and Fran left the store.

Shelley never saw her again—Fran had disappeared for good. Her mother, Patricia, was frantic. On April 9, 1996, three days after Fran was last seen going out for a walk in the evening, Pat Young reported her daughter missing to the Vancouver police. There was nothing they could do, they told her, but after a great deal of nagging on Pat's part they did eventually produce a missing-woman poster. "Fran was last seen on April 6, 1996," the poster stated, "wearing a long black leather coat, blue jeans and a white sweater. At the time of her disappearance, Fran had lived in the Kitsilano area of Vancouver over 10 years."

Tanya Marlo Holyk was the next woman to vanish. Born to an aboriginal family on December 8, 1975, Tanya had lived for a year with her sister Cathy and her husband, Gary Hall, in Klemtu, a tiny fishing and hunting village of 450 people who could get out only on a ferry; they were at least 160 kilometres from a provincial road. Tanya's mother, Dorothy Purcell, who was always called Dixie, had moved to Vancouver years earlier. Tanya left Klemtu when she was sixteen to return to her mother.

"She was really nice, had a lot of energy about her," Tanya's brother Gary Holyk told a reporter later. "I guess that was from living in the city. She just seemed full of drive." Tanya was also a lovely girl of five feet six inches tall; she was slim at 115 pounds, with long black curly hair and deep brown eyes.

Three years after she moved to Vancouver, Tanya, who was using drugs heavily and working as a prostitute, met Gary number three at a club. Gary Silcott was a saxophone player in a band. He turned out to be a man with a history of girlfriends who were prostitutes and drug addicts. A few months after she began seeing him, Tanya discovered that she was pregnant. For the baby's sake she managed to kick her drug habit and she moved out of her mother's house to live with Silcott on Vimy Crescent in East Vancouver. This was, and still is, a pleasant working-class neighbourhood; it's close to Burnaby and about twenty blocks southeast of the Downtown Eastside. When Gary Junior was born in November 1995, Dixie moved into the basement suite downstairs to help with the baby.

Tanya's relationship with Silcott soon fell apart and, intending to clean up her life and stay off drugs, she moved downstairs with the baby to live with Dixie. A few weeks later, realizing that her relationship with Silcott, who remained upstairs, was getting more acrimonious by the day, she moved to Chilliwack, a small city east of Vancouver in the Fraser Valley. She was happy to move someplace where she could make a fresh start and get treatment for her addictions. Silcott was angry about her leaving with their son, so angry that eventually she had to take out a restraining order against him in Chilliwack. But it wasn't long before she returned to Vancouver with her mother and the baby and settled in a house at 42nd Street and Joyce, several blocks south of the place on Vimy. She and Silcott agreed on a joint custody arrangement for their son and he began a new life with another woman, Shannon Arbique, who was also an addicted prostitute. Meanwhile Tanya sought more treatment and counselling, with Dixie's ardent support.

On October 29, 1996, two days before Halloween, Silcott went to Tanya's house to pick up his son; she had asked him to take the baby for three days instead of his usual two because she was going to a Halloween party. Silcott agreed.

When Tanya didn't return home on November 1, her mother felt certain that something terrible had happened. She tried to file a missing-person report with the Vancouver Police Department but they weren't interested. Dixie recalled the experience later for an interviewer with CNN. "Your daughter is just out having fun," she was told. "They said, 'Don't bother us. Don't waste our time,' and hung up on me. I just stood there with the phone in my hand for ten minutes, just looking at it." Dixie pestered the Missing Persons staff non-stop until, two days later, they agreed to let her file an official missing-person report. Tanya's sister, Cathy Hall, sent notes everywhere she could think of, hoping her sister would respond—or that someone would: "I hope your out there and see this please please tell me your okay. I Love You alot!!!!!!!!!!!!!!!"

The last woman from the Downtown Eastside to disappear in 1996 was Olivia Williams, whose family lived in Burns Lake. She was just twenty-two, hopelessly addicted and working as a prostitute; like Tanya Holyk, she lived at the Vernon Rooms. The last time anyone saw her was December 6. She had chubby cheeks and a sweet child's face, with long brown hair and brown eyes. Olivia Williams is one of the least known of the missing women of the Downtown Eastside.

The total count for 1996 was four missing women. Another, Tracey Buyan, almost became the fifth one night in 1996.

"Willie? Everybody knew him," she says. Tracey had lived at the Astoria Hotel for a while and used to see him there all the time. He was a famous john in the neighbourhood, she said; his truck was a familiar sight cruising up and down the side streets.

Tracey's regular spot in those days was the southeast corner of Oppenheimer Park. She was always easy to spot because of her height—she's at least five feet ten inches tall—as well as her deep red hair, usually piled in tumbled curls on top of her head, and her endearing passion for stylish clothes. She always wore high boots, bright jackets and scarves, tight pants or a skirt, and carefully applied makeup. She lived with her husband, an addict like her, in a small room a block away, where he would wait for her to bring home food, money and dope. All she longed for was to kick her habit, get clean and go home to Victoria to see her five kids. If she could stay clean, she promised herself, she might, just might, get them back.

Tracey had a steady list of regulars but Willie Pickton wasn't one of them. So she was surprised when he swung by one night in his truck and pulled over. At first everything was fine, she said. "He picked me up and said he wanted a BJ [blow job] and I told him it would be forty dollars." When she climbed into his truck, the stench almost drove her back out.

"It smelled terrible; it smelled of animals, like barn animals. And then he took me out to his trailer, which was fucking disgusting. As soon as you got in the kitchen, you couldn't go any farther. There were clothes everywhere. The kitchen had a big counter with a sink and a little propane heater. The parking lot was built at the side of the trailer. As you came in, the kitchen was right there, and on the left was the rest of the building. What I could see was just the kitchen. I couldn't go any farther. He said, 'Let's go in there,' but I couldn't get past all the mess.

"So we did our business and then I was getting dressed. I seen him talking . . . he says he can't find his wallet.

"He pulls out this knife. He says I've got his wallet. I pushed him back—he cuts two buttons off my shirt. I got out of the trailer—I just walked out—and he finally comes out and gives me back my purse and my wallet."

Willie drove Tracey back to the Downtown Eastside. All the way back he chattered about how he liked helping working girls and liked helping them kick their drug habit. But he gave them only one chance, he told her. "If they go back to dope, well then, they don't deserve to live. They're useless. They're better off dead."

Tracey paused in her recollection. Her arms were tightly crossed over her chest and her eyes filled with tears. She pressed her fingers against her mouth to stop herself from crying. After a few seconds, her voice steady, she started to speak again.

"Girls were into speedballs . . . girls like Mona Wilson, who was in jail for a little while and was in bad shape. He was picking on the worst ones. He would come and say he would help the girls. Especially the ones in withdrawal. He would talk to the girls downtown. He tried to make friends with them, and they would trust him. He would promise to help you kick the dope. But once a girl tries to quit and doesn't succeed, then they're useless. When they'd go back to dope, he'd say, 'You're useless—just fucking bitches.' One girl was puking and shitting at the same time, she was really sick."

Because she hadn't asked Pickton for drugs and hadn't done any while she was with him, he assumed she didn't do them. He didn't know she had a rule for herself—that she didn't use drugs when she was with a date.

He never stopped for her again. And Tracey never filed a complaint against him for threatening her with a knife. She did tell the women at WISH what had happened, and they added him to their bad-date list.

CHAPTER TEN

LISA YELDS

Lisa Yelds looked at the clock again. New Year's Eve. She had a hunch her son Rocky was out with his pal DJ in his car. Where the hell were they anyway? The kids were underage, and if they got into trouble, well, she'd let them have it.

Life had been hard on Yelds. In the late 1980s, when she finally found a decent little house for rent in Port Coquitlam that was big enough for her and her two boys Rocky and Don, she felt as if her luck was about to change. The school was just a few blocks away and the kids liked it. They were starting to make friends. Lisa spent a lot of time on her own, trying to make sense of the bad years behind her—the sexual abuse in the foster homes she'd been sent to, the drugs and prostitution that became part of her life when she ended up on the Downtown Eastside, a bad marriage, the struggle of rehab. Now, at thirty-eight, she had the pressure of building a new life for herself and her boys. When her older son, Rocky, told her about his new buddy from school, a boy called DJ, she was happy for him and encouraged the two boys to hang out at her place. DJ, she said right away, was "awesome." But she also worried that Rocky, with his dad's wild streak in him, could be a bad influence on DJ.

Tonight the boys had big plans for New Year's and all she wanted was to get them home. Lisa dug around in Rocky's room long enough to find a home number for DJ and then dialled.

"Hello?" A man on the other end of the phone.

"Is this DJ's place?"

"Yup."

Lisa explained her predicament. The boys were out in a car, they were underage, it was New Year's Eve . . .

"I'll take care of it."

And so he did. Willie Pickton found his nephew DJ—Dave's son—and Rocky and brought them home safely.

Yelds was grateful, and before long she and Willie were friends. Not boyfriend–girlfriend or anything like that, more like buddies. But close. And it turned out they lived just a couple of blocks apart on the same road, Dominion Avenue. She was at 1345 Dominion; he was east of her at 963. When he started demolishing a house next to hers, they got to know each other much better, although he was shy for a long time; once when she offered him a soft drink, he blushed scarlet. They started talking on the phone, and one time, just when they were getting to know each other, the conversation lasted for four hours. When she had free time, Lisa would trot over to the farm to help him in the shop or the barns, or just to hang around. She often dropped into the motorhome where he was living and tried to clean it up; it was always a mess.

As for Willie's own hygiene, she was appalled, and never hesitated to say so to his face. In fact, Lisa was the only person who could make him take a bath. "Willie!" she'd exclaim. "You stink, you need a bath, go change your clothes." Or sometimes, more tactfully, "Willie, you're getting a little ripe there. I think you kind of need a bath and a change of clothes here, pal, because you're getting a little rude."

He never took offence when she nagged him. He would just fight back with complaints about her smoking, especially when she smoked in his trailer. "Go outside with your cigarette," he'd snap, waving away the smoke in irritation.

Given his slovenliness, it surprised Lisa that Willie liked having a clean bathroom, clean clothes and the table set properly for dinner, with the knives and forks lined up just so. He wouldn't bother for himself, but when Lisa took the trouble to fix things up for him, he was pleased. She figured it was because she made life more normal for him—he'd told her that being normal was something he craved.

Occasionally Lisa would lie down beside him for a cuddle but there was never a sexual relationship with him. "Don't think that means he can't function with women," she warns, referring to the rumour that he is unable to have normal intercourse. When she woke up with him beside her, he often had an erection, but he never tried anything. She noticed his legs more than anything else about him during those times when he was asleep beside her: they were hairless, bony and white.

"His feet were odd," she remembers. He never cut his toenails; they were about an inch long. But he took good care of his teeth, and every three to six months he went to the dentist to have them cleaned.

Sometimes they'd go to the movies together. Willie loved Clint Eastwood's *Dirty Harry* series. He'd seen all five of them and he got a kick out of imitating the tough cop's favourite line: "Make my day," Willie would growl, then snort happily.

He loved watching movies at home and almost always chose a detective or police story at the video store. Dave liked to come by to watch too and it amused Lisa to see the two tough brothers squirm when the danger was turned up. "They would get so tense that they would rear back on the sofa and push themselves up against the back cushions; they couldn't bear the suspense."

Willie liked shopping and one of his favourite treats was hunting for bargains on Boxing Day. One day he invited Lisa to go with him and let her in on one of his little secrets. "If he saw something he liked and it cost too much he would switch the price tag off another item." He encouraged her to do the same thing. "Lisa," he whispered on their first outing, "if you see something you like, just switch the tag and I will get it through the teller." Although she thought this was funny, she never took up his offer. As a youngster she had been busted for shoplifting and she knew if she got caught again she could end up with a criminal record.

Willie was always generous with her. He gave her meat, as much as she and her boys could use, and sometimes they'd go shopping together at local supermarkets for groceries. He liked Sav-On Foods and Costco, and his favourite was SuperSave. To help Lisa get the best prices, Willie supplied her with a card for Costco and registered it to her as an employee of P&B Used Building Materials in Surrey.

She couldn't persuade him to buy fresh vegetables or fruit; all he wanted was orange juice and milk, potatoes and meat—chicken, beef or pork. Pork was his favourite. Dessert was usually ice cream; for a special treat he'd buy a can of peaches and mash them together with the ice cream. Whether he was in a bar or at home, he never touched alcohol.

Willie liked Lisa because she didn't judge him and she wasn't squeamish. She was welcome in the slaughterhouse when he was working on animals, and he would take her to the knife store in Port Moody when he needed to get new knives or have his old ones sharpened. By 1993 she was working with him, cleaning his trailer and cutting meat in the slaughterhouse. He seemed happy when she agreed to go on errands with him, and sometimes they'd stop at a little restaurant in Burnaby called Uncle Willie's, one of his favourite places to eat.

She'd even go with him when he was filling meat orders at stock-yard sales. "If you wanted meat you phoned him a week or two in advance and he would pick up what you wanted from the auction," she explains. "He'd buy goats, cows, sheep, ostrich, pigs, emu, whatever people wanted." Willie kept track of all the orders in the office in his trailer, where he kept his Rolodex.

"Fraser Valley Auctions would save the culls for him to take home," Yelds remembers. "In other words, the animals that would not sell because they were sick or dying. Plus I have gotten meat from him in about 1992 or 1993 that had abscesses in the leg. It was gross.

"At the auctions everyone called him Bob—he was so different there. He was very country, very polite, unassuming. He talked softly and kept his head down."

By 1995 Willie was going out to the Fraser Valley regularly on errands and Yelds went with him on some of the trips. One was to bid on a vehicle at the Matsqui Institution, the medium-security federal prison near Agassiz. "Sometimes he'd want to visit a used car lot nearby. He got a lot of vehicles there," Yelds says.

Another time they took a two-day drive up into the mountains on the way to Hope, a place near a fish hatchery, to pick up three tons of scrap metal, a job on a government contract. And sometimes they'd drive into the United States just to get groceries and look for tractor parts.

All the time she was in the truck with him, Yelds was aware that he was keeping an eye open for police cars. "I know he was always concerned about the police watching him but I did not know why," she says. "I know that Dave was also worried about cops too, but again I did not know why."

Although Willie liked Lisa and so did Sandy Humeny, Sandy's sister Ingrid Fehlauer, who often stayed at the farm, was afraid of her and couldn't stand her. Neither could Dave Pickton, even though Lisa was the mother of DJ's closest friend. Which was another problem she had with him—she hated the way he treated his son.

"Dave had DJ on an excavator when he was only eight years old," she says. "He worked the pants off that kid. DJ was a sweet kid; he's active, he's awesome. He and I used to have water fights with a hose. But his dad worked him so hard he was always exhausted. One day he had his bike parked up against my house and Dave came looking for him, but DJ hid in a cupboard in my house."

Dave accused her of going through Willie's drawers when she cleaned the trailer. When he saw her on the farm, his usual greeting was, "Hi, you fucking loser, how are you?" Lisa hated this. But she was also afraid of him. When she first started hanging out with his brother, Dave told her he didn't trust her. "I'm gonna check you out," he threatened. "Go ahead," she snapped.

A few days later he told her he had someone with access to her police records check her out and he decided she was okay. Right away she asked herself if Dave was a police informant for the police, and to this day she believes he was. How else could he get into police files? But Willie remained her friend. He liked her because she accepted him for what he was and because she always took his side in any arguments with his brother.

Every morning the brothers would have breakfast together at the Golden Ears, a notorious stripper bar owned by the Hells Angels on Shaughnessy, Port Coquitlam's main street. Dave would lay out the orders of the day.

"Dave was the domineering one," Lisa reflects. "He would bark and Willie would jump."

That all changed one day when Dave, irritated by one of her sharp opinions, tried to trip her. With a bellow, Willie charged his brother and kicked him, knocking him down. Shocked and winded, Dave could only stare at Willie—who fell back against a barn wall, slid to the ground and howled with laughter. It was the first time Lisa had ever seen him get the better of his brother, and it forged a strong bond between the two of them.

For Willie's part, he was fascinated with her. Lisa was the smartest person he had ever met and one of the toughest. She was articulate. She read people quickly and was usually right about them. Once she decided she liked someone, she was ferocious in her loyalty. And she loved fast cars, so she was thrilled when Willie helped her purchase one out at a used car auction place in Surrey.

"You won't like it at first," he told her. "It's red and I know you don't want red, but it's a big Trans Am in good condition. Tell me what to bid and before the week is out it's yours." She suggested he go up to about $1,300, and he was just as pleased as she was when his bid won. Still, he wouldn't let her drive it until he'd done some repairs and tuned it for her.

Lisa surprised herself by loving the car. She'd ridden Harleys for thirty-five years and was part of the local biker scene; for her, until the red Trans Am arrived, nothing was as much fun as a bike. While he was afraid of motorcycles himself, Willie admired her guts. But she also had insecurities he could understand. She didn't trust anyone, she didn't like most people, she drew back when people tried to hug her. She thought she was stupid. And when she would complain to him about not having a driver's licence and that she was sure she'd never get one, it was Willie who told her she could and encouraged her to take the test. "You're not stupid. You can do it. I am going to keep pushing till you go and do it."

She did, and when she raced over to the farm to show it to him, he was the only one she knew who was happy for her. Another time, after she had fallen and cut her leg to the bone, it was Willie who arranged to get her to the hospital right away.

As time went on they'd joke and call each other about ridiculous things. He'd pore over stories about movie stars in the *National Enquirer* and couldn't wait to talk to her about the other crazy people in the tabloid. She remembers the night he took her out for a special treat, a surprise. It turned out to be a children's magic show in New Westminster and Willie was entranced; every trick was amazing to him and he clapped wildly. He turned to Lisa when it ended and said, "I just don't understand how the magician could cut people in half."

But there was a big streak of his mother's practicality in Willie. When Lisa called him once about a problem she was having with her car, he made her describe it and then coached her over the phone till she fixed it herself. "You gotta learn," he said.

During these years Lisa was trying to patch up a bad marriage with her husband, David Yelds, moving back and forth between her place and his. Finally she and her sons settled down for good in the house on Dominion, she and Willie saw each other every day. At some point she realized that he was the blond boy who had been so nice to her at his parents' meat locker when she was a little girl. The same boy who had given her a whole bag of hot dogs.

Whenever anyone asked Willie Pickton what he did for a living, his stock answer was short and simple: "A pig man. That's all I am—just a pig man."

In the 1990s the truth was more complicated. Along with all his buying, slaughtering and selling of animals and his buying, selling and trading of cars and parts, Willie was working with Dave on the other businesses. Among their best little earners in those years were the pig roasts and cockfights they ran out of the back of the slaughterhouse. Dozens of people, most of them from Filipino communities, crowded the farm on Sundays to bet on fights that would run all day and into the evening. The Asians in the crowd preferred a double- or triple-your-money bet and would put down $20 on every fight. The Picktons made their share with steep admission charges, and Dave sold cartons of cigarettes and booze and took a percentage of each bet. These gatherings were the precursor of what was later to become Piggy's Palace, a party barn the Picktons set up down the road.

Dave took no chances at the cockfights. He always had a neighbour or pal act as security as soon as the punters arrived at the gate, people who would let them in and direct them to the barn. And the security worked both ways. "He used a person with a two-way radio to warn if cops came," Scott Chubb said later. "Always on a Sunday. Two to six hours. Depending on how the Asians were betting." If anyone spotted a policeman at the gate, they'd phone down to the slaughterhouse right away and the crowd would scatter. People lined up to do the security job, as they could count on making $90 to $150 a night.

Dave set up the fights and handled the money, shoving thick rolls of bills into his pockets and strutting around as the boss. In the back of the slaughterhouse Willie would help with the birds, which were fitted with vicious silver spurs, and with the mess, which was considerable: feathers, blood, bone. Dave's kids ran around with their friends, watching the fights from the edge of the ring, slipping between the adults to get a better look.

The Picktons' ring was set up just like the ones used for prize fights, and the crowd, almost always Filipino, began drinking right away and placing large bets on the best fighters. It didn't take long for most of the men to get drunk, decide they wanted sex and start groping the women hanging around the farm. The women there were all Pickton friends, not wives—the Filipinos never brought their wives. Occasionally one of the bettors would get lucky, but Willie never let anyone near the women he considered his own friends. "Not this one," he would snarl, if one of the men tried to grab Lisa Yelds.

Some of the men would start fights over not much at all. The drinking, betting and lechery continued late into the evening until most of the birds had torn each other apart.

Pat Casanova was always one of the regulars at the cockfights, and because he spent so much time butchering, scalding and roasting pigs with Willie, he decided to move his three roasting ovens to the farm so they could process between ten and twenty animals each week. He and Willie spent hours together. At first Willie kept the pigs in a small barn near the back of the property, but the roof had rotted badly, and one day a strong windstorm blew down the whole barn. Instead of rebuilding it, Willie began keeping the pigs in a horse trailer that he parked in front of his slaughterhouse.

Willie and Pat Casanova would herd the piglets one at a time down the trailer ramp into the slaughterhouse. The men would grab the pig's hind legs in a noose of knotted rope and pull it tight, then Willie would plunge a knife into its throat. He would attach a hook to the knotted rope and winch the animal up so it would dangle over a metal table and bleed out.

If the animal was too big to handle easily, Willie would coax it into a wheeled cart equipped with what is known as a ratchet lever hoist or "comealong." This is a simple farmer's hoist with a sturdy hook or clip at each end of a chain; the butcher clips the animal's tied hind feet to the chain and pumps the ratchet's handle to pull the animal up feet first. As it bled, Willie would slice through the belly to remove the intestines, which he would toss into a barrel to take to West Coast Reduction.

Casanova, in the meantime, would fill a large tub with water and heat it on a propane burner. When the animal had bled out, he would boil it for about twenty minutes to make it easy to remove the hair. As soon as the pig was out of the tub, Casanova would scrape off the hair and Willie would cut out all the remaining organs. These would also go into the barrel.

The men would clean off the pigs and place them in a walk-in cooler, where they were stored overnight. The following day the men would move the chilled pigs into one of six freezers in the slaughter-house—freezers left over from Leonard and Louise's old pig and poultry business. Over the years, when a freezer rusted or burned out, Willie rarely bothered to have it repaired. By the time he was working with Casanova there were only three left in the slaughter-house that worked.

Food inspectors came around from time to time and, appalled by the unsanitary conditions and sloppy practices, they'd shut down Willie's slaughterhouse for a few weeks. They knew he'd open it up again as soon as they got busy somewhere else. In fact, on at least one occasion they let him finish off what was left in the barn, giving him twenty-four hours to butcher twenty-seven pigs—Willie did it all by himself and did it on time. They also inspected the barn, giving him a checklist of what he needed to do to meet health codes.

Lisa Yelds thought she knew pretty well everything that was going on in Willie's life at the time. But she didn't know another side of his personality, the part that couldn't get enough of life in the Downtown Eastside. The only friend he had who shared this fas-cination was Pat Casanova. After a long day in the slaughterhouse they would often relax by driving into the Downtown Eastside to join the regulars in the bar at the Astoria Hotel. Their eyes feasted on the prostitutes who hung around the bar swapping wisecracks and war stories with one another. Willie was careful to keep this side of his life a secret from Lisa.

What she kept a secret from him was the fact that he reminded her—right from the beginning, and despite her fondness for him—of the infamous American serial killer Ed Gein, who was murdering women in the mid-1950s. Fascinated by the world of serial killers, Lisa read every book she could find on them. She has built up an impressive personal library, covering two walls of her small apartment, of novels, biographies, true crime, anything. She became uneasy about some of the things Gein and Willie had in common.

A rough, uneducated farmer, Gein had lived for years in Plainfield, Wisconsin, with his domineering mother, who ran a small grocery store, and his older brother, Henry, in an old family house. Their father, an unemployed alcoholic, had always been abusive, and Henry bullied Ed, who was shy and unattractive and never fit in anywhere, especially not at school. When Henry died in a brush fire on the property, the police were suspicious of Ed but couldn't prove he had murdered him. After his mother died, Ed left her mummified body in her bedroom. Soon he was digging up graveyards to find human remains fresh enough to skin and dismember. He used the skin to clothe himself and the bones for decorations in the house, but he wasn't caught until he moved on to live victims—including the mother of a local sheriff.

The story of Ed Gein inspired Thomas Bloch's book *Psycho*, as well as the Alfred Hitchcock movie version starring Anthony Perkins. Gein's use of human skin may have also inspired Thomas Harris's *The Silence of the Lambs*.

"I always had this thought at the back of my mind that Willie could be a serial killer," Yelds says now, "but I was never afraid of him myself. I knew he would never hurt me."

Did she ever tell anyone? "Of course not. They would have thought I was crazy. It was just an idea, is all."

CHAPTER ELEVEN

PIGGY'S PALACE

In 1995 Dave Pickton had an idea for a new business, something that came to him as he was demolishing the Boo Pub, a notorious country-and-western bar in a little strip mall in Coquitlam, a bar so country, in fact, that it had saddles on the barstools. Men in cowboy hats, plaid shirts and jeans would gather for breakfast, even though the food was terrible. The Boo Pub's wild reputation came from a nightclub at the back, a haunt for strippers, drug dealers and bikers. Beside it were a wine and beer shop and a Stop & Shop convenience store. Although Dave tore it all out he was careful to keep any material that would be useful for his newest project, a bar and dance hall he planned to build in Port Coquitlam.

If the cockfights could draw a crowd and make money, it stood to reason, he thought, that a booze can and dance bar tucked away on a rural road at the edge of town would do even better. The Hells Angels had established their own hangout a few years earlier, in a grey-blue clapboard house, two storeys, with enough parking for a hundred cars at the back, plenty of parking in the front and a strong chained gate, just down Dominion between Burns and the Pickton farm. Dave was buddies with the guys there. They'd be his best customers, he reckoned.

The sale of the farmland made it all possible. He had used some of the money to buy property on Tannery Road in Surrey for his P&B business office and trucks; it was across the Fraser River from the city of New Westminster, about a twenty-minute drive from the farm. Now, in partnership with Willie, he spent about $200,000 to buy a long, narrow strip of land known as Shiloh Nurseries, on

Burns Road less than a kilometre down Dominion Avenue and around the corner from the farm. Behind a scruffy front yard were a shabby two-storey house, several small shacks and outbuildings and a large corrugated metal shed that stretched across the narrow lot. Previous owners had used it as a riding stable; a small racetrack behind it is still there.

As the lot stretches back, it becomes lank and damp and lumpy with clumps of grass until it reaches the dike that holds back the Pitt River. Eagles fly over the water here and land on the high branches of cedar trees, rocking back and forth until they spy something to eat. Because of the water access at the back of the property, Dave decided to a buy a new motorboat, a big grey one he kept in front of the old house; he told people he needed it for his work.

Dave chose Scott Chubb and Marty de Winter to help him build the new place. What should it be called? Well, he thought, "Piggy" was what some had called his father, Leonard, and it was what almost everyone called Dave behind his back. So let's call it Piggy's Palace, Dave said.

With the basic corrugated metal shed already in place, Chubb and de Winter brought in BobCats and, as Chubb describes it, "pulled out all the horseshit and stuff like that." After framing new interior walls to fashion a dance hall, they installed the bar and restaurant equipment they'd removed from the Boo Pub and the old Metro Centre Hotel on the Kingsway in Burnaby, a notorious biker hangout. These places had yielded enough material to build a long bar, a full restaurant kitchen, a walk-in refrigerator and a raised dance floor. There were even enough tables and chairs to seat more than 150 people. They installed old beer signs, fluorescent lighting, a revolving disco ball and a sound system.

Dave wanted to have food available, so he brought in women he knew to do the cooking. They made cabbage rolls and shrimp; the food, people say, was good. And of course they served Willie's famous barbecued pork, roasted by Pat Casanova at his place.

Bill Malone said later that the idea for the new hall was his. He claims credit for the whole concept, which he has described as a "place for office parties" and a nightclub comparable to any of the big clubs in Vancouver. He also said he managed the whole construction project. "We built proper stages, we brought in everything, we decorated it with beer signs and everything to give it a real home feel. We repainted it all. It would have the full atmosphere of any nightclub. I did it," he boasted. "It was all my doing." It was probably a good thing Dave Pickton didn't hear him say this.

Lisa Yelds got a job cleaning and waitressing at Piggy's Palace, but she still nurses a grudge about the way she was treated. "Dave Pickton was cheap," she says. "He only paid me fifty dollars to work from four thirty p.m. to four thirty a.m."

Scott Chubb was there to do security and collect money from people at the door, who paid ten to twenty dollars each to come in. "I used to walk around with thousands of dollars in my pocket," he remembers. "It was never less than $10,000, and one night I remember we pulled in $43,000."

Everyone was excited about the new business and Willie was no exception. Before it opened, all that the men who worked for Dave could talk about was the women who would be there and the chance for unlimited sex, booze, drugs and partying.

For the first time in his life, Willie thought he might find a steady girlfriend of his own. He thought it was time to stop regretting his failed romance with Connie Anderson and the way Sandy Fehlauer had turned down his marriage proposal. He decided to clean himself up, put his best foot forward, take a chance. He set himself an ambitious program of self-improvement. The first thing he did was get a wig to cover his bald head. He had heard that the Hair Club for Men was the best place to get a realistic hairpiece, so he invested in one that blended perfectly with his own dirty blond hair, hair he kept long, hanging down the back of his neck. Scott Chubb says he nearly dropped dead when he saw the new Willie Pickton.

"We'd just opened Piggy's Palace and a lot of girls were coming in and he wanted to look better. When Willie turned up in new jeans, a new T-shirt and shoes and a new toupee, I said, 'Jesus Christ, you look pretty.' It was the first time I never smelt pig shit on him. Willie bitched that he paid $2,300 for the toupee and that he'd never paid more than three dollars for a haircut in his life."

The hairpiece didn't last long. It hadn't occurred to Pickton that it needed to be looked after. He never removed it and he never washed his own hair, so it soon became filthy. He'd crawl under cars to do work on the engines, ignoring the gobs of grease spattering his head; before long they were stuck to the toupee. Finally he had to throw it out.

And about this time Willie Pickton also decided he needed a new house. He'd outgrown the motorhome and needed space for an office, so he bought a large mobile home clad in white aluminum siding, hauled it to the back of the farm and set it on a concrete slab. A front porch stretched across most of the trailer. The front windows faced down the road towards Dominion Avenue but it was impossible to see the trailer from Dominion; it gave him more privacy than he'd had in the small Dodge motorhome.

There were two front doors. The one on the left was the main door; it opened into a hall. Down the hall to the left was Willie's bedroom, with a bed, closet, nightstand and television. Straight ahead, beside the bedroom, was a bathroom with a tub, sink and toilet. Next to the bathroom was a narrow office with two desks and a phone; it was an open space without a door, and when visitors walked into the trailer, they found the office almost directly in front of them. Down the hall to the right of the front door was the kitchen, and off the kitchen was a laundry and utility area with a washer and dryer, shelving and a small furnace. (The trailer's second front door opened into the kitchen.)

The last room on the right side, the largest in the trailer, was meant to be a living room, but Willie used it as an extra bedroom. This is where various friends and acquaintances would stay, including the wide variety of women who came to keep the place clean, do a little office work and keep him company. Sometimes men working on the property with Willie would bunk in here. Scott Chubb was one of them and all he can remember was the mess.

"There was clothing everywhere," he says. "All over the place. There was clothing in his trailer, there was clothing on the outside of the trailer, there was clothing in the mechanic's shop, there was boxes and boxes of clothing that he used to use for rags and stuff in the back there too. Old curtains and stuff like that that were in boxes they had stored back there that they'd use for oil rags and what have you."

The Pickton brothers incorporated their new business on Burns Road as "Piggy Palace Good Times Society," and it didn't take long for the place to live up to its name. Although they liked to style themselves as community benefactors throwing parties for charitable groups, the fact is that the Hells Angels, the Picktons' neighbours across the road on Dominion, would take over the Palace every few weeks. These parties were always closed, for bikers only, and when they roared out of the parking area on their motorcycles in the early hours of the morning, they'd almost always head back to their clubhouse across from the farm for more drinking, drugs and partying.

Even though it was buried at the back of a large lot on a quiet street of hobby farms, the Palace reverberated all night long with the sound of country music, laughter, Harley engines racing and shrieks and curses. Halloween, Thanksgiving and Christmas were the big times for parties, and then things would slow down a little until Valentine's Day.

"I use Tony of White Knight Security for all my parties," Dave Pickton says. "He's an Angel." A Hells Angel—Dave is very proud of his biker connections. "If I have Angels at my parties I ask them not to wear their colours. I ask them not to scare people. Tony is the best. He's my bouncer, my doorman. All the parked cars are watched. My parties are safe."

"Tony" is Anthony Terezakis, one of the most feared criminals in the Vancouver area. Whether or not he was a full-patch Hells Angel or an associate is unclear, but he was definitely one of the leaders of a large crack cocaine business that operated in the Downtown Eastside and throughout the Lower Mainland, extending into the Okanagan Valley. Terezakis hung out in Vancouver at the American Hotel on Main Street, a place popular with the Angels.

Safe or not, people in the community started to complain about the parties at Piggy's Palace, and after a visit from a Port Coquitlam inspector, the city tried to stop them. It took the brothers to court in 1996 in an effort to end the parties, but the Picktons fought back, insisting that all the profits went to local charities and needy causes. It was very tricky—off-duty police officers attended the parties, and so did city officials. Mike Bowen, a councillor, rented the place for an end-of-season party for a minor league sports team that he coached; he later told Leneen Robb, a reporter for Coquitlam's *Now* newspaper, that it was a good place.

"One of our parents had recommended this hall that we could use to have our wind-up," he told her. "It didn't seem that it was open to the public at that time, but that was my only trip and we went in and we did our thing and we got out and that was it." But Bowen told Robb he found the site unusual: "It was out of the ordinary to go into an agricultural area like that and find this old building in the back forty there that was actually converted into some kind of a half-assed nightclub, clubhouse. It was a bit bizarre . . . but like I said, I was only there for a short period of time and I never went back and never thought twice about it."

Another councillor, Darrell Penner, attended several parties at the Palace, but the most prominent local official to attend was Port Coquitlam's mayor, Len Traboulay. His widow, Joanne Traboulay, told Leneen Robb that they'd been only once and stayed half an hour; they thought the place was tastefully done.

Of course, Dave's neighbours Albert and Vera Harvey were regulars, and so were Cam and Della Grant. The Grants missed only two of the parties at the Palace and wouldn't hear a bad word against the Picktons. Bill Malone was always there too, standing around keeping an eye on everyone.

But the truth is that almost all the people in the community knew the Palace as a wild party place with drugs and prostitutes. And everyone knew that the bikers who attended usually finished the parties at their own place across from the Pickton farm, a clubhouse that had become infamous as a booze can serving alcohol and drugs to members and friends. These places were gold mines, and running Piggy's Palace gave Dave big ideas for other bars. Now he wanted to buy the Wild Duck Inn, a local landmark and former biker hangout on the west bank of the Pitt River, close to the Pickton farm.

It's not surprising that by the end of 1996 the neighbourhood became known in criminal circles as a biker area, one controlled by the Hells Angels. On one occasion, when the Angels were holding a large meeting, they called Don Layfield, then the manager of the eighteen-hole Carnoustie Golf Club, which abuts the Pickton land between the farm and the Palace. A few small houses separate the clubhouse from the Picktons' driveway, but behind these houses the two properties meet. The Carnoustie clubhouse had a back room they rented out for private parties at $50 a head, with soft drinks and sandwiches included.

Layfield got a call from a polite man who said he'd like to rent the room for his club. "Just a few of us," he told Layfield. "Maybe fifteen, sixteen people." Sure, Layfield said.

"So lo and behold," he remembers, "the Hells Angels arrived on their Harleys. Sixteen of them. One of them was carrying their book of rules, which was an inch thick. And they paid me a wad of cash." No cheques, no credit cards from these guys. Layfield was not about to tell them to leave. And they were polite and friendly, not at all like their neighbour across the road.

Willie Pickton drove Layfield crazy. "From the dealings I had with him, it seemed to me that Willie Pickton never left [the farm]. He was always there, being miserable to our golfers. Whenever they were out, they would go after their golf balls and he would yell at them if they came on his land." To get even he would walk horses on the club's putting greens, watching with satisfaction as their hooves dug deep into the grass.

Layfield was not the only person to find the Picktons infuriating. The stench from the pigs wafted over the neighbourhood, and people, especially the ones who had just moved into the new houses being built on former Pickton land, complained all the time. The Picktons ignored them. Just as they ignored the complaints that rolled in whenever Willie would rev up a tractor or backhoe late at night and start digging holes and shoving piles of dirt. Sometimes he went at it for hours.

By this time Lisa Yelds and her sons Rocky and Don had moved again, this time to a house in Surrey, a good hour away from the Pickton farm. (Her middle son, Dustin, decided to move in with his father.) She stayed in touch with Willie, and one day he called her for help. He knew she had a scanner and liked to listen in to police calls, sometimes for five hours a day and sometimes all night.

"He was worried they were going to get busted at the Palace. But I never heard them say they were going to raid it, even though there were a thousand people there. It should have been on the scanner. But the place was full of cops too, lots of them, all in plainclothes."

The whole scene at the Picktons' place made her glad she had moved away. She didn't like what was happening there. "There was all of a sudden a lot of new people, namely hangers-on, coming around the farm. It seems they all smelled money, most of them. I have no idea who they all were but the boys [Willie and Dave] became Mr. Popularity. When Piggy's Palace opened, the place was literally a zoo, there were so many new faces.

"And after they acquired their business, P&B Used Building Materials, Dave used to go downtown or to any job site already under way, looking for anyone who would work cheap. Some people only stayed the day and some stayed longer, but they soon quit because Dave's cheques usually bounced, so half the people were not being paid. They used to camp out at the house, out front waiting for Dave, and many were very angry because they wanted to be paid."

The Picktons soon discovered that they were losing equipment and money from various job sites, including Dominion Avenue, mostly thanks to disgruntled employees determined to get their money one way or another. "If it was not nailed down it was stolen, and that included mail, personal possessions and tools," Yelds remembers. "Vehicles were broken into and many times the work vehicles were vandalized, mobile homes used on the job sites were smashed and the tool sheds broken into.

"That's why Dave had Willie stay at the job sites as a night watchman. The boys were sometimes losing more than they were making in a day—plus they went through workers like crazy.

"It's hard, dirty work doing demolition and salvage, so that's why there were so many strange people around, all trying to cash in on the boys' wealth. You needed a scorecard; there were that many new workers around. And the old workers were ripping off the place and blaming it on the new ones. There was a lot of tension and fights at the farm. No one trusted anyone. The workers were drinking and half the time they were pissed when they went to work. That's one of the reasons the boys owed the ICBC [the provincial car insurance agency] so much money—from everyone abusing the vehicles and getting into accidents."

Dave may have been spending money on land, boats, trucks and buses but his brother was not. "Willie stayed poor," says Lisa. "Lived in the motorhome and then the trailer and did his auctions and farm work while his brother used his [Willie's] ID to go to the States and on holidays." According to Yelds, Dave needed his brother's identification cards because his own would have brought up his criminal record at the border. "What a fucking joke, leaving Willie the way he did."

Willie began to spend more and more time in the Downtown Eastside. He almost always parked his truck or the motorhome in front of the Astoria and would amble in to buy drinks for the girls who flocked to his side. Often he'd pick one to take home.

Sometimes he just drove around looking for someone pretty. He always liked a pretty girl. This was about the time that Gina Houston came back into his life. Lisa Yelds had moved to her new place in Surrey and Willie missed her. Lisa had been a buddy, a pal, someone he trusted.

Gina now took her place. She'd moved out of Vancouver to a basement apartment on Grant Avenue in Port Coquitlam, and a friend of hers named Spirit Littlechild was working for the Picktons at Piggy's Palace. The brothers were hosting a "show and shine," a kind of swap meet where Harley-Davidson owners showed off their prized motorcycles and competed for prizes for the best machines. Given the brothers' biker connections, it was a great success: 1,500 people showed up. Littlechild was selling tickets at the gate and asked Houston to help her. When Dave Pickton ambled by, followed soon afterwards by his brother, Spirit started talking to them and introduced Gina. Clearly Willie didn't remember her from their brief encounter a year or two earlier—when he took her friend Vicky Black into his car for sex on the Downtown Eastside—and they didn't speak.

A few days later one of Houston's friends from skid row, a woman named Georgina Lynn Dickens, asked Houston if she could stay with her in Port Coquitlam for a while. Houston said yes. As soon as Dickens moved in, Houston discovered she too was friendly with Willie Pickton. Before long he began dropping by to pick up Dickens to take her into downtown Vancouver to visit her pals there. Lynn Dickens called him often and he would phone her back or drop by. Right away Gina saw him as a mark, and it wasn't long before he and Gina were best friends.

CHAPTER TWELVE

MAGGY GISLE, CARA ELLIS AND SANDRA GAIL RINGWALD

The first of the Downtown Eastside's women to go missing in 1997 was Maria Laura Laliberté, a fifty-two-year-old Native woman who was born November 7, 1949. Although the last time anyone saw her was on New Year's Day, she wasn't reported missing to the Vancouver police until March 8, 2002, five years after she vanished. Like most of the prostitutes who worked on the Downtown Eastside, Laliberté used an alias; in her case it was Kim Keller. Except for the facts that she was slim, five feet six inches tall, with short, curly brown hair and brown eyes, almost no other information about her is available. Where she came from, who her family were and what happened to her are still mysteries.

Ten days later Stephanie Lane vanished from the area around the Patricia Hotel on East Hastings Street, and far more was known about her. She was twenty years old. She was part Native, part black and completely beautiful; she was five feet four inches tall and weighed 115 pounds. As a teenager she'd been an excellent student, but like so many of the women on the Downtown Eastside, she fell in with a bad crowd and, worse, a bad boyfriend.

"She was pretty and very popular, and I guess I spoiled her," her mother, Michele Pineault, told Bob Stall, a reporter with the Vancouver *Province*. "She was very important to me."

On January 11, 1997, Stephanie used a calling card belonging to her mother to make a telephone call; after that no one saw or spoke to her again. Pineault, who was raising Stephanie's little boy, Stephan, was beside herself. She started hunting for her daughter at a club called Number 5 Orange, where Stephanie, using the name Coco, had worked as a stripper and table dancer. No one knew where she was. George Lane, Stephanie's father, was just as distraught as Pineault. He remembered trying to help his daughter kick her heroin addiction not long before she went missing, an ordeal he described to Kim Barker, a reporter for the *Seattle Times*, as "three days of shaking and puking." Lane wept as he shuffled through a stack of pictures of his daughter and tried to talk about her. Although Pineault says she knows her child is dead, Lane cannot, will not agree.

A month later, on February 14, 1997, the same day women assembled in Vancouver for their annual Valentine's Day march to remember the city's missing women, Sharon Evelyn Ward disappeared. A tiny white woman with a lovely elfin face, brown eyes and brown hair, she was twenty-nine when she vanished from New Westminster.

"The last person she contacted was our mother," said her sister, Donna Jensen, who wrote the following account on the Internet message board the families often used to share information. "Sharon phoned late one night but there was no answer, so she left a message and a phone number. She needed to speak with Mom and that it was important, when my mother tried the number several times over the next few days there was no answer. According to information I have been able to piece together she had stormed out of the house her and a boyfriend shared after an argument. This phone call was the last contact anyone in the family has had with Sharon and has led to no clues."

As Donna Jensen described her sister's life, it was very much like those of the other women who had disappeared. She had had a rough time and suffered from alcohol and drug addiction and, as her sister put it, "many other problems," but her family knew very little about her life. While she was not great about contacting them regularly, she did write or call from time to time. Remembering back, Donna acknowledges that Sharon always kept in touch somehow. Then suddenly there was nothing.

No one linked these women to Willie Pickton.

—

She can't remember the exact date but it was sometime in March 1997 when Maggy Gisle, who was thirty years old, saw her closest friend, Cara Ellis, twenty-five, for the last time. The two had lived in the Vernon Rooms—the "Ho Den"—for years and had become best friends. Maggy and her twin sister, Lisa, Native babies whose parents had left them for dead in a snowdrift, had been rescued and adopted by a white family in Powell River. Maggy developed into a bright student and a talented swimmer with high hopes for the Olympics some day, but she was also a child who was abused by her adoptive father and wound up at fourteen with a boyfriend who turned her on to drugs. She quit school and went to live with him in a squat in Victoria; it wasn't long before he began pimping her to earn enough money for their drugs.

When she was about fifteen, Maggy broke up with the boyfriend and moved to the Downtown Eastside, where she lived for fifteen years, working as a drug-addicted prostitute, thief and pimp. Her street name was Crazy Jackie and everyone knew her. She had hit the bottom on skid row, but she was intelligent and determined. After more than thirty attempts to clean up and get out, she finally succeeded in March 1997, and her ambition was to help Cara do the same.

Cara, who used the street name Nikki Trimble, had moved to Vancouver from Calgary, where she'd worked as a prostitute since she was thirteen years old. Her story was a typical one of troubled teen years, but she never lost touch with her family. Her brothers and their children all adored her because she never lost her love of fun. She kept them all laughing and loved to play with the kids, even joining in spirited games of hopscotch on the sidewalks. But Cara was smart and thoughtful as well; her family remembers how she used to spend hours writing in her journal about her feelings and experiences.

Cara and Maggy had been roommates for seven months in a rehabilitation centre, New Dawn Recovery House, in Surrey, but in the end Cara's addictions pushed her back to the Downtown Eastside. Although Maggy had moved to Langley, a small town in the Fraser

Valley, she often returned to Hastings Street and the Ho Den to look for Cara, who she still hoped could get out of the place.

As Maggy describes it, "The management originally made money principally from rent, in charging ten dollars a head for a girl to turn a trick in the room, but around 1989 management began to operate a drug-dealing business as well, and women could only buy their drugs in the building. They would get hurt if they were doing drugs from somewhere else. They would open the doors and they would check your rooms and you'd get beat up if you had little wrappers [flaps of cocaine] or something like that from someplace else, because you were supposed to buy from the house."

Cara wouldn't abide by the house rules. Doug Vickers, who ran the Vernon Rooms, was a Hells Angel associate whose son was a full-patch member. Vickers accused Cara of stealing from him and ordered one of his thugs to beat her up to teach her a lesson. He suspected she was buying drugs from outside the hotel, not from him. And she'd been sick since Maggy had last seen her; in January 1997 she had a lengthy stay at the Vancouver General Hospital. The hospital discharged her on January 20, when she had a doctor's appointment. She never made it, nor did she return to the Ho Den. Maggy finally caught up with her on March 3.

"It was the day before I went into recovery," Maggy remembers. "She looked terrible. I was so happy to see her. I wanted to help her. She wouldn't go and I cried. I went to an emergency shelter to see if they could help but they didn't know how to help my friend. It hurt so much."

Cara disappeared on March 10, 1997. Maggy went back to look for her in the third week of April but she never saw her again. "I always hoped to find her," Maggy says. "I hoped to meet her at an AA meeting."

Cara's family, who lived in Calgary, began looking for her, although at first they were not too worried. Her brother's wife, Lori Ann Ellis, says her family did not report her missing right away mainly because they didn't know she had disappeared. "It was not uncommon to go for long periods of time and not hear from Cara," Lori Ann explains. "And when she did call and ask the family for money and was told no, she would get mad and not call again for long periods of time."

In August 1997, Lori Ann went to Vancouver to look for Cara and finally called the Vancouver Police Department to report that she was missing. "The police had me on the phone for over an hour asking questions about Cara," Lori Ann posted to a website on the missing women. "I was told that the police would look for her but if she did not want to be found we may not hear. I unfortunately thought that this was the case, that she did not want to be found." She filed a report but never knew that the police did nothing; they did not treat Cara as a missing person. The excuse the police eventually gave her was that because she had not yet married Cara's brother she wasn't considered family, and only family could file a missing-person report.

Lori Ann wasn't buying it. "Part of why this was not looked upon as important enough was because of the style of life she had," she said. "And I feel that was a problem with most of the girls."

Sandra Gail Ringwald had been up all night. She crawled out of her bed in the Cordova Rooms only when the afternoon sun and a craving for a hit of cocaine woke her up. She felt like crap. But she always felt like crap unless she was high. She was thirty years old, five feet six inches tall, skinny and addicted to cocaine and heroin. Paying for her drugs cost her about $200 a day, which meant she worked hard, selling sex from street corners and stealing stuff from any store that would let her through the door. A favourite target was the Army and Navy Store on East Hastings; another was London Drugs on Robson Street. But her signature method of raising cash was breaking into cars that delivered cigarettes to stores, stealing the cartons and selling them herself. She had collected an impressive criminal record of arrests and convictions and done plenty of jail time, and she had tried—and failed—many times to kick her addiction.

Sandra Gail had started using drugs when she was in her late teens, and now, even though she was on a methadone program to wean her off them, she couldn't give them up. Methadone does work for many addicts. While they can't get high on it, it is a strong opiate that calms down users and causes no withdrawal problems. That's why so many doctors prescribe it to help addicts stop using drugs. But methadone wasn't working for her now, any more than the hospital detox program had.

Sandra Gail had two young kids, one eight and the other six, and they had a decent life with their father, Paul Campbell, a fisherman who lived in North Vancouver. She had worked as a cook-deckhand on his boat, the *Ocean Achiever*, for five years when she was younger but hadn't been on his crew since 1994. She desperately wanted to be part of her children's lives. She was also smart enough not to take welfare; she was afraid that if she did the welfare people might start nosing around her kids and she might lose the limited access she now had.

By this time her favourite drug was a speedball, a mix of heroin and cocaine that she injected up to five times a day or as often as she could get it. The cocaine wired her up to feel happy and excited and the heroin calmed her down. This day, on March 22, 1997, she'd had a good sleep and was ready to start her daily hunt for money and more drugs. Once she got going she knew she could be up all night again.

She hit the streets as soon as she was dressed, and after selling enough drugs to get a little grubstake together, she snuck away from her boyfriend and pimp, Stu Jones, and headed for the casino on Main Street at Keefer in Chinatown. She loved gambling but tried to limit her bets to $20 a day. Occasionally she was lucky, but this turned out to be a lousy day. Sandra Gail lost $60 at the tables and was scared; if she didn't make it up fast, Stu would find out and beat her up. She'd have to hit the streets and find some tricks.

But first she needed a speedball, so she ducked in behind the Regent Hotel and rummaged through her stash. She still had several flaps of heroin and cocaine that she'd shoved into the change pocket of her jeans, and a needle in the bag she wore on a belt at her waist, where she also kept condoms. Each flap held about half a point of cocaine or heroin. Sometimes she'd buy it by the cap, which was one point—one-tenth of a gram—and it was always mixed with double the amount of filler, or "buff."

She quickly mixed two papers of heroin with one paper of cocaine, poured them into her syringe and then flicked on a cigarette lighter. Carefully she passed the flame back and forth under the syringe to warm up the drugs, then jammed the needle into a vein in her leg. The drugs chugged into her system fast, and as usual she began to feel frantic and paranoid right away, then ran around the streets for forty-five minutes to calm down. Once she had her breathing under control and her mind cleared of craziness, Sandra Gail, bundled up in a warm jacket against the March winds and wearing hiking boots, went to work at the corner of Princess and Cordova, a block north of East Hastings and three blocks east of Main.

Sometime between ten and eleven o'clock at night, about four hours after her speedball in the alley, a red Chevy pickup truck stopped and the driver's window rolled down. The man driving the truck had shoulder-length dirty blond hair, receding on top. His face was covered with stubble. She figured him to be a couple of inches taller than she was, maybe five feet eight inches, and he was wearing a checked shirt.

"How much for a blow job?" he asked.

"Forty bucks."

"How about a little more?"

"How?"

"Come to my place."

"Where's that?"

"Coquitlam."

"Well, that's a little far. I know a place just down here."

"I'll make it a hundred and I'll bring you back by one o'clock."

A hundred dollars. That would take care of the sixty she had lost in the casino. It was a no-brainer. Sandra Gail hopped in the truck.

For a while the two made a little small talk.

"Everybody calls me Willie," he offered.

"Yeah?"

She looked around and noticed some Smarties and soft drinks on the bench seat between them.

"Can I have some?"

"Yeah."

As Sandra Gail stuffed the candy in her mouth, she noticed something else on the seat: a brassiere. "Whose is this?"

"Some working girl left it in here."

Sandra nodded, opened one of the bottles of pop and took a swig. The two went on chatting. She asked him if he had a family. He said no and asked about hers.

Before long they left the Trans-Canada Highway at the Pacific Boulevard exit to United Boulevard in Port Coquitlam, and then took the Mary Hill Bypass to go around the town to the far end, where the farm is. As always, this route took Willie through the neighbourhood of the original Pickton family homestead, past the exits to the hospitals and penal colonies where his parents had found farmhands.

Just as they reached the Lougheed Highway, Sandra told him she had to go to the bathroom. She spied a Petro-Canada gas station.

"Can you pull over?"

"Well, I'm only two minutes away from my place."

"But I have to go badly."

He didn't respond. The traffic had slowed right down and they were at a stoplight; as soon as the light turned green, he gunned the engine and they hurtled around the corner, past a McDonald's and right to his farm gate. He had to stop the car to get out and open the gate.

Sandra Gail noticed a small white car parked outside the gate, but after he drove the truck in and got out to close the gate again, she saw that there were other cars there too, old ones, as well as trucks, buses and motorhomes on both sides of the dirt road they were on. Then she noticed a brown house on her left.

"Who lives there?" she asked.

"My brother."

As soon as they got to the back of the property, where the trailer was, Willie hopped out of the truck to be greeted by his dog, which was barking on the front porch. Sandra Gail climbed down and followed Willie across the gravel parking area to the dirt patch surrounding the trailer. It was muddy and he slid a piece of plywood under her feet so her boots wouldn't get soaked.

The first thing that caught her eye when she walked into the trailer was a cowboy hat hanging on a coat rack. "That's neat!" she said. "Can I have it?"

"Nope."

She looked around and he walked into the small room he used as an office and pushed a button on the answering machine that sat on his desk. While she waited, Sandra Gail looked into a filthy kitchen on the right and saw a large butcher knife on the kitchen table.

As soon as he'd heard all his phone messages, Willie turned to Sandra Gail. "We're going to the back room."

All she could think of as they walked towards his bedroom at the end of the trailer was how messy the place was. A pigsty, she told herself.

The bedroom was another mess, and there wasn't even a bed in it. All he had was a sleeping bag on the floor, with a thick roll of clear plastic, about eighteen inches in diameter like a piece of rolled-up carpet, lying on the floor beside the sleeping bag.

Willie reached into his pocket, pulled out his wallet and handed Sandra Gail five twenties. They undressed on the sleeping bag and she made him put on a condom. Instead of the blow job he had suggested, they had sexual intercourse. It wasn't anything unusual and lasted about five minutes. Then they got up and put their clothes back on.

Sandra Gail still needed to go to the bathroom and she also wanted to use his phone before he took her back to the city.

"Nope," he said. "Other girls have made long-distance calls on it. If you want to use a phone there's a pay phone at the Mohawk gas station on the way back. I can stop there."

"Okay. But I hafta use your bathroom."

She went in, shut the door and fixed, this time using an equal mix of drugs—a paper of heroin and a paper of cocaine. She was trying to inject the speedball into her leg just below the knee, but she missed the vein and didn't get high. She was annoyed with herself and called out to Willie through the door as she tidied up, "I'll be right out."

When she came out about ten minutes later, she found Willie in his office. "Can I use your telephone book?" Sandra Gail asked him. She needed to call Stu to tell him she'd be back soon. She knew he would be really happy when she returned with so much money.

Willie handed her a phone book and she started thumbing through it, looking for the number of the Cordova Rooms. Her back was to Willie as she leaned over the desk and she could feel him close behind her. Annoyed, she turned around quickly. He grabbed her left hand and began caressing it, stroking the top of her hand and her fingers. And before she could stop him, he had slipped a handcuff onto her wrist.

Her instinct was immediate: fight. Before he could grab her other hand she began to punch and kick and scream. He reacted right away and began to hit her back.

She remembered the knife she'd seen on the kitchen table. As he attacked her, throwing his own punches and slaps, she edged backwards, retreating, retreating, drawing him forward. She backed into the kitchen, and while she punched and clawed with one hand, the other reached backwards, feeling for the table, feeling for the knife. She found it, and when she clutched it, she could feel it slipping through her hand, carving deeply into the fleshy part of her palm. But she kept it in her hand and leapt at him, swinging the knife. She slashed at his throat, then she pulled the knife across his cheek.

"You fucking bitch!" he roared. "You got me good!" With one hand he grabbed a rag and pressed it to his neck, with the other he found a stick and swung it at her. Sandra Gail picked up a plant and threw it at him, and then another, followed by anything else she could grab. While he ducked and swore, she spied a door and tried to push it open; it was glued shut. The only way out was past him and out the door they had come in. She tried to break the door's window and jump through, but it wouldn't even crack. She realized it must be Plexiglas.

He was on her again and they swung at each other and fell on each other, scrabbling, punching, kicking. Sandra Gail blacked out. When she regained consciousness she realized they were both out-side, standing by Willie's red truck. He was over her, bending her back, but she was still holding the knife in her right hand and jab-bing at him frantically.

"Let me go!" she howled. "Let me go! I got a family and they'll pay a thousand bucks if you let me go!"

Willie grunted a response and got the knife away from her. Suddenly he started to slide towards the ground. All his weight was on her, but he was losing consciousness. She slipped out from under him as he collapsed, grabbed the knife and started to run. Covered in blood, she staggered and lurched down the dirt laneway towards the gate, screaming—and saw two houses across the street, both with their porch lights on. Which way should she go?

She got the gate open and ran straight across the road to the closest one and hammered on the door. No one answered. She tried to break a small window in the door using the knife she still clutched in her hand, but it wouldn't even crack. Maybe she could break the big window instead. She swung at it with her elbow and smashed it open.

Headlights suddenly appeared down the road. She ducked down—maybe it was him. She peered at the car and saw two heads, and one was a woman. The car went past but within a minute or two it had turned around and was coming back. Sandra Gail broke another window.

"Help! Help!' she screamed. "Help me!"

The car stopped. The elderly driver and his wife stared at her, appalled. They saw a skinny little woman, terrified, covered in blood. She was almost naked and her guts were spilling out of her stomach. She was waving a butcher knife.

"Don't stab us!" the man shouted.

Sandra Gail threw the knife away. The man jumped out and opened the back door of the car, clearing off the seat so she could lie down. He started the engine and began racing to a hospital.

"Miss, miss, look out your window," Sandra Gail said to the woman in the front seat. "See that little white car?"

"Yeah."

"If anything happens to me, if I die, that's where the guy lives that did this to me, in the trailer . . ."

As she listened to Sandra Gail, the woman was dialling 911 on her cellphone; within minutes they began to hear sirens. As soon as an ambulance and the police caught up to them, the man stopped his car and told the police that the man who had stabbed this woman and who lived in the house at the back of the property had been stabbed himself.

Just before two in the morning, Aaron Paradis, a young RCMP constable with a year and a half in the force, also responded to the call for help. He met the car at the intersection of Coast Meridian Road and the Lougheed Highway, just a couple of blocks from the entrance to the farm. Leaving the couple who had picked up Sandra Gail with another officer, Paradis jumped in the ambulance to accompany her to the nearest large hospital, the Royal Columbian in New Westminster. They arrived just after two a.m. on Sunday, March 23. As soon as the paramedics had rolled her into the trauma room, Paradis gathered some of her clothes from the back of the ambulance and followed her in.

The emergency room team examined Sandra Gail quickly: her hand was badly cut and her lung, they suspected, had been punctured. There were two deep stab wounds in her abdomen. She was losing blood so rapidly the doctors weren't sure they could save her. A few minutes later, doctors moved her to an operating room.

Sandra Gail regained consciousness in the operating room. She remembers swearing at the doctors to hurry up or she would be dead. She blacked out. The next thing she remembers is a nurse rubbing her shoulder and saying, "It's going to be okay. You're going to be okay." And then a doctor was telling her she was going to smell burnt toast and to start counting from one hundred backwards. The last thing she remembers was saying, "Ninety-eight," and that was it, she told people later. While she was under the anaesthetic, the surgeons repaired the massive cuts to her abdomen.

As soon as Sandra Gail was on the operating table, an orderly removed from the trauma room the rest of her clothes and any other bits and pieces she had with her, turning them over to Paradis, who put all of it into evidence bags. By this time everyone knew she had arrived with a handcuff locked to one wrist, with the second cuff dangling from it.

About an hour later Paradis received a call from his boss, Staff Sergeant Paul Giffin, to say that a second stabbing victim, a male, was on his way to the Royal Columbian from the small Eagle Ridge Hospital in Port Moody because they didn't have the facilities there to cope with him. At 3:17 a.m. paramedics rushed Willie Pickton in through the emergency room doors to a second trauma room. Half an hour later, doctors moved him to an operating room.

Paradis pulled aside the curtain of the trauma room, where an orderly, Ollie Smith, was bagging Pickton's clothing in three bags, two for his clothes and one for his rubber gumboots. When Smith went through the clothing to itemize the contents, he found a key in one of Pickton's pants pockets. Looking at it, he thought he'd better give it to Paradis. As soon as Paradis saw it, he took it to the team trying to stabilize Sandra Gail in the operating room. It opened the handcuff that was still on her wrist.

In his notebook Paradis jotted down the time when he had seized Pickton's clothing. It was now 3:50 a.m. but at this point it wasn't entirely clear what had happened. Were both these people victims? Who had stabbed whom? Paradis realized he would need to seize every possible bit of evidence. He talked to the nurse in charge of the trauma room Pickton was in and told her he was seizing the bloody dressings from the wastebasket. At 4:40 a.m. Paradis bagged the dressings and marked them. One of the operating room staff brought back the handcuffs and the key; these too were bagged and logged.

While this was happening, other police officers had descended on the Hells Angels booze can across from the Pickton farm where Sandra Gail had tried to find help. They questioned one man who drove up at about five thirty in the morning. Known as "Biggie" because of his enormous bulk, he was a Hells Angels associate who lived in the house, where he worked as a bartender and caretaker. He had driven his girlfriend home that night; he returned to find police tape across the front of the house and blood splashed on the front steps. Sandra Gail had thrown herself at a bay window and another window, as well as the front door, and they too were smeared with broad bands of blood and her handprints. As the police questioned him, he wondered why they were all over the place.

It turned out to be a long night. By 7:40 a.m. Paradis had logged a knife found at 930 Dominion Avenue, the Hells Angels clubhouse. While the police were talking to a group of neighbours, one told them to try 963 Dominion—the Pickton farm. Paradis guarded the Pickton property while other police went off to get a search warrant; as soon as they were back—about five thirty that afternoon—they searched Willie's trailer and some cars. Just before eleven that night Paradis began logging more items seized by his colleagues, stowing them in exhibit lockers in the RCMP's Coquitlam headquarters. As soon as everything had calmed down, Paradis sat down at his desk, made a flowchart of everything that had happened and filed it away.

The next day was Monday, March 24. When Sandra Gail woke up, it was to find two police officers by her bed. They wanted to know what had happened. She told them everything except how she came to have the hundred dollars Willie Pickton had paid her for sex, because she was afraid they'd keep it. The cops gave her back the money, but what they didn't return were the last flaps of heroin and cocaine she still had folded away in her pants pocket.

Paul Campbell came to visit and she told him what had happened. With his help and for the sake of their kids, she decided to try kicking her drug habit while she was still in hospital; she knew she would be there for weeks and she would have all the medical support she needed. After she left the hospital, she moved in with Campbell and began another methadone program, but it wasn't long before she was back on the street again. This time, though, she gave up on prostitution and stuck to selling drugs to make a living.

In the meantime, Willie was telling his side of the story to Dave. Some bitch had stabbed him, he said. He was bleeding badly but he had made it to his pickup and driven himself to the police station; it was closed. He carried on to Eagle Ridge Hospital in Port Moody, where the doctors treated him for severe stab wounds. However, they decided he needed more help than they could give him, so he was transferred to the Royal Columbian Hospital, just like Sandra Gail. They kept him there for about three days and then told his brother he could take him home.

The *Tri-City News,* the twice-weekly newspaper for the Port Coquitlam, Coquitlam and Port Moody areas, ran a front-page story about the stabbing three days after the attack but didn't name Willie or Sandra Gail. Four days later its Sunday edition had another page-one feature stating that they expected the "49-year-old man" involved in the incident would be charged, but the paper still didn't name him.

Willie was in bad shape but Dave couldn't look after him; he had too much work to do. Then Dave got an idea. He needed the place cleaned up, for sure, because there was blood all over the kitchen and the office. And he needed someone to look after Willie when he got home from the hospital. The first call Dave made to resolve his problem was to Ingrid Fehlauer, Sandy Humeny's younger sister. Ingrid had cleaned the trailer before, but she'd never faced it like this before, with the furniture, walls and floor splashed with dried blood. She scrubbed it away as best she knew how.

Dave also tracked down Lisa Yelds's new number in Surrey. Willie's been hurt, he explained, stabbed by a hooker. "Can you come and take care of him for a few days? I'll pay you."

"I can't," she replied. "It's a bad time for me." She explained that she had been seeing a man who had just got out of prison in Mission and had shot at two small girls behind a fence. She had known nothing about it and was stunned when a police SWAT team converged on her apartment. She was still in shock. And I can't come anyway, she told Dave. "My car isn't insured and I can't afford to buy any insurance."

Dave thought about this for a minute and offered to buy her seven days' worth of insurance on the car. He figured that's all it would take for his brother to get better. After getting calls from Dave's son, DJ, and from Kathy, Dave's girlfriend, who was working at P&B Used Building Materials, Lisa finally said yes. When she got to the farm in Port Coquitlam, the story that she and some of Willie's other friends heard was quite different from the one that Sandra Gail had been telling Paul Campbell and the police.

Willie's version went like this: "I was in Vancouver. Having a little rest in my pickup, and a prostitute knocks on the window. She wakes me up.

"'How much?' I ask.

"She says, 'Two hundred.' So I says, 'Okay.'

"We go back to the trailer. She went into the bathroom and shot herself up. When she came out she wanted . . . well, I had some money on the table. I always had cash on me. I had put $3,400 on the table. There was a knife there. She took the knife and said, 'I want my money up front,' and grabbed for the money. I tried to take the knife away. She starts to stab me so I grab it and try to protect myself.

"She ran out of the trailer and ran to the booze can where the bikers are—she broke a window—an older couple took her to the hospital.

"I drove to the police station—I forgot it had moved. So I went to the Eagle Ridge Hospital and nearly bled to death on the way; I needed over three hundred stitches.

"That woman—you don't hear about her at all."

Lisa Yelds was shocked by what had happened to her buddy but thinks he was exaggerating the number of stitches. When she got there, she guessed he'd had about 150, many of them to repair two long stab wounds in one arm. As well as the stitches, the doctors had stapled the skin on his back to close a six-inch-long stab wound. The biggest job was repairing his throat and jaw. When Sandra Gail first slashed him with the knife she found on the kitchen table, she cut him from ear to ear and then from his ear to his mouth. Not only had the knife entered his mouth, it had cut off the tops of some of his teeth and part of his jawbone, so he had to have extensive dental work done, with bridges to connect the remaining teeth.

"He couldn't chew anything. He tried to eat Campbell's chunky soup and I had to mash it for him. And while he was recovering, the docs had him on Tylenol 3 every six hours. I had trouble to get him on the bed because he was stumbling. He was on straight antibiotics; he would get dizzy and crawl into one of the vehicles and fall asleep."

Yelds stayed with Willie for several days. She cleaned up the trailer, dressed Willie's wounds, made sure he got his antibiotics and painkillers on time and cooked his meals. He wasn't an easy patient, and the hardest part for her was dealing with his rage against Sandra Gail.

"You fool," she said to him, "what were you doing?"

"I want you to find out where she lives," he said. "I'm gonna deal with her myself."

"Let it go, Willie. It's done."

When Lisa finally left the farm, she hadn't looked for Sandra Gail's address and she hadn't been paid. Dave never did pay her for looking after Willie.

But the brothers didn't forget Sandra Gail. After the police charged Willie on April 8, 1997, with one count of attempting to murder Ringwald by repeatedly stabbing her and with unlawful confinement and aggravated assault, he hired Peter Ritchie, one of Vancouver's best-known and most expensive criminal lawyers, to defend him. Willie told people he had paid Ritchie $80,000 for his help. The law firm hired a private detective, the Pickton brothers told close friends, to get as much background as possible on Sandra Gail. His fee, they claimed, was $10,000. A court date was set for January 28, 1998.

Whether she knew she was being investigated or not, Sandra Gail was afraid of Willie. She did not show up in court, and the judge dropped all the charges against him.

CHAPTER THIRTEEN

GINA AND WILLIE AND MORE MISSING WOMEN

As soon as Lisa Yelds had returned to Surrey and Willie was back on his feet, he phoned his new friend Gina Houston, who lived a few blocks from the farm. "I don't want you to get the wrong impression of me by what you're reading in the papers," he said. She assured him that she wouldn't. Even if the local newspapers weren't running his name, all of their acquaintances knew it was Willie who had been charged with attacking Sandra Gail Ringwald.

A week later Gina ran into Willie in the SuperValu, a grocery store on Shaughnessy Street in Port Coquitlam, and she was so friendly that he called later the same night just to talk. Before long Willie was dropping by her basement apartment on Grant Street in Port Coquitlam three or four evenings a week, and he turned out to be the answer to all her problems. Along with the welfare payments she received as a single mother with two children—a son who was eight and a daughter, eleven—Gina was surviving on the money she made as a private foster mother, outside the regulated government fostering system, to at least three children. No government agency would have agreed to let a foster child live with her; she was still a prostitute and a drug addict and suspected of mistreating her own children. But desperate single mothers sometimes need a place to put their children, and they may not have known Gina's history. Finally there was her friend Georgina Lynn Dickens, another sex-trade worker and drug addict, who also lived in the suite and spent a lot of time with Willie Pickton at the farm.

There was never enough money for food. Once Willie came into her life, Gina could count on him to show up with meat from the farm and groceries. He'd invite her and the kids over to the farm to hang around and ride the horses. They talked on the phone every day. She met Dave's kids and girlfriends and other family members, everyone except Willie's sister, Linda, who she'd heard was a "very prim, very proper, very high-class woman who didn't like to get her feet dirty."

About two months after they became friends, Gina was in a panic. Her phone had been cut off because she hadn't paid the bill. Willie liked to help people out. That was his own vision of himself—someone who was a helper, someone who was nice, the kind of guy the neighbours say would do anything for you. He paid the bill for Gina and that was the beginning of a prosperous and happy friendship for her. He started writing cheques for her rent and giving Gina cash, hundreds of dollars a month. Just as he had done with Lisa Yelds, he began taking Gina grocery shopping. They made a good pair; he still liked switching price labels to get a bargain and she specialized in buggy scores: piling up a supermarket buggy with food, manoeuvring it to the store exit and then running like hell out the door with it. Buggy scores work best when there is an accomplice outside, preferably with a car, ready to dump the food inside and race off.

Gina, who took such pride in her skills as a con artist, saw Willie Pickton as a perfect victim. It was still early in their friendship, so he may not have known that she was still involved in a long-standing relationship with a drug dealer named Larry Guthrie. Willie took her to parties at Piggy's Palace and enjoyed having a pretty girl making a fuss over him. Yes, Gina was pretty. She was small and slim; her hair was long and a dark blond. She was also loud and talked so fast it was often hard to understand her. She was quick to take offence, quick to pick a fight and intense in her love for cocaine. What few people knew was that she had snorted so much cocaine earlier in her life that she had to have her nose reconstructed by plastic surgeons. They did a good job; at thirty she was still good-looking. Even though he was in a common-law relationship at the time, Scott Chubb thought he would try his luck with Gina, but to his chagrin she rejected him. She was smart enough to know that Willie wouldn't like her so much if he knew she was sleeping with Chubb, and she didn't want to do anything to upset him.

"I seen her at Piggy's Palace," remembers a woman who was another habitué. "She was hanging all over Willie. Gina was always trying to get into Willie's pants 'cause she seen dollar signs." Dave Pickton, who also suspected Gina was after his brother for the money, tried unsuccessfully to discourage her from hanging around the farm, but it took a lot more than Dave's rudeness to defeat Gina. Very quickly Gina seemed to be controlling Willie's life. She was jealous of other women who dropped by, she wanted to know everything that was going on in the business, and she needed to be the centre of attention.

It wasn't long before Gina was telling people she and Willie were engaged; she even used the name Gina Pickton a few times. But, as she has also claimed, it appears they didn't have sex. What happened was that their friendship morphed into a business partnership. He helped her with money and food. She helped him find women in the Downtown Eastside to bring to the farm—and not just for him. Pat Casanova wanted one or two for himself.

One of Gina's favourite places to trawl for women was WISH, the drop-in centre for prostitutes in First United Church, at the corner of Hastings Street and Gore in the Downtown Eastside. Even though she wasn't living down there any longer, she knew just how to find them. She'd sidle into the drop-in, avoiding the staff, who knew she wasn't a regular and would have tossed her out if they had any inkling what she was up to. She'd head right over to girls she knew.

"I got a friend," she'd say, "and he's got a lot of dope and cash. He's up for a party out at his place and he can take us all." From time to time one or two would agree to go with her, even though many of them were too scared to go; they'd heard of Willie Pickton and they knew his place was far away and isolated and that he was a creep. They knew he was on the drop-in's bad-date sheet.

While none of the women were connecting Willie Pickton to their missing friends, the numbers were frightening—at least five women had disappeared in 1995, four more in 1996. No one had heard from them since; no bodies had been found. People didn't understand how extraordinary such numbers were. For years the rate of disappearance from the Downtown Eastside was about one a year. That doesn't mean one death a year, just one disappearance without a trace. Many Downtown Eastside women died every year and many were murdered, but their bodies were always found. People knew what had happened to them. Beaten, stabbed, strangled, overdosed—at least their families and friends knew. But when the numbers spiked to five disappearances in 1995, terror rose in the community. Now, just six weeks into 1997, Maria Laliberté, Stephanie Lane and Sharon Ward had vanished. The girls on the street started to panic.

That's why what happened to Sandra Gail Ringwald in March shocked them all. She was a familiar face on the street, one of their own, a friend. Everyone knew her and everyone was horrified by the viciousness of the attack. Each one of them had had bad dates, men they'd never willingly go near again. Sandra Gail's experience confirmed the rumours they were starting to hear about the farm—the isolation, the mess, the smell. Handcuffs. The Hells Angels next door. Those parties at Piggy's Palace. Willie.

The word was getting out on skid row. Be careful of Willie, the rat-faced guy with the free dope who asks you to go to his farm. But when Gina came into WISH with her offers of money and drugs, a few thought it was just too good to pass up. After all, she was promising she'd be there too, and she was okay, right? And Willie Pickton's truck was still often parked in front of the Astoria at nights. He was still finding his own dates as well.

On the night of April 23, 1997, when the women of the Downtown Eastside were still warning each other about Willie and talking over the nightmare that had befallen Sandra Gail, twenty-eight-year-old Kellie Little vanished. Kellie was one of the neighbourhood's trannies, born Richard to a Native family on the Island; born small, never to top five feet three inches; with a cleft palate.

As a transsexual prostitute Kellie always had plenty of customers, and soon after she disappeared she had been reported missing to the Vancouver police. They couldn't find her; no one could.

But Gina Houston knew something about Kellie Little. According to sworn testimony she gave years later, she'd met Little at Kent Prison in Agassiz around the end of 1996 or early in 1997. Houston was visiting a friend at the prison; so was Little, who may have been a frequent visitor to the Downtown Eastside but lived and turned tricks in Agassiz. They became friends, and soon Little was yet another person staying with Houston in her crowded basement apartment in Port Coquitlam.

Houston said that Little would go out, turn tricks and bring money back to her; Houston's job was to use it to buy drugs. And Gina testified later that Little told her she had a pair of regular customers she could count on; one, she said, was a guard at Kent Prison who lived in Chilliwack and the other was a Vancouver police officer. Remembering April 23, 1997, the night Little went missing, Houston thought she might be going to see the police officer. "She got ready and she left," Houston said. "And she never came back. Ever."

Houston insisted that she had expected to see Little come back that night. A week later she was reported missing. Not long afterwards, acting on information from neighbours who reported that they had heard a woman screaming in Houston's backyard, police arrived at her house to search the property. Their suspicion was that Little could be buried in the yard. They found no trace of her.

Janet Henry, who was thirty-seven years old, was the next to disappear. The last anyone saw of her was when she was drinking in the Holborn Hotel on June 25, although she talked to her sister the following day. By June 28 the police had filed a missing-person report on her.

Janet was the youngest of eleven children, members of a Kwakiutl band from Kingcome Inlet, in north central British Columbia. Her mother's first child, Larry, was put out for adoption and the second, Richard, died as a baby. Dorothy, Donna and Lavina were next, followed by George, twins Sandra and Stan, then Debbie, Lance and Janet—the baby. When Janet was just a child, her father, a fisherman in Alert Bay, was washed overboard and drowned. "My brother George was with him that day," remembers Sandra Gagnon, Janet's older sister. "He backed up the boat to try to reach Dad but it hit him and killed him. My brother didn't speak for days."

Authorities separated the children, sending George and the older ones to residential schools and parcelling out the little ones to various foster homes. From that point on the doomed family ricocheted from one tragedy to the next. When Lavina was nineteen and caring for several of the younger children, she was raped and murdered by five men in Nanaimo—who each received a five-year jail sentence. "When they brought Lavina's body home, I went to the morgue with my mom," remembers Sandra. "My sister had a white dress on with a big white bow, but what I remember is that her face was all bruised and puffy."

A police car struck and killed Sandra's twin, Stan, in 1990, leaving his widow alone with their children. In 1991 her sister Debbie, who had been brought up in an abusive foster home, swallowed enough pills to kill herself. Her body was found by the railroad tracks in Burnaby. She was twenty-three.

And what about Janet? People describe her as shy and sensitive, but few of them knew that she had been drugged and assaulted by Clifford Olson when she was a teenager. Janet didn't remember what happened to her but the police suspected she had been knocked out by a drop of chloral hydrate mixed into some juice, as other children had been. She was one of the lucky ones—he released her.

After qualifying as a hairdresser, she married Art Chartier in 1984 and had a little girl, Deborah, a year later. They lived in the suburbs of Vancouver, but when Art and Janet divorced in 1988, he moved to McBride, a village in the Robson Valley, in central British Columbia near the Alberta border, taking Debbie with him.

Janet began living with a boyfriend in Vancouver who was taking hard drugs; before long he had persuaded her to try them too, and the next step was prostitution to pay for their addictions. The boyfriend died of an overdose and Janet, by now an alcoholic as well, gravitated to a hotel in the Downtown Eastside. Although Debbie had visited her mother a few times, their main contact now was through letters and photographs, but Janet was in constant touch with her sister Sandra, who lived not far away in Maple Ridge. They were able to see each other often and talked to each other on the phone almost every day. It didn't matter how dope-sick she was or how drunk, Janet could always remember Sandra's phone number.

A few months before Janet disappeared, a neighbour heard her screaming and called 911; when the police arrived they found she had been raped and so badly beaten and choked that she nearly died. John Gary Silvie was convicted of the attack, and the Criminal Injuries Compensation Board awarded Janet $3,500 for her injuries.

Janet called her sister on June 25 and arranged to meet her later at a restaurant. When she didn't show up, Sandra panicked. "I had been stressed because I was looking after her and I was crabby and I had been putting her off. I never got over it." She called 911 to ask the police to check if her sister had overdosed in her room. When they reported that Janet wasn't there and that her rent was paid up for the next month, Sandra checked for herself. She was convinced Silvie had returned to kill her sister.

"But everything was in place," Sandra says. "There was a suit-case packed as though she was going someplace and a little brown bag with toothpaste, toothbrush and two cassettes." Sandra reported Janet missing the next day and began trekking around the Downtown

Eastside's streets with pictures of her sister, asking everyone if they had seen her. No one could help her. Then one of her other sisters told her Janet had confided that she often went out to parties at "Uncle Willie's" farm in Port Coquitlam. "Janet told my sister that she didn't give a fuck about life anymore," remembers Sandra. "She also said that he had little bowls of cocaine set out all over the place."

Not long after Janet disappeared, their sister Dorothy died; a few years after that Sandra's son took his own life, leaving a wife and a baby son behind. Wild with grief, Sandra called Lindsay Kines, a crime reporter with the *Vancouver Sun;* he wrote a story that would run a few weeks later, but he didn't link Janet's case to any of the Downtown Eastside's other missing women.

By the beginning of August, life began feeling normal again, if you can call anything in the Downtown Eastside normal. But then it started all over again. No one knows the exact time or day that month when Helen Hallmark vanished. Helen worked on two well-known strolls, the Downtown Eastside, centred at Main and Hastings, and the Mount Pleasant area, further south on Main around East Broadway.

Thirty-two when she disappeared, Helen had once been a pretty cheerleader with a beautiful smile, hazel eyes and long dark blond hair. She had grown up in Maple Ridge, the small Fraser Valley town just fifty kilometres east of Vancouver on the Lougheed Highway. She was popular in high school and her friends were slightly in awe of her; they thought she was more sophisticated, more worldly than they were. "It seemed she knew a whole world out there, that I didn't even know existed," said one former classmate on the website, www.missingpeople.net. "What I remember the most is Helen always made me laugh. Her eyes would sparkle and her smile was contagious." By her late teens Helen was already into drugs and prostitution. After she had a baby girl, whom she named Chelsea, she soon understood that she couldn't look after her child properly and put her up for adoption.

If there is one tragedy above all the others that haunted the women of the Downtown Eastside, it was losing their children because they could not care for them, because of their addictions. Some gave them up willingly, knowing it was in their best interests, but they never stopped loving them, talking about them, showing off their pictures and bragging about their development and accomplishments. Most tried hard to visit and stay in touch—at least when they knew who had adopted them or was caring for them.

While Helen couldn't change, couldn't cope with rehab and couldn't shake her addiction, she hated seeing other young kids going down the same road. She talked at least one troubled teenager out of taking the chances that had ruined her own life. "I was going through a very confusing, tough time in my life," the teenager wrote on the website devoted to the missing women. "It would have been very easy for me to turn to drugs and prostitution. It was because of several people, Helen being one of them, that I did not.

"When I met her I did not do drugs and she and her friends took me under their wing and basically sheltered me, preventing me from entering the lifestyle. I remember going to her place for dinner one night and we had pork chops and Brussels sprouts . . . She was beautiful. I have gone on to nursing school and I plan to work in the Downtown Eastside when I graduate. I want to help people like Helen and others like her as much as I can. It is my way of paying them back because I could have so easily gone down the same path."

Helen was living at the Vernon Rooms when she disappeared. She was last seen in a Vancouver Police Department paddy wagon, presumably about to be charged with prostitution offences, although the police say they have no record of taking her off the streets or booking her. For years her mother, Kathleen Hallmark, and her younger brother and sister, Shawn and Carrie, tried to find her. No luck.

Jacqueline Murdock, a Native woman who was twenty-seven years old at the time of her disappearance, was the mother of four children. Jacqueline came from a large Carrier Nation family in

Fort St. James, in northern British Columbia. She was last seen at the corner of Main and Hastings on or around August 14, 1997. After she vanished, her mother, Evelyn Murdock, who lived in Prince George, helped raise her children. Her family hunted for Jacqueline and asked the police for help but they have no idea if anything was done.

A few memories from a young niece named Jessie, whose father was Jacqueline's brother, help us to understand her. "I remember how wonderful my aunt was," Jessie later wrote to the website dedicated to the missing women. "And I remember almost everything about her. She was such a funny person [and] she can make anyone laugh."

In another letter that she posted, Jessie gave some of her own painful history and the importance of her aunt to her. "Dear Auntie Jackie, I don't know what happened to you. One day you are with me and Angie and we are just having a great time. Then you disappeared. Your brother my dad dies of a drug overdose. I missed you and I wanted to remember you, I wanted you to tell me stories and tell me you loved me. It's the hardest thing in the world to have lost you, but I promise that somehow in God's hands I will get through such a time as this. I will make you and daddy proud of me. I love you Auntie Jackie and I know once again you are with my father in Heaven. Save a place for me. I love you always and forever. Love always your niece for life, Jessie J."

When the police finally released a picture of Jacqueline Murdock, it showed a handsome young woman with a defiant gaze and a stubborn chin, not yet destroyed by the illnesses, sores and gauntness seen in so many of skid row's women.

It was now the middle of August 1997. So far the Downtown Eastside had lost Maria Laliberté, Stephanie Lane, Sharon Ward, Cara Ellis, Kellie Little, Helen Hallmark, Janet Henry and Jacqueline Murdock. Eight women had disappeared in eight months, a situation unheard of in the city's history. And the year wasn't over.

CHAPTER FOURTEEN

SHERRY IRVING AND MARNIE FREY

One night in mid-September 1997, Renata Bond was working the corner of New Westminster's Twelfth Street stroll near Fourth Avenue. It's in the city's southwest corner, just above the Fraser River and by a large railroad yard. The police were out in force that night in one of their regular anti-prostitution sweeps, and a couple of cops had already stopped by and told her to leave.

When a large car pulled up beside her, she recognized the driver right away even though it had been about ten years since she'd seen him. It was Dave Pickton. The last time she'd run into him was at the Big 6 Café in Burnaby when she was there with her family. She jumped into the car and asked him to pull around the corner because the cops were still hanging around. Dave, dressed in dirty jeans and a T-shirt, clearly didn't remember her but Renata hadn't forgotten him, or how unattractive he was. She got in anyway.

"I'm not a cop," he said, trying to reassure her that he wasn't there to bust her. "I swear it." He undid his pants and pulled out his penis as a show of good faith; after all, what cop would pull out his penis for a hooker? "He wanted to make me feel safe, make me feel secure," Renata explained later. Then he offered her $100 for a blow job, more than twice the stroll's top rate of $40.

"No thanks," Renata said. She tried to look cool, but she was afraid. Stupid, she told herself. *I shouldn't have got into the car. I don't like the look of him, I don't like the smell of him. He looks dirty.* She made up her mind. No.

"I can make it worth your while," he wheedled. Dave pulled out a half-gram flap of cocaine but Renata turned him down again. He repelled her. No way was she going to give this creep a blow job. Especially not for drugs. Renata had a rule: cash only for sex.

"Okay," he said. "Do you know someone else? The date isn't for me. It's for my brother at home." And then Dave promised her the money as a finder's fee, along with the cocaine.

Renata thought for a moment. One hundred dollars? It's a jackpot, she told herself. "I do know somebody. She's at my place and we can go see if she wants to do it."

Bond, who was in her early thirties, was running an informal boarding house for prostitutes in her home in New Westminster. Addicted to heroin and cocaine and a prostitute herself, working under the street name Valerie, she sometimes told people that Gary Leon Ridgway had picked her up on Twelfth Street in 1990 and attacked her, stabbing her so seriously she wound up in the Royal Columbian Hospital. Some of her listeners were skeptical about her claims, but she was only one of a number of Lower Mainland prostitutes who said they had known the Green River Killer.

Renata had been lucky enough to find a roomy basement apartment for herself and her daughter, one that was also large enough to offer other girls a place to stay when they were down and out. She set some of them up with clients and took a share of the proceeds. Was she a pimp? Not technically perhaps, not to the police, but she wasn't offering a place to stay out of the goodness of her heart. She'd met Sherry Irving, a prostitute and addict like herself, on the streets a few years earlier and the two had become good friends, looking out for each other and helping each other when they had the chance.

Now Sherry needed a place to stay. She'd been in trouble with the cops, she told Renata, and had warrants and "no-gos"—police orders to stay out of certain areas—in New Westminster and Burnaby, so she couldn't work on the streets. She'd been convicted the year before of prostitution-related offences and now there was a warrant out for her arrest on a second charge. She hadn't seen her family for nearly a year, and all she wanted was to go home to

Vancouver Island, kick drugs and have a normal, good life. But what she needed now—right now—was a place to stay just for a day or two. Renata was sorry to hear about her troubles. You can stay at my place, she said. I've got room.

Sherry, born on March 19, 1973, was just twenty-four years old. Brought up in the lush Comox Valley, on the central eastern side of Vancouver Island, she had been a popular student at Highland Secondary School and then at Georges Vanier High School in Comox. She was a beautiful, outgoing young woman with long blond hair, dark brown eyes and a gorgeous smile. Like any teenager, she loved rock music and having a good time, but her high school friends liked her because she was cheerful and generous. The ones closest to her also knew she had had a troubled childhood. Her father had been in the air force, which meant frequent moves for the family. When her parents separated, her mother, a member of the Stl'atl'imx Nation, took Sherry and her brothers Chris and Will to live near her Native relatives in Mount Currie, near Comox.

As soon as she left high school, Sherry moved to Vancouver, and by the time she was nineteen she was addicted to crack and working as a prostitute in the New Westminster–Burnaby area to support her habit. Now she was homeless, addicted to crack and burdened with a criminal record.

As he drove Renata back to her place to pick Sherry up, Dave explained that it wouldn't be a big deal for her friend. "My brother is older, a bit of an invalid and probably couldn't even get it up to get a blow job but he likes to have a girl try anyway. So it would [be] an easy date. Easy money. So she's just going out there to try and she'll make a big tip and she can do the drugs. And there's more drugs out there too."

Dave told her they'd be going to a small farm in Port Coquitlam on the way to Maple Ridge. She knew the area well because her parents had a trailer home on the Lougheed Highway in Port Coquitlam. "Even if you have to go [afterwards]," Dave promised, "I'll pay for a cab back."

Renata agreed. "I can't get something better than this," she thought. She figured Sherry owed her money for room and board and this was her chance to get it back. When they got to Renata's apartment, Sherry was there with a friend. He'd arrived a few days earlier to take her back home to Vancouver Island but they'd started doing dope together and he'd run out of money. Now he didn't have enough left to pay for even a pair of walk-on tickets for the ferry to Nanaimo.

Renata took Sherry aside and asked her if she was interested in Dave's proposition. It would be a double date, her and Sherry. You won't be going out there by yourself, she told Sherry. "We each get a hundred dollars and you get half a gram of cocaine, but you owe me money for drugs and stuff, so I'll take sixty of your hundred. That'll leave you enough to buy tickets for the ferry and you'll still have dope left."

Okay, said Sherry. But she needed her friend to come to the farm too, mainly because Renata, who was now hunting for a babysitter for her sleeping daughter, wouldn't let men stay in the apartment. "There's a truck stop on the Lougheed Highway where your friend can wait for you," Dave told Sherry.

As soon as Renata found a babysitter, loaned Sherry some clothes—a blue windbreaker, a sweatshirt embroidered with BCCW (for the Burnaby Correctional Centre for Women), black jeans and some running shoes—and packed the rest of Sherry's belongings, including a bag of laundry, they were on their way. Renata didn't expect to see Sherry again for a while. Besides, she wanted Sherry out of there; she figured she couldn't afford to keep her any longer and she particularly didn't want to go on supplying food and drugs to the man who came to fetch her and wound up staying himself.

After Renata gave the man five dollars to take a bus to the truck stop on the Lougheed Highway, Dave drove the women to the farm and parked by his house. There was a trailer at the back, off to one side of the parking area. To Renata the place seemed huge; in the dark all she could see were the shapes of other buildings. It was by now almost three in the morning.

Dave didn't want the women to go into his house; instead Willie suddenly appeared on the porch. Renata noticed he was wearing boots and jeans but she could never remember later what his shirt was like. He stared at the two women and then nodded his head towards Sherry. Dave handed her the money and she followed Willie as he walked off towards the trailer. Then Sherry, only a foot or so behind him, turned and looked at Renata. "Goodbye," she said to her. "Don't worry; he'll send you the money."

Renata felt odd. This sweet bit of business suddenly felt bad, really bad. Maybe it was shock. She understood that Sherry was telling her she would get the money she owed her from the man waiting at the truck stop. But it was more than that. *I'm never going to see her again*, she thought.

Dave soon spread the word about Renata, and within a few days of Willie's date with Sherry Irving he introduced Renata to an Asian man who took her to the grounds of West Coast Reduction for sex. Others, on Dave's say-so, came looking for her on Twelfth Street. And within a few weeks Dave was calling her regularly. He paid her $100 in cash and added a stash of drugs each time he wanted her to find a prostitute for his brother. Not for himself, he always emphasized; he didn't need hookers himself. He was a biker, and bikers didn't need hookers. It was just for "Willie's losers," he'd tell her. Just find some losers for him, he'd instruct her—girls who will go out to the farm easily, girls who don't care who they go with. Pimping for Dave was no problem.

By now Renata had almost forgotten Sherry. She had a business relationship with Dave, and what he thought of hookers was his problem. As far as she was concerned, Dave Pickton was contemptible. He was a rounder, a biker who hung around with people, who drank. Weird. But, she concedes, approachable. She would describe him as neither fat nor skinny and just a little bit taller than her own five feet seven inches (in fact he was shorter). He had blue or grey eyes and his hair, she thought, was greyish red.

His beard was red and so was his nose, "kind of like Santa Claus," she thought. As for his voice and the way he spoke, he was rude, gruff, rough.

She never forgot the night when a man wearing a full-face helmet drove up beside her on a big motorcycle, a Harley-Davidson, she assumed, although she wasn't sure. Renata hopped on the back seat for a ride, and before she could jump off again, the driver spun the motorcycle around, fought for control and wound up dropping it on the pavement in a blaze of sparks and a grinding of gears. He couldn't get it going again and she had to help him push it. It wasn't until he shoved his helmet visor back that she saw it was Dave. "I didn't know it was him," she said later, "or I wouldn't have got on the bike. He's an idiot."

His brother was different. When Renata tries to describe Willie, she says he was weird too, but skinny and smaller. Even though it was dark she could see he was balding. And he looked evil, she says, evil and mean, and he had beady eyes. She thought he looked hard. And when she finally thought about it—about saying goodbye to Sherry at the farm—she realized she hadn't seen her since that night. And she remembered how she had felt when she saw her friend walk off with Willie Pickton.

"My worst fear was that I would have a child on drugs," Rick Frey mutters. And then he looks back to the time when he watched his little girl, his pride and joy, fall into a pit of dope, prostitution and pornographic movies. He couldn't believe it. He still can't. And he admits he just didn't know what to do. The dear little kid who worshipped her dad had turned into a howling teenager, dope-sick, throwing up, cursing, kicking, whenever he tried to drag her into his car and take her away from a drug dealer's corner.

Life should have been perfect for Marnie Frey. She was popular and exuberant. Her parents had a nice house in Campbell River, a clean, attractive little town of thirty thousand people on the eastern coast of Vancouver Island, just half an hour north of Comox, where

Sherry Irving had grown up. Rick, a big, barrel-chested man with a short, thick beard and grizzled hair, came from a respected fishing family that had lived in this part of the Island for generations. His great-great-grandfather had built canneries in Rivers Inlet, and his father and grandfather had fished together for years around Quadra Island on a legendary boat, the *Western Commander*. "My dad made a very good living," says Rick. "But one day he had a heart attack on his boat. A mayday went out on the airwaves and my brothers and I heard it. But he didn't make it."

For himself, there was never any decision to make about how he was going to earn his living. Rick became a fisherman too and kept his own boat in the port at Campbell River alongside those of all his fellow fishers. In his early years there was still enough salmon in local waters to pay for a decent house in a nice neighbourhood and to give his family a good life. But later on salmon fishing meant sailing north for days to catch the herring fleet and wait for the salmon to appear. Sometimes he didn't get home for weeks.

Rick and his wife, Charlotte, a beautiful young Native woman, rejoiced when Marnie was born on August 30, 1973. They soon had another child, Ricky. Smart, interesting and lively, Charlotte was a good wife for Rick and they were happy until he discovered she was dabbling in drugs. It wasn't long before she was completely addicted. They separated and Charlotte hooked up with another man.

Until she was seven Marnie lived with her mother, but when Charlotte became too sick to look after her, she moved in with her father and his new wife, Penny. When that relationship fell apart, Marnie's next stepmother was her dad's girlfriend Lynn, who took Rick's name even though they never married. In spite of the parental splits, her mother's addiction and the moves, Marnie was a happy, lively little girl. The family lived on Wayne Road in a small brown clapboard house with driftwood piled out in front and wild rabbits dashing around under the wild blackberry that snaked into the yard. Rick's old cork-studded fishing nets are still there, hanging over the back porch.

Marnie enjoyed her years at Ocean Grove Elementary School, and when she was ready to go into the big kids' school, Southgate, she was excited, even though it was an ugly concrete box surrounded by parking lots. In those days Southgate was in the bush on the edge of town; today it's part of a new subdivision about a mile from the ocean. Marnie would run down to the Coastal Highway to catch the bus for her new school—the school where she learned all about using drugs.

Such a gorgeous little town, Campbell River. You can't be there five minutes before you start picking out which house you'd like to buy, which view of the ocean you like best, which beach is the most beautiful. The western side of town, away from the ocean, gets the best view of Mount Baker, to the south in Washington State. Eagles flying overhead are likely to drop down right beside you to snatch a salmon from the water. Deep woods still fill the land beside many of the town's roads; Simms Creek still carries salmon fingerlings out to sea. The big employers are BC Hydro and the Weyerhaeuser paper mill, but a few men, like Rick, still fish for salmon and herring wherever they can find it. People are friendly; life is slow and pleasant.

But its handy little port and the excellent road that connects it with the powerful gang of Hells Angels in Nanaimo, just an hour's drive south, turned Campbell River into British Columbia's heroin capital. The bikers work with the town's Asian gangs, young men who wear expensive sunglasses and drive expensive cars. The police would tell people there had to be about a hundred dealers working in the town.

Rick says it was boys from local Asian gangs who got Marnie hooked on drugs when she was fourteen. She started with pot and quickly moved on to acid. By the time she was fifteen there was just no living with her. Rick and Lynn tried sending her to a Christian school. Rick would drop Marnie off in the school's parking lot; sometimes she'd stay at school but more often she would duck out. She'd head for a grubby little dead-end street called Nootka Gardens, where drug dealers hung out in a row of rundown attached houses and thick cedar hedges hid a lot of the coming and going. Most people believed the area was run by Vietnamese gangs. By the time she got to grade eleven, Marnie had had it with school and had quit. After that Rick and Lynn couldn't control her and they thought it was time for a little tough love. Time to move out, they told her. We can't have you in the house any longer.

Marnie didn't get angry. She understood. She knew she couldn't cope with their rules, or anyone's rules. So she moved around, often staying with Charlotte. All she wanted was a good time. Finally, when Marnie was eighteen, "she went haywire," Lynn remembers. "She had just scored some coke and she hopped on a cop car and was jumping on it. That really pissed off the cop and he arrested her."

As soon as he got the call that she was at the police station, Rick raced over to bail her out. He got her into the car but she struggled to escape. Grabbing her by the hood of her jacket, he forced her back in her seat. Marnie began to scream at him, swearing and crying, and it took Rick a few minutes to realize she was probably coming down from a hit. He tried to calm her down, tried to hold her. She spat in his face.

Rick gave up. He let her go and pulled out his cellphone. By this time they were at the house. "You can go back to jail," he said. He called the police and waited. Within a few minutes a detective, a tiny Ethiopian man, drove up and helped Rick try to move Marnie towards his car. She spat at the cop.

The cop stopped. "Do you have some soap and a sock?" he asked Rick.

"Yes."

The cop told Rick to put the soap in Marnie's mouth. Then he stuffed in the sock, handcuffed her and took her back to the station. She was there all night. The next morning the phone rang in the Freys' kitchen. "Mom," Marnie sobbed. "Mom, come and get me."

And so it went. It wasn't long before Marnie broke the news to her father and Lynn that she was pregnant. She had the baby girl in Campbell River, named her Brittney and lived with her in a small house there paid for by Welfare. It soon became all too clear that she couldn't look after herself, and she certainly couldn't look after a baby. Rick and Lynn agreed to take the child and Marnie moved to the mainland, settling in Coquitlam because she had family there: Lynn's foster sister, Joyce Lachance, who lived there with her husband, Bob, and two children. It didn't take Marnie much time to drift into Vancouver, into the Downtown Eastside, into prostitution and an addiction so fierce that all she could think about was her next fix. Her sunny, bright face disappeared. Now her cheekbones stood out, her hair became lank and thin, her eyes looked dead. And she now had a street name, like almost all the sex-trade workers in the neighbourhood. Hers was Kit Kat, or sometimes just Kit.

Marnie stayed in regular touch with Rick and Lynn, calling them at least three or four times a week and sometimes three or four times a day. Occasionally she would take the ferry over to Nanaimo and they would drive down and pick her up. She would promise to try detox and rehab and they would tell her how they would support her in every way and then she would leave them, saying she couldn't do it . . . not yet. "Soon. Soon. I promise."

Finally, in May 1997 she kept her promise and went into a detox program, which she finished on May 30. By the summer of 1997 her parents learned that Marnie had found an apartment in Burnaby paid for by Social Services, although the officials refused to pay for the bus pass she needed. She was working for the Jamaican pimp Dr. Jay, the man who ran the lives of so many of the Downtown Eastside women, and she told Lynn that she was also making pornographic movies for a group of Vietnamese gangsters who operated out of a house near Burnaby. This may have been where Marnie was actually staying, but no one knows for sure. Marnie told Lynn that, all in all, making "smut films" wasn't so bad because the money was way better than hooking and it was a lot easier.

A few weeks after leaving detox, Marnie fell off the wagon. On August 8 Vancouver police officers took her to the hospital with a suspected drug overdose, and though she survived, her life spiralled into disaster. She told people she was now living at the Regal Place Hotel in Burnaby, so if she had had her own place, she quickly lost it. A couple of weeks later, on August 25, some officers noticed her in a car at the corner of Main and Hastings. Police knew her well; they had had many encounters with Marnie and most of them liked her.

On August 29 a Vancouver police constable stopped her briefly in the 100s block of East Hastings. Marnie's twenty-fifth birthday was the next day, and she called from a pay phone to talk to Rick, Lynn and Brittney. They told her they would be sending her some money and clothes for her birthday. But when she didn't call again soon to tell them that her presents had arrived, they began to worry. They phoned everyone they could think of; no one had seen her or heard from her. Finally, a week after her birthday, they called the police in Campbell River for help.

"Marnie is missing," they said. "We are sure of it." The police told them it was too soon to get so upset. So they called the Missing Persons Unit at the Vancouver Police Department and got the same dismissal. "She's probably on a cruise," the person who answered the phone told them. "Call back again after Christmas."

But unless someone else found it, she was still around in late September, because her monthly welfare cheque was cashed the same day it was issued, on September 24, 1997. That was the last sign that she might still be alive.

Just about the same time Marnie disappeared, another woman from the Downtown Eastside also went missing. Cindy Beck was last seen sometime in September 1997. Like so many of the other women, she lived at the Vernon Rooms, enduring the threats and brutality of the bikers who owned the place. Born in 1965, Cindy had been a beautiful child who had become a lovely woman, athletic, a gifted horsewoman and popular with everyone at school. Tall—she was five feet eight inches—and slim with thick auburn hair, she was the kind of girl who is still remembered with affection by her old girlfriends, many of whom have written to Internet chat rooms with their happy memories of her.

Cindy's brilliant smile in the photographs of her posted on the Internet suggest she was confident in her beauty, but in fact she was never so assured. She and her older brother had grown up in Kitchener, Ontario, the adopted and dearly loved children of a Mennonite couple who had a strong influence on their kids; the boy became a minister, while Cindy's younger sister became a missionary. Cindy was the rebel. Somehow she could never believe she was as special as everyone else thought she was.

In her teens Cindy became pregnant and decided to have the baby, a boy she called Tony. Unable to manage, she had to give up Tony for adoption, which must have seemed to her exactly what had to happen; after all, hadn't she been adopted too? She drifted west and fell into the company of people who used drugs; before long she was working as a prostitute to pay for her addictions. In the summer of 1996 her family travelled from Kitchener to Vancouver to look for her but couldn't find her. By the time Cindy disappeared, none of her old friends would ever have recognized her; she was careworn, sick, destroyed. There was no hope left in her eyes, no tenderness in her smile. She had seen too much and lived too hard and there was no fight left in her.

"Her mother said that when she stopped calling home, which she failed to do on her birthday," one old friend from Kitchener posted to a website, "they knew that something was wrong." When she disappeared, Cindy Beck was thirty-three years old.

CHAPTER FIFTEEN

THE WORST YEAR

Marilyn Kraft was only twenty-two years old when she met Donald Feliks, "a cute blond and blue-eyed Polish-American," as she describes him, who worked in a gas station in Detroit. Each had a lot of history to deal with. Marilyn, who grew up in Vancouver and was working as a secretary, had married an American soldier, moved to Detroit with him, then decided the marriage was a disaster; now she was waiting for a divorce. Don was also trying to get a divorce from his wife, Janet, but there was a big problem: what to do about their four kids, all of them born before Janet had turned twenty. She wanted not only out of the marriage but also out of motherhood. "I'm putting the kids up for adoption," she had told Don.

Marilyn didn't hesitate. "I'll take you and all the kids too," she said. Audrey was the baby, just six months old. Terry was three, Cindy was five and Richard was seven. Marilyn and Don packed up the whole family and moved to Vancouver for a new start.

This marriage lasted only six years. Marilyn discovered that her cute new husband was an alcoholic and a bisexual who decided he'd rather live with his male lover than with her and his children. "We had bought a house in Kitsilano," remembers Marilyn. "We lost it. I had to move out to the suburbs, which were much cheaper." Marilyn found a job at the University of British Columbia and kept the four children with her. Eventually she went to work for the federal government as a senior secretary at Fisheries and Oceans, a good job she kept until her retirement twenty-five years later. By the time Cindy was thirteen, Marilyn had married her third husband and was living in Surrey, still commuting into Vancouver to work.

Even though her son Richard didn't like her new husband, Marilyn maintains that it was still a fairly happy family. She wasn't surprised or upset when Cindy, who was sixteen at the time, suddenly decided she wanted to see her real father again. She tracked him down to a trailer park in Florida and he seemed delighted to hear from her; he even sent her a ticket to come and see him.

Marilyn remembers what happened. "When she got off the plane, he was there to meet her with a mickey of rye and some marijuana and started right away to give it to her. Then he tried to talk her into sleeping with him; he told her that's how a father gets to know his daughter. Next thing I know I get a phone call from Cindy; she's hysterical. Her father has gone off the wall with a gun and is threatening to burn the trailer down. I told her to get the hell out of there." Cindy ran to a neighbour's, who let her stay with her until Marilyn could send the money for a ticket home.

After Cindy got back, it was no time at all before she was drinking and doing drugs with friends in high school. She didn't want to be at home and stayed away for days at a time. She began shoplifting and stealing from Marilyn. The next few years were hell for everyone; Marilyn couldn't control Cindy at all. The girl had become a beautiful young woman, blond and outgoing, with a wide, disarming grin. She had been a competitive swimmer for years but she gave up the sport as she became more and more addicted to heroin. In her early twenties, without a job, Cindy married a car salesman, Terry Mongovius, who loved flashy gold jewellery and drugs. She got pregnant right away, and when Marilyn warned her that the drugs would harm her baby, Cindy paid no attention. Theresa was born addicted; pediatricians in Vancouver General Hospital spent a week gently withdrawing the infant from the heroin her mother was dependent on.

This was the experience that finally forced Cindy to deal with her addictions. She fought hard to give up drugs and succeeded; for two years the marriage was happy and the baby thrived, but when Cindy crashed again, the marriage ended. Theresa was being passed back and forth from one set of grandparents to another. They soon noticed alarming signs of hyperactivity in the little girl and doctors prescribed Ritalin, but by the time she was eight she was impossible to manage.

At about thirteen, Theresa was living with her father and had started to run away as her mother had done. Cindy, now in her mid-thirties, was living in the Downtown Eastside, working as a prostitute and using drugs; she often wound up in jail for short stays. She would promise Theresa that she was coming to see her and then not show up. "The kid would be sitting there, waiting to see her," Marilyn remembers. "And if she did show up it would be with lots of gifts. She tried to buy her way out of guilt." Cindy really loved her daughter, says Marilyn. "She really did. The only thing in the way was the drugs. She never took them to get high; she took them to pass out."

What Cindy liked to do when she was exhausted and sick was come home to Marilyn's house, raid the fridge and then sleep for two days. "She craved sweets—anything sugary," remembers Marilyn. "I remember one time when I was living out in Surrey and a cab pulled up. She was so out of it that she couldn't give the driver proper directions. She asked me, 'What have you got to eat?' and I gave her a big bowl of ice cream. She fell asleep with the ice cream in her lap."

During these years Cindy lived part of the time with a drug addict named John Anderson. Like Cindy, he had been addicted since he was a teenager; he went on to become a career drug dealer who eventually became infected with HIV and hepatitis C. "It happens when you are a kid when you make choices on phoney, bogus information," he told Kamloops reporter Rafe Arnott. "Sixteen-year-olds don't make good choices most of the time anyways. Add drugs and alcohol to the mix—alcohol is the leading drug into all the others." He met Cindy, he told Arnott, "because I was a heroin trafficker and she was a very good-looking, expensive hooker with a lot of money and a big heroin habit." His own habit cost him $1,000 a day and Cindy was paying for most of it out of her own earnings.

Marilyn's family now knew nothing but sorrow. Like her mother, Theresa became a prostitute and a drug addict. Audrey, Cindy's sister, also got into trouble, became an addict and spent a year in Kingston's Prison for Women. She had a little girl who was taken away from her and put into foster care for a few years; today Marilyn is raising her.

The last time Marilyn saw Cindy was at Christmas in 1996. After that there were a few phone calls; the last one was in the summer of 1997, when Cindy had just been released from jail. Other people saw her later that year but she vanished for good on November 26, 1997, at the age of forty-three. Theresa, Audrey, Marilyn and other relatives began calling each other to find out who'd seen her; no one had. Neither had any of her friends in the Downtown Eastside, a close-knit group of people who tried, despite their addictions and poverty, to keep an eye on one another. They started calling Marilyn all the time. "Any word?"

"No. Nothing."

By the time Cindy Feliks disappeared, people in the Downtown Eastside were furious and heartsick. They were also frustrated. They couldn't get the Vancouver police to take the disappearances seriously. Cindy was the twelfth prostitute to vanish that year, following Maria Laliberté, Stephanie Lane, Sharon Ward, Cara Ellis, Kellie Little, Helen Hallmark, Janet Henry, Jacqueline Murdock, Marnie Frey, Sherry Irving and Cindy Beck. Except for Sherry Irving, whose base had been New Westminster, the women all worked around Hastings and Main, although Kellie Little also turned tricks in Port Coquitlam and Coquitlam. In six years of Valentine's Day marches and constant complaints to the Vancouver police and local politicians, no one could remember losing twelve in one year without a trace . . . no explanations, no bodies, no clues. Nothing.

And then they realized, slowly, that a thirteenth woman had gone missing. Nobody could figure out exactly when Andrea

Borhaven had disappeared. Andrea, who was twenty-five, had grown up in Vernon, British Columbia, and had been a high-spirited, cheerful girl. She was about five feet six inches tall and slim, with hazel eyes and brown hair.

Her story is a familiar one—her life at home was unhappy. By her mid-teens Andrea was living in a group home. The manager of the home remembers her as a funny, affectionate girl. "I have very happy memories of Andrea," the woman wrote in a message to the Missing Women message board. "Andrea and I would go out for lunch. She was adventurous and would try everything on the menu. We had our best talks about life when we were on our own. Andrea was always trying to get me to order, 'dum sing.' One day she finally convinced me to order this dish. She of course never told me what it really was that I was eating. She howled with glee when she finally told me I had eaten squid and laughed even louder when I almost threw it up. No more dum sing for us!"

After Andrea moved to Vancouver she gravitated to the Downtown Eastside, where she worked as a prostitute to support her drug habit. One reason it is impossible to figure out when she went missing is that no one ever knew where she lived. As far as most of her friends knew, she was homeless; one person described Andrea as "bouncing off walls." But she always kept in touch with her mother and from time to time would return to Vernon to stay with her. By the end of the year, however, people who knew her realized that, like the other women who had disappeared that year, Andrea was gone for good.

During that year Willie Pickton was a familiar presence in the Downtown Eastside. He couldn't resist the prostitutes even though he blamed them all, Sandra Gail Ringwald in particular, when a doctor told him the reason he wasn't feeling well was that he had contracted hepatitis C. According to Lisa Yelds, he believed it was caused by Sandra Gail's slashing him. He was sure, he said, that he'd been infected by her blood. Very few of the Downtown Eastside women didn't have hep C, so he could have been right.

Although the Astoria remained his favourite hangout, Willie was a regular in many hotel bars, buying rounds of drinks and paying for drugs for others while sticking to soft drinks himself. He found Christmas Eve to be just as lonesome downtown as it was back on his ramshackle farm. If the prostitutes weren't at home with their families, who always made a major effort to provide some happy memories and presents at this time of year, they were enjoying gift boxes and special meals in the community's churches and shelters.

Willie had no special place to go that night so he decided to make his own fun. About seven thirty p.m. he grabbed two gunny sacks, reached into his pigpen at the farm, hauled out two small pigs, dropped each into a sack and put them in his 1992 Chevrolet Cavalier. When he got to Hastings Street, he was grinning with delight at the prank he had planned. He parked in front of a run-down hotel called the Princess, pulled out the squirming sacks and dropped the pigs into the street. Terrified, they took off, careering around, racing down one street and up another until they finally ended up, confused and exhausted, in Gastown, the touristy western end of the Downtown Eastside. Finally someone called the Humane Society and the pigs were taken away.

Willie's eyes twinkled with delight and he chuckled as he regaled an undercover police officer with the tale many years later. "I was an asshole in December twenty-fourth, 1997. I was a really hard asshole. 'Twas the night before Christmas and all through the streets not a soul to be found except two little pigs and two working girls. It was comical for the first little while—until tragedy set in. So what happened is one of the cops chasing the pigs up the hill, the other cop's chasing the pig down the hill, now when he goes down the hill . . . I would love to see him wipe out. . . . Anyways, anyway. Came across there, it was comical for the first little while but I kinda liked it, I liked it. Yeah, how often do you see a pig chasing after a pig? Fucking cop shop. Anyways, this ended in Gastown and I was on the other side of Hastings so anyways I let them go and got the fuck out of there. And then it says the pigs are in the SPCA and we're waiting for the owner to come forward. I said yeah, right. And that was December twenty-fourth, 1997."

Ruth Picknell, a constable with the Vancouver Police Department, is the person who could prove Pickton was there at just that time. Five minutes before midnight she ran a vehicle check on Pickton's Cavalier, which was parked in the 100s block of East Hastings Street, and found that it was registered to him. About the same time, a photographer recorded two frustrated cops trying to round up the frightened pigs.

The day after Willie let the pigs loose in front of the Princess Hotel, Kerry Koski celebrated Christmas with her middle-class family in Coquitlam. Like so many of the Downtown Eastside's women, Kerry had a family that cherished her. They worried about her all the time, and especially now, when she arrived looking as if she was starving to death; she didn't weigh more than ninety pounds. "We'll do anything to help you deal with your addiction and get your life back on track," they told her that day. "Anything. Except give you money to buy drugs."

Kerry had been a beautiful child and grew into a lovely young woman. Michael Whistler, one of her high school classmates, remembers having a crush on her. "I lived a few doors down from Kerry Koski. I was in Grade 10 and Kerry in Grade 9," he said years later, in a posting to the website set up for the missing women. "I thought that she was so pretty, had such a great smile and was so full of life. I wanted to ask her to a school dance but was too shy."

"You would have liked my sister," Val Hughes told the *Toronto Sun*'s Michelle Mandel. "Kerry could dance, and she had a smile that would light up a room." A family photograph shows just how pretty she was: her famous smile lights up her face, and with her well-cut hair, smart button earrings, good necklace and deep pink sweater, she could have been a television anchorwoman. But as Val told Mandel, "She had a talent for picking every bad character who could ruin her life." One lover beat her; another was a manic-depressive who hanged himself. The last one told her heroin would make her feel better. Even though she was trying to raise three girls, Sandra, Lisa and Brianna, and knew how dangerous heroin was, she decided to try it; soon afterwards, she was addicted. She moved from Coquitlam into one of the hotels in the Downtown Eastside.

Kerry was thirty-eight when she came home for Christmas in 1997. She promised her family she would try to kick the drugs. In an interview with Roxanne Hooper, a reporter with the *Maple Ridge–Pitt Meadows News*, Val Hughes remembered what happened next. "I'm sorry," Kerry told Val. "I don't know how this happened." Hughes remembers folding her into her arms. "I just held her and told her we're going to fix this."

A few days later, Val called Kerry and arranged to meet her in Vancouver. The plan was to go for a long walk around the seawall that surrounds Stanley Park and then go for Chinese food, Kerry's all-time favourite. Val called Kerry just before she was leaving her home in Maple Ridge, but when there was no answer she headed straight for Kerry's hotel on Hastings Street. No one had seen her; no one knew where she was. Val began checking the hospitals; they had no record of a visit. She called the police to see if she had been arrested; she asked them to find out if she had cashed her latest welfare cheque. Val soon found that the cheque had not been cashed and there was still money in Kerry's bank account. The best Val could figure out, she told Hooper, was that the last time anyone had seen her sister was on January 7, 1998.

When Val went to the police to report that Kerry was missing, they weren't interested. Don't worry, she was told. "She is probably off partying." Val couldn't believe what she was hearing. Every time she spoke to someone at the Vancouver Police Department the response was the same—dismissive and indifferent. One of the receptionists, Val said later, told her that the women were "just junkies and hookers; don't waste our time." On January 29, 1998, Val finally persuaded the police to list her sister as missing.

Eventually Val had to tell Kerry's children that their mother had disappeared. Brianna looked at Val and said, "You have to find my mom."

"I will never stop looking," Val replied. "I promise you I will find your mom."

Kerry Koski was the last woman to disappear in 1997 and Inga Monique Hall was the first in 1998. Born in Germany in 1952, Hall had emigrated to Canada with her parents when she was four years old. The family settled in Peterborough, Ontario, a pleasant little city 130 kilometres northeast of Toronto, but Hall, a rebellious teenager, left home when she was just fourteen. By the time she was nineteen and living in Prince George, B.C., she'd married a man from Edmonton, given birth to a daughter she named Crystal Kim, and become a heroin addict and prostitute. Her marriage crashed and she had to give Crystal up to the care of her former in-laws.

Very little was known about Inga Hall until Stephanie Levitz, a reporter with the Canadian Press, discovered Floyd Sinclair, the man who fell in love with Hall in Prince George after she and her husband split up. He described a life of doing drugs together, dancing at the local disco and living in hotels, eating fast food. "It was a fast life," Sinclair told Levitz. He also told her how they moved to Vancouver, where Hall gave birth to their daughter, Dianna, in 1978. After staff from the local social services agency threatened to put Dianna into foster care, Sinclair left Hall and took the baby to his sister in Prince George, and later to his mother in Green Lake, Saskatchewan. A few years later Hall came to Prince George looking for her child, but Sinclair's sister told her the baby was with their mother in Saskatchewan.

Hall dropped her search and returned to Vancouver's Downtown Eastside. In 1987 she was charged after trying to rob a branch of the Canadian Imperial Bank of Commerce on Main Street. She had a gun—but it was plastic. Medium in height, medium in build, with long brown hair and green eyes, Inga Monique Hall must once have been very pretty, but her police mug shot shows a woman with the woes of the world on her face.

It wasn't until she was a teenager, Dianna told Levitz, that a cousin told her about her mother, news that her father and grand-mother reluctantly confirmed. Sinclair gave Dianna the only thing left from his years with Hall: a picture of her riding a horse in Vanderhoof, B.C. "I have that and I have her temper and that's about all I've got," Dianna told Levitz. "I know I'm different from her the way I was raised, I wasn't around drugs and I've made better decisions." Her mother was forty-six when she was last seen on February 26, 1998. She was reported missing five days later.

On March 21, 1998, six months after leaving Sherry Irving at the Pickton farm, Renata Bond was alarmed to hear that Sherry Irving had never caught the ferry to Vancouver Island. And remembering her strong sense that she might never see her friend again as she watched Sherry walking out to Willie's trailer, Bond went to the police and reported that her friend was missing. Only the police know if they ever contacted Dave Pickton, the person who had paid Bond to get Sherry out to the farm, to see what he knew about Sherry's disappearance. They haven't said what they learned, if anything.

CHAPTER SIXTEEN

SARAH DE VRIES AND SHEILA EGAN

Bernie Dubois, drug dealer, pimp and flophouse owner, always liked a couple of peach coolers on his birthday. He would tell people he'd given up drugs and booze but his birthday was the exception—two peach coolers to celebrate. "And that's all I drink," he'd say. Dubois was forty-three but looked much older; his back was bent over because of an injury and his clothes and hair were unkempt. His birthday is April 13, and he remembers when his common-law wife disappeared because it was the day after he enjoyed the coolers in 1998.

Her name was Sarah Jane de Vries. Dubois doesn't remember exactly when she left the house; all he can say is that she knocked on the front door early the next morning just as the sun was coming up, looking for something warm to wear because she was cold and had on only a white frilly blouse and black stretch pants under a miniskirt. Bernie handed her one of his own jackets, a black leather bomber that was so big it bagged over the miniskirt. Although she was in a hurry, she promised Bernie she'd be back later; she had missed his birthday and they still had to celebrate. She rushed out, taking her white makeup bag but leaving behind a small black purse on the coffee table. Bernie noticed it almost right away and ran out after her with it, but she was gone. He couldn't see her anywhere.

Other people have their own stories about the last time they saw Sarah, and they start earlier, the day of Bernie's birthday. This was when she had taken one of her regulars, a Chinese man named Sam Lee, to the back room of the tiny grey clapboard house at 396 Princess Street that she shared with Bernie and several other women.

One of them, Shelley Lou-Ann Lessard, who was twenty-nine and called herself Cat, had moved to the Downtown Eastside from the New Westminster stroll and had been one of Bernie's girls for five years. Dubois liked his girls to call him Pappy, but Shelley's memory of his relationship with Sarah was that he "treated her like crap."

Shelley remembers that it was about three in the afternoon and she was "toking up in the front living room" when Sarah started yelling, "Cat! Cat!" Shelley burst into the back room to find Sarah wrestling with Sam Lee. "She had her hands on his pocket and you could see the wallet. And—and then I grabbed him, like, 'Let go of my girlfriend' type thing, right? And she pulled the pocket and she ripped it right out. And then we ran out."

The pair jumped on a westbound Hastings Street bus, got off at the Beacon Hotel, at the corner of Hastings and Carroll, and went upstairs to the room Sarah was sharing with her boyfriend, James "Jay" Zunti, her dealer and sometime pimp. The relationship with Zunti was terrible; he was abusive, and that day he was especially angry with her because he claimed she owed him money for drugs he'd supplied to her.

Sarah was not afraid of him; she'd found $300 in Sam Lee's wallet, as well as a credit card. Relieved, Sarah gave Zunti the cash, prudently keeping the credit card for herself. Zunti sold them a speedball, which the girls "jugged," injecting each other in the neck vein for the fastest hit. About an hour later they left. Shelley says a man stopped his van to pick up Sarah. They'd seen him before: he was about forty-five, balding, with short grey hair and glasses; his four-door van was old and boxy, painted baby blue. Shelley says that was the last time she ever saw Sarah.

Sarah's friend and former lover, Wayne Leng, who worked as an automobile mechanic, tells a different story. A few years earlier Leng, who was divorced and had a grown-up daughter of his own, had picked up Sarah for the first of what would be many paid encounters. He fell in love with her and longed to make her happy. He admits that he often paid for her drugs when she was broke; a fix was what she wanted most, and he would have done anything for her.

Sarah de Vries was exquisite. A mixture of several races—black, aboriginal, Mexican Indian and white—gave her caramel-coloured skin, high cheekbones and a wild, thick tangle of black curls that framed her face. Her large, wide-set, almond-shaped eyes were framed by thick lashes; her broad smile was warm and engaging. Sarah was slender and loved fashion and makeup; she liked to see heads turn as she walked by. And much of her beauty came from her intelligence—she was engaged with the world and with the people she met.

Wayne Leng was heartbroken when Sarah gently told him that all she wanted was to be his friend. They did live together for a few weeks in his tiny apartment in another part of the city, but she moved out to return to the Downtown Eastside, leaving most of her clothes, books, journals and other treasured possessions, at his place. She knew they would be safe there. Leng had accepted her conditions. If friendship was the only thing she could offer, he could live with that; but he called her all the time and saw her often.

The night of April 13 they talked on the phone and Leng arranged to pick her up at the Beacon Hotel. They drove back to his apartment and talked while Sarah picked at a bowl of Froot Loops. She hunted through a dresser where she had left some clothes—Leng had washed them for her—and packed them in an old pillowcase to take with her. Leng fussed about her health and made her take some vitamin pills with her as well; then he drove her back to the Beacon Hotel to go back to work on the street.

"Be cool, my friend."

"I'll call you," she replied.

Other people pick up Sarah's story after Leng left her at the hotel. Up in Zunti's room she hooked up with another friend, Sylvia Carleton. Once again Sarah shared a speedball, then said she had to get back to work.

"I got to go," Sarah said.

"Okay, well, I'll come with you," replied Sylvia. They walked back up Jackson Street to Hastings and east to Princess. Sylvia describes what happened next.*

Sarah stayed on the NW corner by the store. I walked across to the SE corner by the dentist. We stood around for about 15–20 minutes. Several cars drove by, back 'n' forth, around and around—a light blue four door car with a white vinyl roof drove by me a little slower, proceeded east on Hastings—turned right on Hawks and went around the block I presume and pulled up to me on the corner of Princess and Hastings on Princess. He asked me to get in the car and go around the block. I got in.

Sarah and I talked of meeting up after we broke so I looked back to the corner Sarah stood on to see if she got picked up—we were also trying to spot each other—my date and I proceeded around the block and talked business and then agreed to disagree and he turned back onto Princess from Pender to drop me off. I looked for Sarah and saw no one. She was gone. I could see no cars, nothing. I got out of the car on Princess and Hastings all the time looking back and forth.

I don't mean to sound melodramatic but I knew something was wrong. The whole street was empty. No cars, no people, no nothing. It was really quiet. I felt really scared and alone. I knew she wasn't going to meet me. I knew she was gone.

It must have been just a few moments earlier that someone picked her up and stopped long enough at Bernie's place for her to run in and grab Bernie's leather jacket in such a hurry that she left her purse behind. She still had her white makeup bag with her.

Sarah de Vries was the latest woman to go missing from the Downtown Eastside, but unlike Inga Hall she was well-known throughout the area. So many friends and family members were

*Sylvia Carlton is a pseudonym for a prostitute who was interviewed by David Wood for Elm Street magazine in 1998.

watching out for her that when she vanished, they knew almost right away. Leng went to see Dave Dickson, the constable working at the one-man Neighbourhood Safety Office on Hastings Street near Main. "He introduced me to some police officers," Leng says, "and I talked to them about Sarah, but they dismissed it."

Furious, Leng began hammering up posters and calling people; he phoned Sarah's mother, Pat de Vries, at her home in Guelph, Ontario, and her sister, Maggie de Vries, in Vancouver. He walked the streets of the Downtown Eastside asking everyone he saw if they knew where she had gone. Like so many other missing women, Sarah had left behind her most personal and treasured possessions—pictures, letters, her health card, a Money Mart card. And most telling, after being gone for several days, she hadn't cashed her welfare cheque.

On April 21, when the Vancouver Police Department's Missing Persons Unit wouldn't let Wayne Leng file a report because he wasn't a relative, Maggie filed one. A couple of weeks later Maggie talked to Detective Al Howlett, who was working on the Missing Persons desk at the time, but because she didn't know how her sister had disappeared he promised to talk to Wayne Leng. When they did talk, Howlett told Leng he was working on five missing-person cases just then and was pretty sure Sarah was probably just away for a while.

At the time of her disappearance Sarah was twenty-eight and the mother of two small children, Jeanie and Ben. Sarah's father, Jan de Vries, had been a professor at the University of British Columbia; for years he and his wife, Pat, a nurse, had lived with their four children in a comfortable house in West Point Grey, a predominantly white area that was next door to the UBC campus. Their friends were all well-educated professional people, many of them academics; all of them were liberal in their social beliefs. It was perfectly natural that the de Vrieses decided to adopt an eleven-month-old baby girl of mixed-race background. She had been born on May 12, 1969; the adoption was completed on February 10, 1971.

Pat and Jan already had three kids; the first two, Maggie and Peter, were their own, while their son Mark was adopted. This had been the couple's plan—to have two of their own children and then adopt two more. Sarah's new family adored her; it included Pat's sister, Jean Little, one of Canada's best-loved authors of children's books. Pat and Jean's parents had been medical missionaries who worked for the United Church in Taiwan; when they returned to Canada, they had settled in Guelph, Ontario, a small university town. Jean didn't marry or have children, so Pat's children were like her own, and very precious to her.

For Sarah, life at school was difficult; many of her classmates would make thoughtless racial comments that upset her. Her sister, Maggie, has said that Sarah became shy and withdrawn at school. "If we had lived in a more mixed neighbourhood, that would've been better," she has said. "If she had gone to school with kids that looked like her, that would've been better." And when her parents divorced in 1978 after years of acrimony and bitter arguments, Maggie says Sarah, who was still in elementary school, blamed herself.

By the time she was twelve or thirteen, Sarah was on her way to becoming incorrigible. Not only was she picked up for shoplifting in local stores, she would steal small things from the homes of her friends; the parents knew but hated to say anything to the de Vrieses. But they wouldn't have been surprised; as Maggie de Vries has said in *Missing Sarah*, her book about her sister, Sarah's family had to put locks on their doors to stop her incessant pilfering of money, jewellery and other belongings.

By the age of fourteen, when she was a student at University Hill Secondary School on the UBC campus—one of the most exclusive schools in the city in spite of being a public school—she had developed into a beautiful young teenager, attractive to older men, who would tip her well for her time. She would sneak into the Hotel Vancouver on dates with them, only to face doormen who would tell her she was barred from the hotel. She ran away from home again and again and started using drugs. Soon she was spending her time in the Downtown Eastside, telling people she was the black sheep of her family.

By the time she was in her late teens and addicted to cocaine and heroin, Sarah had moved in with Bernie Dubois. They lived on Princess Street, just a few steps from Hastings, in a tiny two-room wooden house—perhaps the smallest in the Downtown Eastside— with a door at the front and one at the back. The house was known as the Crack Shack. It was infamous as a flophouse and a place to score drugs and prostitutes.

Dubois, like Sarah, was addicted to cocaine and heroin, but she was also HIV positive. In 1990 she became pregnant, but Pat de Vries found out only when the hospital called in December to say that Sarah was in labour. Although little Jeanie weighed eight pounds and seemed healthy, the doctors quickly discovered that she had been born with her mother's addiction to cocaine and heroin.

Sarah couldn't cope with the child; she couldn't even look after herself. She left the hospital to get drugs, leaving the baby with her mother; soon afterwards she was once again in jail. With Sarah's agreement, Pat quickly won a court order to keep Jeanie and then worked with the doctors to wean the baby off drugs. They had to put morphine in Jeanie's bottles to prevent the shock of withdrawal from causing serious harm. When Pat de Vries told Sarah and Bernie that she wanted to take Jeanie away and raise the child herself, Sarah didn't object, and neither did Bernie. Like the other addicted mothers in the Downtown Eastside, Sarah knew it was the only way her child would stand a chance.

"Pat took Jeanie from the hospital as soon as she was born," Jean Little says. For a while Pat was caring for the baby in Vancouver while Jean took care of their mother on a farm near Elora, Ontario. After their mother died, Pat and Jeanie moved into Jean's big stone house, which was called Stonecrop and was filled with nearly a dozen pets, including dogs and cats and a big, chatty parrot.

They didn't hear about Ben's birth, on May 1, 1996, so quickly. The father was not Bernie Dubois but a trick who had raped Sarah. Ben was born prematurely in May and didn't arrive in Elora until October. His problems were more serious than Jeanie's; the list included malnutrition as well as an addiction to cocaine and heroin. His blood work showed antibodies for HIV and hepatitis C, but fortunately he never developed either disease.

Jean, who has been legally blind since birth, continued to earn enough money from the sales of her more than thirty books, along with her own pension income and Pat's, to keep the household going and pay for the costly private schools that offered expert help for the hyperactivity and attention deficit disorder present in both Jeanie and Ben. "I got my first baby, Ben, and my first old-age pension within one month," Little tells people. "It's very exhausting." But the sisters always kept in touch with Sarah; so did the kids. And Sarah kept in touch with them. When she disappeared, she had been working on an alphabet book for Jeanie.

Sarah was smart, articulate and thoughtful. She enjoyed a wide circle of friends in the community, men and women she often called and visited. In spite of her addictions Sarah took vitamins, ate carefully and liked to get exercise; many people remember seeing her flying along the streets of the Downtown Eastside on her in-line skates. And she had no hesitation about talking to the reporters who occasionally came to the Downtown Eastside to interview people about their lives. She kept a journal, wrote poetry and sent letters about her life and her feelings to her sister, Maggie. Years later, when Maggie wrote *Missing Sarah*, she said that finding these letters and dealing with them "was the hardest part—having to read them over and over again and copy them for the book and write about them briefly. That little girl in those letters had so much potential because she was full of energy, creativity, and love. And it's too late to do anything differently to give her a better chance."

Sarah's journal, which she left in Wayne Leng's apartment for safekeeping, tells even more about her life, especially the terrifying experiences she had with bad dates. One entry tells of a night when she was feeling drug-sick and needed money to pay for a fix. She hung around in front of the Astoria Hotel, hoping to find a trick. When a car pulled up, "I got in, pulled the door shut and agreed on

40 [dollars] for a BJ [blow job]," she wrote. "His name I don't remember or maybe I just don't want to. Anyway I told him my name, Sarah, and it all started at that moment."

The man started asking her questions about herself. How old are you? Where are you from? he asked. "Sarah this and Sarah that," she wrote. "It started to scare the hell out of me, it was like he was trying to [psych] himself up to do something." Even though he had paid her and "acted like he was the nicest people on earth," he was also driving the car while she gave him oral sex. Suddenly she discovered he had removed the inside door handles of the car and she couldn't get out. He drove to a deserted place, and when she tried to get out of the car, he grabbed her, beat her brutally and left her there to die.

In April 1998 Sarah was twenty-eight; she knew there would be no fairy-tale ending for her life. "Will they remember me when I'm gone," she wrote in one poem, "or would their lives just carry on?" Another poem read:

Woman's body found beaten beyond recognition
You sip your coffee
Taking a drag of your smoke
Turning the page
Taking a bite of your toast
Just another day
Just another death
Just one more thing you so easily forget
You and your soft, sheltered life
Just go on and on
For nobody special from your world is gone
Just another day
Just another death
Just another Hastings Street whore
Sentenced to death

Not only was Sarah terrified by the thought of disappearing as so many of her friends had, she was furious with the police for failing to find the person who was taking them. "If she were some square john's little girl, shit would hit the goddamn fan," she wrote. "Front page news for weeks, people protesting in the streets . . . while the happy hooker just starts to decay, like she didn't matter, expendable, dishonourable . . . it's a shame that society is so unfeeling. She was some woman's little girl, gone astray, lost from the right path."

Although Maggie de Vries and Wayne Leng pestered the police for help in finding Sarah, they had to accept the fact that she had probably been murdered. If so, they wanted the police to open an investigation. Nothing happened, so they turned to reporters for help.

The first reporter to write about Sarah's disappearance was the Vancouver *Province*'s Frank Luba. Although it was a good and frank story about Sarah, it didn't link her to the other missing women, so Leng went to see Lindsay Kines at the *Sun,* who was intrigued by his argument that Sarah's disappearance was one more in a long list. Kines was already aware of some of the missing women because he'd published a story about Janet Henry the year before, in 1997. And when Sandra Gagnon called him on the one-year anniversary of her sister's disappearance, he'd written a follow-up feature about Janet on May 11, 1998. But at the time he didn't know she was part of a pattern of disappearances.

Now, as he listened to this tearful, desperate man spill out the story of Sarah de Vries's disappearance, warning bells were going off in Kines's head. He decided to have a good look at Sarah's history and see if she connected in some way to Janet Henry.

Lincoln Clarkes, a well-known Vancouver fashion and portrait photographer, had taken Sheila Egan's picture the year before. It shows a teenager with a slim body, rich blond hair, clear skin and a beautiful face, the face of a model or a movie star. Clarkes had started taking pictures of the Downtown Eastside's prostitutes in

July 1997. In a sense he was their neighbour. Clarkes lives in a three-storey painted clapboard house in Strathcona, a small area on the edge of the Downtown Eastside that is undergoing serious gentrification. Although Strathcona is one of the few Victorian neighbourhoods left in Vancouver, living there was still cheap because of its proximity to the poorest place in Canada.

As he began to look around the area more closely, photographing the decaying Victorian and Edwardian buildings of the Downtown Eastside, Clarkes had been startled by images he'd never really noticed before—the faces and bodies of the women who lived there. He began to get to know them, to learn who they were and how they had got there, and finally to ask them, one by one, if he could take their picture. Most said sure; in fact, sometimes they would invite friends to join them in the pose. The first woman he photographed, on the steps of the Evergreen Hotel, where she lived, was Patricia Johnson, who was twenty years old; she brought two friends with her, Tiffany Drew and another woman whose identity is not known. Clarkes says the picture he took of the three changed his life. Back home, as he pulled the prints out of the sink in his darkroom, he was shocked: "Here were three heroin-sick women looking right into my eyes. I wept when I saw that photo." What he saw, he says, was their beauty.

That is when he decided to go out every Sunday afternoon to photograph as many of the women as he could. Knowing that he might be accused of taking advantage of them, he made sure they signed a release allowing him to take their pictures and he paid each of them a small amount, about ten dollars. He would bring them water and juice and cigarettes and he took his time, although not too much. "They didn't have a lot of time," he told one reporter later. "I didn't either. I made the most of my moment."

One of his favourite pictures is of Josey Belcourt, a young prostitute he helped. She was homeless, and he persuaded Libby Davies, the New Democrat member of Parliament for the area, to help Josey find a room; soon afterwards, with Davies's help, she was able to

move into the Washington Hotel. Davies used Clarkes's portrait of
Josey on her Christmas card. The picture shows her sitting on a window ledge at the Roosevelt Hotel, combing out her hair. In the photo
Josey is in shock—she's just been in a fight with another woman.
Her shoelaces are gone; the woman ripped her shirt off and another
woman gave her the plaid shirt she is wearing. The spots on her
pants are blood from the fight. In the past she has been both stabbed
and shot, she has been slashed and she's had cancer.

Josey, like most of the women Clarkes photographed, trusted
him. Tall—well over six feet—he is as thin as a rake, his jeans almost
falling off him, his chest almost caving in. His head looks too big for
the rest of him, but he is handsome, with thick black hair, a wide
grin, straight, white teeth and a couple of days of dark stubble. Over
the years he has tried his hand, successfully, at photographing nudes,
landscapes, celebrity portraits and architecture—so successfully, in
fact, that he has become famous in the city. Using an old Rolleiflex
camera that he presses against his chest as he stares down into the
viewfinder, he shoots only black-and-white. When he is outside, he
uses only available light.

In his house the rooms are dark, furnished with old pieces, a
leather sofa, lots of pictures—good-looking but shabby. The walls of
his small second-floor darkroom, about ten by twelve feet, are covered with row after row of his portraits of prostitutes, all hung neatly
from paper clips on tacks. Thirteen or fourteen pictures across, thirteen or fourteen pictures deep. Four hundred of them, in fact, all the
same size, four inches by six inches. "The best way I can help people
is to take their photo," he has said. "Most people avert their eyes if
they happen to see these women in the street. I am taking these photographs so that people can't help but pay attention."

The picture he took of Sheila Egan on the street with her sister
Julie at her side, both standing in front of an upturned mattress,
shows a girl not yet marked by drugs and disease. Dressed in a white
shirt, loose pants, sneakers and a slouchy sweater, she looks like a
model on her day off, relaxed, casual, comfortable. He described her

later as "so fresh and young, she should have still been in school. But she was also a bit of a fashion plate and a party girl who didn't know when to stop partying, I guess." Sheila Catherine Egan was last seen hitchhiking at four o'clock in the morning.

Not long afterwards, Clarkes was showing her picture to another Downtown Eastside woman he was photographing and told her that Sheila was missing. She grabbed the picture, Clarkes says, and burst into tears. "Oh my God, that's my best friend. She's missing?"

She said she knew Sheila was dead because she hadn't called, Clarkes remembers. "That's when I realized something was happening, but I didn't know what." Sheila's police file states she was reported missing on August 5, 1998, although her mother, Shirley Ann Egan, says her family went to the police on July 16, two days after they last heard from her. "We have never had one possible lead from the police," Shirley Ann has said.

CHAPTER SEVENTEEN

A DOOMED INVESTIGATION

What the families didn't understand at this time, in the summer of 1998, was that the police were all too aware that women were going missing from the Downtown Eastside. The problem was that most of the senior officers in the Vancouver Police Department refused to believe a serial killer was responsible. Or they didn't want to believe.

In June 1998, while Lindsay Kines was researching his first stories on the missing women, Doug MacKay-Dunn was a staff sergeant responsible for community-based policing in the Vancouver Police Department's District Two, a central area of the city that includes the Downtown Eastside. One day that month, Constable Dave Dickson dropped into MacKay-Dunn's office. Dickson worked as the community police officer in the Downtown Eastside and knew most of the area's sex-trade workers and addicts well.

"Doug," he said, "there's an unusual number of women missing in my area. There's just too many of these women missing." MacKay-Dunn listened carefully as Dickson laid out his case, describing the sharp rise in missing women since 1995, the fact that the women's families had no idea why or how they had vanished, and the mystery of personal identification, treasured children's pictures, medications and uncashed welfare cheques being left behind in their rooms. He told MacKay-Dunn that he was being called all the time by family members and friends of the missing women. He had searched the bad-date lists kept by women's drop-ins that warned them about dangerous men, giving descriptions and names when possible, but didn't find anything that pointed to anyone in particular. (Willie Pickton wasn't a suspect at this time even though the Vancouver police certainly knew who he was and that he used to invite women to what they called a "party house.")

Dickson also told his boss how frustrated he was because he couldn't interest his colleagues or any officers from the RCMP in this situation. Nor did he have the leverage, he admitted, to make anything happen. "The brass sees me as a social worker down there," he told MacKay-Dunn. "They say things like I've 'been down there too long' or that I've been 'Stockholmed.'" In other words, they believed that Dickson had been in the Downtown Eastside so long he had lost his professional perspective and tended to side with the prostitutes and addicts who lived there. Women who had asked for his help in finding their friends would have been surprised by his colleagues' view of him; they were quite sure he had done nothing to find the women who had disappeared.

MacKay-Dunn heard Dickson out. "I agree with you," he finally said. "Let's get Kim Rossmo in on this. You tell Rossmo the story. I think there is more to this—my gut tells me. But Dave," he cautioned, "here's the way it works. We've got to market this. We've got to build a case so that they will take it seriously." By "they" MacKay-Dunn meant the Vancouver Police Department's chief constable, Bruce Chambers, and his senior deputies.

The two officers knew they would have to wait for a while to meet with Rossmo because he was away most of the summer. In the meantime friends and relatives of the missing women weren't waiting, and they weren't just talking to Dave Dickson; they were now pouring out their hearts to the *Sun*'s Lindsay Kines because they'd heard he was working hard on several angles to the missing women's stories.

It didn't take long for him to discover how many women had disappeared in the Downtown Eastside over the past couple of years, but what convinced him it was a big story was an admission from the Vancouver police that they were alarmed. His investigation resulted in a news feature that ran on July 3, 1998, under the headline "Police Target Big Increase in Missing Women Cases." The statistics he put forward were grim: "The police have outstanding files on ten women who were reported missing in the past two years—including five already this year. By comparison, there is only one outstanding file from 1996, three from 1995, and one each from 1992 and 1996. In total, Vancouver Police have sixteen such cases of missing females dating back more than a decade."

But many more women were missing than the police admitted to. Sarah de Vries was the forty-eighth woman to disappear since Lillian Jean O'Dare had vanished on September 12, 1978. And when the police told Lindsay Kines that ten women had disappeared in 1997 and 1998, they were wrong—in 1997 thirteen women had disappeared; in 1998 Sarah was the fourth to go. A few days after Kines published another story on July 14, Sheila Catherine Egan was the fifth. Her family reported her missing two days later.

Kines missed the three women who had disappeared without a trace in 1992, the five women in 1995 (if you include Jane Doe, whose skull was found in Mission Slough) and the four in 1996. The police didn't even mention the thirteen women who vanished in 1997; perhaps they believed there was a chance, as it was only the previous year, that they would still pop up someplace.

Anne Drennan, the spokesperson for the Vancouver police, told Kines the department had assigned a second officer to the one-man Missing Persons Unit to investigate the disappearances, and that these two people had been told to give the sixteen files "the highest of priorities." But she dismissed any talk of a serial killer. "There is no indication that a serial killer is preying on the women," she said. Instead she suggested that an increasing level of violence in the Downtown Eastside and disputes over drugs were more likely to be the causes. She didn't explain why, if that were the case, none of the women's bodies had been found.

Drennan also told Kines that the police would be following normal procedure in investigating these cases, "interviewing friends, families and acquaintances, contacting welfare offices, distributing posters and entering the descriptions on the Canadian Police Information

Computer. They're the most difficult cases that we ever are called on to investigate," she added. "Even if you can establish murder—most of these are stranger-to-stranger crimes and those are the toughest to solve." The pool of possible suspects was enormous, she added. "There are literally hundreds and hundreds of men cruising in the Downtown Eastside, cruising the streets, every night. So, you'd have to say, it's almost like searching for a needle in a haystack."

Kines listened to Drennan and reported what she said. But he had stopped looking for answers from the police; he could see they were trying to protect themselves and weren't going to tell him anything. Instead he concentrated on an explosive tip he'd just received.

Sarah de Vries had disappeared on April 13, 1998, and Kines's feature interview with Wayne Leng had been published on July 3. Many people phoned Leng to talk about it, but one call, on July 28, was a shock. It came from a man named Bill Hiscox, a native of Campbell River. By this time Leng had started to tape all calls and tips about Sarah, and as soon as Hiscox said he was calling about the *Sun* story, Leng turned on the tape recorder. Hiscox explained that he'd worked for Dave Pickton's company, P&B, in 1997 and earlier in 1998 and had spent a lot of time at the farm. He got to know Dave's brother, Willie, and as he put it to Leng, "He's quite the strange character, eh, very, very strange."

Bill Hiscox is one of the more opaque people in this story. As a child he was taken into care by child welfare authorities and eventually placed in a facility for kids where he got to know one of the other children—a little girl named Lisa Yelds. Years later he would tell people she was his foster sister, which she always denied. "We were never foster sister and brother," Yelds said fiercely. She is no fan of Hiscox, whom she regards as dangerous. "He was put there and so was I and that was it. We are not related in any way." Hiscox has a serious criminal record and a history of petty scamming, so she wanted nothing to do with him.

But over the years they would run into each other, often in the Downtown Eastside, where each spent many years. After he ran into her in 1997 and laid yet another hard-luck story of destitution and misery on her, Yelds gave in and drove him to the Picktons' Burns Road property to introduce him to the brothers. They agreed to hire him to work at P&B.

The way Hiscox remembers the Pickton farm is that after he and Yelds talked about Willie Pickton and all the women's clothing that was strewn around the place, he began to believe that Willie might just be the person responsible for abducting the missing women. It's a strange coincidence, he told Leng, that the police charged Pickton with the attempted murder of Sandra Gail Ringwald in 1997. And that was because of "all the girls that are going missing, and all the purses and IDs that are out there in his trailer and stuff."

"Listen," Hiscox said, "he was already charged, it seems about a month ago, with trying to slash a prostitute's throat, and stab her. And he got off the charges." And, he told Leng, Pickton "has a twenty-five-acre farm, a lot of heavy-duty machinery out there and stuff, you know, easy places to hide things out there. His name's Willie. He's the owner of P&B Salvage here in Surrey. They salvage crap from old houses and stuff like that. He's a really strange character.

"He's got a farm out in Port Coquitlam and, you know, he frequents the downtown area all the time, for girls. Everything started clicking on me, you know, about this guy." On the tape Hiscox can also be heard telling Leng that "Lisa" had told him, "Billy, you wouldn't believe the IDs and shit out in that trailer. There's women's clothes out there, there's purses. You know, what's that guy doing, it is like really weird."

So it wasn't surprising that when he read Lindsay Kines's story about Sarah de Vries and how Leng was searching for her, Hiscox called him. But Leng wasn't the first person he called. Hiscox had also informed Al Howlett at the Vancouver Police Department about what he'd seen on the Pickton farm and of his suspicions. The police told him, he reported to Leng, that they would check Willie out. Years later, in an interview with Victoria *Times Colonist* reporter Kim Westad, Hiscox added that he had told his story to a female constable with the Vancouver police several times but she replied that there was nothing the police could do based on his information. "She said they couldn't really do anything, they can't just go in there based on assumptions," Hiscox said. "The constable wanted to talk to Lisa, but she didn't want to get involved with the police or anything."

Now, in early August 1998, there were more questions about the missing women, and not just from their families. Wayne Leng was pushing everyone he could for answers. Lincoln Clarkes was talking about this with the people he saw. And Lindsay Kines continued interviewing the police, friends, families of the missing women and people in the Downtown Eastside.

Kim Rossmo wasn't due back in his Vancouver Police Department office for three months, not till September 22, 1998. In June, when Dave Dickson was laying out his concerns to MacKay-Dunn, Rossmo was speaking to a comparative crime analysis conference in Bramshill, England, where the British police run a behavioural science centre like the one set up at the Federal Bureau of Investigation's Quantico headquarters in Virginia. Many of Britain's senior geographical and psychological profilers are based at Bramshill. The next stop was New York, where Rossmo assisted police in the Bronx with a serial rape case, and next was an academic conference in Barcelona. After a holiday spent in Venice and Berlin, Rossmo spent part of July at an international homicide investigators' meeting in Zutphen, in the Netherlands.

Later that summer Rossmo was in Washington, D.C., to speak to the country's National Police Foundation, then to students at Hunter College in New York, and this was when he learned of MacKay-Dunn's anxiety over the missing-women situation. Rossmo tried to telephone Inspector Fred Biddlecombe, one of the most powerful officers in the Vancouver Police Department and the man in charge of Major Crimes—a department that includes Missing Persons, Sex Crimes and Homicide—but he was away, so he talked to Sergeant Geramy Field, the acting inspector. They agreed he would study the evidence as soon as he got back to Vancouver.

Kines's second story on the missing women appeared in the *Sun* on September 18, 1998. The police weren't admitting it, but his July 3 story had been damaging because of their apparently half-hearted approach to the problem, and the families and friends of the missing women were becoming more vocal in their criticism of police indifference. Now Kines was reporting that the Vancouver police had set up a working group "to review forty missing women cases dating back to 1971." Sixteen of the women had gone missing from the Downtown Eastside since 1995. But Inspector Gary Greer, Doug MacKay-Dunn's boss, said that the police were still not admitting the possibility of a serial killer running amok. "We're in no way saying there is a serial murderer out there," he told Kines. "We're in no way saying that all these people missing are dead. We're not saying any of that."

At first it looked as if the Vancouver police were serious about finding out why so many women had disappeared. Along with the two-person team responsible for investigating missing persons, the new group would include investigators from Sex Offences and Homicide; Kim Rossmo was mentioned as one of these. Maggie de Vries was one of a number of family members who were happy with the announcement. "I think it's a good thing," she told Lindsay Kines. "It seems more and more as if there's something happening. There's a pattern to this."

But Inspector Fred Biddlecombe made it clear what he thought of the new investigation—it was a total waste of time. There were lots of reasons the women might be gone, he told Kines. "They could have wanted to change their names for any number of reasons. They could have gone to another town with a new identity. They could have gone to the States. They could have married and they don't want anyone to know what's going on." Suicide was another strong possibility, he suggested, "because you find a piece of clothing and a wallet on a bridge. Your suspicion is obviously that it may be a suicide, but you don't have a body. So it still is an open missing-persons file."

Kim Rossmo returned to his desk in Vancouver on September 20 and immediately retrieved all the available files on the missing women. He completed a statistical analysis to see if the disappearances were simply standard events and to determine if there was any possibility that the missing women would be found. He met with MacKay-Dunn and Dickson two days later. Yes, he told them, they were right to be so concerned. Yes, statistically there is something here. There is a good chance a serial killer is at work. "But you have to get on to it before the first body is found," he said. "When the killer is still active—so he doesn't shut down."

Once Rossmo was on board, MacKay-Dunn went to his boss, Inspector Gary Greer, to lay out the case; Greer agreed immediately that they should start an investigation into the possibility of there being a serial killer at large in the Downtown Eastside. The next step up the ladder was Deputy Chief Terry Blythe, no fan of Rossmo's. But he didn't object; he sent Rossmo and MacKay-Dunn to talk to Bruce Chambers, the new chief of police who had replaced Ray Canuel, the man who hired Rossmo and who had recently died of cancer. Hiring Chambers in 1997 had not been the most astute decision—he had been the police chief in Thunder Bay, Ontario, and the Old Boys resented his appointment every bit as much as they'd resented Rossmo's.

"Under Ray Canuel," explained a former VPD officer, "there were six deputies, all protecting their turf, all fussing over office accoutrements." Chambers was in trouble from the start. Treated as an outsider by many of the senior officers, he was constantly fighting insubordination and other political fires and was too distracted to pay much attention to Rossmo and MacKay-Dunn's concerns. Chambers kicked the missing-women problem back downstairs again, this time to Brian McGuinness, the deputy chief constable of Major Crimes; McGuinness in turn sent it down another notch, to Fred Biddlecombe.

And this is where it all fell apart. Almost as soon as Rossmo and MacKay-Dunn sent him their report, with the statistical analysis and their recommendation that the police begin an investigation into the possibility that a serial killer was responsible for the disappearances in the Downtown Eastside, Biddlecombe stormed into Gary Greer's office. "How dare you tell me how to do my job?" Biddlecombe yelled at Greer.

MacKay-Dunn's office was next door to Greer's. When he heard the commotion, he flew out of his office to see what was going on and found Biddlecombe, his face flushed with rage. Rossmo was there; he looked as if he'd been hit over the head by a baseball bat. Greer was horrified. He couldn't believe what was happening. "Fred Biddlecombe was part of the anti-Rossmo group led by Deputy Chief John Unger, and they hated Rossmo," explained a former senior officer who also witnessed the scene. "They thought Rossmo's science was all bullshit." They also disliked Chief Chambers and resented his support of Rossmo.

Biddlecombe's tantrum didn't stop Rossmo; he was used to this by now. He drafted a statement to hand out to the media that said the police were trying "to determine if a serial murderer is preying upon people in the Downtown Eastside." The department refused to release it. The Unger-Biddlecombe group argued successfully that without bodies—the physical evidence—there were no cases. Then they argued that the force had only limited resources available. What they didn't say was that ignoring these victims was possible because they were only addicted prostitutes from Canada's poorest neighbourhood.

No one would have admitted that conflict within the Vancouver Police Department had a major impact on the decision the police made or that Kim Rossmo's analysis was the flashpoint for Biddlecombe's rage. Rossmo's international travel and an admiring batch of feature news stories about him had done nothing to sweeten the atmosphere back home. The news stories, in fact, may have been the last straw. For several years there had been features about his groundbreaking research and international assignments, and in

1997 there had been more stories about him—in the *Globe and Mail, Canadian Geographic,* the *Financial Post* and other Canadian newspapers and magazines, as well as good coverage in the media outside Canada, such as the Chicago *Sun-Times.* He was becoming famous, he was in demand, and the Old Boys' dislike for him only got worse.

"And no one had the guts to tell Biddlecombe, 'Either you do that or we remove you,'" said one officer who supported Rossmo. "The problem was that there was always a feeling within the organization that 'hypes [prostitutes who sell sex to make enough money for their drugs] and whores are disposable.'" The central thing, the most important thing, Rossmo's supporters still believe, is that the VPD's failure to act on the missing-women file is directly related to John Unger's hatred of Rossmo. It was Unger, the most senior of the Old Boys, who led the anti-Rossmo group, not to mention the anti-Chambers group.

"So the key to all of this: Rossmo's analysis," explains a former Rossmo supporter in the department. "If they had followed his analysis and put the best and brightest onto it, they would have saved lives. But they just paid lip service. We had an opportunity to save lives and we blew it. If Kim Rossmo had been given an opportunity to use his science to solve the missing-women case, it wouldn't have been cancelled."

CHAPTER EIGHTEEN

PROJECT AMELIA: A BAD START

Although the Vancouver Police Department wouldn't admit that a serial killer was plucking women out of the Downtown Eastside, it did tell reporters that the new working group, called Project Amelia, was looking at the disappearances of forty women between 1971 and 1998. Sergeant Geramy Field was in charge. Senior officers, including Gary Greer, Kim Rossmo and Al Howlett of Missing Persons, were all lending their expertise, and a young constable, Lori Shenher, was assigned as an investigator. Anne Drennan, the media spokesperson, told reporters that Project Amelia would review the list of missing women to see if any of the files were linked or if any of the women had been found. The group set up shop in a large room at the Main Street police headquarters, organizing the tables and computers in a rough square around the room to make it easier for the group to share materials and discuss the case. Whiteboards went up on the walls, along with posters of the missing women, notes and charts.

Just a few weeks after the group began working together, in mid-September 1998, more women began to disappear. Within three months they had to add six new names to the missing-women list: Julie Louise Young, Angela Jardine, Tanya Emery, Michelle Gurney, Marcella Creison and Ruby Ann Hardy. And two women, Jacqueline Murdock and Helen Hallmark, who had vanished in 1997, were now formally reported missing, Helen Hallmark on September 23, 1998, and Jacqueline Murdock on October 30.

Julie Louise Young was the first woman to disappear after Project Amelia started. Julie came from Hope, the scenic mountain town at the foot of the Fraser Canyon just before the land levels off into the farmlands of the Fraser Valley. It's a popular place for tourists to stop overnight on their way in and out of Vancouver, and it's also a place where everyone knows everyone else. Yet almost nothing is known today about Julie Young, who was thirty-one when she went missing. Her home when she vanished was the Vernon Rooms, the infamous Ho Den. We know Julie had large dark blue eyes and light brown hair, that she was five feet four inches tall and weighed only a hundred pounds. She was pretty—if you could get past the sad, gaunt face. Because Lincoln Clarkes could, he persuaded her to let him take her picture, even though he knew she was heroin-sick. "She was hurting badly for a fix," he said later, "but she still managed to pose."

Unlike Julie Young, twenty-eight-year-old Angela Rebecca Jardine was well-known, both in the Downtown Eastside and in Sparwood, the little community in the East Kootenays where Scott Chubb had grown up. Sparwood wasn't her hometown. She had been born in Sudbury, Ontario, where her father, Ivan Jardine, worked in the mines, bringing home a good salary that paid for a pleasant middle-class life. But as her mother, Deborah, confided to journalist Sally Armstrong in a feature for *Chatelaine* magazine years later, Angela's normal birth had turned into an emergency, with doctors rushing her off to administer oxygen. Her development was never normal and speech came slowly. Ivan and Deborah, whose second daughter, Amber, was born with no complications, began a long and painful parade from one pediatric specialist to another. When Angela started school, teachers couldn't manage her and classmates mocked her; by the time she was eight, the doctors were simply prescribing Ritalin and Haldol to try to control her. Despite caring and loving parents and a move to a special school that made a positive difference, childhood for Angela was a cruel and brutal place.

In 1982 a new job for Ivan moved the family to Sparwood, where life became much more difficult for both Angela and her parents. Here there was no special school and she was at the mercy of classmates who teased her, pushed her around and made her life unbearable. A Calgary specialist even told her parents she needed to be institutionalized. The tragedy of Angela Jardine is that she was capable enough to have a life in the real world, but the real world treated her like a freak. She was attractive, outgoing, cheerful and anxious to please. Too cheerful, too outgoing, in fact—she was often loud and boisterous. She didn't fit in, she couldn't keep up and she was too tempting a target for every bully and mean kid in school. The result, not surprisingly, was frequent emotional outbursts. She simply couldn't cope. Finally, when she was eighteen, her parents arranged for her to live in a foster home in Castlegar, British Columbia. It was a good solution and Angela was happy with Joyce Hillstead, the woman who cared for her. But a year later the government decided she could live on her own, removed her from the foster home and set her up in a motel with an allowance.

But by this time Angela could not manage life by herself. It wasn't long before she was moved into an institution in Haney, close to Vancouver. Two weeks later she ran away. She wound up living in the Balmoral Hotel, on East Hastings Street in the Downtown Eastside, with a new boyfriend who got her started on drugs and was interested only in how much money she could earn as a prostitute. It was a dreadful life, and again and again the Jardines tried to rescue her. They kept in touch by phone and on one occasion took her back to Sparwood to try to look after her. It didn't work out; she couldn't stand to live near the bullies who had tormented her, so she fled, returning to the Downtown Eastside. This was a place where she felt, for the first time in her life, that she fit in.

Still, life was hard for Angela. Drugs, chronic infections and prostitution ruined her cheerful little face. Her health grew worse by the week; she suffered from asthma and needed an inhaler, she was HIV positive and she took sleeping pills to calm down. Her desperate need for money to buy drugs led her to steal, as almost all the other women did, and she racked up a long record of reports and convictions in the police files. But the police records also show that when she was arrested or charged, it was almost always with a drug dealer named Douglas Paul Wright; he boasts an impressive string of arrests over many years and at least twenty-eight convictions.

For a while, good luck came her way. Some people might not call it luck, because she was still on drugs and still working as a prostitute, but she stayed in close touch with her parents and had fine people taking care of her and watching out for her. One was her social worker, Eileen McWade, who saw Angela several times a week, sometimes just on the street to say hello and always once a week for coffee to catch up. It was McWade who loaned her a phone so she could talk to her parents on a regular basis. Others were Mark Townsend and Liz Evans, well-known community advocates who had started a non-profit housing society in the Downtown Eastside's Portland Hotel, on West Hastings just a block from the corner of Main and Hastings. It specialized in hard-to-house people, offered medical and counselling services and received generous government support. They were able to get Angela moved into the Portland, became close to her and tried to help her during the eight years she lived there. Thanks to the care and kindness of people like these, and many more, Angela became involved in the community, often volunteering for various events.

On November 10, 1998, Angela talked to her mother about their plans for Christmas and filled her in on all her news. November 20 was going to be a big day for her, she said, because she was going to volunteer at a big rally at Oppenheimer Park in the Downtown Eastside. That day Angela was up early, pulled on a second-hand fluffy pink prom dress, pushed her feet into high heels, applied some makeup and left her room at the Portland Hotel just before nine o'clock to walk to Oppenheimer Park, four blocks east and one block north.

A community conference with internationally known drug experts had been organized as an all-day event called "Out of Harm's Way," with about seven hundred people present under a large tent. There was plenty of free food and musicians were on hand to entertain the crowd. The idea was to give Downtown Eastside residents a familiar, welcoming space in which to offer the latest and most useful information about drugs and solutions for kicking their addictions. Angela had volunteered to help by ushering people to their seats. By three thirty, however, she had had it; she needed a fix, she was hungry and she was starting to panhandle for money. Liz Evans finally gave her $20, and Angela tottered away from the park in her party dress and high heels, heading east in the direction of the Astoria Hotel, where she often looked for her regular customers. That was the last any of her friends saw of her.

Liz Evans, Mark Townsend and Eileen McWade noticed right away that she hadn't returned to the Portland Hotel, and soon afterwards McWade phoned Ivan and Deborah Jardine. They hadn't heard from her either. People began searching for her immediately, although the Vancouver police remained indifferent to the concerned calls from her friends and her mother. They didn't raise the alarm or look for her until a month had gone by. When Angela hadn't come home or even called by Christmas Day, her parents accepted the fact that she was dead.

Twelve days later, thirty-four-year-old Tanya Colleen Emery, five feet seven inches tall with curly dark hair and large, bright eyes, went missing from the Downtown Eastside. An old high school friend of hers has declared that Tanya was never involved in the sex trade but liked to hitchhike into Vancouver from her home in Surrey and hang out in the Downtown Eastside. Very little is known about her except for the most important fact: she was located alive and well in 2007 in central Canada; she claimed not to have known she was listed among the city's missing women.

Michelle Gurney, another woman who lived at the Balmoral Hotel, was the next to go. Only nineteen, with long black hair and brown eyes, she was small, just five feet four inches tall, and weighed just a hundred pounds. Michelle, a native of the Nisga'a Nation near Prince Rupert in B.C.'s northwest, lived as a child—"the cutest little girl" is how one woman remembered her—with her mother and brothers near Vancouver's Commercial Drive. How she came to be in the Downtown Eastside isn't known, but what is known is that she had a son, Andrew Gurney, who was adopted by Marlene Thistle of Prince Rupert. For a while she lived at the Balmoral Hotel, where she met Maggy Gisle. Maggy had been successful, after a couple of dozen attempts in detox and rehab, in kicking drugs for good, on March 13, 1998. She left the Downtown Eastside that day, although she often returned for visits to old friends and to take part in community events. Years after Michelle went missing, Maggy spoke at a memorial gathering about her old friend.

"Hello, my name is Maggy. I am here today to remember my many friends that are on the missing women's list. Many of you knew me as Crazy Jackie. I lived on and off skid row from 1983 until March 13, 1998. I struggled with drug addiction and have been in and out of twenty-two recovery houses, twenty-two treatment centres and numerous detoxes during this fifteen-year period.

"Michelle Gurney, I met you in 1986 on the streets of Hastings. Under your tough exterior I found a strong, loyal friend. I remember the Christmas we spent in the Beacon Hotel together. We decided instead of ignoring Christmas that we would try to make it a nice experience for ourselves and others that lived in the hotel. Somehow we managed to come up with a little tree with decorations; we made a huge feast of food and we traded clothes and jewellery for presents. We even sang songs around the Christmas tree."

The last time anyone saw Michelle Gurney was on December 11, 1998. She was reported missing on December 22.

And five days later, on December 27, Marcella Creison, or Marcie, as her family called her, vanished sometime between one and two in the morning near the Drake Hotel after being released from jail on prostitution charges. She'd be home soon, she had told her mother, Gloria, in a call from the police station; she was just stopping long enough to pick up some cigarettes. Gloria, other relatives and Marcella's boyfriend were waiting at home with a turkey and presents for a delayed Christmas celebration, but she never showed up. This was not normal behaviour for Marcie, who almost always called her mother every day. Nor did she show up later on for a scheduled court appearance to face drug-possession charges.

Just twenty years old, Marcie stood five feet four inches high, weighed 120 pounds and had light brown hair and brown eyes. Most of what we know of Marcie comes from her uncle Skip Marcella, who posted information about her on the Internet. We learn that Marcie was born in Toronto on June 2, 1978, and moved to British Columbia in 1994 with her mother. She enrolled in a high school in Abbotsford but, according to Marcella, Marcie was already smoking a lot of marijuana and wasn't interested in staying in school.

"By 1997 Marcie was a full blown junkie getting her drugs the only way she could—working in the sex trade in Downtown Vancouver," wrote Skip Marcella. "Many, many times, I almost had her ready to go to detox. But because of the new harm reduction and prevention programs a lot of the detoxes have been closed down, there are only two detoxes in the Vancouver area. Marcie would say things like, 'If it's so bad why are they legalizing heroin and why do they have all them needle exchange programs?' I would just say that it's another way to get you young girls off the streets— 'In body bags'!

"At times I wish I wouldn't say things like that, but she and her sister Melanie were literately disintegrating day by day. Today though, her sister Mel isn't on the streets anymore and she has found a new way to live without getting high and working the streets. Marcie never had a chance to experience what most girls just take for granted. Things like having a job, going to school with girlfriends or boyfriends, wearing that special dress on a date, or even a simple thing like getting a drivers licence."

The precise date of Ruby Anne Hardy's disappearance sometime in 1998 is still a mystery. What we know is that she was thirty-seven years old, that she sometimes called herself Ruby Galloway, that she was just five feet two inches tall, weighed about 130 pounds and had brown eyes and brown hair. We also know that she was a member of the Lake Helen First Nation and Red Rock Band in Nipigon, Ontario. Ruby had a son and two daughters, and one of them, Crystal Hardy, from Thunder Bay, Ontario, remembers her mother well. Years after her mother disappeared from a life of prostitution and addiction in the Downtown Eastside, Crystal posted a letter to a website about her: "I remember my mother as a strong woman who knew how to survive. Despite what people may think, my mother took great care of me and my sister and brother. She always made sure that we had food, shelter and clothing. She was a loving mother that would do anything for her children. She did the best she could with what she had to work with. Despite her problems, I never questioned her love for us. I have come to realize that having an addiction is like having a disease. It takes a long time to get well again. I pray every night that my mother is safe and has started coping with her illness."

Again no one can say what the exact date was, but sometime during this winter of 1998, Willie Pickton invited Giselle Ireson out to his farm. Late one night Giselle, a pretty twenty-seven-year-old with red hair and a temper to match—"a firecracker," as a friend described her—was standing on the street in the Downtown Eastside looking for a trick. She noticed Pickton, dressed in his work clothes, sitting in his parked car and recognized him as a regular in the area. She walked over to talk to him but when she bent down to get in, she spied a rope and a stiletto-heeled shoe in the back seat. She backed off right away.

Willie clambered out of the car in his muddy gumboots to talk to her. He tried to tell her that the other working girls in the neighbourhood knew him and she'd be fine, but she wasn't buying his story. She refused to get into his car. Finally he gave up, gave her some money anyway and took off. Two weeks later she ran into him again on the street and again he gave her money. It didn't work. Giselle was afraid of him, never agreed to get in his car and never had sex with him.

Giselle Ireson was one of the anomalies of the Downtown Eastside. Like Leigh Miner, who disappeared in December 1993, and Diana Melnick, who disappeared in December 1995, Giselle grew up in a sophisticated, affluent family for whom education, travel and career were priorities. As Jane Armstrong documented in a story about her for the *Globe and Mail*, she was born in England but grew up in Ottawa. Her parents had divorced; while Giselle's father stayed in England, her mother remarried and moved to Canada when Giselle was in elementary school. She would return to England regularly for holidays with her father.

Admired by classmates for her fashion sense, Giselle was popular and bright; she learned to speak French fluently and had beautiful manners, and her mother kept their attractive home full of interesting people. But in grade nine Giselle began to rebel. Friends say she was lonely. She experimented with marijuana and it wasn't too long before she was trying cocaine. To her parents' distress she dropped out of school, and within two years she was working in a strip club and sharing an apartment with other strippers. Her parents returned to Europe, and eventually Giselle moved to Vancouver and gravitated to the Downtown Eastside.

"Though Giselle was always scared and alone, she would come across as tough, sure and confident," one of her friends told reporter and former sex-trade worker Trisha Baptie years later. "That is how she made friends . . . she kinda controlled us all. She was the ring leader and the boss and we all followed her." Up to a point. She wasn't able to persuade them that Willie Pickton was dangerous.

"Get Willie off the street to stop the murdering," Scott Chubb told Dave Pickton sometime in January or February 1999. Or that's what he says he told Dave. By late 1998 and early 1999 Chubb suspected Willie was the one taking the women off the streets of the Downtown Eastside. Just adding it all up, it made sense. He knew about Bill Hiscox and his call to Wayne Leng to say Willie was responsible for the disappearances. Like everyone else in Dave's circle and everyone else who hung around the farm, he also knew about Sandra Gail Ringwald's close call with Willie.

And anyone who spent as much time as Chubb did on the farm knew about the women's clothes, the purses and jewellery, the guns and Willie's skills as a butcher. Dave had to know by now, Chubb reasoned to himself. "You can't live on this property as long as he has and not know. Not with all the women coming in—and not leaving." Dave did nothing. He wasn't worried about Chubb; he knew that Chubb not only feared him but needed the work Dave provided.

Besides, Dave had other problems. Piggy's Palace had become notorious. The municipality and the police were fed up with the wild parties there, and the brothers' 1998 New Year's Eve blowout led to a city injunction against them. No one has an accurate count but the Picktons estimated that they had at least 1,500 people crammed into a building zoned for agricultural purposes. "It was a rough crowd," said a musician who played there that New Year's with a band called South City Slam to Vancouver *Province* reporter Greg Middleton. The man, who didn't want his name used, said even the women there were tough-looking: "A lot of leather and denim. It wasn't a cocktail-gown kind of place." And he remembered that many of the men wore their Hells Angels colours and that the people all seemed to know one another. But the money was good: he made $500 for the evening.

Port Coquitlam had tried to close Piggy's Palace in 1996 and again in 1998, when the authorities issued the injunction, but the brothers paid no attention and the Palace stayed open.

Nor did Dave Pickton pay any attention to Scott Chubb's warnings about Willie. On January 16, 1999, a little more than two weeks after the New Year's Eve party, Jacqueline Michelle McDonell disappeared. Just twenty-two, Jacqueline had been born in Toronto but raised in Trail, British Columbia, by her mother and stepfather. Jacqueline was an intelligent, outgoing girl who loved to read everything from novels to newspapers. Life was a fascinating adventure to her. At eighteen, however, she found she wasn't doing as well in school as she wanted, and when she found out that she was pregnant, she quit for good in despair, failing to win the high school graduation diploma she had hoped for. But the birth of a lovely baby girl, Andrea, made up for all the disappointment she felt in herself.

"I remember when she was born, Jacquie was so happy," her friend Willo Bartels told Trevor Greene, a Vancouver writer. "She went overnight from being a loving, fun, caring but kinda flaky girl to being very responsible." Jacqueline obtained social assistance and worked as a waitress to support her child. Her big mistake, one shared by so many of the other women who went missing from the Downtown Eastside, was falling in love with a man who was addicted to drugs. Once he had talked her into trying them with him, she was lost. In 1998 she left him to find refuge with her parents in Victoria; that's when social workers decided to take custody of Andrea, who was almost four, and put her in the care of Jacqueline's parents. Soon Jacqueline turned to prostitution to support her drug habit, and within months she was living in the Brandeis Hotel in the Downtown Eastside.

Jacqueline was a girl everyone loved. She was still young enough to hope that she would kick her addiction, get her daughter back and have a life again. She was smart enough that she could dream of a career. She was alert enough to stay engaged with the world and liked to talk about politics and what was going on around her. Elaine Allan knew her well because she was a regular at WISH, the women's drop-in Allan ran. Allan remembers her as the person who liked to dig through the piles of books donated to the centre to find something new and interesting to read.

"She was the kind of kid who struck me as being the sort that would have gotten a VW van together and would have grabbed a bunch of friends and they would have driven down to Mexico and you wouldn't see them for six months," Allan later told the Canadian Press. "And that's what I thought when I hadn't seen her for a while, I thought, 'She's taken off on some fun adventure.' It was just sickening to think that wasn't the case."

Elaine Allan never believed that Jacqueline would stay in the Downtown Eastside; she was sure she would get out and have a new life, maybe going to university, maybe getting her child back—something. Never this. When Jacqueline suddenly stopped coming into WISH in the middle of January, Allan was frightened for her.

CHAPTER NINETEEN

ROOMMATES

Early in 1999, after another beating from her boyfriend, Ross Contois, Gina Houston took her children and left Port Coquitlam to stay at Sheena's Place, a shelter in Surrey for homeless single women and their children. Because Sheena's Place can keep them for only thirty days, the women, who are free to go out or to work during the day, spend most of their time hunting for a more permanent home and support. Lynn Anne Ellingsen, a single mother addicted to alcohol and cocaine whose son was being raised by her parents, was one of these, there because of a violent breakup with her abusive boyfriend, Ron Menard, one that had landed her in hospital. She made her living doing odd jobs, often as a flag girl on highway construction projects.

Slim and about five feet five inches tall, Ellingsen had thick brown hair, bright eyes and a cheerful dimpled smile that could light up her face. But that smile was rarely seen. Most of the time she was sad and introspective or combative, sure that people were out to get her. At the same time she was always working the angles to get what she wanted, whether it was drugs, money, a place to stay, clothes or food.

It was Ellingsen's terrible luck that Gina Houston was staying at Sheena's Place at the same time. This is because one day Gina received a phone call at the shelter; when she hung up, she told Lynn that it was from a good friend named Willie Pickton, who was a really nice guy. She was going out to meet him; did Lynn want to come? Sure, Lynn said. The women went to a nearby Chevron gas station to meet Willie; after the visit they returned to the shelter,

Gina richer by $50 that Willie had given her to help make ends meet. Once again Gina told Lynn what a terrific person Willie was and gave her his phone number; he was the kind of guy, she said, who would do anything for a friend.

By this time Lynn had been at Sheena's Place for a month; her time was up. She decided to move in with a friend, Susan Calder, in Delta, where Lynn had grown up. Gina too was moving out; she had found a basement suite in Port Coquitlam. But Lynn kept in touch with Gina, and a few weeks later, after a failed effort to reconcile with Ron Menard, she called her new friend in desperation. She needed a place to stay, and because Menard was throwing out everything that she owned, she needed a place to store her stuff. Gina suggested going to Willie Pickton's farm.

"She mentioned that Willie had offered, if I needed a place to store any of my stuff or if I needed a place, that I could go out there," Lynn stated later. "There was jobs, yard cleanup, whatnot that I could do."

Lynn went right away, moving into the spare room in Willie's trailer. This was the room to the right of the front door that would normally be a living room but that Willie used for visitors. It was full of garbage bags and junk when she arrived, so the first thing she did was clean it all out to make room for her own things. Willie's room was at the other end.

Once she was settled, Lynn found she had plenty of work to do. "I would take the faxes that Sandy would fax from D&S, and I would give the truck drivers the order slips. So, instead of them coming in the trailer, I would just receive them out of the fax machine that was in Willie's office and then that way we knew which truck went where." She would give the faxed order to Willie to hand out to the drivers. "I learnt how to drive a dump truck." And, as she readily admitted later, she did drugs—constantly—and Willie would buy alcohol for her when she asked.

Initially the plan was that Lynn would stay at the farm only when there was a problem with Ron Menard, but it wasn't long before she began living there permanently. Willie told her she could stay in return for doing yard cleanup and helping with the orders for topsoil; before long she was also cleaning the trailer, shopping for groceries and doing all the cooking. Sometimes she'd dig through one of the freezers in Willie's sheds, looking for meat to cook. And he went on giving her money for food, drugs and alcohol but paid her no salary. Soon Lynn was a fixture on the farm. The truck drivers working for Dave would drop in at the end of their shift and drink with her; some of them would snort lines of cocaine. Often they would take her out in their trucks and joyride around the farm property, crashing along the paths and through the mounds of dirt. She also began watching Willie and Pat Casanova as they butchered and cooked the little pigs they brought back from the Saturday livestock auctions.

Although she had fled from her abusive boyfriend they kept in touch, and sometimes Menard would visit her at the farm, often staying overnight. This was fine with Willie; people were always dropping by or staying for a night or two. One of the men who stayed over occasionally was Ross Caldwell, a bouncer at the Dell, a local bar infamous for its biker clientele. Another was a young man named Andrew Bellwood, who usually slept in his truck when he was on the property but occasionally bunked down in the trailer.

Bellwood, who came from Nanaimo on Vancouver Island, where he had worked as a logging truck driver and a commercial fisherman, was another one of Gina's lost souls. Then about thirty-one years old, he had a preppy look about him; he was tall and lean with a clean-cut, handsome face, neatly trimmed black hair and owlish Harry Potter–style glasses. But he was a serious crack addict with a criminal record and a troubled past. In 1998 he pleaded guilty to theft, admitting that he had pawned property that belonged to his landlady. His drug habit was so ferocious that he would sometimes spend up to $5,000 on cocaine for three- or four-day binges. But he also knew he was destroying his life. In August 1998 he entered a five-month drug treatment program at a centre in Coquitlam called Inner Visions Recovery Society.

Just as Bellwood was getting to the end of his rehab stint at Inner Visions, he started to worry about where to go next; he had no job, no money and no one to help him. One of the friends he made in rehab was Ross Contois, who was getting out of Inner Visions at the same time; he told Bellwood that he was welcome to stay in his girlfriend's basement suite in Port Coquitlam. With no other place to go, Bellwood accepted the invitation and moved in with them on January 31, 1999. He stayed there for a week or ten days, he said later, but left because of the constant fighting between Contois and Gina. But he wasn't stuck—he'd found a job driving a truck and was picking up shipping containers at the docks. The truck was big enough to have a sleeping cab, so he had a little place where he could bed down each night.

One day Gina, who kept horses, asked Bellwood if he would drive his truck to the Pickton farm to get some hay for her animals. Willie was there and the two men struck up a friendship. Sometimes Bellwood and Ross Contois would drop by to sell Pickton items such as batteries and welding cables. Bellwood often just hung around and watched as Willie slaughtered and gutted pigs to sell to the Filipinos who came by all the time to pick them up for barbecues. Willie, he said, would "dump the pigs into a barrel that was fired by what we would call a tiger torch, heat the water, then the pigs would go onto a table where he would scrape all the hair off, clean them up. The customers that I saw that he had would take the pigs away as a whole."

From time to time Willie would pay Bellwood from fifty to a hundred dollars to help him out with odd jobs. He would also let Bellwood stay in his trailer when he wasn't sleeping in his truck. Years later, when Bellwood was asked to explain where he slept in the trailer, he said that sometimes he slept in the extra bed in Pickton's room and sometimes he slept on a couch in the spare room at the other end, the room Lynn Ellingsen used as a bedroom when she was staying there.

Willie was friendly and the two men got along well together. When it soon became clear there wouldn't be much driving work and Bellwood had to return his truck to its owner, Willie said it would be fine with him if Bellwood moved into the trailer for a while. But first he had a plan. He'd had a good look at the truck Bellwood was using and could see that its tires were almost new. "Willie suggested we swap the tires, which had about 80 percent rubber, compared to some older tires, which only had 40 percent rubber," Bellwood said later. Leaving only two of the original tires, the pair exchanged eight of the good tires for old ones. And then, maximizing the good fortune of having a decent truck at hand, Willie asked Bellwood to help him steal a trailer loaded with lumber, promising to pay him $30,000 for his trouble.

Andy Bellwood wasn't learning any lessons during this period. He'd spent five long months in rehab kicking his addiction to crack cocaine, and he started using drugs almost as soon as he was out again. On February 12, 1999, when he might have gone to jail after being convicted in Port Coquitlam court of fraud, possession of stolen property under $5,000 in value, public mischief and theft under $5,000 in value, he received a very lucky break: a suspended sentence and probation for eighteen months. Bellwood didn't use his good luck to change his ways. Without the truck cab to sleep in, Bellwood moved into Willie's trailer sometime around the middle of February. The arrangement was tolerable for a while. While Lynn Ellingsen and Bellwood were suspicious of each other, a night of doing drugs together worked its magic; once or twice they had sex, an experience each remembers with distaste.

As Lynn Ellingsen and Andy Bellwood vied uneasily for space on the Pickton farm, women from the Downtown Eastside continued to disappear. On February 17, thirty-one-year-old Brenda Ann Wolfe, a Native woman from the Brocket Reserve in southwestern Alberta and one of the Downtown Eastside's great characters, followed Jacqueline McDonell as the second woman to vanish in 1999. Brenda worked at the Balmoral Hotel as a bartender and bouncer; she was liked by many of the other women in the community because of the way she defended them and stuck up for them when they were in trouble. Maggy Gisle, who was a prostitute in the area for sixteen years, remembered Brenda as a woman who could take on two or three men at a time if they were causing trouble in the bar. And because she was large and strong, women on the street sometimes paid her a small amount of money to act as a kind of bodyguard or enforcer, someone to help them sort out disputes with quarrelsome dates. And they also say she would help women for nothing.

This image is at odds with the woman Elaine Allan knew at WISH. "Brenda was a lovely person," she remembers. "She followed the rules, would come in, put her bags down, eat her dinner, smile shyly and leave. Sometimes she hung out with a friend . . . and she had a boyfriend called Ryan who was on parole at the time. He's back in prison now." Brenda also had a son, but few people knew this. In 1985, when she had discovered she was pregnant, she entered a treatment centre to try to kick her addiction to cocaine. A roommate from that time remembers her responding well to the program and "turning into an amazing, wonderful, happy woman. I will always remember her smile and the beautiful son that she had while in recovery." The recovery didn't last and Brenda had to give up this cherished child. One woman who remembers Brenda well is Mary-Lou Wasacase who, years later, explained that they met sometime around 1996, when she sold Brenda some codeine pills. "In the beginning she was always dressed up and clean, and then in the end . . . the clothing, it wasn't clean," Wasacase said. "She wasn't clean herself, in the end."

Brenda had talked to Wasacase about where to find work as a prostitute. "When I knew her," Wasacase said, "she supplemented her welfare with working on the street, for her babies."

Brenda's habits, like those of so many of her fellow addicts in the Downtown Eastside, were fairly regular. She saw her doctor, Ronald Joe, frequently and filled the prescriptions he gave her right away. Her last visit to see him was February 8, 1999, when he treated her for an abscess in her arm, a common ailment among intravenous drug users such as Brenda, whose skin is often badly infected by the needles. Her Ministry of Health records show that she used their services 150 times from August 2, 1992, until February 8, 1999, the day she visited Dr. Joe.

Brenda was also in regular touch with her welfare worker. She was supposed to see her at ten thirty a.m. on February 5, 1999, and didn't show up; she called later to apologize and say she had forgotten the appointment. Five days later the worker stopped production of Brenda's benefits cheques. On February 17, as soon as Brenda realized she'd been cut off welfare, she called her worker again to rebook her appointment, and they settled on March 19. But on February 24 Brenda's worker discovered that she had been evicted sometime earlier and that her two children were living with their father in Toronto. Unable to contact Brenda, the worker closed her file on March 5.

No one can pinpoint the day she vanished, but it was just after her February 17 call to her welfare worker. When Brenda's father, Ray, and her mother, Elaine Belanger, couldn't reach her, they were distraught, as were all the family members and friends in Alberta who cared for her. No one in the Downtown Eastside could tell them where she was. Her disappearance may have saved a friend's life. Maggy Gisle was so upset by Brenda's disappearance that she decided to go back into treatment and kick her drug habit once and for all. If she could do this, she promised herself, she would get her own son back, something that Brenda had never been able to do, something that had broken Brenda's heart.

Once he trusted somebody, once someone was part of his community and he felt comfortable with him, Willie Pickton's gabby nature took over, although he didn't seem to lay out the "poor farm boy" stories for other men. These he seemed to save for sympathetic women and skeptical cops. With Andy Bellwood's drug addiction, his willingness to help Willie steal things and his serious criminal record, Willie probably thought he had found a kindred spirit who might enjoy some of his stories. As Bellwood has related many times, Willie's confidences, spilled during a quiet February evening in the trailer as he stretched out on his bed and Andy slouched in a chair under the window, turned into a gently rolling horror story.

"He mentioned about going to get a hooker. I said no. No, I didn't—wasn't really into getting a hooker. Then he proceeded to tell me what he did with hookers.

"He reached underneath his mattress and grabbed a pair of handcuffs . . . They're just a metal handcuff similar to the looks of police handcuffs. They were under his mattress.

"He pulled out a belt and he pulled out a wire, I believe with a handle on each end of it. It looked like piano wire. And he proceeded to tell me what he did with—with these hookers . . .

"He told me he would pick them up downtown, he would draw them in with drugs or money. He had difficult times getting them to come to the farm because of, you know, they're very—they're very nervous about going out of their area. Yeah, if he could entice them to come to the farm, of course being on—being drug addicts or what-not, it would be a—an easy way to get them to come to the farm . . .

"He would put them on the bed, bring them into his—into his room, from what it was explained to me, do them doggy style on the bed. That would be to have the woman on her knees with her face facing the bed, doing her from behind. He would—he would grab their hands and bring one back slowly, bring the other back, hand-cuff them and strangle them."

And then he proceeded to add some show to his tell.

"He got on the bed and motioned to me as if there was a woman laying there, pretending to stroke her—her hair, and kind of motion-ing with his hand how he would grab her hand and bring it around to her back, although there was no woman on the bed.

"That's about—that's about it. He told me that he was doing them doggy style. He was on the bed on his knees. He would just tell them that it was going to be all right. He kept saying it was going to be all right: 'Things are going to be okay now. That's a good girl,' and things would be over . . . '

"He commented on how much people bleed. From there, I was told they were taken out to the barn and he explained to me how pigs eat pretty much everything of human remains. Anything that wasn't eaten would go into these barrels and taken to the waste plant with the rest of the waste from the—with the pig waste.

"I remember him telling me that he'd hang them in the barn and bleed them and gut them. Whatever the pigs didn't eat, he'd throw into the barrel.

"He would strangle them, gag them. He'd either strangle them with a belt or he strangled them with the—with the wire. And then he'd haul them out to—to the barn."

Breaking into his narrative, Willie again tried to talk Bellwood into going out with him to get a prostitute. Bellwood says he told Willie he wasn't interested.

"'No, I don't want to go get a hooker. I'm broke. I don't have any money to be going to get a hooker.'

"'Well, I can give you a couple of hundred bucks to go get a hooker.'

"'No. No. I'm not into going to get a hooker.'

"He carried on and telling me that I was chicken and scared to go get a hooker.

'Are you scared to go get a hooker, Andy?'

"'No, I'm not scared. I'm just not into—into what you're talking about here.'

"And then it was finally left at that."

Although not for long. A short while later, remembered Bellwood, when Lynn Ellingsen was in the room with them, Willie raised the subject again.

"Andy's scared of going to get a hooker," he told Lynn. Then, turning to Bellwood, he said, "You won't go get a hooker, will you, Andy?"

Bellwood explained, "And I, like, just kind of worked around it to avoid the conversation."

It's clear that Willie regretted his indiscretion with Andy Bellwood. Three days later, on March 14, 1999, Willie told Lynn that he was sure Bellwood was stealing tools from him. Could she call her boyfriend, Ron Menard, for him and explain what was going on and ask him to come over?

As Ellingsen explained later, "Ron said, 'That's not a problem. I'll give Ross a call and we'll come out there.'"

Bellwood had just returned to the farm and it was late, but he dropped in to the barn to find Willie busy cleaning a pig for a Vietnamese customer. Suddenly Lynn and Ron Menard showed up with Ross Caldwell, Menard's friend. "And they asked me to come into the trailer to talk about all the stuff that was missing in the back room," remembers Bellwood. "In the back room meaning where I had slept on the couch. There was some assortment of new tools there, like a circular saw, like a Skilsaw."

They went into Willie's small office at the entrance to the trailer. Lynn perched on Willie's desk while Menard and his friend pushed Bellwood down on a chair and began accusing him of stealing the tools from Willie. When Bellwood denied it, Menard punched him on the nose. Caldwell, coming from behind, hit him on the side of his head.

"No, I never stole nothing," Bellwood protested. "I had kept pleading with them that no, I had not stolen anything. I told them that maybe it could have been Ross, Ross and his friend, because Ross and his friend had been there that day, or I said it could have been Lynn because she kept blaming me for opening up a window I had never opened."

Lynn Ellingsen remembers this just as clearly. "Ross was holding him down, and then I was asked to leave the trailer. I was outside and I could hear him saying, 'Don't hit me again! Don't hit me again! I didn't steal it.'"

Menard hit him again. Bellwood saw his blood splashing on the floor and spraying the walls. He pleaded with Menard to call Ross Contois; when he finally agreed, Bellwood got on the phone and begged him to come over. Contois arrived soon afterwards on his bicycle. The men told him and Bellwood to get Willie's tools back in twenty-four hours, "or we were dead. Before I left, they made me clean up my blood off the floor."

Ellingsen confirms his story. "And then Andy came out and he just left the property, but he was all beat up. . . . He was a mess. Looked like his nose was broke."

As Contois and Bellwood were leaving, they stopped long enough to speak to Willie. "Look, I never took your stuff," Bellwood said.

"Well, one of you did," replied Pickton, "so you better find it. You know, like, look, I helped you guys out, I gave you guys a chance. One of you guys stole from me. I want that stuff back. You better find it."

Contois on his bike and Bellwood on foot made their way to Gina Houston's house, which was about fifteen minutes away. Bellwood remembers that he received little sympathy from her when he told her what had happened.

"I told you so. I told you so. You're not—shouldn't be over there," she remonstrated. "Bad things happen over there."

Bellwood spent the night with them and the following morning Contois drove him to the ferry at Horseshoe Bay. He boarded the ship and got off at the Nanaimo ferry terminal on Vancouver Island and made his way home to his mother's house. As soon as he saw him, his stepbrother, Sean, took him to the hospital, where the doctor told him his nose was broken. Bellwood filed a report on the incident and left the hospital. He never went back to the Pickton farm.

About the same time that Andy Bellwood moved back to Vancouver Island, Lisa Yelds answered the phone in her house in Surrey. To her dismay, when she picked it up, she found herself on the line with Ron Palta, an RCMP officer who wanted to see her. This was the second time she'd heard from Palta. He'd called her almost three weeks earlier, on March 1, 1999, to follow up on Bill Hiscox's information about the women's clothing and identification she told him she had seen at the Pickton farm. Yelds kept the conversation with Palta as brief as possible. Few people have a deeper distrust of the police than Lisa Yelds, and she was not happy about the call or friendly to the police. But she is also not stupid; she knew that if they were going to come to see her there was little she could do to stop them. It didn't mean she had to tell them anything.

Two officers, the RCMP's Ron Palta and Diane McDaniel from the New Westminster police, arrived at Lisa's house on March 19. McDaniel, she learned, had been one of the investigators when Willie was charged with the attempted murder of Sandra Gail Ringwald. The reason for the visit, they explained, was to see what she could tell them about her old friend Willie Pickton. They confirmed that it was Bill Hiscox who had told them she was suspicious of Willie and thought there was a possibility he was the one who was taking the missing women. Another person, a woman who claimed to be a friend of hers, had come forward with the same tip—that Lisa Yelds believed Willie was killing the women of the Downtown Eastside.

Could she help them? Did she really believe Willie was killing women from the Downtown Eastside? What exactly had she seen at the farm? Could she identify any of the women? Lisa was floored. And she was scared to death. If Dave Pickton found out the police had been to see her, she would have a terrible problem on her hands. She was afraid he would kill her. She didn't want to talk to them and was as uncooperative as possible. They gave up and left.

As she thought it all through, Lisa was not surprised. She did believe Willie was responsible for at least some of the disappearances. She knew he could butcher anything; she had watched him—God, she had helped him. Her ex-husband, Dave—whom she hated with a passion that has not abated because, as she puts it, when she left him "he arsoned my red Trans Am, the car Willie helped me buy, and he shot my dog"—was in the meat business. It made her gag to remember that he'd worked with Willie for years, taking away three hundred pounds of ground meat every month to wholesale to small meat shops in several Fraser Valley towns, including Pitt Meadows and Maple Ridge. Lisa believes that some of the meat she ate at the farm or took home as a gift from Willie may well have had human remains in it, and she is convinced that is how she contracted hepatitis C.

Willie Pickton in his slaughterhouse, late 1980s.

Dave Pickton.

Willie hung the head of his beloved horse, Goldie, on the wall of his office.

The original homestead in Coquitlam circa 1911. In 1967, Louise Pickton applied to the city to move the house to 963 Dominion Avenue, Port Coquitlam. It remained on Dominion Avenue until police excavated the site in 2002.

Piggy's Palace, where 24seven, a popular band in B.C.'s Lower Mainland, often played.

The Astoria Hotel at 769 East Hastings Street, home to some of the missing women, was Willie Pickton's favourite hangout. He picked up many women in the bar here.

Elaine Allan and Lisa Yelds in a restaurant near Vancouver.

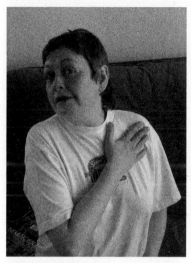

Terrie Gratton, who once fought her way out of Pickton's van, at a lunch party in Elaine Allan's living room, February 2005.

Victim Services worker, Freda Ens, outside the New Westminster courthouse in 2007.

Maggy Gisle and her daughter, Lisa-Marie, 2004.

*Marnie Lee Frey, 24, from
Campbell River, B.C.,
mother of one child,
last seen August 30, 1997.*

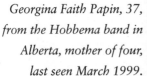

*Brenda Ann Wolfe, 31, from
Lethbridge, Alberta, mother of two,
last seen February 1999.*

*Georgina Faith Papin, 37,
from the Hobbema band in
Alberta, mother of four,
last seen March 1999.*

Andrea Joesbury, 23,
from Victoria, mother of one,
last seen June 6, 2001.

Sereena Abotsway, 30,
raised in Surrey, B.C.,
last seen August 2001.

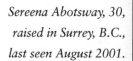

Mona (Ramona) Lee Wilson,
26, from the O'Chiese First
Nation in Alberta, last seen
November 2001.

An aerial picture of the Pickton farm in February 2002, just after the news of Willie Pickton's arrest; media trucks and police cars crowd around the entrance.

Anthropology students carrying their buckets from the conveyor belts where they searched for human remains.

Reporter Lindsay Kines and geographic profiler Kim Rossmo at the Pickton farm in August 2002.

University of Toronto forensic anthropologist Tracy Rogers supervised the students who searched the dirt for human remains.

PART TWO

—

THE MISSING WOMEN

"It is my duty," Wells continued, "to inform you that you have the right to retain and instruct counsel in private without delay. You may call any lawyer you want. There is a twenty-four-hour telephone service available which provides a Legal Aid duty lawyer who can give you legal advice in private. This advice is given without charge and the lawyer can explain the Legal Aid plan to you. If you wish to contact a Legal Aid duty lawyer, I can provide you with a telephone number. Do you understand?"

"Yup," said Willie. "Okay."

CHAPTER TWENTY

WHAT THEY SAW

After Andy Bellwood moved off the farm, Lynn Ellingsen stayed on, doing odd jobs for Willie. She kept the trailer clean and took care of the faxed orders that came into his tiny office. Most of these were for topsoil deliveries that she would give to the truck drivers. During these spring months of 1999, Lynn was doing drugs every day. Willie not only knew about it, he gave her enough money to pay for them, as well as for alcohol, groceries and cigarettes. Sometimes she cooked supper for him; often he made his own, and it was basic fare, usually pork chops and potatoes. Although Willie didn't pay her a salary he did lend her money from time to time; he also wrote successful letters of reference to the welfare office to get assistance for her.

Only twenty-nine years old, pretty and outgoing, Lynn soon made friends with the truck drivers who were in every day. Scott Chubb was still a regular on the farm; and sometimes he would smoke crack cocaine with Lynn; other times he and his wife, Tasha, would play cards with her in the trailer. But like Chubb, Lynn became suspicious of Willie Pickton. Finally she summoned up her nerve long enough to ask Dave if she could speak to him privately. It was about things she had heard were happening at the farm, she told him.

"How I approached him," she recalled later, "was I said, 'Dave, I've been hearing a lot of rumours around here,' and he said, 'What kind of rumours?' And I said, 'Well, I had heard that there were arms and legs in the freezer.'"

"Sure," Dave said. "Let's go in the trailer and talk."

"So we went inside the trailer and he—right against the wall by Willie's desk there's a big bulletin board where all the faxes were—and he pushed me up against the wall, then he slapped me. I went running down the hallway into my room. I tried to close the door; he pushed the door open and he came after me and I grabbed—There was a vase that I had in there with flowers in it. That's what broke the window in that room.

"And then I was told by Willie that Dave wanted me off the property, so when Dave was out and about, to stay inside the trailer."

Almost every time Lynn Ellingsen has described what happened next—"the incident," as she calls it—someone accuses her of lying. There is no question that she does lie occasionally. But in this story her accounts are consistent. What confuses people, including herself, has to do with the date and time the incident occurred, and those details matter. They are important. She says her addictions meant she sometimes mixed dates up. Still, the heart of her story about the incident doesn't change. This is how she has described what happened.

"Ross [Caldwell] had called the house and asked to speak to Willie. I said, 'Well, he's out in the yard.'"

"Well, do you think that you can ask him if I can borrow some money?" Menard asked her.

Lynn said she went out to see if Pickton would be willing to lend some money to Menard, and when he said yes, she told him to call Menard at work and make the arrangements.

"So he went into the trailer and phoned Ross, and so Willie asked me, he said, 'I'm going into Surrey. Do you want to come with me? I gotta go see Ross.' So I said, 'Sure. I'll go in there.' And we got into the Dell—Ross was a bouncer at the Dell—and Willie said, 'Here. Here's twenty bucks. You go get a drink. I gotta talk to Ross for a few minutes.' So I sat there and I was drinking. I had a few.

"And then we left and Willie asked me, he goes, 'Do you want to go out for dinner?'

"So I said, 'Okay.' So we proceeded along. Well, he went over the New West Bridge, over the Pattullo Bridge, and I said, 'Well, we're kinda going the wrong way, like, from here back home.' He said, 'Well, I'm just—we're just going to take a short little drive first.'"

At this point they were driving along Twelfth Street in New Westminster, one of the busiest strolls for prostitutes on the Lower Mainland. It was the same stroll, in fact, where his brother, Dave, had found Renata Bond and persuaded her to take Sherry Irving to Willie's trailer in September 1997. Suddenly a New Westminster police car pulled past them and the driver signalled to Pickton to stop. Constable Jennifer Hyland had been watching Pickton's small pickup truck moving along at just thirty or forty kilometres an hour in a fifty-kilometre zone, but when it suddenly swerved from the centre lane to the curb and back again and then repeated this manoeuvre several times, she forced Pickton to stop. Get out of the truck, she told him. Only when she was satisfied he was sober did she let him return to the vehicle. But when Hyland spoke to Lynn Ellingsen, Lynn readily admitted she'd been drinking. Hyland told them to get off the streets and go home. Constable Hyland's notebook showed that this happened on March 20, 1999.

They didn't go home. Willie told Lynn that first he had to make one stop. He drove straight to Vancouver's Downtown Eastside. By the time they got there, Lynn said later, she was "whining and complaining" about needing some dope; to shut her up, Willie pulled over, spoke to a dealer and bought her some crack cocaine. But he wasn't ready to go home. This is how Lynn remembers their conversation.

"'I gotta go by this one street.'

"'What's goin' on?'

"He said, 'Well, what are you doing tonight?' And I said, 'Well, I wanna get high.'

"So he said, 'Okay. Well, you don't mind if I pick up a girl for the night, do you?'

"And I said, 'No.'

"So he drove around and then he stopped, and I undid my window and he yelled out at this girl. So she came up to my side of the door and we were—She was like, 'Oh, hi!' And I'm, like, 'Hi, how are ya doing?' And she saw my pipe in my hand . . .

"And Willie asked her, 'Do you want to come back to our place for a while tonight?'

"And she said, 'Are you going back there too?'

"And I said, 'Yeah, I live out there.'

"So she got in the truck. We sat there and we got along fine. We were getting high and having a drink and she had long black hair; she had short hair in the front, it was cut short. A nice lady. We stopped and got more drugs. We just stopped and I just asked a guy. I bought—I'm not sure how much exactly I bought, but I bought enough rocks to last us a while . . . We were having a good time, me and this lady."

Willie drove the women back to his trailer; by this time Lynn and the other woman were smoking crack together. As soon as they got inside the woman dropped her purse on Willie's desk and settled in to smoke crack with Lynn while Willie watched them. Finally he'd had enough.

"Let's get this show on the road," he said, according to Lynn, and then he asked, "Who's first?" The woman said she'd go first. So the woman and Willie went to his room and closed his door and Lynn went to her room. Lynn smoked some more crack.

Suddenly she thought she heard a noise outside. A scream. She got up from her bed, opened her door and went over to Willie's room. The door was open and she peeked in. No one was there. She saw clothes strewn around.

"I walked out to the kitchen area and I could see a light sort of out the kitchen window, like where the barn was. The barn was right beside the trailer and that was where he butchered, Willie butchered pigs. I opened up the door and I stood on the porch. The light that was on in the barn wasn't the regular light and I heard—I don't know, just a—like it was a noise, but I—I didn't know what the noise was.

"So I just started walking to the barn . . . As I started approaching the barn, there was a really rude smell. It was awful. I got to the front door, the doors of the barn, and pushed the door open, and all

I could see were these legs, these feet dangling. So I was standing there, I just kind of froze, and I yelled, 'Willie!' and he came from behind the door and he grabbed me. By my arm. I had to go in. Now we walked—walked to the table. It was a really shiny table. I remember it just being, like, bright. There was a light. It wasn't—the light that was on wasn't the normal light. It was a light in the back, back of the barn, kinda just the way it was angled. And he made me stand at the end of the table. I just—I remember feeling really not well. My—I was going to be sick. I had nothing in my stomach. I was just dry heaving. It was . . . the odour was awful . . . I seen these legs. I didn't move my eyes around, I just was in shock. And at my eye level, I could see these legs, toes, red nail polish on them, they were coloured. I seen hair on the table. And I don't know what else was on the table, but it wasn't pretty."

Then Lynn said she had also seen knives on the table. And she understood right away how the body was suspended. "Well, when you walk into that barn, there was a chain that always hung there. It was, as far as I knew, sort of permanent on the roof [ceiling]. And that's what he used when he butchered the pigs.

"Like—she was hanging there. I'm assuming it was the woman that was in the trailer. She had nail polish on.

"He said to me, 'It's okay. She's just like a pig anyways. It's all right. It's going to be all right.'

"He'd cut something and he was pulling something out. It was gross. It looked—I don't know, it looked like stuff, like, from a pig, like, insides. He had a bucket there always. [And] just—it was like a clump of black hair. It kinda looked like a horsetail. He sliced something and it was blood everywhere.

"But, like, he had cut something open, and as he was pulling stuff out, he said—that's when he said to me, 'You say a word to anybody, do anything, this—you'll be right beside her.'

"I was afraid. I said, 'No, I won't. I won't say a word. All I want is my dope and my booze.' I wasn't allowed to leave the barn by myself.

"I told him, 'Don't worry. I'm not going to say anything. I just want my dope and my booze.'

"So he said, 'I'll take ya.' He walked me out of the barn back to the trailer. "I went to grab a bag, just put some clothes in it, or whatever, and I said I'd be back. He said, 'No, no, no,' you know. He gave me a hundred dollars and said, like, 'You can go and buy booze or drugs, whatever you want. I'll pay for a cab, I'll call you a cab, and you can phone me tomorrow and I'll pick you up tomorrow.'

"So he called me a cab. And I must have walked—like, he walked with me right up, like, till I got into the cab to make sure I was in the cab.*

"When I got in the cab, my feet were all mud, the driveway was just muddy. So I got into the cab and I went to go buy more drugs. I ended up back in Surrey. I drank, I got high for a few days.

"I did go back. When I went back, like I called him first and told him that I was getting back together with Ron Menard."

It was a lie, said Lynn, but she told Willie that because she was afraid for her life. Although Lynn told people that she had moved away from the Pickton farm for good, that wasn't true either. Whether she was living there again full-time is not certain, but on March 29 and May 30, 1999, there are records of ambulance calls to 963 Dominion to attend to Lynn Ellingsen, who had overdosed on drugs. Willie was the one who called the ambulance.

The day after Constable Jennifer Hyland stopped Willie Pickton on the Twelfth Street stroll in New Westminster was about the same time Georgina Papin vanished. At thirty-five Georgina was the mother of seven children, the last two being twins born just a few months earlier. At first no one in the Downtown Eastside could

---

*Investigators checked with cab companies in the area and one had a record of a cab being sent to an address on Dominion Avenue close to the Pickton farm at about the right time, but no records with the exact address of 963 Dominion, the Pickton property.

believe she had joined the legions of the community's disappeared. Not Georgina—she was too street-smart, too tough, too well connected. The Papins were a legendary Native family from a wealthy four-band reserve, Alberta's Hobbema Cree First Nation, southwest of Edmonton, and her younger brother Rick was a much-feared criminal, respected and obeyed even when he was doing time in prison. No one dared cross him.

Georgina, who was born in March 1964, was one of nine children; they will admit, with gales of laughter, that almost no one can figure out the family tree. It takes a diagram to remember it all. The easiest way to explain it, they say, is that they all had the same mother but different fathers. That's not entirely true, but it's close.

Their mother, Maggie Rattlesnake, was born in 1942 and had her first baby at seventeen, with a man named Reno Parsons, "a German guy from Squamish," explains Cynthia Cardinal—usually called Cindi—Georgina's sister. That baby, a girl named Debbie, died, but Maggie then met a man named John Ermineskin, of the Hobbema Cree. Cynthia was the child they had together, so she is the oldest. Maggie's next partner was George Papin, and this time she married him; their first baby together was Georgina. Next came the first baby boy, Rick, followed by Tammy.

Not happy with George Papin, Maggie found another partner, a man named Larry; they had a boy they named George Junior. Maggie finally concluded that George Papin was the best of the bunch, so she returned to him and they had three more children, Randy, Elana and Bonnie. Maggie died at thirty-seven, and at that point the children basically had only each other. Although they grew up in foster homes or with relatives, they always made efforts to stay in touch.

Tammy, the fifth in line, did a lot of research to find her brothers and sisters and keep track of them. Rick became the most notorious, but he wasn't the only one who had done time in prison; so had Georgina and Tammy. By 1985 the siblings had connected and arranged a Christmas reunion in a bar in Edmonton. The first thing they did was compare how many children each had; Rick led the way with an admission of "about seventeen," while Cindi and Georgina each had seven. Elana had five, Randy had one and Bonnie owned a puppy (and thought it should count). It was a joyful get-together and all agreed they would stay in touch, which they have done. As they admit, all of them have been at one time or another addicted to drugs. Today, with one exception, they are clean and sober.

To her siblings, Georgina was adorable. "Her face just glowed," remembers Cindi. "She was just about five feet tall, she was ram-bunctious, and if she walked into a room, every head was turned to watch her."

The sisters all look alike: strong-boned faces with high cheek-bones, wide smiles, large, dark eyes that look straight at you. Their hair is thick and black and they all carry themselves straight, with shoulders back. But they decided Georgina was special. She was born to be an artist or maybe a musician. She could draw well. She wove dream catchers and fashioned beautifully beaded jewellery. She could sew strips of leather together to make moccasins nice enough to sell, and taught others, including Maggy Gisle, how to make them. She had a lovely voice and loved to sing for her family and friends; when she was in Oakalla, the women's prison, she wrote songs that women still remember today. And she was a talented cook; one favourite recipe was for bannock and she'd encourage everyone to get involved in making it.

But her life had been just as tough as theirs. Childhood hadn't been just one or two foster homes and institutions; there had been dozens, says her first cousin Sharon Baptiste, who is also a member of Alberta's Hobbema Cree Nation and was particularly close to Georgina. "We grew up together," Sharon says. "I went to Edmonton to stay with Auntie, Georgina's mother, who had moved there; she and my mom were sisters. It was a huge family. All the kids were freckle-faced. Auntie was on drugs so Welfare took the kids away. It was her mom who turned me on to drugs; she injected me the first time with strawberry speed [pink, candy-flavoured crystal metham-phetamine, a devastatingly addictive drug].

"Georgina was in foster care but I was under the radar. I felt my mom didn't want me around. Georgina was short and stocky but she was beautiful. She was very funny. We always used to have a joint together when we were twelve or thirteen."

Today Sharon is a tiny little thing, skinny and lively. She often wears black leather pants and a sweatshirt; her long black hair is tucked up under a baseball cap; her eyes are intelligent and alert. She is an attractive woman with a wide smile and an excellent sense of humour. Bright and literate, with a good vocabulary, she isn't shy and will readily admit to being in the Downtown Eastside for twenty-eight years, and on heroin much of that time, in spite of many efforts to clean up and kick the habit. Sharon moved to Vancouver before Georgina did. "Three years later, who shows up in the Regent Hotel? Georgina! And she has about seven kids."

In 1997, at a Native powwow in Mission, British Columbia, Georgina had another reunion, this time with Kristina Bateman, the daughter she had left behind in Las Vegas ten years earlier. Georgina had been living there with Kristina's father, and when she realized she could not care for her child properly, she left her with Ruth Bateman, Kristina's grandmother. But Georgina never forgot Kristina's birthday and she never forgot Christmas; there were always cards, presents and calls. Ruth would urge her to move back and live with them, but as a seriously addicted woman, Georgina was unwilling to inflict herself on any of them, especially not her child. As for the other women, it was when the calls and letters stopped coming that Kristina and Ruth knew something was wrong.

Tracing Georgina's last days is easier than for many of the other missing women because she was so well-known, because her habits were predictable and because she had so many friends. Maggy Gisle was one of them. By now, having kicked sixteen years' addiction to crack cocaine, Maggy was clean and sober and thrilled to be expecting a baby. Some friends were celebrating the good news with a baby shower and Georgina had said she'd be there too. But they all knew she was distraught. A year earlier, in April 1998, she had found a place to live with the four children still with her; Welfare had paid her rent and moving costs and given her enough money to buy groceries. By October her luck had run out; she had been caught smoking dope and shoplifting that summer, and officials took her kids away and sent her to rehab for a week. In December she had been arrested on a break-and-enter charge.

Georgina turned up at the baby shower in a terrible state; earlier that day a court hearing about the custody of her children had gone against her and now all she wanted to do was head for the Downtown Eastside, find her buddies and get high. Maggy tried to make her stay, to comfort her, but Georgina could not be consoled. Maggy never saw her again. The last time anyone there that night remembers seeing her was March 2, 1999.

What people do know, however, is that Georgina was sitting at a table in the Astoria Hotel with Willie Pickton around this time. He was sipping his usual Seven-Up and paying for beers for Georgina and any others who stopped by. One of these was Sharon Baptiste, who remembers March 2 as if it were yesterday.

"Okay, so this is what happened. Georgina told me on that night that she had a sugar daddy and I should come too; I met her at the Astoria. He—yeah, Pickton—was there and he was ignorant. He was like he owned the place—'Everybody gotta move, get outta my way . . . ' Especially with drag queens—he'd say, 'Listen to him talk!'

"He acted like he ran the Astoria. He'd come in with money and buy everybody a beer. He would never drink himself. At first, when he came in years ago, he was quiet, and then he started flashing the money."

Sharon knows that another man was there with him that night; she just can't remember a name or what he looked like. Just another man.

"He [Pickton] gave me twenty dollars. I was drug-sick but I still had enough sense to know he was weird. He gave me twenty dollars in the Astoria and said to me, 'Go get drugs and come back.' I went to get the drugs but I didn't come back."

The next day she learned that Georgina had left the bar with Pickton. Two nights later Sharon went back to the Astoria and Pickton was there too. As soon as he spied her he jumped to his feet and came right over. "Fucking junkie ripped me off," he hissed to onlookers. As she scuttled away in fright he chased her, drew back his arm and punched Sharon on the side of the head. Down she went, ears ringing, her head on fire. And then he was gone.

Although her cousin Sharon and other friends didn't see her after March 4, Georgina was still around. They had no idea that she had landed in the emergency department of Vancouver's St. Paul's Hospital on March 16 with severe chest pains. The doctors diagnosed pneumonia and a drug overdose and admitted her immediately. It took about five days before she started to feel human again. On March 21 a nurse saw her, tethered to an intravenous line and pushing the IV pole, going to the fourth floor for a cigarette. When she didn't return to her room, staff began searching for her; all they found was her IV pole and tubing in a bathroom. Her medical file states that she left St. Paul's before proper community follow-up for her addiction could be arranged. And that was the last anyone saw of her.

There is a significant difference between Georgina's disappearance and that of most of the other missing women. While her story appears to be incomplete, several people can weave the threads to pull it together. One is Maggy Gisle, who saw how despondent Georgina was at the baby shower. Another is Sharon Baptiste, who agreed to meet Georgina and her "sugar daddy" at the Astoria. And then there is the story that Scott Chubb has to tell.

Chubb is certain that he saw Georgina in Port Coquitlam with Willie Pickton sometime in the spring of 1999. Chubb was with his two-year-old son and his wife, Tasha, on Shaughnessy, Port Coquitlam's main street; they had just parked in front of the Money Mart when they spied Willie's one-ton white Chevrolet flatbed truck "with an orange fender," he said later. Willie pulled up his truck near Chubb's and when he hopped out, the two men said hello. Willie walked into the Money Mart; he kept a mailbox there. While he was gone Chubb had a look in the truck to see who he was with. It was a woman, he said later; she looked rough, as if she "had had a rough life," he said later. He could see that she had long, dark hair pulled back in a pony-tail. He described her as wearing a white baseball cap and a jean jacket over a heavy sweater. Chubb stared at her and she stared right back at him. When he saw pictures of Georgina Papin later, he was sure she was the woman he'd seen in the truck waiting for Willie to come back from the Money Mart.

CHAPTER TWENTY-ONE

WHAT DID THE POLICE DO?

On March 2, 1999, the Vancouver Police Department's chief constable, Bruce Chambers, decided it was time to quash the growing public alarm about a possible serial killer targeting women in the Downtown Eastside. "We keep reviewing this because we hear the concern from the community," he declared, "but we've found nothing that would indicate there's a serial killer involved in these missing people."

That despite the fact that during this period in early 1999, the officers working in Project Amelia, Geramy Field's small Vancouver police unit, were well aware of the rumours swirling around Willie Pickton. They knew who he was, they knew what people were saying and they'd had several tips, including the one from Bill Hiscox. They had looked up his 1997 history with Sandra Gail Ringwald, history that was not in the public eye because the attempted murder charge had been stayed after she refused to show up in court to testify against him.*

"Lori Shenher contacted me in the middle of 1999 about Pickton," says Kim Rossmo. She wanted to bounce ideas off him and hear any advice he could offer her team. Given the fact that he had been frozen out of homicide investigations by the Vancouver Police Department's Old Boys, he was intrigued, and happy to help. He listened to what she had to say about the tip from Bill Hiscox in 1998 and her belief that Robert Pickton was a strong candidate to be the serial killer the VPD didn't believe existed.

---

* A court order had the Ringwald file sealed in 2002, preventing access by the public, including the media.

"We've got this really good suspect—Robert Pickton," she told him. "He's got a wood-chipper. What do we do next?"

The key thing, he told her, was that the police had to mount a surveillance operation against him. "But it's expensive," he warned. "And it takes a lot of people."

Shenher took Rossmo's advice back to her boss, Geramy Field, who agreed but said she was sure their own department wouldn't do it. Instead Shenher asked the RCMP in Coquitlam for help setting up a surveillance team; they assigned a few constables—Grant Wong, Bruce Morwood-Clark and John Cater—to the job (by coincidence, Cater had been one of Rossmo's students in the Criminology Department at Simon Fraser University). They were told to stop Pickton if they ever saw him pick anyone up. And they knew why: he was a person of interest in the missing-women investigation.

After the surveillance team had followed Pickton in unmarked vehicles for two weeks, Cater and Morwood-Clark told their superiors they hadn't seen anything that seemed suspicious, but Cater admitted later that he was sure Pickton had spotted his car on one occasion. Cater and Morwood-Clark tried to be more discreet, staying in the background, but they didn't gather enough evidence to persuade the regional Crown prosecutor, Peder Gulbransen, that they would be able to get a judicial officer to issue a search warrant to see what they could find at the farm. Given Lisa Yelds's assertion that Willie was paranoid about surveillance and continually on the watch for it, Cater was probably right in thinking Willie had spotted him and become more cautious.

Once the police were focused on Willie, however, something else occurred to them. After his arrest in 1997 he had allowed the police to take a DNA sample. If he was a serial killer, they reasoned, he could well be the person who had murdered three Downtown Eastside prostitutes, Tracy Olajide, Tammy Pipe and Victoria Younker, in 1995 and left their bodies in the woods near Agassiz—killings that police had tagged the Valley Murders. The police had been able to obtain the killer's DNA from the women's bodies, and it told them the same man had killed all three. But when they compared Pickton's DNA against the Valley Murderer's, it didn't match.

Was it possible that two serial killers were going after sex-trade workers from the Downtown Eastside? Absolutely not, they reasoned. It was this reasoning that led them to accept Gulbransen's advice that they didn't have enough evidence to justify a search warrant for the Pickton farm. At this point their investigation stalled and the surveillance was stopped.

The families and friends of the missing women felt they had nowhere to turn. The only people who seemed to care about the situation and who were willing to do some digging were reporters, first Lindsay Kines of the *Vancouver Sun* and soon afterwards Peter Warren, an investigative reporter who had an open-line radio show on CKNW in Vancouver.

In early April the families wanted to know why the police wouldn't offer a $100,000 reward for information leading to the arrest of whoever was taking their women.

What had triggered the families' request for the cash reward was a joint decision by the city's police board and the provincial government around the same time to offer a $100,000 reward to find the culprits behind a series of home invasions and garage fires in well-to-do neighbourhoods.

The response from Vancouver's mayor, Philip Owen, who was also the head of the police board, was scathing. "There's no evidence that a serial killer is at work," he told radio reporter Robert Phillips, echoing the party line laid out earlier by Bruce Chambers. "No bodies have been found. They [the police] have a procedure for homicides and missing people, and they are following it. I don't think it is appropriate for a big award for a location service."

It wasn't that Owen wished harm to the missing women, he just didn't think it was the job of the police to locate them when there wasn't any evidence they'd been murdered. And he rejected the families' claims that their loved ones were close to them and kept in touch and wouldn't just vanish into thin air. "That's what they say," Owen snapped. "There's been prostitutes moving around . . . and it never came up before. I didn't get a letter or a phone call from anybody before this and some of these girls have been missing for a year. All of a sudden . . . it becomes a major event."

When Robert Phillips called police spokesperson Anne Drennan, she trotted out the same argument: that there was no evidence the women had been murdered or even that they were dead and that there were no suspects. "It's difficult for us to try to figure out what way a reward would be beneficial and how it would be offered," she stated. "These are missing-persons cases."

Mayor Owen's contemptuous response, especially his reference to a "location service," not only shocked the families and social service workers who had known the missing women, it also upset many British Columbians. The backlash started a wave of public support for a serious investigation into the disappearances. Not long afterwards, the Vancouver police reluctantly began planning to beef up Project Amelia's small team—reluctantly because the top men in the Vancouver Police Department couldn't stomach the thought that Kim Rossmo might have been right.

And, to their fury, he was back in the news, the subject of a long and flattering profile in Britain's *Daily Telegraph* published on April 22, 1999. Explaining that the British police had started to use Rossmo's geographic profiling software to help solve serial-offender crimes, the story went on to say that "by analysing the locations of a series of crimes, the inventor of geographic profiling, Kim Rossmo, can find out a lot about a killer, because the geographic behaviour of humans is easy to understand. 'The offence might be pathological, but the locations of the crime sites are non-pathological,' he says. 'The same patterns that determine how we shop and where McDonalds will put its next restaurant apply to criminals [patterns].' People tend to go about their routine business close to where they live, work or play, giving all of us an activity space which is closely connected to our homes. Needing to bury a body, the places likely to occur to a murderer will fall within the area he is familiar with."

In June 1999 *BC Business* magazine chose Rossmo as one of the most outstanding Vancouverites of the year for his work in law enforcement, noting that he'd used his geographic profiling software in 1,400 cases and trained officers in its use all around the world. *Crap,* thought Rossmo's jealous colleagues. *Just crap.* And these weren't the only stories celebrating Rossmo's genius; about the same time there were features in the *Toronto Star* and *Seattle Times* and on the Associated Press wire service. Rossmo was everywhere. A week after the pieces began appearing, the Vancouver police announced they were adding two senior homicide investigators to Project Amelia.

And none too soon, it turned out. The missing women's families were finally beginning to coalesce into a force of their own. After Mayor Owen's stinging snub, they decided, led by the de Vries family, to hold a rally. To the surprise of city officials and the police, it was a strategic and highly visible success—strategic because for the first time the families were united into a critical mass of people that was impossible to ignore. Between three and four hundred friends and relatives of the missing women, including their children, as well as Native elders, social workers, reporters and some politicians, gathered on May 12, 1999, at a memorial service in First United Church in the Downtown Eastside.

The organizers had arranged flowers on the altar as well as twenty-three candles to represent the twenty-three missing women. The service, a joint one that lasted almost three hours, combined traditional Native practices with First United's Christian service, with a sweetgrass ceremony and a healing circle along with readings, hymns and prayers. The candles were lit one at a time. The congregation sang "Amazing Grace." And many family members spoke out. Stephanie Lane's mother, Michele Pineault, was one of them.

"Today, I hope, is the beginning of a healing process, because my daughter has been gone a long time," Pineault said after the ceremony. "I grieve every day."

Deborah Jardine was too sick to leave her home in Sparwood in the East Kootenays but sent pictures of Angela as well as a letter to read to the other families during the service. "She pursued life with the volume up loud," Deborah wrote. "Her persona was loud and her mannerisms sometimes made the people around her cringe. Each night I ask God to send an angel to watch over our daughter."

Kerry Koski's teenage daughter, Sandra, was there. "I believe God is with my mother wherever she is," she told the crowd. "I hope one day she will come back to us." In a poem Maggie de Vries had written for her sister, Sarah, she said, "May you know somehow and somewhere that you are loved and that you always were." Janet Henry's daughter, Deborah, thanked everyone for coming and for remembering her mother. "I remember the good things she did for me and the smile she had."

Along with the moving words of family members there were protests from community activists, who carried signs declaring that the missing women were not "disposable," underlining the attitude of many politicians and the police towards prostitutes and drug addicts. Criticism of the police was particularly sharp. Tara Khadem, a worker in a rape relief centre, was outspoken: "We expect the police and the RCMP to seriously investigate these women and their cases. We believe the police response to these missing women has been horrible. To say there isn't enough evidence is horrible."

Kim Rossmo agreed. Several months earlier, in the fall of 1998, he had tried to persuade his colleagues that they should be considering the very real possibility that a serial killer was picking off women in the Downtown Eastside. Now, in May 1999, he no longer thought it was possible. He thought it was probable.

This wasn't a guess. Rossmo began his research with a statistical examination of more than eight hundred missing-women cases in Vancouver from 1995 to 1998 to see if there was a standard pattern among them. By the time he was done he thought that twenty of the eight hundred were what he called "statistically significant" and "unlikely to have occurred by chance." In the report that he gave senior officers on May 27, 1999, his forecast was grim: "Based on historical data, we can expect to locate no more than two individuals from this group." His conclusion was more bad news: "While it is not possible with available information to determine with certainty the cause of these disappearances, the most likely explanation for the majority of them is a single murderer (or partner murderers) preying on Skid Row prostitutes."

If the women had all been murdered, he explained, there were three possibilities: they could have been killed by different people, by a single serial killer or by a number of serial killers. But in the case of the women he had studied who went missing between 1995 and 1998, he saw only one conclusion—that a single serial killer was at work, and this person could be part of a team or have a partner. That was because there were no bodies. In most Downtown Eastside violent deaths, he explained, women died in domestic arguments or in drug or alcohol fights. Their bodies were found.

"Similarities in victimology and the short time period and specific neighbourhood involved—all suggest the single serial murderer hypothesis is the most likely explanation for the majority of these incidents," he said. "The single predator theory includes partner or team killers; approximately twenty-five per cent of serial murder cases involve more than one offender."

Based on his belief that a serial killer was responsible for the disappearances, his report offered some other interesting information. He said investigators should consider looking for what he called "cluster body sites." What he meant, he explained, was that it was not unusual "for serial killers who want to hide the remains of their victims to dispose of multiple bodies in one location; using several different sites increases the odds of discovery . . . When a body is found in a cluster dump site, several others can often be located within a range of 50 metres or less." Considering Vancouver's surrounding geography, "potential burial sites are most likely to be in wilderness areas or less likely on the offender's residence or property." And the killer would most likely be a local person, someone who knew Vancouver and the surrounding area well.

Rossmo presented his report to three senior officers, Deputy Chief Constable of Major Crimes Brian McGuinness, Inspector Fred Biddlecombe and Inspector Chris Beach, the new head of District Two, which includes the Downtown Eastside. (Beach was replacing Doug MacKay-Dunn, who had run District Two and had first been approached about the missing women by Constable Dave Dickson.) Although these officers concluded that they still did not have any evidence a serial killer was at large in the Downtown Eastside, they did assign two senior homicide investigators to help the Project Amelia team.

But any special effort the city police were making at this time was completely undermined by vicious internal strife within the force. Rossmo's enemies were determined to get rid of his protector, Chief Constable Bruce Chambers, and in June they succeeded. Two years into a three-year contract, he was fired by the police board, to be succeeded by Terry Blythe. John Unger, Kim Rossmo's most implacable foe, was made a deputy chief.

The Old Boys were now fully in control. But even in power they couldn't ignore the fact that growing public concern about the missing women was morphing into an international nightmare for Vancouver. On July 22, 1999, the popular television show *America's Most Wanted* broadcast a story about the case, asking if a modern-day Jack the Ripper was at large. Although local politicians had decided they had to cooperate with the show, an angry police force insisted that two other Vancouver investigations be mentioned as well. The show's producers agreed, and after more negotiations the show's host, John Walsh, came to Vancouver to announce, together with provincial attorney general Ujjal Dosanjh, a $100,000 reward for information on the missing-women case. "Although police don't have any evidence of foul play, there is a gut instinct that all of us have," Dosanjh said.

"The very best outcome that we could have," John Unger commented at the press conference, "is that every one of these missing women would phone us and say: 'Here I am. I don't wish to make it publicly known where I'm located, but here I am to let you know that I'm safe and sound.'" His message was clear. The missing women didn't want people to know where they were but it would be great if they'd just let everyone know they were "safe and sound."

Still underfinanced and understaffed, Project Amelia struggled along. Officers in the task force knew that most of the senior officers thought their work was a joke. Still, tips continued to pour in to the team. Lori Shenher spent hours with the families, interviewing them, trying to obtain clues about the women's associates, habits, favourite hangouts and anything else they could suggest that would give her a place to start. By the late summer of 1999 she had won their trust and was now a believer, certain that a serial killer was at work.

As they worked, the team tried to come up with methods for identifying women who had died in hospital or on the street without any identification or with only fake identification. The causes of their deaths included drug overdoses, beatings and the diseases so prevalent among the addicted sex-trade workers of the Downtown Eastside: HIV/AIDS; hepatitis A, B and C; pneumonia; infections from dirty needles and skin abscesses. Some of the deaths might have been suicides. While it was possible that some of these women might have been among the missing, without any identification no one could contact their families or even their welfare workers. And because of privacy laws, the hospitals were not allowed to fingerprint them or photograph their faces or identifying marks such as tattoos and scars. Nor did they keep lists of aliases or other information that could help to identify the bodies.

Project Amelia investigators realized very quickly that an important goal for the police was to obtain fingerprints, hair for DNA samples, and dental records from women in the Downtown Eastside so they could be identified later if their bodies were found. A macabre goal, to be sure, but many of the sex-trade workers were not against it. They were already starting to work with staff at DEYAS—the Downtown Eastside Youth Activities Society needle exchange—which was now urging them to call in before they left the area for any length of time.

The police team also began to see before them a vague image of the person who might be responsible for the disappearances. In the late summer of 1999 Lori Shenher took her colleague Constable Al Arsenault through the efforts she and her colleagues had gone through in trying to find out what had happened to these women. Arsenault was finishing *Through a Blue Lens*; given Shenher's experience, she was a good person for him to interview. But the conversation inevitably moved to the work she and the rest of her group were doing to find out what had happened to the missing women.

Arsenault had brought with him his colleague and fellow Odd Squad member Constable Toby Hinton, who would manage the video camera while he interviewed Shenher. They met in the large Project Amelia room in the Main Street police headquarters. Shenher, who is slim and attractive, with a ready smile but the wary eyes of a seasoned cop, was wearing a black V-necked pullover and slacks, her long, dark hair pulled up in a bun, her only jewellery a pair of gold hoop earrings. She had plenty to say.

The person taking these women, she believed, had to be a man. She saw him as someone with enough social skills to instill trust in his victims, "in order not to have to use violence to get at them." And she believed he would be an "organized type," one with "set fantasies with his victim that he sets up ultimately to kill them." And by this time, familiar as they were with the files, she and her colleagues were assuming they had at least thirty-one victims.

Shenher understood that the missing women and their families had been essentially marginalized, but she was defensive about the criticism of her force and thought the media had a lot to answer for. "Sandra Gagnon [Janet Henry's sister] didn't have her calls returned two and a half years ago by the press," she told Arsenault. "The media reflects society's values and the police are being lumped together with the media, but the police cared for these women from the get-go. They've done good work, and now a national story comes out and only now it's important to the media."

And she felt her group was getting somewhere. They had sifted through two-thirds of the missing women's files, Arsenault noted during their conversation, and "had documented it, and had five hundred pieces of information over and above the files on the women, and they are working on a 'person of interest.'" By October 1999, she predicted, the team's focus would be much narrower.

After all those months of studying the files, Shenher had plenty of general conclusions. The victimization of sex-trade workers was an economic problem, she declared. "It's one of poverty. The closure of Riverwood, the former mental hospital in Coquitlam, had thrown many women on the street that should have been institutionalized. The women need proper medical care, to start with. Many of them were on medication without supervision and many ended up taking more drugs to dull their pain, and this leads to victimization.

"They are highly victimized and vulnerable and are not making good decisions. And they will do anything to get drugs. They go for the drugs against their gut feelings because they want to believe that the guy offering them drugs and clothes will be nice to them. They can be made street-smart and given cellphones, but there will still be males out there to hurt them, sex offenders who are released without treatment who know where to find these vulnerable victims. And every girl—*every* girl—has numerous threats on their lives."

Shenher and Arsenault talked about the kind of men who would do this and they also talked about the myths arising in the Downtown Eastside community from all the talk and fear. Many men who would do this don't have criminal records, declared Shenher. A good example was Brian William Allender, a married family man, hockey coach and first offender who killed a prostitute, then cut off her breasts and genitals. As for the urban legends, the most prevalent was the belief that the missing women had been taken onto ships in Vancouver Harbour and dumped at sea. "The fear of dying [among women in the Downtown Eastside] is almost palpable," Shenher said.

The good news was that she and her team were beginning to win the trust of the women in the neighbourhood. They were starting to get calls from street women despite their worry about being "branded as a rat," as she put it. These personal connections, Shenher told Arsenault, would eventually break the case.

As they talked, Arsenault went back to a broader view of the case, one that sought comparisons with other places, other cities. Do we have more missing women here in Vancouver, he wondered, than in other major cities across Canada? Shenher had asked herself the same thing. Using the Canadian police messaging system, she'd sent out a note to forces in large Canadian cities, and the response was surprising. "Only four places had a missing-persons section," she told Arsenault. "Toronto didn't know of such a trend. Vancouver is the only problem centre for missing women in Canada."

If you compared Vancouver's missing women to the Green River Killer's forty-eight victims in Seattle, Washington, the most important difference was that in Seattle the police had the dead bodies. In another case, in the small city of Poughkeepsie, New York, eight women had gone missing over twenty-two months; police found their bodies stuffed in the rafters of a man's house—a man who had used fifty of the community's seventy prostitutes. In Vancouver, there were no bodies.

By the time they finished their lengthy interview, Arsenault and Shenher were feeling more relaxed. "When all's said and done," Arsenault asked as he began packing away his equipment while Toby Hinton kept the tape rolling, "what is your gut feeling on this case?"

Shenher paused. Suddenly her earlier certainty about a single killer's being responsible seemed to her too fantastic. Experience had taught her how rare such a person was. "One-third were probably killed by drug activity, one man per each girl. One-third probably died in hospital under an alias. One-third were probably murdered by several serial killers." She thought for a minute. "Still . . . That's my gut feeling today—but it changes."

While Hinton filmed cutaways of Shenher and Arsenault together, along with long shots of the room showing the whiteboards with the names of the missing women grouped under dates, Shenher hesitated again. Arsenault waited. His tape recorder was packed but Hinton's video camera was still on and picked up her comment. It was just a throwaway line, an afterthought.

It was about her plan to go to Port Coquitlam the next day.

"There's a guy in PoCo," she confided. "We're being pretty quiet about this. He's a real freak. A pig farmer who has guts rendered offsite. I've had a source on him since July and this is the third source, and apparently he's a real loner, a tough guy to get close to." She stopped. The interview was over; Arsenault and Hinton were about to leave. And then she blurted, "Yeah, we're pretty quiet about this. We're doing some work there tomorrow."

She didn't mention that RCMP officers had followed the pig farmer for two weeks earlier that spring and that they had tried, unsuccessfully, to obtain a warrant to search the farm.

Who might have been the source mentioned by Lori Shenher on September 2, 1999, in her conversation with Al Arsenault? Bill Hiscox, Wayne Leng and Lisa Yelds had already been interviewed by the police, thanks to Yelds's initial talk with Hiscox about the women's clothes on the Pickton farm and her suspicions about Willie. But neither of the men was able to give the police solid leads, and Yelds, the original source, had refused to cooperate at all. Still, given Pickton's record with Sandra Gail Ringwald, the police knew he would have to be high on their list of "persons of interest." There is only one possibility: in the summer of 1999 Lynn Ellingsen became a fourth source.

After her experience in the barn and Willie's threats to kill her if she ever told anyone, Lynn was terrified. But she did talk about it to close friends. In July 1999 she went to live with a man named Gerry Loranger, sometimes described as a counsellor for Alcoholics Anonymous. Lynn was herself an alcoholic and frequently sought help from AA and other agencies. She told Loranger of the rumours about human body parts stored in Willie's freezers. Loranger wound up in jail not long after she moved to his place, and may have talked to the police about Lynn's stories. Within a few weeks of leaving Loranger's place, Lynn was living with Randy Maleschuk, a friend of her former boyfriend Ron Menard. His sister, Connie Maleschuk, was close to Lynn and had helped her move some of her belongings out of the Pickton trailer. Lynn appears to have told both Maleschuks about what she saw in the barn at Willie Pickton's farm.

But living with Randy Maleschuk was a mistake. He was tending a marijuana grow-op in the basement of the house and running up large hydro bills in her name just to keep the lights on for the plants. After she accused him of stealing from her they had a wild fight and he wound up knocking out her front teeth. He moved out.

It was just a few days later, on August 8, that the police came to see Lynn about Willie Pickton. Rumours had reached them that she'd been telling friends about being in the barn when Willie was slaughtering a woman. She denied it. No, she said, she had not seen him doing anything like that in a barn that night. That was the night, she stated, that she had left the farm and met Ross Caldwell, an old friend of hers, in a bar; she also claimed that he had driven her back to the farm later that night. The next day she was taken to the RCMP office in the Whalley area of Surrey for more questioning.

Lynn's story stayed the same: she hadn't seen or heard a thing. We heard you witnessed a woman hanging in a barn, the police said; she said no, it wasn't true. But she did say that Willie hit her. On August 26 two different police officers questioned her again. Ellingsen told them she never saw Willie hurt anyone; they were sure she was lying. As Lori Shenher suggested to Al Arsenault just a few days afterwards, Lynn was considered an important source, and they had a trip planned to see her the next day, on September 3.

Lynn Ellingsen was terrified. Not of the police—she had spent much of her life trying to outwit them. She was afraid of the Pickton brothers. She thought Willie might kill her if she talked; if he didn't, Dave might. She wouldn't be honest with the cops, but Willie would have to pay for her silence. Two months earlier, on June 7, he had already asked Sandy Humeny, the bookkeeper for P&B Building Supplies, to make out a cheque to Lynn for $350. The following month, on July 9, Willie made arrangements for a second cheque for Lynn, this one for $150. Sandy Humeny didn't ask any questions; she just did exactly what Willie asked her to do.

CHAPTER TWENTY-TWO

CLOSING IN ON WILLIE

Although Lynn Ellingsen was talking to the police about Willie Pickton during the summer of 1999, the information she gave them didn't interest them enough to spend any more time on him. The police had him under surveillance for two weeks, he'd spotted them, he didn't murder anyone while they were watching, and they couldn't get a search warrant to look around his farm. They had no bodies and his DNA had proved he wasn't the Valley Murderer. End of story. The officers working for Project Amelia were discouraged. Family members were beseeching them for help, for information, for action, but they had little to offer—the unit was still understaffed and senior officers in the Vancouver Police Department continued to regard the effort as a colossal waste of time. Geramy Field, Lori Shenher and the rest of the team did the best they could but they were frustrated, again and again, by the lack of resources and by the negative attitude towards the whole exercise from the top brass.

To be fair, it was not a good period for the city's police force. Ever since 1993 the city had been whittling away at its budget and the only recourse seemed to be to cut staff. Forty-two officers had been laid off since 1993 even though there was more work to do every year. That meant that the officers who remained on the force were having to work overtime, and the cost of all those extra hours was prohibitive. But the news for Vancouver's chief constable, Terry Blythe, wasn't all bad. In November 1999 the International Association of Chiefs of Police honoured him for his leadership—for the work of Kim Rossmo's geographic profiling unit, a particularly ironic twist in view of the fate of the unit in the days to come.

Later the same month, on November 27, 1999, Wendy Crawford disappeared. Born on April 21, 1956, Wendy was forty-three when she was last seen. Photographs of her show an attractive woman with a weary but still handsome face, with high cheekbones wide set, watchful eyes and a nimbus of curly yellow hair, her best-remembered feature. When she was little, her parents, who had four other children, moved back and forth across British Columbia, Alberta and the Yukon, but they ended up in Chilliwack, where Wendy spent most of her life. The family went through very difficult times when two of her brothers died, one in 1982 and the other in 1990.

Wendy, who was in her teens when she began sniffing glue and trying drugs, later struggled as a single mother to look after two children, a son and a daughter. Wendy's biggest problem was her health. Not only did she have diabetes but she was also diagnosed with Crohn's disease, which causes serious inflammation of the intestinal tract. It's painful, exhausting and debilitating and requires a careful diet and strong medication. With very little money, Wendy was forced to raise her children on welfare. It was a tough situation. Although the family lived in a mobile home in Chilliwack, Wendy's sister, Susie Kinshella, is adamant that while Wendy worked as a prostitute, she never abandoned her family, her friends or her kids. They always knew where she was.

"She was a mother of two beautiful children," Kinshella stated in a powerful letter she wrote to the *Vancouver Sun* years later, after reading a story that she felt had denigrated Wendy. "My sister did not have a history of disappearing. She had a family to raise, but as the kids grew and Wendy was freer to roam, she would go off and do her thing. But someone, be it her children or other family members, would usually have a basic idea of her whereabouts. Yes, she did travel the streets of Vancouver . . .

"She owned a mobile home and paid pad rental. The most important issue in this case is the two beautiful children she did her best to raise with what cards life dealt her. Reporters never walked a mile in the shoes of any of these women who suffered tragic deaths, but you quickly label them prostitutes and drug addicts. My sister raised her children on a welfare budget and anyone who has experienced that can understand that such a minimal amount of money does not always pay the bills and put enough food into their mouths every month.

"Yes, my sister sold her body on the streets. However, something is drastically wrong when you can call my sister a prostitute for trying to feed her children while other participants in this act are men who keep their good standing in society. Are they not prostitutes as well? She was a sister and an aunt, as well as a great-aunt and a friend. She was not on the streets every day selling her body and she did not take drugs all the time. Something is drastically wrong when you can call my sister a prostitute for trying to feed her children."

There are still few details available that explain her disappearance, but a young neighbour, who gave her name as Jennifer, posted a note to a website that may contain a few clues. Jennifer said she was fourteen years old when Wendy vanished. "I remember the last day that any one saw Wendy alive," she wrote. "I was on my porch getting my dogs leash on to go and check the mail. (we lived in a tralor court) from my porch I saw Wendy get into a truck with . . . an ugly looking man. About 2 weeks after that date, nurses had been coming to Wendys trailor as she needed medication. After so many unanswered attempts the police were called. I walked down to talk to the police. (My mom told me it was the right thing to do as I had seen her last.) when I began talking to the officer all I got out was 'I saw Wendy about a week ago get into' and I was rudly cut off with a 'Your just a kid you dont even know what your talking about.' To this day it hurts so bad to think that maybe if I had just stood up and said what I new maybe we wouldnt be reading her name under the headlines."

Wendy Crawford was reported missing by her worried family on December 14, 1999.

Almost two weeks later, two days after Christmas, twenty-eight-year-old Jennifer Furminger also vanished. Born on October 22,

1971, Jennifer was an aboriginal baby put up for adoption by her parents. The date isn't certain but she was probably about two years old when a couple in St. Catharines, Ontario, adopted her. By all accounts she was a very happy little girl with loving parents, a child who especially enjoyed fishing outings with her father. In public school from grade two on, she was part of an inseparable threesome that people called the Three Musketeers. Those years were the happiest of Jennifer's life. "I remember going from Brownies to Girl Guides together—when you fly up from one to the other," one of the friends, many years later, told Alison Auld, a reporter for the Canadian Press. "It was the three of us and she was really excited about that."

Jennifer was pretty, bright and talented. She loved to sketch and paint, her friend told Auld. "She had an awesome talent." And she appeared to be very happy at home. Everything changed when Jennifer went to high school. With her dark skin she felt out of place. She was fighting with her parents and confused about the reason for her adoption. She became withdrawn and sad. But in grade nine she made a new friend, a girl named Kelly Gilby, who eventually asked her parents if Jennifer could come and stay for a while because she was so miserable at home. The Gilbys agreed and for a while everything went well. "When she moved in with us," Gilby told Auld, "she was able to smile, she was more relaxed. I think she finally understood what it meant to have fun. I remember going out shopping, chasing guys, having fun and giggling—just the usual fifteen-year-old stuff. In school, she applied herself. She was kind of serious about high school. I think she really wanted to better herself and wanted to give herself something to look forward to in the future."

But then the two girls had a spat and Jennifer moved out. They lost touch and Jennifer ran away from home before she finished grade ten. Her family and friends saw her from time to time, but after she moved to Vancouver most of them lost touch with her. If you think about this short time between quitting high school, leaving home and landing on skid row, it seems shocking that no one was able to break her fall. But by 1989 Jennifer was living in the Downtown Eastside.

Her new friends all remember her as smart, funny and outgoing, and they all remember the cat she had tattooed on her shoulder. Some of them knew she'd had a baby boy but they assumed she had put him up for adoption, because he wasn't with her.

It didn't take long before Jennifer had become just another addicted girl on the street, selling sex to pay for her drugs, coping with bad boyfriends. In 1999, after one of these boyfriends locked her out of their apartment, she was taken in by fifty-six-year-old Noel Paris, a retired construction worker who had been disabled by an accident. Paris and Jennifer had known each other for years and had become friends; eventually, despite their age difference, she became his sometime girlfriend—sometime because she had another boyfriend who lived in the Fraser Valley. "We stayed friends and [our relationship] would come and go," Paris—who described Jennifer as "genteel"—told Chris Miller, a reporter for the *Vancouver Courier*. "I'm not a possessive man and I knew what she did. I'm not naive. She was very feminine and playful and she was very, very mellow. Jennie's idea of a good time was to sit cross-legged on the couch and read a book."

Noel Paris watched Jennifer standing on her corner at Cordova and Dunleavy in the Downtown Eastside on December 27, 1999. Although he saw a police car stop and heard a cop speak to her, asking how she was, he didn't see the man in the car that picked her up shortly afterwards. Three months went by. Jennifer had always come and gone as she pleased and she did have that boyfriend in Abbotsford. Still, by this time Paris knew something had to be wrong, so he went to the police at the end of March 2000 and reported that she was missing. They began to look for her. Seven months later, in October, they added her name to the list of missing women.

Four days after Jennifer Furminger disappeared, the Picktons' annual New Year's Eve party at Piggy's Palace was in full swing, Willie relishing every minute of it. Whenever he described it to a police officer later, his voice was high and tight with excitement and his eyes, shining with remembered pleasure, blinked rapidly. "There was some really good times. That night we had seventeen hundred people in the place. People had a grand time. We hired security guards, oh yeah."

But then the police arrived. For Willie, as he described it, the raid seemed to be as much fun as the party itself. "It was the biggest bust I've ever seen . . . There were fifty or sixty cars of cops." But the police didn't shut the Picktons down; the fire marshal did. "That was it," Willie said. "No more. [They say] they can't have a nightclub, there's no nightclubs in the city of PoCo, they don't want any nightclubs in the city.

"It was the biggest party: seventeen hundred people. It was a beautiful, beautiful party. People were having a grand time. It was the best time they ever had. So much money was donated for kids, so, so much. Our nightclub holds about three hundred people—seventeen hundred was a lot of people. The police didn't know nothing about it until the party was half over. There were some good times, some real good times."

That's for sure, but the good times were over at Piggy's Palace. To make sure the brothers didn't run another party in the barn, the RCMP obtained a court order against the Picktons' company, the Good Times Society, that said the police could arrest and remove anyone attending public events there. And just to tighten the screws, the Good Times Society lost its non-profit status in 2000 for failing to provide mandatory financial statements.

The police in Port Coquitlam may have finally succeeded in closing down the Palace, but the cops working in Project Amelia's Downtown Eastside office were finding their job impossible. With dozens of women now missing, with families calling every day for news, with reporters hounding them for progress reports and with their best lead, Willie Pickton, dismissed, it was difficult to keep up morale. And because it was no secret that the top brass held the project in contempt, it was difficult for its members to see their time on Project Amelia as a career-enhancing experience. Months earlier, in July 1999, Mayor Philip Owen had issued a press release trumpeting the city's strong response to the crisis: "The women's families and friends, and the entire Downtown Eastside community need to know what has happened. We're doing everything we can to get answers."

Perhaps the mayor didn't realize that wasn't happening. And it wasn't because the officers in Project Amelia weren't trying. The reasons behind their failure were complex and remained secret until a *Vancouver Sun* investigation uncovered some of them two years later. Although the police team had nine members in 1999, for example, it turned out that most of them were only working on it part-time or were working on two jobs at the same time. Geramy Field, the sergeant in charge of the investigation, "was essentially doing the work of two or even three people," the *Sun* story said, "supervising an on-call homicide team of eight officers, overseeing the coroner's liaison and missing person's units while leading a probe into a possible serial murder case rivalling that of the Green River Killer in Washington State."

The paper's reporters, Lindsay Kines, Kim Bolan and Lori Culbert, unearthed other problems. Despite the fact that Headquarters had given Field two homicide investigators, they were expected to help with new, unrelated cases at the same time. Another two officers were junior and inexperienced. No one on the team had received any training in major case management from the Canadian Police College, the standard requirement for a complicated assignment like this one. And infighting among the team members had poisoned the workplace. The *Sun*'s team reported allegations "that at least two members of the team were withholding information from other officers and running parallel investigations without alerting the others. The *Sun* has learned that the situation was so bad that some investigators refused to sit in the same room with each other."

Some of the problems were simply administrative. Not enough data-entry people, for example; data getting lost in the computer system. Staff burnout was another major issue. Despite all these setbacks—which were not known by the families at the time—Project Amelia had some successes. For instance, reported the *Sun* journalists, "detectives located four of the women by following up leads, monitoring bank accounts, e-mailing pictures to psychiatric hospitals, border crossings and police departments; and checking databanks across the country for medical, social service, vital statistics and coroner's records. Two of the women were located alive, while two had died—one of a heart condition, the other of a drug overdose."

The team struggled along into 2000, recording hundreds of tips and trying to talk to prostitutes in the community to get their ideas about who might be involved in the disappearances. Unfortunately the police simply didn't have enough people to follow up all the leads or analyze all the information.

On January 19 the RCMP's John Cater, who had been part of the surveillance team on Pickton a few months earlier, actually interviewed Pickton about his experience with Sandra Gail Ringwald in 1997, hoping to gain some new information that might help the team. It didn't work, but Pickton did mention one interesting thing. He said the police still hadn't given him back the clothes he was wearing when he was questioned the night he got into the knife fight with Ringwald, after he'd tried to handcuff her. He'd been rushed to hospital and his clothes, including his gumboots, had been taken away. The police noted his comment but didn't return anything to him; it seemed like a long time ago, the case had been concluded, and everyone forgot about it.

Pickton knew by now that he was a person of interest to the police and he became cautious. While he may have known that Lynn Ellingsen was the biggest threat to his security, and he may have suspected that she'd already talked to the police, he couldn't be sure. But he knew she was dangerous. And what was more exasperating, she was expensive. Willie told Scott Chubb one day that she had cost him about $10,000 so far. Exactly when the pair had this conversation is unclear. Chubb has variously stated that it was in early 2000, in the summer of 2000, and even in 2001. What he is much clearer about, though, is what Willie said to him.

Chubb, who was broke and needed cash right away, had called Willie to see if he had any work for him. Okay, said Willie. When Chubb arrived at the farm he found Willie with a pile of lumber from a demolition site. One large pile consisted of plywood flooring that had been covered with Arborite, and Willie needed to pull off the Arborite and remove all the nails before he could take it back to P&B's Tannery Road site for resale. A tedious job, but the two men worked agreeably alongside each other for hour after hour, filling the time with aimless conversation. And then, recalled Chubb in interviews with the RCMP, "It just kind of came out of nowhere. Willie offered me a thousand dollars to hurt Lynn.

"He said something to the effect that—that Lynn was costing him a lot of money and that he was looking—basically he was looking for somebody to go talk to her or hurt her or something. He was telling me, you know, different ways that you could probably get away with hurting her. He explained to me that him and another partner of his, or somebody had taken a syringe of anti-freeze or window-washer fluid and had injected somebody with it and they died right away, and that if the RCMP were to find the bodies, that they wouldn't really know the difference because usually they were junkies and that there was track marks that, you know, you wouldn't know whether or not she died from that or from heroin or a drug overdose."

Chubb didn't take up Willie's offer. Broke as he was, much as a thousand dollars would have been a godsend just then, he wasn't a killer.

But then Chubb had another encounter with Willie Pickton that would prove to be just as significant as their conversation about getting rid of Lynn Ellingsen. Scott Chubb had often seen firearms on the farm; in fact, Willie liked to show them off to him. And Chubb remembers that Willie kept them in the laundry room of his trailer. "The ones I seen," he explained later, "was a .38 Browning, a nickel-plated .44 magnum and there was another magnum there. And I think there might have been a Mac 10 there, I'm not exactly positive . . ."

When Chubb asked Willie if he could borrow the .38 Browning for a short while, Willie agreed right away and even threw in four free bullets. Although Chubb returned the gun soon afterwards, it wasn't long before he asked Willie if he could borrow it again. And again Willie said yes.

Although in 2000 Willie Pickton still cruised the streets of the Downtown Eastside, he wasn't bringing many women back to the farm. And fewer women were disappearing. In 1997, the worst year, thirteen women disappeared. In 1998 there were eleven; in 1999, when Willie realized he was under surveillance, there were four. But women in the Downtown Eastside were terrified and the lower total for 1999 was no comfort. Their friends had been disappearing for years and years; the official estimate was now acknowledged to be thirty-one, but they all knew it was much higher.

The Downtown Eastside is a village. Dysfunctional, yes. Poverty-stricken, certainly. Ugly and sad, almost everywhere. But it is still a community where most people know one another, and it is still a place where love and respect and generosity and laughter are present in surprising and gentle places. Five nights a week, Monday through Friday, one of these places was the drop-in for women in the sex trade at First United Church. About a hundred women a night tried to arrive in time to get a hot dinner, have a shower and wash and curl their hair, try on any new clothes they found in the donation bins, put on their makeup to be ready for work later that night, and maybe, if they felt they had the time, watch their favourite television shows. They sat on sofas in the crowded little space the church provided; they gossiped and showed each other pictures of their children and talked over their worries. And regularly, in a file kept in a safe place, they would enter the names and descriptions of bad dates they'd encountered, men who had beaten or threatened them, who had perverse or dangerous sexual demands, men who refused to use condoms or stank or were weird. Men who seemed to be dangerous. Willie Pickton was one of the men listed in the file.

The drop-in is called WISH, which stands for Women's Information Safe House, and is open to sex-trade workers only. No men were allowed, not even the cook, a cheerful Nova Scotian named Woody who came in early to get meals ready for up to a hundred women. He'd play golden oldies tapes while he prepared the things they liked best, which basically meant anything with pasta. He made sure the women had fresh vegetables and fruit, and while they all loved fish, he knew enough not to make the one thing they hated—tuna casserole. The only item on the menu he didn't have to think about was dessert; all the desserts, which might include cookies and squares, donuts, cake and fruit, were donated. The favourite meal was shepherd's pie with Rice Krispies squares and cakes. How he managed it was a miracle, because the centre received only $26 a night for groceries; the rest of the ingredients came from a food bank.

Volunteers came in to serve the food because Woody was out the door before six o'clock every night. That was when the girls started to pound on the door demanding to be let in, and WISH was a male-free zone. Once in and fed, the girls would do their makeup and hair; they used hairspray and lots of shampoo, conditioner and towels. "The girls would stay one to two to three hours," remembers Elaine Allan. "All the regulars ran for the TV and they hogged the best places on the couch. We closed up at ten and I often drove girls home if they were dope-sick and couldn't go out to work."

Elaine Allan was the coordinator of WISH from 1998 to 2001. A communications graduate from Carleton University who'd worked for the federal Conservatives in Ottawa and for various companies in Vancouver and Los Angeles, Allan had started at the centre as a volunteer in 1997, brought in by a friend. Right away she loved the work and the people she was helping. It was never easy to find people with the skills and the passion for social justice needed to work in such a tough environment; the chair of the WISH board, an Anglican minister named Cathy Campbell, asked her if she would be willing to replace the outgoing coordinator. It would mean a drastic cut in pay but Allan agreed. She had found her place in the world. She knew she could help, she knew she could make a difference and she knew she would never find a better job.

And she wasn't alone. There were experienced volunteers to help, as well as a legendary street nurse, Bonnie Fournier, who had graduated as a psychiatric nurse from Riverview Hospital in Coquitlam, had worked in the holding cells at the Vancouver provincial courthouse in the Downtown Eastside for years, and now saw sick and troubled men and women every night on the street health van. Fournier, often accompanied by home-care nurses, came into WISH every night at six-thirty to give flu shots and to clean and dress deep skin abscesses caused by needle infections. When they saw serious medical issues, Fournier would make arrangements to get the women into hospital right away or refer them to doctors or clinics if their problems weren't emergencies.

"Other agencies treated the missing-women crisis as a nine-to-five thing," Fournier says, "but we started on the van every afternoon between one thirty and two thirty and ran till two thirty in the morning. We were out there when they were out there." By "they" she means the women who worked the streets until the early hours of the morning. "We knew them all. They were kids. We knew them from juvenile to adult court."

By this time Fournier had become a legend in the Downtown Eastside. In 1970 she had become director of a street program that was dealing with narcotics in the brand-new Raymur Social Housing Project, on East Hastings near Clark Drive at the east end of the Downtown Eastside. "I was on twenty-four-hour call," Fournier says, "and those were the acid years, when the psychedelics would call me, and I'd spend a lot of time standing in doorways with a paper bag." The bag was to hold the cotton balls soaked in airplane glue that the distressed kids would hand over.

In 1994 Fournier moved a bit further west for a new job but remained in the Downtown Eastside. She began working in the holding cells of the provincial courthouse on Main Street, where she did all the admission medicals; here she was the only full-time nurse employed by Sheriff's Court Services in British Columbia. After retiring in 1998 she moved to the new job with the health van; its base was the Portland Hotel on East Hastings, just two blocks from First United Church. Few people knew the women in this community better than Bonnie Fournier, and no one cared more for them than she did. In Elaine Allan she found a kindred spirit, someone who liked and appreciated the women, someone who believed they were worth all the love, help and time she could give them.

Two other women felt the same way. One was Ruth Wright, the minister at First United Church, which, like the Carnegie Centre, just another block east on Hastings Street, was a haven and resource for the community. The other was Freda Ens, a Native woman from Haida Gwai, also called the Queen Charlotte Islands, north of Vancouver Island. Ens was the executive director of the Police and Native Liaison Society, working out of an office in the Vancouver Police Department's Main Street headquarters, right beside the courthouse where Bonnie Fournier worked until 1994.

Picture it: four women, all working with addicted women in the sex trade, all working within a block or two of each other on skid row. They compared notes, they shared information, they helped each other. All of them were outraged at the lack of action on the missing women. And each would play a major role in the unfolding story.

It's important to know that, of the four, only Elaine Allan worked exclusively with the women. For the other three, their community included the men who lived in the Downtown Eastside, men who crowded into First United for breakfast every morning and who slept off their drugs and booze in the pews of the sanctuary. Men who needed clothes and a place to pick up mail and an address for government cheques or help writing their Christmas cards or a phone to make a call. Men who landed in the holding cells at the courthouse, where Bonnie Fournier would check them over, or who stopped by the health van in later years, where she offered her medical experience, a warm hug and a few jokes. Men who drifted into the Native Liaison office to ask about their kids who were missing or who were in care or who needed Freda Ens's advice on where to find rehab or housing or drug counselling.

Elaine Allan, Ruth Wright, Bonnie Fournier and Freda Ens made a close team, a unique one. Wright had come to First United from eastern Canada, where she worked as a minister in some small parishes, including the conservative little eastern Ontario town of Vankleek Hill, east of Ottawa near the Quebec border. The mother of four adopted daughters, Wright has two doctorates, one in theology and one in education. Along with teaching at the Vancouver School of Theology at the University of British Columbia and serving on its board, she freelanced as a business consultant to raise money for First United's programs. Her specialty was unusual for a minister: she was an executive coach—a person brought into the executive offices of large companies to study and advise on the leadership effectiveness of top managers, usually the chief executive officer. Such specialists are famous for their "360" assessments, which involve confidential interviews with all the employees who work with the leader to determine his or her strengths and weaknesses.

The fourth member of this unofficial team, Freda Ens, is a diminutive woman, not more than five feet tall, with short, dark hair, large, watchful eyes and a dimple in her cheek that deepens with each wide smile. And when she smiles, her face lights up—it's the puckish, lively face of a confident and happy woman. She speaks with a soft and gentle voice, but she is as brave and strong as any Native warrior celebrated in Haida legend. Her own story is as horrendous as that of many of the women.

Because her birth mother was unable to take care of her, Freda was given as an infant to another Native woman in Haida Gwai. Her new mother would have nine children—six girls and three boys—after Freda arrived, children who were treated far better than she was; to her adoptive family she was nothing more than a servant. She tells of being beaten and sexually abused by her father from the time she was still in diapers, but he wasn't the only one. A cousin also molested and raped her; so did an older man, who bought her from her drunken mother when Freda was nine years old. The price? A bottle of beer. She couldn't believe her mother wouldn't protect her, that she wouldn't stop the sexual abuse. Much later she found out that her mother had tried. She had begged the local minister, the nurses and the doctors for help, but they told her it was a family issue and the family had to solve it. "And so, having ten kids in a remote reserve—what are you going to do?" Freda asks. "She did the best she could. The police were not interested in child abuse in those years."

Freda's story, in the context of the stories other women tell in the Downtown Eastside, is not unusual. What is unusual is that she survived. "I came to a place where I could let it destroy me or I could go on and fight," she said in an interview published in the newspaper *Native Drum*. "I made a choice that I was going to come out the other end. As much as I despise what happened to me and what I went through, I had to stop and realize that, when you look at our communities and our Native people, many of them are the product of residential schools. My dad went to a residential school. He was a victim; my mom was a victim. The same thing with my uncles and cousins."

Like so many women who ended up in the Downtown Eastside, Freda ran away from home when she was a teenager. She wound up with a foster family for two years and then attended a bible college in the United States. Afraid of men, wary of relationships and commitment, it was difficult for her to make the decision to marry one of the few men she had learned to trust. But marry him she did, when she was twenty-one, and they soon had a boy and a girl. Her worst fears were realized when he eventually turned on her, berating her for being damaged goods, her virginity stolen by her father.

Freda Ens went on welfare, took courses and graduated from a community college with a diploma in counselling, then did enough volunteer work to earn a job as a victim services worker with the Native Liaison Society. Only a few years later she was the director. She knew most of the aboriginal community in the Downtown Eastside; one woman she was especially close to was Mary Lidguerre, the woman beaten to death on Mount Seymour in 1995, who had designated Freda as the official guardian of her little boy. Another was the mother of Tracy Olajide, one of the three dead women left in the woods near Agassiz in 1995 by the unknown killer in the Valley Murders.

While Freda was able to forgive her mother, she made a much tougher decision about her father, the man who had raped her as a toddler. She knew he had also abused the other children in the family, the boys as well as the girls. He had moved to the Downtown Eastside himself, and when she discovered he was volunteering as a babysitter at the Carnegie Centre for women who needed an evening off, she decided to take action. She laid charges against him; he was convicted and spent six years in prison.

"There were twelve victims in the family," she told *Native Drum*. "Four of us testified against him. But the most important thing was the sense of validation I got from the court case; the recognition that what had been done to me was really a crime. After he went to jail all my nightmares stopped."

And so did the cycle of violence and abuse she had known. It ended when she had her own children. Freda's daughter, Juanita, is one of the most talented young artists in the Native community; she is a gifted jewellery maker working in silver, gold and argillite, and her work is shown in Vancouver's leading galleries. Freda's son, Bill, is just as talented as his sister; he is a young chef who apprenticed in some of the city's finest restaurants and who now works as a senior chef. He still lives with his mother and sister in a small, pretty house close to a park—but near the Downtown Eastside—cooking them meals of fresh salmon and halibut and brewing up cappuccinos on his own machine in their tiny kitchen.

Freda Ens forgave her father. After he got out of prison she made an effort to seek him out, visit him and talk to him. She makes no excuses for what he did to her and to her sisters and brothers, but she understood his past well enough to tell him this and to tell him she had forgiven him. He died not long afterwards.

CHAPTER TWENTY-THREE

ANOTHER CLOSE CALL

Katrina Murphy looked at herself in the mirror. Not bad, she thought. She leaned closer to pat a little more concealer under her left eye, where an old powder burn still showed like a fading bruise. But her skin was still firm and clear, and with rose pink lipstick, shadow to deepen her dark blue eyes and plenty of mascara, her makeup was perfect. Her yellow scoop-necked T-shirt was tight to her slim body; her new beige jeans fit like skin. Reluctantly she gave up her original plan to wear a pair of high-heeled boots; she might have some distance to walk, so she tied on comfortable sneakers.

A few minutes later her girlfriend Diane picked her up outside her apartment building in Surrey, a working-class suburb southwest of Vancouver, for the forty-minute drive to Kent prison in Agassiz. It was Thursday, visiting day at Kent, and the women were on their way to visit their husbands, who were both locked up in protective custody.

Katrina Murphy and her husband, Blair Cody, are outlaws. They rob banks. Katrina, who is sometimes called the "Ma Barker of British Columbia" by awestruck cops, has nineteen heists to her credit. Blair has twenty-nine. It was only dumb luck that Katrina—who is thirty-five but looks younger in spite of bearing two children and having an addiction to cocaine and heroin that began when she was fourteen—wasn't in prison herself; she was out on bail, awaiting trial. Blair, however, was not so fortunate: he was doing twenty years. And Kent is no country club. It's the only federal maximum security prison in B.C., and it's reserved for murderers, bank robbers and other violent offenders.

As soon as Blair saw her swing into the visiting room, his eyes lit up. "You're beautiful," he said. They talked about her upcoming court date and about the chance that with his record he might be shipped to Quebec, to serve the rest of his sentence in an even tougher prison than Kent. To cheer themselves up, they also talked about the earliest possibility for his parole. Katrina was disappointed when Blair looked at the clock and told her she'd better get going.

"No way. It's only eight o'clock. Visiting hours last till nine."

"It'll be dark soon, honey. I don't want to worry about you. How are you getting home anyway? You got a ride back?"

"No. Diane is staying in Agassiz overnight. But one of the wives in the waiting room here says she can take me as far as the Trans-Canada. Then I'll hitch."

Blair didn't like the sound of this, but Katrina said, "I'll be fine. It's still light out and I can take care of myself. C'mon, you know that."

She was right. Katrina was tougher than half the guys at Kent. "Okay. Take care. Love you."

About half an hour later, Katrina's ride let her off on the Trans-Canada Highway at the Bridal Falls exit. It's right about here that the road from Vancouver to Calgary begins to move from flat river plain to the mountains of the interior. Going west towards Surrey and Vancouver, the Fraser River rolls along the right-hand side of the highway; on the left side of the Trans-Canada, the mountains, rising from the river plain, are cut here and there by thin fissures of waterfall. Bridal Falls is the longest and most beautiful of the falls on this stretch of highway, and it was a good place for Katrina to get herself a ride, as drivers often slow down here to admire the scenery. With luck she'd be home within the hour.

By now the sun was setting. It was late August and the evenings were getting chilly. Dressed as she was in sexy clothes to please Blair, she was starting to shiver. Thank God I wore the sneakers, she thought. But she didn't have to wait long. A van shot past and then slowed down. It stopped and backed up; Katrina ran to meet it.

Then something about the van made her hesitate. It was filthy, with thick streaks of mud and dirt crusting the grimy sides so that she could only guess its colour. White maybe. Maybe grey. She couldn't see into the windows, which were painted black. As she stood there, the passenger door swung open. Oh, what the hell, she thought.

As Katrina hopped up onto the passenger seat and pulled the door shut, she knew immediately that her first impression had been correct. Inside, the van was as dirty as it was outside, and it stank. She nearly gagged at the smell. Like bad meat, she thought, or dirty clothes. Or shit. But it was too late; the van was moving and the driver's head was looking left as he quickly pulled into the traffic. Then he turned to look at her and smiled. "Hi," he said.

Bozo the Clown, she said to herself. My God, it's Bozo the Clown.

Although most of the top of his head was bald, the man had a long, matted mess of orange-brown hair that hung down onto his shoulders and stuck out around his ears. Untidy stubble covered his cheeks and jaw. A thin, wide grin split his face and a pair of bright blue eyes twinkled at her. He was wearing a grubby black T-shirt with a Hells Angels logo and dark, grease-stained sweatpants tucked into the tops of a pair of heavy black gumboots, encrusted, like everything else in the van, with dirt.

At first Katrina worried more about her new pants than about the driver. Noting the garbage stuffed between the two front seats and behind them, she wondered what she was sitting on. She couldn't tell what was in the back of the van because a large piece of cardboard was in the way. When she looked more closely, she could see that it not only went up to the ceiling of the van but was folded to wrap around the inside walls behind her. Its presence meant she couldn't see into the back of the van at all. The sliding door panel was on Katrina's side, but because the window was painted over she knew no one could see her inside. And she couldn't see out.

"How far you going?" she asked.

"Port Coquitlam."

"Great. I get out in Surrey; just let me off at 152nd Street."

"Okay."

"So, what do you do?" she asked.

"Carpet-layer."

"What's the smell?"

"Took some stuff to a rendering plant up the valley."

"Oh."

There was silence for a while. The man broke it first. "My name's Willie," he offered.

Katrina said nothing. She knew he was looking at her and she was uneasy.

"You're pretty," he said, smiling at her again. "Where you comin' from?"

"Kent," she said.

"Do you want to smoke a joint?"

"Okay." Katrina thought it might relax her. Willie reached up to the visor and snapped off the rubber band holding a cigarette package; it was full of rolled joints of marijuana. He removed a twist and handed it to her. She took a drag and gave it back to him, but he didn't want any so she smoked it all herself. It didn't help. She was still afraid, and when she looked around for a way to escape, she was shocked to discover that there was no handle on her door. She wouldn't be able to open it.

Maybe if I look out the front window, she thought, maybe if I can get someone's attention, someone will recognize me if I get murdered. They'll say, "Oh, I seen her driving down the road."

"So your husband's in Kent, eh? So he wouldn't miss you if you didn't get home tonight."

"No, he phones me every night. And I got lots of people who care for me. Look, we're coming up to 152nd—it's my stop. Here's where I get out."

But Willie was in the Trans-Canada's fast lane and he didn't move over to let her off.

"Hey! That's my street," she yelped.

"I'll double back. I'll drive you right home." By this time, though, he was hurrying along the Trans-Canada towards the Port Mann Bridge, which spans the Fraser River between Surrey and Coquitlam. When he didn't slow down at 104th Street, the last exit before the bridge, Katrina knew she was in trouble. Her hands trembled as she quietly opened her purse, which was resting on her lap; as Willie crossed the bridge, her fingers felt through the contents looking for anything to use as a weapon, anything at all. Nothing. There was nothing.

"You try anything," Katrina hissed, "and I'll fucking kill you."

Delighted, Willie looked at her and began to laugh.

Moments later he took the first exit off the bridge to Number 7 Highway, spun the van around to go under it and backtracked west towards the Mary Hill Bypass, which avoids Coquitlam's congested roads. Instead it takes drivers along the northern bank of the Fraser River straight into the small town of Port Coquitlam. But just before he entered the bypass, Willie swerved into a small industrial park. Still searching through her purse, trying to keep her fingers as quiet and motionless as she could, Katrina finally felt a pencil. It was a good size and had an eraser on the end. Making sure the pointed end was facing in Willie's direction, she wrapped her fists around it and sat still, desperately looking for a way out. Maybe I can break the window with my elbow, she thought, but I'll probably just break my elbow instead.

Willie was hesitating now. He'd made a mistake by turning into the industrial estate—the only thing ahead of him was a cul-de-sac. He had to turn around. Katrina waited. As soon as he slowed the van down to move it into reverse, Katrina struck, stabbing the pencil into the side of his neck, snapping off the tip deep in his skin, and gouging his eye with her left thumb. She hurled herself across his lap, pushed open the door handle and dove out the door to land face first on the gravel at the side of the road.

She felt nothing. She jumped to her feet and started to run back along the cul-de-sac, expecting to be tackled at any moment. But all she could hear was his laughter, which was loud and merry.

"Haw haw haw," he howled. "Haw haw."

She glanced back. He wasn't even trying to chase her; instead, he just stood there beside his van, his gumboots planted on the gravel, watching her run, laughing his head off.

He's a mental case, she thought. He's crazy. Up ahead, just a block away, she could see the lights of a gas station, and she ran faster until, within a minute or two, she had collapsed by the pumps. There was one young man, about seventeen, working at the full-service pump; another was inside at the cash register.

"Holy shit, lady, you okay?" the kid at the pump asked.

"I was attacked . . . He's right back there . . . He's crazy," she gasped. She could see that Willie had started up the van. She could hear the grinding of his engine and the sound of the driver's door slamming.

"I'll call the cops. You're bleeding bad."

The kid ran into the gas station and Katrina stood up. She didn't think she was hurt, but when she looked down, she could see that the front of her pants and T-shirt were covered with dirt and grease and blood. The gravel had scraped skin off her chest, collarbone, face and arms; her hands were lacerated; blood was soaking through her clothes. Dirt and stones were embedded in her skin.

It didn't take long for an officer from the local RCMP detachment to arrive. Concerned, he wanted to know everything that had happened. "Wait here," he said, as she finished. "I'm going to report in."

When he returned a few minutes later, he was brisk. "Okay," he said. "We see you have a record. But we're going out after him." He got into his police car and left.

The youngsters manning the gas station didn't know what to do next. They had a woman standing there, shaking, bleeding, distraught, but the cop had turned his back on her and there was no one else to help.

An old man who had come to buy gas at the self-serve pump watched her for a few minutes and came over.

"Are you okay?"

"Not really. Would you be able to give me a ride?"

"I guess so, but I'm going to New Westminster. Is that on your way?"

"That would be great. I'll get a friend to pick me up there."

That is what happened to Katrina Murphy in late August 2001. A few weeks after she escaped from Willie Pickton's van, Katrina Murphy was back in prison, convicted of armed robbery. She never found out if the Mountie who came to the gas station ever followed up on his promise to go after Willie. But at least Katrina survived. Sereena Abotsway was last seen the same month, on August 1, 2001. Diane Rock was last seen October 19, 2001. Mona Wilson was last seen on November 23, 2001. They are all dead, and Willie Pickton killed them.

CHAPTER TWENTY-FOUR

DEADLY GIRLFRIENDS

Elaine Allan was close to most of the women who worked the streets in the Downtown Eastside, but there were a few she dreaded seeing come through the church doors. One was Willie's pal Gina Houston, who would come in from time to time to fish out women so desperate for drugs and money that they'd agree—unhappily, fearfully—to go out to the Pickton farm with her. Everyone knew Gina, everyone was afraid of her, and most of them knew the farm was bad news. Friends who had been there swore they'd never go again; they whispered fearfully that it was a filthy, terrifying place and that Willie was a weird, sick man. A few would agree to go anyway; the money and the dope were, they calculated, worth it. But whenever Allan saw Gina hanging around WISH talking to a woman, she would chase her out the door.

Gina Houston wasn't the only person trying to lure women out to the Pickton farm. By this time, early in 2000, Willie Pickton had a new best friend. Just as he had replaced Lisa Yelds with Gina Houston, he was easing Gina out in favour of a dangerous addict named Dinah Taylor, a Native woman in her late twenties from Thunder Bay, Ontario. Taylor, who had a substantial criminal record, mostly for drug trafficking, was about five feet six inches tall, weighed no more than 115 pounds, and had long, dark hair, often held back by a bright cotton bandana, her signature accessory. She'd been in the Downtown Eastside for about twenty years and usually lived at the Roosevelt Hotel. Sometime in late 1999 she began staying at the farm for days and weeks at a time.

On one occasion, according to a story Lynn Ellingsen told,

Dinah called her, saying she was with Willie. Would Lynn meet them? Lynn refused; she was terrified that Willie wanted to kill her.

Just as Gina had found WISH a rich hunting ground for desperate women, so did Dinah. Stephen Arsenault, the doorman at the Roosevelt, watched her trying to convince other residents to come to the farm with her, offering free drugs and good money. He saw how she would talk to the women, how she told them she had an uncle and then tried to coax them into coming out with her. As soon as they agreed, and many did, Taylor would use Arsenault's phone to call Pickton to come and pick them up. Sometimes women turned her down. Valerie Hewlett was one of them, more because she disliked Taylor than because she knew anything about Pickton.

If Dinah couldn't get any takers at the Roosevelt, she'd cross the street and head one block east to WISH, at the corner of East Hastings and Gore, to troll through the crowd. Usually someone would agree to go. Bill Malone, the Picktons' neighbour in Port Coquitlam who kept a watchful eye on their farm, remembered seeing her getting out of a van at the farm on several occasions, always with a few other people; she would ask him if Willie was around. Malone didn't say who was driving the van or if the people in it were women gathered by Dinah to party with Willie.

Not everyone disliked Dinah. Cheryl Shalala considered herself Dinah's best friend; they'd known each other for fifteen years. Dinah was like an older sister to her, she told Suzanne Fournier, a Vancouver *Province* reporter, years later. "When she wanted to get away from Willie for a while—because he could be very controlling—she'd come and crash at my house. But then the phone would ring and it would be Willie wanting to know where Dinah was. He adored her and he'd do anything for her, give her money, clothes, whatever she wanted. She used him as a sugar daddy," said Shalala. "She knew his bank code and she knew he always left money lying around the trailer."

Dinah used to bring Willie to visit Shalala, but he rarely spoke during these visits. He'd just sit and listen. "It was kind of eerie,"

Shalala told Fournier. "But no one was scared of him, we all thought he was harmless, just kind of sitting there in the same old dirty vest and gumboots he always wore." And he endeared himself to Shalala's parents with his customary bread-and-butter present, a freshly slaughtered pig, which they would get cut and packaged at a local supermarket.

Whenever Elaine Allan spied Dinah Taylor whispering to one of the women at WISH, she'd race over and throw her out, just as she did with Gina Houston. She knew these women were trouble. But there were times when she didn't know they were there.

One night Allan was getting ready for the dinner rush at WISH. The doors were still closed; it was just before six o'clock. She heard pounding on the church's side door on Gore, the door that opened directly into the large foyer used for the dinners. It was a young Fijian woman named Aschu (or sometimes Ashwan). She was crying and trying to talk but too upset to make much sense. Allan let her in and tried to calm her down, but Aschu was wild with worry. "Tiffany didn't come home last night," she sobbed, hanging on to Allan. "Something's wrong. We had a system."

Tiffany Drew, Aschu's best friend and roommate, lived at the Hazleton Hotel, less than a block from First United. Because they were afraid of disappearing as so many of their friends had done, they had worked out a buddy system to make sure each knew where the other was at all times. Other women in the area had adopted the same practice.

Allan remembered seeing Tiffany at WISH the night before. Right away she paged Constable Dave Dickson at the nearby Community Policing Office; she'd been told that all calls about missing women had to start with him. Dickson was unconcerned. I'll come and see you, he told Allan, but Tiffany always does this: she'll go off with a john. It's just something she does, so I'll have to wait to see if she picks up her welfare cheque. Allan remembers Dickson telling her that even if Tiffany was with a date she'd still try to access her welfare cheque. "Tiffany does this all the time," he repeated. "There's nothing I can do till welfare day." Dickson took no notes, remembers Allan. He remained dismissive for months, even though Aschu came into WISH night after night pleading for help in finding her friend and hounded Dickson. After several weeks of this he finally admitted to Allan that he still hadn't checked with welfare about Tiffany's money.

Months later Allan nagged Dickson once too often, and he said he needed to talk to her privately. When they were alone, he said this was a little awkward for him but he felt he had to tell her—Tiffany was fine, she was in a safe place, a recovery centre, in fact, but she didn't want to talk to Aschu or to Allan. Tiffany was afraid, he said, that she might start using drugs again if she saw people from her old life. Neither Allan nor Aschu was buying his story. It didn't ring true; Allan *knew* it couldn't be true. Why would Dave Dickson make this up? She couldn't understand it.

Allan remembers Tiffany as a creature of habit. "She'd come in, plug in the curling iron, get all her shower stuff, go in and have her shower, come out and do her hair and makeup. She looked terrific; she wore blue eye shadow and lots of mascara. And she would panic if someone unplugged her curling iron. She was saucy and had a lot of attitude. She was also sweet and beautiful and she took good care of herself."

Like her friend Aschu, Tiffany was tiny, just under five feet tall. She weighed about ninety-five pounds and she was twenty-five years old when she disappeared. She had grown up in two towns, Port Alberni, on the west side of Vancouver Island, and Nanaimo, not far away on the east side. Beautiful places both of them, but full of terrible memories for both Tiffany and her sister, Kelly Prado. Their parents had split up and the sisters lived with their mother, an alcoholic who showed them little affection and poured invective on them when she was drunk. "Mom would go out and spend the welfare money on booze," remembers Prado. "Tiffany and I would be so hungry . . . I remember once we only had a can of green beans to eat."

Tiffany, who was quiet and shy, had few friends in school, her sister said. But she had one good friend, Sylvia Lalonde, who later

posted notes about Tiffany to a website for the families of the missing women. Lalonde said that Tiffany had been her best friend in
Redford Elementary in Port Alberni, and they stayed best friends
until they were about fifteen. "We both loved to party hard," she
wrote in one of the notes. "But you know I was the real wild child,
not Tiffany. The last time I talked to her was New Years Eve 1993.
Both of us promised to get together soon. And we never spoke again.
I wish we had not lost touch . . . Maybe I could have helped."

Tiffany's mother kicked out both of her daughters when they
were still in high school. Later she told Kelly that the worst mistake
she ever made was not having an abortion when she was pregnant
with her. "She tried to slit her wrists. She would take the welfare
cheque to the bar." The girls moved in with their father, did whatever
they felt like and stopped going to school. Kelly Prado remembers
her sister as beautiful. "I was always so jealous—she was so beautiful; she had big boobs, blond hair, bright blue eyes. So beautiful . . ."

Kelly married, moved to Bellingham, Washington, which is just
south of Vancouver, and had three children. Her life was on track;
she felt settled. Things were good. But not for Tiffany. Kelly remembers visiting her in Vancouver when a winter blizzard hit; the women
were in a laundromat and Kelly told Tiffany she had to drive home
to Bellingham right away before the storm got worse. She wanted
Tiffany to go with her. Kelly had discovered that her sister was
drinking as heavily as their mother used to, and she was desperate
to help her. Tiffany finally agreed to go, but she didn't stay long.
Despite promises to get counselling, soon she was back in Vancouver.
What Kelly didn't know at the time was that her sister was also a
drug addict and a prostitute.

When she couldn't track her sister down after several calls,
Kelly panicked and called the Vancouver police to report her missing. She explained that Tiffany hadn't called their aunt, who was
raising Tiffany's daughter, and hadn't called her father. She usually
kept in close touch with both. And her family had just learned that
she was a prostitute.

The reaction from the Missing Persons office was blunt, remembers Kelly. "What do you expect?" the woman said. "She's a prostitute."

Kelly Prado says she decided to look for her sister herself. She found a picture of Tiffany when she was clean and healthy, before she started using drugs, and went back to Vancouver's Downtown Eastside. She passed the picture around but no one there knew who it was. Only later, she told Mary Lane Gallagher, a reporter for the *Bellingham Herald,* when they were shown a photograph of an identity card of Tiffany's that had been found in a crack house, did they recognize her "sad-eyed, drawn face."

The actual date of Tiffany's disappearance is still up in the air. At first the official date was December 31, 1999, but later the police changed it to March 2000. Others say it was later that year. No one knows for sure.

The exasperation shown to Tiffany Drew's frantic relatives by the staffer in the VPD Missing Persons Unit was standard operating procedure. Addicted prostitutes didn't rank very high on their list of priorities. The phrase on everyone's lips in cases like that was the same: "These girls made their own choices."

An internal audit done by a retired VPD inspector, John Schouten, and unearthed by *Vancouver Sun* reporter Chad Skelton showed that the Missing Persons Unit was a disaster. "Overworked officers, inadequate supervision and shoddy record-keeping," as he described them, were only part of the problem. There was only one full-time officer working in the unit and one part-time, a civilian clerical worker, completely untrained, who would often go to crime scenes. Cases were assigned to phantom officers who hadn't worked there in years. And that led, Schouten wrote, not bothering to hide his fury, "to a concern that investigative leads that could have been pursued were abandoned and continuity of the investigation is lost."

It could take several days to assess a missing-person call, and even after someone paid attention to it there was "little active investigation of files," Schouten reported. And there was also almost no follow-up, which, he warned, "had the potential to embarrass the Vancouver Police Department and could possibly result in civil liability."

The shoddy record-keeping also meant it was almost impossible for investigators to put together enough information to look for people or to judge whether a serial killer might be at work. Nor were there any guidelines to determine when a disappearance should be considered a homicide. "In those cases where suspicious circumstances are involved," wrote Schouten, "it is imperative that the police conduct a thorough investigation, at the earliest opportunity, so that no evidence is lost."

At that time the Missing Persons Unit was in much deeper trouble than anyone suspected. The officer responsible for Missing Persons, John Dragani, spent most of his time working with the force's pipe band; when he wasn't busy with music, he was trolling for child pornography on his home computer (Dragani was suspended in 2005, arrested in 2006 and convicted for possession of child pornography in 2007).

The families knew none of this in the years when their loved ones were disappearing; all they knew was that the Missing Persons Unit was incompetent, indifferent and a heartbreaking waste of time. Some of them turned instead to Dave Dickson for information and comfort, but he too, while pleasant and courteous, had little to offer. They believed they had no one else to help them because Dickson, who had so enraged Elaine Allan with his reaction to Tiffany Drew's disappearance, had an enormous amount of power in the Downtown Eastside. People, including the area's sex-trade workers and addicts and Elaine Allan, were told that if they had any complaints or concerns, whether they were about bad dates or missing friends and relatives, they had to start with him at the Community Policing Office. This was a small office that he shared with Deb Mearns, who was in charge of it.

Mearns was married to John Turvey, the former heroin addict who ran DEYAS, the needle exchange. A final member of this informal but powerful group was Judy McGuire, who ran WISH and was

Elaine Allan's boss. To hem in Allan even more, both McGuire and Mearns served on the WISH board. She soon found out that her advocacy on behalf of the women and her aggressive questioning about how hard anyone was looking for the missing members of their community wasn't earning her any friends among this foursome. Before long her job would be on the line.

CHAPTER TWENTY-FIVE

ROSSMO OUT

During this period in 2000 the police didn't go to Kim Rossmo for help, at least not officially. In January 1999, when he sent a form to the inspectors in charge of major crimes and special investigations, asking them to let him know how many requests they would have for geographic profiling in 2000, one inspector never replied, while another put down zero next to every category.

The new chief, Terry Blythe, was not as hostile to Rossmo as other members of the Old Boys group, but because he was their leader they felt they had his unwritten permission to freeze Rossmo out. His fiercest enemy was still John Unger, who, having failed to be named chief, was promoted to deputy chief in March 1999. "When Unger didn't get the chief's job, he tried to be nice, and he smiles and says to me, 'I want to make it work,'" Rossmo remembers. "And then he came back with a two-year offer. It was a slap in the face. I wrote a note back: 'What does this mean?' I was short of getting to my pensionable age, which I would have had if the contract had been renewed for another five years."

By this time Rossmo was so inured to the enmity of these men and busy with a number of interesting cases that he simply pushed the contract issues aside for the moment. He was getting positive press from a serial rape case he'd been working on in Cincinnati, Ohio, with the local police. An Associated Press story about the case that ran across the United States and Canada noted that he had worked on 1,700 investigations worldwide. The *Cincinnati Post* reported that local police were impressed with his skills, as was the prosecutor, Mike Allen.

"There's no question that his work will help us," Allen told the reporter. "We hope he will be able to narrow down significantly the geographic area where the offender may live, work or possibly, but hopefully not, where his next strike could be." Allen also pointed to what he called Rossmo's "unbelievable" success in a Louisiana serial rape case. "He pinpointed a four- or five-block area where he thought the rapist lived," Allen told the reporter. "The rapist turned out to be a deputy sheriff who lived right in the center of the area that had been pinpointed."

In spite of the Old Boys, Rossmo still had many friends and allies within the Vancouver Police Department. They made sure he knew what was going on. The City had decided the Department had to shed 3.5 positions. Gary Greer, now a deputy chief constable, had warned him that Alex Muselius, the VPD's director of human resources, was making a case for killing off the geographic profiling unit, arguing that it didn't make financial sense; in fact, he had already suggested that Rossmo make a presentation to justify the cost of his office. Rossmo complied on December 1, 1999, and held his breath.

Greer talked to Rossmo about his situation at a private meeting on May 3, 2000. Look, Greer said, your five-year contract was signed in May 1996 and it's going to end on December 31, 2000. Eight months away, sure, but worth thinking about right now. They're going to shut down your geographic profiling program, he warned. And they're going to offer you a new job at a constable's rank.

Rossmo knew that he should speak to a lawyer—right away. The first person he called, employment lawyer Dick Hamilton, was considered one of the best in the city, but he couldn't take him on. His excuse was a good one: he was acting for Blythe and Unger in another dispute. Someone else suggested Murray Tevlin, who ran an employment law practice with his partner Dan Gleadle; Tevlin said yes. They set up an appointment for the following month, on June 6.

But a few days after Rossmo called Tevlin, on May 8, the police board went over a new plan directed by the City, in which

Chief Terry Blythe cut three positions from the force. One of them was the geographic profiler. The board agreed and made it official on May 31. Days of discussion followed as the police department's top brass, human resources staff and board members tried to figure out how to manage what they knew was going to become a messy situation. Finally a letter was crafted, approved and, on July 6, sent to Rossmo's office.

The problem was that Rossmo wasn't there—he was on one of those trips that so infuriated his enemies even though they were approved by his department. He'd left for Australia on June 12 for a speech in Sydney and then a conference in Perth on June 17; his next stop, on June 22, was a case in Singapore that needed his expertise. He flew back to North America for a conference in Florida, attended another one in Germany and then went to England, where he had three events to get through. The first, on July 5, was a geographic profiling presentation before a group at Scotland Yard. Once he got back to his hotel he started to work on another presentation, for a meeting of the Forensic Science Society in Harrowgate, Yorkshire, on July 7.

"My secretary, Cheryllynne Drabinsky, knew where I was and left a message. I returned the call and she said she'd seen a letter for me, which was signed by Unger, and wanted to let me know right away. She was very upset. It was not good news but I wasn't very surprised." Unger's letter, which was actually signed by Alex Muselius, stated that his contract wasn't being renewed for budgetary reasons and that he would revert to his former rank of police constable. Unger wanted to see him on July 17, as soon as he was back from his trip.

What Rossmo remembers from that day was that the London weather was sunny and warm, the city was beautiful and there was nothing he could do except focus on the meetings and presentations he had planned for the week. He also knew it was crucial that he pay attention to Murray Tevlin's advice not to react at this stage. So he made his presentation to the Forensic Science Society, wondering as he finished if these people would still be his colleagues and peers in whatever new work he was forced to take. The society, an international professional body that sets standards and accreditations for forensic science, was his kind of intellectual world. Most of its 2,500 members in sixty countries around the world were scientists, but there were also many police officers and crime scene investigators.

Two days later Rossmo was in Bramshill, Hampshire, to make a presentation at the Police Staff College, the United Kingdom's main police training college and a centre very much like the FBI's training school at Quantico, Virginia. Bramshill is also part of the European Union's police training system that specializes in serious crime analysis, training, operational support and, as they put it, "the development of new policing technologies and skills." Rossmo also had a working session planned with Bramshill's geographic profiler, someone he had trained a few years earlier.

Those days were surrealistic for Kim Rossmo. He was completely engaged by the work he was doing, but in quiet moments he thought about what was happening to him. His career destroyed, financial distress, humiliation . . . and he would have to start all over again somewhere else. What would he do? Where would he go? He kept pushing these worries away in order to put up a strong front before his British colleagues, but he was deeply wounded. And he was angry.

He called Murray Tevlin, who once again briefed him carefully about what to do about the meeting with Unger that was scheduled for as soon as he got back. Tevlin's advice was succinct: "Go into the meeting. Listen to what he has to say. Don't argue. Make notes."

Rossmo met John Unger in his office at 312 Main Street in the Downtown Eastside on July 18, 2000, and learned just how grim his situation was. "Unger wanted to take away some of the things I needed for my contract," he told friends later, "including my computers." Kim Rossmo had two computers. One was a Sun UltraSPARC that he used for his geographical profiling work; at that time a normal PC couldn't run the profiling program, given the mathematical and imaging work that it required (today a good laptop would find it quite possible). The second computer was an ordinary PC that he used for his writing, his cases and all his correspondence. Unger also told Rossmo he was cancelling his budget for the two conferences a year the department paid for. (In the case of all the others he attended, the host police force or organization covered all the costs.)

That was just the beginning. Unger wanted Rossmo downtown in the headquarters at 312 Main, not in his office at the old headquarters on Cambie Street. The Cambie office was a large corner space that Rossmo loved, with large windows on two sides offering a spectacular view of the mountains. He had a large L-shaped desk, big enough to lay out all his papers and books and graphs. There was always a criminology graduate student volunteer working there; he or she had a desk at the end of the room. There was a side office off the entrance for Cheryllynne Drabinsky and even a room for the people he was training, usually officers from the RCMP, the FBI or the British police who came for four months at a time before completing the training back with their home forces.

The worst news was Unger's decision that Rossmo's new and much smaller quarters at 312 Main would be right beside his own.

So eager was John Unger to humble the globetrotting profiler that he failed to clear his action first with the police board. Some board members were so upset that they protested loudly and leaked stories to the media. They were angry that Unger had sent the July 6 notice of Rossmo's dismissal without clearing it with them; they also said that Unger hadn't followed their instructions to him about dealing with Rossmo. Unger's excuse for his intemperate behaviour was that he'd had legal advice that he needed to act quickly to give Rossmo some kind of notice. Then he blamed communication glitches.

This debacle was embarrassing, unpleasant and potentially harmful for everyone, including the board. They finally told Unger that Rossmo would stay in his own office with his own staff, equipment and budget until his contract ended on December 31, 2000. By the end of July Mayor Philip Owen was wanting to know all the details of the situation. He was beginning to realize that Unger and Blythe hadn't reviewed the legal issues around Rossmo's dismissal, or even debated the value of the geographical profiling unit.

By early September the *Vancouver Sun* was also all over the Rossmo story and Rossmo was confirming it. He and Tevlin held a news conference on Tuesday, September 11—what Rossmo called the saddest day of his life—to confirm the news that he was suing the VPD.

The VPD tried to respond that nothing had been decided yet. Lindsay Kines was not having any of that. "Earlier this week," he reported on September 15, "Vancouver city police media liaison Constable Anne Drennan said senior management had advised her the department was in negotiations with Rossmo over the possible renewal of his contract, which expires at the end of the year. Asked if a decision had already been reached, she said: 'No, not at all.'" Kines demolished her statement by printing a chunk of the letter Rossmo had received from the VPD in July, stating his contract wouldn't be renewed beyond December 31.

And Murray Tevlin pointed out to Kines that the contract had also said that if Rossmo wasn't "renewed as a detective inspector, his employment would be terminated. So they are not reading the contract accurately. They say they're going to bust him down to constable. What for? I don't know what for."

A week later Tevlin and Rossmo confirmed that they were suing for wrongful dismissal for what Rossmo "alleges was malicious and high-handed treatment by the police board and deputy chief John Unger," reported Glenn Bohn for the *Vancouver Sun*. "His lawsuit claims that Unger was among a group of senior officers who disagreed with Rossmo's sudden promotion five years ago from constable to detective inspector, which leap-frogged him several job levels." And Tevlin told Bohn that the VPD had fired Rossmo without the authority of the police board.

The day after the story ran, the *Sun* weighed in with a tough editorial offering Rossmo wholehearted support and declaring that his firing "once again raises troubling questions about the management of the city police department." The paper ran through his brilliant résumé, from his time on "the toughest beat on the Downtown Eastside" to his doctorate in criminology and "his invention of the geographic profiling software that had generally done much to burnish the international image of the Vancouver city police."

The editorial also pointed out the commendation he'd received from his chief and all the job offers he'd received. It also made sure readers understood that the Vancouver police had created the new position for him, so he wouldn't leave. "But police managers need to explain why an officer whose skills are sought around the world suddenly isn't wanted by his own department," the newspaper thundered. "They also need to explain why Mr. Rossmo was apparently notified before the decision was ever finalized by the police board. And finally they need to allay concerns that he is a victim of the nasty office politics for which the department has become known."

This editorial was the last thing the VPD needed. It was already under constant fire for neglecting the missing women and for its inability to find out what had happened to them, and the bad publicity around the Rossmo scandal was a disaster. The media got hold of Rossmo's statement of claim for his lawsuit, which stated that the board and Unger had breached his contract, damaged his reputation and publicly humiliated him. Until his case went to court, however, he was through with the Vancouver Police Department. The Old Boys had won. Defeated, sore in heart, mortified, he had to start looking for a new job.

The Rossmo mess wasn't the VPD's only problem. Their demoralized, understaffed officers in Project Amelia had run out of steam. A few weeks earlier, on August 8, 2000, the police had announced cutbacks to the investigative team, from nine people to six. "There wasn't enough to keep everyone busy anymore," media relations constable Anne Drennan told the *Vancouver Sun*. Remaining were two homicide detectives, a missing-persons detective, a sergeant, a constable and an administrator, but the writing was on the wall. Their best leads, especially the one that had pushed Willie Pickton to the top of their list of suspects, had gone nowhere.

What was astounding at this stage in the investigation was that the number of missing women had dropped back to almost, but not quite, the normal levels of disappearance in this community of impoverished, addicted sex-trade workers. By October 2000, ten months into the year, there had been only one disappearance—Tiffany Drew. Was it possible that the nightmare was over? VPD chief Terry Blythe and his cadre of senior officers wanted to think so. Overall, they pointed out, the numbers were moving down each year. In 1997, for example, there were thirteen disappearances. In 1998 there were eleven. In 1999 there were five. So far in 2000, knock on wood, there had been only one. Blythe and his colleagues in the VPD's executive offices decided that the threat was over and the "missings," as people called them, had stopped. It was time to disband Project Amelia and send the officers back to work on more important investigations.

Not everyone agreed with this decision. Doug Henderson, a staff sergeant in the RCMP's Unsolved Homicide Unit, wasn't happy about it; he thought the missing-women case was too important to be dropped. Henderson's unit was working on the still unsolved 1995 Valley Murders of Tracy Olajide, Tammy Pipe and Victoria Younker, deaths they continued to believe might be connected to the missing women of Vancouver. So he sent an email to his colleague Don Adam, who was a staff sergeant like himself and an experienced homicide investigator, to see if he and his fellow investigators could do anything to help the stalled investigation.

Don Adam, a member of the Serious Crime Unit, was a good choice. Born in Wynyard, Saskatchewan, a small town north of Regina, he'd gone straight to "Depot Division," the RCMP training academy in Regina right after graduating from high school. He'd become a polygraph examiner, a specialist in interviewing and interrogating people suspected of serious crimes such as murder. He'd been there five years before moving to the RCMP headquarters in Langley, a small city about forty kilometres southeast of Vancouver, where he worked for the Major Crime and Street Unit, training younger members. Between 1999 and 2000 he had pulled together a small, informal group of RCMP officers who had also become skilled at interviewing homicide suspects, and at this time he was working on a plan to turn the team into a permanent full-time unit with a home in the RCMP's Special Projects group. In 2000 it looked as if this was going to happen; Superintendent Gary Bass brought Adam back to the Surrey headquarters to work in Major Crime—Special Projects.

What Adam didn't realize was that there had been some meetings involving the VPD's Project Amelia team, an RCMP Major Crime team from Chilliwack that had investigated the Valley Murders, and Margaret Kingsbury of the RCMP's Violent Crime Linkage Analysis System (ViCLAS). Because this group believed that the same killer was responsible for the missing women and the Valley Murders, Kingsbury insisted that the RCMP needed to coordinate the investigations of both as one major investigation. She persuaded Doug Hunt, who was in charge of the RCMP's Unsolved Homicides team, to try to talk Adam into postponing his plans for the interview team and see if he couldn't help with this joint investigation.

"Hunt said we should meet to see if there was anything the RCMP could do to help out," Adam remembers. "But behind the scenes, Margaret Kingsbury was pulling the strings. She'd been having meetings about the Valley Murders and the missing women and neither investigation was succeeding."

Adam was a popular officer, liked by his colleagues for his ready grin, wry sense of humour and quick intelligence. He seems utterly at ease most of the time. Thin and about six feet tall, he has greying brown hair and a long, bony face, yet there is something about him that remains boyish, eager for a new adventure. And

Adam thought Henderson's request to help with the missing-women file was reasonable. He knew the Vancouver police thought the missing women had been murdered; the question was still how many killers they were looking for. Adam decided he needed new people, fresh to the case.

Adam and Margaret Kingsbury had worked together before, but in 2000 ViCLAS was not a priority with the B.C. government, which didn't see the importance of it and was not willing to commit the resources. As a result the ViCLAS office was understaffed, but Adam knew that, with her encyclopedic memory for the smallest details, Marg Kingsbury would be an essential addition to the team.

Paul McCarl, the investigator in charge of the Valley Murders case, was Adam's next choice. At this point, because Olajide, Pipe and Younker had come from the Downtown Eastside, few officers knew more about the area than he did. Since the RCMP and the Vancouver police still believed there had to be some kind of connection between the two cases, Adam also asked Geramy Field, the officer in charge of Vancouver's failed Project Amelia, to work with the new group.

At the beginning, this was very much an ad hoc kind of group pulled together to look at the twenty-seven cases Project Amelia had identified as the most suspicious. At first they thought the work Project Amelia had done was adequate. Without human remains, without a tight time frame for the disappearances, without DNA in most cases, it might take years to find anything new. But the more they looked at the twenty-seven cases, the more they began to see weaknesses in the original investigation and areas that needed more work. It wasn't always the fault of the investigators. When people reported that loved ones were missing, "there was no mechanism in place to collect and store DNA so that it could be checked against crime scenes or recovered remains," Adam explained later.

The coroner's service at the time was keeping the remains of about 130 people but there was no proof they'd met a violent death, nor had any DNA been collected from most of them. Most of the remains, the police believed, were old, quite possibly from First Nations graves. Finally, though the Vancouver police had collected familial DNA—from family members such as parents, siblings or children—from about nine people, there was no place to store it and no matches had been made.

Adam's little team, designed as a joint force of RCMP and VPD investigators (although the RCMP members outnumbered the VPD), was now formally called Project Evenhanded (British Columbia is the RCMP's E Division, and all special projects begin with that letter), or the Missing Women's Task Force. Their starting point was to acknowledge what the Vancouver police had refused to accept: a serial killer was responsible for the disappearances. This decision was key. It meant going well beyond the old plan to investigate only the missing women. It meant looking at the files of men suspected or charged with sexual assaults.

"We decided to go back into the past," Adam explains, "and operate from the hope that that person had committed lead-up crimes or botched crimes, wherein they may have left their DNA and they may have left a trail which would lead us to them." But given that there was no DNA identification system in place for the missing women, how would they make a match if they found remains?

The team set that problem aside for a while they tried, during November and December 2000, to figure out where to start. Finally they began with a file review: looking for their killer by plunging into thousands of pages of files of old solved and unsolved murders and sexual assaults, as well as murders of hitchhikers, because, as Adam put it, "these were people who would get into a vehicle." The team believed that the killer they were looking for would certainly have a means of taking the person out of the Downtown Eastside.

Soon the pool of possible victims grew much larger as the team began looking beyond the Downtown Eastside to other areas of British Columbia. But they had no way to link these victims without actually travelling to each office to review the evidence, a job that was beyond this small group. Then the team hit more roadblocks:

the various coroner's offices around the province didn't keep records in databases that they could easily access. And there was no police database at this time that had linked the cases.

Project Evenhanded's four-person team also started sorting through the 1,300 tips that had come in, most of them men's names, as well as files collected by their predecessors. The net was wide enough; Adam was fairly sure their killer was within this group.

The next step was to divide the work into phases. The first was to collect DNA from previous crimes to see if they could connect any of it to the Valley killings or to the missing women. The next phase would narrow down the field of suspects; to find them, the police would look for what they called "lead-up crimes" or previous crimes. Over time the group collected the DNA of twenty-two such suspects. The last phase of their work would have them working with the DNA to get a match with a victim.

CHAPTER TWENTY-SIX

PANIC ON SKID ROW

There was no question: the numbers were down. In 1997 thirteen women had disappeared. It 1998 it was eleven. Five vanished in 1999. Getting close to Christmas 2000, it looked as if the tally might be only one so far—Tiffany Drew—a normal number for women from skid row. And Tiffany Drew wasn't really considered to be missing by the police; Dave Dickson had told Elaine Allan that she was in a recovery house and didn't want to see people from her past, especially not Allan. She wasn't really gone at all.

But women in the Downtown Eastside didn't believe for a minute that the threat was over. The feelings of dread and panic during much of 2000, feelings that had just started to recede after the reassurances that Tiffany Drew was alive, began to creep back in as the year was drawing to a close. Abruptly, late in the year, Dawn Crey, Debra Jones and Sharon Abraham vanished, and the fear washed back in full force. By now the community suspected that Christmas and New Year's was a favourite time for the maniac who was taking their sisters from skid row, and they were right—between 1984 and 2000 at least fifteen women disappeared during the holiday season.

Thirty-five-year-old Sharon Nora Jane Abraham was one of them. Her picture on the missing-women poster shows a handsome young Native woman with wide-set, cautious eyes, a straight nose and an unsmiling mouth; her shiny brown hair is pulled back but bangs flop over her forehead. She was about five feet six inches tall. Very little is known about her, although her name and photograph appear on many Native websites and in all the lists of missing women. For years all that was known about her was that she disappeared in December 2000. Recently, however, an old friend of hers, a woman named Theresa Hardy, contacted Lori Culbert at the *Vancouver Sun* with information. In 1989 she and Sharon had met in a transition house on the Lower Mainland, she told Culbert, and when they left they shared a place together. Sharon had been in an abusive relationship and had left, taking both her daughters, a baby and a toddler.

"She never drank when she was with me, never did drugs," Hardy told Culbert. "We didn't go to bars. We did things with the kids. She always made sure the kids had diapers. She wasn't out buying cigarettes and beer. She always made sure the rent was paid and there was food in the house." A year later, in 1990, Sharon moved with her kids to her own apartment; Hardy didn't know she had disappeared. "The three of them were such a happy family unit," she told Culbert. "I'd like to tell her kids some day that their mom was pretty cool. It breaks my heart because she loved them so much."

Although no one knows much about Sharon's disappearance, many people had a very good idea of when Dawn Crey was last seen. While Don Adam's team was combing through old files, Dawn Teresa Crey was just trying to get through each day on the street. Everyone knew Dawn, a sweet-natured woman whose face had been ravaged by acid thrown over her many years before. As a child she was famous for her gorgeous smile, bright, eager eyes and big dimples; now her face was twisted and scarred and in her eyes there was no hope left. There had been a time when she was beautiful. There had been a time when she was happy. But there had never been a time in her forty-three years on earth when her life was carefree.

Dawn was one of seven children in a well-known Native family that had settled in Hope, 150 kilometres east of Vancouver. The Crey family belonged to the Sto:lo Nation, and like so many children of his generation their father had attended a residential school, St. Mary's, in Mission. He'd married young and had a family but that marriage ended; he married again, this time a much younger woman from a leading family of the Cheam reserve. Both he and his new wife, Minnie, were alcoholics. Although they were sober for a few years, her father died at fifty-seven when Dawn was just five years old—he collapsed after a massive heart attack and died in her arms. Minnie went back on the booze almost right away.

"This was the dissolution of my family," explains Dawn's older brother Ernie Crey, who was thirteen when his mother started drinking again. "I was sent to a reform school on Brannon Lake near Nanaimo, on Vancouver Island. I was sentenced for petty thievery. All the other brothers and sisters? They were farmed out to non-Indian foster homes."

Dawn's first foster family was a disaster. Sent to them with her sister Faith, Dawn was just nine years old when authorities discovered she was being abused; they pulled her out. Fortunately her next home was a safe haven. Dawn was placed with Jake and Marie Wiebe, who had five children of their own and who grew to love her as if she was one of them. Here, at last, she was happy. One of her foster brothers, Wes Wiebe, later described her as "a beautiful girl who always liked clothes and fashion and always liked to look her best." But when she reached her teens, she was rebellious and difficult to manage. She spent most of her time with a boyfriend, got pregnant and at sixteen had a baby son she named Jonathan. Sometimes she took him with her when she worked with Marie Wiebe in the fields picking berries, and on one occasion she ran into her sister and the baby of the family, Rosalee, who was also berry-picking. It was a strange experience because the Crey children hadn't seen much of one another after they were taken from Minnie's home.

"We were strangers, except for those who lived together," Rosalee told Seattle reporter Mike Lewis many years later. "But we would see each other, we'd make eye contact and we would just know. I didn't want to talk to her. I was so nervous. I was afraid of the situation. My mom talked to her. She asked her all sorts of questions about my family." Still, as the years went by Rosalee and another sister, Lorraine, kept in touch with Dawn. They knew, as all the siblings knew, that Dawn had been unable to look after Jonathan and had to leave him in the loving hands of the Wiebes. They also knew she had moved to the Downtown Eastside in search of cheap and plentiful drugs. And they knew that to pay for them she made money the only way she could—selling sex and the goods she shoplifted from stores. She also collected used clothing from a church and sold it to women out of her room in the Roosevelt Hotel.

Dawn was a creature of habit. She ate lunch at the Women's Centre and had supper at WISH. She showered and curled her hair, fixing it to hide as much of her ruined face as possible, but she didn't have to count on street trade. Like a few other fortunate women, she had a few older clients, nice men she saw in her room at the hotel, and tried not to look for business on the street. "She didn't like the idea of standing on a corner getting into cars. That scared her," Lorraine Crey told the *Vancouver Sun*'s Lori Culbert.

People in the community were fond of her. Dawn didn't have an enemy in the world. "I lived just down the hallway from Dawn in the Roosevelt Hotel a few years back," wrote Diana Govenlock to Wayne Leng's website, www.missingpeople.net. "I remember Dawn as being very nice to everyone. No matter how little she had she was always willing to share."

As Christmas Day 2000 drew near, Rosalee, who now lived with her husband and children in Bellevue, Washington, and Lorraine, who managed a Native housing co-op in Vancouver, wanted Dawn to spend Christmas with them. When they tried to contact her, they found that she hadn't been seen for a while; in fact, she had moved from the Roosevelt to the Balmoral Hotel without telling them. In some ways her absence didn't surprise Lorraine, who had looked for Dawn for weeks until she discovered she was living in the Balmoral. She knew her sister was afraid of someone in the Roosevelt; Dawn had told Lorraine someone was trying to kill her. She was terrified that she was going to become one of the missing women.

On December 21 Dawn's caseworker at the methadone clinic told Rosalee and Lorraine that the last time she had seen their sister was in November. They also discovered that Dawn's doctor at the clinic had reported her missing when she failed to show up for an appointment on December 11. She hadn't picked up welfare cheques since November. She had also failed to respond to a summons to appear in court in November on a shoplifting charge. And now no one at the Balmoral knew where she had gone. When Lorraine searched Dawn's room, she found all her things, including bags of used clothing she hadn't yet unpacked to sell, but no clue where she might have gone.

"No way Dawn would ever go away without telling me," Lorraine Crey told the Vancouver *Province* six weeks after her sister disappeared. "Even if she had the money, which she didn't. The last time I saw her she was terrified, talking about all the missing women and how she feared she would be next. She'd never said anything like that before."

There was one person, however, who had certainly seen Dawn before she disappeared. Dinah Taylor, who scooped women up from the Roosevelt and from WISH, admitted she had known Dawn and seen her recently. Women in the neighbourhood whispered that Dinah might have been able to coax Dawn into going with her to see Uncle Willie.

The second woman to vanish at Christmas 2000 was Debra Lynne Jones, an attractive woman with short blond hair, beautiful eyes and a sad, weary face, who was last seen around December 25. Debra, born in December 1957, was also forty-three and had four brothers and sisters—and they missed her immediately. She was reported missing on December 29. After she disappeared her sister, Kathleen Anne McKenzie, wanted people to understand that her beloved sister was much more than a junkie prostitute from the Downtown Eastside; this was a talented musician with a great voice, she said. "She sang like Janis Joplin and she played guitar, piano, dreamed of going to Nashville one day. She was a mother, a niece, a loving sister and a daughter to a mother. [There] was much more to her than drugs. She was a poor woman who had nowhere else to live but downtown so her medicine could be given to her." Kathleen also insisted that Debra had cleaned up and wasn't working as a prostitute when she disappeared.

No particular alarm bells went off in the police community when Debra Jones disappeared, but that wasn't surprising: Project Amelia was moribund and the Missing Women's Task Force was only just starting up. As far as the Vancouver police were concerned, the killer, if there was one, was out of business. The number of women who had disappeared so far this year was about par for the course.

What jolted everyone out of their complacency was the news that Patricia Rose Johnson had disappeared.

Patricia Johnson was twenty-seven years old when she was last seen in February 2001. Her friends and family called her Patty, and when they try to explain what she was to them, the words tumble out: *A golden girl. She could light up the room just by walking into it. Fearless and strong. A beautiful girl with a gentle heart. Her beauty was inside and out. Kind, sweet woman. Very decent human being. Goofy, full of life. Just a kind, happy, caring person.* Her school friends remember the sleepovers and parties to this day. And her family remembers her, from the earliest days, as a sunny child. "All she wanted was to be loved," her aunt, Angela Johnson, has said.

Her mother, Marion Bryce, a single woman who worked as a waitress, adored her little girl and did the best she could for her. But her own life had been full of trauma and grief, and she is the first to admit that she didn't have the parenting skills and stability her child needed. She and Patty's father were only teenagers themselves when their daughter was born. "I'd lived in a foster home most of my life," Marion confesses, her lips trembling and tears leaking down her weathered cheeks. "I have three kids and no husband. My last boyfriend just left—he was abusive to me."

Patty quit school early, when she was eighteen, and got a job in the same mall where her mother worked. That was when she began to experiment with drugs, and her fall was fast and merciless. By the time she was twenty she was a full-blown heroin addict, working as a prostitute to pay for her drugs and living in the Evergreen Hotel in the Downtown Eastside. She had two children by her boyfriend, Chris, and they had a relationship for a few years, but she was—like every other mother on the street—unable to care for them, even though she had fought to stay off drugs and alcohol during each pregnancy to make sure the children would be born without problems. When they were two and three years old, Chris took custody of them; a year later, when he realized he couldn't cope, his mother, Laura Tompkins, an immigration lawyer, gained custody of them. It's not easy for Marion Bryce to admit she cannot take them herself, but she is grateful they are in such good and loving hands. "Laura is doing a wonderful job with them," she says, still crying.

The children were as bright and eager and cheerful as their mother had been when she was small. Patty never missed their birthdays; she was always full of plans for Halloween, Christmas and St. Patrick's Day; she called all the time. And she dreamed of sobriety. Even though she had returned to the street, Patty loved her kids, saw them often, spent time with them. They meant everything to her. And because of the children, she tried many times to kick her habit.

Lincoln Clarkes noticed Patty in July 1997 and was stunned by her beauty, despite the ravages of drugs and illness. "Patty was beautiful but she didn't know it," Marion Bryce says. "She didn't dress up; she just wore jeans and flannel shirts. She didn't go round as if she thought she was beautiful."

Clarkes asked if she would let him take her picture. She agreed right away, and he took a picture of her from the back as she looked to her left; one shoulder is bare, displaying two rose tattoos with the names of her son and daughter. Because she brought two friends in on the adventure, he took a second photograph, of the three heroin addicts together. The result was the photograph that changed

Lincoln Clarkes's life. The women—tragic, defiant, stunning—are looking right into the lens in what has become one of the most famous portraits of the women of the Downtown Eastside. Patty is on the left, a woman called Tiffany is in the middle—her last name is not known—and Kim Point is on the right. After this Clarkes began to photograph other women in the Downtown Eastside and eventually published *Heroines,* a book of photographs of the community's addicted women.

By early February 2001 Patty had a plan. Her uncle, Marion's brother, was looking after her because she was homeless. He did more than just let her stay at his place; he offered to help her fill out and deliver the correct application for a rent subsidy from Welfare. If it came through they would be able to rent a place together and she'd have a real home for her kids to visit. That was the plan—a nice place, a safe place, a place where she could get clean and, most of all, a place where her kids could come and see her.

Patty made a date with her uncle to meet him downtown on February 27 to fill in the form the welfare office gave her. The way it worked was that if the landlord agreed to rent to her, he would sign the form, which would go back to her welfare worker; the worker would then send the rent cheque directly to the landlord. Welfare cheques were due now, so Patty was in a hurry to make it happen. And her uncle had cooked a special dinner for her to celebrate.

She never turned up. "He was really worried because she was staying with him," remembers Marion. "It was not her style."

Patty's son's birthday was March 4, and he expected his mom to call as she always did. He expected she would come by with a present. He was waiting to talk to her about what he would wear for St. Patrick's Day later that month—he knew his mom hated him to wear anything but green. He would get to tell her about his music and how he was learning to play the violin, and he wanted to tell her all about how his fencing lessons were going. Sometimes he played in a band with his sister; she played the West African drum, and he knew his mom would be excited about that too. She would be excited about everything they were doing. He simply expected her, as she always did, to light up his life as soon as she came through the door.

When Patty didn't show up, everyone knew something was wrong. Patty would never miss her boy's birthday. Never. Marion went to the police with her sister-in-law to lay out their concerns before Sandy Cameron, a civilian employee in the Missing Persons Unit.

"Patty didn't pick up the last time I called," Marion told Cameron. "The last time I spoke to her was February 21. She was supposed to take the SkyTrain at eleven, but I said no, it's too late. February 23 was the day she should have picked up her welfare cheque but she didn't pick it up. February 27 was the day she was supposed to take in the 'intent to rent' form." And then, Marion explained, on March 4 she missed her son's birthday and didn't call.

Soon after the women had reported Patty's disappearance to Cameron, a police officer, Ron Palta, joined the conversation. Marion was told that Patty had gone to Montreal. That couldn't be true, Marion thought in horror. In her whole life Patty had never left Vancouver except for a visit to Lake Cowichan, on Vancouver Island. The police had to be lying to her. She was sure her child was the victim of the serial killer who was taking women from the Downtown Eastside.

Patricia Johnson was last seen near the corner of Main and Hastings. She was five feet four inches tall, had blond hair and blue eyes and weighed about a hundred pounds. When her description was circulated, it said she had two rose tattoos on her left shoulder, one for each of her children.

Within a week of Patty's disappearance Don Adam added three more members to his growing task force. On February 26, 2001, Jim McKnight and Phil Little from the Vancouver Police Department moved over to the new unit; two days later, on February 28, Wayne Clary, a senior RCMP officer, joined the group. All these officers were experienced homicide investigators. The group at this point was still small; with Adam and Marg Kingsbury, it was now just seven people. Although they were absorbed in the file review and the tips received by Project Amelia, they were all aware that Willie Pickton was a prime, or "priority one," suspect, and they were all aware that he had been interviewed by RCMP officer John Cater a year earlier. They all knew he'd been under surveillance; they all knew about the failed search warrant effort. But they still thought Pickton was a non-starter for the missing women.

"When we started this review in late 2000, early 2001," Adam said later, "it was believed that the disappearances had ceased in or around, I believe, 1999." But very quickly the small task force got a rough awakening. Within one month, from March 2 to April 1, 2001, three more women were missing. Now there could be no doubt, especially after the disappearances of Dawn Crey, Debra Jones and Patricia Johnson (Sharon Abraham wouldn't be reported missing for another three years), that the disappearances had definitely not ended.

If there was ever a child less likely to land on skid row, it had to be Heather Bottomley. She was a cute kid, a lively girl who made friends easily, who did well in school, who had loving, sensible parents. Not so different, in fact, from a number of other girls who climbed into a truck and disappeared for good from the dark streets of the Downtown Eastside. In Heather's case, it wasn't abuse at home that sent her off the rails; it was another common nightmare—an abusive boyfriend who soon had her hooked on drugs.

Born on August 17, 1976, Heather had grown up in a nice neighbourhood in New Westminster, where she attended Connaught Elementary School. Her parents loved her and Heather's friends thought they were great. Her mother loved to cook for her friends; her dad, Barry, coached the girls' basketball team at school. Heather was a good little athlete as a child—baseball was her favourite sport—but she wanted to be an actor when she grew up.

"She was so funny," her friend Danielle Montreuil told *Globe and Mail* reporter Jane Armstrong years later. "She had the most off-the-wall sense of humour. She was always doing little skits in her back yard." Young as she was, she became a fan of David Letterman. In a posting to www.missingpeople.net, Montreuil shared other memories: "As kids, Heather and I would pretend that we were Jake and Elwood Blues from the movie *The Blues Brothers* (of course, Heather was always her favourite actor at the time, John Belushi). Sunglasses, going to Chicago."

As soon as she got to New Westminster High School, things began to change for Heather. Her parents divorced and she felt lost and alone, especially as she found living at home with her mother's new husband very difficult. Heather was pretty, with wide-set hazel eyes, a mischievous, engaging smile and thick, curly hair. And she was tiny; just over five feet tall and little more than a hundred pounds. She found a boyfriend in grade nine but he wasn't a catch; both were immature, dropping out of school, and far too young for the baby daughter that Heather gave birth to at seventeen. The boyfriend had also turned Heather on to drugs. Danielle Montreuil ran into her years later and was distressed by the change in her old friend. "She was not happy. She looked stressed out," she said later. Heather was then living in a basement apartment and pregnant with a second child. "Out of all of us," Montreuil told Canadian Press reporter Alison Auld, "she was the last one you would have thought this could happen to."

By the late 1990s Heather was in the Downtown Eastside and was well-known to the social workers, police and medical personnel in the area. She had acquired a minor criminal record during her short stay in the neighbourhood; on February 7, 1998, she was picked up by the police for failing to pay for a cab ride, strip-searched, charged with unlawfully obtaining transport and sent to jail for a day. When her effects were listed, they consisted of her identification, some condoms, a ring and a lighter. She had no money on her, and the officer noted that she had two black eyes from a previous injury; he also noted that she was a "violent suicide risk."

Heather was last seen on April 17, 2001. She was twenty-four years old.

Four or five weeks later—no one knows the exact date, but it was between March 16 and 21—thirty-three-year-old Yvonne Marie Boen disappeared. Family members remember that the last time they saw her was on March 16; they reported her missing on March 21. At five feet ten inches tall, with blond hair and brown eyes, she had been a beautiful young woman; even in her thirties and with a history of serious drug addiction she remained beautiful. But as with almost every other woman in the Downtown Eastside, the story of her difficult childhood points the way to what happened to her in later life. Some children survive these traumatic years successfully; others carry them forever. Yvonne carried them forever.

Born Yvonne Marie England in Saskatchewan on November 30, 1967, Yvonne never had what you'd think of as a normal childhood. When she was only four months old, her father was killed in a car accident. Her mother, Lynn Metin, married again and had two more children, but as she told the *Vancouver Sun*'s Lori Culbert, she parted with her new husband because he was abusive. Metin, a trained nurse, was able to support her children, and for a while Yvonne's childhood in Melfort, Saskatchewan, was happy.

Melfort, an old pioneer town in the northeastern part of the province, was originally settled in the 1880s; today it is a prosperous city of about five thousand people. Yvonne made many good friends at Brunswick School and at Melfort Regional Division 3 School; she learned to ride horses and she took part in school sports. She was always pretty and popular, but when she was thirteen she turned into a rebellious kid, refusing to go to school or obey any rules.

Nothing very unusual about this behaviour. The problem was that no one was able to get her back to school, back on track. At fifteen she married Gerald Boen, a man ten years older than she was, and by the time she was eighteen she had three children, all boys:

Joel, born in 1984; Troy, born in 1985; and Damien, born in 1986. But Yvonne and Gerald separated before Damien's birth, and when she found herself unable to manage the three children by herself, she left them in the care of her mother.

This became her tragedy—her children not only lost their mother, they had to be split up. Joel went to live with his dad and his grandmother; Troy stayed with his other grandmother, Lynn Metin, who moved to Kelowna, B.C., and Damien grew up in a foster home. "Letting family members raise her children was out of love for her children and not because they were a burden to her," posted one of her closest friends, a woman called Hank, to a website after Yvonne went missing. Hank said she met Yvonne when they were both eighteen. "She cried many nights over her children, no one will ever know what she went through. The only reason she never took them back is because they were stable and happy where they were and she didn't want to take that away from them."

Yvonne moved south, to Moose Jaw, but she began working for a travelling carnival when she was twenty-one and spent the next ten years on the road with them, moving from one town to the next. The life seemed to suit her. She made a close friend during that period, a woman named Debbie Benning, who has said that in ten years of working together with the carnival she never saw Yvonne use drugs. "She was a travelling girl," Benning told the *Vancouver Sun*'s Lori Culbert many years later. "She loved to move. It gave her a sense of freedom. Everybody out there is one big happy family."

By the mid-1980s Yvonne was based in Vancouver. She tried to stay in touch with the boys, and their memories of her are affectionate. "She was actually a really cool mom," Joel told a reporter later. "She went her own way and that is okay with me . . . There are lots of good memories. We didn't see each other too much but when she was around she was the best, she was awesome. I enjoyed my time with her so much." But Troy, the middle son, remembers being "tossed around from family member to family member for years," as he told the Kelowna paper, the *Daily Courier*.

According to her friend Hank's posting, Yvonne had started using drugs only two years before she disappeared. Debbie Benning told Lori Culbert about the time in 2000 when a tearful Yvonne arrived at her door to admit she had become addicted to cocaine. "I'm in it a lot deeper than you think," she told Benning. "I'm scared and I don't know what to do."

Yvonne had been staying with Hank, but when she found that she simply couldn't manage without drugs, she walked out of her friend's house, leaving behind her wallet and personal belongings, and never returned to get them. Hank believes this was because Yvonne was so disappointed in herself. "That way, she didn't have to face me."

Troy and Yvonne's mother, Lynn, were the last family members to see Yvonne, when she visited them in Kelowna in March. When she left on March 16, she and Troy had made arrangements for him to come to stay with her the following week during the March school break. Troy couldn't reach her and she never phoned, so they reported her missing to the Vancouver police. But the family kept hoping she would call. Every time there was a birthday or a holiday they would wait for the phone to ring.

Rumours about Yvonne's whereabouts began to surface right away, and they weren't pleasant. Her family knew that she had spent some time with Willie Pickton in the past, and Troy Boen even remembered meeting him twice when he was a youngster. In an interview later with the Kelowna *Daily Courier*, Troy described him accurately: "He didn't shower. He was really smelling. My mother and my aunt met him because the Pickton family had a little bar." What Troy was talking about was Piggy's Palace in Port Coquitlam. His father, Gerald, knew for several years that Yvonne had spent time with Pickton.

And the family soon learned that she may have taken Willie to a barbecue at a squalid crack house known variously as the "House of Horrors" or the "House of Pain"—one of the most notorious drug dens in the small community of Whalley, in Surrey, an area often compared to the Downtown Eastside because of its poverty, sex-trade workers, crime and drug dealers. Yvonne seems to have been a regular at the crack house, and people remember one day when she turned up with a date who, as Debbie Benning described him, "had a ponytail, dressed really grubby and smelled bad."

CHAPTER TWENTY-SEVEN

THE FILE REVIEW

Yvonne Boen's disappearance, just ten weeks into the new year, was the third so far in 2001; two weeks later, on April 1, Heather Chinnock's disappearance was the fourth.

One of the tragedies of these women is that the pictures we have of them, the ones you see on posters and websites and in news stories, are almost always police mug shots, taken when they were arrested for some infraction of the law. Most of the time in the case of the women from skid row, the pictures show them at their most vulnerable: unkempt, afraid, sometimes defiant, sometimes resigned—and sad. Heather Chinnock's mug shot shows a woman who has given up. It shows a thirty-year-old who looks at least forty, whose hair is tangled, whose eyes are without hope.

Heather never thought of herself as a prostitute; in fact, she often declared that she absolutely wasn't one. That despite the fact that she had been charged twice for soliciting for the purposes of prostitution. Her arrest records show that she served two sentences, one for three days in jail and one a nine-month suspended sentence. However, she would maintain with some pride that she earned her living as a shoplifter or, in the language of the streets, a "booster," who stole from department stores, grocery stores, drugstores—you name it—and sold the stolen goods to pay for her addiction to drugs and alcohol. Maggy Gisle, who lived in the Downtown Eastside during the years Heather was there, remembers her as someone who would steal to order. "I really liked her because she was straight up," Gisle once told Steve Mertl, a reporter for the Canadian Press. "Like, 'What do you want? I'll get it for you.'"

Born in Denver, Colorado, on November 10, 1970, Heather was in her teens when she moved to Marysville, a little town in the Kootenays, after her mother married a Canadian citizen. What happened to Heather to make her so unhappy during these years isn't known. What is known is that she left home during her teenage years and wound up, like so many other troubled kids, in the Downtown Eastside, where she soon became deeply addicted to cocaine and heroin. And just like almost every other young woman there, she had children, two of them, children she could not care for, children she loved—but who had to be raised by other people.

In her late twenties Heather had started dropping into WISH occasionally to have supper and look for some clothes and makeup, but she wasn't a regular. When she was there, she was quiet and pleasant, never causing any trouble. But during this period her boyfriend, a musician named Gary Bigg, knew that she was spending time at Willie Pickton's farm, and he didn't like it. He believed the place was dangerous, and that was because of the hair-raising stories Heather would share with him after her visits there. As well as telling Bigg that she was sure Gary Leon Ridgway, the man who confessed to the murder of forty-eight women in Seattle many years later, was among the people who partied at the farm, Heather told him that biker gangs were bringing drugs and pornography onto the property.

"She seemed to think it was a fun place to go," Bigg told Darrow MacIntyre, a reporter for CBC Television, years later. "Like, she obviously didn't figure any harm was going to come to her. She said the guy was a bit strange, right, in some ways, but she could control him . . . so I think that means he liked kinky sex, right, but she could control, you know, what she would do with him and what she wanted to do with him."

But Heather, who came from the aboriginal community, also thought there were evil spirits on the farm, he said, "spirits of people that she figured harm had come to. At the time, I wasn't sure. It didn't make any sense to me at the time. I thought maybe it was just a little ploy so I would say, 'Well, don't go out there, Heather; I'll go to the liquor store and I'll buy you a bottle,' or something like that, right. I think she was trying to tell me more than what I got out of her, and maybe she was trying to tell me something, and maybe it was my fault for not listening, right."

Bigg knew that Heather was afraid of other men who hung around the farm, especially the ones with connections to the Hells Angels. She even talked to him about her fear that a prostitution ring was operating there. And, he said, talking about what she saw on the farm always made Heather cry. To someone as addicted as she was, however, the enticement of free drugs and some money was worth the risk.

In the spring of 2001 Heather was living not in the Downtown Eastside but in an apartment in Surrey with Bigg. They had an argument the night of April 1, and after calling a cab, she left. Bigg never saw her again. "She was depressed," he explained later, "because she had no money for booze and drugs." Gary Bigg's memory of what happened next seems hazy; he tells a vague story of leaving Surrey to go to Florida for a while and then spending time in Phoenix, Arizona. When he finally got home again, Heather still hadn't returned. No one knew where she was. Frightened now, Bigg reported her missing.

In the spring of 2001 Patricia Johnson, Heather Bottomley, Yvonne Boen and Heather Chinnock vanished right under the noses of Don Adam's new task force, which was still trying to figure out how many women in all had gone missing. Still, as police officials said again and again, the task force wasn't investigating possible crimes; all they were doing was reviewing files assembled by the officers who had worked on the now-defunct Project Amelia. Responsibility for investigating any actual crimes fell to the individual police forces where the victims lived or where they disappeared. The largest burden fell on the shoulders of the Vancouver Police Department because most of the victims had lived in the

Downtown Eastside. Although Don Adam was ramping up his file review by adding more officers, the VPD still had only two officers working on all their missing-women cases. And these officers were also working on other missing-persons cases, not just the Downtown Eastside's missing women.

At the task force Don Adam brought in two experienced RCMP officers: Ted Van Overbeek in May and Carole Hooper in June. The group, still small although it had grown to ten officers, continued sifting through more than 1,300 tips about possible suspects that had come in from the public. In August 2001 Adam's team had been churning through the old cases, collecting DNA and adding to the suspect list, but they also focused on police files from smaller cities on the Lower Mainland—files of missing women that the Vancouver Police Department had not considered part of their list of twenty-seven. Adam's team soon realized, not just from their slog through the files but also because new information was rolling in, that more women were missing than anyone might have predicted. Eighteen more, to be exact.

"The eighteen were in police files; they just weren't being looked at in the right way," Don Adam remembers. "We very much wanted to know exactly how bad the situation really was. By the first few days of September, I went back to RCMP and VPD management to say that we needed to aggressively investigate these eighteen new names. If they were truly missing then we had an ongoing serial killer operating in the DTES. Then I upped the numbers on the task force to deal with this new potential.

"Right from the outset of our investigation we believed there was a serial killer. What we had been told by Project Amelia of course was that the missings (and what I believed were murders) had stopped in 1999. What the new eighteen meant, once we investigated properly to ensure we weren't being Chicken Little again, that we weren't crying wolf and then we found them alive, is that the killings were ongoing in the here-and-now."

It was now, in the summer of 2001, after so many years of

women going missing, that Don Adam's group knew it was time to go looking for the killer. They needed more resources, so Adam laid out his case before the top brass at both the RCMP and the Vancouver Police Department and pushed his team to scour the files on suspects, or "persons of interest." As they did this they began dividing these persons into three groups: priority one, priority two and priority three.

"Priority one," Adam explained later, "was a person that is or was charged with murder or attempt murder of a sex-trade worker or aggravated sexual assault of a sex-trade worker that was in some way associated to the Downtown Eastside, either by living there or having been located on the regular strolls. In that category would also be dangerous sexual offenders that resided in that particular area, the Downtown Eastside.

"Priority two was very similar. It's an individual charged with an offence against a sex-trade worker who had a history of violence towards sex-trade workers, not necessarily murder, that was found [in] or could be associated to the Downtown Eastside, or had a history of violence towards a sex-trade worker but lived outside of Vancouver."

Adam's priority-three group consisted of people who didn't fit into the first two categories but needed to be looked at anyway. These might be people who were, as he described them, "active participants in attending the stroll area or had vehicles, for example, that would be equipped with restraining devices, or vans." Or they might be people who had been named in such situations as an attempted abduction "where we felt," said Adam, "based on the registered ownership of the vehicle, that they may be heading out to the valley area—the Fraser Valley area of Vancouver."

Very quickly the team had between thirty-five and fifty names set aside as priority-one suspects. Sometimes after they had studied the files and discussed them, names would move from priority two to priority one. Right from the beginning, because of his history with Sandra Gail Ringwald in 1997, because of the frequent tips about him, because of his access to vehicles and because of his isolated farm property, Robert William Pickton's status was in no doubt—he was priority one and he stayed there.

Despite this progress, no one had yet authorized a real investigation. The task force was still just doing a file review and the Vancouver police wouldn't add any more officers to their two-person Missing Persons Unit. It stayed that way for months.

During this period, Willie's personal fortunes were improving. In March 2001 the Pickton siblings sold off another chunk of the family farm to developers for $769,469. The new townhouse development, called Heritage Meadows, overlooked Willie's trailer, although a massive pile of dirt gave him some privacy from curious new neighbours. This muddy, filthy property, crammed with rusting machinery, collapsed sheds and skeletal remains of cars, heaped with piles of landfill and dirt, many covered with black plastic tarps, would soon be crowded on two sides by crisp, neat, freshly painted homes, on the third side by woods and a golf course, and on the fourth, where the road was, by a sprawling shopping centre of big-box stores. The shopping mall faced the farm and its closest neighbour on the south side of the road, separated only by a parking lot, was the Hells Angels clubhouse; it too faced the farm.

The Picktons appear to have used some of the money from this land sale to buy a suburban house for $257,000 at 22810 113th Avenue in Maple Ridge, about eleven kilometres east of Port Coquitlam. From all accounts this became a rental property, another of several bits and pieces of real estate they owned jointly, either by inheritance from their parents or by investing. Linda didn't own any of the Piggy's Palace property but she certainly had an interest in it, as she had given her brothers a mortgage on it when they bought it.

Willie was fifty-two now and the days were long past when he was bullied by his brother, Dave. He ran his own pig-butchering business with Pat Casanova's help, he bought and sold vehicles and auto parts and he sometimes worked with his brother on demolitions.

He'd also help out at Dave's headquarters on Tannery Road in Surrey, a property as untidy and ramshackle as the farm itself, where Dave kept many of his trucks and heavy equipment and a battered metal-roofed shed that was his office. Sandy Humeny, commuting from Maple Ridge, worked there, taking orders, managing the payroll and keeping the books. Willie loved Sandy and was always happy to be around her. But there was always plenty of time, he found, to take his regular trips to the Downtown Eastside.

On June 1, 2001, five weeks after Heather Chinnock vanished, Andrea Joesbury disappeared. Born November 6, 1978, she was twenty-three years old. "She was the cutest, the most stubborn, the most opinionated—and the kindest little girl," remembered her grandfather, Jack Cummer, a retired businessman who had spent most of his working life designing and building small boats, with a specialty in commercial dinghies. His daughter, Karin, had married a man named Kevin Joesbury, a drywaller who had emigrated to Canada from England; they settled in Victoria and, although they had two children, Andrea and her brother, Sean, the marriage was a disaster. Kevin Joesbury turned out to be violent and abusive, beating his wife so badly on one occasion that he wound up serving four years in prison. Karin had suffered so much in the marriage that she was too frail to manage the children, and Andrea became close to her maternal grandparents, Jack and his second wife, Laila.

"After he [Kevin] got out of jail, Andrea wanted a father so desperately that she didn't object when he wiggled his way back into her life," Cummer said. Another child was born, a sister named Heather, but the Joesburys' family life never recovered. Although Jack and Laila gained custody of the three children, Heather became severely depressed and Children's Aid placed her in foster care—"in five different homes," snorted Jack in despair. "She hated being a ward of the court . . . the stigma of it."

Andrea attended Victoria's Craigflower School, where she was well-liked by both her classmates and her teachers, but by the time she was fourteen or fifteen she was losing interest in school. She was a stunning girl by this time, tiny and slim, with a gorgeous smile, long blond hair and a sweet nature that enchanted everyone who met her. What people didn't understand about Andrea was her deep longing for a normal, happy family; the disruption and pain caused by her father had been devastating for her. She had seen so much abuse, alcoholism and mental illness in her own family that she was easy prey for men who pretended they cared for her and for the drugs they offered.

One day, when she was about sixteen, a girlfriend introduced Andrea to a man named Mohammed Khogaini, who was, according to Jack Cummer, an Afghan refugee.

"He was a Muslim, about thirty years old," he said, "and she phoned me to tell me how much in love she was with him." Cummer knew Andrea longed for a father figure in her life, but this relationship frightened him. The new boyfriend gave Andrea a garment that covered up her body and told her he was going to marry her. "She told us," said Cummer, "that she was going to go back to Afghanistan with him."

In fact, Mohammed had no such plans. Although she was living with him in Vancouver and had a baby girl with him, and although he kept promising to marry her, everything he had told her was a lie. Khogaini was a pimp and a drug dealer who had had three children with another woman. His plan for Andrea was to keep her on drugs and keep her turning tricks; her youth and beauty made her a highly prized commodity. Andrea resisted; she loved her baby daughter, was taking good care of her and was staying off drugs.

But one night when she was breastfeeding the baby, said Cummer, Children's Aid came in and took the child. Mohammed wasn't there. "We think he reported her," Cummer said. "He wanted the baby adopted. He needed to keep her on the street. All she wanted was a baby; all her life that was all she wanted. A family. And after that everything went downhill for her. She was lost, like a zombie. She started to take drugs again and Mohammed got Andrea back."

Even worse was the news that Andrea had tested positive for HIV. And she suspected she was pregnant again. Her family tried to rescue her. Karin Joesbury got her home once but not for long. Andrea returned to the Downtown Eastside and her second-floor room at the Roosevelt Hotel, the same hotel Dawn Crey lived in, the same hotel where Dinah Taylor hunted for women to take to the pig farm. But then things got a bit better. Mohammed Khogaini was arrested on a long rap sheet of charges and safely stowed away in jail. Andrea began a methadone program; she started seeing counsellors; she had a sympathetic new doctor she trusted named Susan Burgess; she went to WISH every night at six o'clock for a good dinner and a shower and stayed till it closed at ten. She felt safe there and people kept an eye out for her. "Andrea was just the sweetest girl," says Elaine Allan. "Although she was quiet and gentle she didn't like it when people pronounced her name *Ann-drea*. She was quite firm about this. Her name was to be pronounced *Awn-drea*."

The last time Andrea spoke to Jack Cummer was on Saturday, June 2, 2001, when she called to tell him she had been invited to a party. "She was thrilled to be asked," remembered Cummer, "thrilled to be going to this party."

On June 5 Andrea visited the Downtown Community Health Clinic to have an open sore on her foot cleaned and dressed, but she failed to turn up later that day for her regular methadone treatment with Dr. Burgess. This was unusual; Andrea was always careful to make her methadone appointments. Dr. Burgess had often visited Andrea in her room at the Roosevelt. "She was very sweet and young in terms of naïveté," she later told the *Globe and Mail*'s Jane Armstrong. "Like an optimistic child, she had hopes and dreams for herself. She was quite beautiful. She loved to wear rings and jewellery. She was very shy, actually. She was vulnerable, in the trusting sense, and probably saw good when there was not good."

Dr. Burgess called Jack Cummer right away to say that Andrea hadn't come in for her appointment. Andrea's brother, Sean, immediately went to the Downtown Eastside to look for her; when he couldn't find her, he went to the police. They couldn't help; all they could do was confirm that Mohammed was in jail, so he hadn't harmed her in any way. The only people who knew anything at all were two men who worked at the Roosevelt Hotel. When she was leaving the hotel that last night, it was raining hard, and Chi Sing Leung, the manager of the hotel, said later that he had been worried about her. "I advised her not to go out because of the weather. She said she was going to Coquitlam."

Stephen Arsenault, the hotel's part-time doorman, was fond of Andrea and considered her one of the nicest women he knew; he gave her the same advice—stay in tonight. He also heard Dinah Taylor on the phone at the hotel's front desk, setting Andrea up with Willie Pickton. Dinah told him later, said Arsenault, when they were talking about where Andrea might be, "Oh, I saw her in Port Coquitlam going on a date. Never heard of her since."

On June 8 Kelly Goodall, a street nurse, was worried because Andrea hadn't shown up to have the dressing on her foot changed. She reported her missing to the Vancouver police.

A few months after Andrea disappeared, the police interviewed Khogaini; in an interview with the Vancouver *Province* he claimed to know nothing. He explained that he had been in jail when she disappeared and after he got out he had hunted for her. "I looked around everywhere," he told reporter Adrienne Tanner. "I went to the methadone program and she wasn't there. I had bruises on my feet from walking." Khogaini also told Tanner that he hadn't wanted Andrea to work as a prostitute. "He said he stole in an attempt to finance Joesbury's drug habit," Tanner reported. "But it never seemed to be enough. 'I told her a thousand times not to work the street, but she didn't listen to me.'"

Andrea's teachers in Victoria were deeply distressed by her disappearance and called Jack Cummer to tell him and Laila how sorry they were. As he told this story his eyes filled with tears that slid down his old, lined face. "They said to me, 'You had the most beautiful grandchild.' Yes, I did."

CHAPTER TWENTY-EIGHT

DO SOMETHING

The summer of 2001 was an embarrassing period for the Vancouver Police Department. Clearly the belief that the disappearances of sex-trade workers in the Downtown Eastside had abated and that the killer, if there was one, had left town was a fantasy. The families of the missing women were angry and becoming more proactive; not only were they calling the Missing Persons Unit all the time, as well as officers working in Don Adam's joint task force, many of them were talking to reporters, especially to the *Vancouver Sun*'s Lindsay Kines. He had written most of the stories so far, challenging the Vancouver police again and again about their failure to investigate these cases.

The VPD didn't need another big scandal on the boil, but they had a dandy: their dismissal of Kim Rossmo and his subsequent lawsuit demanding lost pension benefits as well as damages for what his lawyer described as "malicious, high-handed and insensitive treatment" by the police board and Deputy Chief John Unger. The force might have hoped he would simply disappear; he'd found another job and it looked like a good one.

Rossmo was now director of research at the Police Foundation in Washington, D.C., a private non-profit organization doing research and training for U.S. police forces. His new salary was substantially higher than the $120,000 a year he had been making in Vancouver, and the foundation, which had been set up with Ford Foundation money, was glad to have him. The foundation's president, a former Newark, New Jersey, police chief named Hubert Williams, couldn't have been warmer in interviews, telling Lindsay Kines that Rossmo "brings a number of very outstanding credentials to the police foundation. He has not only had experience as a high-level police official, he has been working for police organizations and the FBI for many, many years doing work that is very much related to what we're doing. In addition to that, I think that we got a very solid individual. Kim is a delightful person to work with. Everyone really has great respect for him, and he fits like a hand-in-glove in the Police Foundation." Williams made it clear that the foundation had no problem with Rossmo's dispute with the Vancouver force. "Whatever his issues are with Vancouver, that's his issues, they're not our issues."

Although Rossmo was working in Washington by this time, he spent many weeks preparing for the civil trial scheduled to begin in June 2001. As his lawyer, Murray Tevlin, told Kines, "What we're saying is that the issue in this trial wasn't really about money or budgets or even whether geographic profiling works or not—because everybody knows that it works—it was a matter of putting this upstart, over-achiever constable in his place. That's what's going to be interesting about it. The human dynamics of the case are going to be interesting." Exploring those dynamics, everyone knew, would include questioning some of the Old Boys who had made Rossmo's time at the VPD so difficult.

When the trial began, under B.C. Supreme Court Justice Marion Allan on Monday, June 18, in the Vancouver Law Courts, the testimony did not disappoint those hoping for sensational revelations about the force. In his opening statement Murray Tevlin was blunt. "The reason why he [Rossmo] worked too hard is maybe because he was too smart and achieved too much," he said. "He put John Unger's nose out of joint and when John Unger became his boss, he exercised his temporary power as acting chief to terminate Rossmo's contract the first chance he had."

The first witness, former chief Bruce Chambers, had strongly supported Rossmo. In plain words he said that the Old Boys' group in the top ranks were stubbornly committed to old-fashioned methods of policing, that they were obstructive and that they did whatever it took to belittle new techniques such as Rossmo's geographic profiling. "What I saw," he testified, "was passive-aggressive behaviour and obstruction on their part." They also opposed his own efforts to modernize the department, Chambers added, "and were doing everything to derail it."

During the trial a number of officers who supported Rossmo had their own stories to tell. Sergeant Grant Smith, for example, testified that, given Rossmo's PhD and his new rank, he had once joked around about how to address him. The response from Unger was swift and vicious: "I don't care what you call him, he'll never be an officer of this force and he'll never be a member of the officers' mess."

Smith described the way that four senior officers who had supported Chambers, including himself, were treated shabbily by Unger and Chief Terry Blythe; he himself had retired early because he grew tired of fighting them. Chambers's only mistake as chief, he declared, was not getting rid of at least one of the troublemakers. Smith told the judge, "I think he should have taken a harder line, instead of being a gentleman, and fought back with all he had."

One of the most interesting witnesses was Inspector Ken Doern, a senior officer who had respected and liked both Chambers and Rossmo. The only way he would agree to testify was to insist on being subpoenaed; that way he would not look as if he had volunteered—his career had suffered enough. And his story was a sad one. He told the court that he had been pulled off a project he'd been working on to plan the VPD's requirements for facilities and officers for the next twenty-five years. His new assignment? On orders from Chief Terry Blythe, he would be organizing the Gay Pride parade and the law enforcement torch run and doing fundraising. "Police officers unfit for regular duties were assigned those tasks in the past," he explained.

What was worse was that when he went to see Blythe about the demotion, Blythe said it was because he had supported Chambers. Later Unger told him that at least twenty-five officers had come by to tell him they'd seen Doern having lunch with Chambers. Doern was flabbergasted. "Is Chambers evil? Or has he been accused of a crime?" he had demanded of Unger. Unger was not amused. Doern told the judge that what he had gone through was "devastating." Not long after the trial, after thirty-one years with the Vancouver Police Department, Doern, then fifty-eight years old, resigned to join a private security company.

When Kim Rossmo finally had his turn on the witness stand, his testimony was a shock. Instead of rolling through a litany of the insults he'd suffered from the Old Boys, he went straight to the heart of the crisis: in 1998 he had told his superiors that he believed a serial killer was taking women from the Downtown Eastside and that the police needed to issue a public warning about it right away. Rossmo described Fred Biddlecombe's temper tantrum at the time and the immediate rejection of his suggestion, as well as the fact that the police issued a news release saying they *didn't* believe a serial killer was terrorizing the area.

Murray Tevlin took Rossmo through his history with the force, his education and the fact that he was the first police officer in Canada to earn a PhD, his development of the geographic profiling software and the reason for his being assigned the rank that so enraged the Old Boys: a competing and very tempting offer from the RCMP to join them as a detective inspector and set up a geographic profiling unit. After a lengthy matter-of-fact outline of what had happened to him in the grim years he'd endured under Blythe's command, Rossmo summed it all up by stating that he should have spent most of his time working for the Major Crime Unit, which includes the Homicide and Sexual Offences squad, but Major Crime asked him for help only once, while the sex offences group asked only a few times.

Just before he left the witness stand, Rossmo couldn't help letting his anger show. Not only did he call John Unger a bully, he laid much of the blame for his dismissal on him. "I think he played a significant role and interfered in contractual negotiations," he declared. "My belief is John Unger sabotaged the renewal of my agreement."

Most people reading the newspaper accounts of what was going on in Justice Allan's courtroom were horrified, but no one was more upset than the relatives of the missing women, who were quick to connect the dots. When Angela Jardine's mother, Deborah, learned that the police had refused to issue a warning about a possible serial killer, she was deeply distressed. "I think it might have made a difference," she told the *Vancouver Sun*'s Bruce Morton. "The women would have taken extra precautions, including my daughter. I was told it wasn't a serial killer, that she just disappeared and started a new life somewhere. I've said all along it was a serial killer or killers."

As the days went on, officers from the Vancouver Police Department tried to rebut the statements of Rossmo and his supporters. Deputy Chief Gary Greer did his best to paint the force in a good light, objecting strenuously to Rossmo's statements that the police had refused to issue a public warning and failed to set up a proper task force. "I think that's an outrageous statement," Greer said. "Our men and women in the police department are very concerned." As for the charges that the envious members of the Old Boys' Club hated Rossmo, he dismissed those as well. Getting rid of the geographic profiling unit had been done for financial reasons. "It wasn't cost-effective," he said. It was costing $700,000 a year and had served its purpose. As for the demotion back to constable, well, Rossmo's rank was tied to the position and the unit, and once they were gone so was the rank.

It would be months before the case was finished. It had already run through its allotted court time, and at the end of June 2001 Justice Allan called a halt. She and the lawyers had other commitments and wouldn't be able to resume until sometime in the fall. Kim Rossmo went back to Washington, his case unresolved.

The trial's revelations so far had been disturbing to many Canadians, not just to people living in British Columbia. As the summer wore on, an increasingly restless and angry community of relatives of the missing women, community workers and ordinary citizens demanded action from the police. Neil Boyd, a respected professor of criminology at Simon Fraser University, was among many who spoke out about the very real possibility of a serial killer at work. "One of the features of serial murders is that the victims have similar characteristics," he told one reporter. "They might be all children, as in the case of Clifford Olson. They might be teenage girls, as in the case of Paul Bernardo. Or they might be all prostitutes. I think the facts of the Downtown Eastside case disappearances certainly do raise legitimate questions about the possibility of a serial killer."

The response from the Vancouver Police Department spokesman, Scott Driemel, was that just because the women were addicted prostitutes from the Downtown Eastside wasn't proof of anything. "Other than the fact they were missing, that was all they had in common . . . To actually go and say there is a serial killer lurking in the Downtown Eastside that's picking off dozens of women? We have no evidence of that." Driemel made these comments at the end of June 2001.

This was just the kind of remark that made street nurse Bonnie Fournier crazy. She has never forgotten the day she was in a restaurant and, overhearing her conversation, the waitress asked her if she knew Patricia Johnson. "I said yes," remembers Fournier. "She said, 'I'm her mom. I haven't heard from her.'" She hardly knew what to say to the broken-hearted Marion Bryce.

Like so many people who worked in the Downtown Eastside, Fournier knew that there had to be a serial killer, and she was fierce in her efforts to protect the women she saw every night in the Health Van (its official name was the Mobile Access Program, or MAP, but everyone knew it as the Health Van and Manny Cu was the driver). "One night Manny and I were driving along Cordova past Oppenheimer Park heading to Heaton Street," she remembers. "There were no street lights. Up ahead we see a truck and saw it pulling an arm . . . It looked like it was pulling someone . . . and we floored the Health Van and leaned on the horn and he let the arm go and sped off. The girl, she got in the van and she had a chunk of hair pulled out. She was hysterical.

She said this guy wanted a date and hauled her in by the hair when she wouldn't go with him."

To this day Bonnie Fournier believes the driver was Willie Pickton, probably aided and abetted by Dinah Taylor. Because she had always believed that Taylor was evil, luring women to the farm, she nicknamed her the Witch of Endor, after the infamous sorcerer said to have been consulted by King Saul before his battle with the Philistines. She believes that Taylor took women to the House of Horrors (Fournier always called it the House of Pain) in Whalley and would then take them from there to the Pickton farm. "If they [the police] had started listening to us six years earlier, these women wouldn't have died," Fournier says.

Night after night the same faces appeared at the van, and every night Bonnie knew Sereena Abotsway would be one of them. "Hi, Mom," Sereena would chirp as she spied Bonnie. She seemed to know that Bonnie had a special place in her heart for this affectionate, extroverted young woman who had been diagnosed with fetal alcohol spectrum disorder (FASD). Sereena and Bonnie would also see each other earlier in the evening, as Bonnie arrived at First United to set up her nursing table at WISH. "Sereena would be in the back of the sanctuary playing cards with the old guys," Bonnie remembers, "waiting for WISH to open up."

Sereena, born of aboriginal parents, was twenty-nine that summer of 2001. She had been just four years old, traumatized by severe sexual and physical abuse, when social workers delivered her to her new foster parents, Bert and Anna Draayers, in Surrey in 1976. They came to love her right away, as did their own children and the other kids they fostered; she was pretty, bubbly and very sweet. They have described her as "a lovely girl with a lot of good in her. She always had a good word for someone. She was very caring."

But she wasn't an easy child, and because the teachers couldn't handle her the Draayerses tried to teach her at home. It was their best shot in a difficult situation and it worked for several years. It was only when Sereena was in her mid-teens that they began to find her disruptive and unmanageable. Finally, at seventeen, when they felt they couldn't cope with her any longer, she was moved into a group home. Sereena never held this against them; she phoned the Draayerses every day for the rest of her life.

It wasn't long before Sereena's story became much like that of most of the women in Canada's poorest postal code. She became addicted to drugs, gravitated to the Downtown Eastside, started prostituting to make enough money to pay for her fixes. In 1997 one of her dates beat her so badly she wound up in a coma with a fractured skull; she nearly died, and surgeons had to insert a steel plate into her head to keep her alive. But she did live and she returned to the street and to her suppers at WISH and her nightly visits to the Health Van. She even attended church, as her foster parents had always done, where she loved to sing the hymns. Sereena asked Cheryl Bear Barnetson and her husband, Randy, who ran a street church at Main and Hastings, to baptize her; they obliged with a service in Crab Park and a dunk in the ocean at the park's edge. "It was good to see how the Lord was beginning to touch her and move in her life," Bear Barnetson later told Canadian Press reporter Dirk Meissner.

The spring and summer of 2001 were hard for Sereena. She was on several medications, including corticosteroid inhalers for asthma. On April 30 Welfare paid for her to take a cab from Surrey Memorial Hospital to Helping Spirit Lodge; the lodge couldn't keep her and sent her the same day to Evergreen Transition House. She wasn't there for long; soon she was being treated at St. Paul's Hospital in Vancouver and was sent the same day to another transition house. She was evicted on June 8 from yet another shelter and moved into Triage, a centre for the homeless and addicted in the Downtown Eastside. A week later she was living on the street, until welfare workers persuaded Triage to take her back.

The St. James Community Service Society managed Sereena's welfare benefits, and workers there were worried when she failed to pick up her money on July 18. But on July 16 and 19 her pharmacy received inhalers for her and she picked these up, probably on the nineteenth. Around that time Bonnie Fournier remembers seeing Sereena at the Health Van close to midnight; she was wearing a red leatherette skirt over a longer black skirt, a sheer ruffled black blouse, black net stockings and high heels. Her lipstick was a startling bright red. "Well, don't you look nice!" Bonnie exclaimed.

"I'm going to a party in Whalley." Sereena grinned happily, thrilled by Bonnie's approval. "They're going to pick me up in Victory Square." And she danced off.

"Be a good girl." Bonnie laughed as she waved goodbye, but she wondered. Normally Sereena did not dress like that. Suddenly she felt anxious. Sereena was so easily taken in and so fragile, not like some of the other girls, like Cindy Feliks and Georgina Papin, who had been much more street-smart. And then the image of Dinah Taylor came to her. Had Dinah lured Sereena to some terrible place—like the House of Pain in Whalley? Troubled, Bonnie packed up the van and went home for the night, the image of Sereena in her red skirt, high heels and bright lipstick fixed in her mind.

Bonnie Fournier never saw Sereena again, but another woman remembers running into her in the Downtown Eastside later that summer. Yolanda Dyck, who was working at WISH, saw Sereena looking for tricks at the corner of the Fraser and Broadway stroll in the summer of 2001. Sereena usually worked downtown, on Hastings Street, so Dyck was surprised to see her there. Sereena told her she was "going to the country." Dyck remembers the man who was with her: he was wearing jeans and rubber boots; he was of medium build, balding and blond.

In Surrey, Anna Draayers waited for Sereena to call. She always called. Every day. They were expecting her home at the end of August to celebrate her birthday. She never called and she didn't show up. Ever since that time the Draayerses have wondered if Sereena knew what could happen to her. In the last year of her life she wrote a small poem she called "In Memories of My Sisters," about the women she'd known who had disappeared.

You were all part of God's plan,
He probably took most of you home
But he left us with a very empty spot.

Losing Sereena was a shocking blow to Bonnie Fournier, whose heart raged with anger and grief. She thought about all the other girls she had looked after, all the stories she had heard, the wounds she had dressed, the laughter they had shared. The hugs, the promises, the pain. And the images of the mothers and sisters and children of the missing women filled her head. She remembered Leigh Miner's mother, always elegant and polite, always so sad, coming in again and again to ask if she'd seen Leigh anywhere. She thought about eighteen-year-old Diana Melnick, the former private-school girl, sitting in a holding cell in the courthouse when she'd worked there. And she thought about Andrea Joesbury arriving on the dot of six every night at WISH. She thought about Marnie Frey and Patricia Johnson; she was certain "there was no way these girls would ever get into a car with a stinky man." Then she would see Cindy Feliks's face—a girl who could be so confrontational but who would talk to her for hours about her life. Face after face, story after story, crowded her brain. Bonnie couldn't help herself; she cried and cried for all the lost girls.

And she thought about all the complaining she had done as well. To the police, to everyone she could think of, to Larry Campbell, the coroner, who had tried to help. And what good did this ever do? Elaine Allan had teamed up with Bonnie to demand action. Look, they yelled, the bank accounts haven't been touched for months, the rent hasn't been paid, they haven't picked up their drugs. Do something! Please, do something . . .

CHAPTER TWENTY-NINE

A NEWSROOM LEADS THE WAY

By mid-September 2001 three reporters at the *Vancouver Sun* were finishing a series of eleven stories on how the Vancouver police and the new Downtown Eastside Missing Women's Task Force had responded to the disappearances of so many women on skid row. Lindsay Kines, the original reporter on the missing women, who was also covering the ongoing Kim Rossmo fiasco, had been working with Kim Bolan and Lori Culbert for several weeks to get the series researched, written, edited and illustrated in time for the launch date of Friday, September 21.

When it began appearing that Friday morning, the series shocked the city. First of all, people learned that the numbers of missing women were much higher than anyone knew. Don Adam's new joint task force, they reported, had concluded there were forty-five women missing, not twenty-seven as the Vancouver police had been saying. Forty-five? This figure blew the case up into one comparable to the infamous Green River Killer case in Seattle, with its forty-nine victims.

Because of these findings, the *Sun* team reported, the police were finally taking the missing women seriously. On Thursday, September 20, the day before the first story ran, the Vancouver police brass, scenting a scandal, were in full damage control. A last-minute interview with the *Sun* for this first story had Chief Terry Blythe and Deputy Chief John Unger announcing that they were beefing up the joint task force with four more Vancouver police officers and that the RCMP would be adding another two, for a total of sixteen. Despite underplaying the tragedy for many years, Blythe told the reporters he would be asking Vancouver City Council for enough money to cover the cost of these additional officers for four years.

Blythe was defensive about the VPD's role in the past, pushing the blame as delicately as possible in the direction of the RCMP. "Right from the beginning, I think we've acted very responsibly and we've done as much as we could with the resources we had and with the information we had," he said. "The other thing that really annoys me is why we're taking the brunt of this. These are people"—referring to the missing women—"that may have gone through Vancouver, but they were obviously from elsewhere in B.C. and other provinces. I mean this is not solely our investigation, and I don't think we need to be blamed for it."

And then Unger, who brushed off questions from the *Sun* about why he and his boss were finally onside, blandly took ownership of the case. "Without revealing the investigative leads that we have, I can't really go into that," he said, referring to the conversion from hostility to support for the case. "But I can say that we've made significant progress. What I can tell you is that we are looking at a number of other missing women."

For the next week the stories plastered the front pages of the *Sun,* each one more damaging than the last, leaving the Vancouver police looking inept, slipshod and worse. The reporting laid out the infighting within the force, its lack of experienced officers, the outmoded computer systems and the data-entry mistakes on the files of the missing women. What small effort the VPD had made in its investigation of the missing women, the newspaper proved, was flawed, poorly coordinated and understaffed.

Not surprisingly, the families of the missing women—the people who had been calling Lindsay Kines and other reporters for years—were beside themselves. One after another they voiced their anguish and fury. Vancouver Island's Erin McGrath said in a *Sun* story that she had been asking Vancouver police for a year why her sister, Leigh Miner, had not been added to the missing women list; why had she never been given a straight answer before now? The VPD's Missing Persons Unit had never called or updated her family, McGrath told the *Sun.* "People are so welcoming to pets, to dogs, but to the people who have these terrible problems that take their lives, we treat them like they are sub-human. They really didn't seem interested in my sister's case. When somebody lives a lifestyle like my sister, they really are looked down upon. It felt like she just didn't matter, and we didn't matter. We were marginalized because of my sister's addictions." Erin also discovered that they had lost her sister's file, and had been lying to her for years about looking for her.

Other family members were just as outspoken. Angela Arsenault's mother, Margaret Kennedy, was stunned to find out that the police hadn't included her daughter on their official list of missing women. They had dismissed Angela as a teenage runaway, she told the paper. "Girls will be missing and before they are officially deemed missing, it could be a year later," Kennedy said in an interview. "Any chance of getting quick leads is gone with that kind of delay. I can't believe the way the whole thing was handled right from the beginning. They just didn't seem to care. I can't believe that she wasn't already on that list."

Patricia Johnson's mother, Marion Bryce, also spoke out, stating that the police had done nothing to solve Patty's disappearance, nor would they add her name to the missing women list. "Nobody's called me. Nobody cares," Bryce told the paper. "I have to phone them. They don't call me. They don't care about these girls who have gone missing from the downtown."

In the next few days the *Sun* team ran short, moving profiles of many of the missing women, including Patty Johnson, Leigh Miner, Angela Arsenault, Georgina Papin, Sereena Abotsway, Heather Chinnock, Wendy Crawford, Cindy Felix, Sherry Irving and Andrea Joesbury. Angela's grandmother, Pat Arsenault, probably spoke for all the other family members when she told the newspaper from her home in New Brunswick, "I know she's dead. But please find her so we can have an end to this. It's in my heart every day. Every day."

The issue of police neglect was very clear, and nothing the VPD chief constable or anyone else on the force could say mitigated the damage. As the stories rolled out each day, it got much worse. A feature on the VPD's botched investigations described completely dysfunctional and incompetent management. Just a few examples cited in the story that ran on Saturday, September 22 (dwarfed by the larger news of the terrorist attacks in the U.S.), included the small, overworked staff, many of whom were working on two jobs at once and two of whom had never done homicide investigations before; the ugly infighting within the team; the way team members withheld information from each other; the fact that officers became frustrated and asked for transfers out of the unit; and the fact that once they seemed to be making progress, the investigation was scaled back. The paper stated, "Investigators looked at 1,348 tips, but a number received only cursory treatment and still required more analysis and follow-up by the time the team was scaled back."

Remarkably, the reporters were able to get a frank and emotional interview from Project Amelia's leader, Geramy Field, whose words said it all. "In hindsight, if we'd had more people, we could have done a better investigation—a faster investigation. But there weren't enough people to do that. I would have liked to have had time to meet with the families on a more frequent basis," she said. "But there wasn't enough time."

Until the newspaper printed the information, no one knew that Field was still working in the homicide division and was supervising eight other officers. "I see the articles in the paper or I get a call and I get this little pang," she admitted to the reporters. "It's important to me. The case is important. Everyone there was dedicated. It wasn't a perfect investigation and I think we've all learned things. But nobody's ever investigated a case like this. The investigators that are working on it now know what they have to do and, unfortunately, it's going to take a lot of money and manpower to do that," she said. "I just hope they get the support to do it."

Vancouver's chief constable, Terry Blythe, continued to find it difficult to admit he'd made any mistakes. "We can't just do things willy nilly overnight and tell somebody well, we need this or that," he told the reporters. "We've got to be able to justify very clearly why we're doing what we're doing. It may have been under-resourced. But I don't want anybody to believe that we didn't think it was serious. We've been hit with this criticism so hard that it's tough to defend yourself. But right from the beginning, I think we've acted very responsibly and we've done as much as we could with the resources we had and with the information we had."

Blythe soon found himself without many of the allies he had counted on in years past. Defensiveness, stalling, refusing to accept any responsibility—these tactics insulted not just the public and not just the people who had loved the women who had disappeared; they were swept aside by other officials and police officers who spoke openly about the failures. Rich Coleman, for one. The province's solicitor general, himself a former police officer, began using words such as *merger* and *integration* and *regionalization,* words that threatened many officers in the Vancouver police, who foresaw the RCMP's taking over all the big cases. Just merging the Lower Mainland's major crime and forensic units would be one good step, Coleman said, adding that the RCMP was already at work on a plan to amalgamate some police services. He told the *Vancouver Sun* in response to the first five stories in its series, "There is no question we would like to see some form of regionalization." He was talking about setting up effective methods of communication, sharing information and sharing cases—all anathema to many small forces, and certainly to the Vancouver police. They were the top dogs in the country's third-largest city and they were used to calling the shots.

The *Sun* investigation exposed the problems of police forces that couldn't work together, and not just because they were threatened and not just because they were territorial. Sometimes the problems were purely technical. Computers couldn't talk to each other; having different systems in each jurisdiction slowed down investigations and often made them almost impossible. It was time to integrate the province's computer systems, Coleman told the newspaper. Then there was the issue of a DNA bank. One had been promised but it was postponed. Why? Because, Coleman said, it should be done by the federal authorities. He conceded that the police had not done anything so far to compare the small number of DNA samples they had been able to collect.

Rich Coleman wasn't the only one demanding change. So was Wally Oppal, a B.C. Supreme Court judge, who told the newspaper that it was "absolutely asinine that we have twelve municipal forces and all the detachments of the RCMP." It's not as if he hadn't tried before. Seven years earlier Oppal had released a seven-hundred-page report recommending the regionalization of certain police responsibilities across the province. And setting up a major crimes unit to serve the different areas was a good place to start.

Vancouver's mayor, Philip Owen, found it painful to endorse the new calls for cooperation and regionalization. Not only was he the chairman of the police board and a strong supporter of Terry Blythe, he had also approved the firing of Kim Rossmo. He hedged on the issue of providing more money for the Missing Women's Task Force that Don Adam was running and he made it clear he would take his direction from Blythe on all these issues. Voluntary cooperation already exists between forces, he told the newspaper. "We look at the whole picture and look at the best expenditure of rather limited public resources these days, that are not going to increase in the next two or three years." Owen and Blythe were far from squawking alone; other municipal leaders were just as reluctant to merge their forces with others or to spend money on computers that could talk to each other.

Don Adam was staying away from the sound and fury drummed up by the *Sun*'s revelations. He believed a serial killer was taking women from the Downtown Eastside. His Missing Women's Joint Task Force had determined there were eighteen more missing women than anyone had expected. He wasn't going to wait around until the various police forces and municipalities got their acts together. It was time to take control of the investigation and do what he thought was necessary.

Looking for some guidance, Adam called police officers in nearby Seattle, Washington, less than two hundred kilometres south of Vancouver. They had carried out a hunt for the man who had murdered at least forty-five women, most of them prostitutes, and left their bodies by the banks of the city's Green River. Because the Green River Killer, as he became known, appeared to have gone on a three-year murder spree that lasted only from 1982 to 1985, many police officers had almost forgotten about him. If they thought about him at all, it was to assume he had stopped. But he surfaced again in 1999, when another woman was found dead by the Green River.

Within a year the Seattle police were beginning to develop new DNA tests that linked killer to victims. Their hope was that these tests would allow them to charge Gary Leon Ridgway, who had worked for thirty years as a truck painter; they were almost certain he was the killer. Ridgway had been the prime suspect since 1983, but no one had ever been able to build a strong enough case to charge or convict him. In 1984 he took a lie-detector test and passed. In 1987 the police asked him to bite on a piece of gauze to get his saliva for blood typing, and he agreed. There was still no proof he had killed anyone. It wasn't until 1997 that DNA matching became elegant enough to compare samples accurately, and by this time the samples had degraded too much to test. Be patient, the scientists told the two police officers still chasing Ridgway. Science will improve. We will get there.

And they did. In April 2001, with new DNA tests available, the Seattle police set up a new Green River Task Force to try one more time to catch the killer. On September 10 new tests matched the DNA from the gauze Ridgway had chewed in 1987 to DNA found on two victims. This was happening just as Don Adam was thinking through DNA issues for his own task force, although the Ridgway news was not yet public and he had not yet been arrested.

Adam knew enough about the Ridgway case to see that it had many similarities to his investigation. The Vancouver case had stretched from as early as 1991, he thought, to the present 2001. At least forty-six women were missing. Almost all the missing women were prostitutes and drug addicts and most of them had been living in the Downtown Eastside when they disappeared. In Seattle the time period stretched from 1982 to 2001, which was much longer, but there also most of the victims were prostitutes; the killer was picking most of them off the highway near the Seattle-Tacoma Airport. Adam also knew that the police had had a man in their sights for many years but couldn't catch him. The time frame in the Canadian situation was similar enough to the Green River case that Adam knew the Americans' experience would be invaluable.

A second case in Washington State was similar enough to the missing women case to make another call worthwhile. Police in Spokane had hunted for years to find the man who had been killing prostitutes from the city's skid row district since 1977. In 1998 they finally caught Robert Yates, a highly decorated U.S. Army helicopter pilot who had served in Germany and Somalia before becoming a civilian pilot. Yates pled guilty to thirteen counts of first-degree murder and was sent to prison. He was now under investigation for two more murders that had happened in 1975 and in 1998, just before he was caught. (Both Ridgway and Yates avoided the death penalty by admitting to their guilt in all the murders.)

The police in both Washington State cities shared their information, insights and advice with Adam and the other officers, a group that included a forensic biologist and a crime analyst. Two years later, Adam described how the Americans had helped and how they had, as he called it, coached their Canadian counterparts. "What we learned from them," he said, "is that a standard investigation, the way we had started ours out, would always be behind an active serial killer, because the carnage that they can create following up on all the tips, tasks and what have you will expend all your energy—so they'll be in front of you. What we needed to do was get in front of them—by being in the area where they prey on their people. Which in our case would be the Downtown Eastside.

"And the realization that we had an ongoing killer operating led investigationally to another step—the potential [exists] that the person will make a mistake and if you follow up the right leads you're going to encounter them. And so we made sure that we would watch for any investigations that had the potential of being a lead-up crime."

And not just watch—they planned to become actively involved in any case that looked remotely like a lead-up crime, "to make sure that the investigations were done right and that we knew what was going on."

Finally, Adam also contacted Margaret Kingsbury's former colleagues in the RCMP's ViCLAS unit to help his team compare characteristics found in violent crimes, including serial murder, that had been logged in their database, and then help identify prime suspects from these linkages.

During the fall of 2001, adding more and more officers to the task force, he moved quickly on all three fronts. The team set up a proactive group of twelve officers in the Downtown Eastside to talk to the women working on the streets, to get to know them, to make them feel comfortable enough to pass on information. They wanted to know who the bad tricks were. Most of all, they wanted to know the prostitutes well enough so they would know right away when one went missing. "Just not to be so far behind the killer," as Adam put it.

The second step in this plan was to begin gathering DNA for matches. Working with the families and the women's friends in the Downtown Eastside, the police were gathering familial DNA where possible and DNA that came from hairbrushes, say, or other belongings of the missing women. They asked families, usually mothers, fathers or children of the missing women, for samples scraped from the inside of their cheeks to compare to DNA they hoped to find later from victims. This DNA from family members is often described as secondary DNA.

For primary DNA—samples from the women themselves—the investigators went to see Dr. Jasenka Matisic, a pathologist at the British Columbia Cancer Centre, on West Broadway in Vancouver.

Every day Canada Post and other carriers deliver about 2,500 slides to the centre, each one bearing the Pap smear of a woman in British Columbia. These are tested for cancer cells and saved; the positive tests are stored indefinitely and the negative ones are kept for seven years. These smears from their bodies contained their primary DNA, which could not be questioned or doubted, DNA that could definitively identify the missing women should the police ever find any trace of them. Their DNA might be found in blood on a jacket, a body part, a tooth, lipstick or underwear . . . the smallest thing that might contain a trace of blood, saliva, a hair root, marrow from a bone. So many of the women had been gone for so long that the police knew they might not find much left of their bodies.

Many people find it surprising that the Downtown Eastside's prostitutes and drug addicts would have Pap smears to start with, and that their samples would be at the cancer centre. But that's because people don't understand how much sense it makes. With an intensity that few other women could understand, the women of the Downtown Eastside worked hard to stay alive. Almost every one of them had an alphabet soup of hepatitis, usually A, B and C. Many of them were HIV-positive and some had full-blown AIDS. Most had skin lesions and sores; their immune systems were shot. The result? They lined up in clinics for prescriptions for painkillers, antibiotics for infections and dressings for abscesses. They picked up their methadone every day from pharmacies when they were trying to kick their heroin addiction. They visited the Health Van every day for medical attention. They went to their doctors regularly. They were often in hospital, usually brought in by ambulance or taxi, to be treated for beatings, overdoses, malnutrition or cocaine psychosis. When they went missing, it was often a doctor or a nurse who alerted their families first because the woman had not turned up for an appointment or to pick up a prescription. No one should have been surprised that these women, sex-trade workers all, also made sure they kept their appointments for regular Pap tests.

What Adam and his team feared most, knowing what they did

now, was "someone being able to wear a mask of being normal, someone without a criminal record. That was our worst-case scenario." So the next major job, the third in their overall strategy, was building a big list of suspects. They began by looking at lesser crimes such as sex assaults or attempted murders. In all, Adam's team reviewed four thousand sexual assaults and obtained DNA for many of them.

Their biggest concern was making sure they cast their net wide enough to capture the killer. "If the killer was outside it," Adam told people, "all the police efforts would be to no avail." And what they needed to watch for, what they needed to expect, was that their killer would make a mistake. If we follow the right leads, Adam told his team, we will find the mistakes.

Despite the valuable advice they had received from the Green River team and the progress they made as they implemented it, the challenge was still grim. As the British Columbia task force members buried themselves in the evidence and the data, they felt overwhelmed. There was no centralized provincial police computer system that could cross-reference information. They had to deal with six municipal police forces and several RCMP detachments on the Lower Mainland, without any formal, structured way to work together. After reviewing the existing records of 107 murders of sex-trade workers in British Columbia, task force members counted 52 as unresolved cases. Along with these were a number of what Adam called "hitchhiker murders"—people who had been willing, like so many of skid row's prostitutes, to climb into a stranger's car. As they examined the files of possible suspects and moved them into the piles designated priority one, two and three, Willie Pickton's name was moved into the priority one file. He had not been put there previously because the police had eliminated him in 1995 as a suspect in the three Valley Murders, and they couldn't bring themselves to consider that more than one serial killer might be at work. As Adam said later, "He didn't rate higher than the others." But now, when they considered his attack on Sandra Gail Ringwald and the suspicions of Project Amelia investigators such as Lori Shenher, he was upgraded to priority one.

Some members of the task force continued with the file review of old cases, but, heeding the advice of the American police to get ahead of the killer, Adam moved the rest of his team to ongoing crimes. They watched all new missing-person reports closely. When they decided their own group could do a better job of investigating the new disappearances, they would be "right on the front cutting edge of those investigations," Adam said. "If they were homicides, we might turn something up that the City, being resource-strapped, wouldn't be able to turn up." And each time, he added, they would be alert "to anything that looked like a lead-up crime to the abduction of a woman and her potential murder."

Just as important as the investigative steps the new team had taken in the fall of 2001 was Don Adam's decision to make peace with the victims' families. It was time, he decided, to meet with them—all of them, even families whose missing women were not on the official list. In early October the task force contacted forty-three families to plan a get-together for October 14 at the Delta Vancouver Airport Hotel in Richmond, just across the Fraser River from the Vancouver Airport. RCMP sergeant Wayne Clary explained the reasoning behind the meeting to the *Sun*'s Lori Culbert. "As we move along in this file it's getting bigger and bigger," he said. "And [the meeting] is a bridge that had to be crossed, as far as the victims' families go. So, what we've decided to do is maintain contact with them. We wanted to just have a meeting to introduce ourselves—this is who we are and this is what we are doing."

It was a watershed decision. From that moment on the task force was in touch with the families on a regular basis. Not that all the meetings were friendly, or even cordial; they were always full of tension, tears, dread and hope.

This first meeting, with fifty family members and ten police officers, lasted four hours. No reporters were allowed in. After the officers introduced themselves to the families, they brought them up to date on the state of the investigation. The biggest surprise was the news that the police had identified six hundred possible suspects and were now tracking down evidence for each one of them. This meant they would need to bring more officers into the investigation. Although several family members vented their anger and frustration during the long session, most left the meeting feeling reassured, believing that the police finally cared about the missing women and were determined to find the killer.

Dawn Crey's brother, Ernie, said he had asked if the Vancouver police and the RCMP were working together and if this was a serious investigation. "And I left reassured, for now," he said, "that that seems to be the case, that it's going to happen, that they're going to do a good job."

Sarah de Vries's sister, Maggie, also left the meeting feeling better than she had when she arrived. "I believe them that they are going to do everything they can to find the person or persons responsible for the murders of the missing women and to find out what happened to the women and where their bodies are," she told Lindsay Kines. "I was afraid that it was going to feel today like being patted on the head . . . but I didn't really feel that. It's encouraging that they are, truly, all of them working full time on this case only. And that was never the case before."

On October 15, 2001, the day after the meeting at the Delta, the Vancouver police and the RCMP made the announcement that the families and, indeed, the city had been waiting to hear for years. They were treating the disappearances of forty-six women as murders.

CHAPTER THIRTY

POLICE ON TRIAL

All anyone in Vancouver could talk about in October 2001 was the sensational *Vancouver Sun* series. It shocked the city and it frightened a number of police officers who feared more media scrutiny. Some worried the situation would go beyond bad publicity to dismissals, charges being laid, careers ending in disgrace and financial ruin. It also galvanized the missing women's families into demanding action and it gave Don Adam's task force the publicity and legitimacy it needed to move ahead quickly. But the series may also have given the city a sense of false security. There had been no disappearances since Sereena Abotsway vanished on August 1, and it seemed almost as if the public had turned a page on the case. It was over. Now it was time to clean up the police force and bring the killer to justice.

It also seemed as if the timing couldn't be better for resumption of Kim Rossmo's wrongful dismissal case against the Vancouver police—better, that is, for Rossmo. Catastrophic for the police. In fact, it was not good for either side. Ultimately Rossmo didn't succeed in his attempt to win back his job and receive compensation for his legal costs. Justice Marion Allan concluded, later that fall, that under contract law the police had the right to refuse to renew his expired contract as a detective inspector. Nor did they have to pay his lawyer's bills. But because he had emerged with his reputation intact or even, as most people would argue, enhanced, and because he was now working for the Police Foundation in Washington, he had a highly paid job with plenty of prestige. The Vancouver Police Department, on the other hand, emerged from the trial with its reputation badly damaged. And some of that had nothing at all to do with Rossmo.

It began with a story the *Sun* had run in August about Murray Phillips, a VPD detective who in 1998 had worked for three weeks in California with two American policemen; it was a murder case involving a defendant who had an apartment in Vancouver. According to documents filed in a U.S. court by the defendant's lawyers, Phillips had broken the law several times while he was there. He had, the documents stated, withheld evidence when he asked for a search warrant; used cocaine during a search of a suspect's apartment and fell asleep there; used an expired search warrant for a telephone records search; and had sex in a karaoke bar with a prostitute.

After an internal investigation by eight officers and a sergeant, the VPD suspended Phillips in August 1998; he went on administrative leave and then on medical leave. This much *Sun* readers knew by October 16, 2001, when Deputy Chief Constable Gary Greer took the stand in the Rossmo case. What Greer did, under questioning by Rossmo's lawyer, was expose the sweet secret deal that protected Phillips's pay and pension. Chief Constable Terry Blythe had agreed, he testified, not to fire Phillips or to take any disciplinary action against him; instead Phillips would be allowed to use up all his sick leave until he qualified for his pension and retired.

As Murray Tevlin pointed out to Justice Allan, the sordid tale showed the difference between how the two officers had been treated. A man who had been on the force for twenty-two years and had acted discreditably was allowed to stay on sick leave for another four and a half years, until he could retire quietly with his full pension. Another man, himself a twenty-two-year veteran, who had brought international recognition and praise to the VPD was dismissed five years short of the time he needed to earn his full retirement benefits. In the days that followed these revelations, Mayor Philip Owen, who was still the chair of the police board, and Chief Constable Terry Blythe blamed each other for the fiasco. Blythe testified that the non-disclosure agreement he had with

Phillips prevented him from discussing the situation. Despite an avalanche of public criticism, media commentary and demands from Rossmo's lawyer, neither Blythe nor Owen would reveal any details of the deal given to Phillips.

Fighting on another front, Blythe said in court that Ken Doern, one of Rossmo's supporters, had lied earlier in the case when he testified in June that Blythe had punished him with demeaning assignments. In court the following day, Rossmo's nemesis, Deputy Chief Constable John Unger, also accused a fellow officer, Sergeant Grant Smith, of lying in his testimony when he gave evidence in June. That was when Smith said he'd joked about Rossmo's new PhD and Unger had said, "I don't care what you call him; he'll never be an officer of this force and he'll never be a member of the officers' mess." When Murray Tevlin asked Unger about this event, Unger said he never said that and that Smith was lying. Hour after hour, the denials and accusations flew back and forth in the courtroom. Justice Allan was asked to allow a new witness to testify, an officer who had read that Unger denied making such a statement to Grant Smith. This new witness was prepared to swear that Unger had told him he would lie if asked about the comment. Justice Allan refused to hear the witness.

It took Allan two months to deliver her judgment on the case. It had been a sensational inside look at a dysfunctional police department that had made a disastrous hash of the missing women file and had fired the officer who warned them a serial killer was on the loose in the Downtown Eastside. Accusations of lying had been hurled from both sides. It had not only been ugly and a public relations nightmare but in the wake of the missing women fiasco it made the police look criminally irresponsible. But Allan did not give Kim Rossmo the verdict he hoped for and expected; the police had the right not to renew his expired contract, and they did not need to give him a reason.

"I find that the board neither 'promoted' Kim Rossmo to the substantive rank of Inspector nor 'demoted' him at the conclusion of the [contract]," she wrote in her decision. And there was a sting in one comment she made about Rossmo, when she stated that his lawyer offered evidence that was, as she put it, "more relevant to his apparent desire to embarrass the VPD than to a determination of the legal issues of this case."

While her comments were a major blow to Rossmo, Justice Allan saved her toughest words for the police. Deputy Chief John Unger's behaviour in Rossmo's case had been "inappropriate," she said. And she believed Sergeant Grant Smith's story about Unger's outburst against Rossmo. "I prefer Smith's version of events," she wrote in her judgment. "Sergeant Smith, who had no reason to fabricate such a story, gave his evidence in a forthright manner, without embellishment. Unger was unconvincing in his denial that he had an animus towards Rossmo." The judge was sharply critical of Unger's actions on other occasions, especially in his efforts to fire Rossmo just as two of his supporters were leaving the police board and would not be able to argue against the dismissal.

In fact, Justice Allan was so critical of John Unger that she issued a judicial rebuke to him and told the police board they would have to pay legal costs for the trial. She spared Rossmo his own court costs although he still had to pay Murray Tevlin's bills, which were $200,000. It was almost impossible for Kim Rossmo to see her decision as anything but a humiliating defeat and a financial catastrophe. He took no comfort in the words she wrote about the police, but in later years they would stand out. Other officers were jealous of him, Allan declared. "Almost immediately after Rossmo's appointment, dissension surfaced in the officer ranks. This resentment meant many senior officers did not make full use of geographic profiling—an internationally recognized tool—to fight crime in Vancouver. In one case, Rossmo sent out a survey to other inspectors asking how often they thought they would make requests of his new unit. One Inspector returned the form with zeros in every category and another Inspector declined to respond at all," wrote the judge. "That resistance was unwarranted. Rossmo's skills and expertise were under-utilized locally for the types of criminal investigations that were particularly suited to geographic profiling."

The fact that this bitter case had been fought in open court while the biggest serial murder case in Canadian history was finally under investigation by a large, skilled team was not lost on anyone. Kim Rossmo's geographic profiling skills could have made a difference much earlier—years earlier—but he was never asked or encouraged to help in any way. Instead he worked on cases in foreign countries where the police were glad to have his expertise; he also trained geographic profilers in other countries and jurisdictions so they could help find serial predators. His software was sophisticated and mathematically driven but his thesis was simple: serial predators, whether they be killers, bombers, rapists or arsonists, peeping toms or child molesters, all tend to work in the areas where they are most comfortable, where they are most at home. Put together a list of your top suspects, plot the places where the crimes happened and the place where the suspect lives, and the software will show you the prime suspect: the person whose home is nearest the probable crime scene. It allows the police to eliminate many suspects and focus on the most likely ones, the ones at the top of the list. And almost always the computer's first choice is the right person.

How could this have helped identify Pickton? He wasn't killing women in the Downtown Eastside, where he picked them up. But most people in the neighbourhood, including the police, knew he was taking them to his farm in Port Coquitlam. That was never a secret. And they knew he had nearly killed a woman in his house, because he had been charged with attempted murder back in 1997 of Sandra Gail Ringwald after she arrived at the New Westminster hospital with no pulse and almost no blood left in her body. The night they found the key to the handcuffs in Pickton's pocket.

And the police had been tipped off by at least three people, Bill Hiscox, Lynn Ellingsen and Scott Chubb, that Willie Pickton took prostitutes from the Downtown Eastside to his place. By Kim Rossmo's standard—by anyone's standard—that was where Pickton felt most comfortable, which is why the police had mounted surveillance on him and why they'd tried to get a warrant to search his place.

The only good thing about the police failures, people believed now, as the Rossmo court case was over and the Missing Women's Task Force was steaming ahead, was that the killer, whoever he was, had stopped. Six women had disappeared since January 2001; the last one, Sereena Abotsway, hadn't been seen since August 1. The Downtown Eastside community hoped—almost dared to assume—that all the publicity had frightened the man off. Then they found out that Diane Rock, the mother of five children, had vanished from her room in the Marr Hotel in October, just as the Rossmo case was winding up. Nobody had seen her or heard from her since October 19.

Her former boyfriend, a thirty-four-year-old longshoreman named Vince McMurchy, told people he knew she had disappeared right away, because his birthday was October 20 and she hadn't called him to wish him a happy birthday. Even though he'd kicked her out of their home months earlier, told her she'd be better off dead, told her she was a piece of crap and never to call him again, he remained convinced that because she didn't phone him on his birthday, well, she had to be dead. Picking McMurchy for a boyfriend was just one of the bad choices Diane Rock had made in her short life.

Diane was a beautiful woman with a tender heart, adored by her family and by almost everyone who ever met her. Born to a teenager in 1967 in the small southwestern Ontario town of Welland, which lies between Hamilton and Niagara Falls, Diane arrived at Ella and Denis Marin's house when she was about four weeks old. Her teenaged mother had asked her girlfriend, the Marins' fourteen-year-old daughter Denise, to babysit Diane for a little while. But when Ella, who worked as a nurse's aide, realized the baby had a bad cold, she insisted that mother and baby stay with her family for a few days until the baby was better. The young mother gratefully accepted

Ella's help and the few days turned into two years. The Marin family, including two older children who had moved out before Diane arrived, worshipped her; she was a cheerful, sweet child with dark curly hair, large almond-shaped eyes and a gentle disposition. They wanted her as part of their family forever. Ella and Denis, who were devout Roman Catholics, knew the young mom couldn't take care of her properly, and finally the girl agreed they could adopt her.

"My mom spoiled Diane," remembers Lilliane Marin. Everyone did. It was a big family in a small working-class city, with plenty of aunts, uncles and cousins, and no one could resist her. Only when she reached her own teenage years were there problems; Diane was strong-willed, full of mischief and fun. And history repeated itself when, at sixteen, she had a baby girl of her own, a lovely child she named Melissa. The Marins set her up in an apartment in their house and helped her take care of the child.

A year later Denis Marin, who had worked as a crane operator most of his life, died, and times became tougher for the family. Diane dropped out of school; soon she was expecting a second child. She decided to marry the father, and after a traditional church wedding with a garden reception at home, Diane couldn't have been happier. She called the second baby, a boy, Donnie. And soon she had a third baby to take care of, a little girl she christened Carol-Ann. Soon her marriage broke down; the father took off and Diane was left with three children to care for. But Diane had no education to speak of, no real work experience and no money until Ella was able to get her a nurse's aide job in the nursing home where she was working. It still wasn't enough. What could she do to earn enough money to look after her kids?

Finally she chose one job she could do after the kids were in bed, looked after by relatives. She began working nights as a table dancer. "Diane was dancing in bars to make a living," states her sister Lilliane, who had married a man named René Beaudoin and settled in Welland. "She was even dancing when she was seven months pregnant, just to make a living; she never showed much."

She began using drugs; they were easy to come by in the bars where she worked. But she was smart enough to know she needed to fix her life. She moved with her kids to nearby Brantford, but things weren't much better—more bars, more drugs, more worries. She met a man there named Darren Rock and fell hard for him. They married and decided to start a new life together in British Columbia; his father ran a paving business there and had plenty of work for his son. For Diane this was the fresh new start she'd prayed for. The family moved to Vancouver in 1992 and she and Darren had two boys, Darren and Justin, tow-headed little guys just like their dad.

Diane looked for work right away and found a job in Abbotsford, a small Fraser Valley city sixty-four kilometres east of Vancouver, with the Mennonite Central Committee, looking after mentally handicapped adults. Her managers liked her and described her work as exceptional. A few years later, in 1998, Diane left to do a similar job with the MSA Society for Community Living in Abbotsford; at the same time she was studying part-time to qualify as a registered nursing assistant. But by 2000 Darren wasn't working very often, and once more Diane was trying to manage two jobs. Soon, with the strain of five kids, exhaustion and too little money, the marriage was falling apart. Darren and Diane separated and Diane started using drugs again.

Diane's daughter, Carol-Ann, was only twelve when she realized that her mother was on crack cocaine. Within a year Diane was sometimes staying out all night, leaving her little boys, five and ten, in Carol-Ann's care. Carol-Ann couldn't cope and called her father; Darren immediately took the boys to live with him. Melissa and Donnie, Diane's two oldest children by her first husband, had been on their own for some time; Carol-Ann was the only child from that marriage still at home.

"She was a good woman," Carol-Ann told Cheryl Stepan and Jocelyn Bell, reporters at the *Hamilton Spectator* who interviewed her years later. "She was a very, very good woman. She took care of us very well at first. She couldn't handle the drugs. She was not capable of taking care of anybody—not even herself—at the time." Carol-Ann stayed with her mother as long as she could stand it; eventually she moved back to Welland, where she felt safe with her large and welcoming family of aunts, uncles, grandmother and cousins.

Diane was falling faster and faster. In March or April of that year, Janice Edwards, a close friend and co-worker at the MSA Society, got a phone call; it was a desperate Diane begging her to come and get her in Port Coquitlam. Edwards raced in from Abbotsford, and while she can't remember exactly where she picked Diane up, when she found her she'd been roughed up and her body was covered with bruises. Diane didn't want to talk about what had happened; all she said was that she had been at a party on a farm and now she just wanted to go home.

Soon afterwards, in May 2000, Diane was hanging out in a popular New Westminster bar called Chicago Tonight; it shared space with Mugs and Jugs, a second bar in the College Place Hotel on Carnarvon Street, just a short block from the Supreme Court building. This is where Diane met Vince McMurchy. They started seeing each other regularly; his story is that after she poured out her troubles to him, he invited her to live with him and have the kids come too. Finally she agreed and moved in with him in October 2000. But McMurchy was bad news; Diane's friends believed him to be a drug dealer and they blamed him for getting her back on drugs.

For years Ella Marin had visited her daughter in B.C. When she arrived in February 2001, she was horrified by Diane's deterioration. Losing her children had nearly destroyed her; she missed days of work, her need for drugs had taken over and she even stole money from Ella to buy them. Janice Edwards was distressed to see her show up at work with bruises on her arms; there were times, Diane admitted, that she'd leave McMurchy and look for help at a women's shelter. Vince was threatening her, she told Edwards.

"He said he should just put her in a body bag and dump her body somewhere, that she would be better off dead," Edwards said later. "And Diane had told me before that he had threatened

to put her in a body bag and dump her body in Ladner somewhere." She added that McMurchy had actually driven Diane out
to Ladner, a Vancouver suburb on the south bank of the Fraser,
and showed her where he would dump her body. Edwards was so
angry that she phoned McMurchy and demanded that he stop
giving Diane money. Her reasoning was that if Diane didn't have
money she couldn't buy drugs. Maybe that would help her get
into recovery. McMurchy's response, said Edwards, was that this
was his way of controlling her. "And if he couldn't have her, no
one else would."

But McMurchy hadn't entirely given up on her. One night in
June 2001 he took Diane to a bar in Burnaby, a place just off the
Lougheed Highway. They ran into one of McMurchy's friends,
who suggested they move on to an after-hours booze can in Port
Coquitlam; it turned out to be the Hells Angels blue wood-frame
clubhouse on Dominion Avenue, right across the road from the
Pickton farm. Youngsters outside directed their car into the large
parking lot behind the house; when they walked into the house the
music was bouncing off the walls and the place was crammed with
at least a hundred people dancing, drinking and smoking dope.
And they found a large bar—drinks at five dollars a shot—with
bartenders rushing to keep up with the demand.

Whether McMurchy finally threw Diane out, which is what he
says, or she fled of her own accord isn't known, but leave him she
did, with no place to go. For a while she stayed with a friend but
soon, drug-sick and desperate, weighing just over a hundred pounds,
she wound up in the Downtown Eastside. She found a room, first at
the Biltmore Hotel and then later at the Marr Hotel, the infamous
drug-infested dump owned by the Hells Angels on Oppenheimer
Park. And that is when Diane began to prostitute herself to make
enough money for her drugs.

In August 2001 Janice Edwards's phone rang. It was Diane and
she was hysterical. Come and get me, she begged. I'm in Port
Coquitlam. I'm at the gas station across from the mall.

It's only a twenty-minute drive from Abbotsford to Port Coquitlam. Edwards headed for a small strip mall where the Lougheed Highway meets Ottawa Street, the north–south street that bisects the mall. Diane told Janice she would be in a white van and that she would be dropped off at the gas station near the corner of Ottawa and the Lougheed.

When Diane tumbled into Janice's car, she was almost incoherent, but gradually she was able to tell her story. "I made a really big mistake," she sobbed. "I went to a party out at this farm where the girls got free drugs. And I ended up in a room and I was raped by these guys. It was a lot of different guys. I was pretty high myself. I got locked in this room somewhere. For two or three days. The windows in the room were blacked out. It was in a basement . . . a room with blacked-out windows. And I was raped by all these guys."

As Diane spilled out her story, all Janice wanted to do was get her to a hospital. She could see that her friend's lip was swollen and her arms were badly bruised. So were her legs. And her blue summer dress was ripped, filthy and ruined. "It looked like she had a lot of restraints or burns or whatever around her wrists," remembered Janice. "She had a lot of marks on her arms. She was wearing a short-sleeved dress so she was a mess. Her dress was torn in the back and she was a mess, literally. Her hair didn't look like it had been combed in a day or two and she looked pretty bad. In all the time I've known her I've never seen her look like that."

So Janice argued with Diane: You have to go to the hospital now. No, Diane said, no. "She was very afraid," Janice remembered later. "She wouldn't go to the hospital and she wouldn't go to the police. She said she couldn't. And I asked her why and she just . . . she . . . we cried a lot."

Diane soon returned to the Downtown Eastside, but when her daughter Carol-Ann went looking for her in the summer of 2001, she couldn't find her. Carol-Ann was only fourteen years old when she travelled to Vancouver from Welland and started searching through the streets of the Downtown Eastside, showing pictures of her mom to crackheads and street people. "It was really scary down there," she told Cheryl Stepan and Jocelyn Bell in the interview she gave them the following year. "But I wanted my mom back. I couldn't live without her . . . They didn't want to stop and talk to me. It was the worst place I've ever seen in my life. I've never seen so many faceless people." Carol-Ann never found Diane, and Diane didn't find her either.

But Diane saw Vince McMurchy again, twice. Once was when he met her to turn over her welfare cheque; these went to McMurchy's mother's house and she would hang on to them until Diane could pick them up. McMurchy wanted her to cash it right away so she could pay him back money he claimed she owed him.

The second time was in mid-September 2001, when they met at the SkyTrain station in Surrey, the last stop on the line. Diane, as McMurchy told the story, wanted to come back to him. "She wanted to change and she wanted another chance, and I said no, and she said, 'I guess I'm some other guy's problem now.' And I said, 'I guess you are,' and she gave me a hug and left on the SkyTrain back to Vancouver. That's fine with me. I had—I had no feelings for the woman at that time."

By now Diane had lost her children, her home and her job. She had even lost the journals she had kept over the years; they were with her things in McMurchy's house and, after reading them, McMurchy threw them all out. Diane's welfare cheques continued to pile up at McMurchy's mother's house. She never called to ask for them. She phoned her son Justin on October 17 to wish him a happy birthday, and after that no one in her family heard from her again. She was last seen on October 19, 2001.

CHAPTER THIRTY-ONE

THE LAST WOMAN

Because Diane Rock was a relative newcomer to skid row, her disappearance passed without much comment in the community. They simply didn't know her. The regular routines of an addicted sex-trade worker—visits to the medical staff at the Portland Hotel, meetings with welfare workers, meals at the Women's Centre, stops at the Health Van, even conversations with the neighbourhood cops—hadn't yet become Diane's routines. But a month later, when Mona Wilson didn't come back from a date, people knew right away.

Mona, who was twenty-six years old and used the street name Stacey, was a fixture in the Downtown Eastside. The last time anyone remembers seeing her was November 23, 2001; she was reported missing seven days later, on November 30. Still, it was her failure to contact her family at Christmas that finally convinced her sister, Ada Wilson, that something had happened to her.

Mona was the youngest of five children in an aboriginal family from Alberta's O'Chiese First Nation. Ada was the second youngest, and they were always close. When Mona was only six years old, social workers found her, beaten and terrified, in the corridor of an apartment building; they removed her right away and placed her in a youth treatment centre. Two years later she moved into a foster home, but by the time she arrived there, according to members of her new foster family, she had been through more trauma and sexual abuse than any other foster child they had ever known. "She had never been to school," her foster brother Greg Garley told one reporter. "All she knew was profanity." And on one occasion, he said, Mona's mother had even tried to hang her.

The move to Norma and Ken Garley's hobby farm in Surrey couldn't have been more successful. Mona was happy there. Loved and cared for at last, sharing treats and holiday trips, she began to trust people and she began to learn how to be a child. Despite having four of their own kids and several foster children to look after, the Garleys had become the parents she needed. They enjoyed her tomboy nature, her love of the farm animals, her eagerness to join in family activities and her pleasure in the simple routine of going to school every day.

Summer camp, according to a girl who knew her then, was another treat. In a posting to a family members' website, a woman named Dawn wrote that Mona "was so much fun at camp because she got to be a kid. She was so curious and full of spunk. She loved to challenge the adults who were caring for her but also had good connections with some of them. When she didn't get her way she would take off through the woods and the staff would have to follow her to make sure she was safe. She would run through the woods laughing because she enjoyed it when the staff chased her."

Another poster, a woman named Helen Campbell, wrote about being a good friend of Mona's in grades five and six at school in Surrey. "I always remember her and thought of her often and always wondered where she had moved to . . . We had some good times together did some terrible things and also some good things. LOL."

But Mona's life was to follow the same sad pattern endured by Sereena Abotsway and Angela Jardine. Though she was easy to deal with when she was young, Mona, like Sereena and Angela, became unmanageable in her teen years. The Garleys believed she was tormented by memories of the sexual abuse she had suffered as a child. They tried to comfort and understand her; they tried to make sure she stayed in touch with a brother and sister who had been close to her. But when she reached her teens they couldn't cope; she wasn't just disobedient, she also became violent.

Just as Bert and Anna Draayers had been forced to do with Sereena, the Garleys finally had to tell child-care workers that they didn't know how to manage Mona. A hard decision followed, one that must have been as traumatic for the Garleys as it was for Mona, who was sent to live in the care of a new foster mother with a teenage son. This transition, during which Mona was very unhappy, lasted for two years, until she turned sixteen; at this point she was allowed to live independently in East Vancouver with some assistance from social services. But the new arrangement—one very much like the arrangements made for Angela, who was eighteen when she was settled into an institution in Haney, and Sereena, who was moved into a group home when the Draayers could no longer manage her—failed, just as Angela's and Sereena's arrangements had failed. And like the two other girls, Mona began using heroin. She quickly became a serious addict.

By her late teens Mona, now a young woman with thick dark hair, large, expressive eyes and a warm smile, was living in the Downtown Eastside, prostituting herself to pay for her drugs. She had no trouble finding dates but she was unlucky in her choice of boyfriend. His name was Steve Rix, and Elaine Allan came to know him when he accompanied Mona to WISH every night, waiting outside until she had showered, eaten her supper and dressed for work. Rix was an obnoxious, aggressive bully. He would stand outside WISH and yell for Mona, and when she stuck her head out the door, he'd screech, "You fucking bitch! Get out here! And bring me something to eat."

"She fought with him every day," Allan remembers. "It was just part of going to work. And we were always telling him to get the hell off the [church] stairs, be respectful . . . and sometimes we would have to call the police." Allan finally had to keep Mona out of WISH for a while just to get rid of Steve. But that didn't work.

"Then he was barred altogether from First United to put pressure on him to chill out," Allan remembers. "Mona would come in and talk to me and cry. He used to make her walk five paces behind him. I helped her get into a safe house in Richmond for a while but it didn't last. She had problems getting along with other girls and she was depressed. By the time she disappeared her teeth were all rotten. She would have been a lovely girl if she hadn't been so drug-addicted." And Mona had desperately wanted to kick her habit. She begged Allan for help getting into a detox centre and following up with rehabilitation, but Allan could never find a space for her.

This was nothing new. There never seemed to be any spaces for the women who asked Elaine Allan and Bonnie Fournier to help them kick their addictions. All there was in the Downtown Eastside was a small room in the Salvation Army hostel, a room with four cots separated by thin cotton sheets strung on a line and an adjoining closet with just enough space for two more cots. Once the women had gone through detox here—which usually took about four terrifying days of sweating, chills, throwing up and diarrhea—they were dumped back on the streets, because it was even more difficult to find a rehab centre for follow-up treatment and counselling. Lacking immediate rehab, they would leave the Sally Ann shelter with no place to go except their old life on the streets and the desperate desire for a fix.

Even when welfare workers could find a centre to take them in right away, these were often run by vicious owners working on contract for the government. One favourite trick was to take the welfare money and then find excuses to throw the women out a day or two after they arrived. The money was never refunded, of course. Treatment was often a joke; some of the centres enjoyed a brisk trade in drugs and the women would be hooked again, instantly. But sometimes the centres were caring and helpful and sometimes they did help women kick their addictions. Mona, unfortunately, never found such a place.

Steve Rix says he was the last person to see her before she disappeared; it was the night of November 23, 2001. Mona was just getting into a car with two men who said they didn't want to have sex with her but would pay for her time. Rix told people that the men chased him off with a piece of wood but he couldn't remember who they were.

Who knows what bits of truth were in Steve Rix's statements? After all, he tried to suggest they had a happy, cozy life together. "We had a place . . . for two months before she went missing," he told the *Vancouver Sun*. "We had a nice place. A warm apartment in a basement suite with a nice bed and TV. We weren't homeless."

He couldn't resist painting himself as her guardian, her protector, her knight in shining armour. "She didn't want me to control her, so I said, 'Okay, fine, I'll spot for you,'" he jabbered on to the *Sun*. "'Anytime you go out I'm coming' and I looked every bastard in the eye when she got in a car and I made sure they knew I knew who they were. I told her, 'The reason you're alive is because I'm here. If I wasn't here, you'd be dead.'"

Elaine Allan doesn't believe a word Rix says. "Steve was a parasite and he didn't do anything to support himself or his drug habit. If Mona hadn't disappeared she would have dropped dead from being worked to death by Steve." Now he was forced to support himself, which he did as a squeegee guy who sometimes worked on Robson Street but was more often to be found harassing drivers at the corner of Main and Terminal.

When Mona Wilson was reported missing a week later, on November 30, 2001, the police paid attention. Don Adam assigned John Cater to her case and asked him to concentrate on possible suspects. Mona had been missing for only a few days and the trail seemed fresh.

Maybe, if this had been Cater's only job at the time, he might have been able to follow up with all of Mona's closest associates in the Downtown Eastside. As it was, he was still working on a system for storing exhibits. There was just too much to do. Information was beginning to flow in from the twelve-person proactive team in the Downtown Eastside. They were also collecting the DNA of the missing women. By this time it would have been only human for the task force members to sympathize with their overworked, understaffed predecessors on Project Amelia.

By this time the task force had about a hundred suspects at the top of their list after reviewing the files of six hundred possible men, all of whom had been convicted of violent assaults against women. They eliminated many of those simply through tedious fact-checking, such as combing through arrest records; these showed whether the suspects were in jail or out of the area when the women disappeared.

To do this very picky work, they needed good computer programs. The RCMP had something known as E&R, for Evidence and Reports, but Adam didn't like it because there wasn't enough technical support available to make it a practical system for his task force. He wanted a big-league computer system. The Vancouver Police Department was using a program called SIUSS, or Specialized Investigative Unit Support System, which had been developed in the United States; the task force decided this was better for them. They sank $100,000 into buying a licence and training people on it, but it proved to be a frustrating choice. "It moved at a snail's pace," complained Adam, "and it wasn't a product that could travel at the speed we needed." Still, that's what they had, so for a while they made do with it. Once all the information about each suspect had been entered, the program could analyze the data and show if the suspect had any connection to the case they were investigating. Soon, however, the task force became so frustrated with SIUSS that they went back to their old Evidence and Reports system.

Adam also asked Keith Davidson for help. Davidson, an RCMP inspector, had been trained as a criminal profiler, that much-reviled species of expert held in contempt by so many police officers.* There were very few in Canada at the time, and only the RCMP's Ron MacKay and the Ontario Provincial Police's Kate Lines had been trained at the FBI's headquarters in Quantico, Virginia. MacKay had trained Davidson, and if the task force hadn't been desperate—after all, he was a friend of Kim Rossmo, also a profiler, albeit a geographical profiler—they probably would have ignored his skills.

---

*Keith Davidson helped organize the ill-fated Project Eclipse exercise in Vancouver in 1991.

But like Marg Kingsbury, he was also a believer in ViCLAS and had even helped design the software, so his technical knowledge would be a godsend.

She doesn't remember the exact date, but sometime late in 2001 Terrie Gratton climbed into Willie Pickton's truck. At the time Terrie was living in a tiny, immaculate room on Powell Street in the Downtown Eastside, just a couple of blocks from the waterfront. Terrie's kids lived in Alberta, and her room was decorated with snapshots of them and mementoes—notes, cards, little gifts. An intelligent, well-read and funny woman, Terrie loves to show off her children, and it tore her apart that she couldn't be with them; her face twists with grief when she talks about what a mess her life is. A long-time drug addict, Terrie also suffers from serious asthma; although she later had to use a portable oxygen tank, in 2001 she could still manage to get around without one, as long as she stopped frequently to catch her breath.

Willie Pickton had one or two other women in his truck the night he stopped to see if she'd come too; despite the warning bell that went off in her head again and again, the usual promise of free drugs and decent money proved too good to pass up. Terrie agreed to go to the farm with him for a hundred dollars. She remembers him well, and she remembers his truck. "It was a brownish yellow thing, a pickup, and he used to park in the side streets and watch all the girls."

When she got into the front seat, however, the smell of the animals that had been carried around in his truck was so pungent and thick that she couldn't breathe. "I smelled it right away," she said. "It stunk of dog—wet, dirty dog—and it stunk like animals. And my asthma got worse right away . . . the truck was awful." As the full asthma attack hit, Terrie screeched so loudly to get out of the vehicle that Willie finally stopped, but he belted her across the face before she could get out. Gasping and crying, she staggered home.

Terrie decided against reporting the attack to the police. What good would it do? She'd tried that before—on March 12, 1999, to be exact, after she had been savagely raped and beaten for nearly two hours by a Burnaby truck driver named Lance Dove, who had picked her up late on a Friday night. When he let her out of his car, she managed to memorize most of his licence plate number and took it to Elaine Allan at WISH. Elaine immediately called the police. Three hours later an officer got back to them. The police were eventually able to track down Dove's cellphone number and phoned him twice over the next six months to ask him to come in for questioning. He didn't bother. On August 3, 1999, the day he received the second call, he picked up Kimberly Ann Tracey, a twenty-eight-year-old mother, in a bar in Burnaby and offered to walk her home. Instead, he raped her in a vacant lot and beat her to death, punching and kicking her so ferociously that the police had to use her fingerprints to identify her body.

Terrie was racked by guilt when she heard about Kimberly's murder. Even though she knew she was not to blame, she still believed, deep down, that it was her fault. If the police hadn't phoned Dove again that day because of her repeated requests for them to do something, Terrie thought he might not have taken out his rage on an innocent young woman.

CHAPTER THIRTY-TWO

THE ROOKIE COP

During the last few weeks of 2001, events began to overlap. Mona Wilson vanished. Terrie Gratton survived a close call when she scrambled out of Willie Pickton's van. And Don Adam's team was working feverishly to narrow down the key suspects in what they all knew had to be the biggest serial killing case in Canadian history. This one, they thought, could even be bigger than the Green River case. Public pressure was intense; reporters from Europe and the United States were beginning to follow the case closely. The police needed a break. When it came, it was almost by accident.

To say that Scott Chubb and his common-law wife, Tasha, weren't getting along is an understatement. By November 2001 they had been separated for months and Tasha was living in Port Coquitlam with their son, Cody. Although Chubb had worked hard to kick his addiction to cocaine and now had a job driving for Trans West Logistics, a Port Coquitlam trucking company, it was only part-time and he was $11,000 behind on his child-support payments. Tasha was furious with him. One night when he was visiting his son, Tasha flew at him in a rage and Chubb called the police.

It was the middle of the night and the Coquitlam RCMP detachment on Guildford Way dispatched Nathan Wells, a uniformed constable, whose thick eyebrows and solemn face couldn't dispel a pink-cheeked youthfulness. Wells, who hadn't been on the force more than a year, had been assigned to the Port Coquitlam area. As soon as Wells and his partner arrived at Tasha's place, Chubb, who was drunk by the time they got there, was beside himself. He seemed to have forgotten about his failure to make child-support payments; instead he was full of accusations against Tasha. "He was upset at the drugs his girlfriend was using, specifically cocaine," said Wells later, "and he was sick and tired of the drug problem in Port Coquitlam and he wanted the police to do something about it."

Scott Chubb had good reason to be angry. He had made serious enemies among some people in one gang; he always claimed they were Hells Angels and he was probably right. A short while before this encounter with Nathan Wells, several men who were either gang members or associates delivered a brutal thrashing to Chubb in the parking lot behind the Golden Ears Hotel, their favourite hangout in Port Coquitlam. Chubb ended up in hospital; he claims he needed 160 stitches and suffered memory problems for a time. (An odd coincidence is that a close relative of Tasha's—her grandmother—had helped to establish the Hells Angels chapter in Nanaimo, on Vancouver Island, then considered one of the most dangerous and powerful chapters in the province.)

After talking to Chubb for half an hour, Wells realized he might be a useful source and he ended the visit by establishing something of a friendship with him. "You get back in touch with me," Chubb told Wells. "I'll make you famous." He didn't explain what he meant. Wells just assumed that here was someone who might help him identify drug traffickers in the area. He gave Chubb his name and phone number. "Please give me a call when you get a chance," he said. "I'd like to talk further to you about this." Chubb said he would.

A few weeks later, on January 1, 2002, Nathan Wells moved into a new job in the Coquitlam RCMP's drug section. When Scott Chubb called him on January 25 to suggest they meet, Wells knew he needed some advice. Constable Richard Kim, an officer with far more experience in drug enforcement, briefed him on how to handle Chubb and went with him in an unmarked police car to meet Chubb a few blocks from his home in Port Coquitlam (he had reconciled with Tasha and they were living together again).

Chubb climbed into the car and it was clear he was upset. I just lost my job, he told the officers. His rent was due in a week and he was desperate for money. Could the police pay him for the information he had? More confident now than he had been, thanks to coaching from Kim, Wells told Chubb they were interested only in real news, not gossip, not old stories.

Chubb was prepared for this. He could provide the names of three local cocaine traffickers, he said, as well as the name of a man with a marijuana grow-op. Not good enough, they said. The RCMP already had the cocaine traffickers' names and had taken action against them. As for the grow-op, there were so many in the area that the Mounties weren't willing to pay much for information like that. He'd have to try harder.

Stung, Chubb tried to explain his motivation for helping them— it wasn't just the money. "He starts talking about his criminal background and all the things that he had done before and that he actually legitimately felt bad for them," recalled Wells later. "He had changed his life around, he has children now, he has a common-law spouse and that he really wanted to clean up his life. He was sick of drugs. He said drugs had ruined his life. Yes, he was hard up for cash, but on top of that, he was also motivated that this was something he felt he needed to do to feel better about some of the wrong that he had done."

At some point during this meeting in the car, the men drove past the house with the grow-op that Chubb wanted to show them. It held three hundred plants, he explained, and the man renting the house paid a percentage of his take to the owner. Chubb had the cell and pager numbers of these people; he could give them to the police but they would have to pay him $700 to $900 so he could pay his rent. Once again the police told Chubb the information on the grow-op just wasn't worth $700.

Chubb wasn't really surprised. It had been worth a try, but he had another card up his sleeve. Would they be interested in illegal, unregistered firearms? This time the Mounties perked up. As long as the information was solid, as long as it could lead to an arrest, as long as there were seizures or, as Wells put it, "as long as something is obtained at the end of the day," they were very interested. Information like this was definitely worth money. But, Wells cautioned, "if you're motivated financially, there is nothing to gain by providing false information, 'cause you're not going to get anything until the end of the day when seizures are made, arrests are made, charges are laid."

Chubb said he understood. The conversation was over and the officers dropped him off near his home. In the meantime, Wells went over Chubb's criminal record at headquarters to better understand what kind of person he was dealing with. The list of offences he found was impressive. Going back to 1985 in his hometown of Sparwood, it began with breaking and entering and forcible confinement and progressed over the years to assault with intent to commit robbery, more break-and-enters, theft, possession of an unregistered restricted weapon, possession of a firearm or ammunition while prohibited, forgery, failure to attend court, failure to comply with probation order, possession of property obtained by crime, impersonation with intent, and drunk driving. His record ended in 1997. Most of it had been petty crime, but it was still an impressive list.

A week later, on February 1, 2002, Chubb called Wells again. His rent was due that day and he had to have some money. It was time to talk. Wells found another officer, James Petrovich, who was free to go with him to meet Chubb. Petrovich, a seven-year veteran with unruly hair and mournful eyes, acted as the driver and observer; Wells did the talking. In a conversation that lasted only half an hour, Chubb told them that Willie Pickton had three guns in his trailer at 963 Dominion Avenue, including a Smith & Wesson Mac-10, a .38 and a .44, possibly hidden in the laundry room. "You can see them if you pick through the laundry," he told them. "And there is ammunition in the trailer. But I don't know if the guns are loaded." Then he reminded them of his perilous financial situation. He really needed the rent money. Wells and Petrovich promised to get it to him the following week. Would that work? Yes.

The deal was on. But Wells made Chubb understand that he would have to get a search warrant to go into the trailer, and to do that he had to be sure the information was credible. As Wells explained later, "I need reasonable grounds to believe that these items that I've specified that I'm looking for are going to be in that said place at the time that I execute the search warrant. So I need to be satisfied that the information is credible, it's compelling, it's corroborated and that it's there and that the information is recent enough that I believe it's still there. I don't think that it's been sold or moved or so on, that it's still there.

"This was still a very new area for me. The issue of invading someone's privacy by executing a search warrant on their residence was a significant invasion of privacy. I wanted to make sure that I had gathered as much grounds as I believed that I could get."

Chubb understood. I'll check to see if the guns are still in the trailer, he promised. But what he didn't tell the policemen was how he knew about the guns; later he said that Willie had told him about them. "The ones I seen was a .38 Browning, a nickel-plated .44 Magnum and there was another Magnum there. And I think there might have been a Mac-10 there, I'm not exactly positive . . ."

Chubb had wanted to try them out. He claimed he needed them for "home protection," which was not all that far-fetched, given the beating he had taken from the bikers. So Willie let him borrow the .38 Browning and gave him four bullets. A few days later Chubb brought it back with three bullets. Willie couldn't resist showing off the other guns, so he brought them outside. Chubb borrowed the .38 Browning again but he didn't bring it back; instead he took it to Wes Baker's gun shop in New Westminster and sold it to him for $300. Given that Chubb was terrified of Baker and that Baker probably sold the gun to Pickton in the first place, it was a risky move, but Chubb had needed the money.

After they dropped off Chubb, Wells, who was born and brought up in Port Coquitlam, said he knew Pickton's name. But it was Petrovich who knew Pickton's history. He told Wells that he had worked on the investigation in March 1997, when Pickton had picked up Sandra Gail Ringwald in the Downtown Eastside, brought her back to the farm and tried to handcuff her, the night she fought back with a knife she found lying on a counter and stabbed him first. On duty that night, Petrovich had met the driver of the car that picked up Sandra Gail on the Lougheed Highway, and he had stayed until the ambulance arrived to take her to the hospital. Pickton was charged with attempted murder, Petrovich told Wells, but the charges were dropped after Sandra Gail refused to testify against him. The Ringwald incident was a reason, Petrovich told Wells, that Pickton was a person of interest in the Missing Women's Task Force investigation.

This is a Coquitlam file, explained Petrovich. You can pull it and review it. Wells hustled back to the Coquitlam headquarters and did just that. When he ran a background check on Pickton, the Canadian Police Information Centre (CPIC) revealed that Pickton was in what they called the "surveillance category." It said that he was a person of interest and that any information about him should be forwarded to two detectives with the Vancouver police. "I noticed that this entry had been entered by Coquitlam detachment in 1998," recalled Wells. "I remember thinking that it was odd that it would be the Coquitlam detachment entering information to contact the Vancouver city police."

After Nathan Wells finished reading about the Ringwald incident, he knew he needed to talk it over with Staff Sergeant Brad Zalys, the commander of the Coquitlam detachment and the person in charge of all the plainclothes jobs, including the Serious Crime Section as well as the Drug and Property Section. Wells figured it could wait, so it wasn't until Monday, February 4, that he went to see Zalys. He described his surprise that an old CPIC entry in the system was telling him to send queries about Willie Pickton to two Vancouver police officers. Zalys explained it was because Pickton had been a person of interest in the missing persons investigation. Phone Sergeant Wayne

Clary at the Missing Women's Task Force, he told Wells. Let him know you're preparing this affidavit for a search warrant.

But before he could do this, Wells discovered that the task force already knew that the Coquitlam force was looking at Willie Pickton. While the young constable had been poring over the files, his supervisor, Corporal William Mulcahy, who knew about the Pickton brothers through the many contacts they'd had with the local police, had called Clary. "I phoned him," Mulcahy stated later, "because I knew he was on that task force and advised him that it looked like we might be able to obtain grounds for a search warrant for that property, for that person, Robert Pickton, and asked him if that would interfere with anything."

Clary said no; he was fine with Coquitlam's going ahead with a search warrant. But as soon as he hung up he phoned Don Adam to say that Willie's place finally might be searched. When he called, by coincidence, Adam was already in the RCMP's Coquitlam headquarters, interviewing a suspect in a sexual assault; he interrupted the interview to listen carefully to Clary's news. What Don Adam calls his "spidey sense" told him this could be it. He had to insert his Project Evenhanded team into the operation. "Nathan Wells tells us he's going to search the farm," he reasoned. "We can't afford to let someone get on the farm and miss our opportunities. We know the current names that are missing; the names mean something to us. We are positioned to win."

Up to this point Nathan Wells had been working in a vacuum, which continued for a few more hours. He didn't know much about the task force; all he knew was that he had to start drafting an application for a search warrant to look for the guns. After some hasty research he learned that the Smith & Wesson Mac-10 semi-automatic pistol was a prohibited weapon under the Criminal Code; he also discovered that the other guns Chubb mentioned were restricted. He had another talk with Chubb at about one o'clock that afternoon to get a few facts straightened out; at two, when the afternoon shift started and his colleague Richard Kim came in, he went back to him for more help. He also talked to Wayne Clary and Don Adam, laying out Scott Chubb's information, and they advised him on the wording for his affidavit for the warrant. Richard Kim helped as well. He actually knew Willie; before he became a plainclothes investigator in Port Coquitlam he had dealt with him on a traffic violation.

For Clary and Adam, Wells's news was a major break in the missing women case. If a judge granted the warrant, it would be the first time that a police officer had gotten a chance to get onto the Pickton property and make a search, regardless of how limited that search might be. Clary asked Wells if he'd mind having one or two of the task force members come along. No, said Wells.

The two RCMP offices were half an hour apart by car. The Coquitlam RCMP headquarters are in a new building on Guildford Way, on the north side of the city, and the task force was in an RCMP building at 12992 76th Avenue in Surrey, about thirty kilometres south and across the Fraser River. No matter how fast you drove, it was such a congested area that it took time. Clary began thinking through the timing and who should be sent.

Then they received more good news. Scott Chubb called Wells to say the guns were still there. He may not have told Wells exactly how he knew this, but not long afterwards he confided to another person that he had sneaked into the trailer late Saturday night, on February 3, when Willie was out. Chubb found the Smith & Wesson; if he saw any other guns he didn't say. And it was in the laundry room, just where he thought the guns were kept. But while he was searching he heard Willie come back in his truck. Panicked, Chubb searched for a place to hide; he pulled out a bed in the room at the other end of the trailer from Willie's room and crouched down behind it, dragging it back as far as he could towards the wall. He prayed that Willie wouldn't look in and notice the bed was not flat against the wall. He was in luck; Willie staggered in, went into the bathroom, peed loudly into the bowl and then dropped into bed.

Hours later, as soon as he was sure Willie was asleep, Chubb crept out. (This was Chubb's story, but the police don't believe it and they don't believe he went back to check. They believe he didn't know for certain that the guns were still there.)

By three thirty, Phil Little, the detective on loan from the Vancouver police, and RCMP constable John Cater, who had just called his wife to say he might be late getting home that night, had arrived at the Coquitlam RCMP headquarters to meet Wells. As a couple they were a study in contrasts. Cater is thin and preternaturally perky, with ramrod posture, a gaunt face and a habit of using formal police jargon—"my brother officer" is a common modifier when he refers to a colleague in court testimony. Little's worn face with world-weary dark eyes and his slouched posture and rumpled clothes speak of long years spent on a major city police force. *Seen it all,* his body language telegraphs. Both were experienced officers. Cater, who had put in eleven years with the RCMP, had been working in the Coquitlam detachment before joining the Missing Women's Task Force, while Little had been a homicide detective with the Vancouver police for several years.

The men didn't talk much; it was just a hello-how-are-you greeting. Wells was too busy drafting his application for the search warrant to chat. Richard Kim was helping him; it was only the second time Wells had done a search warrant application and he wanted to get it right. Little and Cater decided not to hang around while Wells laboured so they drove over to the Pickton farm. Just as they were going by the front gate on Dominion, a man drove out. At first they thought it was Willie, so they ran the licence plate to check; it turned out to be Dave Pickton on his way up Coast Meridian, probably to Murphy's, his favourite neighbourhood diner, which was in a small strip mall at the corner of Coast Meridian and Prairie, about ten minutes away.

"We were frustrated by the lack of activity," admitted Cater. "We were curious, but we didn't hear anything." To kill some time, the pair stopped for a quick coffee on their way back to the farm.

By five o'clock in the afternoon Wells had completed the "Information to Obtain a Search Warrant," and because it was now after hours and no judicial justice of the peace (JPP) or judge was available in Coquitlam, he faxed it to a JJP in Vancouver. It didn't just mention the trailer; it included all the outbuildings, leaving out only the old family farmhouse.

Just after six thirty Wells received a call from the JJP, Candace Rogers, who had turned down his application because she was concerned about one of the paragraphs in the request. She wanted to know how the informant would know what a Mac-10 was and how he would be able to describe it. Wells looked over his request again and told Rogers the informant had a strong knowledge of firearms. She asked if the informant had a criminal record and Wells said yes. Wells redrafted the application, faxed it off again, and Rogers's permission to execute the warrant arrived at 7:40 p.m.

Within ten minutes Mulcahy was meeting with the rest of the team that had been chosen to make the search. It included Constables James Petrovich, Richard Kim, Vince Sebastiano, Grant Wong and Howard Lew. As the team leader, Mulcahy, whose thick black eyebrows made a startling contrast with his pale silver hair and who usually took the trouble to dress formally, took the group through the ground rules for the search and doled out the jobs.

Kim was to take a battering ram to knock down Pickton's door and he was to take pictures of everything as it developed. Bruce Morwood-Clark, who was a little older than the others, with dark grey hair, tanned skin and pink cheeks, was also there to take photographs. Petrovich was to be the exhibits person, responsible for logging and seizing any firearms, ammunition, and licences, documents and receipts related to firearms. Howard Lew was going to search the trailer as well. Grant Wong would guard the farm gate at the main entrance on Dominion. And the lead person, Mulcahy told the group, would be the man who had obtained the warrant, Nathan Wells—the youngest and most junior man on the team.

It took them until eight thirty to notify Phil Little and John Cater, who were still drifting around, on standby for the task force. We're going to meet now in the parking lot of the elementary school just north of the Pickton farm, they were told. Timing was very tight. There was no written operational plan. At this point the raid was not a task force operation; it was simply a search for illegal firearms.

We have to be aware of the place we're searching, Mulcahy warned them. Let's look for what we're after—the firearms—but take care not to disturb the rest of the stuff. We don't want to damage or destroy anything that might be part of another investigation. No one spoke of the missing women, but each man knew exactly what the stakes were in this search.

The warrant had to be executed by nine o'clock. It was well after eight now, but the farm was only two miles away and several officers had been on the property over the years and had a good idea of where things were. Mulcahy and Wong left early to check on the best access to the property, while the rest of the team stayed behind to make the final decision on who would guard the perimeter of the farm and who would search the buildings. These jobs went to Sebastiano and Wong; they would get help, if needed, from the other men on the property.

They were ready. The group moved out of the Coquitlam headquarters in marked police cars, driving east with the headlights on but without sirens. Morwood-Clark drove a Chevrolet Savana van. They stopped in the parking lot at Blakeburn Elementary School, the designated staging area. Once everyone had gathered there, Morwood-Clark led the searchers to the lane at the back— the north end—of the Pickton property; a berm of earth between the trailer and the road would prevent anyone from seeing them coming in. Two other officers hovered close to the front entrance at the south, as inconspicuously as possible, waiting to secure the entrance if necessary. Little and Cater drove around the area in a wide perimeter but close enough to get into the property in a hurry.

It was now just after eight-thirty and they had less than half an hour to serve their search warrant. They had no idea if Pickton was at home. The entry team to the north stopped their cars and got out. Silently they crept forward and then froze—they could see truck lights down the old laneway, near the front gates. They crouched down and no one said a word. A muddy pickup truck bounced forward and stopped in front of the trailer. Willie stepped out, shut the door and walked up the front steps to the trailer's porch. He opened the main door and went in, closing it behind him. Lights went on inside. The men quickly moved forward again. Mulcahy stayed at the rear corner of the trailer, facing the lane.

Five officers—Wells, Wong, Lew, Petrovich and Kim—climbed onto the porch and huddled by the door they'd seen Willie open; they didn't yet realize there was a second door several feet to their right. At a nod, Petrovich stood aside as Kim stepped forward and slammed the door open with the ram, yelling "Police! Police! Police! Search warrant!"

Suddenly the second door opened onto the porch and Pickton's head popped out. "Hey!" he protested. "What's happening?"

"Police!" someone yelled.

Willie slammed the door shut.

With guns drawn, the officers, led by Howard Lew, swarmed in through the rammed doorway and met Willie in the middle of the trailer. They threw him to the floor so that he was lying face down, then pulled his arms behind his back and snapped cuffs on him.

"I am arresting you for possession of prohibited and restricted firearms," Wells said to him. "Do you understand?"

"Okay."

"It is my duty," Wells continued, "to inform you that you have the right to retain and instruct counsel in private without delay. You may call any lawyer you want. There is a twenty-four-hour telephone service available which provides a Legal Aid duty lawyer who can give you legal advice in private. This advice is given without charge and the lawyer can explain the Legal Aid plan to you. If you wish to contact a Legal Aid duty lawyer, I can provide you with a telephone number. Do you understand?"

"Yup," said Willie. "Okay."

"Do you want to call a lawyer?"

"Not right now."

"You are not obliged to say anything, but anything you do say may be given in evidence. Do you understand?"

"Yes. Yeah, okay."

It was now thirty-six minutes after eight o'clock. Wells pulled Willie to his feet, led him outside to one of the cars and pushed him into the back seat. As Wells got into the car, he had a final question.

"Is there anything we should know about in your house?" He explained that officers were searching the premises and he didn't want them to be hurt in the process. Were there any booby traps? Anything there that could harm an officer?

"I have a .22 in the barn," replied Willie.

Satisfied, Wells started the car and drove down the muddy lane to Dominion Avenue, heading back to the RCMP headquarters in Coquitlam with his prisoner in the back seat.

CHAPTER THIRTY-THREE

TWENTY-FOUR HOURS

As Nathan Wells was driving Willie to the police station on February 5, 2002, it was just after eight thirty, and the police had less than half an hour to serve their search warrant. The men remaining at the farm prepared to start the search. Petrovich cleared the trailer to make sure no one else was in it, and then Morwood-Clark, the photographer for the search, went in with Lew and Kim, who were going to help with the search for firearms. There were six rooms in all. The police later designated them as Room 1, the spare room on the far right; Room 2, the kitchen; Room 3, the laundry and furnace room; Room 4, the office; Room 5, the bathroom; and finally Room 6, the last room on the left and Willie's bedroom.

They'd been too distracted with taking Willie down to notice it when they first crashed in, but now, as the men went back in and faced his office across the hall from the front door, they were unnerved by the sight of an immense tan horse's head and neck, mounted and hung on the wall. They knew right away it was real but they didn't know that this was Willie's beloved Goldie. The other thing that overwhelmed them was simply the mess—clothes, junk, paper, dirt. Everywhere.

Petrovich snapped on a pair of latex gloves. He had planned to start his search with Willie's bedroom, but suddenly he remembered that Scott Chubb thought there was a gun in the laundry room, and that room, which contained a washer, dryer and small furnace, was the other way. "Curiosity got the best of me and I went in to have a look," he said later. On a shelf over the washing machine he found a case with a gun in it. That's all he cared about—the search warrant was safe. He let his team know. Now the place to start was Willie's room.

It was just after nine o'clock. Back at the police station, Pickton was safely stowed in a cell, so Wells hustled back to his office to listen to the police radio and follow the search of the property. He was nervous; what if Scott Chubb was wrong? What if the search warrant was wrong? This would be a fiasco. To his relief he soon heard a voice on the radio saying that they'd found a gun.

When Petrovich and Morwood-Clark entered the bedroom, they saw a double bed to their immediate right. A dark wooden headboard with shelves was behind the bed, against the wall between the bedroom and the bathroom. It was on a shelf in this headboard that Morwood-Clark found his first photograph of the search: it showed a pair of handcuffs, covered with fake tiger fur. Nesting beside them Petrovich found several pieces of women's jewellery, a picture of a woman, some pieces of paper with Dinah Taylor's name on them, and a woman's purse. Right away he radioed the rest of the team with the news and Morwood-Clark took more pictures.

There were a couple of nightstands near the bed. Petrovich opened the bottom drawer of one and found a blue box with a flare gun inside. When the gun was examined later, they discovered it had been adapted to take twelve-gauge shells. And there was another pair of handcuffs, these ones covered with red fake fur. There were also several large cable ties, more commonly called "zap straps" by police and criminals, both of whom use them to tie recalcitrant people. And two dildos.

Right next to the nightstand, on the floor, was a box; when Petrovich opened it he saw a collection of kitchen knives, all different sizes. Then he moved to a television stand. There he found a mess of videos and papers; among them were books and a paper with Heather Bottomley's name on it.

Petrovich and Morwood-Clark moved back to the laundry room. Petrovich reached for the box he'd found earlier and opened it again. He took out the gun, a silver Smith & Wesson .22 revolver with an etched black grip. But the gun was wrapped in plastic, and it looked really weird. Something was attached to it. Suddenly the men realized what it was: a curved plastic dildo pulled over the barrel. The cylinder was loaded with five live bullets and one spent shell casing. "I never fully removed the dildo from the barrel," Petrovich said later. "I only moved it enough to get the bullet out of the chamber."

As they searched, the men found the crowded space difficult to manage. Richard Kim found a glass container containing women's hair barrettes, but he was frustrated by the cramped quarters. He's six feet four inches tall and weighs 240 pounds, and Petrovich is even bigger; they kept bumping into one another. Kim tried to stay out of his way but it was almost impossible, so he went outside to look around.

While Petrovich was working his way through these first rooms, Howard Lew was searching Pickton's office and the bathroom. Lew had been with the RCMP in Coquitlam since 1996 but had never had any contact with Pickton until now. There was nothing in the bathroom, but when he got to the office he found a small holster and an unspent .22 calibre shell. Lew continued to Room 4, Pickton's office; here, under a chair, he found a grey Solomon ski bag, and inside it a pair of women's running shoes. It also held an orange inhaler containing Flovent, a medication used by asthmatics. On one side was the patient's name: Sereena Abotsway.

As soon as Lew saw Sereena's name on the inhaler he radioed Mulcahy. Now, along with Heather Bottomley's name on the piece of paper, they had two solid pieces of identification linking Willie Pickton to missing women.

Up to this point the search was still a Coquitlam RCMP operation. But while Lew and Petrovich were searching the trailer and Morwood-Clark was photographing their finds, Mulcahy called John Cater and Phil Little, who had been waiting on a road nearby, to invite them onto the property. As they locked their car and walked onto the farm along a muddy path, they heard the radio squawk; it was Petrovich telling the rest of the searchers about the firearm with a dildo attached to it. Just as they reached the trailer, Petrovich emerged carrying a piece of identification with the name Dinah Mary Brigid Taylor on it.

"We just stood around," Cater remembered. "We never entered the trailer."

Suddenly they all heard Richard Kim's voice on the radio; he was in an outbuilding, talking about finding something "strange." Cater and Little hurried over to see a small grey trailer full of live, squealing pigs pulled up beside the slaughterhouse. There was no light, just that from Kim's flashlight, but when they went into the building they were able to make out a large hook suspended above a table. Kim shone the light around on the floor and they saw two skinned pigs, along with several drums of animal remains.

They had been in the slaughterhouse for only about three minutes when everyone heard Wong's voice over the radio, this time from the mechanical shop (later known as Site C). He'd found some women's things. Cater and Little walked over to have a look. Wong was upstairs in a loft, and when the two men climbed up, he had his flashlight on a pile of three purses and some shoes. There were some papers on top of these, and on one piece they were able to see Lynn Ellingsen's name. Cater said later he wasn't worried about this because he'd seen her name in the Pickton files; while he thought she was a former girlfriend, he knew she was still alive.

While they were searching the men were startled to hear a car coming up the lane from Dominion Avenue. It was an old Camaro and the driver identified himself as Ross Palmer, one of the Palmers who worked with Dave Pickton's crews. He was just coming in to pay Willie back some money he owed him, he said to Howard Lew, who had motioned him to stop. Lew shooed him off the property.

By now it was 9:53 p.m. The next voice they heard was Vince Sebastiano's, telling them about the piece of paper from Willie's bedroom with Heather Bottomley's name on it.

Cater listened, stunned by the news. "What kind of paper?" he asked.

"ID," Sebastiano replied. "And a birth certificate." Then Sebastiano told them there was more. "I have another name," he said. "Sereena Abotsway."

"What's that name on?" Cater asked him.

"An asthma inhaler. The date is July 19, 2001."

Cater knew that Sereena Abotsway had been last seen on August 1, 2001. "I felt physically sick," he remembered later. "I was shocked."

After hearing the names and then the news of purses, shoes, women's clothes, a gun with a dildo, the inhaler and more, he said, "We were all completely shocked. I recall . . . everyone standing around, very solemn. They couldn't believe what [had] happened. They've known me for a number of years and they'd never seen me like that."

No wonder Cater was so rattled. No wonder he felt sick. He'd followed Pickton for two weeks in 1999 before his superiors had called off the surveillance. He'd interviewed him in January 2000. He'd tried to get a warrant to search the farm and had been sent away to start again. The surveillance and the effort to search the farm were both part of the missing women investigation, the investigation that had gone nowhere.

Don Adam was still at the Coquitlam headquarters interrogating a suspect, so Cater called Wayne Clary to let him know what they were finding. Stop the search right now, Clary told them. Seize the property. And then get back here as soon as you can.

It was five minutes after ten o'clock. Cater and Little told everyone to stop searching. But the Coquitlam officers weren't quite ready to walk away. Morwood-Clark had been steadily snapping photographs and there were more to take. With help from Petrovich he took a picture of the gun with the dildo in the laundry room. Then he needed to get a shot of the television in Willie's bedroom, because the documents with Heather Bottomley's name were on it. He moved as quickly as he could. Morwood-Clark and the other

Coquitlam officers then left the property at 10:45 and went straight back to Coquitlam headquarters.

Don Adam was still there. He'd already been briefed on what had happened at the farm and had made arrangements to have the place sealed off and guarded by police. He knew he was taking a chance.

"We couldn't continue with the weapons search," he says. "To get the maximum potential for success we had to lock down the farm." And he did this based on Heather Bottomley's ID and Sereena Abotsway's inhaler.

When he thought about it later, he winced at the risk he had taken that night. "I was pulling that trigger on two pieces of ID."

Adam's next step was to call his colleague Inspector Doug Kiloh; they made arrangements to have an undercover officer, known as a cell plant, placed in Pickton's cell, which happened about four in the morning. They also made sure the cell was wired for audio and video. Cell plants aren't allowed to question a prisoner, but if a prisoner confides in them or even confesses to them, those statements can be used by the prosecutors in court.

At 6:50 on the morning of February 6, Adam contacted Kiloh again, this time to start the paperwork for obtaining emergency wiretap authorization to listen to Pickton's calls. They talked about what grounds would be needed for it and how the whole thing would come together. Margaret Kingsbury made a to-do list and went out to get it started.

Twenty minutes later Adam was on the phone to Peder Gulbransen, the regional Crown prosecutor based in New Westminster, to tell him what had happened and to find out what John Cater would need for a second warrant to search the farm. They agreed that, for the moment, Gulbransen would continue to be their contact person.

By seven twenty Adam was meeting his team, none of whom had slept all night. "We're going to be on that farm for three months," he told everyone. "Now it's time to deal with logistics."

He tried not to second-guess himself. "We have to do it right," he said. "It's right to seize the property and do a correct search. It would be wrong to keep going on all the other initiatives."

Dealing with logistics turned out to be easier than he had dared to hope. Quite simply, everyone wanted to help. Once Gary Bass and the Vancouver police found out what the task force had, their question for Adam was simple: "What do you need?"

Adam tried to figure it out. People. He needed people and he needed a lot of them. Right away the Vancouver police promised twenty-seven officers and Bass arranged for nearly a hundred more. Overnight, the Missing Women's Task Force had nearly 130 new members. More logistics: where would they put them? Let's get some double-wide trailers and set them up as offices in the parking lot, someone suggested. Great idea. Someone else took responsibility for organizing those.

But no one was really prepared for anything like Pickton. When Don Adam pulled the trigger on two pieces of ID, *Pickton* stopped being the name of a man; it became the name of a shocking, massive emergency. No one had expected this. Yes, they were hoping to catch the serial killer who was taking women off skid row, but the police had always thought that, when it did happen, it would involve a car or a truck—the man would be in a vehicle with a woman. They'd even prepared for something like that. "We created the protocol and had the tools ready," Adam says. A farm had never occurred to them. With dread they started to understand what they could be facing.

Adam decided he needed to just sit quietly for a while and analyze the whole situation. "Who do I need in charge?" he asked himself. "How big is this? What are the tools I need? Resources? What are the obstacles? What help do we need to get past those obstacles?"

Then he needed to do what he calls a "time-frame breakdown" to start producing results. "That night I broke it down to ten different things and gave each person about three hours to figure out how to manage. I called in everyone and I told each one, 'You own this problem. And here's what I want to know.' I knew I was going to do it right. This file had lots of chances to do it wrong, but I wasn't going to let that happen."

The citizens of Port Coquitlam already knew on the night of February 5, 2002, that something big was happening up on the Pickton farm. Police cars patrolling the property from nearly nine o'clock Tuesday night through to the next morning. A dog barking. Officers standing at the gates to keep people out. A large trailer, borrowed from the RCMP's Burnaby headquarters, hauled in to serve as a mobile command centre near the barn.

But on the morning of February 6, things were still relatively calm on the farm itself. Morwood-Clark spent most of the day following one of Dave Pickton's trucks taking a load of debris to North Vancouver.

Calls began pouring into newsrooms; reporters, photographers and television camera crews raced to get to the farm. Networks set up satellite trucks while news helicopters buzzed back and forth over the property. More police officers were posted around the perimeter of the farm and at the gates to prevent anyone trying to enter the property. The task force media spokesperson, RCMP constable Cate Galliford, as well as Corporal Pierre Lemaitre, an RCMP officer from Coquitlam, were besieged by the news teams that were besieging the gates of the farm, standing around in the mud hour after hour trying to get hard information.

Police officers began phoning members of the missing women's families to tell them that they finally had a suspect in custody, calls that went on for several hours. Except for the few facts given out by Galliford and Lemaitre, at this stage there was very little, so the reporters began calling family members as well to find out what they knew. When one officer reached Leigh Miner's mother, Doreen Hanna, she told a CBC reporter, he had said "they had a suspect that looked like a good suspect"; Leigh had disappeared in 1993.

Ernie Crey also received a call, about his sister, Dawn, who had disappeared in 2000.

"They seem to feel they have some reason that's going to keep them on that property for some length of time," Crey told the CBC, "so I know we're going to be sitting on tenterhooks anticipating what's going to come next."

Ross Contois, Gina Houston's boyfriend, hustled right over as soon as he heard, and was happy to share his thoughts with the *Vancouver Sun*'s Lindsay Kines, telling him that the police had already questioned Willie about the missing women. "These guys are totally on the wrong trail," Contois told the *Sun*, although he also admitted that rumours about Willie were not new. "It's been going on for years."

As the hours moved on and daylight approached, families in British Columbia and across the country were learning with relief, then horror, that the suspect was a pig farmer in Port Coquitlam and that his place was the focus of a massive search. Few needed to be told about pig farms; they knew that pigs will eat human flesh.

In Campbell River, on the northeast coast of Vancouver Island, Vince Sturla and Keith Morrison were in the middle of an interview with Rick and Lynn Frey. Sturla is a producer with NBC's *Dateline*. Morrison is a journalist from Saskatchewan, the former host of CBC television's current events show *The Journal* as well as a former anchor on CTV's nightly news; he was now living in Los Angeles and was a host on *Dateline*. And NBC was only one of the many networks to take an interest in the missing women story in Vancouver, now that it looked as if a serial killer could be responsible.

Sturla and Morrison had been in B.C. for several days working on the story, and the Freys had agreed to talk to them about Marnie. Cameras and sound equipment had been set up in the Freys' living room and everything was ready.

"We were in the middle of taping an interview with the Freys when they received word that there was to be some sort of televised announcement," said Sturla. They turned on the television "to hear members from the joint RCMP and Vancouver police department announce Pickton's arrest." The NBC team kept everything rolling, picking up the stunned reaction of Lynn and Rick Frey as they stared at the television. What they had hoped for, what they had prayed for, had happened. They were long past expecting Marnie to come home again; all they counted on was that her killer would be found and punished. Maybe this news was the beginning of that.

Adam's old friend Corporal Margaret Kingsbury is someone he likes to call the conscience of his group. He knew her as a warm-hearted, clever woman; outsiders see her as a small, thin person with careful eyes, short grey hair, a calm demeanour and, very occasionally, a wide smile. Overnight she became the go-to person for almost everything because of her common sense, a legendary memory for the smallest details and a clear view of the whole investigation.

John Cater briefed Kingsbury on what they'd found on the farm before turning his attention to the job of preparing an affidavit to obtain a new warrant so that members of Project Evenhanded could start a thorough search on the farm during daylight. The rest of Don Adam's senior team—people who hadn't slept all night—began to divide the remaining tasks. At that point it was almost minute-by-minute, seat-of-the-pants thinking.

Corporal Carole Hooper, admired for her administrative skills, was another task force member. In 2001 she'd been in charge of the file reviews of people of interest—the men involved in sex-trade murders, assaults and assaults on hitchhikers. Now Adam asked her to become the surface-search coordinator, planning the best way to process the exhibits they were finding in the trailer and on the rest of the farm property.

As soon as they thought of calling Bob Stair, it became clear that everyone understood the farm could be a graveyard. Stair, a good-natured retired RCMP officer and former British Columbia coroner who had managed the province's forensic identification unit, was needed for advice on body recovery over a wide area. He had all the experience they could hope for. A formidable international reputation

kept Stair in demand; he had worked on the search for and excavation of human remains in war crimes investigations in several
countries, including one in Kosovo, in the former Yugoslavia, that
produced dozens of bodies and evidence of atrocities. He'd also
helped with the identification of remains in New York City after
the terrorist attack on September 11, 2001. Between 1998 and 2000
Stair had even worked as a forensic consultant on twenty-three
episodes of *Da Vinci's Inquest*, a TV show whose hero was also a
coroner. (Lori Shenher, one of the Vancouver police investigators in
Project Amelia, was also an advisor on *Da Vinci's Inquest*; she worked
on twenty-five episodes of the show between 2001 and 2003.)

Though it was still early in the morning on Wednesday,
February 6, Adam asked Carole Hooper to call Jack Mellis right
away. A staff sergeant with the RCMP's Vancouver laboratory of
the Regional Forensic Identification Support Service, Mellis had an
international reputation and was the province's top crime-scene
investigator and bloodstain pattern analyst. There was a ton of work
to do and they needed to get at it right away, Hooper told him.
Could he come in at four o'clock that afternoon for a meeting? Of
course, he said. Hooper explained that the priority would be examination of Pickton's trailer and the vehicles on the property, especially the motorhome.

Once he was off the phone, Mellis began calling around to
put together a team of forensic identification specialists as well as
the equipment they would need for crime-scene work: lights,
alternative light sources and everything else they'd need to properly process the scene. Mellis knew this investigation was going
to require dozens of people.

He also knew he'd need space for the exhibits they collected, a
room much larger than the one being used now in the Surrey office,
and there would also have to be room for a lab.

John Cater, "a great doer," as Adam calls him, was asked to figure out the best way to log and track massive amounts of exhibits
and material—such things as every item the search team had found

in Willie's trailer. Cater had an answer for them right away: a new computer program called, appropriately, Exhibit Tracker, which included a system of bar codes for each exhibit.

Cater's affidavit for a new search warrant for Dominion Avenue was ready by 2:15 that afternoon, so he and Doug Kiloh drove to New Westminster to see Gulbransen, to make sure it was in order before they took it to a judge for approval. They also needed him to vet a second warrant, to place wiretaps on Pickton's communications, and a third that would allow the RCMP's Special Operations Unit, or "Special O," to organize constant surveillance of Pickton once they were ready to let him out of custody. Gulbransen found the warrant application to be in good order and shortly afterwards a judge approved them. They were set to go.

"The file," said Adam, "had massively, exponentially, exploded."

Just as important as all the organizational chores the police were thinking through was the star of the show, Willie himself, still sitting in a jail cell in Coquitlam. He was charged with storing a firearm contrary to regulations, possession of a firearm while not being holder of a licence, and possession of a loaded restricted firearm without a licence. The police released him on bail at about one o'clock on Wednesday afternoon, about sixteen hours after he'd been arrested at the trailer, but told him he would not be allowed back on the property until they had finished searching it. Pickton said he was worried about his pigs; they needed to be fed. Okay, he was told, he and Dave could feed the pigs, but then he would be off the property until they said he could go back.

Just before three o'clock Willie and Dave arrived at a gate on the farm's west side to avoid all the police cars and reporters at the Dominion Avenue entrance. They wound up chatting with Corporal Mike Coyle, who was there to prevent the curious from coming in. He had filled a million yards of backfill here over the past twenty years, Dave bragged, but it would take another 250,000 yards to get it up to grade with the properties to the west of their place. Willie paid no attention to the chitchat; he just wanted to get into the Dutch barn near the west gate to feed the pigs and his dog.

"You don't understand," Coyle said, exasperated. "You cannot walk about this property." Turning to Dave, Coyle made the situation clear: "Listen, you're responsible for your brother. It's from the front gate to the residence and that's it. If he's anywhere else, anyone anywhere else, you're going to be arrested."

"I'll try," Dave said. "But he's his own person."

Another police officer, Constable Jeff Levine, went with Willie into the Dutch barn; they stayed just long enough to feed the animals. The brothers left the property but within minutes Dave was back; this time he wanted to get his pickup truck, which was parked near the farmhouse. When Willie left, he didn't come back. The police didn't want him interfering with the search so they fed the animals themselves.

Dave had moved away from the farm a few years earlier, into a house in Port Coquitlam, but now was living in a new, well-kept ranch bungalow on Burns Road, two doors away from Piggy's Palace. He told his brother that he could stay with him till things got sorted out and that Willie would work for him on job sites while he waited for the police to leave the farm. No one was even talking about what was going to happen with the firearms charges. At this point they were almost an unnecessary distraction, but they had served their purpose: they had got them onto the farm.

By four o'clock that afternoon Don Adam's team leaders and a number of invited experts were gathering in the Surrey task force office to take stock and to parcel out more jobs. Adam asked Phil Little to manage a small group of investigators that began at twenty-five members and would quickly rise to sixty. Little would be assigning tasks and reviewing them and making sure the members had everything they needed, including vehicles, notebooks, computers and phones. He realized he also needed to develop processes for the examination of each area on the farm, and that led to a large knot of questions and issues.

Carole Hooper had been looking at ways to process and manage evidence; now she had to speed everything up and get them into place immediately. By the end of this meeting she had become the on-site coordinator, making sure everyone had all the material and staff they needed. Staff Sergeant Randy Hundt, a long-time Major Crimes officer, was chosen as the site commander, while Corporal Wade Lymburner was given responsibility for excavation of the site. Mike Coyle would manage the search technicians on the site and Constable Bev Zaporozan would manage the exhibits.

They also discussed the perimeter of the search. What should it be? The farm had shrunk to about fourteen acres; were they going to search all of it or just the areas around the buildings? The decision didn't take long: all of it. From the front, on Dominion, along the east-side ditch as far back as the townhouses to the north, along the north side to the western border, where new houses were also under construction, and back down to Dominion. All of it.

Okay, if that was the plan, what was the best way to search such a large space? That generated even more discussion, but finally the group agreed that the best way was to break it down into different sites. First of all, the team had to learn about the farm and its buildings. Then it needed to decide which places, buildings and vehicles to search first and in what order. So they gave each site a letter with the idea that they would search them in alphabetical order. Willie's trailer would be Site A, the primary site, because of what had been found with the search warrant for weapons. Then they drew up a list:

Site A   Willie's trailer, a two-bedroom mobile home set on a concrete slab

Site B   the slaughterhouse

Site V-3   the motorhome, a small Dodge DeSoto recreational vehicle that was no longer driveable

Site C   the mechanical shop, which had a loft upstairs

Site D   the garage and workshop

Site E   the barn
Site F   the original Pickton farmhouse

The priority now was to get a fence up right away and to get it electrified as soon as possible to alert the police to any intruders; Coyle took that on. In the meantime, twelve members of the Coquitlam RCMP were maintaining security around the perimeter; several of them belonged to the force's ERT, the highly trained Emergency Response Team. Cameras and lights were about to be installed. And because of the muddy conditions on the property, they also decided to take a van in right away to keep evidence safe and dry.

Meanwhile, the CBC reported, the City of Port Coquitlam was providing maps and aerial photographs of the area, while the fire department had brought in lights, generators and tents.

As the hours ground on, the planning in the task force offices in Surrey continued, systematically and carefully. Outside it was a different story. Outside it was wild. Members of the missing women's families began to gather at the Dominion Avenue gate of the Pickton farm; determined to keep a vigil and frantic for information, they refused to leave. By Thursday, February 7, people in Port Coquitlam knew that Willie Pickton was now a suspect in the missing women case. They began connecting him to the mysterious event in 1997, when a naked woman had run off his property bleeding and screaming.

A man named Don Daly told reporters that the neighbours had never forgotten the incident. "About 3:00 in the morning she was stabbed, came running out of the house naked or something," Daly told reporters. "That's all that happened, but there wasn't any follow-up that happened in the news." This was Sandra Gail Ringwald, who nearly died of stab wounds that night. A few days later a *Vancouver Sun* story identified Sandra Gail and ran an interview with her mother who confirmed that her daughter had nearly died that night of a stab wound.

What made the story even more sensational was that this presumed killer was in fact a wealthy man. The farm had just been assessed as worth more than three million dollars.

And then there were the parcels of land the Picktons had already sold. Some of the land had been made into a community park. One parcel now had an elementary school on it. Another parcel, to the north, was part of the new Riverwood subdivision, with dozens of new condominium townhouses on it; another to the west, also part of Riverwood, was crammed with upscale single and semi-detached homes, many still under construction.

Not surprisingly, people began asking if there might be bodies under these parcels of land. Simone Blais, a reporter with Coquitlam's *Now* local newspaper, found out that the teaching staff at both Terry Fox Secondary School and Blakeburn Elementary School, both in Riverwood, were trying to calm worried parents; their younger children were in some cases being questioned by the police and their teenagers were hanging around the farm trying to find out what was going on. The principals told Blais they believed it was important to give the children accurate information, to encourage them to stay away from the farm so the police and forensic people could do their work, and to provide counsellors if needed.

Brian Fichter, the principal of Terry Fox Secondary School, decided to ignore media requests for yearbook pictures or background information on Willie or David Pickton. "We talked to staff about visitors, journalists, media people coming in trying to access old annuals and that kind of stuff," Fichter told *Now* reporter Angela Mackenzie. "We have information in those annuals which is specific to grads and I believe under the Protection of Privacy Act, I don't think it's in their best interests to be handing out that information. We did have reporters from major newspapers and we shooed them away. We have no desire to entertain any of them."

Some reporters tried to interview residents of the new subdivision crammed up against the north and west sides of the farm; not surprisingly, they couldn't think of anything to say. Not at this stage.

But everyone knew they must be wondering if there were bodies under their homes.

Across Canada, around the world, people learned that Willie Pickton might be the most prolific serial killer in North American history. They learned that the Vancouver police had dismissed talk of a serial killer years before and had fired their own expert on the subject, a star officer named Kim Rossmo, whose work was valued in many countries—just not in Vancouver. "We all have a right to expect that our police forces will do the job that they're there to do, and we don't accept that they'll do any less," Ernie Crey, Dawn Crey's brother, told CTV News. "The lifestyle that [Dawn] pursued should never have figured into whether police did a serious job."

CHAPTER THIRTY-FOUR

THE LARGEST CRIME SCENE IN CANADIAN HISTORY

On Thursday morning, February 7, Carole Hooper and a few other officers made their first drive-through of the Pickton farm. Hooper's vehicle was a Budget cube van she'd rented earlier that day so there would be a safe place to store exhibits. They began by making sure the gates at the front and back of the farm had security teams with a logging system in place so that supervisors would always know who was on the property and when they'd left. No one would be free to wander around. Hooper's determination to control access to the farm and know who was on it at all times was wise; by this time there were already between fifty and fifty-three cars and trucks on the property and she could see that the numbers were escalating every hour. They had to know who was there, and why.

The administrative issues were thought out carefully. Down the road, they knew, there could be a major trial, and the team had to start as they meant to go on, tracking and recording every item, every person, every detail, leaving no unexplained gaps for a defence team to run through. Before the rest of the team searching the site even left the task force headquarters in Surrey, they had all watched a video about forensic evidence collection; they also knew what to look for, from a briefing based on the search two nights earlier when Pickton had been arrested and soon after released.

To keep track of what they found, task force officers quickly decided the VPD's SIUSS system was too slow and cumbersome. Usually the RCMP worked with evidence-tracking software called E&R, for Evidence and Reports, and they changed to this familiar system. E&R had been developed in 1985 by RCMP corporal Cal

Smith after a plane crash in Gander, Newfoundland, that killed 256 people. Smith, a forensic identification officer from Nova Scotia, designed a common-sense numbering system for every piece of evidence, a system refined after the Swissair crash near Halifax in 1998, when 229 people died. The new system began with establishing areas of responsibility, "from pathologists to fingerprints, dental and DNA specialists, morgue examination teams, pathologists, and forensic identification specialists. Once these were set, every area of the morgue—medical, dental, DNA and fingerprinting—used the same numbering system," explained Joanna Kerr, a writer for the *Gazette*, an RCMP in-house magazine, in 2001.

The forensic identification work on the Swissair crash victims— the largest DNA recovery case in Canadian history—managed to identify almost everyone on board from thousands of body parts. The scientists failed in only one case: they were unable to differentiate between a pair of identical twins, who shared the same DNA, but at least they knew they'd found both of them.

The Swissair work also taught the scientists that hairbrushes, toothbrushes and razors are the best personal effects to use when trying to find victims' DNA for comparison. For the missing women, the pure DNA from the Pap smears at the cancer centre was proof positive. However, Pap smears were not available for all of the women, which is why Adam's team had gone to the families as well. The Swissair disaster also proved the value of new DNA collection kits, made with a special paper that bonds with biological samples; this paper protects the sample from contamination and allows it to be safely handled, shipped and stored.

One of the most useful characteristics of the RCMP's E&R software was its ability to create a barcode for each sample and exhibit. That made tracing and identifying them easier and far more accurate. When the Pickton case "exploded," as Don Adam put it, these modern scientific advances became a godsend.

The protocols for the searches were carefully planned as well. The logbook of people on the site would come in every day to Carole

Hooper and Sergeant Randy Hundt, who shared an office. The lab reports would go to Wayne Clary, with copies to Hooper, and the exhibits forms would be entered into the E&R program.

Jack Mellis had also studied the property that first morning and realized immediately what the task force was facing. There were not only cars, trucks, Willie's trailer and the slaughterhouse to search but many other sites, including a garage, a mechanic's shop, a motorhome, several old sheds, a barn and the old family farmhouse. They needed more people right away. Doug Kiloh called in an eight-person unit from the Provincial Auto Theft Task Force to help; one of its members, Constable Steve Vrolyk, was given the job of standing at the Dominion Avenue gate to take tips from civilians who showed up, as well as to answer their questions. There were plenty of both.

At one thirty the first search team assembled at the Carnoustie Golf Club, next to the farm, while Jack Mellis and Randy Hundt explained what was going to happen and what they expected of each member. Mellis told them how the searchers would work. Each team would have a member of Project Evenhanded; these people were familiar with the names of the missing women and the circumstances of their disappearances, so they would recognize relevant material. Another member would come from the Biology Section of the RCMP's Evidence Recovery Unit and would be responsible for collecting DNA. The third would be a specialist from Forensic Identification Services, someone trained in attending crime sites, taking fingerprints, collecting physical evidence and photographing everything.

It took time to get started. One delay after another meant that the search team didn't leave for its destination—Willie Pickton's trailer—until after four p.m. Mellis led the way in a police van filled with officers, each dressed in a protective white Tyvek suit, latex gloves and paper booties. He drove to the front gate on Dominion but to his consternation found the road crammed with people, from police officers, curious gawkers and neighbours to grieving family members and media. The way in through the north is clear, he was told, and it's much closer to the trailer. Mellis reversed and drove around the farm, entering the north laneway from the construction site where new townhouses were going up. He advised the people in the other vehicles to come in at the north end as well.

Vancouver police constable Daryl Hetherington, who had joined the task force in October 2001, and the RCMP's Margaret Kingsbury were the designated searchers for Willie's trailer. Though Mellis had brought two search teams, each with a forensic identification officer as well as two people to videotape and photograph everything, he wanted to wait until the first team was done so he could assign each of them to a new team. "Whenever we added more new people," explained Carole Hooper, "they were always teamed with people who'd already done it."

Once all the members of the search team had arrived, they set up a perimeter using police barriers, then the two officers photographed and videotaped the trailer and the area around it. By the time they finally got started in the trailer, at four thirty, it was crowded with people.

The first search that afternoon took more than four hours, even though it was just a walkabout of the trailer and the other sites nearby; they weren't taking out any evidence that day. Mellis, wearing surgical gloves and kitted out in a Tyvek suit and booties like all the other searchers, didn't touch anything, nor did he take notes. Instead, as he guided the others inching through the site, he dictated his findings into a tape recorder.

One of the first things they did was gather all the clothing they found—and there was a lot of it—and sort it into piles. The Evidence Recovery Unit separated any women's clothes with stains on them into another pile and set them aside in the north bedroom, known as Room 1.

Bev Zaporozan, as the exhibits person, stayed in the centre of the trailer, receiving the items as they were found and formally seizing them. And thanks to the photographs taken by Morwood-Clark two nights earlier, as well as the description of what the police officers had seen, these new searchers knew what to expect. First of all they were looking for the ID for Heather Bottomley and the ski bag and inhaler that seemed to have belonged to Sereena Abotsway.

The search, which began in Willie's bedroom (Room 6), turned up many more of Heather Bottomley's possessions. Here they found a spiral-bound notebook with several documents inside, some of which had her name written on them. The notebook was found beside the television on the TV stand in the corner. Inside it were a photocopy of a paper with a partial social insurance number on it; a copy of a hospital card; a birth certificate with Heather's name on it; a document in the name of Heather Bottomley stamped by the Ministry of Social Services and dated March 22, 2001; and a cheque stub for $175. They also found a blank rental application form and a red plastic wallet containing various papers, including handwritten notes about pregnancy tests. There was a copy of a provincial identity card in Heather's name, and a piece ripped from a Zig-Zag cigarette rolling paper. Tucked inside the spiral notebook was a silver notebook with some writing inside, and attached to the book, maybe wrapped around it, was a pink ponytail elastic. Everything was noted and photographed.

As expected, they found Sereena Abotsway's grey Solomon ski bag and her orange Flovent inhaler in Willie's office (Room 4). But when they looked through the bag's outer pockets, they also found two syringes, filled with a blue liquid that looked like antifreeze.

Because they had started so late, it was beginning to get dark. Daryl Hetherington left the trailer to inspect Site B, the slaughterhouse beside Willie's home. The searchers knew that there were live pigs there, in an animal trailer, and they needed to know what the situation was. Hetherington, a tall, strikingly pretty woman with long blond hair, was a twenty-three-year veteran of the Vancouver police. Because she lives on a farm outside Vancouver and raises pigs herself, she was asked to look at the condition of the animals. It was horrifying.

THE LARGEST CRIME SCENE IN CANADIAN HISTORY 415

The pigs in the animal trailer had neither food nor water. One sow had recently given birth to a litter and was now "in such a condition that she could not stand"; her piglets had slid into the muddy yard and were dead, and Pickton's pit bull was tossing around one of the bodies. Two sick pigs were lying on top of a third; when Hetherington looked more carefully at the pig underneath, she found that one of its hooves was infected and rotting off. She called over another police officer, who contacted a veterinarian; three of the pigs were put down. On the west side of the slaughterhouse Hetherington spotted a decomposed sheep's carcass, more pigs' carcasses and barrels full of animal carcasses and entrails.

When she went inside the slaughterhouse, it was worse. A walk-in cooler and three freezers were in there, as well as three other freezers crowded together on a raised platform. A pig's head lay on a butcher's table. Hetherington had a closer look. There was a hole between its eyes that she thought must have been made by a nail gun. There were rotting pigs' carcasses in the room, including one still hanging by a hook from the ceiling, and more in the freezers. Hetherington didn't search the freezers on the platform or go through the slaughterhouse carefully; this was more of a look around. But she was so distressed by the filth and the neglect of the animals that the next day she brought food from her own farm for the survivors.

At some point during this first day of searching, as they listened to the officers talking on their radios, Don Adam and his senior colleagues started thinking ahead. Where was this going to go? Cautious as Adam is—as they all were—the gut reaction was that this was the guy. They'd got their man. Willie Pickton. He'd been an on-and-off suspect for years, although eventually eliminated when the police discovered his DNA didn't match that of the man who had killed three women in the Fraser Valley. Now what? If they were right—and they couldn't be sure until much more of the farm had been searched and more evidence found—they would need to get ready to question him.

The person Adam had in mind was Staff Sergeant Bill Fordy, a close friend and young protégé of his. Fordy had been chosen as one of twelve officers Adam had trained for the interview team—the polygraph unit, as it was also called—that he'd set up in August 1999. None of the members were full-time interviewers; they had other duties in the Major Crimes section. But they were a tight group, most of them living near one another and socializing as families, and Adam and Fordy were considered the leaders.

The night before this meeting, Adam had called an old friend, Sergeant Jim Hunter, the head of the RCMP's polygraph unit in Vancouver, to make sure he could be there too. Hunter and Adam had worked together before, but that had been a long time ago, and Hunter hadn't been involved in the missing women case. Not till now. Nor had he ever met Dave or Willie Pickton.

Fordy seemed like a good choice to interview Pickton. One of the force's rising young stars, he was handsome—tall and slim, with a rugged face, thick, dark hair and eyebrows and a quick grin that could charm almost anyone. He knew how to make people comfortable, his sense of fun was contagious and his passion for his job and dedication to his colleagues were absolutely clear.

That night, February 7, both Don Adam and RCMP superintendent Larry Killaly, the head of the Surrey offices on 76th Avenue (the "Surrey satellite"), where the Major Crimes offices and the Missing Women's Task Force were headquartered, called Fordy, who was on assignment on Vancouver Island, to tell him to get ready to do an interview soon with Robert Pickton. Fordy returned right away. He'd never had anything to do with the missing women file, but on the following morning he was immersed in it. He was briefed on the case as well as the raid on the Pickton farm and told he had full responsibility for interviewing Willie Pickton. He learned that Willie, who was now under constant police surveillance, was not allowed on the farm and was working at one of his brother's job sites near Steveston.

Everyone knew the interview would take a lot of thought and research. As for when it would happen no one was sure, but it would be soon, maybe later that day. Other members of the team who had gathered with Fordy to learn about the case took on a variety of jobs to help prepare him, including listing key witnesses to research and interview. Some prepared background material and "interview aids"; these included photographs, maps and information about the missing women. Dana Lillies, a nine-year veteran who was studying to be a criminal behavioural profiler, was the team's most junior member; she was also asked to prepare for interviews with Lynn Ellingsen; Willie's sister, Linda Pickton Wright; and Sandra Gail Ringwald.

Fordy had his own lengthy to-do list after the briefing. He asked the RCMP's Drug Intelligence and Field Operations office for help with an undercover operation—he needed a police officer who could be placed in Pickton's cell after the arrest. Another cell plant, in other words, and he had to be very skilled. The best they could get.

Fordy made another call, this time to RCMP superintendent Glenn Woods, a criminal profiler who ran the Behavioural Sciences Branch in Ottawa. Would he be able to provide some insight into a person like Pickton? Woods told Fordy that nobody had ever successfully opened up a person like Willie Pickton. In fact, Fordy said later, Woods told him that he "could not refer me to anybody in particular."

The next call went to the RCMP's Special I Section, which is responsible for electronic surveillance; Fordy wanted to make sure that both Pickton's cell and the interview room were wired for sound and video. And he wanted it done at the RCMP's main headquarters in Surrey, several miles south of the Surrey satellite offices. The headquarters building had cells, which were not available at the Surrey satellite, and interview rooms, so he thought this would be a better place for questioning. He also asked Special I to install recording equipment in an unmarked police vehicle.

Finally, the last two people on his list were two forensic psychologists, Dr. Nicole Aube and Dr. Myron Schimpf, who often helped the interview team try to understand the people they were questioning. After his call, Jim Hunter took Aube, an expert on serial killers, on a tour of the Pickton property to get a sense of who Willie was and what his life seemed to be like. Hunter, who had toured it earlier that day, had compared the new police photographs of Pickton's trailer with those taken after the attack on Sandra Gail Ringwald in 1997. The trailer today was far messier, far filthier, he told Aube, than it had been five years earlier.

Although the psychologists quickly put together their conclusions on Pickton, Fordy said later that he didn't find the information particularly helpful. "It was just a personality profile," he said. "And quite frankly, it wasn't anything that I would not have thought myself. So I had the information, but it's hard for me to say if I used it or not. It was just knowledge."

Later that day Fordy finally went to see the farm for himself. He was appalled, as everyone had been, by the filth and the mess, but he was also shocked by the size of it. "It's the perfect place to kill people," he told his colleagues.

But the more they thought about it, the more Jim Hunter and Don Adam realized it was too soon for Fordy to question Pickton. The search teams needed more time on the farm to find evidence. And Bill Fordy needed more time to get ready.

On February 7 Tristan Walker, a civilian member of the RCMP who worked in the force's Evidence Recovery Unit out of Vancouver's Heather Street headquarters, and Marg Kingsbury had been working their way through Willie's bedroom in the trailer. They had uncovered his treasure trove of sex toys that had been photographed by the searchers two nights earlier. There were several vibrators, including a "Ms. Lady Flexible Multi-speed Stimulator." The drawer beside the bed held more vibrators, as well as a box with the label G-SPOTS on it. There were the plastic cable ties, or zap straps, often used to restrain a person's hands and feet, that had been spotted earlier, as well as the steel handcuffs with fake leopard skin attached, stained with what was later found to be blood. There was also a tube of lubricating gel. They found three belts; one appeared to be a man's black belt while the other two were women's—one was beaded, the other was white—as well as a hairbrush and some syringes. Walker pulled Pickton's bed apart and cut out stained sections of the mattress and sheets. Then they tore out a panel from the bedroom wall because they found stains on it they suspected were blood.

In Willie's office (Room 4) they found a woman's leather jacket, stained on the collar and sleeves. Up in the wet, leaky loft above the mechanical shop (Site C), Hetherington found a white purse with a lipstick in it, among other things. A black purse containing condoms, a toothbrush and cosmetics was in the same area; there was also a used condom in it. The slaughterhouse yielded many items, including a woman's watch. Of course, none of the searchers at this time knew if the stains they had found were blood. They didn't know who owned the purses, clothes, shoes and bits and pieces of cosmetics and jewellery. It would take months, then years to identify the people who had died there. But what they did know, after a day in Willie's trailer and his slaughterhouse and his loft, was that they were in a killing ground, even if they had not yet found any bodies.

As they worked, all dressed in the Tyvek suits, booties, gloves and, after the first day, masks, the searchers would bag the item, seal the bag and put their names on it and then the name of the item and where it was found. These would be collected by another member of the team, usually Bev Zaporozan, and sent to the lab for numbering, bar-coding and examination. Each time the searchers left the site and returned, they would put on fresh suits, gloves, booties and masks. And so it went, day after day.

But everyone knew the search had to include the ground itself, not just the buildings and vehicles. After his work for the International War Crimes Tribunal in The Hague on mass gravesites in former Yugoslavia, Bob Stair, also a former RCMP member and chief coroner for the province, knew better than anyone what the ground can yield. The entire farm, about fourteen acres, had now been declared a crime scene, the largest in Canadian history. The problem now was that the task force managers weren't sure how to proceed with a ground search that size. While they had a pretty good idea they'd be sifting the soil for bones, teeth, hair and body parts, as well as for such identifying materials as buttons, cloth, leather and jewellery, they weren't sure how to do it.

And what should they do about all the large stones, pieces of concrete, old tools, junk metal? How would they sift dirt on fourteen acres? How do you put that kind of dirt through machinery? Clearly it was a job the Picktons themselves had done, because they were in the topsoil business. They took in truckloads of dirt, even contaminated soil from the old Expo site in Vancouver, removed the rocks and debris, mixed it with other soil and delivered it to farms and market gardens in the area. The Picktons had used an old screener, now rusted and abandoned, that took the dirt in through the top, let it fall into a bin, shook it through bars and screens and let it fall out as reclaimed soil, with all the garbage held back by the bars and screens.

Randy Hundt suggested his friend Gerry Murdoch from Cranbrook. Murdoch's company, BA Blacktop, built and paved roads and bridges. He knew what equipment would be needed, where to find it and how to use it. He also understood the complicated process of setting up contracts with the federal government's public works department, which, because the RCMP is the national police force, would be paying for most of the investigation. Bev Busson, the deputy commissioner of the RCMP in British Columbia, called Murdoch to make the offer formal.

"So I talked to my wife," remembers Murdoch, "and packed my truck and left." As soon as he arrived in Port Coquitlam, just over five hundred miles from home, and took in the size and demands of the job, Murdoch rearranged his Cranbrook schedule and rented a house in nearby Pitt Meadows. The plan was to commute home every other weekend; on alternate weekends his wife would drive down to Pitt Meadows.

Bob Stair walked the farm with Murdoch, who listened carefully to the coroner's requirements. "He told me his vision of what he wanted," Murdoch said. "My job was to make this happen." The first thing to do, Stair decided, was make a grid of the farm; they estimated it would be made up of 220 twenty-metre squares, each one numbered. Once that was done they would dig each square of the grid, one at a time, down to undisturbed soil. How would he tell if it was undisturbed? Two ways. Experienced excavators can tell just by feeling the dirt. "You pick up a piece, like a brick-sized piece, and break it in half," says Murdoch. "If it breaks in a line, it's undisturbed. But it's just a feel . . . otherwise you get a specialist from a professional engineering firm to do a test."

Once the digging begins, a backhoe chews and scrapes up the dirt, rock, gravel and topsoil from the grid square, clawing down, down, until it reaches undisturbed earth. Even if the soil on top is damp or muddy, it doesn't make any difference to the screening process; they dig straight down, and the dirt is always dry below the surface. The dirt gets dumped into a truck that carts it to the screening area. There it goes into a Grizzly, a large vibrating machine that shakes the dirt down from a bin onto the screeners. It then falls through the screens to a conveyor belt. As the dirt first enters the machine, steel bars—and these can be set to any width—stop pieces of rock, metal, cement and other large chunks of debris from entering the bin. The operators can change screen sizes in about fifteen minutes; the mesh ranges from a quarter-inch to two inches to allow screening of different materials such as rock, sand, gravel and topsoil.

Stair and Murdoch then discussed the sizes of conveyor belts they'd need. They realized they had to start working backwards. "What do you want to see here?" Murdoch asked.

"Anything from twenty-five millimetres down," Stair replied.

That's about five-eighths of an inch. Stair recommended using two search belts, or "picking belts," one for the very fine five-eighths-inch screen and one for a slightly larger one-inch screen that would let larger chunks of soil through. The dirt that was like powder would go through the finest screen to simply pile up; anything left on the screen would be put in a box and examined as well.

Once Stair had made it clear what he needed, Murdoch began working with the federal public works department to order the equipment needed on site. The list was long and expensive—in the millions of dollars. It took several weeks, and in some cases months, for the necessary equipment to arrive, get set up and start operating. Hazco Environmental would be supplying all the trucks, Grizzlies, screeners, backhoes, front-end loaders, tents and what everyone called the "ATCO village."

The "village" comprised the vast collection of ATCO trailers that would soon be strewn around the property; it included the command post, staff trailers and trailers for the people working on the conveyor belts, or, as they came to be known, the "picking lines." The trailers were equipped with microwave ovens and refrigerators, although there was no commissary. Even if people could stomach the idea of meals cooked on the farm, there wasn't room; they would either bring in a packed lunch or leave for the coffee shops and chain restaurants scattered around the mall across Dominion Avenue, all within easy walking distance. Contractors hooked up the ATCO trailers to the Port Coquitlam power and sewer systems so there would be electricity and heat as well as toilets and showers for both men and women.

And then there were the "reefer trucks"—refrigerated trucks to hold the biological samples until they could go to the labs. There were also many tents ready to set up for exhibit storage and testing, especially in bad weather. And the weather was bad: rainy, damp, cold. It was still winter and the work was bone-chilling. The ground was muddy, with pools of water everywhere. But once in a while the sky would clear and the sun would come out, lighting up the snow-topped Coast Mountains in the distance behind the farm, a glowing reminder of the splendour of what had once been wild and beautiful countryside.

CHAPTER THIRTY-FIVE

SCOTT CHUBB

While Don Adam's team continued to delegate jobs on the Pickton farm, tips were flooding in at the main gate on Dominion Avenue and by phone to the task force office. Reporters were fanning out across the Downtown Eastside and Port Coquitlam to talk to anyone who knew Willie, Dave or their family. Peter Warren was handling tips every day on his radio show. The police realized that one of the key people to see as soon as possible was the man whose information had led them to the farm four days earlier: Scott Chubb. Because Chubb was Nathan Wells's source he was assigned to talk to him, but he went with a more senior officer, Corporal Ted Van Overbeek. They met at about eleven thirty on the morning of February 9, with Van Overbeek taking the lead.

The first thing Chubb wanted to talk about was Lynn Ellingsen. "Hey, listen," he said. "I was thinking about this shit yesterday . . . there's this girl named Lynn. She had something over Willie, right? When Willie was paying her fucking big bucks, like, once a month, I believe—five, six grand a month. It just showed up, right? So if you can find her, I bet you can find something that's gonna help you."

Chubb told them that Lynn had started blackmailing Willie for what she knew about him and missing women. He described her to Wells and Van Overbeek: "She's a coke slut. Willie had her out there, for about six months—"

"Like a girlfriend?" asked Van Overbeek.

"No, it seemed more like a roommate. Like, maybe she was doing him once in a while, kinda, maybe, I'm not sure—but I was looking at the paper and all during that time Lynn was out at the farm."

Chubb rattled on about borrowing a gun from Willie and that he had mentioned if "someone wanted to get rid of bodies he could take care of that . . . stuff like that."

"How did that conversation come up?" Van Overbeek asked.

"I was trying to borrow one of his guns off him to shoot gophers," Chubb replied. "And we had a conversation about that . . . he said something to the effect that him and a buddy or something, you know, they'd get hookers . . . I don't remember the exact conversation, but he said something about windshield-washer fluid or radiator fluid . . . something to the effect of taking windshield-washer fluid and shooting them up with it and if the cops were to find the body, it wouldn't make any difference—because they were junkies, right?"

Chubb did most of the talking at this meeting. He told Wells and Van Overbeek that he'd been reading the papers and thought he recognized a couple of the missing women from pictures; he also thought he had seen one of them with Willie at the Money Mart on Shaughnessy in Port Coquitlam. Van Overbeek listened, then told Chubb he wanted to do a formal taped interview. Right away Chubb bristled.

"I won't go to court," he said.

"No?"

"No."

"I'm just asking."

"You're putting me in a real bad position. If I go to court that means, I mean, fuck, you guys would have to put me in the witness protection program."

"It's certainly something we can discuss, certainly," said Van Overbeek.

"I'm not prepared to do that."

Scott Chubb was terrified of Dave Pickton. What would happen to him if Dave found out he was talking to the cops? "Dave has nothing to do with this shit," he said quickly. "I mean, it's always been said between the truck drivers that Willie is fucking weird."

For about forty minutes, with an occasional interjection from

Nathan Wells, Van Overbeek questioned Chubb, trying all the while to keep the tone buddy-buddy friendly. But he wanted to squeeze out of Chubb every possible witness or lead that he could. He began by taking Chubb through his own background in Sparwood and his history with the Pickton brothers, including driving a truck for Dave and building Piggy's Palace.

"Willie doesn't really talk too much," Chubb said. "He's a pretty quiet guy, pretty much sticks to himself. It took me ten years to become a friend of his. But all the truckers know he has whores at the farm on weekends and shit like that.

"Like I said, she [Lynn Ellingsen] had something on him real bad," he went on. "I don't know what the fuck it was, because he was paying a big ton of money every month. He wasn't very impressed. He was asking around to find out if I could, if I knew someone that would fucking kill her."

Chubb told them how Willie killed his pigs. "He'd slit them by the throat, hang them up inside the barn, let them bleed to death. He'd save the blood. A lot of times he'd sell the pigs down to the Chinamens downtown." Dave's drivers had talked about a woman named Shelley, who sold Willie his sex toys, including a life-size blow-up doll for Dave's fiftieth birthday and an inflatable pig—known generally as the "fuckable pig"—that Willie kept on his desk.

"Doesn't everybody have a fuckable pig at home?" responded Van Overbeek. Nathan Wells started to laugh. "Any other weird shit out there apart from the fuckable?" Van Overbeek continued. They all chuckled.

Van Overbeek wanted to know if Chubb had ever seen any bodies when he was working on the farm. No, he replied. He told them about the cockfights, the bikers who hung out at the booze can across the street from the farm. Van Overbeek pushed Chubb for every name he could think of, every detail that could help him understand Willie Pickton. And Chubb told them again that Willie had asked him if he would be willing to kill Lynn Ellingsen.

Although the conversation lasted for only about half an hour, it had given them some good leads. And they weren't finished with Chubb; if they were lucky, he could be their guide into Willie Pickton's world. Van Overbeek left and Nathan Wells finally gave Chubb his $750 so he could pay the rent.

Later that day in the task force office, Don Adam and Jim Hunter met with Bill Fordy and other members of the interview team to decide how the major interviews ahead should be handled. Two other Vancouver Mounties, both profilers, had been invited: Keith Davidson and Scott Filer. A former sex-crimes investigator in North Vancouver when Ron MacKay had been in charge of Major Crimes, Davidson had developed a skill in analytical work and years later was trained as a profiler by his old boss. With Glenn Woods, he'd also attended a seminar in Quebec given by Roy Hazelwood, one of the most famous FBI profilers ever. And, of course, he'd worked with MacKay to set up Project Eclipse, the 1991 police workshop in Vancouver that looked into twenty-five unsolved murders of women in the Lower Mainland—the workshop that concluded there was at least one serial killer at work and perhaps as many as three—conclusions that were ignored or mocked by the local police.

Davidson had also worked with Kim Rossmo and Ron MacKay on the famous Abbotsford Killer case in the mid-1990s. That case resulted in the arrest of Terry Driver, who had murdered one woman and sexually assaulted several others. It had involved seventy-five investigators and more than nine thousand interviews, and it cost more than two million dollars. Jim Hunter wanted Davidson at the meeting because of this experience with serial killers over the years. As he put it, he thought Davidson could tell them something about "this kind of person."

Scott Filer was an RCMP geographical profiler trained by Kim Rossmo, and Davidson had asked that he be present at the briefing. But the two had little to say, if records of the meeting are anything to go by. And all that Jim Hunter offered about Davidson's contribution to the discussion, in the notes he wrote later, was "Keith gave an overview of the scene and the subject. His opinion is that the pigs are surrogates for women, that there appears to be a sadistic component, ante- and post-mortem. Not necessarily is the act the same every time."

After much discussion, Adam and Hunter decided it would be a good idea to have two interview teams, one to question Pickton and the other for Dinah Taylor, whom the police now suspected might have been a participant in the crimes. Hunter decided to ask Danielle Campbell, a senior RCMP member in Edmonton, to work with Fordy on the Pickton interview. Hunter thought highly of her, describing her as "a skilled profiler, a dynamic interviewer, strong investigator, very good with people." Besides, he thought, it might be a good idea to have a woman doing the interview. After all, he said later, "Pickton had been involved with . . . all these women, obviously women have a strong impact on his life. We had learned that there was a relatively strong connection with his mother, so we felt that a woman could have an impact in that interview." But why not use Dana Lillies, who was already a member of Don Adam's interview team? Hunter believed she wasn't experienced enough. None of this sat well with Bill Fordy. Like so many of his colleagues, he had no use for profilers and psychologists.

Danielle Campbell flew out to Vancouver right away. She discussed the case with Keith Davidson, and their strong recommendation was to bring in Roy Hazelwood, who, with his colleague John Douglas, had created Quantico's famous Behavioral Science Unit, which specialized in serial killers, bombers, arsonists, pedophiles and other dangerous criminals. Hazelwood, now a private consultant to police forces all over the world and a mentor to Ron MacKay, was an expert on sex crimes. The missing women case was now so notorious, possibly even bigger than the Green River murders, that it might tempt him.

Hazelwood by this time was one of the most famous profilers of serial killers in the world. He'd just published his second book,

Dark Dreams: Sexual Violence, Homicide and the Criminal Mind,
the successor to his first bestseller, *The Evil That Men Do: FBI
Profiler Roy Hazelwood's Journey into the Minds of Sexual
Predators.* He was best known for his work on three famous
cases: the "Lonely Hearts" murders, when Hazelwood forced the
police to look at several seemingly unconnected murders that all
turned out to have been committed by Harvey Glatman; the Paul
Bernardo–Karla Homolka murders, for which Hazelwood was
often attacked for concluding that Homolka was a "compliant
victim"; and the Atlanta child murders, when he was the first
police officer to suggest that a black man was probably the killer
of many black children in the city.

Although Adam agreed to invite Hazelwood to come to Canada
to meet with the team, Fordy still wasn't enthusiastic. He had the
typical contempt for profilers that Ron MacKay and Kim Rossmo
had come up against in their work. He didn't think that a profiler,
even one as renowned as Hazelwood, could help him prepare for
the interview with Willie; as far as he was concerned, profilers were
inexperienced academic types who hadn't worked on the ground
investigating real killers.

However, another police officer, Tim Sleigh, an RCMP forensic crime-scene and fingerprint expert from the Burnaby RCMP
detachment, was warmly welcomed when he joined the team on
February 10. Sleigh knew the Pickton farm and he knew the
brothers, thanks to his 1981 investigation on the stolen cars found
on their property. He had known then that they were involved in
a chop shop for a biker gang, and he remembered that it was
Willie who had showed him where he and his brother had buried
the cars to hide them. Years later, in 1995, Sleigh was the investigator at the RCMP's Vancouver headquarters who had examined
Jane Doe's skull, the one that had been found in Mission Slough,
and who had determined she had been murdered.

Coming back to the farm after so many years, now as a search-
team manager assisting Jack Mellis, Sleigh was stunned when he

saw the mess. "To be honest," he said later, "it probably took two days to get over the feeling of being overwhelmed." His new job was to help Mellis supervise, assign tasks, and find and buy supplies for the forensic identification team. These were highly trained officers who gathered the evidence at the search sites, who swabbed surfaces for blood, who delicately, carefully removed stained clothing and other objects and bagged them, sealed them, numbered them and sent them to the labs for testing. Sleigh and Mellis would never find all the people they needed for this job in Vancouver, or even in the Lower Mainland; what they did was recruit volunteers from other RCMP detachments who came in for three to six weeks at a time. Many of these forensic identification officers would come in for their three weeks on the farm, go home for three weeks, then continue this pattern on and off for years.

Two search teams were now at work. Each one had a member from the RCMP's general investigation service or a detective, as well as a forensic identification officer, someone from the Biology Section's Evidence Recovery Unit, to look at potential biological and DNA evidence. And as the search ramped up, the people in Willie Pickton's world were apprehensively waiting to find out what would happen to them. Scott Chubb, meanwhile, was cooperating with the police—and turning out to be a gold mine of information.

Lynn Ellingsen was another matter. She was living in Surrey with a friend when the police took over the farm. They were aware from interviewing her earlier, in 1999 and 2000, that she knew a lot. But what the police wanted to know now was her involvement with Pickton. Did she lure women to the farm? Was she an accomplice? They drove to Surrey to pick her up. When they arrived, she was high; in fact, they found her walking to a neighbour's house to borrow some baking soda to cook up a little crack cocaine (its simple ingredients are powdered cocaine, water and bicarbonate of soda; once it dries into little "rocks" it can be smoked for an instant high). The police took her to the Surrey headquarters, put her in a room that had photographs of the pig farm arranged around it, and told her she was under arrest and would be charged with conspiracy to commit murder.

Two officers hammered her with questions. As Ellingsen explained later, she was high and could remember very little of this lengthy interview, but she did remember crying and phoning her father to come and help her. The police reminded her that she'd been interviewed about Willie Pickton in August 1999 and that she had denied then that she'd seen him kill anyone. They reminded her about a second interview, when she once again denied any knowledge of Pickton attacking a woman. She remained obdurate. Frustrated, the police removed her from the interview room and put her in a cell for a few hours to let her think about her situation. You could go to jail for twenty-five years for conspiracy to commit murder, they said. It was time to tell the truth. "The circle is closing around you right now," one of the officers said. "Those are the facts of the case and it will bury you."

Although she was afraid and in tears much of the time, Ellingsen wouldn't help them with any information. When she finally asked for a lawyer, one was supplied; in exasperation, the police released her without charges.

Gina Houston blamed Ellingsen for all Willie's troubles. Gina, like her common-law husband, Ross Contois, had been hanging around the farm gate after Willie's arrest, and she told people that it was all the fault of an addicted prostitute. She was lying, Gina said. "She phones the police and tells them that she watched him and I doing that there one night, she said it was one of the missing hookers from the Downtown Eastside, but it was just a pig," Gina told anyone who'd listen. Willie Pickton, insisted Gina, was a "nice, caring man" who was a good friend to prostitutes.

As the army of police and evidence-recovery experts grew larger every day, so did the gathering of relatives and friends at the farm's

Dominion Avenue entrance. Several of them refused to leave. Neighbours, employees and friends of the Picktons also hung around, along with reporters, photographers, camera crews, satellite trucks and cars. Every so often the police would send out a media spokesperson to offer a bit of news, but it was never enough. "We could be here for a matter of days," Cate Galliford, the RCMP spokesperson, told the journalists. "It's more likely we'll be here for weeks or even months."

One day a reporter, standing amid the thick scrum of journalists desperate for news, suddenly spoke up loudly: "Look! A shoe!" All eyes turned to where he was pointing to see a lone sneaker in the ditch by the road. Cameras swung to get footage. Everyone stared at it. Then some of the reporters began to feel silly. It was just a shoe. But everyone was spooked. Were there bodies under the ditch? Under the townhouses? Was it true, as some people were saying, that the Picktons fed women to the pigs? Was it true that Willie had a wood chipper and disposed of bodies that way, like in *Fargo*?

Realizing that the families gathered at the gate with the reporters needed privacy and a place to talk to each other and to counsellors and victims' services workers, Hazco Environmental loaned a square white tent for them to use. It was erected on a small piece of land directly across from the farm gate, land owned by Home Depot, between the store's parking lot and the Hells Angels clubhouse. As soon as the tent was up, with a floor and some tables and chairs inside, family members began placing candles around and lighting them. A woman named Dawn Sangret lit a candle to remember Elaine Dumba, who had disappeared in 1998. "I'm here for her today," Sangret told a Vancouver *Province* reporter, "and just want to find out what happened to these poor women."

Workers from BC Hydro, who had been putting in power lines around the farm to run the ATCO trailers, came across the road to pay their respects. "They stood by the candles and they were shaking like leaves and crying," remembers a counsellor who was there

to help the families. "They said they had been working in Site A*
and that there was a bad feeling in there." The tent, soon known as
the Family Tent or the Healing Tent, was off limits to the press.
Within days it was festooned with photographs of the missing
women, notes, ribbons and flowers.

When the police called Doreen Hanna, the mother of Leigh Miner,
who had disappeared in 1993, she was glad to hear that they had a
"good suspect." But Leigh's sister, Erin McGrath, told a reporter that
she was now filled with a sense of dread "that my sister could be
there—and what a terrible place to end up, in a field. It's just so sad."
Sandra Gagnon talked to CTV News about her sister, Janet Henry,
who had gone missing in 1998. "I hope we can find my sister's remains
and bring her home because it has been a long, long road." Maggie
de Vries went out to see the farm for herself, knowing that this might
be the place where her sister Sarah had died. "I wanted to make it real
to myself, and I wanted to see the police looking," she told a reporter.
Some of the task force officers met with a few family members on
Sunday night, February 10, to tell them how the investigation was
progressing, but most could not be comforted, nor could they be
distracted from what they saw as police negligence.

The *Vancouver Sun* tried unsuccessfully to find Sandra Gail
Ringwald to see what she might have to say about Willie's arrest.
Her mother said she never understood why the charges were stayed
after he nearly killed Sandra Gail in 1997. She also said that her
daughter knew how lucky she was to be alive.

Along with reactions from family members of victims, reporters
were chasing any information they could wheedle out of the tight-
lipped investigators at the farm. When they began reporting that
the belongings of two of the missing women had been identified,
senior task force officers made it abundantly clear to everyone
working on the search site that no one was to speak to the media

---

* *Willie Pickton's trailer*

at any time. This didn't stop journalists from digging into the Picktons' finances and family history; to their surprise they found that the muddy, junk-filled fourteen-acre property was now worth more than $3 million, and that the Picktons had already made millions by selling off half their land for development.

And, inevitably, reporters also started writing about the disastrous decisions made by the police over so many years, decisions to ignore the missing women from the Downtown Eastside. As Suzanne Jay, who worked for the Vancouver Rape Relief and Women's Shelter, told a CBC reporter, "Our rape crisis centre has spoken to people who have identified the farm and identified the farm to police." They had long suspected, she said, that "there was some connection between the missing women and the farm and the men who ran the farm."

Scott Driemel was the Vancouver Police Department officer who was picked to speak on behalf of the force about the missing women and the Pickton investigation. Although he must have been doing what he was told, his combative, blustery style and his endless denials disgusted ordinary citizens. As for the families, almost everything he said made them angry. "Information that was received by police, whether it be by the Vancouver police or whether it be from another agency, that information was shared and whatever information could be acted upon was," Driemel told one reporter. Well, given the *Vancouver Sun* series that had run just a few months earlier and the extraordinary revelations about the pig farm, few people took Driemel's spin seriously. Family members of the victims were furious, as were workers with social service agencies in the Downtown Eastside. And so were hundreds of thousands of people in Vancouver and the Lower Mainland. They didn't believe that "the information was acted upon." Ever.

The issue before people now was the search of the Pickton farm. Why were the police giving briefings without saying anything about how the investigation was developing? Cate Galliford's explanation was that the police had to preserve the "integrity of the investigation." Why didn't the police seize the farm years ago, when several people warned them about it, even fingering Willie for the disappearances? Again Driemel wouldn't admit the police had done anything wrong. "We're not about to discuss what was said, when it was said, how it was acted upon or anything of the nature. You can be assured that information was received, that information was evaluated and a decision was made as to what we can do with that information at the time."

Vancouver's mayor, Philip Owen, refused to accept any criticism about the police. He rejected calls for an inquiry into the way the Vancouver police had handled the missing women case and continued to defend them. "I think it's been handled in an expeditious, very serious way," he said. "And I don't think there's any intention or effort to ever duck it or avoid it."

Within a week of Willie's arrest the task force was sifting through four hundred tips from the public. One of them came from Renata Bond, the New Westminster prostitute who had, at Dave Pickton's request, taken Sherry Irving to Willie's trailer on the farm in April 1997. Bond kept most of the money Dave paid her, giving Sherry just enough to buy a ferry ticket back to her home on Vancouver Island. She had planned to return to the Island as soon as she left the Pickton farm; her boyfriend, who was going with her, was waiting at a nearby truck stop.

Before Willie was arrested, Bond had seen a picture of Sherry in a newspaper story about the missing women. On February 11, soon after she heard about the arrest, she left a message on the tip line to tell the task force what had happened. RCMP corporal Jay Buckner called her back the next day. It took many more months before they would have the full story.

On February 12 the police got a major break in the case—Carole Hooper was able to confirm that DNA tests on the Solomon ski bag and some of the inhalers found in and around Willie's trailer were positive in their identification of Sereena Abotsway. She had been there; the items were hers. It was good news, but the test results weren't enough to bring murder charges against Pickton.

The next day, four days after their first interview with Scott Chubb, Ted Van Overbeek and Nathan Wells sat down with him again, this time in a room at the Executive Plaza Hotel on North Road in Coquitlam. The men ordered lunch from the Copper Club downstairs, and while they waited for it to arrive, Chubb told them about his childhood in Sparwood and his family: he was thirty-four and had a seven-year-old boy and twin girls who were sixteen. He didn't know where his girls were, he said; he'd met their mother when he was much younger and was just getting out of prison. After splitting up with this woman he had moved to British Columbia, and that's when he began working for Dave Pickton. He talked to Van Overbeek and Wells about helping Dave tear down old bars and nightclubs and building Piggy's Palace on the Burns Road lot. And he filled them in on the relationship between Dave and Willie, and what Dave Pickton had been thinking since Willie's arrest. "Actually, I talked to Dave the other day about work and he doesn't want to stick any of his trucks on the road," Chubb said.

Once again Ted Van Overbeek was the lead interviewer; he asked Chubb why Dave was doing this. Because the company name, P&B, was on all the trucks, Chubb explained. "Their name's printed all over the . . . everywhere, 'P&B' written everywhere," he said. "Stick a truck out there—he doesn't know if one of these women's relatives or whatever, you know. He's pretty sombre. He wasn't too talkative." Chubb also told them that Dave was trying to stay away from the media, hiding out at his girlfriend's place in Burnaby.

A waiter arrived with lunch: club sandwiches and pop for the two policemen. Chubb wasn't hungry. The men chatted about driving trucks and hockey while the officers ate their lunch. Finally Van Overbeek got down to business. The information you've given us has value, he said, and the police want to make a deal with you. But first we need to make it clear that we have other sources just as good as you are; you are only one of many. Nor can we pay you for information, because, as Van Overbeek put it, "if it ever comes to the point where that, we need that, our Crown cannot say to a court,

'Listen, we have given this person X amount of money and then he told us the story.'

"And I know it's not fair for you. I know your situation and that money's tight for you right now. That's something we can certainly help with. If we ever do need that information we can take care of other things, other needs for you and for your family." This meant that the witness protection program was an option, and if it came to that, he and his family would be well looked after.

"Now the only other thing I need from you and want from you," Van Overbeek added, "is total honesty, and like I said, I don't believe this, but I'll put it out to you anyways because I have to. If you were ever involved with anything with him in regards to that shit, any and all, tell us up front. We'll know about it up front and it's something we can deal with. If we ever have to go to court with this, the last thing we ever want for you is to be embarrassed. You never had any type of thing to do as far as the broads go?"

"No," replied Chubb.

"Thank you," said Van Overbeek. "I suspected as much but I needed to ask you that."

Relieved to have that out of the way, he assured Chubb again that they would be fair to him. But Chubb wasn't really listening. Now that he was on the team, he wanted to share more information. Al Trautmann, he told them, had worked for Dave for nineteen years. "And I had a conversation with him the other night and Trautmann told me that Willie told him that he had helped get rid of two bodies out there. That's what Willie told Al straight to his face."

"Okay," said Van Overbeek. "Let me go there again. Willie told . . ."

"Al."

"Al Trautmann?"

"Yeah, that he had gotten rid of some bodies out there."

Van Overbeek was taken aback. When he pressed for more information, Chubb explained that Trautmann, who lived in Port Coquitlam, belonged to the close-knit circle of old friends that hung around the Pickton farm. When Van Overbeek realized that Chubb knew all the Pickton friends and connections, he asked him how Dave actually ran his business. Chubb said that Sandy Humeny was Dave's ex-wife and did the company books; he also went through the family history to show how Sandy's parents had originally owned P&B before Dave bought it from them. And not only did Sandy work for P&B now, but so did their children, Tammy and DJ.

But something was bothering Van Overbeek: this source was so good that maybe he was too good to be true. Before he got sucked in by a load of lies from a guy with an impressive criminal record, he needed to reassure himself that Chubb was telling the truth. Once again he asked about his relationship with Willie. "As far as anything criminal that you and Willie did together . . . did you ever do anything criminal?"

"Nothing."

"Good, okay, good, but you understand I have to ask that question."

"Yeah, no problem."

"And when we do go on the record, I'll ask you that question again . . . I've been in these situations before where things come back to bite."

"No," Chubb reassured him. "I've never done nothing weird."

As they talked and Chubb began telling Van Overbeek about women he'd seen with Willie, the officer stopped him. There was too much here to digest. He had to make sure he was getting all this information accurately, and he explained his reaction. "In most investigations . . . murders I've been involved with," he told Chubb, "there's usually one thing or one person. And I don't believe that's going to be the case in this particular case. I think you're going to have a series of people like yourself who give us little pieces and we are dealing with this magnitude . . . it's just so huge. I mean, it's the biggest thing I've ever been involved in, I can tell you that; probably the biggest thing I ever will be involved in. So that's why people like yourself are important."

It was time, he said, to start formally taping Chubb's statements. The two Mounties set up a camcorder, and while they did that, Chubb said he would have to talk to his wife about what was next for them. He knew they would need to move out of the area; for the sake of his son, he thought a small town would be best.

Once the camcorder was working, Chubb described seeing Willie in Port Coquitlam with a Native woman in front of the Money Mart where he picked up his mail. He saw another woman, a blond girl—he couldn't remember just where but he thought it had to be at the farm—whose picture had been in the paper with other missing women. And then he told the Mounties that he and Willie had been pulling nails from boards at the farm one day, sometime in 2000, he thought, when Willie asked him to hurt Lynn Ellingsen because she was costing him so much money—$10,000 so far, he told Chubb. It would be easy to get rid of a junkie or a hooker, Chubb said Willie told him, by injecting her with windshield-washer fluid or radiator coolant. "And, you know, put it in your arm, and fucking she's gone, just like that. He was basically asking me if I would do something like hurt Lynn."

But Willie didn't ask him again, said Chubb. That was the only time. Their relationship was cordial but not close—Willie was a good mechanic and would fix his car when needed; he even loaned Chubb money from time to time. "He was a lot easier to get along with than Dave," Chubb said. "He was a lot more approachable."

And when the policemen wanted to know what Willie was like, Chubb summed him up fairly succinctly. "Well, basically he just putters around. That's basically what he does. If he shows up at a job site he's always getting in the way or, you know, if we were working and then he wants it done this way but we were already doing it one way already and it was working . . . he'd come in and throw a fucking monkey wrench into the situation."

What kind of temperament has he? the cops asked. Misunderstanding the question slightly, Chubb answered, "Little temper, really quiet person . . . but when he got angry he would snap—usually it would come to violence. One time him and Dave got into an argument out back in the garage, and I don't know what the argument was about but they were screaming at each other, and the next thing I know fucking Willie just went right off and punched him in the nose."

It was time to wrap up the conversation but Van Overbeek was curious. He had a last question. "Were you ever with him when he killed pigs?" he asked.

"Sure."

"How did he do it?"

"He'd bring them in, he'd hook them up to a hook, he'd put a little slit in the back of their calf right at—"

"Like through the Achilles tendon?"

"That's right, yeah. And then he'd stick the hook up there, crank them up like with an engine hoist. And then he'd hold them up and then, you know, I always thought this was kind of weird, he'd grab them by the crotch and kind of stroke their pecker for some reason. I don't know why the hell he'd do that."

"Ha, ha," responded Van Overbeek.

"It was kind of weird, you know. And then he'd just take a knife and cut their jugular and let them bleed out and then, after they started bleeding out he'd take a nail gun or something like that—I'm not exactly sure, or an old .22—it was like a little .22, fuck, shell that went into something . . . you know what? It was a Hilti."

"A Hilti gun?" repeated Van Overbeek.

"Yeah. That's it. Right."

"Concrete, with the .22 charges?"

"Yeah, that's it. Right. And then he'd nail them with the nail or a concrete nail right in the head, yeah."

"After he slit their throats?" asked Van Overbeek.

"After they slit their throats, yeah. And then he'd throw them in boiling water and scrape them down."

"And he did this all by hand?"

"Yeah."

"Okay, and then he's—all the guts and everything would fall to the floor after he cut them open?"

"That's right."

"And what did he do with that?"

"He stuck them in barrels, blue barrels."

"Did he have any type of machine to process this goop?"

"No."

"It just goes right into barrels and that type of thing?"

"That's right."

"Would he kill pigs all hours of the night?"

"All hours of the night. Always at night. It was never during the day that I'd see him kill a pig."

Across the road from the Pickton farm: the families' Healing Tent (front) and the Hells Angels' clubhouse (behind) with the Home Depot parking lot (right).

Families taped pictures and mementoes of their loved ones on the sides of the Healing Tent.

Families were invited to witness Dave Pickton's house being knocked down, that last building to be searched and demolished, on July 26, 2003.

Two of Pickton's defence lawyers, Marilyn Sandford and her husband, Richard Brooks, leave the Port Coquitlam courthouse after the preliminary hearing ended in June 2003.

Chief Crown prosecutor Mike Petrie (centre) walks to the courthouse with Adrian Brooks (left) and Richard Brooks (right) of the defence team, in 2007.

July 9, 2003: Willie Pickton is momentarily guileless as he smiles and waves on seeing his friend Pat Casanova take the witness stand.

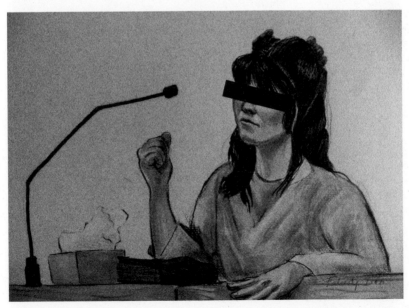

During the 2003 preliminary hearing, Sandra Gail Ringwald shows the court how Pickton held the knife as he stabbed her in 1997. She was not allowed to testify at the 2007 trial.

Court TV reporter Sue Sgambati reporting from the trial early one December morning in 2007.

January 22, 2007: Peter Ritchie and Patrick McGowan arrive at the courthouse before dawn on the first day of the trial.

The only eyewitness, Lynn Ellingsen, on her way to testify at the trial, June 25, 2007.

Key Crown witness Andrew Bellwood testified against Pickton during the trial on July 16, 2007.

Scott Chubb, another key witness for the Crown, testified at the trial in June 2007.

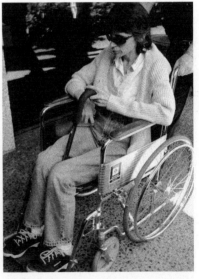

Weak with cancer, Gina Houston, Willie Pickton's best friend, testified at the trial in July 2007.

The Crown team at the trial included (back row, from left) Geoff Baragar, Derrill Prevett, John Ahern, Jay Fogel and Mike Petrie and (front row) Satindar Sidhu, Jennifer Lopes and Crown staff Annie Martin, Carol Martin and Carol McClure.

Missing Women's Task Force head, RCMP Inspector Don Adam, with Laura Isberg, the sister of Debra Jones (one of the missing women), after the trial.

Senior Missing Women's Task Force officers, Margaret Kingsbury and Wayne Clary of the RCMP, at the press conference after the verdict.

An unhappy Bill Fordy, the RCMP sergeant who interviewed Willie Pickton, speaks to reporters after the verdict, December 11, 2007.

RCMP profiler Dana Lillies interviewed Pickton for hours before he was formally charged with murder.

Bill Hiscox and Wayne Leng at the trial, December 2007.

In a post-verdict prayer circle, second from left are Rick and Lynn Frey, Troy Boen, an unknown man, Bonnie Fowler, Elana Papin, Bonnie Fournier, Cynthia Cardinal and Elaine Allan (partially obscured by camera).

PART THREE

—

ON THE FARM

"They had their own lives, regardless of their lifestyles," he said. "They were known to have certain things in their lives that were important to them. Some of them were known to regularly phone or visit loved ones, and then inexplicably stop doing so." These women abandoned residences, personal belongings and children without any explanation; they didn't pick up prescriptions; they didn't go to their doctor appointments; they didn't pick up their welfare cheques. "In short," Prevett told Judge Williams, "there was a complete end to the pattern of living without any known reason."

CHAPTER THIRTY-SIX

GETTING READY FOR WILLIE

Two weeks after the raid on his farm and his arrest, Willie Pickton, who was under constant RCMP surveillance that included wiretaps on all his phone conversations, was working for Dave in the yard at P&B's headquarters on Tannery Road, as well as on a job site in Richmond. By now people around the world were reading stories about a possible serial killer in British Columbia by the name of Robert William Pickton; no one even tried to pretend that he was the subject of an investigation into possession of illegal firearms.

On the morning of February 13, in an effort to understand him and his family background, Dana Lillies was in Vancouver interviewing his sister, Linda Wright. Although Lillies may have been the most junior member of Don Adam's hand-picked interview team and was the only woman on it, she was no neophyte. She'd been a member of the RCMP for nine years and was working towards her profiler's qualifications. Young, slim and attractive, with long, tightly curled dark hair, a soft voice and a gentle smile, Lillies had become an excellent interviewer with a sympathetic manner. Although Linda Wright for many years had had as little to do with her brother as possible, unless she needed his signature on a real estate deal, she was willing to help. She talked openly to Lillies about her family and her brother's life, telling her what a difficult time Willie had had in school. She also said that Dave dominated Willie to the point that he would tell him when it was time to go to bed.

But as Lillies and Linda Wright were meeting in Vancouver, the whole case changed abruptly. At eleven thirty that morning Daryl Hetherington received a message to go immediately to Site V-3, the

Dodge Fargo DeSoto motor home. On her first look around it seemed very messy and dirty, so dirty that it looked as if rats had been living in the vehicle. But the searchers in the motor home told her they thought what they were looking at in several places was blood. With another RCMP officer, Joy Kearsey, Hetherington formally seized the vehicle. Within half an hour they had found what they were sure was blood—on the wall just above one of the beds, on moulding, on socks and shoes and on the edge of a plywood kitchen counter. They continued to search and bag evidence, and when they returned the next morning, they found even more staining that they were sure was blood. They seized cigarette butts, a used crack pipe and nine syringes found in a woman's black jacket, as well as a broken green Growers cider bottle, a full cider bottle, a cardboard box that had contained handcuffs and another woman's jacket with a syringe in it. There was one puzzling object that they seized as well: a long white metal-mesh hose, also stained, with a showerhead attached to it.

They were certain that the staining they had found on most of these items was blood. And they were also sure that someone had been using the motor home very recently, because it was dry. Fairly fresh food was still in the refrigerator and cupboards, and clothes and bedding were strewn around, including a sneaker with blood on it. It was hard to conclude anything else other than that someone had lost a lot of blood in that motor home and that it had happened in the recent past. They had no idea at this stage whose blood it might be, but the site became the immediate priority for testing.

While the forensic team worked in the motor home, Stephen Vrolyk had been working with forensic identification technicians outside Willie's trailer; they were taking pictures as he examined the items one by one. Rooting through a garbage can, Vrolyk found four inhalers, one wrapped inside a piece of yellow paper that turned out to be a prescription receipt made out to Sereena Abotsway for salbutamol; a bronchodilator, bought at Garland Pharmacy on East Hastings in Vancouver; and two other inhalers, one for Flovent and another for Nasacort, both with Sereena's name on them.

On this same day a third search team, led by two Port Coquitlam RCMP sergeants, Mike Connor and Gary Moore, was searching two lockers that Pickton had rented at Imperial Self Storage in Port Coquitlam's industrial park, a convenient place to drop stuff off, as it was a five-minute drive from the farm. Willie had packed them full with clothing, tools—including saws and power tools—a briefcase containing documents with Ross Contois's name on them, a woman's black belt and an envelope full of teeth.

Other task force members spent the day working with witnesses. One of these was Renata Bond, who gave the police a six-hour taped interview about Sherry Irving's time at her place in New Westminster, telling them how Dave had hired Sherry for Willie and what happened the night she took Sherry to the farm. The police decided it was time to become more proactive, more aggressive with Pickton. They'd just found blood in the motor home, more of Sereena's medicine, tools and women's clothes in a storage locker, and had listened to Bond's chilling story. After some discussion they came up with a plan: Danielle Campbell would visit Willie the next day to serve him with a summons to appear in court, a summons based on their finding illegal weapons two weeks earlier. She would also tell him that the police had found a woman's finger on the farm, and while that wasn't true, Canadian law allowed her to do this in an effort to gain information. But her main job was simply to talk to him, to see how Pickton would respond to her as a woman.

A few hours later, after she returned from interviewing Linda Wright, Lillies joined a number of the other team members to meet with star profiler Roy Hazelwood. After an urgent request from the task force, he had travelled from his base in Virginia to give the interview team his best advice. Danielle Campbell and Keith Davidson, who had met Hazelwood before and knew his work, had suggested asking him to help, arguing that this was one of the best ways they could think of to help everyone understand Willie Pickton and to get beyond his surly indifference when the time came for a formal interview. As long as they could send him plenty of background material, he'd be happy to help, was Hazelwood's response.

Bill Fordy was skeptical about this plan and he objected to the cost of bringing Hazelwood to British Columbia. The only reason he agreed was that neither Davidson nor Scott Filer had experience with someone like Pickton, and they wanted Hazelwood there. "At the end of the day, I said yes," Fordy said later. "I did not recommend Mr. Hazelwood, but at the end of the day, I'm the one who said, 'Yes, bring him out.'"

The meeting with Hazelwood began at six thirty. Jim Hunter was there and Fordy, of course, and Lillies; so were Campbell, Davidson and Filer, as well as Paul Stader, who was learning how to be a profiler, as Davidson's understudy. Fordy remained convinced that this whole thing would be a useless exercise and was also worried that Hazelwood might take a role in the interview. "I saw his value as such that I did not need him to come," he said later. "I did not request that he come out for the interview. In other words, I felt there would be no value added by his presence."

The meeting did not change Fordy's mind about what Hazelwood and his fellow profilers could bring to an understanding of how to deal with Willie Pickton. "They didn't have any experience with serial killers," he said. "Some of [their ideas] I see as common sense and some I guess I see as [having] less value. I guess that flows from the perspective or the—what my teammates and I bring as experience that is operational in nature. The perspective that the profilers bring is based on reading articles. And when I say 'operational' I mean like hands-on, frontline experience. They do not have that experience."

The difficulty about Fordy's antipathy towards Hazelwood's presence was that, like so many good criminal investigators and so many who were senior and respected, he was as uneducated about profilers as Kim Rossmo's colleagues in the Vancouver Police Department had been. Despite the negative publicity the VPD received over its disgraceful treatment of Rossmo, especially when he was proved right about the missing women, many senior police officers in British Columbia continued to see profilers, even world-famous, experienced cops such as Roy Hazelwood, as nothing more than a joke. "Voodoo science" they continued to call their work. Not for real men.

How much did Bill Fordy really know about Roy Hazelwood, other than that he was famous? Did he know that he had served with the U.S. Army's military police in Vietnam, where his main focus was investigating sexual assaults and where he was in charge of the army's criminal investigations division training for new agents? Did he know that by 1968 Hazelwood was a major, that he went on to study forensic medicine and, after leaving the army, joined the FBI in 1971? He had been investigating the Italian Mafia in New York State when he was reassigned to the Quantico headquarters as a manager. Soon afterwards he moved to the new Behavioral Science Unit, joining, among others, the legendary Howard Teten, Bob Ressler and John Douglas—all very experienced police officers who had worked on many homicide investigations and serial killer cases—because they were looking for a sexual assault investigator. When Hazelwood let Teten know that he was also interested in profiling, Teten himself became Hazelwood's instructor.

. It was Hazelwood who established the distinction between "organized" and "disorganized" killers—standard definitions that have been used all over the world since 1980—and he soon became recognized as one of the FBI's most experienced officers anywhere on sex crimes. In the course of his work he had interviewed hundreds of murderers, including serial killers and sexual sadists.

When Fordy did agree with what Hazelwood had to say, it was because, he explained, it was just common sense. He also admitted that he agreed with the assessment of Hazelwood and the other profilers that Willie was a psychopath. But he had no more respect for the RCMP's profilers than he did for Hazelwood. After the general meeting with them that day, Fordy had nothing positive to say about their advice. "So prior to the interview, it's hard for me to assess the value they added," he said later. "Certainly in retrospect, I don't feel that they added much value to the interview process in a custodial situation." Hazelwood, he added, "provided a background on Mr. Pickton and identified some potential themes that could be used in the interview— some basic interview strategy like room setup, mike quality, et cetera. I don't want to disparage Mr. Hazelwood, but I walked away with no more understanding than when he started." And when asked if he had been "assisted at all by his theories," Fordy's reply was a firm no.

After the meeting, Don Adam told Jim Hunter that Fordy's interview with Pickton was off for the time being. They weren't ready. Roy Hazelwood returned to Virginia.

The next day, February 15, the team decided to deliver the summons to Willie to appear in court on the firearms charges; it was just an excuse to try to talk to him. But it set off a difficult discussion about Danielle Campbell's usefulness. Keith Davidson thought a woman wouldn't be able to connect with Pickton, and that asking her to deliver the summons and try to talk to him and win his confidence was "a complete waste of time," as Fordy said later. "I don't think he saw any reason to involve a female in this." Two hours after Davidson's comment, Jim Hunter and Dana Lillies dropped Campbell off at the Vancouver Airport to catch a flight home to Edmonton.

Lillies and Hunter left the airport for a brief meeting with Bill Fordy in a nearby Starbucks, where they worked out a plan to go to Willie's job site so Lillies could deliver the summons to appear in court. But when they got close to the site, the RCMP surveillance team keeping an eye on Willie alerted them that Dave Pickton was there too. Knowing he would interfere, the officers decided to try again the next day. And the next day luck was with them: Dave was on another job. Jim Hunter had coached Lillies on what to say to Willie: Tell him we've found a ventilator in a red car. Tell him we've found a woman's fingertip. Tell him the media are waiting for an explanation for all of this.

Fordy made sure Lillies was wired up with an Eagle micro-recorder, powerful enough for police work but small enough to be virtually invisible when it was clipped to her belt. For her own safety, because she would be alone with Pickton, he also gave her his cellphone; this was a flip phone she could also clip to her belt and leave open, on and connected to Jim Hunter's cellphone. Dressed in plainclothes, driving an unmarked black four-door Pontiac Grand Am, Lillies headed to Willie's job site for the day, near the corner of Number 1 Road and Moncton Street in Richmond. Several miles directly south of the Vancouver Airport, the site was near the mouth of the Fraser River, where it empties into the Strait of Georgia, the body of water that separates Vancouver Island from Vancouver and the rest of the mainland. Lillies drove alone but she was protected. Jim Hunter and Bill Fordy were nearby in another car, and Special O had sent a vehicle as well. They weren't conspicuous, just drifting, always nearby. No one was taking any chances.

When she arrived, Lillies found the work site surrounded by a chain-link fence that she had to open before she could drive the car in. She parked the Pontiac, leaving her documents in it so she could keep her hands free, and got out. A man was on a clattering white BobCat moving pallets around. She recognized him from pictures—it was Pickton. Lillies took out her badge and waved it at him.

"Are you Mr. Pickton?" she asked over the roar. The man shook his head and kept his foot on the Cat's accelerator.

"You look an awful lot like Mr. Pickton," insisted Lillies. "Can I see some identification, please?"

Pickton paid no attention to her. He turned in his seat, reached behind it and pulled out a hammer. Then he tried to put the BobCat into gear.

Lillies asked him to turn the BobCat off. He did. "Are you Mr. Pickton?" she asked again.

Yes, he nodded.

"Did you think that I was the media at first?"

Pickton nodded again.

"There's nothing to be alarmed about," she said quickly. "I just have some paperwork I need to serve you with."

Gesturing towards the black Pontiac, Lillies began walking over to it and Willie ambled along beside her. Lillies opened the driver's door and indicated that he should get in the passenger side. He hesitated, then pointed to a building nearby. "No," she said. "My paperwork is in the car. This won't take long."

Willie swung himself into the front passenger seat but only perched on it, leaving his legs outside with the door open. Ready to run, if he had to. But Lillies was calm. She told him that even though she was wearing regular clothes she was a police officer, and that nothing he said to her today could be used against him. He nodded as if he understood. And when she asked him if she could see his driver's licence, just so she could be sure he was Willie Pickton, he got it out and showed her his valid licence.

The two of them chatted for about twenty minutes about all the negative press he had been getting. Lillies' gentle style made Willie feel comfortable, and he confided, with tears welling in his eyes, that he felt like Princess Diana because he was being hounded by the media just as she had been. When Lillies finally handed the summons to him, he didn't look at it; he simply folded it across his left knee and continued to talk about his problems. He was just a poor farm boy, he told her. Then he started in on the story of his life. It wasn't long before he'd hauled his legs into the car and pulled the door almost shut. Soon rain started to pelt down, and for two hours they sat there while Willie, staring straight ahead through the windshield, talked about his life. Occasionally, when he thought she wasn't looking at him, he would glance at her quickly, then return to looking straight ahead. He refused to make eye contact.

"He wasn't fully acknowledging my presence," Lillies said later. "And then when I asked how he was dealing with the media, he did become emotional. And at several periods during the conversation he became quite emotional and had his head down and I could see tears dripping from his face onto the floor mat. At some points there were gut-wrenching sobs . . . I was able to see his chin trembling with the emotion of his tears." It doesn't matter what happens now, he told her, my life is over. "I'm screwed and tattooed."

His stories as he poured them out to Dana Lillies that afternoon were more or less the same ones he rolled out for anyone who would sit and listen to him. As Lillies remembered later, "they were about the people that he had helped along the way who were down and out, saying that, you know, when you help people, then they'll be there to help you.

"He talked about his childhood and gave me numerous dates that—that sort of jumped from one date to the next. He mentioned the first trip that he'd ever taken to the States and he repeatedly mentioned that he had only two hundred dollars in his pocket. He mentioned that several times. He mentioned that he had a number of pen pals that he talked to regularly and that while on his trip to the States he met with a female whose name I couldn't recall immediately following, but I believe was Connie. And [he] said that he had been engaged to this female. And he said that he had wanted to marry this female, but she had been unwilling to leave the United States and he had been unable to leave the farm." And why couldn't he leave the farm? Because there was a clause in his mother's will stating that he was to remain on the farm until he was forty years old, he confided with resentment (later, though, he told Lillies that he hadn't known about this clause until after his mother's death). He also told her a story from his trip to the United States; it was his uninformed yarn about Americans eating cherry pie, something he found disgusting. As Lillies told her colleagues later, he clearly didn't understand the Presidents' Day holiday, when Americans eat cherry pie in honour of George Washington.

And Willie told Lillies all about his favourite black and white calf that he had picked out as a child, and that he had gone out to the barn one day to find that it had been slaughtered. He told her about a black bear that killed pigs on their farm and he told her about a dog he'd had called Toby. He rambled on about his parents and when and how they had died. He complained about Dave, calling him an asshole who was greedy and always took more than he needed. "He'd only ask his parents for fifty cents because that was sufficient to buy what was needed, a pop and something else," said Lillies later when she repeated his comments to her fellow officers, "whereas his brother would ask for two dollars." Willie said he had once slaughtered forty-three pigs in one day and, showing Lillies the scar under his chin where Sandra Gail Ringwald had stabbed him, he told her how he had nearly died. He told her as well about being attacked by wild boars.

Willie even tried to explain why he could never have killed any of the women at the farm. He had given Gina Houston a truck to use, he said, and had not expected anything from her in return. He had given another woman $700 to pay a phone bill and had not expected anything in return. "If I'm a killer," he asked Lillies, "why didn't I kill one of them?" Willie was having such a good time rolling through his good old days on the farm and all his built-up resentments that it was hard for Lillies to get a word in edgewise. The guns on the farm were ones he'd inherited and he needed them because the farm was a dangerous place. He had no use for drugs or alcohol. Nor for computers, cellphones and modern technology.

Finally Lillies had had enough and began asking him tough questions. What about the inhaler the police had found in a red car? Willie said it must have been in one of the cars he bought from police auctions. And when she told him a woman's finger had been found on the farm, he wanted to know where it had been found. Lillies said she wasn't sure; it might have been the barn—had there been any industrial accidents on the farm? Yes, he said, but none that he could remember that involved any women.

Her final item of business was the summons regarding the three firearms offences. If you don't show up in court, she warned him, you will be charged with failure to appear and a warrant will be issued for your arrest. Willie said he understood. Did he have to be there in person or could his lawyer go for him? Ask your lawyer, Lillies replied. "And make sure you know if you need to attend for fingerprinting."

At one point during the conversation Willie noticed Bill Fordy's cellphone on her belt. "Is the tape recorder working okay?" he asked. "Yes, it's fine, thanks," said Lillies. In fact it wasn't. Lillies had no idea that the battery on Jim Hunter's phone had died, which meant that he and Fordy, hiding nearby in their own vehicle, couldn't tell if she was in trouble. They assumed, because the conversation had gone well so far, that she was safe.

"It's been nice speaking with you," Lillies said finally, "but I have to get back to work." They shook hands, but Willie didn't want to let her go. He continued chatting to her even after they stopped to move her car away from the gate to let a large truck onto the site. Before she left, Willie asked her for a business card; when he looked at it, he told her that his lawyers had cautioned him against speaking to anyone and he would be telling them about talking to her. The police won't find anything on the farm, he added. They can dig up the whole property but they won't find anything.

As soon as she got back to headquarters, Lillies discovered that Jim Hunter's phone had died and that the Eagle recorder had not been working while she talked to Willie. No one could download the audio files, so Lillies hastily made notes and debriefed her colleagues at a meeting in the early afternoon. Later, through the rest of the afternoon and early evening, she worked through these notes, adding more and more detail as one topic after another triggered her memory. Later, Bill Fordy said that he must have turned off the recorder by mistake.

CHAPTER THIRTY-SEVEN

MIKE PETRIE WANTS THE JOB

It was now February 16, 2002, and Willie Pickton still faced only a comparatively minor charge of possessing illegal weapons. Growing numbers of experts were picking through the buildings on his farm, seizing evidence, while Bill Fordy, sure that Pickton would be charged with multiple murders, was preparing to interview him.

People were being cautious. The slightest mistake could stall everything. The evidence they collected had to be strong enough to charge him with murder and keep him behind bars until he went to trial. That meant Don Adam's team had to be able to convince Peder Gulbransen, the regional Crown counsel in New Westminster, that they had a good case against Pickton. They hadn't forgotten that Gulbransen was the same regional Crown who had sent John Cater back to obtain more evidence to support his application for a warrant to search the Pickton farm in 1999.

Adam admitted to his colleagues that the waiting was difficult. "We were having lots of trouble hanging on to Mr. Pickton, so we were very frightened," he said later. He and his colleagues met with Gulbransen and laid out the case—no paper, just talk. Gulbransen was collegial but blunt. Don't charge too soon, he advised. The case was still too weak and the investigation was incomplete. "So, in essence," remembered Adam, "we were just going to have to try and contain Mr. Pickton and keep going." Pickton knew he was under surveillance and he knew that his phones were tapped.

Adam's challenge now was to present enough evidence to Gulbransen—everything the police had, including any information they knew of that might contradict their position—so that a judge could review the documents and make a decision about whether there was enough evidence to lay charges. Because these decisions are often contested after the fact, the idea is to have the Crown vet the documents to ensure that they convey the information and to prevent any errors or omissions that might later result in a successful application to override the authorizing judge's decision. The Crown counsel usually goes with the police when they turn the documents over to the judge for review.

As these discussions were going on in the New Westminster Regional Crown Office, one of the prosecutors working there was fascinated. A few weeks earlier when he had the radio on, Mike Petrie had heard task force spokesperson Cate Galliford talking to Vancouver broadcaster Peter Warren. For several years Warren, a well-known investigative journalist in Vancouver, had been running interviews, commentaries and tips from listeners about the missing women case. As Petrie remembers it, the interview was "all about how they had put together a joint RCMP–VPD task force and I remember thinking that was a good idea."

At forty-eight, tall, broad and balding, with bright blue eyes, a wide smile and a goatee, Petrie was a senior Crown in New Westminster. It was just a few days after listening to Warren's interview with Galliford that he heard the news about the police seizure of the farm. Petrie was intrigued. He lives in Coquitlam and could even picture the property. As soon as he got to work, he dropped into Gulbransen's office.

"Is this our case?" Petrie asked.

"Yes."

"Is there anything to it?"

"Yes, there's something to it."

It would be their case because Pickton's trial, if there was to be one, would be held in the Supreme Court building that housed their own offices. While Port Coquitlam had its own courthouse, it was a provincial court. If murder charges were laid, the preliminary hearing to listen to the evidence would be held in that courthouse. But if the provincial court judge decided there was enough evidence to send Pickton to trial, the trial would normally take place in New Westminster.

Petrie listened carefully as Gulbransen laid out what he knew about the new case. "Oh," he said, fascinated, "I'll put my dibs in on that!" Which is how a lawyer who was born and brought up in a Vancouver housing project for poor people and spent much of his childhood at the Salvation Army mission in the Downtown Eastside wound up running the longest, most expensive, most complicated and highest-profile criminal prosecutions in Canadian history.

Although he was named Michael Shannon Mahoney when he was born in New Westminster in 1954, Petrie's parents divorced, and he soon took the name of the man who brought him up, Daniel "Sax" Petrie—called that because he played the saxophone. Mike Petrie's real father, a drinker, a rounder and a man who had served time in the penitentiary, had seen nothing but trouble all his life and would die an alcoholic. When he was truly down-and-out he would go to Harbour Light, the Salvation Army mission on East Cordova in the Downtown Eastside.

When Mike Petrie was a child, his mother, who supported her kids by working as a switchboard operator at St. Paul's Hospital, would take him down to Harbour Light to visit his dad, and the staff would babysit him. It was his introduction to the Downtown Eastside and to Sax Petrie, who worked there. Sax married Mike's mother when Petrie was six and his sister was eleven; he left the job at Harbour Light for a better one, as maintenance man at the Georgian Towers Motor Hotel on Georgia Street. The family lived in a small townhouse in Orchard Park, a neighbourhood of subsidized housing several blocks south of the Downtown Eastside. "We always called it the Project," remembers Petrie. "It was at 41st and Nanaimo in southeast Vancouver; it was part of B.C. government housing that included Orchard Park, Little Mountain and Raymur, which was down on Hastings and Skeena, near Broadway and Boundary.

"Back in those days, if people moved they went to another housing project," Petrie explains. "To get in, there were financial requirements. You had to have at least two kids. You were always under a certain financial bracket. There was a lot of social engineering going on then, putting low-income people into middle-income neighbourhoods, but it didn't work. There was a lot of crime." And in the Petrie family there were soon four kids, too many for their tiny three-bedroom row house. Lack of space was only one of the pressures the Petrie family faced. "There was no money," he says. "So there was no hockey, no tennis, no skiing . . . well, it was an interesting youth."

What there was all through these years was the Salvation Army. Petrie attended services there with his family every week until he was seventeen. Although he was a good student, both in elementary school and at Killarney High School, after graduating in 1971 it never occurred to him to go to university. It wasn't just the money; it was because there was no tradition in his family of going to university. Instead, because he knew he needed some kind of education, he studied economics for two years in a diploma program at Langara Community College. What he'd do after that, he had no idea. Look for a job probably. But one day he ran into an old friend who had been the Killarney student council president. He told Petrie he was picking up an admission form to law school.

"What's that all about?" Petrie asked. The friend explained and Petrie thought it sounded pretty interesting. "So I decided I would do that too. I didn't know bugger all about law but I always thought it was good to have options open."

Petrie took the LSAT exams with his friend, and when he discovered how well he'd done, he transferred from Langara to the University of British Columbia (UBC) for his last two years. Although he had always secretly hoped he'd work in the music business, he wound up studying psychology and thought about becoming a clinical psychologist. Then he considered going on in English literature, or maybe theology. Theology? "I have never abandoned the spiritual side . . . my faith is very important to me," he says today. "It has never abandoned me—but church? No."

His choice finally was the law. He started classes at UBC's law school in 1975. "I always had a good sense of right and wrong. A lot of kids in the Project would go into the police or the military. I thought about it too—the money was good." But in the end, law school was the right decision. He found it exciting, especially criminal law. The years at UBC were interesting, joyful ones for him. But Petrie had to work harder than most of his classmates. From high school through to the end of his law school years, he worked part-time for up to twenty-eight hours a week. He never had a car. He lived at home until he was twenty-three. Yet he always knew, even if he lacked their advantages, that he was well-liked and as bright as the other students. Years later when one of them, now a successful Vancouver lawyer, was asked what people thought of Mike Petrie, the poor boy from the Project in a law school dominated by kids from well-to-do families, the reaction was immediate. "Mike? They thought he was adorable."

In the summer between his second and third years, Petrie couldn't find a job and wound up having to take out a student loan. It was a drastic move but it proved to be a good one; for the first time in his life he had a little free time. And luck came his way. Out at the law school one day, he looked at the postings on the notice board and saw one looking for a student to work in Cranbrook, a small town in the beautiful mountainous British Columbia interior. The man who posted the job notice was Dana Urban, a brilliant young defence lawyer from Saskatchewan who had already had a fascinating life; his career by this time had included being a machine gunner with the U.S. Army in Vietnam and a member of a railway tunnel crew in the United States. Now he was doing legal aid work.

Petrie got the job, loved working in Cranbrook and was inspired by Urban's passion for the underdog. Years later, like coroner Bob Stair, Urban worked for the International War Crimes Tribunal in The Hague; he served as an international prosecutor in the case against Bosnian Croats for crimes against the Muslim population in Bosnia-Herzegovina.

The day after he was called to the bar in 1979, Petrie returned to Cranbrook to article with Melnick and Carlgren, a firm of defence lawyers whose partners, Tom Melnick and Don Carlgren, went on to become judges. Once again Mike Petrie was fortunate in his choices, not just because his bosses were outstanding mentors but also because he quickly learned what his own strengths were, and for him that meant being in a courtroom. "I always wanted to make a difference," he says. "I hated being in the office. I hated managing. I liked being in the courtroom."

It was in the courtroom that he met a young broadcast reporter, Erin Hoole, whose family owned the local radio station as well as stations in nearby Fernie and Trail. Petrie had planned to return to Vancouver, but meeting Erin changed everything; they married and he worked happily as a Crown prosecutor in all the small towns in the East Kootenays, including Sparwood, Fernie, Creston, Invermere, Elkford and Cranbrook. Again Petrie was blessed with talented colleagues who went on to high-profile jobs: Richard Kierans, who would become a prosecutor on the Air India case; Dirk Ryneveld, who would become B.C.'s police complaints commissioner; and his former boss Don Carlgren, who became a judge.

In 1988 Mike Petrie and Erin Hoole, now the parents of two boys, Geoff and Alex, moved to Coquitlam; she had a new managerial job with CKWX Radio (and eventually became a vice-president of Rogers Broadcasting). Petrie continued to work as a Crown prosecutor, now based in New Westminster. Eight years later Petrie and Hoole separated amicably, although they have never divorced.

"One of the things I have always felt was that I had one foot in the world I grew up in and one foot in the other world," says Petrie. "Erin's dad had a plane. They went out for dinner. Never in the entire time I lived with my own parents did we go out for dinner. I was twenty-three before I ever had a dinner outside my own house.

"When this case came along I felt a connection to that part of my past, the part that relates to people who live in this environment. I had one foot in that world and now I had a chance to do something about it. There was a girl, the daughter of a woman who grew up across from me. She was murdered." Many people in the Project dealt with violence all their lives, he said, "and there, but for the grace of God, go I. Taking the Pickton case was a way of reconciling what I'm doing now."

Like everyone else at this point, all Mike Petrie could do now was wait to see if the Mounties could pull this off. John Cater was toiling on new affidavits that would meet the Crown's requirements for an arrest and murder charges. The pressure on the police was intense. By now the story that the police had finally found a prime suspect for the disappearances of dozens of women was making headlines around the world. The wails of family members were seared into the memories of television viewers. If the police could lay murder charges against Pickton, it could easily be North America's largest serial killer case. The task force was bringing in more helpers every day; two weeks after Willie's arrest there were eighty-five people working on the farm, including forty-five forensic identification specialists. Every day new tents, new awnings, new ATCO trailers were brought in. Soon there was a swipe-card system in place at the main gate so that the command centre knew exactly who was on the site at any moment; without a swipe card, no one was allowed in.

Though the police remained silent about what they were finding in their search, news was leaking out, some of it from Bill Malone, who had appointed himself the family spokesman. He talked to reporters about an inhaler the police had found, as well as "shoes, women's clothes, men's clothes, identification . . . you won't believe what gets left behind." But these items came out of vehicles the police had sold at auction, he said, out of vehicles that had been seized and held in a police compound, most of which were in rough shape. It was only natural that they would be stuffed with clothing and junk. Malone also told reporters that the Picktons knew they were being watched by undercover police.

The brothers assumed, quite correctly, that their phone calls were also being recorded. On February 18 Jim Hunter listened to a tape of the brothers discussing Dave's friendship with a couple of Vancouver city police officers who were working for the task force. He also heard Willie ask Dave for his opinion about bail, the charges he might be facing, a possible release date and whether or not he had to obey Dana Lillies' summons to show up for fingerprinting. The next day the police brought Willie in for a lineup and asked Renata Bond if she recognized the man who was waiting for Sherry Irving at the Pickton farm in September 1997. Bond picked out Willie right away. He knew he was in deep trouble.

"I'm going to go bye-bye," Willie told Dinah Taylor. "I'm tired of the whole life." Was he threatening to kill himself or bluffing? Jim Hunter decided it was time for Dana Lillies to see him again; Willie had already opened up to her and maybe she would be able to get even more out of him. On February 19 Hunter and Lillies drove to the Steveston work site; the excuse she would give Willie this time was that the police didn't need him to come in after all to be fingerprinted and photographed, because they were fine with the prints and picture they had from his arrest on February 5. She would also tell him that there had been far too much media attention, and the police would contact his lawyer the next time he needed to come in. Hunter gave her another Eagle recorder, as well as a backup digital voice recorder, and this time he made sure they were working.

Willie was in a building when she arrived, and another worker called him to come out.

"Are you Connie?" Willie asked. Lillies was puzzled. Connie? No. Later she realized he might have been thinking of his long-lost girlfriend Connie Anderson, the pen pal from Pontiac, Michigan, he had once hoped to marry. The girl who didn't want to leave her job for a farm in British Columbia.

This time their conversation lasted less than ten minutes. Lillies gave him the good news about the fingerprinting and picture. But he was morose. He blurted out that he wanted to die. He said it was a

bad scene. Lillies attempted to placate him. "I got yelled at for talking to you so long," she began.

Willie listened to her but his mind was elsewhere. "Finger this or
that . . . way over my head . . . one day at a time . . ."

"How did the rest of the weekend go?" Lillies asked.

"Busy, busy, busy, busy."

"Other jobs on the go now?"

His response was inaudible. Lillies decided to wrap this up. "It's
a great idea to talk to you, but I'm not the one in charge." She
needed to let him know she had no say in what was going to happen
to him.

"Thank you," said Willie. "I really appreciate that."

Lillies drove off but Jim Hunter decided she should try again the
next afternoon, which was February 20. Once again she headed to
the Richmond work site equipped with an Eagle recorder and a
backup digital recorder. This time her job was to give Willie some
more good news—the finger she'd mentioned to him a few days
earlier was not, in fact, that of a woman; tests had shown it was a
man's. And then she was to show him a poster prepared by the task
force with numbered pictures of forty-eight missing women and ask
him what he knew about them. The poster was one of the several
dozen "interview aids" prepared to help Fordy with the interview he
expected to do with Pickton.

Followed at a safe distance by Hunter, who remained out of
sight but in touch through an open cellphone, Lillies found Pickton
at about twelve thirty that afternoon. Willie didn't hesitate to climb
into the front seat beside her. And there he stayed, for two hours.

At first Lillies apologized for the cluttered car. "It's a little
dusty . . ."

"No problem," Willie said. "When this is over, I'll buy you
supper."

"We had word back from the lab today," Lillies said. "I told you
about the fingertip. You know about DNA. I've got great news. It's
male DNA."

"It's way over my head," said Willie. "Can't believe all this. So somebody lost their prints? Where did they find it?"

"In the barn."

"Was it all split up, deteriorated?"

"It was a significant chunk."

"Thank you. I really appreciate this."

At this point Lillies unrolled the poster she'd brought and showed it to Willie. "There were a lot of coming and going from the farm— can you tell me which of these women would have been here?"

He stared at the faces in the poster. "Well, they're sure ugly, aren't they? See them . . . none of them . . . this one here looks like somebody . . . not sure . . . not at my place . . . I might have seen her downtown . . . I know a *lot* of women . . . number fourteen . . ."

"I don't want to rush you," Lillies said.

He picked out one face. "Seen her around someplace . . . not at my place . . . she looks awful pretty . . . there are *some* that are pretty . . . are they all missing?"

"Yeah."

Willie had moved on to another face on the poster. "She was pretty too. Look at them marks on her face, eh? I got to tell you, I don't know none of them, eh . . . can't see anything here, and I got a good memory. The one that knifed me, she's not in here neither."

"No," Lillies agreed.

Willie stared at the pretty woman's face on the poster. "Not seen any of these around my place. If I remember right, I seen her around the Patricia . . . they got a little parking lot there and they say, 'You want a date?' and I say, 'No, no' and I give them twenty bucks or so . . ." He began to ramble. He mentioned Dinah Taylor. "Dinah was with me eighteen months or so; [she is] handicapped . . . said she'd never walk again . . . on crutches . . . worried about falling down . . . If I can help somebody I will try and help. If I can see some better pictures. These are not the clearest pictures."

By now Willie had lost interest in the pictures of the missing women. He knew he was in deep trouble. "Don't know where it's all going to end up. I hope I come out clean in all this. I'm nobody. Now my whole life is gone. I honestly don't know what's going on."

Lillies listened patiently to his complaints before asking him if he'd been by the farm lately. "I have a friend that's working there now," she told him. "It's a huge task. It will take six months. They are digging right down."

"Oh really? I never thought I'd be this popular. Six months, eh? Somebody told me it could be two years."

"They're even talking about going in under the new condos there," Lillies said.

"What! How can you do that?" Willie exclaimed. "There is nothing there. We did a ton of work there and had machines there day and night. Some places we were down eighteen feet. All structural fill. We had it for a dump site. Had to bring it up. Nothing out there. One time I buried a llama there; it fell off the truck and hanged itself. West Coast Reduction only takes pigs. Won't take goats, lambs. There's nothing, but nothing, around the townhouses, nothing but nothing. Behind the piggery I buried a llama. I can do a map if you like."

"Sure," agreed Lillies.

"If it helps at all . . . I'm trying to help if I can." He sighed and started to draw a map of the farm on a piece of paper. "The piggery is all gone now . . . uhhh, right around there."

"What's that?"

"Maybe chickens . . ."

"You got live chickens walking around there?"

"No, they're buried there—anything buried, it's right there."

"How many chickens?"

"Say a hundred."

"You were telling me about the llama," Lillies said. "Where was the llama buried?"

"I honestly don't know. Should be buried right around here . . . don't know."

"Is the piggery still standing?"

"No, it's all gone now. I do have a pile of bones here, three feet long, a pile of them here. In the barn. You got it—you go in—it is right behind the cooler. I know where everything is. If you can set it up, I will go in and show you where everything is, if it would help. I'm not trying to hide anything. Right in this area here." He fiddled with his map. "The doorway is here . . . the bones are three feet long. You'd be interested in looking at them."

"Bones of what?" asked Lillies.

"If you were to see them," answered Willie, "you'd think they were human." At this point Willie's mind wandered back to Christmas Eve of 1997, when he drove to the Downtown Eastside with the two black piglets. "I had a little Chevrolet Cavalier, black," he remembered. "I had two little pigs . . . I wanted to do something with them Christmas Eve. I took two little pigs to Vancouver and let them go on Hastings; comical for the first little while. Right before Christmas, nothing to be found but two working girls and two little pigs. Little guys. They were pets around the house. That happened in 1997."

Then Willie returned to the map he was drawing for Lillies. "These ones here, these leg bones, they would be . . ."

She tried to understand. "You said they are—" but Willie interrupted.

"Only thing I ever kept were leg bones. They're two-legged. I'm going to be nailed to the cross, I tell you. There's one doorway there, one doorway there, one doorway there . . . if they wished me to, I'd like to go in and show them for—possibly one bone is right there . . . these are two-legged—if they are human I'm nailed to the cross."

"Are they going to come back as human, Robert?" Lillies asked gently. "You should tell me if you want to. I'm not going to judge things, Robert."

"If you wish me to," Willie said, "I'll go on a lie detector. If there is anything . . ." But his mind wandered again. "Lost three receptical [reciprocating] saws in the last few months. Why would they steal my reciptical saw? I use it for cutting meat. I lost a cutter, my plasma cutter, second one; I lost tools like you wouldn't believe."

Dana Lillies tried to bring him back on track. "My mind's open to you," she said. "How did the bones get here?"

"I put them here," said Willie. "And if they're human I'm nailed to the cross. They're mine, the leg bones down there, they should not come back as anything but animal, but if they come back as human, I'll be glad to admit to it."

Lillies was quiet for a minute. "I think you know we're gonna find out these are human bones," she said. "These are humans."

"They should be inside the wheelbarrow," said Willie. "If they are human I'll admit to it—they are two-legged animals as far as I know—animal, and I put them there."

"How many are there?"

"Three sets. Five and one over here. Maybe four with one over there . . . closest thing to human. If that helps, anyway. Myself, they should be sitting inside a wheelbarrow."

"What's over here?" Lillies asked, trying to keep him on track.

"Chickens. I got to see the autopsy on that."

"Where did you find them?"

"They're two-legged animals?"

"Can't you think of any?"

"They're probably . . ." Pickton's attention had drifted again. "Don't know anything . . . My sister don't know nothing, my brother don't know nothing—I'm about the only one who knows anything. Nothing but nothing but nothing. If they come back as human bones I am screwed."

"You already know what's going to come back," Lillies said. "You know they're human."

"You got me thinking," said Willie. "Could be female or could be male—it's gonna to be interesting."

"You already know what they're going to be," she said. "They're going to be human . . . I am not here to judge you."

Willie recovered quickly. "The bones are not human. If they are,

I'm in deep shit. The freezers—long time ago—that was not human parts in the freezer as far as I know. May have been one or two quite a spell ago but not human parts."

"Just bone at that point?" she asked. "Or did they have flesh on them?"

"Oh yeah, oh yeah."

"Did you do that?" she pressed.

"Oh yeah—I was making stuff up with them." Suddenly Willie became cagey again. "I should probably tell you what they are. The bones there are ostrich. I had three of 'em. My plan was . . . I couldn't do it. If I didn't do it they couldn't go after me."

While Lillies talked to Pickton and tried to make sense of his scattered responses, events were moving quickly on the farm. The forensic technicians in the motor home found a blood-stained orange cushion and foam mattress, and Jonathan Faris, a technician in the lab, also found semen and hairs on them. Search techs gave the lab many more items from the motor home, including the silver mesh hose with the showerhead; the lab found that the staining on all of these things was human blood. But whose blood? Feverishly the lab looked for the answer. It came in at 3:15 the next afternoon, February 21, 2002, when the lab called Marg Kingsbury and told her the DNA tests on the bloodstains in the motor home had tested positively for the last woman to disappear. Mona Wilson.

CHAPTER THIRTY-EIGHT

THE CELL PLANT

As soon as the lab confirmed that it was Mona Wilson's blood in the motor home, Don Adam went to see Peder Gulbransen in New Westminster; within an hour Adam had his approval to arrest Pickton and charge him with first-degree murder. Adam couldn't help feeling stunned by how quickly everything was happening.

"I could not, in my wildest dreams, have thought that I would be seizing a property like that and have that situation occurring right under me in real time," Adam now says. "I didn't know how big the investigation was going to be. It was unfolding literally by the hour. Information was coming at us quickly from all directions and it was difficult to keep it all straight."

But just before he left to see Gulbransen, Adam alerted Fordy and the rest of the interview team to get ready for Pickton's interrogation the next day, February 22, 2002. Since November 2001 they'd been rehearsing interrogation strategies for the suspect, whoever he might turn out to be. Now it was time.

At eight o'clock that next morning, Adam gathered together both the interview team and the investigative team to hear the news: Phil Little, Ted Van Overbeek and Jim Hunter would be arresting Pickton later that day. As soon as the meeting ended, the three men huddled together outside the room to read Hunter's handwritten script, which Little was to follow when making the actual arrest. They wanted to be sure it was right. Soon afterwards, a three-page typed version of the script was ready and once again they read it carefully. Adam had chosen them to do this job and Little to make the actual arrest; no one wanted to mess it up. After Little had approved and initialled the script, the men, all dressed in plainclothes, headed for an unmarked police van. Van Overbeek was driving, Little sat in the front passenger seat and Hunter stayed in the back; he was managing a recorder hidden inside his briefcase that would tape the arrest. They drove to the site in Steveston where Pickton had been working for the past several days, the place where he'd talked his heart out to Dana Lillies. Two or three blocks before they got there, Van Overbeek stopped the van long enough to allow Hunter to activate the recorder and make sure it was working.

Later, Phil Little described what happened. "We turned into a demolition site on the south side of Moncton Street just across from the community police station in Steveston, drove southbound into this building site or demolition site. At that point, I could see a flat-bed truck just off to my west. We proceeded past that to the end of the site down by the river. I recall asking a work—a work individual if Mr. Pickton was on site. They directed us back to the truck that we passed on the way in. Van Overbeek turned the van around, we approached the truck. I could see, slouched down in the driver's seat, what appeared to be the back of a male, the back of his head."

They thought the man might be sleeping. Little climbed out of the van, approached the truck and peered in the window. He saw that it was indeed Willie Pickton, and if he had been dozing, right now he was wide awake. Little explained that he was a police officer, showed him his badge and asked him to step out of the vehicle. Willie, who was wearing work clothes—damp ones, and filthy as usual—did what he was told.

"You're under arrest," Little said. Willie was silent.

Then, when Little took Willie to the back of the flatbed truck where Van Overbeek was waiting with a pair of handcuffs, Hunter stepped in. "That won't be necessary," he said.

Van Overbeek put the cuffs back in a pouch. Willie didn't say anything, even when Van Overbeek patted him down for knives or guns, even when he walked with the police officer to the rear seat of the police van. As soon as the four men were in the van, Little began reading the arrest script they'd brought with them, charging Willie with two counts of first-degree murder and noting that he was also under investigation for the murders of another forty-eight women.

Finally Willie spoke. "You mean I murdered every one of them?"

"I don't know; you tell me," replied Hunter. ·

"Yeah, no kidding. I'm shocked myself."

"Are you?" asked Hunter. "You kind of knew it was coming, though, didn't you, Willie?"

"No. Fuck, I can't believe this."

"You have to know that something was going to come pretty soon with all the work that's going on at the site there at your home," Hunter said. "You had to know something was coming down the pipe. And one of our guys is going to explain that all to you. I would prefer that."

"Fuck," Willie repeated. "I can't believe this."

"Why do you say that?" Hunter asked.

"It's not true."

"There's an awful lot of evidence that says it is true."

"I was at the lawyer's a couple of days ago," Willie said. "And he said something about Sereena Abotsway . . . and he says they found a bag or whatever and that was found on, uh, the bed in, uh, Nancy's room, and uh, there's a girl that, uh, brought over all the stuff to me. She was supposed to do all the washing at my place."

"Yeah, well, you know what?" said Hunter. "You know what though, Willie? We know that's bullshit. See, we know that. That's not true."

Hunter asked Willie if he wanted to call his brother. When Willie said yes, Hunter called Dave Pickton on his cellphone and told him that Willie was under arrest for two murders and was being taken to the Surrey cells. He handed the phone to Willie and the brothers spoke briefly. Hunter spoke again to Dave, who said he would call Willie's lawyer right away.

The drive from Steveston to the Surrey Municipal Centre on 57th Avenue took about half an hour. When the van arrived at the

Centre, it entered a long, straight avenue with the RCMP Surrey detachment on the right, the provincial courthouse on the left and Surrey's city hall straight ahead. The complex is set in a large area of parkland and landscaped with lush flower gardens, mass plantings of trees and shrubs and sweeping acres of neatly cropped grass. Many visitors would be surprised to learn that it also contains jail cells and courtrooms.

Except for the exchange with Jim Hunter, Willie hadn't spoken much during the drive, and the other officers made no attempt to talk to him. Van Overbeek pulled the van around the back of the RCMP building and drove down into a locked bay; it opened into a large, modern cell block. The officers took Willie to the counter, where the guards booked him in. The records show that he was fifty-one years old, his phone number was 604–941–2690, he was charged with murder, the time was 1:33 in the afternoon and the details were being held for the Major Crimes officers. Guards placed him against a grey wall and took his mug shots, then led him to a cell. During this process, Hunter, who knew that Willie's lawyers were at Ritchie Sandford—the firm that had represented him when he was charged in the attack on Sandra Gail Ringwald in 1997—phoned them; the office promised they would alert Marilyn Sandford immediately.

During the afternoon of February 22, members of the investigative team gathered in a large room off the booking area. It was a big moment; every one of them would remember this for the rest of their lives. Phil Little would remember that he was the one who had arrested Willie Pickton on two counts of first-degree murder, just as Nathan Wells, who had returned to regular duties in Coquitlam, would always know that he was the one who made the first arrest, on the night the police raided the farm. Little had no assigned duties left that day but he stayed anyway. Bill Fordy wasn't there; he was concentrating on the interview ahead of him.

Several officers were assigned to contact members of the missing women's families to tell them an arrest had been made on two counts of first-degree murder. Others were dealing with a newcomer to this case, an undercover member of the RCMP brought in to share Pickton's cell, which was wired for both sound and video. A highly trained cell plant can take on a new persona and talk to a prisoner in the hope that he will make admissions about his crimes, or at least provide information that will help the people doing the interview. Although cell plants are usually well briefed, they're not allowed to try to interview the prisoner. Innocuous questions, yes. Anything more, anything that appears to be eliciting information, is not allowed.

But sometimes—and this is what happened in Willie Pickton's case—the officer has been placed in the cell on such short notice that he has to work by his wits, without much background information. All this man had to go on was a fact sheet that said "the suspect aged 51 has a criminal record for violence," and that he had just been arrested on two counts of first-degree murder. The only other information was a copy of Pickton's booking-in sheet. Because the cell plant wouldn't be able to write notes during his conversations with Willie, he would be working with a "cover officer," a person stationed down the hall, out of sight and out of hearing. This officer would remove him from the cell to give him any new intelligence that came in, evaluate the progress being made and offer suggestions. The cell plant's main job during this break was to make fast, accurate notes on the conversation he was having with Willie. To leave the cell without arousing Willie's suspicions, he would use the excuse that his lawyer was outside and had to talk to him. The police would play their role by banging on the cell door to tell him his lawyer was there.

The police had taken away Willie's filthy work clothes, tried unsuccessfully to make him take a shower ("I was raised to take a bath, not a shower," he complained) and dressed him in a pair of dark grey jail-issue sweatpants, a matching fleece hoodie with a white T-shirt underneath and a pair of dark socks. Now nearly bald, what hair he had left was brown with some red still showing, but it was wild, frizzy and matted. Thick stubble covered his cheeks and chin. His hands and nails were filthy, his breath foul. He arrived at the cell to find a roommate, a scowling, tough-looking man lying on the centre section of a narrow U-shaped concrete bench attached to the walls that served as three bunks. The cell, which was about ten feet square, also held a toilet and sink on the fourth wall, beside the door that opened out into the hallway.

"Hey, where's my fucking lawyer? I pay my fucking lawyer," snapped the man as the guard led Pickton into the cell.

"He's coming," replied the guard.

"Fuckin' yeah," the man said angrily as he climbed off his bed. "I don't fuckin' share cells here. What's going on?"

The guard paid no attention to the man; he clanged the door shut and left. Now the two men stared at each other.

Willie sat down on the bunk on the left wall. "It's not fuckin' bad enough," he muttered. "I don't have a clue. Holy shit. I'm gonna use the washroom here." He got up, walked over to the toilet and peed into the centre of the bowl. The roar of urine splashing into the toilet reverberated around the cell and went on for a full minute or two. He didn't wash his hands. He pulled a mat off the floor, slid it onto the bench and folded a blanket into a pillow. He lay down, head on blanket, legs crossed at the ankles, one arm under the back of his head.

"So, what are you in here for?" he asked the other man.

"Well, for my health . . . It's fuckin' bullshit."

"What's your charges?"

"Hey?"

"What are you charged with?"

"Fuck me. It's fuckin' warrants from back east."

The guard was back, carrying some blankets for the men. The cell plant glared at him. "Want to fuckin' check on that call?" he snapped, referring to his lawyer.

"Yeah."

"That's fuckin' bullshit. I've been waiting all afternoon."

"Yeah," the guard said. "We'll be waiting to alert you, sir."

"That's the problem when you're dealing with back east," the man told Pickton. He explained his arrest warrants from eastern Canada: "Yeah, fucked up there and from six months ago."

"That happens," Pickton said. "It happens. Fuck, I can't believe this here."

"What's up?"

"I was just driving, pulled me off the road."

"Why they want to fuckin' throw you in jail for driving . . . not where I come from."

"Oh yeah, I know . . . They said they got attempted murder. I got murder charges against me. Two murder charges."

"You?"

"Well, fuck me," said Willie. "Fuckin' a working kinda guy—not a kinda, I've been working all the time, fuck. Anyways, they're trying and I don't know what's going on."

"He told you very much or just fucking with you?"

"He says that they are gonna charge me for murder one on two counts." Willie told his new roommate he'd been set up by the police.

"Do you think?"

"Fuckin' right. These are cops and dirty at that . . . They got me up for murder one, two counts . . . And I know nothing about it . . . I didn't do it, but the trouble is it's not the answer."

"Don't worry about it. You'll be out of here before you know it."

"Maybe. Maybe. Maybe never, either."

"Won't you get a good lawyer?"

"Yeah," said Willie, "but that's not the answer. Lawyers can only do so much."

It didn't take long for the cell plant to have Willie eating out of his hand. Look tough, talk tough, sprinkle *fuck* and *fuckin'* into almost every sentence (150 times during their hours of conversation) and he had Willie dying to talk.

"What am I sharing with, some fuckin' celebrity here or what?" he said when Willie told him the news media were hounding him. By now Willie was enjoying himself. He had someone to impress. The tape loop in his brain that switched on when anyone seemed interested in his story—the tale of the poor little farm boy who became a plain ol' pig farmer—began to play. How he had to stay on the farm until he was forty. How the police took his guns and were looking at him for fifty murders. How he was charged with two so far.

"This one fucking bitch," confided Willie, "I had about two— about a month and a half ago. About a month and a half ago this fuckin' bitch—she lives, ah, she had no place to stay or anything, she stays inside a van. She brought all of her ID over to my place and everything and all her clothes. The only problem is now I'm charged with her murder and they found her ID at my place."

"I think you're being set up. Any call [from the lawyer] yet?"

"Not yet . . . I can't believe this, I can't believe this. Now they want to interrogate me for the next twenty-four hours or forty-eight hours or whatever."

Willie seemed proud of how famous he'd become. His town, he told his new best friend, was called "Pork Coquitlam now, not Port. Pork. I heard of mad cow disease," Willie snickered. "Now you got fuckin' pigs eating people . . . the whole fuckin' world knows me. All the way to Hong Kong, to everywhere."

"Fuckin', I never knew you were world-renowned," the under-cover man said. "You're an all-star!" When he flattered him by comparing his fame to O.J. Simpson's, Willie briefly switched gears.

"O.J. Simpson. I don't know what happened to him. Is he okay?"

"He's a fuckin' free man. Out there wining and dining all the time. Out swinging a golf club."

But then Willie was right back to how badly the police had treated him, throwing him off the farm, charging him with two mur-ders. Fortunately for the cell plant, Willie's lawyer, Marilyn Sandford, arrived; as soon as Willie left the cell to talk to her, the man hustled out to make his notes. Gone only twenty-five minutes, he was back just before Willie returned to carry on with his poor-farm-boy his-tory as if there had never been a break.

He told the story of his knife fight with Sandra Gail Ringwald five years earlier. "I got charged with attempted murder. The prob-lem is I got knifed. I got $3,400 on me. And the bitch wanted my money. So I got slashed from here, my chest, across my throat, through my tongue, right through my bottom jaw. Took the whole top of my tongue off."

"No shit."

"And across the back," said Willie. "That bitch nailed me in both arms. And now I got a murder charge, two murder charges, and forty-seven pending. I just can't get over this here. My brother told me not to go to the job site because they knew [where] to find me."

"You should have fuckin' went back east," the cell plant commented.

"They told me to."

"But you gotta cover your own ass, I'm telling you."

"That's what my brother said to me."

"Well, it sounds like your brother is a pretty smart guy, been around a lot."

"He warned me."

"Well, you should have hopped to the plane down like in that Cuba somewhere."

"I'm just a plain pig farmer."

"Not anymore, my friend."

"The whole world knows me now."

"That's right, you're a fuckin' legend."

"Really, I am now."

It was his childhood he wanted to talk about now. The deprivations of life at the homestead on Dawes Hill. Living in a chicken coop, getting fresh water from a stream under the house, no fridge, working hard all his life, milking cows before and after school, slopping pigs . . . which reminded him how angry he was that the police had thrown him off the farm after the raid two weeks earlier. "I can't go in there and feed the pigs," he ranted. "They starved them for five days. Fucking police wouldn't let anyone on the place or anything else. Tough titty, said the kitty. They don't get anything, don't get water, don't get nothing for five days."

By now his mind was jumping around. So much to share. "Did

THE CELL PLANT   477

this, did that. I was a meat cutter for six and a half years. Those are working hands. Those have not just been born yesterday. It does not overnight. Those are working hands and they're hard-working. I've been in for fingerprints: he says open your hand up and you can't open your hand because your palm of your hand doesn't flatten out—so, so hard. Now I'm up for murder I'll lose everything. I lose everything. Everything I worked for. But I'll still do it tomorrow. The same thing. Help people, everything else. I won't change myself much, I won't change myself very much. I have my life. Now they're trying to bury me. I told them about the horses. I enjoyed my life. I worked hard."

At a loss for words after these scattershot grievances, all the cell plant could say was, "You're a smart guy."

"No, I'm screwed, tattooed, nailed to the cross, and now I'm a mass murderer. Now they're coming after me, fuckin' pig man, because they say my pigs ate people." This was interesting. So far since his arrest, no one had said anything to him about his pigs eating people or that they believed he had killed many women.

Willie talked about the plan to sell the rest of the farm property for a subdivision. Where would he live? the cell plant asked.

"On the other one." He meant the Piggy's Palace site on Burns Road, where neighbours knew Willie was building a new house for himself behind the Palace.

And he talked about the friends who would stand by him; one was "Dinah" [Taylor], his current girlfriend. "I'm just a pig man," lamented Willie. "I'd like it to be just the way it used to be."

The cell plant empathized: "I'm behind. I'm just not prepared for the modern stuff. This stuff is way, like I said, I'm behind now . . . That's my crime here. I know I fuckin' done a lot of shit in my day."

Willie agreed. "That's why I'm here. I'm stupid. I'm not with the times. I don't have a computer. So I'm a murderer, mass murderer now? I got a murder charge and forty-eight more against me. Now about a hundred policemen on the case. I got America Most Wanted there. I hit the big time. I'm in so deep I can't see outside."

The cell plant wondered about bail. "You got cash on you or something to borrow against?"

"My brother's trying to arrange something. I can't believe they charged me for two and they said we have forty-seven or forty-eight more to come."

Along with the charges and his bail worries, Willie needed to talk about how the guards had tried to make him take a shower when he came in earlier. "I said I don't have a shower, I have a bath." His cellmate thought that was funny but told Willie it was customary to allow prisoners to shower before they went before a judge. Willie agreed; the guard had told him the same thing. But he said he refused. "I told him no. If I can't have a bath I don't want a shower. I don't, I won't take a shower."

"Well, you got a fucking phobia of showers or something?"

"What's that?"

"You afraid of showers or what?"

"No, I'd rather have a bath . . . [it's] the way you're brought up and now you don't change yourself. You don't."

"Yeah, I hear you."

"If I want to smell like . . . whatever, that's the way I want to be . . . fuck . . . if I can't have a proper bath the way I want to have it done. I've got my rights, haven't I?"

"Good attitude," said the cell plant.

Bored with the shower/bath issue, Willie switched gears to consider whether the police might be watching him right now and listening to his conversation in the cell. "Is that a camera?" he asked, pointing to the bubble in the ceiling.

"Oh, fuck yeah! You think those lazy guards are gonna get off their fat ass and walk around all the time?"

"I thought it was an ornament," said Willie, forgetting that he'd recognized it as a camera earlier. He got up and peered at it again. "Well, I'll be God-darned . . . I see something in there but I'm not sure, it could just be a reflection."

"No, that's the motherfucker," said the cell plant. "I'd say it is, no doubt in my mind. That's why you don't see the guard all the time."

The reality of the camera, of microphones, finally triggered Willie's fury. His voice pitched high in anger, he said he knew what was happening on the farm; he knew the police had brought in loads of gravel fill, presumably for parking their trailers and vans; he knew they expected to be on the property for two years; he knew members of the RCMP were coming in from all over the country; and he knew reporters were crowding around the farm and working throughout Port Coquitlam to get his story. And he knew that the general public was coming by to sightsee. All of it enraged him.

"Sounds like they made it into a freak show," the cell plant said.

"Fuck. Come one, come all," replied Willie. "And I think they spent around two million dollars over it, for nothing. They're going to nail me to the cross."

"You're famous."

"I still don't have to settle for a shower. I wish I could do something in here . . . taking something apart, destroying it, doing stuff." Which reminded him—he was doing stuff on December 24, 1997. In fact, he said, he was a real asshole that night, "a really hard asshole." That was the time he let loose the two little pigs in the Downtown Eastside and watched them run into Gastown, the tourist neighbourhood next door. And he had made an even better plan for the following Christmas Eve, in 1998, he said, which was to release three large ostriches—the kind he bought occasionally at livestock auctions for customers who liked their meat—in the Downtown Eastside and let them run. But that's not all. He would put on a tuxedo, rent a room at the Vancouver Hotel—one of the best hotels in the city—and release two suitcases full of bats into the elevator shaft. "That would have been a real good one. That would have been fun to see. Still want to do that. I was so close."

Trying to follow the train of Willie Pickton's thoughts must have bewildered the undercover cop. His tale about the planned ostrich caper reminded Willie of something else and he was off on another tangent. Ostrich bones. He'd told the woman cop, he exulted, that there were bones on his farm and he'd told her where to find them. He knew the cops would dig them up immediately and figure, because of their length, that they were human bones. But then they'd find out they were ostrich bones. Willie was beside himself with glee.

And inevitably he told his cellmate about Goldie, the horse he'd bred, trained and finally had to put down. "I got him March 20, 1977; I put him down December 21, 1981, at five thirty in the afternoon." He'd trained many horses, he said, but because Goldie was the best one, he had his head and neck cut off and stuffed. Maybe, if he did go to jail, he could get permission to have the stuffed animal head in his cell.

"I'm just plain little ol' me, little farm boy. Little farm boy, that's all I am." Then this little ol' farm boy moved on to tell the cell plant that he had plastic explosives he could use to make small bombs, ones he could simply tape to a door. "Light the fuses and blow the door, blow the door locks." It's not hard to get the material, he said.

The cell plant was astonished. "Fuckin' military shit. Do you have a licence or some shit like that?"

"Yeah, I have something like that. You can get anything you wanna get if you want it bad enough."

Pickton wandered along memory lane to describe the parties at Piggy's Palace, including the New Year's Eve bash in 1999 for more than fifteen hundred people that drew fifty to sixty police cars to shut it down. "The fire marshal shut us down," Willie said. "That was it. No more."

Finally Willie had run out of things to say. He pulled a blanket over himself, turned onto his side and closed his eyes. Soon both men were sound asleep.

Late Friday night the police held a news conference to announce that they had charged Willie Pickton with two counts of first-degree murder. "We believe now we have answers regarding the disappearance of two of the missing women, but this is a case involving dozens of missing women," Cate Galliford told reporters. "There are a lot of questions still unanswered. The investigation is not over. The detailed inch-by-inch search of the farm property will continue for many months to come." She confirmed that evidence found on the farm had led to the charges and that forty officers were now combing the property. But Galliford cautioned the reporters that there were still other suspects in the investigation—"hundreds of suspects."

Her caution was ignored by most of the media. The story that went around the world was that a serial killer, a pig farmer from a small town in British Columbia, had been arrested and charged on two counts of first-degree murder and was suspected of killing as many as fifty prostitutes. This could make him North America's most prolific serial killer ever.

Dave Pickton went to see Willie's lawyers, Marilyn Sandford and Peter Ritchie, at their downtown Vancouver office later that night. It shouldn't have surprised him that the media had been sent there too, but when he saw Al Stewart, a CBC journalist, homing in on him, Dave tried to grab his video camera. He then closed in on Stewart and broke the journalist's glasses, but Stewart kept on filming. The scuffle appeared on the television news shortly afterwards.

CHAPTER THIRTY-NINE

THE FORDY INTERVIEW

When Willie woke the next morning it was Saturday. No one seemed in a particular hurry, and after breakfast he sat around waiting for something to happen. His hair was still greasy and uncombed and standing out in a wild frizz at the back of his balding crown. Finally, at 10:16 a.m. a guard arrived and took him from his cell to an interview room nearby; a few minutes later the undercover officer also left the cell to make his notes. When he was done, he went home for the rest of the day.

The interview room, wired for sound and video, was small and narrow, with only enough room for two office chairs. A filing cabinet sat against the long wall; two baby palm trees, both dead, sagged over the edges of their pots onto the floor. Three larger rooms nearby were taken over as monitoring rooms for observers watching the interview. The first, a small room often used for interviewing children, contained the recording equipment for the interview, which was being managed by Sergeant Richard Konarski. The second, a conference room, was crammed with people, including Don Adam, Jim Hunter, Doug Henderson, Baltej Dhillon, Rob Angco, Brad Marks and Dana Lillies, all senior task force members, as well as the psychologists, Myron Schimpf and Nicole Aube, there to assess Willie's state of mind, and two RCMP behavioural science profilers, Scott Filer and Keith Davidson. A third monitoring room, also a conference space, had been set aside for the investigative team. All the rooms were now full as everyone waited to watch Sergeant Bill Fordy interview Willie Pickton.

Fordy believed he was ready. Over the past week he'd reviewed volumes of evidence reports, Willie's statements, his talks with Dana

Lillies, and victims' statements. He'd read everything about Willie's encounter with Sandra Gail Ringwald in 1997; he'd pored over interviews with people who knew the Pickton brothers well. Fordy told people that, though he rarely worked from a step-by-step plan in interviews, he had written some general notes about his approach to Pickton on his laptop.

This morning Fordy had put on a grey wool jacket with a starched white shirt, a dark silk tie and black slacks. While he waited in the room to meet Willie for the first time, Fordy looked into a camera and apologized to the families of the missing women. Knowing that the interview would eventually become public, he admitted that he would be saying "awful things about their loved ones," but it was part of his effort to find the truth. Seconds later, Willie shambled into the room and sat in one of the chairs, tilting it back until it rested on the wall, stretching out his long, thin legs.

Fordy started the conversation. He wanted Willie to call him Bill; was it okay if he called him Rob? Willie said he was okay with that. Fordy promised respect and said that no one would hurt him. Willie didn't respond but just stared at him.

"You've been arrested for a couple of murders," Fordy said.

"That's what they say, yeah," Willie replied, examining his legs and wiggling his feet. "I was charged yesterday but I was told about them today."

"Police are also investigating fifty missing street workers."

Willie laughed and rolled his eyes.

"I can't imagine how you feel—you've probably got a ton of questions. Lawyer gave you some advice . . ."

"No kidding," Willie said. "The advice from my lawyer is 'Don't talk to the police.'"

"Under the law you don't have to talk to me." Fordy waved his hands around.

Pickton said nothing; he just cleaned out his ears and wiped the wax on his pants.

"You're being investigated for up to fifty murders. Can you describe what that means?"

"It's hogwash," declared Willie, grinning.

"I don't think so. You're bigger than the Pope, for chrissakes."

"I've been set up."

Fordy tried to explain the seriousness of the situation. "This investigation is huge," he told Willie. "It's massive. It's real important to me that you understand. In your own words, why am I here talking to you?"

"I'm mind-baffling," replied Willie. "And I'm just a working guy. Just a plain working guy, that's all I am. I'm just a pig man. That's all I've got to say. I'm not a bad dude."

The interview was not going well. Willie had been questioned by police before; he knew what he was doing. As Fordy struggled to find a footing in the conversation, there was a knock on the door. Willie's lawyer was on the phone, waiting to talk to him. He left to take the call and was back in the interview room a few minutes later.

"Everyone might say, 'Don't talk to the police,'" Fordy said to him. "That decision is yours. I can't make you say anything you don't want to say."

"I can't say. Don't know anything."

"I'm not gonna force you. Nobody can do that. It's your choice."

Willie gnawed on a fingernail. "I'm the same as you," he blurted. "Both use a washroom . . . That's life. Life goes on. If I could turn time around, change things that I did wrong, I don't think I did anything wrong. I wouldn't change much."

Fordy tried a new tack to establish rapport. He understood what it was like to fail, he said. He could have been a professional hockey player but he broke his knee. "I've never achieved the goals I had in life."

Willie didn't react. He was not interested in Fordy's hard-luck story.

Fordy tried again. "What's the worst thing that ever happened to you?"

That was a question worth answering. It was in 1997, when he was charged with the attempted murder of Sandra Gail Ringwald, he said.

"So if I was holding a mirror and said, 'Describe yourself as a person,' what would you say?"

"Same clothes, same shoes, different sizes . . ."

"Tell me about you on the inside."

"Which way?"

"Any way."

"We eat the same food, use the same toilet . . . same washroom, everything else . . . same people."

"My mother died of cancer," Fordy offered.

"So did mine. April 1, 1979."

"What kind?"

"Spreading cancer."

"How did you two get along?"

"Two peas in a pod."

"Do you miss your mom?"

"Tit for tat."

"I'm a really hard worker," tried Fordy. "I give all that credit to my mom. She's the person I respect most in the world. Who do you respect most in the world?"

Willie paused for several seconds. "My mother."

"What qualities did you like in her?"

"Strong. Strong mind, strong willpower." Willie's fingers were laced across his stomach. His face was turned away. He looked only at the wall or at his hands, never at Fordy.

"Were you able to be there with her when she died?"

"I don't know where I was." But he quickly recited his parents' vital statistics: father Leonard, born in England in 1896, died of "old age" in January 1977; mother born in 1912 in Raymond's Creek, Saskatchewan, died in 1978.*

"How do you want to die?" Fordy asked.

---

* According to her will, Louise Pickton was born in Alberta.

"I don't know. I really don't know. Old age, hopefully. We're here as long as we're here for. There's always a reason for everything."

"What do you think the reason is that you ended up here today?"

"Don't know. Don't know. Don't know."

Fordy then asked Willie about the best thing that had ever happened to him, and right on cue Willie launched into his familiar story of the one and only holiday of his life, when he was twenty-four and ended up in Pontiac, Michigan, engaged to a girl named Connie Anderson. "She's probably married off by now. Kids. It was a long time ago. I had to get back to the farm. I enjoyed myself. I never got down to the States again. Well, that's life."

What about the rest of his family?

"Linda, she went to a Catholic school. Me and Linda never was close. She always liked the high lights—she likes to go out, go here, go there—went to school—right up to university and everything else. Think it's good. Some people can make it up to school and some people can't. She never worked at the farm, no."

"Isn't that bizarre?"

"Nope. She's just herself. No problem with that." As for Dave, said Willie, "He is a hard-working guy. We have the odd quarrel— everybody does—I enjoy his company."

By this time Fordy had succeeded in getting Willie to talk, but it was the same family and personal history he told to anyone who'd listen. His early childhood; experiences with pets and farm animals, including the deaths of his pet calf and his horse Goldie; accidents on farm equipment; buildings he'd torn down or put up.

Fordy decided it was time for lunch and offered Willie a submarine sandwich. "I'm pretty flexible," Willie replied. "Don't eat lettuce or celery or vegetables." But he wanted to talk about butchering, not lunch.

"Most I ever butchered at one time was thirty-four pigs— December 23 right through December 24. It was '77."

"Fastest you ever did it?"

"There's nothing fast about it," Willie said. "You gotta do it respectfully 'cause people have to eat it. I have seen people butcher lambs and goats and don't care . . . I do a clean job. This is for the public. If the water temperature is not right it takes that much longer; some weeks I was doing up to 150 a week."

"For someone who wasn't raised on a farm," said Fordy, "give me a free lesson on how you do it."

"Got to make sure the pot has right temp of water; that's very important. Half the battle. Half the battle is the water temperature." He fell silent. Two minutes later he yawned.

"So what do you do then?"

"Put the pig in the water until the hair comes off, then you strip the hair."

"Is the pig still alive?"

"No. You get a handgun, a .400—did some boars—biggest one I ever did was 980 pounds."

"Wow. So you've told me you like working. What do you enjoy most about the pig farm?"

"Nothing. I want to get out."

The talk about butchering animals went on for a few more minutes before Fordy abruptly switched tack. He started to tell Willie about all the experts working on the farm. "There's bone, forensic anthropologists, blood-spatter experts," he said. "The forensic anthropologists are bones, the etymologists are bug [experts], blood-spatter, special lights—fluorescent—the whole property is secured now, twenty-four hours a day. They will be there a year."

"A year?" said Willie. "A year?"

"Yes. And they are going down twenty-five feet from the surface. They have some of the same stuff the U.S. had over in Afghanistan looking for Bin Laden—ground-searching equipment. They're looking for evidence of your involvement, trying to understand you. Some of the people who were associates of yours, people who were close to you—friends—now have a better understanding of what is going on."

"What is going on?"

Fordy finally turned to the poster board with forty-eight head-shots of the missing women. "I'm not saying you killed all fifty of those girls. I wouldn't believe all those people. Only person I'd believe is you."

The police were interviewing everyone who knew him, Fordy said, and while they hadn't wanted to talk before he was charged, now they did. Some were negotiating their interviews with the police. And some of the best police officers in the province were working on the case, he added. They were looking for DNA evidence.

"Yeah—what's that got to do with me?" Willie asked. He slumped against the side of the chair, one hand tucked between his knees, the other holding up his head.

Fordy reached over to the poster and began hitting each photograph with the side of his fist—a short, sharp *thwack*—"Do you know this one, Rob? No? Well, do you know this one? Has this one been at your place? No? What about this one? Has she been at your place? Could you give me an explanation of why some of these women were at your place?"

"No way," said Willie loudly. "No way."

"You don't know any of these girls?"

Willie shook his head.

"Ever had sex with any of these girls?"

Willie stared at the pictures. "Did I? Not that I'm aware of."

"Have any of these girls ever been in your car?"

"Never had a car."

"Okay, a vehicle of transportation."

"No."

"Ever been in the house?"

"No."

"Ever had sex with any of these girls?"

"No."

One at a time, Fordy led Willie through the pictures of the missing women. Eventually Willie acknowledged that some of them might have been at his place and he recognized a few of them, but he certainly hadn't had sex with any or partied with any or known them very well. As he looked at the pictures he made the occasional comment, usually to say in his nasal twang, "She's pretty."

"You're telling me that none of these women have been at your place?" demanded Fordy.

"I don't know any of these women."

Pickton admitted he had sex with some "working girls" but not any of these women. The first time he had sex with a prostitute was with Sandra, he said, the one who knifed him in 1997.

"What's your favourite way of having sex?" Fordy asked. "Will you have sex any way?"

"Doesn't matter. I'm not fussy. Haven't had it for a while, maybe a year."

"What went wrong with you? What about first sex with a girl?"

"There's not much to say. When I went to school, a lot of the girls weren't interested. Never had sex with Connie neither—that was the first girl I got interested in."

"Do you remember your first prostitute?" Fordy asked. "Everybody does; it's normal."

Once again Willie said, head back, yawning profoundly, it was "probably" Sandra Gail Ringwald. "The one that knifed me. I had $3,400 on me. The first time was when I got knifed there. The first was Sandra and the second was Roxanne.* Is she missing? Dead? I hope not. Haven't seen her for a while."

"None of these girls have ever been to your place and none of them have ever had sex with you?"

Willie didn't reply. Fordy was going nowhere fast.

A few minutes later Dana Lillies arrived with lunch; while she was unpacking it, Fordy left the room. Willie took a long pull from his

---

* "Roxanne" was the street name of Monique Wood, a sex-trade worker who did visit Pickton's farm and eventually testified at his trial. Pickton never harmed her.

drink. "Jesus Christ," he muttered. He studied the poster. As soon as Fordy returned he began picking all the vegetables out of his sub; then Willie simply stared at him, knees crossed, eyes blank.

"What do you make of all the media?" Fordy finally asked.

"Out to lunch. Out to lunch."

"Pretty spectacular. You're like the Pope," said Fordy. For a few minutes Fordy talked about the press reaction to Willie's arrest.

Willie shrugged. "Can't believe anything you read in the media. They'll put anything in the paper."

When Fordy, changing the subject, asked him how, aside from his farm work, he made money, Willie told him that he bought cars for scrap from the Vancouver Police Department. Willie would buy the wrecks from "Wild Bill" Henke, a well-known auctioneer and car collector who lived in Fort Langley. Henke bought them in large lots at police auctions and sold the ones he didn't want to Willie, who took them apart for scrap.

One time, Willie said, he found a single-bladed axe with blood all over it in a 1989 Chevrolet Astro van that had blood over the back seats as well. "Whatever took place, I haven't a clue," he said. "But life goes on." He would buy about 150 cars and trucks a year, he said, and they were always full of junk, including needles, bras, tops and inhalers. "It's outrageous," he said. "Innocent people can go to jail too. People can be set up. I'm sorry about the way I am, but I'm still going to help people."

When Fordy reminded Willie that he had been charged with two counts of murder, his reply was quick: "I'm charged. That still doesn't make me a murderer. I just don't remember any of these people. You can do whatever you want. Nail me to a cross. I'm just a plain little farm boy. I'm just myself. I'm sorry for living."

Fordy decided it was time to go over the evidence. "Huge amounts" of DNA from the missing women were all over the farm, and blood-spatter experts said Willie had killed them. The investigation was costing a million dollars a month just to do the digging. "This is the biggest crime-scene investigation in the history of Canada.

This is a snowball that will not stop. It's indisputable. Irrefutable evidence. It's not just a little piece. This is a freight train. A super freight train coming down the tracks. This is just after two weeks. After a year, I can't imagine."

Willie shifted slightly in his chair. "I'm in the paper today too?" he asked.

Fordy paid no attention. The investigators have found blood, semen and saliva, he told Willie, showing him pictures taken in the motor home. And when they analyzed the mattress in the motor home, it too had human blood on it. There was human blood all over the place, especially Mona Wilson's blood—and Mona had her shoes on when she was killed. Someone took them off and put them in a cupboard in the motor home.

Willie heard him out. "So my picture's all over the front page?" he asked. "Shit. I didn't do anything."

"It's all over," Fordy said. "So why not just say what happened and give the victims' families a bit of peace of mind and closure?"

"Shit, it's in the paper and everything else?" asked Willie. "I can't go to the fucking courthouse or anything else."

Fordy forced him to talk about the motor home. "I haven't been in there for quite a spell," Willie replied. "Quite a spell. Quite a spell." Then, looking at photographs of Sereena Abotsway and Mona Wilson, he denied hurting them in any way.

Fordy had another card to play. He turned on a television monitor and played a videotape of Scott Chubb talking to the police. He'd seen Willie with Georgina Papin, "a dark-haired Native girl with curly hair," in Port Coquitlam, Chubb told them. He'd seen them together on Shaughnessy, close to the Lougheed Highway. Chubb told the police that Willie had explained to him how easy it was to kill a junkie: all you have to do is put windshield-washer fluid in a syringe or use radiator coolant, inject it—and people would think the woman simply overdosed on drugs.

"Scott Chubb?" Willie asked. For the first time he seemed rattled.

"He's going to give evidence," Fordy replied.

"After everything I helped him with!" Willie stared at the images on the monitor. "Why would he . . ."

"Did he say he had done it before?" the officer in the video asked Chubb. "Try and give me exactly what he said."

"To get rid of a junkie or a hooker," Chubb explained, "get some windshield-washer fluid or coolant and put it in her arm . . . and she was gone. Women were dirty, rotten pigs. He looked at them as a commodity."

Pickton yawned.

"You get the idea, right?" said Fordy. "You have a friend called Andrew Bellwood. He's being interviewed today. I want you to listen to this." He pushed the Play button and Willie heard Bellwood tell the police that he'd met Willie, whom he called Rob, through a mutual friend, Ross Contois, Gina Houston's boyfriend.

"The first encounter was with my friend Ross," Bellwood said. "He used to stay at Rob's house . . . went there a couple of times with Ross, he introduced me to him . . ."

"Out to lunch!" Willie snapped.

Bellwood's voice droned on: "I go there by myself after that. Seemed to be an upright guy—I worked, stayed in the trailer, never did much for him; it was cash and a place to stay. One evening me and Rob were sitting in the trailer and he talked to me about getting a hooker and proceeded to show me how he would kill her—he would handcuff her, reaching behind her back, and then would proceed to strangle her with a belt, then he told me after he killed them he took them to the barn."

"What is that?" Willie exclaimed, suddenly alert, listening intently. "Whoaaa!"

Fordy stopped the tape. He began to walk Willie back through his lies. There was the $400 asthma inhaler in a shiny case that Willie claimed to have found in a car he'd bought at a police auction—which is why it was in his trailer. But the police found it in Sereena Abotsway's tote bag, Fordy told him, and the date it was sold to her was the date she disappeared.

"This is the most important day of your life," Fordy said. "Sereena disappeared on July 19, the day she picked up the inhaler, and the thing that's interesting about the inhaler being in your house is that Sereena's DNA is all over your house and your DNA is mixed with hers. You're done. Your DNA is mixed with Mona's. You're finished on this."

In addition, he said, the police had found the DNA of eight other women in the trailer. "There's hair there that looks like it's been pulled out at the roots. There's Mona's and yours and Sereena's and yours and the DNA of eight others and the hair of who knows—that was torn right out of the scalp. It's interesting that the guy who phoned in says you told him you fed the bodies to the pigs."

"Crock of shit," muttered Willie.

"The fact is that they're willing to spend millions of dollars to get to the truth, to look under every rock. We have an exhibit-tracking system specially designed for this investigation."

By now Fordy was pumped. He badgered Willie a little longer, demanding to know if he killed little kids too, like Clifford Olson. And then he moved to close in on his pitch: "Now, you're probably sitting there asking yourself, 'How can I possibly come out of this situation?' You've had a pretty rough life. Shit happens. You are a survivor. You have been attacked by a bear, by wild pigs, by crazy hookers. You've never had an ounce of recognition. You will survive this. You are a survivor. You're asking yourself, 'What is the upside here?' You can go to jail with respect or you can go to jail with no respect. I wonder what you're gonna do.

"You lived your whole life with no one ever having respected you. This is the first time in your life everyone's even recognized you. You're as big as the Pope. You're as big as Bin Laden. You can have respect.

"This investigation is costing one million dollars a month, so in addition to having respect you can save us a lot of money by taking us to where those girls are. I don't think you killed all fifty. You can see the situation—you need to deal with what's best. You can deal one way. Stand up and be brave. Was it just hookers or was it the hookers and the little kids? People might say Robert Pickton was a hero: when he knew his day was over he had the decency to end it quickly."

"I didn't do anything."

"You did! Explain how Mona's blood is mixed with your blood."

Willie refused to answer. He sat there, staring at the floor, his hand sometimes covering his eyes. Finally he tried to answer. "I dunno. I don't know how I got set up on this here. It doesn't look good, does it?"

"No policeman in the world would try to set you up. Rob, this is the most important day of your life. One way, you have respect. The other way, you're just a dirty little liar."

Willie yawned.

Fordy pressed on. "You need to get self-respect. You need to say, 'Bill, this is what happened.' Very matter of fact. Very businesslike. If you think being quiet is going to help you through this—you need to look forward to the rest of your life. It's crystal clear what the right thing to do is. You need to ask yourself, Rob, what kind of killer do you want to be? Because you are a killer. There's no question about that."

"I haven't killed any kids. I haven't killed anybody. So I'm being charged with two murders, right?"

"Yep. For now. How does that make you feel?"

"It makes me feel sick."

Bill Fordy had pushed Willie hard for five and a half hours but he hadn't got anywhere. The officers watching the interrogation were concerned.

"Nothing that was being said to Willie had any effect whatsoever on him," Jim Hunter said later. "It was time to move Willie into the evidence that the police had gathered, and Bill had not really moved into that as yet." Hunter, Adam and another senior officer, Doug Henderson, argued about what to do. Hunter decided it was time for a new approach, and he told an astonished Dana Lillies to go in and try her luck—she was replacing Fordy. Lillies hadn't made any preparation for this.

Fordy was furious. He stormed out into the corridor, where

Hunter met him to explain. "Bill and I had a—quite frankly, it was a bit of a shouting match in the hallway about that," Hunter admitted later. "He was upset that he was taken out." Adam and Hunter tried to explain how necessary it was to start telling Willie about the evidence they had. Fordy would not be mollified.

In the meantime, Lillies tried to get somewhere with Willie. He tried to make her feel sorry for him. "I should be on death row," he said. "I'm finished. I'm dead."

Lillies paid no attention to his whining. Mona Wilson's DNA was found on a dildo that had been attached to the end of a gun, she told him. Willie's DNA was on top of Mona's.

"But that doesn't mean I did it," said Willie.

"Yes, it does."

There were long silences while Willie brooded about his predicament. Lillies waited. Finally he said to her that he couldn't get over Scott Chubb's statement to the police. And he decided to try to explain the dildo on the end of the gun. "I put it on there for shooting pigs or hogs. I used it as a silencer."

"That sounds a little unusual," replied Lillies. "How did Mona Wilson's DNA get on there?"

"I don't know."

"Yes, you do . . . When you kill a woman, are you understanding what you're doing or does it just happen?"

"I didn't do that."

"Yes, you did, Robert. We both know that . . . Like I said, Robert, the evidence does not lie, and there's a mountain of it. And there's more building every day."

It wasn't long before Lillies left and Fordy was back in the room, energized and bristling with damning facts to put before Willie. Lynn Ellingsen, to start with, had told the police she'd seen him skinning a woman, he said. Dinah Taylor had brought prostitutes to the farm for him.

"The truth is, Willie, you're probably going to be the largest serial killer in Canadian history. You're going to be a famous guy.

You will have achieved something. You have eluded police for years, but now it's over."

Willie remained obdurate. He simply didn't respond to Fordy's bluster. Finally Fordy tried appealing to his conscience, to his sense of remorse—a tactic that Roy Hazelwood had warned wouldn't work. He's a psychopath, Hazelwood had said. He won't respond to that.

"Do this for your mother, who is watching you from heaven, Rob!" Fordy pleaded. "Do this for DJ and Tammy! You have a chance to be a hero!"

Willie stared at Fordy. He didn't blink; he said nothing.

Suddenly the door opened and Don Adam walked into the room. "Hi, Bill," he said. "I'm just wondering if I should spend—come in and spend just a couple of seconds with Willie. I don't think he's quite got the whole picture of what is going on here."

"Absolutely. Do you want me to leave you with him?"

"No, no, I just want to lay this out for him. Hi, Bob, or Robert—which do you prefer to be called?"

"Doesn't matter," Pickton muttered.

"My name is Don Adam, by the way." He shook Willie's hand. "Have a seat. I have heard some people say you prefer to be called Robert. I knew you as Willie. I used to be stationed in Coquitlam back in the early '80s with John Pearson and all those guys back in the days when, ah, you guys were burying equipment and doing that kind of stuff.

"Bob, I'm in charge of this investigation. Bill's gone over some of this stuff, but I think that maybe you need to hear sort of the overall picture, and I'm not going to spend a lot of time with you but I want to just set things out, sort of crystal clear as to how this comes together."

Fordy quietly left the room.

CHAPTER FORTY

DON ADAM TAKES OVER

Watching Willie Pickton's comfortable attitude while an experienced interviewer floundered and put forward incorrect information was what had brought Don Adam to his feet. Fordy had been making mistakes in his facts about the DNA evidence, and as Adam looked ahead to the trial and a tough cross-examination from Willie's defence lawyers, he realized he'd better move in fast. While the law allows police to lie to suspects during an interrogation, Adam knew that at this fragile moment his case hung on only two pieces of evidence: Sereena Abotsway's inhalers and clothes and Mona Wilson's blood in the motor home. The searchers hadn't yet found any bodies, or any body parts. The evidence could be shredded by any competent defence counsel. It was essential to do this interrogation with as few mistakes as possible, and Adam believed he had a better grip on the evidence than Fordy.

"Okay, the first thing you need to know is this," Adam told Willie. He spoke firmly, like the professional he was, but always with a kindly expression, as if he didn't feel bad about having to be in the same room as Pickton. "Right now we can associate you to twelve of these women, and that's two weeks into the investigation. Twelve of them. Next you need to know that, relative to Sereena Abotsway, we have Linda Dyck, who will state that last summer she met you and Sereena together and Sereena introduced you as Robert and that Sereena said you were going out to your farm."

Willie shook his head.

"No, no, no, just wait and listen. Never saw her again, that will be her evidence. The next evidence is that I have got my people tracking every movement of Sereena Abotsway. Sereena Abotsway was no good with money, Robert. What happened is that every three days she would have to go to welfare to get money. They would give her, I think, $35. I could stand to be corrected on that, but she was no good with it. [But] she was always in getting her asthma medicine, all right.

"Here's your problem. We have statements from people, including your brother, where you say, 'Yes, it was a shiny case; I brought it into the house.' Willie, that's going to be the evidence. 'A shiny case I brought into the house.' You discussed it with a whole bunch of people—and we have that. That inhaler was not found by itself in your house; it was found in a tote bag belonging to Sereena Abotsway. Inside that tote bag are her shoes, her clothes, a needle—and on that needle is her DNA and your DNA together. Additionally, when we went out into the garbage—we found layers of garbage—we found her second inhaler that she got on the nineteenth, in your garbage."

Again Willie shook his head.

"No, no, no," Adam insisted. "This is a fact: in your garbage we found two more of her inhalers. Yeah, we got four of them. Willie, you told a lie to try and justify how that inhaler got into your house."

Once again Willie shook his head.

"Oh yeah, Willie. Listen to me so you know what the evidence is. Only by knowing where you are, Willie, by knowing exactly how locked in you are, how the lies are dragging you down like a stone. If you pick up a great big boulder, Willie, and step into a deep lake, what happens to you?"

Willie pressed his fingers against his eyes, pushing away tears.

"You go to the bottom, don't you? And the lies that you've told, the little cover-ups you've tried to create, are stones that are going to carry you to the bottom, Willie. All right, so you need to listen to me, 'cause I am not here to lie. Bill got a bit of the evidence confused, all right, and I'm going to straighten out that confusion right here and now.

"Sereena Abotsway. You will be convicted of that, all right. On the tote bag, Willie, is her blood. And Willie, you are locked in to all of your stories about finding that one inhaler, Willie—one inhaler. Not a tote bag with blood. Not extra inhalers in your garbage, not any of that stuff, Willie. You are completely finished on that case."

Adam stayed pleasant and relaxed, almost parental, as he laid out the evidence. "Mona Wilson. That is a murder site inside that motor home. We have got tons of witnesses talking about you in that motor home. I've got forty-five guys out taking statements and I've got a roomful of statements, videos, Dictaphone taped statements, everybody talking about you. It is coming down on you like an avalanche, okay? And you've helped bring it down by your little stories, all right.

"Mona Wilson. That's a murder scene, no doubt about it. There's drag marks where you dragged her out of there. There's the fact that you've got the dildo with the gun and your mixed DNA with hers on that dildo. How do you think a jury is going to look at a dildo on the end of a gun, Willie, that's got DNA of you and her connected with a murder scene?

"It doesn't end there. We've got the ID of Heather Bottomley there. Your friend [Scott Chubb], he likes you; he talks about liking you. But he is not willing to sit by, Willie, when you murder somebody. And, you know, he talks about the needle with the windshield-washer fluid."

Willie roused himself. "I don't know nothing about that."

Adam smiled. "You don't know anything about that? Absolutely not? Well, Willie, I got bad news for you, because inside your entertainment unit or whatever it is, guess what's there? A needle with windshield-washer fluid. Yes, Willie, absolutely."

"I know nothing about that," Willie insisted.

"Willie," Adam said gently, "tell me your story."

"I'm honest with you," Willie whined.

"Well, you want to know something? I haven't even started, but you want to know how bad it is? Your brother, Dave, is talking to Mark [Chernoff] and Bruce [Wall], those two policemen he's been dealing with. He told them today, 'I know it's over for Willie. I know there's bodies.'

"Willie, maybe you didn't kill every single one of those; maybe Dinah Taylor is involved in some of it; maybe you were getting blackmailed. We know that Lynn Ellingsen was blackmailing you. If you've been used, Willie, if you've been drawn into this by people, maybe pressured, you need to explain that. Okay? But it's coming down.

"Dinah Taylor, after she told what she knew, went back to the reserve in Ontario. We flew some policemen out there and they went to her house with her mom and dad. [They] talked her into co-operating and she said that she had phoned you and tried to cook up a story with you about some sort of a duffle bag, that it came from some hotel, the Cobalt."

"That's true," Willie interrupted.

"Yeah, well, she did phone you, because she told us that."

"That's true," repeated Willie. "It did come from the Cobalt."

"No, no, no." Adam smiled. "She told our people that was a story you guys agreed to tell. Lynn Ellingsen is now negotiating with her lawyer to give you up right now so she doesn't go down for whatever her involvement was.

"Willie, do you know who Paul Bernardo is? Paul Bernardo killed two young girls back in Ontario, okay, and he killed them with his wife; her name is Karla Homolka. And they're famous here in Canada because it is sort of the first man–woman team that we're aware of where they were involved in serial killings. Now running this file, Willie, I can tell you that I don't know how involved or uninvolved Taylor and Ellingsen were with you. I know they were bringing girls out to you. I've got tons of evidence of that. I know that Ellingsen has talked about blackmailing you. She talks about coming in when you were skinning a girl, hanging on a hook."

"That's not true."

"Well, Willie, you know how bad it is."

"That's here nor there."

Don Adam continued in this vein for some time. He told Willie he must have been angry that one of those girls gave him hep C, that one of them stabbed him. "If it's a situation where you weren't thinking straight," he went on, "that your anger at being stabbed, that you're upset over being sick because of that caused you to make these mistakes, give people a chance to understand. Because you know what, you do not want to be hated and despised for the rest of your life.

"Okay, so you gotta start thinking longer-term. We're not offering you any deals, Willie, because we don't have to. Do you know what's in this for us, why we care? Two reasons, Willie. Number one is that I know these families. I met them, I know them, and I know that these ladies you knew, their lives went wrong. I know that you have nothing but contempt for them, and I know that in my life, before I got involved in this file, I would just ignore them. I wouldn't think about it.

"But I've met their families, and they didn't end up wanting their kids to be that way, and your mom and dad didn't want you to end up being a serial killer. Your brother doesn't want you destroyed. Now I tell you what, though—half of my investigators think Dave is fully involved; they think that the two of you were involved. There's other people that think the Hells Angels are involved with you."

Willie shifted in his chair.

"Okay. Willie, you know how big or how small this is." Adam moved closer and leaned in. "You know whether it's just you and the girls, and you know whether it was you and Dinah, you know whether it's you and Lynn. You know what that is, Willie. You know whether it's you and Dave.

"But if you're looking for why you should deal with this thing, deal with it up front, I can tell you a number of really good reasons. By explaining, giving people a chance to understand, it's going to make a huge difference in how you are treated for the rest of your life. It's going to make a huge difference in how you are seen in that prison environment. The truth is, Willie, you're probably going to be the biggest serial killer in Canadian history. You're going to be a very, very famous guy. You will have achieved something. You know you eluded police for years and years, let's face it. It's pretty amazing. But it's over.

"Willie, there are some people who think you hate your sister. There's people who talk about how Dave treats you badly, that he yells at you and you know, and that you're hostile towards him. Is that true?"

Willie shook his head no. Soon he launched into his old story of taking a holiday to visit his pen pal Connie Anderson in Michigan. Adam didn't let him wander there for long; instead he hauled him back to the frustration Willie must have felt, chained to the farm.

"How old were you then?"

"Twenty-four."

"Twenty-four and your whole life ahead of you, right. Willie, that was your chance to get away . . . We want options, we want to be able to meet somebody we care about, not prostitutes, Willie. We've got lots of statements from prostitutes about the fact that you turn them over and you have sex with them; you never even look at them. You won't ever look at them."

"Yeah."

"Pardon?"

"Never had much sex with them."

"You never had much sex with them." Adam thought about this. "But sometimes you did. I've got statements from them. I've read 'em, Willie. And you had the girls bring them out, right? Did Lisa ever bring out girls for you?"

"Who?"

"Lisa Yelds, a blond-haired girl; she used to be married to Blackie the biker."*

---

*Rick "Blackie" Burgess, an infamous member of the Haney chapter of the Hells Angels. He was never married to Yelds but had known her since she was a child. Yelds (whose hair is actually black) says he was always very good to her: "he didn't treat me like a dummy." When Yelds bought her

"Yelds, Yelds . . . Lee," Willie murmured.

"Yeah, did she ever bring girls out for you, or is your relationship with her not that?"

"Lee's nice."

"But did she ever bring girls out for you?"

"No."

As the hours dragged on, Willie never tired. He rejected offers of food and bathroom breaks. He listened to Adam's entreaties for information, sometimes with a smile, sometimes with interest. Dinah Taylor might be making deals with the police? It didn't seem to worry him.

Adam was fed up. "Well, you're not going to be able to talk to her," he said. "Our people are going to be negotiating with her over the next little while and they'll come to some agreement. Dave is saying, all right—Dave told Mark and Bruce this morning that it's all going to be over, that there are bodies, and that you didn't kill them all."

This got Willie's attention. "There are bodies?"

Adam veered away from this question—no bodies had been found yet, and he didn't want to admit it—to return to Lynn Ellingsen. Abruptly Willie agreed with Adam; yes, she had blackmailed him, "time and time over." But when Adam added that Ellingsen had told the police she'd walked in on him skinning a woman, Willie was scornful. "Oh yeah, right."

Adam persisted. "You're finished, Willie . . . You know whether you are the worst monster to ever come down the pike here in Canada . . . You know whether you've killed fifty women or more. Blood's all over your place. Not just Mona Wilson; there's other blood in there that's going to probably [be from] other kill sites. Do you know what's going to happen? They're moving the lab right on site! We're actually putting up a lab there right now; there are nine [police] trailers on your property.

---

first Harley-Davidson motorcycle, at sixteen, she bought parts for it from Burgess. His abandoned car was found in January 2002 in the Downtown Eastside; he was declared missing, and his body was never found.

"They're going to be able to separate, rapidly, the pig blood from human blood. They're going to be moving into the slaughterhouse. Willie, I absolutely believe we're going to find human blood in there."

Adam continued to hammer Willie with the fact that Lynn Ellingsen was blackmailing him and urged him to get revenge by telling him the full story of who had died on the farm. "Your bargaining power is disappearing. Because in the end, if you choose not to tell, the investigation simply keeps rolling, the search continues, unfortunately the families, they have to live with uncertainty for another year as we dig and find the DNA and the teeth and the hair and everything."

Willie laughed. "I don't think you'll find anything."

"Pardon?"

"You won't find anything. You won't find anything 'cause there's nothing there."

"Well, Willie, I don't believe you. Look me in the eyes. We'll find it."

Pickton shook his head no.

"Willie, we'll find it. Are you so foolish that you can't see what we're going to do? You can't see the millions we're going to spend, we're going to fine-tooth comb . . . We've got your trailer, we've got your mobile home. We know that you lived in the basement before that. We don't know whether you started killing back in the '80s [or] sometime in the early '90s. I'm thinking at a minimum by '97 you were full-blown into it. Okay. And we can associate twelve to you already and we have just started. We took down the wallpaper that had the blood on it, and now in behind was the old wood panelling, but we're going to go over every square inch of that, all right, and that blood gets in there, it dries up and it would last there for five hundred years in that state and, Willie, we'll just pull it out . . . You changed the carpet, do you remember?"

"No." But Willie was listening intently now. He was taking in everything Adam said. And it was obvious that he liked Adam, who was cheerful, relaxed and treating him more like a colleague, sharing information he knew would interest him.

"We've got the person who changed that carpet. We're going to go in, we're going to take up the floor, and the blood and stuff from all the girls is going to be there, Willie . . . All you can do is end up losing, Willie, because the only power you have is right now. Right now people care about your story. But once the deals have been made with Lynn, and the deals have been made with Dinah, and the deals have been made with the other people, you'll have no bargaining power anymore."

Adam also tried to show that he understood what might have happened to Willie when he was younger. "Willie, our lives are made up of things that change and alter us. Okay, we think we're heading in one 'direction and other things happen. When you were young, [you] start to get interested in sex. You know, you never got involved with girls. Whether you were shy, whether the fact that the farm . . . working farm kids, sometimes they go to school and we still smell of the farm. I grew up in the Prairies; I know about farms, okay? And people laugh at us. Did they laugh at you, Willie? Did you feel separate from them?"

"Yeah . . . I don't know. Not really."

"Different."

"Uh-huh."

"You worked on the farm, but did you hang out with other kids?"

"No."

"No. And we both know that we all need to belong, Willie. That's why you paid these girls to come out and spend time with you, even if you weren't going to have sex with them. We need to belong, don't we? Willie, I don't know you, I don't know what's inside your head, okay, but I know that you need people. We all do. And I don't believe that right into the core of your being you are as much of a monster as people are going to portray you to be.

"So Willie, the mistakes that you made, they're driven, I think, by anger and stuff that's happened with you. But you're not at a schoolyard, Willie, are you? You're not trying to grab little girls off the street. There's absolutely no indication you have ever done anything like that, and if you tell me that you haven't I will believe you. Can you look me in the eye and tell me, 'Don, I have never done anything like that'?"

"I haven't done anything like that." Willie remained wily in his responses; he was volunteering nothing, admitting nothing.

"You're thinking," said Adam, "what's in it for you to tell the truth? Whether or not you say a word, it's over for you. You know right now if Dave is involved."

"No, he's not."

"Anyone ever helped you do it?" Adam asked. "Any more involved that you're telling us?"

"I shouldn't be talking without a lawyer present."

"Are bikers involved?"

"Don't know."

"We're looking at you and three prostitutes bringing prostitutes out to you," Adam said. "Is this bigger than we think?"

"I don't know."

Adam thought for a few seconds. "Willie, I believe you are almost like two people—kind to your friends, [but] the other you is keyed by rage. Either one of two things: that happens to you or else you fantasize to do it—almost like [the way] the girls are driven to drugs. It's almost like a drug—you kill one and you're okay for a while, [but] when it happens it's never as good as the fantasy. All of a sudden it starts building again. Willie, did you keep them alive and torture them?"

"I shouldn't answer. We're not in court right now."

"Willie, look at me," implored Adam. "The families need to know. I'd like to know."

"I've made my own grave."

"Tell me this is not a situation where you chained them up and tortured them and they screamed . . ."

Willie sighed deeply. "Pigs, they go quickly. I gave them money for drugs and everything. What they did was up to them."

"Is this going to be a story of tortures, of cutting fingers off and cutting vaginas out?" demanded Adam. "This is important. Only you can tell me how much these people suffered."

"I don't know," Willie replied. "We're going over our heads here. I'm not supposed to talk about it."

Adam by now needed a break. He needed to talk to his colleagues, see what they thought, then decide if he was ever going to obtain a confession. Was this the best they were going to get that day? As he got up he asked Willie if he needed to use the washroom. No, replied Willie. Adam smiled. Willie had been sitting in that chair for hours without a break.

"You're quite the guy," he said. "Want something to eat?"

"I don't deserve to eat."

Adam abandoned all thought of a break. Was Willie ready to talk? He sat down again. "How bad are the deaths?" he asked. "Are you a sadist? Can we be open with each other for just a minute? Willie, what are you good at?"

"Whatever. Anything. Building. Tearing down."

"You know, Willie, there's a part of you that likes killing. You crossed the line between killing pigs and killing women. Killing . . . sex and loneliness and anger against these women. I don't know. I am not a shrink but maybe we could unravel all this together."

"I am not a bad guy," Willie responded.

Adam returned to Willie's childhood, to his mother's will that forced him to stay on the farm, to the ongoing investigation, and finally to the floundering Port Coquitlam police, who had missed him entirely. "They're going to take a lot of heat for that. You led them on a merry chase for years. There you sat, right under their noses for months, and they didn't have a clue. What you've done is impressive. Horrible, but impressive. If you're over fifty, you're the biggest serial killer in North America. Sandra Ringwald—that incident started you on the road to killing. Tell me the truth—that there was nothing prior to her. Shake my hand."

Pickton shook his hand.

Cheerfully, matter-of-factly, Adam continued. "Could be a couple before her or not? How did you start?" Pickton just shook his head.

"Was it by accident? What would happen? You'd just start to rage inside? What would happen?"

"Don't know."

"We've come a long way. The first ones—you caught them trying to steal—or was it just anger and rage that took you over?"

"I dunno. I dunno."

"Was it hard to do at first and then it just got easier and easier? Did you feel bad afterwards, at first?"

"Dunno."

"I think you do. How come you spared some?"

"Nice people."

"The nice ones you let go?"

"I'm not supposed to talk to you."

"Right. It doesn't matter what I say; it's over. I'm asking for a chance to understand. Prior to Ringwald, what happened? I'm asking for the truth."

"I'm not the only guy."

"How many do you think you've done?"

"Dunno."

"You have a good idea. Fifteen? Twenty? Thirty? It doesn't matter. Tell the truth. Well, I can put about twelve to you right now."

Now Adam leaned back in his chair, looking relaxed. He began to count backwards. "You did Sereena. Let's start from that."

Bill Fordy entered the room and wordlessly handed a picture of Sereena to Adam.

"Let's take little steps, all right?"

Willie started to laugh. "You're making me more of a mass murderer than I am. What's going to happen if I say something I shouldn't say? I don't have a lawyer present. So what's gonna happen?"

"Willie, that's fair," Adam said. "I know I can convict you on three. I know you. I know there's some full bodies buried in here."

Willie smiled. "I wish you luck. If I tell you what you want to know, will you pull the fences down?"

"I'll be straight with you—no."

"Why don't you go to the higher-ups?"

"I am high up."

"If I tell you everything I know . . . If I admit to everything, will you pull the fences down?"

"What kind of numbers are we talking about?" Adam asked, fascinated.

"And let everything die off . . ." Willie continued.

"I'm not making a deal!" exclaimed Adam.

"I'm only asking. [So we can be] getting lives back together again."

"Give me a number," demanded Adam. "I'm not lying—I don't want to negotiate at this stage."

"I'm just asking you."

"I'm not prepared to deal."

"Anyways, think it over," Willie offered. He wasn't ready to give up yet. "Everybody go back to normal. Go back to . . . I know all the numbers . . . not here or there."

"How can you help me find them, then?" Adam asked.

Willie continued to try to make a deal. "I got no lawyer here or nothing. I'm getting nailed to the cross. I know the position I'm in—burying myself."

"We're going to start digging," warned Adam.

"I know the situation. I'm screwed. I'm screwed." By this time Willie was more relaxed. He was making eye contact with Adam; both his legs were swung over the arm of the chair and he was leaning back, looking very much at home.

"You're cagey as a fox, Willie."

Willie smiled. "What do you want me to say?"

"'Don, I don't know how many women I killed . . .' Every one of those kills is a special moment in your life."

"No."

"You mean, like, it's nothing?"

"Not really."

"It's a big deal to you? Or is it like killing one of the pigs? Or is it somewhere in the middle?"

"Dunno. Dunno. Dunno what to say, either."

"Was there anyone you killed that you regret? That you shoulda let her go? Ever had those thoughts?"

Willie thought about that for a few moments. "What do you want me to say?"

"The truth."

Willie wasn't ready for the truth. He still wanted to make a deal. "Like, I asked you a question already."

"If I negotiated a deal," said Adam, "then nothing we say is admissible in court. You would like to make a deal. That doesn't mean there aren't ins for you if . . ."

"If what?"

"Dave not involved?" Adam asked.

"True."

"Not involved in anything?"

"True."

"You told Dave that Dinah killed some of them."

"I don't want to commit myself to her," Willie replied.

Adam thought about this. "She has two choices. To own up that she killed some too. Even without you she killed some too. Even without you she killed some of the girls."

"No comment."

"Why not?"

"Guilty of murder then. Am I going to take the blame for . . . I'm not going to walk. The problem is that everybody has to get their life back together. I'll take the fall and everything else."

"For Lynn too?"

"I gotta speak to Dinah."

"Let's put Dinah aside. Are you gonna take the fall for Lynn? I don't see you owe her any loyalty. You're in a good, powerful position."

Willie considered this, but he was hedging his bets. "Still gotta talk to Dinah first. I'm the head honcho, right?"

"Yes."

"You got me," he said. "A lot of people are coming down with me."

"Now that's more interesting," Adam replied. "Give me some hints."

"I'm going to take the fall," Willie said.

Adam pushed for more information. "We've had a report about blood sports out there—a group of guys . . ."

"No! Ha, ha, ha, ha! Other people involved—not naming names."

"How were a lot of other people involved?"

"This is way over your head," Willie said. "I'm the head honcho and you got me now."

Adam decided not to push. "You hungry now?" he asked.

"I don't deserve to eat," muttered Willie.

"Want a pork sandwich?"

Willie realized he was being kidded. "I did tell you a few stories," he admitted slowly. "You got me, right?"

Adam returned to the one question that everyone—police, families, journalists, the general public—was asking. "Is it true Dave is not involved in anything?"

"True."

"It started after Sandra Ringwald?" Willie nodded.

"Definitely afterwards?" Willie nodded again.

"Gotta whiz," said Adam, who stood up and left the room, closing the door behind him.

The discussion outside was brief but intense. Every man and woman watching in the three rooms was aware of the time; Pickton had been in the interview room for nearly eleven hours. He hadn't left to go to the bathroom, he'd eaten nothing, he'd drunk only a small bottle of pop. Adam was getting somewhere, but he was running out of time. They couldn't question Willie much longer without facing accusations of mistreatment and failure to let him talk to his lawyer again. But they also knew Adam was close to obtaining a confession. Willie liked him. It was beginning to look as if he wanted to tell him everything.

In the interview room, Willie only yawned. A few minutes later Adam was back. This time Willie did ask to use the washroom, and Adam took him out. When they were back in the interview room, Adam put forward a proposal that Jim Hunter had suggested. If Willie would agree to tell them what he'd done—and how he did it—it could mean that the investigators could be off the farm property sooner than they had planned. But Willie wasn't buying.

"That's not what I asked for, is it?" he said.

Adam was surprised. "What did you ask for?"

"You got me, right?"

"Yeah."

"I'm the head guy, right? And I'm fucked anyways?"

"Yeah."

"The only problem is . . ."

Adam had had enough. "Robert, you killed Sereena and Mona, agreed?"

"I won't admit to anything yet."

"Well, it's a simple question."

"Okay, but I won't admit to anything yet but, but go ahead."

"All right, so that's the girl, that's the one with the inhaler?"

"Um-hum."

"Did you kill them by yourself or was Dinah involved in them, in those two?"

"No comment . . ."

"Which kinda tells me that she was involved."

"But there'll be other people coming down too," Willie said.

"Without naming names, give me an idea of, of how they're going to come down, so I can understand."

"There will be other murderers or whatever, other people charged, but that's not here nor there."

"Men or women?"

"A man."

"Man. One other man."

"Um-hum."

Willie was talking about Scott Chubb. Although he had admitted to Adam that he was shocked by the videotape Fordy had shown him of Chubb describing how Willie had talked to him about killing women, it was nothing more than "a lot of gossip." Lynn Ellingsen too, he said, was just telling the police more gossip. Adam dismissed Willie's stonewalling and began to talk to Willie as if he had admitted to the murders.

"Was there any, ah, were there any snuff films made or anything like that, Willie?"

"No."

"Nothing like that?"

"No."

"Nothing shocks me, right. I mean, I've been a cop for almost thirty years. When you finally open up, are we going to be talking about torture and stuff like that?"

"No," Willie said. "Nothing like that."

"When you finally decide to talk about this, are you, do you know why you were killing them, like, in your own mind, do you know what it was?"

"No. I mean, I won't, ah, no comment at this stage. 'Cause I gotta talk to Dinah first."

For a short while both men were silent. Finally Adam told Willie to look at the foam board covered with pictures of the missing women.

"How many do you recognize?" he demanded. "If you were free to talk right now, how many could you reach out and touch?"

"You can touch 'em all." Willie pointed to the board.

"No, I mean that you killed."

"You make me more of a mass murderer than I am."

"Well, you're saying you haven't killed forty-eight?"

"Hmmm."

"You've killed women that are not on here too?"

"Forty-what?"

"Well, there's forty-eight, right?"

"Yeah."

"Okay. So my question is—that there's women you've killed that aren't on here . . ."

"No, no, no, no comment."

"Why not just answer my questions?"

"Because if they're not on there [the poster board], then I'm not charged for it, right?"

"Yeah, but what's the difference between two or twenty? It makes no difference to the sentence."

"Whatever other ones that are not on there, I am not charged with?"

"That's right," Adam replied. "You are only charged with two that are on there. But you will be charged with more, obviously. Willie, the DNA is pouring in. I gotta tell you, I am thinking to myself, 'Why am I even having this conversation with you?'"

"That is what I am asking you," Willie said. "I feel the same thing, but the problem is, like I said, I am the head honcho, the head guy."

"So without you, none of these murders would have happened is what you are telling me? Is that true?"

Willie dodged Adam's questions. He tried to suggest that other men were involved in the murders but refused to say anything more than the fact that "there be guns involved here."

Adam was frustrated. "You need to explain that more. I need to understand that."

"Okay, well, I mean myself. If I commit, there will be at least one extra gun involved."

"That you have used to kill a girl?"

"Mm-hmm . . . other things."

"Oh, wait—are you hinting there could be dead guys there too?"

"Uh-huh."

"How many? Are they Angels?"

"No, no, no!"

"How many?"

"One anyways. Somebody else did it."

"You were there?"

"No."

"Body?"

"He didn't . . ."

"Bring you the body? Well, we're certainly travelling, Willie."
Adam brushed aside Willie's meaningless sallies. "We do have information on Dave picking up girls and bringing them to the farm," he
said. "Willie, you didn't do a good job of cleaning up the girls'
blood. Like, you got to agree with me."

"That's right. I was sloppy."

"Yes, you were. That sums it up."

"That's what I am, I'm sloppy."

"Did you change the carpet because of the blood?" asked Adam.

"No," said Willie. "I went vinyl. To keep it clean." Just a pair of
guys talking about keeping a place neat and tidy. Willie was enjoying
himself. This was a conversation between equals. He liked Adam's
cheerfulness and the respect he was showing him.

"With everything that was going on, how do you think you
managed to avoid getting caught for so long?"

"No comment."

"How long you got—it's just bad police work or, you know, like
what?"

"Carelessness on my behalf," Willie said.

"As a policeman," Adam ventured, "I look at Ringwald."

Sandra Gail Ringwald appeared to be one person Willie didn't
mind discussing. "I was gonna take her back the night she went
bananas," he confided. "She'd made arrangements for me to meet
her pimp. I said no way, no way . . . I had $3,400 on me. She wanted
more money."

"Everything I see about you . . ." Adam said. "You have a great
memory. I am sure you can remember the details of each murder.

Each and every death, the details, the disposal. Willie, if you would really like us to shorten our time at the farm . . ."

"Be my guest," Willie said. "I don't care if you dig under the townhouses. Be my guest."

"We hear there are rumours about mass graves."

"Wish you luck again."

"If you could take us to a spot—"

"If I could, I would."

"—we could do our job."

Willie felt he had the upper hand at last. "Bad policing is why it took you so long," he said.

"Did you ever think of quitting?"

"Yeah. It'll all come out."

"Did you have fantasies of killing?"

Willie said nothing, just shook his head.

"No? It was not like that? Serial killers have fantasies of what they'd do."

"No."

"Anger? Well, you sort of said it was anger. Would I be right in saying, Willie, that you had reached the stage where you just no longer, sort of, really viewed these girls as being worth anything?"

"Uh-huh."

"And you killed . . ."

"But, uh, no, no. That's—I had one more planned, but that was—that was the end of it. That was the last. I was gonna shut it down. That's when I was just sloppy, just the last one."

"You were gonna do one more?"

"That's—that was the end of it. That's why I got sloppy, because I never got that far."

"Like, why didn't you just drag that mattress that—where you killed Mona?" asked Adam. "Why didn't you just drag it out and burn it? Did you not realize that there was blood underneath it? Like, you don't have to say anything. But like, if you'd have burnt it, Willie. Just sloppy."

"Sloppy, like I just told you."

"Let me ask you a question. Did you keep trophies?"

"No."

"So when you kept the women's ID in your place, that was just, again, sloppy?"

"Yeah."

"Jesus, Willie, you must be kicking yourself, like—it must piss you off."

"I know, I know. Sloppiness."

At this point Adam decided to ask him about Mona Wilson. "You know what they call impact blood?"

Willie looked puzzled. "No."

"When you were hitting her—it cast off blood."

"No."

"How do you explain that there's bloody palmprints—did you use a hatchet?"

"No."

"A hammer?"

"No."

"What, then? Tell me! Come on man, I'm dying to know! I've investigated this for a year. You're dying to tell me—I can see it in your eyes. What did you use?"

"Sloppiness."

"Did you ever think about cleaning up?"

"I was too busy at the job sites." And then, suddenly, Willie started to laugh. "Ha, ha, ha, ha," he chuckled merrily. "Ha, ha, ha."

Adam didn't see the joke. "Why did you take her to the motor home? Why not do it in the trailer?"

"No comment."

"Too messy?"

"No comment."

"Willie—give it up and come on . . ."

Willie looked at him almost fondly. This was fun. "You've done your homework," he said.

"Did you do most of the killings in your motor home?" Adam was pushing him now, hard. "You killed Mona on the [mattress], we agreed." The door to the interview room opened and Bill Fordy walked in carrying another large foam board with a picture on it, an aerial shot of the farm. "Bill has just brought in a picture."

"That's nice," Willie said, looking at the photograph with interest.

"How many other girls died in there?" asked Adam.

"How many others you got?" Willie asked, still staring at the picture. He was curious, so Adam began to tell him what he was looking at. "There's $50,000 worth of gravel along with power and water in there, Willie. You're very large—most notorious guy in Canada now. I can see it in your face. You're not happy with what trouble you are causing your family."

"True."

Adam was pointing out various farm sites on the picture. "How many girls in there?" he asked, pointing to one building.

"One for sure." Willie stared at the picture. He was relaxed, his legs still slung over the side of the chair.

"How many?"

"Two. Maybe three."

Adam smiled sympathetically. "You gotta be—you gotta be saying, like, why? All you would have had to do . . ."

"I know."

"Is go through that, clean up . . ."

"I know."

"And you'd still be on the street."

"I know."

"Oh, it must piss you off."

"I know."

"It must, eh?"

"I know."

Adam showed Willie where the motor home was on the foam-board picture. "How many girls in there?" Adam asked.

"One, for sure."

"Trust me, you used the dildo on her," Adam said. "Was she alive or was she dead?"

"Alive."

"Did you shoot her?"

"What?"

"Whatever you did caused a lot of blood," Adam told him. "This is one way we can test your truthfulness, Willie. If you're truthful with me and you go, 'Well, Don, you could find up to five different women's blood in there,' and we do find it, then we can sit there and say, 'Okay, you know, now we can start to believe what Willie says.'"

"Uh-huh."

"All right. So my question is how many?"

"I'd say two, probably two, maybe three."

"No, no, no!" exclaimed Adam. "You hear me out. You're the one who's asking me, and you're asking me to believe you."

"I already told you how many's in the trailer," Willie replied. "Probably maybe up to as high as three in that, in the motor home."

"All right."

"That was as far as we got," Willie said.

"Right."

"Possibly."

"Why did you use the motor home instead of the trailer?"

"Well, I don't know what you got on there," Willie said, eyeing the photograph.

"Mona Wilson disappeared around the end of November, December last year," Adam said, smiling at Willie. "When did you get her out there? You're done. Come on, cough it up. You used the dildo on her when she was still alive?"

"Yes," Willie admitted. "She didn't want to have sex. Didn't want to do anything. No comment." And then he laughed, a long whinny. "No comment. No comment at this stage. I'm not supposed to talk to you. I'm nailed to the cross."

"That's true," Adam agreed. "Do you remember when you killed the other girl, with the inhaler?"

"No comment."

"Would I be right if I guessed the slaughter area? Or was she dead when you brought her there? Come on, Willie!"

"No."

Both men stared at the picture for a few more minutes.

"You're the one who's asking me about the farm," Willie whined.

"In the motor home?" Adam asked.

"I told you up to three."

"What about a ballpark on the trailer?"

"I gotta talk to Dinah."

"Okay," said Adam, backing off. "When you talk about three— is the girl with the inhaler in there?"

"You're off. No comment."

"Willie, Willie, Willie. Think it over."

"Possibly two more," admitted Willie.

"You're finished with the inhaler girl."

"No."

"You're caught."

"No."

"Willie," said Adam, "look at me for a second." Willie stared at him, enjoying the moment. "What are you giving me to take back to my people? You've told me already other people were involved."

"Why should I tell you that?" Willie snapped. "Tit for tat."

"Let me step out for a minute," said Adam.

"I'll let you sleep on it," Willie said. He was the big man now. He was in control and it felt good.

Once again Adam asked him if he needed to use the bathroom. No, Willie replied. Adam smiled. "Frankly, you got more zip in you than I do. Why not give me everything?"

"Why should I do that?"

"For the families," Adam answered. "They need to know."

Willie didn't bat an eye. "Not my problem," he said. "Shit happens."

Adam was, for once, almost at a loss for words. "Well," he said at last, "you certainly sum up how you feel about it. My sole reason for being with you here is to do something for these families."

Pickton shrugged. "I'm nailed anyway, so what?"

"What if this were your niece or nephew?"

"They were in the wrong place at the right time. The only thing they can do is shoot me. I'm nailed to the cross. So what can I do?"

"Do the right thing. You're not willing to do anything for these families?"

"What can I do?" Willie asked. "I'm nailed anyway, so it don't mean nothing."

"Willie, I hear you. You sit here with a complete lack of care. Can't you respect them for worrying about their offspring?"

"At my stage now I haven't got nothing to say."

"Do you remember Clifford Olson?" Adam asked. "You are exactly the same personality as Olson."

"No, I'm not."

"I need to leave you with this, Willie—think it over. I sit here and try and see things from your eyes. I have to try to understand you. And all the time I'm seized with the fact that these people— their hearts are broken. And for you it's just a chess game. I just want to get lives back together."

Adam walked out of the room. Willie was alone. It was now 9:47 at night. He leaned forward to look at the foam board. He studied it and then looked behind it. He leaned back and looked at it some more. Finally he grabbed it, set it up closer to him on the floor and stared at it with his chin in his hand.

Five minutes later Bill Fordy returned to the room. "Your lawyer came. She's gone for coffee. Do you want to phone her? It's up to you."

"Don't matter."

"It's up to you if you want to see her."

"Don't matter."

Fordy laughed. "Okay. I'll phone her, see where she is."

It was now 9:54 p.m.

CHAPTER FORTY-ONE

BACK IN THE CELL

When Willie returned to his cell, his friendly roommate was waiting. "What time is it?" he asked.

"Ten," said Willie.

"Holy fuck, you've been gone all day. Fuck, they beating you up in there or what?"

"Yeah, they nailed me to the cross. They got three or four murders on me already. The rest of my life, without parole."

Just then a guard arrived, interrupting his account of what had happened; Marilyn Sandford was waiting to see him. Forty-two minutes later Willie was back. He peeled off the hooded sweatshirt he'd been given and sat down in his sweatpants and T-shirt. His hair was still sticking up, wild and dirty and frizzy; even his wispy beard looked unkempt.

"I can't believe this," he moaned. "I can't believe this. Interrogation, tough. Fuck. I didn't need that. Fuck, they're sure putting me through the wringer again. Like a fuckin' nightmare in hell. A nightmare in fuckin' hell. Oh God, what a fuckin' day."

"That's a fuckin' long day, yeah," agreed his new best friend. "Fuckin' right. It's ten thirty out there."

"And I've been out there since ten o'clock this morning. And even my lawyer says that's a fuck of a long time." His lawyer, who had been waiting since five that afternoon, had told him that he was facing thirty or forty murder counts.

"Fuckin' bring it on, eh?" responded his cellmate. "Bit of a fuckin' hunting trip, was it?"

"No shit. No kidding. I guess they want me real bad." His mind wandered to the search of the farm. "They put in five hundred yards of gravel. Ten buildings. Whew! Now I'm all over the paper. Make the headlines—whoo, pig farmer charged with murder, first degree. In all the front pages, every fuckin' paper is, right across the fuckin' headlines."

"You're a fuckin' all-star."

Willie told his new friend that he'd tried to bargain with the police saying he wasn't the only one involved in the murders. "If I go down, a lot of other people go down. I was just telling them left and right, left and centre, that's the way it is and that's it," he said. Then, as he often did, he switched abruptly to another subject. This time it was the cost of his lawyer—"one of the most expensive lawyers in Vancouver"—who had charged him, he said, $80,000 to act for him when he was charged with the attempted murder of Sandra Gail Ringwald.

"But it was worth it, right?" asked his cellmate.

Willie didn't reply to this; all he said was that the case had now come back again.

"But you did walk then, right?"

"This time, no," replied Willie. "This time I'm not gonna walk. I won't even come up for bail." His lawyer had told him that bail was up to the judge but she doubted he would get it.

Now, as Willie gobbled down a late meal—bread served with a heap of baked beans—the conversation shifted to his cellmate's legal worries. He told Willie that he had talked to his own lawyer and would have to appear in court the next day on three attempted murder charges. Willie put his plate aside and smiled. He held up his right hand, five fingers spread wide, and then pointed to the camera. Still smiling, Willie spread his fingers wide again and then closed them to make a large zero with his thumb and forefinger.

"Five?" asked the cellmate.

"No."

Willie held up the five fingers of his right hand and then again formed his left hand into a circle.

"Fifty?"

"Yes."

"Fuck you. You're full of—you're shitting me."

"Camera," Pickton warned, pointing to the dark glass bubble on the ceiling.

The undercover officer began talking about how he had killed his own victims. The first one he did, he said, was with a pickaxe. In the back of the head. "Hardly any mess, no fuckin' blood and fuckin' hard to detect, eh. Takes the cops a while to figure out what happened to the guy." To get rid of the bodies, he went on, he threw them in the ocean. "Do you know what the fuckin' ocean does to things? There ain't much left."

"I did better than that," said Willie through a mouthful of food. Carrying his plate, he got up and moved over to sit on the bunk right beside his new buddy. "A rendering plant," he said, grinning.

The man was startled. "Hey?"

"A rendering plant," repeated Willie.

"Ha, ha. No shit. Ha, ha. That's gotta be fuckin' pretty good, eh? Can't be much fuckin' left."

Willie swept out his arm to show that there would be nothing left. "Only I was kinda sloppy at the end too, getting too sloppy," he said. "They got me, oh fuck. Gettin' too sloppy. I was gonna do one more, make it an even fifty. That's why I was sloppy. I wanted one more, make the big five-oh."

The cellmate hardly knew how to respond but he worked hard at it. "Make the big five-zero." He laughed. "Fuck. That's fucked. Fuckin' five-zero. Fuckin' half a hundred."

Cheered by the impression he'd made, Willie giggled and scraped the last bits of his dinner off the plate. "Everybody says, 'How many of those?' Wouldn't tell 'em. Talk about half, about one-quarter. Talking about all of them. I says no. I wouldn't tell 'em."

All his cellmate could do was laugh uneasily. But Willie was on a roll now. "You know, they got forty-eight on the list," he said. "I think I'm nailed to the cross, but if that happens there will be about fifteen other people are gonna go down."

He admitted that he was upset when the police showed him video-taped interviews with Scott Chubb and Andy Bellwood, men he'd considered to be friends. "They even says I filled the syringes up with antifreeze and you inject the stuff and you're dead in about five to ten minutes. They got a lot of stuff on me. That's only part of it. They're gonna nail me to the cross. I made my own grave by being sloppy."

Willie began to get ready for bed. He was tired but he was also enjoying himself now, with someone to impress. "But, you know, it pisses me right off," he said. "Really fuckin' pisses me off. I was just gonna fuckin' do one more, make it even." He pulled off his pants and climbed onto his bunk wearing only a T-shirt and underpants. "Bigger than the—these—bigger than the one in the States," he said. He was talking about Gary Leon Ridgeway, the Green River Killer, whom Don Adam had mentioned a few hours earlier.

"Fuckin' looks like you got the record," said the undercover man, laughing.

"It's big, it's growing," replied Willie. "They say they want to dig."

"Yeah."

"They want to dig, they are—they're gonna dig for a year." Willie snickered. "Let 'em dig. Have fun. Play in the dirt." He snickered again. "Teeth, we're gonna find fingernails, bones. Yes, oh yes!" Lying on the bunk, he looked at the ceiling. "Mr. Sloppy. Sloppy at the end. Just at near the end, just sloppy. But I sure racked their brains, I'll tell ya. Now they didn't know what to say."

"Hee, hee, you stumped them, eh," said his cellmate, chuckling.

"Oh fuckin' yeah, I had 'em going. I was sitting in the fuckin' chair and everything else," Willie said. But he returned again and again to the fact that the police had him on four murder counts for sure. If he had been more careful he'd never have been in this mess now. And he had had a plan, he confided. Once he'd done fifty he was going to take a break for a while. "Then I do another twenty-five, twenty-five new ones." He laughed merrily, and soon his pal joined in.

By now Willie had cheered up. He grinned at the camera and waved to it. "Hello!" he said. He wasn't sleepy yet; he needed to talk. The police had caught him because of his guns, he said. He had a Mac-10, a ten-millimetre pistol, a forty-five and a thirty-eight, he said. Plus more than a hundred rounds of hidden ammunition for each. "They took the walls out of my trailer . . . so I don't know if they found it."

There was silence for a while.

"Forty-nine," Willie finally said.

"Almost made it," said his cellmate. "Almost made it."

"I haven't done fifty yet." Willie laughed. "And the pigs are baffled, the pigs are baffled."

"Baffled?"

"Pigs—cops," Willie explained. "Now they're going to dig in the manure and see if the pigs shit out human remains."

"They fuckin' wouldn't eat human remains. Fuckin' pigs don't eat that."

"I know that but you can't tell 'em that," Pickton said. "They never seen nothing like this ever before."

Just before he fell asleep he talked happily about the impression he would make on his fellow prisoners once they knew who he was. "There would be a lot of people: *Hey, congratulations!*" he said. "*I can't believe it, I mean I can't believe it, I'm with the fuckin' pig man!*"

His cellmate laughed. "Sign autographs."

"That's bigger than the Green River," murmured Willie. He knew he could cut a deal with the cops, he added. He just needed them to bring a friend of his out from Ontario so he could talk to her privately first.

"Hey, what do you got to lose?" his cellmate responded.

"I have nothing to lose," Pickton said.

The men were silent for a few minutes. Each was exhausted. Finally Willie stopped pretending. "Ah, I think I'm dead," he muttered. "It's obvious. So, so, so, so, so close."

The police officers in the three monitoring rooms were stunned. Forty-nine. Did Willie really say forty-nine? What some of the officers had thought might be a search for as many as a dozen bodies had suddenly blown up into a massive search, one they realized right away was going to take much longer and cost far more than anyone had ever dreamed possible.

Just before midnight the undercover officer left on the pretext of talking to his lawyer. Willie was lying on his back on the bunk with a grey prison blanket rolled under his head. A few minutes after he heard his cellmate going down the hall, he reached down into the front of his underpants, pulled out his penis and began masturbating. Suddenly he heard voices and a lock turn and a door slam. He reached up behind his neck, pinched a corner of the blanket and threw it over himself like a matador flinging his red cape at a bull. Covered top to toe with the blanket, Willie thrashed around on the bunk. He stopped the second his cellmate walked back in. Both men fell fast asleep and barely moved until someone came with their breakfast.

CHAPTER FORTY-TWO

TAKING WILLIE TO THE JUDGE

While Willie spent a quiet Sunday alone in jail—his friendly cellmate having gone for good—Sergeant Richard Konarski and Corporal Baltej Dhillon pulled Lynn Ellingsen into the task force's Surrey satellite headquarters and signed a deal with her. She was no longer under arrest; now she was a witness.

"This is to confirm with Lynn Anne Ellingsen," her deal read, "that our interest in her is as a witness in the homicide investigation where Robert William (Willie) Pickton has been arrested and charged. He is also a suspect in other murders. We understand that Lynn Anne Ellingsen has indicated that she has not participated in any of these murders. We understand that she has knowledge of some of these events and that she wishes to voluntarily provide her version of these events and to participate as a witness. We understand that Lynn Anne Ellingsen agrees to tell the truth and that telling the truth is a condition of this agreement."

In spite of the signed agreement, Lynn remained so terrified that Pickton would somehow get bail and be back on the street that she still refused to tell the police everything she knew. To make matters worse, she couldn't think clearly; she was high on drugs. But Ellingsen did admit that she had told her boyfriend, Ron Menard, the whole story. He was not surprised, she said; in fact he had told her that he already knew Willie was murdering women. "He said, 'That's not his first,' and I'm like, 'Well, uh, if you knew that, why are you allowing me to stay there?'" she told the officers. "He goes, 'Because you're okay. You're not a prostitute so he'll leave you alone.' And I said, 'It doesn't matter. If he's capable of doing it to one human, I'm sure he can do it to—it doesn't matter.'"

The police weren't discouraged by her inarticulate answers to their questions. They had time to help her become clean and sober, and she was well worth it. Their hunch was that, so far, she was their single eyewitness to murder.

The following morning—Monday, February 25, 2002—sheriffs escorted Robert William Pickton to the provincial courthouse on Mary Hill Road in Port Coquitlam. The courthouse, designed by Vancouver architect Arthur Erickson and built in 1996, is probably the most beautiful building in this small city. From above, the red-brick structure is triangular in shape and three storeys high, but anyone climbing the broad, shallow steps from the street to the wide terrace across the front of the building and the main entrance gets the impression of a low, wide rectangle framed by shrubs and trees. This morning the steps and terrace were crammed with friends and family members of the missing women, curious local people, and about forty reporters, photographers and camera operators; behind them, filling the street, were television vans with satellite equipment. But none of them saw Pickton arrive because the convoy of sheriffs' vans took him through a side entrance into a secure basement parking area, walled off from the public parking lot, with an elevator to bring him up to Courtroom 2.

Courtroom 2 is just one of several courtrooms on the ground level, which also houses a coffee shop in a central atrium with several tables for the public, as well as the registrar's offices, where the records are kept, and the offices of the Crown counsels who handle the cases flowing into the various courtrooms. The third floor contains another row of courtrooms that open onto a corridor overlooking the atrium.

On a normal day it is simple to enter the courthouse. Not this day, however. Armed sheriffs at two gates searched every person who came in and put them through a metal detector. The police were taking no chances that a grief-stricken family member, a possible Pickton accomplice or a crazed vigilante might try to kill him. The lineups were long and many people were turned away. Courtroom 2 had room for about a hundred people but it quickly filled up. One person who couldn't get in was Steve Rix, Mona Wilson's boyfriend; he told reporters he was angry about not being able to look at Pickton "face to face."

Judge David Stone, one of nine provincial court judges working here, had been assigned the Pickton case. In his mid-forties, he was experienced and well-liked by court staff and other lawyers for his calm nature, common sense and compassion. But he wouldn't be the judge for Pickton's murder trial. His job today was simply to listen to the charges and send Pickton to jail until his preliminary hearing began. When the hearing took place, he would be the presiding judge. There he would listen to the evidence presented by the prosecutors, as well as cross-examination of witnesses by Pickton's lawyers, and rule on whether or not there was enough evidence to send Pickton to trial before the British Columbia Supreme Court.

When Pickton walked into Judge Stone's courtroom, still dressed in his grey sweatpants and hooded top, his hair as wild and filthy as it had been when he was arrested, there was almost no time for the crowd to react. The charges were read out: one count of first-degree murder in the death of Sereena Abotsway, twenty-nine, between the eighteenth day of July, 2001, and the fifth day of February, 2002, at or near Port Coquitlam, and one count of first-degree murder in the death of Mona Wilson, twenty-six, between the first day of December 2001, and the fifth day of February 2002. Judge Stone quickly remanded Willie into custody until his next court appearance, on April 12.

Willie was led out of the courtroom and driven to the North Fraser Pretrial Centre, a large, modern provincial jail in an industrial park on Kingsway Avenue in Port Coquitlam, no more than a mile from the courthouse. Prisoners are kept here until they come up for trial; if they are found guilty they are usually sent to a provincial or federal prison. Until that happened—if it happened—Willie's new home, as the crow flies, was halfway between the courthouse and his farm.

Outside the courthouse, reporters swarmed Peter Ritchie, Pickton's lawyer. Although he had little to say, Ritchie asked them not to pester Willie's family and said that, yes, he expected Willie to apply for bail. "This is very early in the investigation here," he cautioned them, "and I would ask that no one leap to any conclusions at this stage." "Mr. Pickton" was "completely shocked" by what had happened, he added. "Our client hasn't been told very much about this case against him yet."

The police were not much more communicative, although RCMP constable Cate Galliford, spokesperson for the task force, briefly outlined what was ahead: "We believe we now have answers regarding the disappearance of two missing women. But this is a case involving fifty missing women. There are a lot of questions still unanswered. We will not rest until those answers are found. Let us be very, very clear—the investigation into the missing women is not over. The detailed, inch-by-inch search of the farm property will continue for months to come."

Fifty women. If there was any takeaway from her carefully structured comments, this was it. The public did not hear what Pickton had confessed to his cellmate. But they did hear that the police saw Willie as a serial killer, and fifty would make him bigger than the Green River Killer across the border in Seattle.

When it was his turn to say something, the Vancouver Police Department's spokesperson, Scott Driemel, who was now working with Galliford, was defensive about his team's record of failure in the case. He wasn't going to discuss the VPD's investigation of Pickton at this time, Driemel told them, but he did add, "I think there's a ton of misinformation out there. I wish I could sit you down, show you the entire timeline, every meeting and everything that was done, right from the inception of this whole process. I feel pretty good about it, but . . . it's tough, we just can't make it public. If you armchair it and quarterback it now, is there things we could have done or should have done or might have done more of? It's pretty hard to put today's judgment on an issue that was there yesterday. But from what I've seen, it looks like we were reasonably diligent as far as how we dealt with the issues with the resources that we had available and how it unfolded.

"If we would have got the break sooner, we would have had the breaker sooner," Driemel added. What he meant by "the breaker" no one was sure, but he didn't stop to explain. "They haven't even shared with me what the type and style of evidence was that has led them to be able to go and provide a first-degree murder charge," he confided. "They're being real careful with it."

As Galliford and Driemel briefed reporters on the front steps of the courthouse, two teams of officers were picking their way through Willie's motor home a couple of miles away. Along with another one of Sereena Abotsway's inhalers, they had found a silver metal shower hose stained with blood; the head looked mangled and the hose appeared to have been used as a whip. The blood on it was so dry it was falling off in chips. They had also found a broken green glass cider bottle thick with dried blood. In fact, almost everything in the motor home seemed to have blood on it—a space heater, newspapers, a mattress and a waterbed heater were just a few of the items. They could only imagine the savage attack that must have taken place in this space. It wasn't long before they concluded that most of the blood belonged to Mona Wilson.

Very quickly the police realized they were going to have to swab the surfaces of every item in the motor home, the trailer and the slaughterhouse, a process that required highly trained forensic technicians and scientists. The technicians would have to go over every inch of every surface in every building: every floor, wall and window; inside every drawer and closet; every piece of furniture; every tool; every piece of machinery; every vehicle; every appliance. It meant dividing each space—a room or part of a room—into distinct search areas. The searchers began wherever possible to further divide these areas into grids of one-inch squares. Each tiny grid square had its own identifying letters and numbers to pinpoint exactly where the evidence was found.

As they worked, the technicians would note in a carefully organized logbook the date, location and other identifying information for the items they had swabbed. They would also outline, using a special silver pen with black ink, the grid squares they had swabbed. Later, back in the lab, they typed up their findings. And they photographed everything they did. During this process the technicians wore masks, full Tyvek suits, booties and gloves; every time they left the site they were working on, they replaced their gear before they went back in—new gloves, suits, masks, booties.

The actual swabbing meant dipping a sterile cotton-topped stick (like a long Q-Tip) into sterile water and then gently wiping—using one turn only—the surface of the grid location. Each stick was placed in a sterile container called a Spin-Eaze tube; if the tiny square required more than one swab, each stick became a separate exhibit and was put in a separate tube. Frequently the search technicians would find blood as they searched, or stains that they believed could be blood. In those cases they would first use paper strips called Hemastix to find out if the stain or drop was indeed blood; in the presence of blood the paper turns green. Later, a further test kit, called HemaTrace, would indicate if the blood was human or animal. If the blood was human, the sample was sent to the RCMP's forensic biology lab for DNA testing.

Within a week of Pickton's arrest the police had torn out walls from his office and bedroom in the trailer and had moved them into a tent to test them for bloodstains. They also drained the ground around the slaughterhouse, pumping the water into children's plastic swimming pools—which were used as holding tanks so the water could be tested later—and placing filters on the pumps to trap evidence. When they moved into the slaughterhouse itself, they divided it into two sections with two teams; each team looked at every item in their section, photographed it, recorded it and decided how important it was. Then the items were moved to two tents set up outside, with DNA workstations and light stations in each.

As the technicians worked they found significant evidence. One searcher discovered six hairs with roots on a hairbrush, blood and scalp hair in the hinges of handcuffs, and some human blood on a vibrator. Another found night-vision goggles in Willie's laundry room with DNA belonging to Pat Casanova, the Filipino butcher who so often worked with Willie; Willie's DNA was on the strap of the goggles. Casanova's DNA was also found on a rubber apron hanging in the slaughterhouse. Sereena Abotsway's DNA was found on black lingerie in Willie's bedroom closet; her tote bag, which contained her Bible, some running shoes, a pair of pumps, three books and an inhaler, was soaked with her blood. And they found Andrea Joesbury's DNA in a garbage bag in the slaughterhouse.

By the end of February the investigation was running on two separate fronts. One was the forensic search of the farm, and this was managed entirely by the RCMP. Jack Mellis had been in charge, but because he was the regional head of forensic identification and needed to return to his regular job, he was replaced by Sergeant Brian Andrews. Andrews was there only a few weeks before being promoted and moved out; Sergeant Martin Thompson then stepped in. Reporting to him were four forensic identification managers: Corporal Tim Sleigh, Corporal Ed MacKenzie, Corporal Ross Spenard and Corporal Fred Nicks. MacKenzie and Spenard were the search team leaders, but because Spenard had made a specialty of digital photography and photograph record-keeping, that became his job as well.

The other half of the forensic work—the digging and sifting of soil—hadn't started yet. Gerry Murdoch, the sand-and-gravel man from Cranbrook, was still organizing the site, setting up the ATCO trailers, ordering the required refrigerator trucks and vans and getting the site hooked up to city water, sewers and electricity. There was also a third area of investigative work, but this happened off the farm: following the hundreds of tips that had come in from the public, as well as interviewing Willie's friends, relatives and acquaintances.

Bill Malone was high on the list. Malone, who had set himself up as the unofficial Pickton family spokesperson with the media, was busy spinning the story in a positive way. The police were furious when, a few days after Willie's arrest, he told a television interviewer that the orange inhalers found with women's clothing on the farm were there simply because they'd been in vehicles Willie had purchased from police auctions. And that the Pickton brothers were "hardworking boys who had nothing to do with any of this." Malone later said that he was only exercising his right as a Canadian to free speech.

Malone's statements paled beside his treatment of Baltej Dhillon, one of the officers who tried to interview him. Malone demanded that Dhillon, an Indo-Canadian, remove his turban before he would talk to him; the officers could hardly believe what they were hearing. Later he defended his stance: "This is my country," he blustered, "and I do not wish to have everybody who comes to my country changing the rules. The rules must be respected." He refused to cooperate with any kind of police interview, but he didn't hesitate to interfere when the police tried to interview Sandy Humeny and another employee at the P&B Tannery Road building. Malone insisted on staying in the room—his role was to report back to Dave Pickton about everything they said.

Other people were more cooperative. Janice Edwards talked to the police about her friend and co-worker Diane Rock, whom she had picked up, hysterical and bleeding, at a gas station in Port Coquitlam in August 2001. Diane had described being raped repeatedly in a cellar at the Pickton farm, Edwards told them; she shared everything she could remember about their conversation. Constable Sandra Lavallee drove her to the gas station where she remembered having picked up Diane.

Scott Chubb was another significant witness. Despite his lengthy conversations with the police before Willie's arrest, he was now questioned even more closely. Dana Lillies and Nathan Wells picked up Chubb for a formal interview at the RCMP's Langley headquarters, but it was Sergeant Brad Marks who interviewed him. When he told Chubb that everything he said would be taped and recorded on video, Chubb's response was fast: "Get the son of a bitch off the street."

Even though Pickton had been charged with only two counts of murder, Marks explained, a massive investigation was under way. "Things are just beginning."

"I don't regret coming forward," replied Chubb.

"Sometimes when people come forward," Marks warned him, "it turns out they are part of the offence."

"That ain't me," Chubb said.

Marks didn't budge. If you've done anything, the police will come after you, he said. "Anything you say can be used in evidence and you don't have to talk to me."

Chubb said he understood. And once again he went through his history with both Dave and Willie Pickton, describing the kind of trucks he drove, where they worked, the projects he worked on, the equipment they used. Willie he described as a weirdo, a loner, someone who loaned him money, and he talked about how Willie had paid Lynn Ellingsen "big bucks to keep her mouth shut." He repeated the story about seeing Willie at the Money Mart with a woman. They were in Willie's white truck; later, he said, when he saw the woman's face in a newspaper story, he recognized her as the woman in the truck.

And he returned to his tale of stripping nails from wood with Willie at a workbench beside the trailer in the late summer of 2000. This was when Willie had asked him to hurt Lynn Ellingsen and had suggested injecting her with windshield-washer fluid. "The police would never know and she'd be dead in a couple of minutes. Willie said Lynn was a crackhead and she was costing him a lot of money. I came to the conclusion she had something on him. He mentioned it had already cost him ten grand. It was an everyday conversation, normal. No big emotion."

Chubb also admitted that Willie had loaned him money and had bought junk cars from him. Once again he listed many of the people who hung around the place, including some of the men who worked for Dave; they included Al Trautmann, Tim and Clarence Palmer, Scott Baker, Marty de Wolfe and Myles Nord, better known as Pancho.

"Had any contact with Dave?" Marks asked Chubb.

"Yes," he said. "I called about work and Dave was perturbed and said he'd heard I'd given a statement and that statement was the only thing sinking Willie and I was going down . . . Did Dave get this from Willie's lawyer?"

"Probably," Marks said. "They get everything."

"I'm gonna have to get my friggin' family outta there."

"That seems reasonable," Marks said. "You have a three-year-old, I understand."

"Yeah, and an eight-year-old by another woman."

Finally Brad Marks levelled with Chubb. The case is going to go on for years, he told him. Everything will come out. Chubb couldn't lie to them. "If you know something more about this investigation, the time to tell me is right now. Stuff does have a way of coming out. You know you have a criminal record, and believe me, when you get on the stand that's going to come out."

"That was ten years ago. I'm a changed person."

"I want an honest answer. Did you have any part in the deaths of these women?"

"No. Of course not."

"Why should I believe that?"

"Well, I don't know. How am I supposed to convince you? I'm a family man. I don't need that shit in my life. And I sure as hell ain't a murderer or a rapist or a skinner . . . Just look at my MOs—it was in property shit and, you know, I was a badass, but it's over now."

Marks got up and brought Chubb a cup of coffee. They went over the whole story one more time, and Chubb remembered that Willie had offered him $1,000 to kill Ellingsen. He also remembered that he borrowed Willie's .38 Browning and sold it to Wes Baker, the New Westminster gun dealer and Scott Baker's father.

Marks had other things on his mind. He played a bit of conversation between Willie and Sandy Humeny that the police had taped after his appearance in court.

"This guy Chubb is putting a big load on me too, eh?" Willie said.

"Oh?" replied Humeny.

"Oh yeah, big time. I can't believe the fuckin' dink. I mean, I got enough to put him away for twenty years."

"And he's comin' forward and talking about you?"

"Oh yes, big time."

Listening to this, Chubb was upset. "I don't know what the hell he's referring to."

"Scott, it's really important," Marks said. "If there is something else, we gotta get it on the table."

"There's nothing to tell you guys. I don't know what he's talking about."

Marks rolled through Chubb's criminal past and conversations he'd heard about him; Chubb seemed to be able to convince him that the stories people told were exaggerated. But then Marks asked Chubb about his relationship with Patricia Johnson, who had gone missing in March 2001, almost exactly a year earlier. Chubb said he didn't know her.

"All right, Scott. Would you be willing to take a polygraph test on the issue of have you killed anybody?"

"Sure."

"What will it show us?"

"It shows I'm not lying. I've never killed anybody. I almost killed somebody in 1986."

"Tell me a little bit about that."

"Well, I was charged with attempted murder. I was a young kid, eighteen years old; we got drunk with this little Frenchman kid and we damn near beat him to death, and I was just a kid. We robbed him and took him out to the bush and dropped him off. I feel really bad about it. I haven't looked back since then."

"Charged and acquitted, then?"

"No. I was charged with attempted murder, forcible confinement, robbery, assault with intent, a bunch of other charges. I ended
up doing two and a half years—I think they convicted me on robbery and some other, lighter assault."

"Two and a half years. That's pen time, right?"

"Yeah—Mission, and they sent me to a camp. I was eighteen."
Chubb meant the Mission Institute, a federal penitentiary near Stave
Lake in Mission.

Marks had heard enough. He believed him. He let Chubb go
and Nathan Wells drove him home.

The next day it was Lynn Ellingsen's turn. So far Don Adam's team
knew that Chubb and Ellingsen were their most important witnesses.
They needed to grill her over and over, as they had with Chubb, to
make sure she was telling the truth. On March 2 and 3, 2002, the
police talked to her again, saying they wanted to know everything
Ellingsen could tell them about the woman Willie had picked up
with her, the woman she claimed to have seen hanging on a hook in
his slaughterhouse.

"She had lots of makeup, beautiful long nails, chipmunk-like
cheeks, and her nose was wide," Ellingsen remembered. "I was high,
she was high. I don't know about Willie, but she kind of had big
cheeks, little chipmunk cheeks. Her nose was wide. She had beautiful nails, really long nails. Oh, I'm getting a headache."

Ellingsen admitted that she had taken money from Willie after
she moved off the farm. "Never did I ask him for money," she
insisted. "Never did I ask him for money. When I asked him for
money, that's when he bought my washer and dryer from me. I said
to him that I was broke and that I'm in the midst of moving, and he
goes, 'Well, what are you taking?' And I said, 'I'm taking only what
is necessary,' and, like, I left a lot of stuff behind. Willie came out
and he gave me—I believe it was $150 for my washer and my dryer,
and that was it. Like, I've asked him to borrow money. I was still
into drugs then."

But later in the interview Ellingsen said she had asked Willie for money on other occasions. "I'd ask him and he said no. He said, 'I've got no money.' Or when I—when he'd hear my voice on the phone, right, he would sort of insinuate that, you know—he'd say, 'I'm broke. I've got the hep C. It's costing $800 every two weeks.'"

After being questioned, Ellingsen went to the Pickton farm with Corporal Baltej Dhillon for a walk around the property. As she moved from building to building, it seemed that deeply buried memories were rushing back. There was nail polish on the toes of the woman she saw dangling from the hook in the barn, she told Dhillon. And on the metal table beneath the hanging woman she remembered seeing a dark ponytail.

"Like, I was—when I walk in—I froze, like instant. 'Oh, Willie,' I yelled, 'Willie!' And he was right behind the door. He wasn't near her at the time, 'cause he grabbed me as soon as I open that door and I go 'Willie,' and he came right around and he grabbed me on the side of my arm . . . This table was really shiny, really shiny, and I just see knives. Now he walks me in. He held me there for a minute and he told me I had to watch. It was just like doing a pig." The woman's body was hanging by her neck, she told Dhillon. "I just—I just see a naked body. I didn't really—didn't really look. I just see her hanging."

Ellingsen's revelations stunned the police. They believed her; they knew she was intelligent, and if they could keep her sober and healthy she could well be their star witness. But she was deeply addicted to cocaine and alcohol, she had a criminal record, and she spent her time with men who encouraged her drug and alcohol use. Her parents were raising her son and despaired of being able to help her recover. It was going to be difficult to manage her but the police knew they had to try, so RCMP constable Sandra Lavallee was assigned to be her contact person and help her manage any crises that could threaten her ability to testify against Pickton.

Managing witnesses like Chubb and Ellingsen was one thing, but trying to manage the families of the missing women had become just as important. After being ignored and dismissed for so many years, they were now becoming media celebrities who did not hesitate to blame the police and the government for the tragedy. Leading the group were Rick and Lynn Frey, who still lived in Campbell River on Vancouver Island, and Ernie Crey, the Sto:lo leader from Chilliwack. Marnie Frey, Rick and Lynn's daughter, was last seen August 30, 1997; Dawn Crey, Ernie's sister, was last seen on November 1, 2000. Reporters found the Freys and Crey eager to talk. Other family members and friends of the missing women also stepped forward.

Once again the task force needed people who could help the families and friends stay informed and make arrangements for meetings when necessary. This job fell to Victim Services workers, a group of trained people, most of them women and many of them Native. On March 10, 2002, they helped when the police called a meeting of family members to ask for any information they could offer about their loved ones.

CHAPTER FORTY-THREE

IN THE WORKSHOP

Three weeks after the police charged Willie Pickton with two counts of murder, Gina Houston told Darrow MacIntyre, a CBC Television reporter working for *The National* news, that the police believed she was involved with Pickton in the murders of the missing women. MacIntyre, who is affable, empathetic and smart, had succeeded in winning Houston's trust where few others could. He had tracked her down in the first place simply by hanging around outside the North Fraser Pretrial Centre in Port Coquitlam, because he knew she often visited him there. Although she refused to be interviewed in front of a television camera, Houston met him several times and poured out her heart to him. Some envious reporters said she had a crush on him, which was probably true.

The police were following her, she said. "They've been making my life a living hell." MacIntyre wasn't sure he believed her until he realized that one or two plainclothes officers were sitting nearby every time he met Houston in a coffee shop.

"These days," reported MacIntyre on March 23, 2002, "Gina Houston lives a kind of hunted existence, hiding from media, hounded by police. She says Robert Pickton, whom she calls Willie, is a very close friend. She and her three children may be closer to him than anyone. Her youngest daughter calls him 'Daddy Willie' even though she isn't related. Since his arrest, Houston has regularly visited Pickton in prison, where he's awaiting trial."

She also told MacIntyre that the police had searched her locker at a storage facility and taken away everything, including furniture, children's toys and personal belongings. "I've been under investigation for four years," she told him. And when he asked her why, she said, "Let's just say I used to hang around with a group of girls and now there's only two left alive and I'm one of them. Well, the others, I should say, are missing."

"Are they on the missing women list?" asked MacIntyre.

"Yes."

If MacIntyre had thought Houston was paranoid he soon changed his mind. Gina had gone to the jail to visit Willie and was shocked to find that he was furious with her. "What the fuck are you doing?" he had asked, handing her a list of calls she had made to MacIntyre. This was how Gina found out that the police had placed wiretaps on her phone and were listening to her conversations with MacIntyre. Now Willie didn't trust her and refused to see her again. Upset, Gina stopped talking to MacIntyre and accused the police of harassing her. Two days before the story went to air, he tried to talk to her again but she was hostile. "You are a fucking cop," she hissed.

She wasn't the only one under investigation. Dinah Taylor told CBC Radio that the police were treating her as a suspect also and that she'd moved outside the province to get away from them. Even though she'd returned to her native band in Ontario to live with family members, she couldn't escape the task force, which sent two members east to talk to her. Before long she was back in Vancouver, hanging around the Downtown Eastside, staying with anyone who had a couch to crash on and successfully ducking the police at every turn. And Ian Donaldson, one of Vancouver's best-known criminal lawyers, who was acting for Dave Pickton, was also full of complaints. He told reporters that their interest in the case could jeopardize a fair trial for Dave's brother.

In March 2002 the task force members weren't paying much attention to the squawking of Houston, Taylor and Donaldson; they were scrambling to get investigators and equipment in place on the farm and following up on the continuing avalanche of tips flowing in. Jim Hunter put Scott Chubb through lie detector tests; Chubb passed the first polygraph, during which he was asked if he'd helped Willie get rid of bodies, but the second test, when Hunter asked him if he'd participated in the killings, was inconclusive.

On March 27 the police announced they were adding a new name, that of Ruby Hardy, to the list of missing women from the Downtown Eastside. Ruby, a Native woman with brown eyes and long brown hair, just five feet two inches tall, was thirty-seven when she was last seen in 1998. The day before they put Ruby's name on the list, searchers found Jennifer Furminger's black Digitech watch in Willie's slaughterhouse. It was only one of several women's watches that Willie had stowed away in little hiding places.

During these same weeks the forensic search team led by Jack Mellis and Tim Sleigh was inching ahead through the buildings on the Pickton farm. They'd started by having close-up aerial photographs taken of the property and giving each building or search site a letter, sometimes with a number. With help from Gerry Murdoch, who was still setting up all the ATCO trailers, they had a command post and a staging area where the search technicians could put on their Tyvek suits, booties and gloves. This staging area was also the "safe zone," a place to have meetings and make notes without contaminating the search areas.

The searchers were all highly trained forensics experts from the Evidence Recovery Unit (ERU) of the RCMP's Identification Section or scientists on loan from the Biology Section of the Vancouver Forensic Laboratory. The first priority was Willie's trailer, so that's where they started. As they worked they began to understand the huge scale of the search, so they broke down each site into individual rooms and each room into individual zones. What they were looking for, Sleigh said later, was any biological evidence that suggested a misadventure or even an assault or a death. That meant evidence of blood and DNA, fingerprints, jewellery, clothing—any items at all that might be traced back to the victims.

By the end of the month they'd found so much blood and DNA evidence in Willie's trailer and motor home that they were sure three of the missing women—Jacqueline McDonell, Heather Bottomley, and Diane Rock—had been killed there. They found Jacqueline McDonell's blood on handcuffs in Willie's bedroom, Heather Bottomley's blood on Willie's mattress and Diane Rock's blood and clumps of her hair in the motor home.

On Tuesday, April 2, 2002, Willie appeared in the Port Coquitlam courthouse by video link from jail to listen as the Crown laid three more first-degree murder charges against him. With Mona Wilson and Sereena Abotsway, the total had grown to five. Aside from blinking occasionally, he showed no emotion—something that upset Mona Wilson's sister, Ada Wilson, who was there in court that day and disappointed that Pickton wasn't in the room. She started to cry as soon as he appeared on the video screen, reported the Canadian Press's Terri Theodore.

"When I seen him it just kind of, I've been waiting for this for a long time and I've been holding it in," Ada Wilson told her. "But now it's time. I wanted him to see how the family is reacting to all of this." Theodore found another heartbroken family member, Kathleen Hallmark, whose daughter Helen had disappeared in June 1997.

"I didn't know he was even alive there until he blinked," she told Theodore. "The man doesn't show any, anything, no expressions."

Even though they were expecting something like this, the news shocked other people who had known these women, not the least of whom was Elaine Allan, who had taken care of them at WISH, the Downtown Eastside drop-in centre she ran. "It's very hard," she told Michael Friscolanti, a *National Post* reporter, when he mentioned Jacqueline McDonell. "I know she's been missing for a long time, but this makes it very real. She's not going to show up. She wasn't on a road trip to Mexico [the excuse one police officer gave when he waved aside Allan's demand that the police look for her]. This confirms it. She didn't seem like a hard-core addict, at least not yet. That's what's so tragic about her. She looked like she was going to bounce in and then bounce out of the scene."

———

Two days later, on April 4, the police searchers had finished working on the trailer and two teams moved on to Site B, the slaughterhouse, sometimes called the barn. One team worked forward from the main entrance along the west wall while the second team worked along the east wall.

But something was worrying Tim Sleigh. It was just a niggling feeling that bothered him from time to time, and it was about the electricity on the farm. He knew there were at least nine freezers* scattered around the property, probably old ones used by Leonard and Louise when they were running their meat locker in Port Coquitlam. He suspected there could be evidence in those freezers. They'd get to them in time, but he fretted that the power on the farm wasn't reliable.

"We were having electricity problems and intermittent power failures on the site," he explained later. "We were bringing our own auxiliary hydro onto the site to feed electricity to the equipment for the search teams, as well as the command-post equipment and the computers and everything else on site." But it wasn't working well, mainly because the property was below sea level, close to the Pitt River, and very wet. It was the middle of a B.C. winter and the rain never stopped. The result was a series of interruptions to the RCMP's power supply. Sleigh worried about losing the evidence that might be in those freezers. He'd posted two night lights at Site D, the garage/workshop, one for each of the two freezers in there; the night lights were clearly visible, and their constant flickering told him that the power to that site was only intermittent.

The garage/workshop was essentially two buildings joined together and contained three rooms. The garage, with two rooms, was closer to the slaughterhouse and Pickton's trailer, while the one-room workshop on the south side was closer to Dominion Avenue. The garage was made of wood and had a sliding door across the front; it opened out to the roadway that ran from the Dominion Avenue

---

*The police eventually uncovered twelve freezers.

entrance to Pickton's trailer. Inside, in the largest space, was a small truck that Pickton was taking apart; strewn around it were car parts and tools as well as tables and workstations against the walls. The second room was smaller, and so crowded with shelving and equipment that only a small walkway allowed access into the main area of the workshop. The two chest freezers were in the workshop, pushed against the back wall; the police called them XD-1 and XD-2.

On the morning of April 4 Sleigh walked by the garage/workshop at about twenty minutes after eight. He wondered why such a stink was coming from one of the freezers, the one labelled XD-2. Maybe it was something going bad inside, maybe a result of insufficient power or because the freezer itself was old and in disrepair. Sleigh decided to take a look. But power tools and automotive equipment were piled on the lid, and he had to ask his colleague Corporal Fred Nicks, a forensic identification specialist with thirteen years on the force, to help him pry it open without disturbing the stuff on the top. When the men bent down and peered in, they saw several wrapped packages, all heavily frosted over, as well as a large chunk of solid ice. On top of this pile, lying on their sides, were two white five-gallon plastic buckets. One, a Clout detergent bucket, was frozen solidly inside the other.

Gently Sleigh tipped up the buckets and shone a flashlight into the frozen mass in the Clout bucket. God almighty—a head. Half a head. He asked Nicks to have a look and verify what he was seeing. Yes, Nicks said, it's a human head.

Clearly visible under the frost and ice was the top portion of the back and side of a head. They could see some long, matted hair lying in stiff strands, as well as an eyebrow, a cheek and an ear. It looked, Sleigh said later, "as if the head were looking away from me." Carefully the men closed the freezer lid and left the building. Go back to work, Sleigh told Nicks—and be quiet about this.

Sleigh went straight to the command centre to talk to Randy Hundt and Carole Hooper, the RCMP officers who were managing the site. They realized they would have to change their search plan immediately. All three went to the slaughterhouse (Site B), where the two forensic identification teams were working, and told two members, Corporal Ross Spenard and Constable David Richard, to continue working there. Everyone else was to move to Site D, the workshop, immediately. This group now included a forensic pathologist, Dr. Daniel Straathof, a slim young man with closely cropped hair, a light beard and serious eyes, who was now a central player in the Pickton investigation. Along with having a fine international reputation as an academic researcher, Dr. Straathof was a clever forensic detective when it came to working on human victims.

The team began by hauling away all the junk lying around the sliding garage door and then setting up a tented staging area in the newly cleared space. Next they opened a route through the garage and storage spaces into the freezer area; that also meant carefully lifting all the tools and equipment off the freezer lids without losing any evidence on those items. As soon as the way through was cleared, the forensic team photographed and videotaped everything in the spaces before they began taking anything out of the freezers. Finally they began searching the inside of each freezer and removing everything in them. After photographing the pair of buckets they tugged them apart, gently pulling the Clout bucket out of the plain white one.

"Look at this," Sleigh breathed. Straathof and the others crowded closer. They could see a human head in the plain white bucket as well. Like the other one, it had been cut in half vertically, down through the face and through the back of the skull. It was lying cut side up; carefully placed inside the cranial cavity were what looked like two hands. Under the hands were two feet. Neat and tidy. From what they could see, the contents of the Clout bucket were much the same: a bisected head, with one side containing a pair of hands and the other a pair of feet.

The time was now 3:29 in the afternoon. Corporal Mike Coyle, who had been working on the property since Pickton's arrest and was now a member of the search team, was asked to buy two large camping coolers right away and bring them to the workshop. Back at the site within half an hour and dressed once again in a Tyvek suit with fresh gloves, Coyle lifted each bucket out of the freezer and gently placed it in a cooler. He was on his way to the morgue at the Royal Columbian Hospital in New Westminster.

The next day Sleigh, Staff Sergeant Jack Mellis and Corporal Ross Spenard, representing the forensic identification team, and Brian McConaghy, a specialist in forensic firearm and tool-mark examination at the Vancouver Forensic Laboratory, met in the morgue to watch Danny Straathof perform the autopsies on the body parts found in the buckets. Aside from the heads, hands and feet they'd seen the day before, they didn't know what else might be in there.

Two metal gurneys, each covered with a blue sheet, waited for them in the room. The first gurney held five items, all of them found in the outside white bucket. Three of them were the feet that had been in the bucket as well as a portion of a heel; the others were the two halves of the same human head. Each was resting ear down on the sheet, and lying inside the cranial cavity of one of them was the pair of human hands. Everything, while recognizable, was in an advanced stage of decomposition. A few teeth were also found. And a bullet was discovered as well, lodged in the back of the neck just where it joined the spine.

Later that evening Sleigh helped Spenard take fingerprints from the two hands; to their relief, eight of the ten prints were usable. Based on the fingerprints, they concluded that these pitiable remains belonged to Andrea Joesbury, the twenty-three-year-old who had disappeared ten months before, on June 6, 2001. Dr. Straathof told them she'd been shot in the rear right side of her head and that the bullet had come out through her left eye.

The second bucket, the Clout bucket that had been inside the white one, was next. This one had also been emptied; the sad little pile of remains was even more decomposed than the other set. They appeared to be a left and right foot and two halves of a human head with matted hair—all that was left of Sereena Abotsway. The head had been severed between the second and the third vertebrae. Like Andrea Joesbury's, the back of it had been cut in a vertical line that stopped on the right side of the forehead above the eye. The second cut was made through the front of Abotsway's face until it almost met the cut that came through from the back.

Like Joesbury's skull, Abotsway's also had a bullet hole in the back, as well as one through the ear. This second bullet, a .22 calibre, was lodged in the lower part of the skull; they found the first one in the bucket. Three teeth and some nails rested in the bottom of the bucket. Only after he'd had X-rays taken of the remaining mass in the cranial cavity was Dr. Straathof able to state that these were a pair of human hands.

The tool-marks expert, Brian McConaghy, couldn't see any marks on the hands or feet that had been caused by a tool such as a saw or an axe. In his judgment, the bones had been taken apart carefully "where they naturally join," as he put it; *disarticulated* was the word they all came to use. The heads, however, were a different matter. These, McConaghy decided, had "significant tool marks and firearms damage." He would look at them more carefully later.

Three days later, on April 8, McConaghy began to investigate the heads. He started with Andrea Joesbury's. Given the damage, it was clear to him that a bullet had entered the right rear of her skull and had probably exited through the left eye socket, which was why they hadn't found it. As for the way the head was cut in two, McConaghy decided it had been done "with two vertical cuts performed with a reciprocal power saw which went up through the chin, through the palate, up through the forehead, stopping centrally at what could best be described as the high forehead. Another cut was performed through the rear base of the skull, rotating up to the top of the head. The two saw cuts did not meet in the top. There was about perhaps an inch of skull that was not cut. It was then fractured. So it had been split open, the last remaining portion." How had the head been detached from the body in the first place?

McConaghy's conclusion was that the killer had simply used a hand-held reciprocating saw here also and had cut it off between the first two vertebrae below the skull.

The remains of the second woman were identified by the RCMP forensic lab as those of twenty-five-year-old Sereena Abotsway, who had disappeared on August 1, 2001. McConaghy found that she had been treated very much like Andrea Joesbury. Her hands and feet had been disarticulated and the head cut in half vertically with a reciprocating power saw. The main difference was the bullet that he found. "This skull also had bullet damage," he reported. "The bullet on this occasion has entered above the right ear and passed in a downward direction into the left side of the skull and was found in the skull on the left side. It was still in situ when noted at autopsy." Willie had already been charged with the murder of Sereena, and now here was proof.

When he finished examining the two skulls, the police asked McConaghy to look at a third skull, the one Bill Wilson had found in Mission Slough on February 23, 1995. Jane Doe's skull. Tim Sleigh had never forgotten working on her case, and he asked McConaghy if he'd mind taking a look at the skull—or, more precisely, half-skull, because the second half had never been found—because he couldn't help but wonder if it had been cut the same way. Would you see if there are any similarities? Sleigh asked him.

When he looked at it, McConaghy could see that it was the right side of a skull with a bit of the first vertebra attached to it. "The damage to this skull was consistent," he reported, "and the tool marks were produced by a reciprocating saw that travelled up through the forehead, through roughly the centre of the face, stopping in the very high forehead area, and then another cut passing through C1, the vertebra, and then through the base of the skull and rotating right up over the top and actually overlapping the cut slightly in the forehead area where it came apart." As he expected, the cuts didn't meet up. Although he couldn't find any bullet damage, it was just like the others.

On April 9, 2002, the day after the autopsies of the two skulls, the police charged Willie Pickton with the first-degree murder of Andrea Joesbury.

Had the turning point for this case been the discovery of Sereena Abotsway's inhalers eight weeks earlier? Or Mona Wilson's blood in the motor home in February? Was it when Willie Pickton admitted to Don Adam that he had been sloppy and hadn't cleaned up properly after killing a few women? Or was it when he told his cellmate that he had killed forty-nine women and was aiming for a total of seventy-five? Was it when the police added the three new charges—for Jacqueline McDonell, Heather Bottomley and Diane Rock—based on DNA matching? No. The turning point had been the moment when Tim Sleigh found the buckets with the heads in them. This was when the police knew for certain that Don Adam hadn't been wrong when he "pulled the trigger on two pieces of ID" and arrested Willie Pickton for murder.

Now they needed nothing more to be sure. Two murders with physical evidence from Willie's freezer, in his workshop, on his property. The count might now be seven, and while no one working on this case doubted that Robert William Pickton was their serial killer, the critical mass of numbers would now convince any skeptics. Yes, these remains might well belong to the same women whose blood had already been found. It hardly mattered; the fragments would help the police understand how the women had died.

These last cases also changed everything. They were both a breakthrough and a new challenge: the first victims whose physical remains had been found. Bones, flesh, hair, teeth, skin, nails. Finding the human skulls and other body parts changed the search strategy on the farm. Instead of methodically marching through the search sites from the north to the south of the farm, working alphabetically through Sites A, B, C and D, the team stopped searching the slaughterhouse (Site B) and the mechanical shop (Site C) to focus on Site D, the workshop.

For the moment the forensic team left the remaining packages in the freezers, closed the lids and fixed the electrical connections so that power to the site was secure. They put in thermometers and did regular checks to make sure the contents stayed frozen. And then they returned to the two five-gallon buckets. Working with the Evidence Recovery Unit biologists, the forensic identification technicians gridded each bucket inside and out with one-inch squares and then swabbed each square for DNA. Then it was time to empty the freezers and let them thaw out. The teams photographed every item and every surface and then gridded and swabbed each surface inside and out. When they saw a stain, they would circle it and make a notation instead of swabbing it.

Although it was now late in the British Columbia spring, there had been, as usual, a lot of rain, and parts of the farm, especially just west of Site B, the slaughterhouse, had been flooded. This was where the Picktons, when they still raised their own animals, had once had a piggery—essentially a long shed that housed the pigs. It had collapsed years earlier, and all that was left was the concrete foundation, the floor with some troughs in it and a large mound of dirt, branches and flooring pieces piled up along the south foundation wall. The troughs had been used to collect manure, which would have been hosed or pushed into an old cistern, now called Site B-2, at the end of the old piggery.

The police had originally decided to search the cistern later, but the flooding now made it a priority. They brought in pumper trucks from a sewage removal company to clean it out. It should have been a quick job, but after the men pulled back the cistern's concrete lid, dropped a hose in and began pumping, it took four days to empty it. Willie had probably never bothered. Stinking and filthy as it was, the searchers went through all the muck by hand. They found animal bones, pieces of silverware, scraps of fabric, hair, razor blades, a used sanitary napkin, a copper ring, a glass bottle and several unidentified metal objects. They put these things into a pail at the screening table; the next step was taking them to a tent for processing.

During the time it took for the pumpers to empty the cistern, Fred Nicks was working close by in what was left of the old piggery building. Even though they were using a BobCat to move the debris, they still had to go through it—first with a rake and then with their hands—to see if there was anything significant in it. Nicks had been on duty since eight that morning; it was now just after two in the afternoon and he was tired. But as he picked through the mess with a rake and then lifted small heaps of it onto a colleague's shovel, he suddenly realized he'd found something solid—something covered with dirt and pig shit and garbage, but solid. They peered at it. It was a jawbone with teeth in it, but Nicks wasn't sure if it was human. A few minutes earlier he'd shaken a small animal vertebra out of his rake, and now this new thing . . . he couldn't tell.

As soon as Tim Sleigh took a look at what Nicks had found, he was sure it was a human jaw with some teeth attached. He found a toothbrush and gently cleaned it—there was a filling in one of the teeth. In a case like this one, teeth are always extraordinarily significant finds. After visual identification and fingerprints, teeth are the most useful sources for identifying a victim; they last longer than any other body part after death. Of course, obtaining X-rays of the victim's teeth before death, usually from a dentist, is important, but it's not as essential as it was just a few years ago. Today dentists can extract DNA from the pulp that remains in teeth. They have to be careful, though; the act of grinding a tooth to extract DNA can destroy its usefulness for further testing. That's why forensic odontologist David Sweet was a key person on the identification team. Well-known internationally, he was considered a brilliant forensic dentist, and given the challenges of this investigation, they were lucky to have him close by. The bone and teeth told him that the jaw had been bisected in the same manner as the two skulls he'd examined earlier.

It wasn't long before DNA tests identified the jawbone and teeth as those of Brenda Wolfe, who had disappeared almost three years earlier, on February 1, 1999. Later, searchers would find her DNA on a leather jacket and two lipsticks in a closet in Willie's trailer. More of Brenda Wolfe's DNA was found in a green duffle bag the searchers uncovered in the loft upstairs in Site C, Willie's mechanical shop. The duffle bag also held a handcuff key, handcuffs, two handguns, leg cuffs and jewellery, all with her DNA on it.

The discovery of Brenda Wolfe's jawbone in the piggery was significant. The police had already known how complicated the search was going to be, but finding her remains in a pig trough underlined the necessity of searching every crack and crevice in every location. They dated back to 1999; there was a chance they'd find evidence from even further back.

On May 8, the day after Nicks found Brenda Wolfe's jawbone, the forensic team determined that one of the bones they'd found in the manure from the cistern, a bone that was tiny and dark and shaped like a diamond, was human. Much later they would find that this little fragment was all that was left of Wendy Crawford, who had disappeared on December 14, 1999.

Less than two weeks later, on May 22, 2002, the police charged Willie Pickton with the first-degree murder of Brenda Wolfe, adding her name to those of twenty-six-year-old Mona Wilson, twenty-nine-year-old Sereena Abotsway, twenty-three-year-old Jacqueline McDonell, thirty-four-year-old Diane Rock, twenty-five-year-old Heather Bottomley and twenty-two-year-old Andrea Joesbury. Wendy Crawford would have to wait a little longer.

CHAPTER FORTY-FOUR

THE FORENSIC TEAM

Carole Hooper and Randy Hundt, the two RCMP officers in charge of managing the pig farm site, knew it was time to start digging. Gerry Murdoch had been working flat out to get the equipment and services ready—the mobile labs and reefer (refrigerated) trucks, the ATCO village, electrified fencing, electricity, water, sewers and telephones, and all the large excavators, including front-end loaders, BobCats and backhoes. Then, to cope with all the dirt they planned to dig, move and search, there were dump trucks, Grizzlies, screeners and conveyor belts.

Although the task force had known from the beginning they would have to dig down to undisturbed soil, it wasn't until Tim Sleigh found the skulls and bones in the buckets that everyone understood exactly how important the soil search was going to be. When Willie told the undercover officer in the cell with him that he'd taken remains to a rendering plant, it had seemed possible that blood evidence and the belongings of the victims might be all they'd find on the farm itself. The discovery in the workshop cancelled that possibility. Willie had kept remains. Where had he hidden them? How much could they expect to find? How many years back would they go? Were they all in freezers or were some buried in the ground?

Recovering and identifying bones like the ones found in the freezer meant that the team would need a forensic anthropologist—someone trained to conduct the search, recovery and analysis of human remains and to decide if the person had died as a result of a crime. There were not many forensic anthropologists in Canada at the time. The one best-known to Canadians, crime novelist Kathy

Reichs, would have been too busy; she divided her time between two labs in two countries: the Laboratoire de sciences judiciaires et de médecine légale in Montreal, and the Office of the Chief Medical Examiner in Charlotte, North Carolina. The main character in her fiction is a forensic anthropologist much like herself and the inspiration for the U.S. television series *Bones*.

Fortunately for the task force, the person who came to mind right away was someone they'd worked with many times—Tracy Rogers, a scientist who had earned her master's degree from McMaster University in Hamilton, Ontario, before going on to do her doctorate at Simon Fraser University in Burnaby, British Columbia. While she was still at Simon Fraser she was working on cases for the provincial coroner's office, reporting to three different people. One was Larry Campbell, a former RCMP officer who was then chief coroner for the province and the inspiration for the title character in CBC Television's popular show *Da Vinci's Inquest*. Another was Bob Stair, the former member of the RCMP, who had recently returned from working on graves in Kosovo for the United Nations War Crimes Tribunal on the former Yugoslavia. And the third was Chico Newell, an identification specialist with the coroner's forensic unit.

Rogers, who had moved back to Ontario when she was offered a job teaching at the University of Toronto, was a specialist not only in human bones but also in crime-scene analysis, and she had plenty of experience testifying in court. That part of the job, she told her students in Toronto, is essential. "In my classes you're going to have to look for evidence in the field, you're going to analyze it and, finally, you're going to present it in a mock trial. If the evidence can't sustain the attacks from defence counsel because it is too weak, poorly handled, and even badly delivered, the judge may throw it all out. Or a jury might not believe it."

Rogers had been following the Pickton story closely. Finally she picked up the phone one day to call Brian Andrews of the RCMP's Forensic Identification Service. "I asked him if they had a forensic anthropologist for support and advice. I thought they needed me."

Yes, Andrews admitted, they did need her. When she signed on in early May 2002, Rogers didn't know that she already had a connection with the Pickton case, one that stretched back seven years to the 1995 discovery of Jane Doe's skull in Mission Slough. Tracy Rogers had been asked to try to reconstruct Jane Doe's face so that a police artist could draw her as she might have looked when she was alive. No one ever responded to the poster, and Jane Doe's skull had remained in a police evidence locker.

Soon after the university term ended in Toronto, Rogers went to Port Coquitlam; when she heard about the severed heads in the freezer, she thought right away of Jane Doe's bisected skull. Although she and Tim Sleigh did discuss how the evidence on Jane Doe's skull could fit with this investigation, her first priority was to find people who could work on the conveyor belts—people who could pick through the excavated dirt to find bones, teeth, hair or any other human remains, or personal belongings such as buttons, jewellery, identification, even shreds of clothing. Word went out to university anthropology and archaeology departments to say that the task force needed students with some background in forensic work. As the applications rolled in, Mike Coyle and another RCMP officer, Dan Almas, did all the hiring.

The first hurdle for the students was passing police checks; after that Rogers helped choose the best candidates based on their training. Rogers agrees that the definition of a forensic anthropologist can be confusing. "In Canada," she explained, "a forensic anthropologist works on the scene and the body: searching for, recovering, excavating and analyzing the skeleton or the remains." Scientists who only do recovery are called forensic archaeologists, she said; "They know how to excavate and some are familiar with bone but do not really know what to expect from a forensic scene." And finally there are students with osteology training. As Rogers explained it, these students are "familiar with dry bone but not the soft tissues, decomposition, or scene work."

Students from all three specialties came to work on the farm, but they didn't arrive all at the same time. The task force began with only a couple of dozen at first, just enough to handle the growing flow of material and to determine the best speed for the conveyor belts. The ones who were chosen knew it was going to be tough; they had been told quite bluntly there would be no hand-holding. Shifts began at eight o'clock in the morning and finished at eight o'clock at night. Twelve hours a day, five days a week. And they had to find their own places to live. Some commuted from Vancouver; some shared modest apartments in or near Port Coquitlam; some boarded with police officers. But the applications came in steadily; ambitious students knew what an opportunity this was.

Along with the students, Tracy Rogers had two experienced forensic anthropologists to help her, although they weren't able to be there full time. Professor Richard Lazenby, a medical doctor and expert in skeletal biology from the University of Northern B.C. in Prince George, was on call, and so was Owen Beattie, from the University of Alberta in Edmonton. Beattie was famous for his ten-year study of the disastrous Franklin expedition to find the Arctic's Northwest Passage; in 1984 he found and exhumed the perfectly preserved body of a member of the ill-fated ship's crew. Ernie Walker, a well-known professor from the department of archaeology and anthropology at the University of Saskatchewan, was a special con-stable with the RCMP and an expert on identifying human remains; he also came to the site to help with the belt searches. Then there was Bob Stair, who had gained valuable experience in ground searches working on the graves in Kosovo. In February 2002 he had visited the site of the devastated World Trade Center in New York with some of the other investigators to get ideas for the conveyors they planned to use on the Pickton site. After the attack in New York, bone fragments had been found on rooftops as well as the ground, and all were used to try to identify victims.

By the time Rogers arrived at the farm, the whole property had been divided into 216 twenty-metre squares, with stakes marking the corners of each square. (The police also established grid-search lanes going from west to east across the entire farm; each lane was defined by wires fifty metres apart holding small flags attached with wire pins.) Each square was assigned a number on the grid map. The plan was to start digging any grid squares that didn't have buildings on them. Squares with buildings on them, such as Willie's trailer, the slaughterhouse, the barn and even the original family farmhouse on Dominion Avenue, would wait until the buildings themselves—which were the first priority—had been searched, taken apart and removed.

Allowing for the delayed ground searches under buildings, Gerry Murdoch's original plan had been to march ahead systematically from one grid square to the next. But the makeup of the farm made this impossible, and he had to rethink the plan. At least four of the grid squares were well below the water table and had to be pumped out; other wet areas had dangerous sinkholes in several places—on at least one occasion officers had fallen into them and needed to be rescued. And the area set aside for the police command centre also needed work; it had to be built up to take the weight of the ATCO trailers and vehicles.

Once the ground search actually started, a backhoe or a BobCat would begin by clawing at the surface of the grid square. As its bucket lifted the dirt into waiting dump trucks, a team of students would stand carefully around the edges of the hole. James O'Dwyer, the site's senior health and safety officer, had taught them all how to work around heavy industrial equipment, including exactly how far back to stand to keep from falling into the hole. When the trucks arrived at the conveyor belts—which had been set up at the north end of the property, far away from the sightseers on Dominion Avenue—they dumped the dirt into the Grizzlies to start three levels of sifting. Each belt had its own Grizzly vibrator, which would shake down the dirt until only rocks and large pieces of wood, glass or metal remained. Although the sifted material that landed on the conveyor belts was small enough to search, the teams took the precaution of doing an even finer sifting as well, into a pile that was set aside and searched carefully for the smallest items, items such as human teeth and shards of bone.

Working on the "picking belts" wasn't easy. "Some of the health and safety issues were ergonomic," explained Rogers. "There was back strain from standing, so we provided mats for their feet, but there were also height problems at the conveyor belts. And people on the belts often felt seasick." Senior identification technicians were always nearby to help the students decide if an item was significant. After forty-five minutes on the belts, the students would take their buckets and go through the contents with Rogers or a forensic specialist.

The first things they set aside were any bits of metal or stone, anything they called "mechanical." Next they set aside anything they deemed to be "biological," whether it be animal or human. This material went into another set of buckets, which the students would walk, in single file, to a large tent nearby for further examination. There it was sorted into paper bags, marked for identification and set aside in a special box for Rogers's examination. Her job was to decide which bones were human and which were animal. When she wasn't able to be there, Richard Lazenby made the call.

Making these decisions wasn't difficult; they could tell the difference between animal and human bone fairly quickly. "When I opened up the bag, if it turned out to be animal, I would fill out the paperwork indicating that the material was animal and then I would bag it back up, put it in a box and store it. It would go into Exhibits when the box was completely full of animal bone." If it was human bone, Rogers would tell Jim Coyle, and a forensic identification technician would come to the tent, photograph the item, seize it formally and give it an exhibit number.

The dirt that was left over from the belt search was collected and carted to a holding area, dumped and carefully covered with a tarpaulin until it was possible to return it to its original space. So the work progressed, one grid square at a time: one big hole, one set of belts, one set of buckets, one tarp-covered hill of dirt.

Sometimes Rogers or Lazenby would have to go to the grid site itself. This would happen when the operator of an excavator, assisted by a search technician, peeled back the surface of the earth to find a pile of bones. When that happened, the procedure was clear: they stopped working right away and called Rogers or Lazenby as well as a forensic identification technician, who would photograph the pit, measure everything and note what was "mechanical"—in other words, not flesh, not bone. They'd also call a safety officer to make sure it was okay to take the students into the pit, which could be as deep as thirty feet. Just getting down the sides of one that deep was tricky, but not nearly as dangerous as the biological hazards of actually working in it. (There weren't separate teams of student searchers for the pits and the conveyor belts; they took turns on these jobs.)

Rogers and her colleagues had suspected that the Pickton farm would be full of bone pits. This wasn't unusual; farmers routinely dug such pits on their property to use as dumps for "deadstock"— the carcasses and bones of slaughtered animals. Although they knew Willie took dead animals to the West Coast Reduction rendering plant in the Downtown Eastside, they also knew they would find animal remains on the property as well. And they did, between thirty and forty bone pits. Some pits had just a few bones; some were crammed with them—more than enough to frighten everyone.

Rogers had asked a forensic veterinary pathologist about the biohazards they might find in these pits and the news was grim: "They included salmonella, bacterial types of infections, and a possibility that there could be animal-borne diseases that humans could get, like bovine tuberculosis," she said later. "Some of this buried material may have included chickens, and the salmonella bacilli might still be active. And there were a lot of cows in the pits. They might have had bovine tuberculosis. What would the risk be? How viable are the tuberculosis bacilli after death? I was trying to focus the techs on working with care. In order to protect ourselves from any of that kind of biohazard, we wore Tyvek suits, double gloves and usually HEPA respirators when attending these."

The process for searching a bone pit was always the same. "We peeled back the top layer of earth," Rogers said. "Once the dirt was peeled away I could see the extent of the bones and I tried to see if there was anything human in there. When they first exposed the bones in the pit, there was a bit of adipocere, and we tried one process of peeling back a layer of the bones. It was very difficult to do. We tried a couple of different things but we ended up taking the whole mass of bone out and putting it through machinery. It was too thick. It was a biohazard and messy and we had to clean everything afterwards.

"Most of the bones were animal bones but there were human bones as well, like the vertebrae in Pit 23. One pit had human bone and animal bone. The pit team would never know when they would hit human bone." Another pit they found had only human bone in it. "I was aware that we were dealing with human remains," admitted Rogers.

The HEPA respirators were essential any time they were working around cow manure or decomposing tissue. Dust masks were mandatory the rest of the time. Though everyone knew how careful they had to be, the forensic anthropology students had more experience with this kind of work than the archaeology students, who were, as Rogers put it, "less experienced in the potential of decomposition." That made it difficult emotionally. "The forensic students managed quite well, while the archaeology students found it harder—and internalized it differently." Bob Stair, Rogers and the members of the task force had known this work would not be easy. They provided counsellors to work with the students, and that helped, but a few were too distraught to continue working on the site, and they went home.

"There was a briefing at the beginning and the end of each day, and every couple of weeks we would say something to keep everyone on track," Rogers remembers. "People came and went. There was almost constant hiring. People got injured and had to leave; a lot of it was ergonomics. They were sorting by hand and breaking down clumps of dirt and they'd get tendonitis. They would get put on other duties until they could return to the belts. But for some, it was just too much physical work." Still, a great camaraderie developed in the group as more and more students arrived. They hung out together after work, they tossed Frisbees around during their lunch break, and many became close friends.

CHAPTER FORTY-FIVE

TALKING TO THE FAMILIES

By the end of May 2002 it had been almost four months since the searching began on the farm. Although the search was going to continue for at least another year, the police had already found thousands of personal items they believed had belonged to the missing women. It was time to ask for help from relatives; maybe they could identify some of these things. But Don Adam also knew it was time to give the families another briefing.

This time more family members met with the police, Crown counsel, coroners and duty officers on Sunday, May 25. People had many questions but again were frustrated by receiving very few answers. And again that was because the police knew that several of the relatives talked to reporters all the time. Still, the investigators were forthright about the most important question they heard: "Will we get our loved one's body back?"

The answer was blunt. No. "They said we shouldn't expect them to find any bodies, but we can expect them to find fragments," Rick Frey told reporters. "I think it was the coroner [who] said it was like a massacre. A lot of people couldn't stand it. They broke down and it was tough," he said.

Another question on everyone's mind was the adjoining land, former Pickton farm property now covered with recent subdivisions, a park and a school. What chance was there of expanding the search to these areas, even if it meant tearing the houses down? The police had no answers to this one, nor would they make any promises.

Aside from bringing people up to date and giving them a chance to ask questions, the main purpose of this four-hour meeting was to have family members look at photographs of about three thousand items collected from Willie's trailer, the loft above the mechanical shop, the slaughterhouse and other locations. Could they recognize anything? Anything at all? It turned into a heartbreaking exercise. Family members strained to identify familiar objects. Could that be their sister's necklace? Her keys? Was that her ring? Could it be her purse? Her shoes?

Laura Tompkins remembers turning the pages of hundreds of pictures trying to find anything that might have belonged to her daughter-in-law, Patricia Johnson. "It was very difficult from just looking at pictures," she says. "Almost impossible."

Rick Frey drew another conclusion from the pictures. "It's going to be hard on people," he told the *Toronto Star*'s Daniel Girard. "If they found 3,000 exhibits on top [of the ground], who knows what they'll find underneath?"

The families left the meeting with mixed emotions. They appreciated the effort made by the task force to keep in touch; they were glad to have the opportunity to help with identification of belongings. But they still felt resentful that no one would tell them anything. The only news was that the site would yield no bodies. And they were irritated by the long wait for this second meeting. They also had another, dangerous question that remained unanswered.

Ten days before this meeting, CBC News ran an interview with Kim Rossmo, who was by then working in Washington, D.C., as head of research for the Police Foundation. Back in 1999, he told the CBC, Willie Pickton was on the top-ten list of suspects in the missing women case. "I heard about him from the investigators looking at the missing persons case, and the number of those individuals that I heard about was probably five or less," Rossmo said. "So that's why I'm saying you look at him as being one of their top ten." If he'd been asked to use his system in 1999, Rossmo told the CBC, "there are two geographic facts that might have given police more cause to look at the pig farmer. One is he had a place that allowed him to dispose of bodies, and two, he made regular visits to the

Downtown Eastside for the purpose of going to the rendering plant."
And the CBC made a final point in its story. Why wasn't a search
warrant issued to search the Pickton farm in 1999?

What the CBC didn't know was that the Vancouver police had
tried to obtain a warrant in 1999 but were told by Peder Gulbransen,
the regional Crown counsel, that they did not have enough evidence to justify a search. No justice of the peace would have issued
a warrant based on what they had, but it shouldn't have surprised
anyone that the families were upset and angry after hearing
Rossmo's allegations.

Eight days later, on June 3, CTV broadcast a story that went
around the world: Willie Pickton's freezers held the body parts of
missing women. There had been a rare leak, cited by CTV as a
"police source" who had told them that "the feet, hands and heads
of two females were stuffed into several freezers. That discovery,
made months ago, has only now been revealed." The leak was only
partly correct—the remains were in one freezer. When CTV talked to
Dave Pickton, he admitted that the police had seized five or six
freezers used on the farm to store unsold pork, and one of them had
contained the body parts. But Willie didn't do it, he insisted; it was
"a former employee who had planted them to frame his brother."
When another reporter tried to get Dave to talk about this bombshell
statement, Dave backed away quickly. "I never talked to anyone
today," he snapped. "What the hell are they saying? I don't know
what the hell you're talking about."

Dismayed by the leaks, the task force issued warnings to its
team: Do not respond to questions from the media. Direct them
instead to our official spokespersons, Vancouver police officer Scott
Driemel and the RCMP's Cate Galliford. The families felt stone-
walled, and so did reporters. A prominent defence lawyer tried to
explain to the *Vancouver Sun*'s Kim Bolan the reasons for the tough
stance on sharing information.

"That type of coverage clearly has a grave potential to impact
on this man's ability to get a fair trial," Michael Tammen told her.

"I believe on this case that the task force and the media liaison people are well aware of that and that is why they are trying to walk the tightrope they are. I think they have done a reasonably good job of that—keeping the families informed on the one hand and telling the media what needs to be known while still preserving, as best they can, the fellow's right to a fair trial."

The following day, on June 4, two searchers, Constable Dan Christiensen and Corporal Dan Swan, were working around Site B, the slaughterhouse. This should have been the second site searched after Willie's trailer, but when Tim Sleigh found the heads in the workshop freezer, the slaughterhouse had been put on hold until the workshop search was finished. When they finally got to the slaughterhouse, Christiensen and Swan were appalled by the smell. They tracked it into the building, through the central butchering area with the metal table Lynn Ellingsen remembered—the table over which she said she'd seen Willie butchering a dark-haired woman with red nails—and then farther back, behind the main wall, into a small corner space that not so long ago had been a pigpen. Whatever was causing the smell was in there.

The men looked around and spied two plastic garbage pails behind some pieces of wood. When they looked inside one of the pails, a green one, they realized it was crammed with human remains (the other one held animal offal). Right away the men called Daryl Hetherington, who took the pail to the Royal Columbian Hospital for the contents to be autopsied. Once again Dr. Straathof conducted the autopsy while forensic odontologist Dr. David Sweet and Brian McConaghy, the forensic firearms and tool-marks examiner, assisted.

What the searchers had found was another human head, sawn in half just like the ones found in the workshop freezer, as well as two feet and two hands. Very quickly, DNA tests showed that these were the remains of Mona Wilson. In some ways it wasn't a surprise; her blood was all over the motor home and Willie had been charged on February 22, 2002, with her murder, as well as that of Sereena

Abotsway. Like the two women whose remains had been found in the workshop freezer, Mona had been killed by a bullet to her head.

When the experts looked at the way the head had been sawn apart, they concluded that a reciprocating saw had been used, a type of saw with a long, narrow blade often called a sabre saw or known by the brand name Sawzall; it is often used by door and window installers because it is designed to make vertical cuts. By comparing the marks, Brian McConaghy concluded that the same reciprocating saw not only had cut in half the heads of Mona Wilson, Andrea Joesbury and Sereena Abotsway but was also the saw used to bisect the skull of Jane Doe found in Mission Slough in 1995.

The saw cuts were all done exactly the same way. The first cut began under the jaw at the front of the face and moved up through the face. The second cut began at the base of the head at the back and moved up, but none of the cuts met at the top. McConaghy found fractures at the top that told him the skulls had been simply snapped apart or split at this point. The cause of death for all three heads found on the farm was a gunshot wound to the head. Police found a reciprocating saw in the slaughterhouse but they couldn't connect it with hundred percent certainty to the marks on the four skulls.

About the same time in early June, Stephen Kozak was working in the slaughterhouse with Dan Swan; their job was to move three more chest freezers from a raised platform, get them on a truck and take them over to a work site for examination. In front of the freezers was a three-foot-long wooden panel that separated the freezers from the pigpen; this panel had to come out before the men could haul out the freezers. When they began cutting and pulling it out, they also uncovered a pile of dirt and manure, a small knotted rope, a shell casing and what looked like bones.

After moving out the freezers and breaking for a brief lunch, the men went back to the platform with a five-gallon bucket and trowels and began removing the muck that had been under the panel. Kozak dropped piles of it into the bucket and Swan carefully spooned it into a sifter. And they did find bones, about fifty small ones. All of them went to Tracy Rogers, who examined them to determine if they were human. They were; tests later showed they were the hand bones of Georgina Papin, who was thirty-seven when she disappeared on March 14, 2001.

While the forensic teams scoured the farm for evidence, police officers in Vancouver and the whole Lower Mainland were following up on tips and old leads. They hadn't forgotten Lisa Yelds; in 1999 two officers had tried in vain to get her to talk but she was so hostile they backed off. Late one afternoon, on June 20, 2002, RCMP member Beverly Csikos, based in the Surrey detachment, tried again. Yelds wasn't much more cooperative this time, although she did allow Csikos to take a swab from inside her cheek for a DNA sample.

Everyone was giving DNA samples by this time, including every officer, student and visitor on the Pickton property. With this information—what they call a "known DNA data bank"—the police could quickly identify and eliminate those people as they searched for traces of the missing women. At the same time they were still collecting DNA samples from family members. Because the DNA of every person is made up of fifty percent of the DNA from their mother and fifty percent from their father, when there is no body, it is possible to identify a victim by comparing DNA from blood or tissue samples to that of parents, siblings or children. The pure DNA supplied by the BC Cancer Centre, from the Pap smears of many of the victims, was the fastest and most reliable way of identifying or eliminating the samples found on the farm, but the familial samples were also helpful.

By June 26 the police had four new DNA profiles. They were able to identify the one that belonged to Helen Hallmark very quickly. She had disappeared on September 23, 1997. Task force members visited her mother, Kathleen, right away to tell her; her reaction, she explained to the *Vancouver Sun*'s Kim Bolan, was relief. "It is good to know. I have had some really rough times in the last few months," she explained. "They have been really, really rough. But I am looking to change. I need my life back. That is what I am looking for now."

What was disappointing, though, was the news that they had not yet found enough DNA or evidence to charge Pickton with Helen's murder. It was the same situation for Patricia Johnson, who had disappeared on May 31, 2001; the police found her DNA as well but there was not enough evidence to lay charges. As for the remaining DNA, the samples that had been connected to two other missing women, the police were not yet ready to say anything publicly.

Early in July the task force decided to start searching the Picktons' Burns Road property, home of Piggy's Palace. Except for finding that Willie had begun work on the site of a new house for himself there, behind the Palace and hidden from the prying eyes of anyone driving past, they found no significant evidence. But in mid-July there was another important discovery in Willie's slaughterhouse. Stephen Kozak was swabbing one of the chest freezers he'd removed from that site a few weeks earlier when he was called back to the slaughterhouse. The searchers there needed his help removing the platform that the freezers had rested on. As soon as they pried it off they found a cement floor with old timbers across it; mice were running in and out of nests and pathways they'd made in the wood. Mixed into this debris, the searchers found a green toothbrush, a braided string friendship bracelet and a human bone. The DNA tests showed that the bone had also belonged to Georgina Papin.

The Pickton story was now an international sensation. Newspapers and broadcasters from the United States, Great Britain and Europe sent reporters to Port Coquitlam to see the site for themselves. Camera crews roamed the alleys and streets around the corner of Hastings and Main, much to the irritation or bemusement of the local citizens, and took ferries across the Georgia Strait to visit families living on Vancouver Island. Some went to see families in the interior of British Columbia. They came away with more than a horrific tale of a sex killer who may have been responsible for the deaths of dozens of women, and who appeared to have fed their butchered bodies to his pigs or tossed them into the furnaces of a huge rendering plant. They also came away with stories of a drug-infested, filthy and poverty-stricken neighbourhood crammed with prostitutes, dealers and addicts in the heart of one of the most beautiful cities in the world.

Hardened journalists couldn't believe it. Nor could they believe what they heard about the way the police forces, including the RCMP but most especially the Vancouver police, had ignored the missing women case, denied anything was unusual, lied about it and covered up their failures. Kim Rossmo's blunt interviews from his senior position in Washington made things even worse. Vancouverites weren't used to bad publicity like this. They were embarrassed, angry and desperate for someone to fix the situation. They demanded accountability.

Terry Blythe, Vancouver's police chief and the man in charge when the Rossmo fiasco blew up, had known for a while that his position was untenable and just getting worse. In April he had announced his intention to step down, and now, with his departure expected at the end of July, the Vancouver police board still hadn't named a new chief. The original list of candidates included nineteen names; among them was that of Larry Campbell, a former member of the RCMP's drug squad, which he had joined in 1973. After twelve years with the force, Campbell had set up the city's first district coroner's office in 1981; in 1996 he was appointed chief coroner for the province. It wasn't long before he had become one of the best-known people in the city, as a coroner who fought for the rights of the addicts, prostitutes and poverty-stricken people of the city's Downtown Eastside. In 1998 Campbell's career inspired Vancouver television producer Chris Haddock to create *Da Vinci's Inquest*, the gritty, realistic and compulsively watchable CBC series about a crusading coroner. The Downtown Eastside was the series' most familiar location, and Campbell became involved in the series as a consultant and screenwriter himself.

Now, however, to the surprise of many people in the city, Campbell was out of the running for police chief. He had made the short list, but his fame, his twelve years of experience as a member of the RCMP and another ten years as a coroner were set aside; the police board was nervous about him. He had been too outspoken on the issue of the missing women. He had even told the police to look for a person who had access to a pig farm, a rendering plant or a crematorium. "As it turned out," he said later, "the person had access to two out of the three." He was also a strong advocate for the city's new harm-reduction drug policy, which involved safe injection sites so that addicts could inject their drugs in a clean, safe place instead of in skid row's filthy alleys and hotels.

After Campbell was dropped by the board, probably because of his vociferous criticism of the Vancouver police for their lack of action on the missing women case and because he was no longer a police officer, the list was down to two men: Inspector Bob Rich, a long-time Vancouver Police Department officer—the inside candidate; and RCMP superintendent Jamie Graham,* the head of the force in Surrey and former head of the RCMP detachment in North Vancouver—the outside candidate. He was seen as a smart, popular and efficient manager, with nothing to connect him to the missing women fiasco.

While people waited to see which man would win, Terry Blythe said that his force was reviewing their work on the missing women case and that they had started the review in late May or early June. But he wouldn't admit that the VPD had done anything wrong. Instead he told the *Vancouver Sun*'s Lindsay Kines and Kim Bolan that the main purpose of the review was to make sure the department had its house in order rather than to correct problems with the initial investigation. "It's not a review, as such," he told them, "to say why didn't you do this or why didn't you do that, and we better do it now. That isn't the point of the review at all. To me, it's normal process. With all the media coverage and with the accusations that have been made that we may not have done something or

Jamie Graham is the author's second cousin; they share the same great-grandparents from Belleville, Ontario.

we overlooked something . . . I wanted to just reconfirm with myself that we'd done all the right things so nobody's looking foolish at the end of this. So far, I believe we're looking very good in this."

The police board didn't agree. Given the public outrage boiling up from the discoveries at the pig farm, it was time to bring in an experienced outsider to clean up the mess. They chose Jamie Graham. It didn't take long for Blythe's cronies to scatter; notices of resignations and retirements became routine.

On July 15, 2002, Detective Constable Mike McDonald, a Vancouver police officer who had been working on the farm since the end of February, was asked to help RCMP constable Dan Christiensen search two more old chest freezers, at the back of the workshop/garage known as Site D. Lifting the lid of the second freezer and looking inside, they saw three plastic bags packed in what looked like melting ice, along with a sheet of plastic. Although they could see that there was ground meat in the bags, their only job now was to take out the bags and put them into a large Tupperware container to be stored in a refrigerated truck on the property.

It would take another four months before someone examined the bags and discovered that their contents included ground human tissue. The DNA recovered from it matched that of two women: Inga Hall, who was forty-seven when she disappeared on March 3, 1998, and Cindy Feliks, who was forty-three when she disappeared on January 8, 2001. When the task force realized that ground human remains had been in a freezer on the property for more than four years, they knew they needed to talk to provincial health officials and perhaps even warn the public. It was entirely possible that Willie had been selling the meat to butchers in the area. After all, he had been working with Dave Yelds, Lisa's ex-husband, to grind, package and sell up to three hundred pounds of ground meat every month to small butcher shops in the Fraser Valley. No health warning was issued until March 2004.

CHAPTER FORTY-SIX

WHAT THE DEAD REVEAL

By the thirty-first of July the task force had added nine new names to the list of missing women, which brought the official total to fifty-four, although most of them had been reported missing years earlier to the Vancouver Police Department. Along with the names the police gave the dates when they were last seen, including: Lillian Jean O'Dare,* September 12, 1978; Yvonne Marlene Abigosis, March 1984; Sheryl Donahue, August 1985; Teresa Louise Triff, April 1993; Richard (Kellie) Little, April 1997; and Tanya Colleen Emery, December 1998. And the list was going to grow, warned Constable Cate Galliford.

When he saw his half-sister's name on the list, Eli Triff was shocked. He told the *Vancouver Sun*'s Lindsay Kines and Kim Bolan that he and his sister had never been close; they had different fathers and had been raised in different provinces. He hadn't seen her since 1989 and he wasn't the person who reported her missing. But in the last hour and ten minutes since he'd read the list of names, he said, "I've found that I've had more immersion into this whole situation than I have in the past several years. There were some times where I was thinking, jeez, we gotta try to go to the police and see. It just never really got there. Had our relationship been maybe closer, it might have been a different story."

*In 1989 Lillian O'Dare's skeleton was found in the basement of an old house in the Downtown Eastside but wasn't identified until a DNA match was made in 2007.

A few days after announcing the nine new names, on August 8 the province's solicitor general, Rich Coleman, told the public how much the investigation had cost so far: ten million dollars, paid by a special contingency fund. That was just the beginning, and British Columbia was going to need money from the federal government. "We're committed to do the investigation in its entirety, however long it takes," Coleman promised.

Later that same afternoon, two police officers drove to Maggie de Vries's house. They'd called first to make sure she was home but didn't say what they wanted to talk to her about. They didn't need to. Her younger sister, Sarah, had disappeared in April 1998, when she was twenty-eight years old, and now Maggie de Vries was sure the investigators had found some evidence that Sarah had been at the farm. "I knew that was what they were coming for," de Vries told Kines and Bolan. "I was trying to prepare myself that it might be something else. But I knew it really wasn't something else."

However, when they arrived at her home, all the officers told her was that Sarah's DNA had been found on an item at the farm. They didn't tell her that it was on two tubes of lipstick found in her cosmetics bag, and they didn't tell her that DNA matching Willie Pickton's had been found on a used condom near the white bag. Nor did the police say that Sarah was dead.

"All it literally means is something Sarah touched was on that property," she told the reporters. "So it doesn't even mean she was ever there. She could have lent her jacket to somebody, or her hat, or her shoes, which she did all the time." Still, de Vries wasn't fooling herself. "Now I'm not going to be waiting to know anymore," she said. "I'm going to be settled with this. So that's a good thing."

The news about Sarah de Vries, one of the best-known of the missing women, was widely publicized; she was one of the most interesting and high-profile victims of the street. It wasn't just her beauty or the poetry she wrote or the brutally honest diaries she left behind. It was also because of the articulate interviews she had done with journalists, and the prominence of her family, which included

Maggie; her father, a university professor; her mother, who had been a respected senior nurse in Vancouver; and her aunt Jean Little, the famous writer of children's books.

Another well-known missing woman was identified soon afterwards, thanks to the work of one of the students working on the farm. Amy Brienne Deforest had just finished her honours bachelor's degree in anthropology at the University of Alberta. Having graduated with first-class standing, she was one of the students chosen to work on the farm in the summer of 2002. Brie, as people called her, had specialized in human bone work and taken part in two field schools in forensic archaeology. She was so impressed by Tracy Rogers that she had already applied to do a master's degree under Rogers's supervision at the University of Toronto.

By August 21 Brie Deforest was experienced in both searching the bone pits and working on the picking belts. As usual, she had started at seven fifteen in the morning and was standing at what was called Screener Number 1, her eyes raking the dirt and debris slowly moving past her on a medium belt. Normally there would have been three more students on her side of the belt and four on the other side, but today was different: five students were on each side of the belt. They'd been told that the searchers were digging in what they called a "high-potential area"—a large bone pit, thirty feet deep, with what looked like human bones in it. The material was due to come along her belt this morning and she was determined not to miss anything.

At first it felt just like any other shift. "I pulled multiple pieces of bone and other materials and just put them in my bucket," she remembered later. "At the end of the shift, I was walking back up towards our group wash area, where we write up any items of interest. And I looked in my bucket and realized that one of the pieces of bone that I had pulled during the shift looked like it had potential to be human. I washed my boots* and then took all the material straight

---

Anyone entering an evidence tent had to wash off their boots first so they wouldn't track in any biohazards or dirt.

to Dr. Rogers . . . Personally, for me, it was the teeth. I find human teeth look pretty distinct and pretty easy to tell from other animals, relatively easy to tell. It was just a fragment with three teeth attached into it, still socketed. It was dirty, it had been in the dirt, and it was broken."

Normally Deforest would have filled in a form and given the bone and the form to a technician to bag and stow away for examination later. But this time she took it directly to Tracy Rogers, who confirmed that it was indeed a partial human jaw with three teeth. The front and left side were gone, and the remaining right side showed some damage that could have been made by the Grizzly as it went through the sifting process. Rogers thought it had been in the ground for two or three years. A more detailed examination later found that the jaw had been sawn in half vertically, which explained the missing parts. It also meant that it was what was left of a severed head. Not surprising by this point—they knew now how Willie Pickton had been butchering the women. Exactly the way he butchered his pigs. Exactly as Scott Chubb had described it.

To identify a human being from these sad fragments, David Sweet would have to grind or crush the teeth—preferably these would be molars, which would still have some DNA-rich pulp left in the core—and blend the powder with frozen nitrogen. Luck was with him on Brie Deforest's discovery; these fragments proved to be all that was left of Marnie Frey. But Rick and Lynn Frey, Marnie's birth mother, Charlotte, and her brother Ricky wouldn't be told for another three months. The scientists needed to be sure about the test results.

The day after Brie Deforest found Marnie Frey's jawbone on the picking belt, other searchers found a human left rib and a heel bone just beneath the surface in another bone pit behind the slaughterhouse, close to the site where Marnie's remains had rested. Right away they called Tracy Rogers. When she hurried in with Bob Stair, they first looked on the surface of the grid square for other human bones but found none; that meant they could let an excavator continue scooping material out of the pit. Rogers brought in some extra students to help search by hand, telling them first to make sure they wore biohazard suits and to bring some five-gallon buckets and hand tools. Rogers was right about the importance of this area; it also contained a calcaneus, or heel bone, that revealed the Achilles tendon had been cut through to remove the foot, as well as a scaphoid bone, which is part of the human wrist.

Then another grid square close by produced four pieces of human vertebrae. When she examined them carefully, Rogers found that two were from a human neck and fit together perfectly; the other two pieces, from a spinal column, also fit together. They had all been cut vertically through the spinal column, almost certainly with a reciprocating saw. The body had been severed into two long halves, exactly like the procedure Pickton used to butcher pigs.

DNA testing proved that the wrist bone belonged to Georgina Papin; it fit perfectly with her hand bones that they had already recovered. But the real shock came after DNA tests on the heel, neck and rib bones. They belonged to Jane Doe, the woman whose skull had been found by the whirligig man in Mission Slough in 1995. And the tool cuts on these bones had been made by the same saw. The implication for the task force was clear: they would have to search the slough.

Gina Houston had told people that Willie would take her to towns in the Fraser Valley when he was working, but he never took her to Mission. The only thing the police could assume was that Willie didn't want Gina to see what he was doing there. His problem was clear to the investigators: a victim's hands and feet, a victim's skull are instantly recognizable as human. Willie couldn't take the chance of throwing them into the vats at West Coast Reduction. Regardless of how sloppy their intake and surveillance might be, a glimpse of a human bone would be disastrous for him. Those pieces he would bury or hide around his own place. Or maybe chuck into a slough.

But what did he do with the long bones from the bodies, the leg and arm bones? No one knows for sure. They might have been easier to take to the rendering plant because they are less distinguishable as human. Wherever he took them, he made sure to remove them from the farm—the forensic anthropologists never found any human arm or leg bones in any of the pits.

Rick Papin was at home in Wetaskiwin, Alberta, forty-four miles south of Edmonton, on the Monday night, September 16, 2002, when the RCMP drove up to his house. As soon as he saw them, he too, just like Maggie de Vries, knew why they were there. DNA evidence, the police explained to him, had proved that his sister Georgina's remains were on the farm. "She wasn't just a prostitute; she was a mother too," Papin told Global Television the next day. "She could light up a room just by coming in. She made a mistake."

Three days later, after the families had been informed, the task force announced four more charges of first-degree murder against Willie Pickton, although they didn't say what the evidence was. The four included thirty-year-old Jennifer Furminger, last seen on December 27, 1999; her blood was found on a watch in the slaughterhouse, on a hoodie in Willie's laundry room and on another jacket in his office next to the laundry room. Another was Helen Hallmark, thirty-two when she was last seen on June 15, 1997; her blood spatter, caused when some unknown object struck her body, was found on a panel in Willie's bedroom. The third was Patricia Johnson, twenty-seven, who was last seen on March 3, 2001; her projected blood was found on a plywood sheet in the slaughterhouse. And the fourth was Georgina Papin, thirty-seven, last seen on March 21, 1999, whose wrist and hand bones were found in the piggery. Their names were added to those of the other seven Willie had been charged with killing: Sereena Abotsway, Heather Bottomley, Andrea Joesbury, Jacqueline McDonell, Diane Rock, Mona Wilson and Brenda Wolfe.

By now ninety-one men and women, including the anthropology and archaeology students, were working on the pig farm and at the Piggy's Palace site on Burns Road. Sightseers watched the dump trucks moving dirt from grid-square sites to the Grizzlies and screeners at the back, but even those with high-powered field glasses and zoom camera lenses couldn't see, from any approach to the property, what was going on at the picking belts or in the laboratory tents erected by each search site. Electric fencing and entry through the gates only for pass-card holders helped guarantee the security of the crime scene. Gerry Murdoch also took special care with the picking belts, making sure that screens were set up around them to protect the dignity of the dead. He also put up a soaring metal roof to protect the students as they worked on the belts, and the human remains they found, from the driving rain of the West Coast.

What curious onlookers could see was surrealistic: hawks, eagles and the occasional heron, refugees from the marshes of the Pitt River nearby, drifting over the site; a tangle of wrecked cars and trucks and rusty machinery piled at the sides, displaced by tarps, tents, reefer trucks and the chaos of Gerry Murdoch's crowded ATCO village; the green haze of new grass covering many of the twenty-foot-high mounds of dirt, seeded by Murdoch to make the place seem less like a moonscape. Ditches full of filthy brown water. Prim new clapboard houses in pastels edging the property on three sides. The Home Depot across the road beside a rickety tent full of sorrowful mementoes. The Hells Angels clubhouse facing the farm entrance. And as a backdrop to all the bustle and mess and horror, the Coast Mountains rising to the east, dense green forests growing up their sides to the snowline.

Fred Maile couldn't resist it. The retired Mountie, who had hunted down Clifford Olson in the 1960s and built a prosperous private investigation firm in the 1990s, had to be there. He volunteered, putting on his work clothes to drive a front-end loader on the farm for three months. For Maile, as for most people, the focus was the farm: finding the remains, identifying them, informing the families. Nobody knew better than he did how agonizing the wait was for these people; he had had to deal with the families of the eleven children Olson abducted, tortured, killed and buried in the woods. For other officers, the focus was outside the property, on trying to put the whole story together. They interviewed witnesses, followed leads, chased tips. And some took care of the challenging task of babysitting key witnesses such as Lynn Ellingsen.

Ellingsen was the Crown's single most important witness, the only eyewitness to a killing, and even more valuable because she had been along for Willie's entire trip—the drive through New Westminster's skid row looking for drugs for Lynn and a woman for him, when he was stopped by the police and then continued on to the Downtown Eastside, where he picked up a woman. Her story was always that she was in the truck when he brought them back to the farm, remained in the trailer and wakened later, when she heard a scream. That she saw him in his slaughterhouse with the woman hanging on a hook, dead, gutted, red-painted fingers and toes dangling. That he told her never to tell or he'd kill her too.

Ellingsen was a serious addict, desperate for money and drugs, and her police handler, Corporal Sandra Lavallee, found her to be a handful. So did the officers who continued to pump her for more information. On September 22, 2002, she met again with Corporal Baltej Dhillon. She told him about her friendship with a woman called Angel, a heroin addict she'd met at a safe house in Surrey, a year or two before Willie's arrest; both were staying there in an effort to get through a drug rehab program. When Angel discovered that Ellingsen sometimes stayed at the Pickton farm, Ellingsen told Dhillon, she said she'd been there too. "She was a little girl," she told him. "Like, she was littler than I was. She had not very good skin, like scabs on her skin. She was a nice girl. She had—some of her teeth weren't all there. And brown, I think, shoulder-length hair. A lot of the time in the house she had her hair up in a ponytail." It was a fair description of Andrea Joesbury, who was known as Angel on skid row.

Ellingsen's information about Andrea Joesbury and other women was useful to the police, but it was her testimony about Pickton that they needed most. Looking after her, however, was a nightmare because of her addiction. Her moods skipped from tearful and querulous to demanding and angry to penitent and charming. She surprised the police by admitting she had slept with Pat Casanova during her time at the farm and that he'd been good to her; even now, she said, she was seeing him from time to time—Casanova was generous and she needed money. The police also learned that Lynn wasn't the only woman Casanova had fancied during his visits to the Pickton farm. He had sex with several others but his favourite was Andrea Joesbury; later he told police that he had paid her about thirty dollars for a blow job in Willie Pickton's bedroom in the trailer, probably in 2001.

On Wednesday morning, October 2, the police announced they were charging Willie Pickton with four more counts of first-degree murder, based on evidence found on the farm. When they made their announcement, the police did not give any details about the evidence they'd found that allowed them to lay the charges. The victims included Heather Chinnock, who was thirty-one when she disappeared on April 15, 2001. Investigators had found Chinnock's ring in the same pigpen where they found Georgina Papin's hand bones, as well as her DNA on the handle of a Clout detergent bucket in the workshop/ garage. The second charge concerned Tanya Holyk, whose DNA was also found in the workshop/garage. She had been only twenty-one when she disappeared six years earlier, on October 29, 1996.

Sherry Irving was the third, twenty-three years old when, in April 1997, Dave Pickton picked her up in New Westminster and drove her to Willie's trailer; she was never seen again. Her DNA was found in a freezer in the workshop/garage. And the fourth charge was for the murder of Inga Hall, at forty-six one of Pickton's older victims, who disappeared on February 26, 1998. Once again a freezer in the workshop/garage had yielded human DNA—the investigators had found hers in a bag of frozen ground meat that contained human flesh.

It was at this point that Peter Ritchie demanded more money for Willie's defence. Although he'd already placed a $375,000 lien on the Pickton farm property—a common practice among defence lawyers to make sure they get paid—Ritchie announced officially that he would have to quit working on the case. He and his partner, Marilyn Sandford, couldn't afford to do it, he told Associate Chief Judge Pat Dohm in the province's Supreme Court on October 9, 2002. He had also filed an application for legal aid known as a Rowbotham application, he told Dohm, but it had been turned down.

"It became clear as the counts were being laid," Ritchie said, "that it's absolutely impossible for two people to deal with this case." There were more than 200,000 DNA samples and he needed at least six lawyers to help. He also told the judge how difficult such cases were: the public was quick to vilify lawyers who defended accused murderers in sensational trials. Even the lawyers' families would be subject to outbursts of anger; it was hard on marriages. And even if he did receive legal aid, the fees were far too low to convince decent lawyers to take these cases.

Dohm listened sympathetically. After the hearing, and behind closed doors with Ritchie and government officials, the judge agreed on a rate that was acceptable to Ritchie; the amount has never been disclosed. But the deal infuriated several family members of the missing women. Ritchie's statements and his lien on the property prompted Georgina Papin's brother, Randall Knight, to speak up for them. "It seems like the guy [Pickton] has some money tied up in property," he said. "It doesn't seem fair that it should go to the government when the government didn't do their job in the first place." Pickton's assets should be held in trust, he said, and divided among the families.

But the deal meant that Ritchie was able to add more lawyers to his team. He and Sandford quickly brought in fifty-one-year-old Victoria lawyer Adrian Brooks, best-known for his strong defence of Kelly Ellard, the teenager accused of killing Saanich teenager Reena Virk, who had been swarmed, tortured and beaten by six girls and two boys under a bridge near Victoria on November 14, 1997; she was finally held underwater until she drowned. Ellard was convicted of the murder. A native of Victoria but a graduate of Osgoode Hall

Law School in Toronto, Brooks had articled under Toronto defence lawyer Eddie Greenspan before moving back west. As Brooks's reputation for careful and clever work grew, he was in demand as a prosecutor brought in by the government to take on special cases. Low-key and courteous, he was well-liked by the legal community across the province. Brooks had to think hard before accepting the offer from Ritchie and Sandford. Defending what appeared to be Canada's most prolific serial killer? Perhaps even the most prolific in North America? He lived on Vancouver Island, and commuting back and forth to the mainland for a long period would be difficult. He calculated that the case would last two years, maybe two and a half. But in the end, it proved an irresistible challenge.

The last visible member of the defence team during this period was Patrick McGowan, a 1997 UBC law school graduate who had served as a law clerk in the B.C. Supreme Court. He had joined Ritchie Sandford as an associate, was still young and had none of the easy geniality of Adrian Brooks, but he was clever and ambitious. Then there were the invisible members of the team working on Pickton's defence, including private detectives whose job was to locate and research the backgrounds of all the Crown witnesses; a retired judge and volunteer Dodie Holmes, the daughter of one of B.C.'s most famous defence lawyers (later a judge himself), Angelo Branca, who worked completely in the background.

Mike Petrie, the man in charge of prosecuting Pickton, was also adding to his team. Soon after he took the case, when there were still only two counts of murder, Nanaimo Crown prosecutor Derrill Prevett, who had conducted forty homicide prosecutions and realized, as he said, "that DNA would play an important role in the investigation," volunteered to help. Prevett's knowledge of forensic DNA analysis was encyclopedic; in fact he is the co-author, with Cecilia Hageman and Wayne Murray, of *The DNA Handbook*, a manual for the Canadian legal profession.

Like Peter Ritchie, Prevett did his undergraduate degree at the University of Western Ontario in London. Today Ritchie is a skilled banjo player who often plays in Vancouver bluegrass groups, but in those days he played the trumpet in the university's marching band while Prevett played clarinet, flute and saxophone in Western's concert band. Prevett had worked for a local law firm while he finished his undergraduate studies. As soon as he graduated he moved to Vancouver to attend the UBC law school. Coincidentally—Prevett was the prosecutor in the Kelly Ellard case—he knew what it would be like to go up against Adrian Brooks.

Ellard had not been Prevett's only high-profile case. There had been many, but none more horrifying than that of Jay Handel, an abusive husband from Quatsino, on northern Vancouver Island, who got even with his wife for threatening to leave him by killing their six small children. He then burned down his house with the children's bodies inside, forcing his wife to watch. Handel was found guilty and went to prison. Prevett was also involved in three heartbreaking cases of young girls murdered in brutal sexual attacks in British Columbia: eleven-year-old Carolyn Lee in woods just outside Port Alberni in 1977 and sixteen-year-old Cathy Pozzobon in a farm field in Maple Ridge in the summer of 1978. Twenty-one years later, in 1998, Prevett prosecuted Carolyn Lee's killer, Gurmit Singh Dhillon, and Andrew Wayne Larsen, Cathy Pozzobon's killer, in New Westminster in 2000, twenty-two years after she had been strangled. In both cases, forensic DNA analysis that was not available in the late 1970s, when the girls were killed, was central to identifying the killers. But it was another murder of a small girl, another DNA case, that he remembers most often. A man called Roddy Patten murdered a little eleven-year-old girl at a ball park in Port Alberni. Only after hundreds of men gave DNA samples did the police finally get a match when they eventually got DNA from Roddy Patten, who had been avoiding them. "What he did to Jessica States was sickening," Prevett said. "Afterwards, he buried her body in a ravine at the edge of the park. He claimed to be under the influence of several drugs, but when they looked at all the evidence, the jury didn't buy it. There is a monument to little Jessica in the park. She is known as

'Our Angel In The Outfield.' People leave little tokens, stuffed animals etc. there. I will never forget that case either.

"At the end of the case, everyone was crying," he said. "The judge was crying, the court clerk was crying and there was only one stinking box of Kleenex in the whole place. The sheriffs were crying, the jury was crying, and as we passed around the one box of Kleenex everyone was crying except one hard-hearted bastard—me. One CBC person came to me and asked me why I wasn't crying too. I said, 'We're Crown counsel. We cry at night. We have to steel ourselves so we can function properly.'"

On May 1 a former RCMP member, John Ahern, also joined Petrie's team. No two people could have been less alike. Ahern, a lean man addicted to running marathons, had been born to wealthy parents, who raised him in Bermuda and sent him to a private school in Switzerland. When he was eighteen, he started classes at the University of Toronto but dropped out for a job as a customs officer. Police work appealed to him, and two years later he joined the Peel Regional Police, north of Toronto; he stayed there seven years before leaving to train as an RCMP officer in Regina. Ahern spent the next eight years on postings in Alberta, but finally, when he was thirty-three years old, he decided to go to law school in Victoria. He did well there and upon graduation was chosen to clerk for Judge Carol Huddart of the B.C. Supreme Court. For a time Ahern practised as a litigator with a Vancouver law firm but, restless once again, decided to become a Crown counsel in 1994. He's remained one ever since, serving in Vancouver and the Fraser Valley and teaching part-time at UBC's law school and New Westminster's Douglas College, as well as working on an automobile fraud task force. When he was given the chance to work on the Pickton prosecution team, he jumped at it.

Petrie and Ahern worked out of the Crown Counsel Office on the third floor of the New Westminster Courthouse. Ahern's main responsibility at that time was managing the disclosure of evidence gathered by the police to Peter Ritchie and his colleagues on the defence team. After Ritchie had concluded his presentation to Judge Dohm on October 9, Ahern came down the courthouse steps with an amused smile on his face, pondering Ritchie's plea for more hardship money. "I make $82,000 a year," he said, to no one in particular, before walking off down the street.

CHAPTER FORTY-SEVEN

WILLIE GOES TO COURT

"In this city," thundered Larry Campbell to approving cheers from the crowd crammed into Vancouver's huge Library Square, "no one is disposable!" With this statement, Vancouver's new mayor—elected on November 16, 2002, with a massive majority of 80,772 votes to his opponent's 41,936—was giving voice to the shame that people across the city, regardless of their income or status, felt about the gruesome deaths of so many poor, addicted women and their neglect by the city police. Campbell's opponent had been alderman Jennifer Clarke, who represented the more conservative forces in Vancouver. She had not been able to persuade voters that she cared about the issue of the missing women and the problems of the Downtown Eastside.

In contrast, Jamie Graham, the new police chief, and Larry Campbell, the crusading coroner, had promised to make changes, to clean things up, to take responsibility, to manage with more compassion. The Old Boys' club of senior officers, the men who had damaged Kim Rossmo's career in Vancouver and ignored or covered up their failures with the missing women, melted away into retirement, with unlisted phone numbers, or took new jobs un-related to police work. Some consulted lawyers, worried that they might be facing difficult questions at a public inquiry into the failures of the Vancouver force.

In Port Coquitlam, where the nights were now coming early and winter rain had turned the Pickton property into a muddy mess of potholes, the students—a group that had doubled in size to 102—laboured on, along with the police and forensic specialists. Backhoes and dump trucks chugged around the holes and the huge mounds of dirt while new townhouses sprouted around the edges of the farm. Reporters rarely came by anymore. Across the road, families of the missing women came to the Family Healing Tent from time to time and a small group of victims' mothers and sisters worked on quilts or made beaded pins to commemorate the women. In the town, people gossiped about who had really killed all the women. The most popular theory was that Willie Pickton was just the disposal man, not the executioner. These girls, the theories went, were killed by their drug dealers, by the Hells Angels or by Asian criminals making snuff films.

Although Dave Pickton insisted that his brother was innocent, their sister, Linda Wright, was much tougher in her assessment when she heard what he was saying about Willie. "It's ridiculous to say he's not guilty," she snapped, when asked about how she was coping. The body parts alone that were found in Willie's freezers, she said, would convict him. But she could understand why Dave was still defending Willie. Rob, as Linda Wright calls Willie, had never told Dave what he was doing because he didn't want Dave to be angry with him. "Just like my dad," Wright said. "Robert didn't want Dad mad at him. Rob was always lazy and had never worked a day in his life. Maybe if he had worked at a real job he wouldn't have done this. If Rob had any conscience at all he would plead guilty and get it over with."

Wright was also upset to find out that Dave was talking to the media. "Dave talks too much. I've suffered enough," she said. "I'm a victim. My family has been victimized. David has been hurt and his family has been victimized as well." Furthermore, Willie's problems had nothing to do with her. "PoCo was another life and I've put it out of my memory. I've made a good life for myself. My kids have done well. One has a PhD, another has his master's degree and the third is in college."

And she had no use for Peter Ritchie, who, she claimed, hadn't told her anything about what was happening. "He's Rob's lawyer.

I haven't spoken to him for four or five months." The only news she could get came from Kim Bolan at the *Vancouver Sun*, who spoke to her often, kept her informed about court proceedings and was, she said, the single journalist she could trust. Linda Wright admitted it was true that she didn't visit Willie in prison; neither did Dave. They were afraid of the reporters hanging around waiting for them to show up.

Dave, like Linda, was willing to talk to some reporters privately. When he did, he would brag about his connections to the Hells Angels, the private parties they had held in Piggy's Palace over the years and his close relationship with Tony Terezakis, the notorious Angel who ran a drug ring out of the American Hotel in the Downtown Eastside and had worked as Dave's security chief during parties at the Palace.

On one occasion Dave Pickton told a reporter who wanted an interview that sure, he'd cooperate, but first she had to find Scott Chubb for him. At the time she didn't know why. Only the task force investigators were supposed to know that Chubb was the informant who had led the police to arrest Willie Pickton. But the reporter soon found out that Dave Pickton was well aware of Chubb's role and was already on his trail. His inside knowledge of Chubb's whereabouts came from provincial government records: social insurance files and Chubb's driver's licence details. "Have you found him yet?" Dave would ask her with a sly grin, and then offer a hint: "We know he's cashing his social insurance cheques in Chase [a small town in eastern British Columbia near Little Shuswap Lake]."

"That's when I started getting scared," the reporter said. Feeling threatened, she went to see an old friend on the police force. There are two possible endings here, he told her. "Either you're going to find Scott Chubb and tell Dave where he is and he'll be dead, or you'll find Scott Chubb and not tell him. And if you don't tell him where he is, you'll have bikers on your doorstep." Soon the reporter discovered that Dave Pickton was playing the same game with two CBC reporters, and they were also hunting for Chubb.

Within a few weeks the reporter began to notice clicking sounds on her cellphone each time she made or received a call. She didn't think the police were tapping her phone—their equipment was too sophisticated to reveal itself like that—but she believed that Dave Pickton's friends could do it. And then someone stole the phone. She replaced it. A few weeks later a woman called her, leaving a message to say that some hitchhiking teenagers she'd picked up had left the phone in her car, and she could have it back. Although the reporter did not return that call, there were others from people purporting to know a lot about Willie Pickton's activities; nobody ever showed up when she went to meet them. Then Dave Pickton let her know he had her address and knew all about her small children, including their ages and where they went to school. That was the last straw, and she didn't hesitate. With her employer's blessing, she took a year's leave.

"Dave has protection," she says. "He's done so many favours for the boys [the bikers]. He wants to impress them. He wants his [gang] colours. And the police cannot help me." What she didn't know at the time was that the police were actively working to protect her. They were well aware of Dave Pickton's intimidation techniques and took them seriously. He soon stopped calling her, but Scott Chubb was another matter. Chubb was so terrified of being found that he was begging the police to put him in the witness protection program. They said they'd think about it.

By this time Mike Petrie and Peter Ritchie were appearing before Judge David Stone in the provincial courthouse in Port Coquitlam to prepare the ground for the preliminary hearing. Ritchie had an extraordinary demand to make of the judge. A preliminary hearing—held to determine if there is enough evidence to proceed to trial—is always subject to a publication ban if the accused person asks for it. This means that no one—not journalists or members of the public or victims' family members or the lawyers themselves—may repeat what they hear in the courtroom. If the judge decides the evidence street from the courthouse, and tried to keep warm as they waited for the sheriffs to open the doors.

Pickton arrived unnoticed, in a van escorted by armed sheriffs in cars in front and behind. The vehicles rolled down the ramp under the courthouse to its secured parking area and he was transferred to a holding cell to wait for the proceedings to start, at ten o'clock sharp. At about nine o'clock the doors opened to the public. Sheriffs dressed in khaki uniforms and bulletproof vests, armed with batons and guns, carefully picked their way through wallets and handbags and passed metal-detecting wands over each person—reporter, family member or curious citizen—who entered. Anyone found to have a camera or a cellphone with a camera had to surrender it until he or she left the building. Only lawyers and court officials were allowed to go through without a search.

In Courtroom 2, the small main-floor room where the pre-liminary hearing was starting, Pickton's place was a chair inside a rectangular bulletproof glass box at the front on the left. Witnesses would give their evidence from a box at the front right.

About twenty reporters, including two from Seattle, and the two courtroom artists sat in the front rows on the right side; on the left, halfway back, were a few family members of the missing women, accompanied by Freda Ens and Marilynne Johnny, the Victim Services workers. More armed sheriffs, all wearing bulletproof vests, stood around the room.

Two court-watchers, Russell MacKay and Art Lee, both retirees, also showed up. MacKay, a grey-haired, pink-cheeked man in his sixties who wore jeans and a warm jacket, had been a welder who'd done some work on the farm; he knew the "Pickton boys" and couldn't resist the spectacle. Lee, a small businessman who fixed radios in Coquitlam, had grown up in the Downtown Eastside and was also following the case with interest.

Four seats had been set aside for Willie Pickton's family and close friends. People speculated in whispers about the possibility that Dave Pickton would come, or Linda Wright, or maybe Sandy

is strong enough to proceed to trial, the ban stays in place u
trial ends.

In this case, however, Peter Ritchie startled Judge St
everyone else in the courtroom when he said that a publica
alone was not enough. Ritchie wanted Stone to restrict th
room to lawyers and witnesses only. He did not want any
of the public allowed in, and that included reporters, Pickt
members and the victims' families.

On December 6, 2002, Judge Stone turned down
request. "I am not prepared to accept," he said, "that at th
the proceeding the justice system is so fragile that appro
rective measures cannot be taken so as to ensure that ar
right to a fair trial is not jeopardized." The prelimina
would be held in open court.

And so it began, under high security in a small co
Port Coquitlam, on January 13, 2003. Given that this
gest serial killing case in Canadian history and perhaps tl
North America, and given the predictions of media fren
at the courthouse that morning was a surprise. A few
and trucks were around and a couple of dozen reporter
the radio and major television networks (CBC, CTV a
well as the *Globe and Mail*, the *Toronto Star*, Ca
Maclean's magazine, Associated Press and Reuters. F
came from the local papers, the *Vancouver Sun* and
and three or four were from newspapers and televisi
Seattle, Washington, drawn by the similarity of this
their own Green River Killer. Two court artists wer
Felicity Don and Jane Wolsak, packing large bags
sketch pads and pencil crayons. And there were a fe

But the expected crowd never showed up, no
folks from Port Coquitlam, not any of the Pickton:
bours or employees, not even Bill Malone. Most pe
by eight thirty to make sure they would get a seat i
they grabbed coffees and muffins from Lattay's I

Humeny, who had a soft spot for Willie. Or maybe Vera and Albert Harvey, the blueberry farmers who had been so close to Louise Pickton and such strong supporters of Willie after his arrest. But the seats remained empty.

Peter Ritchie, immaculately dressed as always in a dark suit, white shirt and silk tie, his thick white hair neatly barbered, arrived with Patrick McGowan and Adrian Brooks to defend Willie Pickton. Marilyn Sandford wasn't there; she was working back in the offices the defence team had rented in a building across from the courthouse. Brooks and McGowan, like Ritchie, wore dark suits. Their faces were expressionless as they walked in. Prosecutors Mike Petrie, in a brown suit and gold tie, Derrill Prevett, in a navy blazer with grey flannels and a silk tie, and John Ahern, in a navy suit and silk tie, were there for the Crown; they seemed far more relaxed than the defence team. The crowd in the gallery stood as Judge Stone walked in, then everyone sat down and waited for Pickton to enter the glass box.

By now the charges of first-degree murder had grown to fifteen: Sereena Abotsway, Mona Wilson, Jacqueline McDonell, Diane Rock, Heather Bottomley, Andrea Joesbury, Brenda Ann Wolfe, Jennifer Lynn Furminger, Helen Mae Hallmark, Patricia Rose Johnson, Georgina Faith Papin, Heather Chinnock, Tanya Holyk, Sherry Irving and Inga Hall. In early December the task force had told Marilyn Kraft, Cindy Feliks's stepmother, that they'd identified her remains on the farm; she'd heard nothing since then, and Cindy's name wasn't among the fifteen counts.

Judge Stone, now sitting at centre front, clean-shaven, with dark hair, a grave face and sad, careful eyes, seemed too young for such a massive case. He looked out at the people before him. He didn't smile, but then no one did. The room fell silent. There was one door at the back of the prisoner's box, in the courtroom wall. It had a small window, and suddenly the face of a sheriff appeared in it; then the door opened. Pickton shambled in and sat on the chair; a sheriff came in and sat behind him. Pickton wore a grubby, stretched-out grey sweater and dark pants. His lank rusty brown hair, scraped away from his shiny bald pate, fell almost to his shoulders. His face was expressionless but feral, with a long, bony nose, protruding cheekbones and a thin slash of lips.

If this had been a normal preliminary hearing, Mike Petrie would have started things off with an opening statement giving an overview of the case. But because the lawyers and the judge were worried that the reporters from the United States and other countries might violate the publication ban, they had decided to let Petrie start his presentation by playing the videotapes of Pickton's time in the Surrey holding cell after his arrest. The tapes would begin with Pickton's conversation with the undercover officer on February 22, 2002, and then go to his subsequent interrogations by Bill Fordy and Don Adam the following day. Dana Lillies' very brief interview with him was also included. The tapes ended with Pickton's last conversation with the undercover police officer the same day.

Marilyn Sandford, who had arrived to cross-examine witnesses on the DNA evidence presented for each count, complained bitterly that she and her colleagues couldn't keep up with the material sent to them by the Crown prosecutors and that they couldn't read the material sent on computer disks.

"We have thirty thousand pages of DNA material," she told Stone, "and five hundred pages of expert-witness material—we have sixty binders of material!"

Mike Petrie was annoyed. "When we set the dates here [for the preliminary hearing], we had only two counts." Now there were fifteen, and most people had heard that more were coming. "It's going to take three or four months to lay out the evidence," he continued. "We have six hundred pages of exhibits and ten thousand pages of reports: seven gigabytes in total." And for the last ten months, he said, he had been giving the defence lawyers everything—all the evidence, all of it indexed and bookmarked—as he received it.

"Now, ten months after they began to receive material, this is the first time they've said they had problems!"

Sandford didn't back off; instead she complained that the defence team couldn't read the PDF documents on the disks being sent over. Judge Stone had heard enough. The software to read PDF files was easily available, he snapped. Sandford scowled and sat down. The exchange seemed trivial but it was a foretaste of things to come; the same complaints from the defence came forward frequently during the preliminary hearing.

Although it took nearly five days to play the videos, the people in the courtroom did not hear everything. The tapes had been heavily edited after an agreement was hammered out with Pickton's defence team. What was missing? Significant sections of Willie's interrogations by Fordy and Adam and equally important chunks of his talk with the undercover officer. When the reporters first heard about this on January 15, two days into the preliminary hearing, they were disappointed. The scuttlebutt was that the tapes contained Pickton's confession, and now they wouldn't hear that portion. They had no idea what else they were missing, but they guessed that whatever it was would be sensational.

What the spectators in the court were missing were Pickton's admissions to the undercover officer in his cell that he'd killed forty-nine women and disposed of their remains in a rendering plant or given them to his pigs. They also missed his admission during his interview with Don Adam that he'd killed some of the women. But they did hear Andy Bellwood and Scott Chubb talking to the police about Pickton's admissions to them about how he killed women, either by garrotting them or by injecting them with windshield-washer fluid.

As soon as the tapes were finished, Mike Petrie questioned each of the RCMP officers involved in Pickton's interrogation, including the undercover man in Pickton's cell, Bill Fordy, Dana Lillies and Don Adam. They were followed by police and forensics experts who had searched the farm. By this time Peter Ritchie was no longer attending the hearing; Adrian Brooks was usually on his own in court to cross-examine the witnesses.

Bill Fordy testified that the police had been wiretapping Willie's phone even before he was arrested, and that on several occasions

Willie had told his caller that he was "bigger than Bin Laden." Dana Lillies told Brooks that she had only three minutes' notice before going into the room to speak to his client. No one had instructed her on how to talk to him, she testified. "I just related to Mr. Pickton as I had on previous meetings. I didn't have any script."

Day after day, police officers, forensic specialists and other experts testified about their roles in the Pickton case: the initial investigation, the arrest, interviews and discovery of evidence. Willie Pickton sat in his glass booth with a long memo pad attached to a clipboard and made notes; occasionally he would ask the sheriff sitting behind him to pass the notes to his lawyers. When Pat McGowan was there, he would look briefly at the notes and set them aside. During noon breaks Adrian Brooks would occasionally visit his client downstairs in the holding cell while Pickton ate his lunch—always a sandwich, a cookie and juice or a soft drink, put together by Irene Thompson and her sister Lou Ferguson, who worked in the small coffee shop in the courthouse foyer. They made the lunches for all the prisoners being held in the cells downstairs between appearances in court.

Family members of the missing women would visit the court-room throughout this period. Those days were difficult for every-body. Victim Services workers made the arrangements for most of the family members according to guidelines set down by the gov-ernment. The government would pay for only two of them, for example, and they would be put up in a modest motel or hotel chosen by the workers. Each family could use up to $3,000 to visit the court, for the preliminary hearing or the trial itself. For anyone coming from eastern Canada or even from Vancouver Island, that money would disappear very quickly in airfares, ferry tickets and meals. The rules drove the family members to distraction; many found them mean-spirited and unreasonable, and they blamed the Victim Services staff for being unyielding and unfair. What about a mother with three or four children? Who would stay home? What about Georgina Papin's nine brothers and sisters? They were shocked to discover that the two designated family members included Papin's daughter, who lived in Las Vegas and had no plans at all to come to British Columbia.

The Victim Services workers were upset; they were simply following the bureaucrats' orders, and agreed with the families' complaints. Lunches were a major issue. One father came several times with his three children; their mother was a victim. Some came with sisters, friends and others not on the lists prepared by Victim Services. What were they supposed to do at lunchtime, when the allowances would cover only approved family members? Many of these people were poor; they couldn't afford to stay in motels or eat in restaurants. So they bunked in with those on the official lists and shared rations. It was a bad situation. Finally a local church came to the rescue. They'd heard about the problem and arranged for a group of churches in Port Coquitlam to make lunches for the families; these were served in a private room in the Terry Fox Library, near the courthouse.

Marilyn Kraft, Cindy Feliks's stepmother, had one of the worst experiences of any family member. She lived in Calgary and was bringing her granddaughter, Cindy's teenage niece, whom she had raised. Victim Services had agreed to pay the airfare for her and her granddaughter, and also to pay for a rental car. Kraft paid $663 for their expenses; Victim Services told her later that the task force wouldn't reimburse her for more than $74.81—Cindy's teenage niece, Dallas, wasn't considered a relative and the money would have to be saved for Cindy's teenage daughter, Theresa. Kraft was livid. "I am a retired single parent living on a fixed income with a teenager to raise with no outside help," she said later in a letter to Vancouver police chief Jamie Graham, adding that the families had been promised reimbursement of up to $3,000 for expenses to attend court hearings.

But it was what happened in court that upset Kraft more than the financial problems she faced. She arrived on March 24 without any idea of what had gone on there a few days earlier. A police officer named Julie-Anne Lanctot, a member of the task force, had testified that in late November 2002 she had pulled packages of wrapped meat from one of Willie Pickton's freezers. Some of the meat was ground, some was in solid pieces like a roast. The packages were wrapped in clear plastic bags, supermarket plastic bags or brown butcher's paper. Lanctot had drilled core samples out of each one. Tests on the fourteen meat samples showed that eight of them were human tissue. Six bags of ground meat, she testified, came from the body of Cindy Feliks, and two bags came from the body of Inga Hall. The ground meat was pale and fatty, like cheap hamburger; it was also maggoty.

While Pickton had been charged with the murder of Inga Hall, he had not yet been charged with the death of Cindy Feliks. When Marilyn Kraft arrived in court four days after Lanctot's testimony, Derrill Prevett was questioning David Morrissette, a senior DNA scientist working in the RCMP's forensic laboratory in Vancouver. He was going through the DNA testing done on the samples described by Julie Lanctot. Kraft sat there listening to the scientific evidence, all of which must have sounded rather arcane to an untrained ear. But anyone would have understood when Morrissette began answering Prevett's questions about "samples taken from ground meat or tissue found in freezer XD-2." Kraft sat there rigid, surprised, shocked, not at all sure what they were talking about, but nervous.

About an hour later, after the morning break, Morrissette listened to Prevett's statement that when he was dealing with a bucket from the freezer, "there were human remains inside, as well as [from] swabs taken of the handle. In both instances, the DNA there was tested and you are able to attribute the DNA profiles there to Abotsway."

"That's correct," said Morrissette.

"In addition," Prevett said, "from this freezer, ground tissue was located which was tested: 67230B and 67239B. The DNA from those you are able to attribute respectively to Feliks and Hall."

"There were a total of nine samples there. It's 67230B through 67239B."

"Yes, I beg your pardon. Yes, collectively."

"Yes."

"And these were attributed, then, to Feliks and Hall?"

"Yes."

Marilyn Kraft's eyes widened and she gasped. Her fingers shook as she pressed her hand against her mouth, trying not to cry out. Colour drained from her cheeks. It was clear she wasn't hearing anything more now; she was trying to absorb the horror of what she had just heard. As soon as the court adjourned for lunch, she got up from her seat and crept out the door.

No one had prepared her for what she might hear. At first she was shocked, but later she was furious. "This is atrocious!" she stormed in the letter she sent to Jamie Graham. There was no warning for her, nor any counselling ahead of time, she said. "How can the VPD treat the families of the victims in this regard?" And in an email to family members—they had soon begun to share experiences through email and Internet message boards—she described what happened to her in court that day. "They had to know that the witness that day would be the DNA expert . . . they did not advise me as to what the witness would be doing. When the Crown [Prevett] asked the DNA expert about #19 (which was my daughter, Cindy) I perked up as I had not been told anything about remains, bones, or what DNA was found. When the Crown asked the DNA expert about blood found in a freezer and whose it was and he replied Cindy Feliks I was fine, but when he asked about ground meat found in another freezer (like hamburger meat, 6 packages of it) it was like knocking the wind out of me." The Victim Services workers didn't try to comfort her, she said; they didn't put their arms around her or even look her way. "I have to wonder how they were picked for this job and why?"

Marilyn Kraft was not the only woman with a grievance; other families felt the same way: neglected, kept in the dark, pushed around, patronized and ignored. The two main Victim Services workers, Freda Ens and Marilynne Johnny, were not able to explain their side of the story to the families. The simple facts were that they were badly paid contract employees, pressured by the civil servants in charge of dealing with families, forbidden to discuss the case with them and without the authority or the budget to offer anything more than they were doing. Anytime they tried to do more, they were slapped down. The bureaucrats took credit for the churches' helping the families during the preliminary hearing, even though it was Freda Ens who had made it happen. She had not wanted her bosses to know; she was sure there would be a reprimand for exceeding her authority. On the other hand, although their civil-service masters were petty and fearful and mean, the task force investigators loved Ens and Johnny. The women always accompanied the police when they were breaking bad news to family members and they were on call at all times. And for many of the police officers, the relationship stretched back to the years before 2003 when Freda Ens, working with Marilynne Johnny, was still running the Native Liaison office out of the Vancouver Police Department's Main Street headquarters.

Despite security worries, because of the publication ban the preliminary hearing motored along efficiently without incident. News outlets couldn't publish any of the testimony, so most of them pulled their reporters out of the courtroom and reassigned them to other stories. CTV tried to keep student interns there, but only rarely were there journalists from the daily press. Some of the major news outlets pooled together to order court transcripts of each day's proceedings. A sensible move, maybe, but the reporters would miss the drama of testimony from key witnesses. All of the reporters were unhappy about being pulled out; they didn't want to miss a thing.

For Peter Ritchie's team, and setting aside the devastating forensic evidence—weapons, blood, bones, flesh, hair, DNA, personal identification documents and belongings such as clothing, jewellery and medication—there was no question that the most dangerous witnesses would be Lynn Ellingsen, Sandra Gail Ringwald and Scott Chubb. Ellingsen arrived in court on April 7 to tell her story to Judge Stone, and this time some reporters were there to hear her. Slim and pretty and about five feet five inches tall, she wore her thick dark blond hair in a short, shaggy bob just above her collar. The deep dimples in her cheeks appeared during the very occasional times when she smiled. On the first day she wore a long sweater over black pants; when she was sworn in, her voice was low and clear.

There was another newcomer in court that day: a tall, well-dressed man in his late fifties or early sixties, balding, with white hair, glasses, a large nose and a face devoid of expression. He walked in with Adrian Brooks, Patrick McGowan and Peter Ritchie and sat with them at the defence table. This was the first time the defence team had brought in a new member; he was introduced to the judge as Richard Brooks. A few reporters perked up; his reputation was well-known to anyone who covered the crime beat. Brooks was married to Marilyn Sandford and had acted for a wide range of criminal defendants, including members of the Hells Angels. "He's the guy they bring in when they need to destroy a witness," someone said. "He'll kill Ellingsen."

Pickton looked up as Ellingsen was sworn in, and she shifted in her chair trying to avoid his steady glare. Her panicky eyes darted everywhere until she decided to focus on the judge himself. Under gentle questioning from Mike Petrie, she told Judge Stone that she was thirty-two and that while she'd been off drugs for a year now, she'd used cocaine and alcohol for a long time and had a criminal record for dangerous driving. She described befriending Gina Houston at Sheena's House, the women's transition house in Surrey, meeting Willie Pickton through her and eventually moving to his Port Coquitlam farm because she had nowhere else to go. While she was there she cleaned the trailer and cooked Pickton's meals. "I always cooked for both of us," she said, "but I never ate meat from the farm."

As she answered the questions, Pickton would grin and shake his head. When she began to weep as she talked about the time Pickton had hired her former boyfriend Ron Menard to beat up Andy Bellwood, Pickton smiled. From that point on Lynn Ellingsen was an emotional wreck. "Andy was a mess," she sobbed, "and there was nothing I could do."

Her next story was the account of driving with Willie to New Westminster and then to Vancouver to pick up drugs for her and a prostitute for him. As Mike Petrie took her through her story, she stumbled and cried; again and again Judge Stone told her to compose herself, take a drink of water, start again. When Petrie asked her to tell the court what happened after they returned to the farm, Ellingsen began to dab at her eyes again. Soon she broke down completely. "I can't . . ." she wept. Petrie tried to help by breaking down the story into small sections. "Was she carrying a purse?" he asked. "Did you leave the room at any time?"

Ellingsen tried to think. She cried harder. She wiped her eyes and blew her nose. Finally she said that Willie had told her, "Let's get the show on the road. Who's first?" and then took the woman into his bedroom. Ellingsen said she went into her room and smoked the crack they'd bought in the Downtown Eastside when they picked the woman up. Quietly but firmly, Petrie guided her along the narrative line of her story. The judge waited patiently while she blew her nose and dabbed at her eyes. The spectators in the room sat silent, afraid to breathe, the only sound the soft scrape of pens and pencils racing over reporters' notebooks.

Finally Ellingsen said that she'd heard a noise, a noise like a scream, and when she walked out to see what had happened there was no one in the trailer. The only light was coming in through the kitchen window from the slaughterhouse, which Ellingsen called the barn. It was where they slaughtered the pigs, she explained. "I walked to the barn . . ." She blew her nose and began crying again.

"I know this is difficult," Petrie said gently. Everyone waited.

"So I started to approach the barn—there was this really rude smell . . . awful . . ." The sobbing began again. She stopped for a minute and stared at the wall behind the judge. She took a deep breath. "I got to the front door of the barn . . . pushed the front door open . . . and all I could see were these legs . . . feet dangling . . ."

Willie Pickton smiled. The courtroom fell completely silent. The only sound was Lynn Ellingsen's weeping.

Judge Stone was patient with her. He offered her water and breaks and kind words, but he was unyielding. "Just have some water and we'll give you a few seconds. You're going to have to get through this, so you might as well start right now. There's some water there. Just take a drink."

Ellingsen would stare at him, pull herself together and continue with her testimony, describing the blood, the smells, the black hair on the metal table, the pile of human entrails she'd seen. And she talked about Willie Pickton threatening her if she said a word to anyone. It was difficult for her and it was difficult for everyone else sitting in the courtroom. People had little to say to one another during the breaks. When Petrie finished taking Ellingsen through her testimony, he asked if her life had changed since that time.

"Yes," she replied. "I'm clean over a year now. I can work now— it's been nine months—and I'm good at my job. I can maintain myself and see my son. What I seen was wrong. Very wrong. It could have been me." Once again, as she looked at Judge Stone, the tears began to roll down her face. "I was more fortunate than the other ladies. Than the one that I seen. It was terrible. I live with this every day."

After a ten-minute break Richard Brooks got to his feet. Keeping his hands in his pockets, occasionally rocking back and forth on his feet, he quickly broadcast his strategy in a high, strident voice. Because she was an addict and had been on drugs during the period she was describing, she was "addled," her recollections were "muddled," she was in a "drug-fog"—altogether a completely unreliable witness. Pickton watched, his arms folded across his chest, smiling. One by one, Brooks tested her on the statements she'd made to the police about her experiences with Willie Pickton.

"You told Corporal Dhillon you were not in Willie's room," he said. Petrie jumped to his feet and forced Brooks to read out her whole statement. What she meant, said Petrie, was that she had a room of her own and never slept in Willie's room.

The sparring between Ellingsen and Brooks went on. After Willie's arrest, she had said, she held information back from the police because she was afraid he would be released. She had admitted again and again that she was an addict but she refused to agree when Brooks hissed at her that she had been hallucinating, that she hadn't seen what she claimed to have seen. "Everything was in a fog?" Brooks asked, sneering.

"Not everything, no," she replied.

Again and again Brooks attacked her for her addictions. And one by one he went through a list of people who had taken drugs with her—all the people, from former boyfriends to other women she knew, even Gina Houston. "Have I left anybody out?" he demanded.

"I'm an addict. You probably left out a few," she retorted.

By this time the reporters and others in the courtroom were watching this pitched battle with fascination. Although Ellingsen wept, would look only at the judge and needed frequent breaks for water and tissues, she did not give in to Brooks's tactical bullying. Although he was doing the best job he could for his client, who was smirking in his glass box, Brooks lost the respect of his audience. Ellingsen was a fighter, and she displayed a certain feisty dignity that had people rooting for her.

"You were hospitalized as a result of drug use," he sneered.

"I was in hospital because I was beat up," she retorted. After arguing over the reasons for her being in hospital, Brooks said he should have been given her medical records. He wanted them now. Petrie objected right away and Judge Stone asked Ellingsen to take a break. A police officer took her out of the courtroom while Petrie argued against Brooks's demands for her records. When Judge Stone sided with the prosecutor, Ellingsen returned to the witness stand.

"Do you recall telling Gina Houston, either at that time or at some later time, that you were—that you had been institutionalized because you were experiencing paranoid delusions and cocaine psychosis as a result of your crack usage? Do you recall telling Gina that?"

"No, I don't," replied Ellingsen. "That wasn't part of my life that I liked to share with people. That was pretty confidential."

"You recall telling Ron Menard that?"

"Ron Menard I was with for twelve years. Yes."

For three days Lynn Ellingsen tried to deal with Richard Brooks's questions. He took her, minute by minute, word by word, through everything she had told the police and others about what she had seen in the barn, about her past use of drugs, about her sexual relations with several men, about her history of theft and her criminal record, about her failure to be a good mother to her son, about her parents' inability to cope with her addictions, and more. It was excruciating for her and for almost everyone in the room, except for Willie Pickton, who was enjoying every minute of it. But she never backed down about what had happened the night she and Pickton drove into Vancouver, picked up a woman in the Downtown Eastside and returned to the farm. Nor did she back down on what she saw in the barn later that night.

At the end of the third day, Brooks made one last attempt. "And you would agree with me, because you were so high when you went into that barn, that there is a possibility—perhaps a slim one, but nonetheless a possibility—that because of all this crack that you smoked and the alcohol that you consumed, that you're mistaken about what you think you saw that night in the barn. You would agree with that, that that's a possibility because you were so high that you're mistaken about what you saw. You would agree with that, wouldn't you?"

Ellingsen looked at the judge. She still had some fight in her. "I wouldn't, Your Honour."

It was over. She shuffled out of the courtroom in tears, escorted by a policewoman.

CHAPTER FORTY-EIGHT

TELLING TALES: ANDY BELLWOOD, SANDRA GAIL RINGWALD AND GINA HOUSTON

A few minutes after Lynn Ellingsen left the courtroom, Andrew Bellwood, now thirty-two years old and still looking like a well-heeled college student, was in her place, swearing to tell the truth. Once again Mike Petrie started the proceedings by taking him through his story for Judge Stone to hear: his criminal record, his drug use, his friendship with Ellingsen and the few months he stayed with Willie Pickton at the farm. Bellwood recounted the story of Pickton trying to talk him into going to find a prostitute and how he had refused; he also repeated Pickton's story of how he killed women by garrotting them with a belt or wire and then disposed of their bodies. Finally he described the beating he received from Ellingsen's boyfriend, Ron Menard, and her ex-husband, Ross Caldwell, after Pickton accused him of stealing tools. He explained that he had gone home to Nanaimo, on Vancouver Island, where his mother took care of him, and he talked about his efforts to kick his drug habits and find work.

Bellwood unknowingly revealed the small world that revolved around Willie Pickton and the farm. After he recovered from the beating, he had found a job on a fishing boat in Nanaimo owned by a man named Paul Campbell, whom he described as "Sandra's husband." Sandra? That would be Sandra Gail Ringwald, who followed him on the witness stand a few days later.

Petrie finished with Bellwood near the end of the day. To the relief of the people in the courtroom, Adrian Brooks began the cross-examination. Tough, probing, repetitive to the point of putting many in the courtroom to sleep, Adrian Brooks was still a welcome change from the other Mr. Brooks.

Bellwood explained that he had worked with Paul Campbell between 1993 and 1998 and he remembered talking to Sandra Ringwald. Although Ringwald told him that she'd had an altercation with Pickton, "she did not describe it as an assault," he assured Judge Stone. He saw her once more in Vancouver about a year later. Bellwood testified that she did not appear to be under the influence of drugs when he spoke to her, nor did the farm come up in their conversation.

Brooks took Bellwood through the details of his problems with the police, the charges against him and his history as a cocaine addict, and tried valiantly, over several hours, to make him admit he was wrong in his statements about Willie Pickton. Bellwood was often upset. His eyes would occasionally well up and he'd have to stop to compose himself. Sometimes he was angry. But he didn't back down on his story: He was staying in Willie's trailer in March 1999, and one night, while he and Willie were watching television in Willie's bedroom, Willie suggested going to get a prostitute. Bellwood testified that he was sitting in a chair and Willie was lying on his bed. Willie reached under the bed and pulled out a set of handcuffs. He put those on the bed, reached under it again and brought out a dark brown leather belt. The third time he retrieved a piece of piano wire—"a fine-grade wire, fine braid, goldish . . . greenish," Bellwood said—spliced at each end to make loops. And he described the way Pickton had showed him how he brought the women's arms behind them, handcuffed them, put the belt around their necks, put the end of the belt through the buckle and then pulled it tight. He had also demonstrated how he strangled them with the wire, Bellwood said.

Pickton's preliminary hearing usually ran from Monday through Thursday; Friday was a day off so the lawyers could get ready for the next week and deal with issues that had come up in court. So it wasn't until the following Monday, April 14, that everyone was back in front of Judge Stone. The first on his feet was Richard Brooks. A new statement from Ellingsen had come in from the police, one they'd taken from her four months earlier, and he was outraged that he hadn't seen it before cross-examining her. He wanted her back right away and he wanted to question her again.

Mike Petrie jumped up to object. New material was coming in all the time, he said, and it went to the defence as soon as it was transcribed. In this case he had given it to Pickton's lawyers immediately, but it had nothing in it they hadn't seen before. To bring Ellingsen back from out of town, especially when she had been so traumatized by the questioning a few days earlier, was unreasonable. This was a preliminary hearing, not a trial. The judge didn't need every scrap of information, only enough to decide whether or not to send Pickton to trial. "So, with the greatest of respect, it seems to me that to have this particular vulnerable witness come back and be subjected to further cross-examination . . . would be inappropriate in this preliminary hearing," he said. "It simply doesn't advance the process."

Judge Stone seemed to agree with Petrie, but then he said, "The difficulty I have is that the witness is not an ordinary witness. The witness is an eyewitness to a murder in the slaughterhouse and the evidence that she gave, as chilling as it is, is very, very important from the point of view of this case." A few days later Stone ruled that Ellingsen should return for further cross-examination. It never happened. Other witnesses, other events intervened, and Lynn Ellingsen did not see Richard Brooks again during the preliminary hearing.

Without question Ellingsen was a key witness, perhaps the most important of all. But it would be a difficult call if she were put up against Sandra Gail Ringwald, who came in next on that same morning. This time a new lawyer who had joined the prosecution team, Geoff Baragar, would begin; Peter Ritchie, for the first time since the prelim-inary hearing had started, would handle the cross-examination.

Baragar had graduated from McGill University and obtained his master's degree from the London School of Economics before going on to study law at UBC. A bright student who'd won several awards, he'd articled with the province's Supreme Court as well as with a firm in Melbourne, Australia, on a Commonwealth Scholarship law program. From 1992 to 1998 he'd been a Crown counsel in Port

Coquitlam before moving to the provincial attorney general's commercial crime section, where he spent six years working on an automobile insurance fraud investigation. His colleagues on the team considered him their best legal scholar. Murder was something new for him when he joined Mike Petrie's trial team in 2003. Like Peter Ritchie and Adrian Brooks, Baragar is competitive and loves the outdoors; he is a sailor, a ski instructor and a licensed pilot, among other things. Managing this next witness was another challenge for him and a significant event in his career, but he looked relaxed as he chatted to his colleagues, waiting for Ringwald to arrive.

When Sandra Ringwald walked in wearing a blue sweatsuit with a pink and blue tie-dyed T-shirt on underneath, little plastic clips holding back her long brown hair, she looked like a teenage waif. As soon as she sat down she began to swivel back and forth in her chair. In contrast to Ellingsen and Bellwood, she seemed interested in what was going on around her. And as Baragar took her through her date with Pickton on March 21, 1997, there were no tears, no hesitation. It was only when she began to describe the moments after Pickton handcuffed her wrist that her voice sped up, becoming ragged and hoarse. Pickton listened carefully to every word and just shook his head.

Baragar took her through the rest of the attack. She told him how Pickton had tried to calm her by stroking her wrist and how she had fought him and inched backwards into the kitchen to reach for the knife she'd seen earlier. Still swinging back and forth on her chair, she looked at Baragar and said, "I slit his throat."

It was time for a coffee break. Outside at the snack bar, where sisters Lou and Irene were handing out cookies and making change, people were smiling and shaking their heads. What this case had lacked so far was a hero. Now they'd found one.

When everyone came back into court, Peter Ritchie was up, ready to start asking questions. He began by asking her about her drug use. Ringwald replied that she was on a methadone program and took it once a day.

"When was the last time you had methadone?" Ritchie asked.

"Yesterday . . . about eleven—ten thirty, quarter to eleven."

"Today is Monday. When did you last do heroin?"

"When did I last do heroin? Probably late Saturday night." Ringwald explained that it cost her $20 every time she bought a point—"two-tenths of a gram"—and she paid for it by selling cocaine. She no longer worked as a prostitute.

"When did you start doing heroin?" Ritchie asked.

"Probably in the early '90s."

"So would you say you've had a heroin addiction now for well over ten years?"

"Off and on, yeah."

Ringwald told Ritchie she'd made money when she worked on a fishing boat and by shoplifting, but she hadn't shoplifted since 1988, when she went to jail for it. Ritchie wanted to know more. "What sort of theft? Is it only shoplifting we're talking about here?"

"Yeah. And we used to break into cigarette cars."

"I beg your pardon?"

"Break into the cars that deliver the cigarettes to the stores."

"You would steal cigarettes from cars."

"Yeah."

"Any other ways that you supported your habit?" asked Ritchie.

"No."

"Okay. Now, you mentioned that you were in jail. When were you last in jail?"

"I got six months, I think it was in—I'm not even sure which year, '99, 2000. I'm not sure which year."

"Okay. What jail were you in?"

"BCCW [Burnaby Correctional Centre for Women]."

"How long were you in jail?"

"Six months."

"Okay," said Ritchie, "and what was that for?"

"Theft over, stealing a police car and dangerous driving."

"Stealing a police car. Okay. Did you get methadone when you were in prison?"

"No."

"Did you have an addiction when you were in prison?"

"My first six months I didn't have an addiction but I did do drugs. My second time, no."

"You did the drugs heroin and cocaine?"

"Just heroin."

"Heroin is in the prison."

"Yeah."

"Okay. And when you do heroin, do you do the same and usual amount or does the amount that you take vary?"

"I usually do the same amounts."

"And that amount is what?"

"About a point."

"And how many times a day would you do a point?"

"Sometimes one, sometimes four."

"And when you do heroin, do you mix it with cocaine?"

"Sometimes. Not—not like I used to. Not very often. Maybe once a week I might mix it with coke."

"Maybe once a week you'd mix it with coke."

"Yeah."

"Explain how you do that."

"Like, what do you mean?"

"How do you fix it up? How do you mix it with coke and how do you fix it up? It's a speedball. The prosecutor referred to a speedball here. That's what you're talking about here, isn't it?"

Ringwald stared at him. She was getting a kick out of this conversation, and if Pickton's lawyer wanted her recipe for a speedball, she was happy to oblige. Her new fans in the courtroom watched this performance carefully. She was a character, cute and interesting for sure. But when was Pickton's lawyer going to take her apart? He seemed to be in no hurry.

"Just dump 'em both into the needle," she answered. "Shake it up and do it."

"Okay. And how much heroin, how much cocaine do you put in the needle and how do you mix it?"

"About a point of heroin and a half a point of cocaine."

"Okay. Do you warm it up at all or you do not?"

"Mm-hmm."

"How do you do that?"

"Well, when it's in your syringe, just take the lighter to it and warm it up."

"Sorry, once in the syringe you take the lighter to it and—?"

"Take the lighter to it and warm it up."

"Okay. And what part of your body do you usually inject it on, or is there a usual anymore?"

"My leg."

"You did a speedball when you were at the Pickton residence."

"Mm-hmm."

Peter Ritchie was one of the most experienced criminal lawyers in British Columbia. He had defended Willie Pickton in 1997 when he was charged with attempted murder for stabbing Ringwald. He had billed Pickton $80,000 for his work at the time. But now, in this small courtroom in Port Coquitlam, he seemed more interested in getting to know this woman than in destroying her on the stand. While he kept a poker face, he was well aware of the slight twitches on a few lips, including Judge Stone's, as Ringwald answered his questions. Ritchie had a hard time keeping from smiling himself. Finally he took her to the period in the New Westminster hospital when she was recovering from her fight with Pickton.

Ringwald told Ritchie she had talked to the police again in 2002, right after they arrested Pickton on February 5. They had tracked her down at the Wings Hotel in the Downtown Eastside. And this is when it was clear to everyone in the room that she had been a valuable asset to the police.

Ritchie returned again and again to her drug use, trying to wring from her an admission that she had been too high to be sure of her facts. She didn't back down. While she was still in hospital, she said, she'd told her husband the same story exactly. "But not every little detail." That didn't take place until she was back with Paul Campbell and their two children at his home in North Vancouver. Ritchie went back to her drug use, and when she admitted she sometimes felt paranoid, he saw his chance.

"You do crazy things when you're paranoid once in a while?"

"Sometimes I did, yeah."

"What kind of stuff?"

"Steal a police car."

"Steal a police car? What did you steal the police car for?"

"I was running from him."

"From who?"

"I thought he was after me. Willie."

"You thought Willie was chasing you, so you stole a police car to get away?"

"Yeah, I'd do anything to get away."

"And, in fact, he wasn't chasing you. It was the speedball?"

"It was the psychosis, yes."

"Yeah. Okay. How far did you get with the police car?"

"A block."

"Then they stopped you and arrested you?"

"No, I hit a wall."

"Had the police stopped you to ask you questions or something like that? Or what prompted you to steal it?"

"I was running out of the alley down the street yelling, 'Help me! Help me!' And I guess I ran towards them and they were ignoring me, so I jumped in." The police, she explained, were searching a man, and they ignored her. So she jumped into their car, sped down the alley and hit a wall. She woke up in the hospital with a broken ankle.

It was all because she was paranoid about Pickton and was doing speedballs.

"When did you stop?" asked Ritchie. "Was it after the police-car incident, that that was sort of the end of the line, or did you do speedballs after that?"

"It was the second," she said, in a matter-of-fact tone. "The second cop car."

"The second cop car? You better explain that."

"Well, I stole two, twice. It was after I got out from doing the six months from the second one when I basically quit doing speedballs. I did the odd one, but not too often."

"I just want to see if I've got this straight here. You stole two police cars. Are these both in Vancouver?"

"Yes."

"And the incident that you were thinking that you were running from Willie here, was that the first incident or the second incident you stole a police car?"

"That was the second one."

"The second."

"But the reason I stole the first one was the same reason."

"So the second incident, did you have to go to jail for six months as well?"

"Yes."

By this time Ritchie must have realized he'd made a mistake. No one was shocked by Ringwald's stories; instead, by now most people in the courtroom had broad smiles on their faces. Willie was laughing, and even Judge Stone was having difficulty keeping a straight face. Sandra Gail Ringwald had won the hearts of everyone in the room, and Ritchie tried hard to wrest back his control of the cross-examination. He failed. All of his questions elicited the same kind of short, straightforward answers. The break couldn't come soon enough for him, and officials whisked this cheerful little witness away.

After they returned to the courtroom, she continued to tell her stories about various trips to the hospital, her efforts to get the police to help her and her drug use. Mercifully there was a lunch break, but she was back on the stand in the afternoon. Ritchie tried again to wrest control of the interview away from her.

"Ms. Ringwald, did you tell the truth about everything this morning?" he asked.

"Yes."

In order to take Ringwald through the experience she had with Pickton in his trailer, he began with the moment Pickton had picked her up in his red truck at the corner of Princess Street and Cordova in the Downtown Eastside. It was around ten or eleven at night, she said. Ringwald talked about her day, her visit to the casino and how she had lost money there and was hoping to recoup her losses. When Pickton came along, she saw her chance. Even though she balked at going as far as Port Coquitlam with him, she finally agreed.

She described having sex with him, noticing the big roll of plastic sheeting beside the sleeping bag they were on, getting dressed, using the bathroom and finally trying to use his phone to call her current boyfriend (she was separated from Paul Campbell) to let him know she was on her way home. She told Ritchie about how Pickton tried to stop her making the call, how he put one handcuff on her and how she then began to fight.

"Can you generally describe what you did?" Ritchie asked. "Did you try to hit him, did you claw him, kick him?"

"I don't recall. I just went nuts, I guess."

"You went nuts. Well, there's no way that you can describe the manner in which you fought him?"

"No. I was throwing things at him, keeping him away from me."

"Okay. This is inside the trailer?"

"Yes."

"Was he fighting back?"

"Yes."

"How?"

"He had a big long stick."

"Was he hitting you with it?"

"Trying to."

"Did any blows land?"

"I don't recall."

"Do you know what stuff you were throwing at him?"

"I know I threw a plant."

"Okay. Anything else?"

"I don't recall what."

"And then what was the next thing? You grabbed the knife?"

"Yes."

"And when you had the knife, did you try to slash his jugular, his throat?"

"I didn't try, I did."

"Well, was there lots of blood when you did that?"

"I believe so. But he covered it with a rag."

"Okay. Do you remember events clearly after that? Because I don't understand when you answered the prosecutor's questions and you said you blacked out, or something similar. I'm trying to figure out when that was."

"It was—it was after I slashed his throat, and I remember struggling again, and then that was it." When she regained consciousness, she told Ritchie, she found Pickton's arms around her; he had collapsed and was unconscious. "I just slid out from under him," she said. She knew she was badly hurt; all she could think about was getting away. She described staggering down the lane to the main road and trying to get help in the house across the road; she remembered the couple driving by and coming back to help her. "I asked them to help me, to get me to the hospital, that I'm bleeding to death."

"Did you ever speak to those people ever again?"

"No."

"And what did they say when you asked them to help you?"

"I remember him saying, 'Don't stab us,' and then that's when I threw [away] the knife. And then he got out and she got on the—the cell, and he was cleaning out the back seat. Like, I think there was a briefcase he was putting in the trunk and that."

"Okay. So you got in the back seat of the car, right?"

"Mm-hmm. And he told me to lie down."

"Can you remember those things pretty well, or were you too upset to remember things?"

"No, I—like, I basically remember them."

"You'd say, given the circumstances, you were pretty calm, or do you think you were very excited?"

"I was probably—I was probably, like, not really badly excited. I was more—I was more concerned about dying."

The only thing she could remember later on was waking up in the hospital. "I remember screaming and yelling at the doctors and swearing at them, telling them to hurry up, I was going to die," she told Ritchie. "And then I blacked out. I went out. And then I come to again, and then the nurse was rubbing my shoulder, saying, 'It's going to be okay. You're going to be okay.' And then I remember the anesthetic, or the doctor, whatever, told me I was going to smell burnt toast or something, and he said, 'Count from one hundred backwards,' and I remember saying 'ninety-eight' and that was it."

Ritchie asked Ringwald a few more questions but no one was paying attention; they were looking at this little person, still swinging back and forth in her chair, who had captivated every one of them for many hours. It was the first time there had been someone to cheer for, someone who had, without realizing it, brought a sliver of hope and humour to this long-running nightmare.

Anyone going by the Pickton farm in mid-April could see that there were now great bald patches on the property. As the searchers took apart each building and shed, the debris was carted away. The soil under the building would be removed, sifted and searched and then hauled back to its original location. Pickton's trailer? Gone. The workshop/garage? Gone. The slaughterhouse, a place where even the hardiest souls shuddered as they worked, had also been torn down and, on the last day, after workers had hauled away the debris, demolished. The searchers gathered at the site for a brief ceremony of remembrance while a piper played a lament.

When these buildings disappeared, the picking belts, now staffed by 102 students, were much more visible from the road. Bright lamps strung overhead helped the students see better on gloomy days and into the evenings; the huge roof kept them dry. Gerry Murdoch continued spreading grass seed on the mounds of dirt in an effort to make the place less terrifying, keeping the trucks moving and working with municipal contractors, who were putting new drains through the property and building up the road surface in front, on Dominion Avenue. There were constant demands for more storage and work space. When the ATCO trailers used as offices filled up, the RCMP moved double-wide mobile homes into the parking lot behind the office building in Surrey that housed the task force headquarters. Then they outgrew that space as well and moved into a building next door.

Pickton's preliminary hearing had been running nearly four months but it was time to stop for a while. Both sides needed to digest the latest lab reports from the task force. The Crown needed to get its next round of witnesses prepared; the defence team needed to get ready to destroy the Crown's arguments and its witnesses too. Judge Stone agreed on a two-month break, but before they could leave Courtroom 2 there was a pair of witnesses to hear: Gina Houston and Scott Chubb.

Houston came in on April 16, 2003, the day after Sandra Gail Ringwald completed her testimony. Houston spied Willie Pickton right away and waggled her fingers at him in a flirtatious hello. Pickton smiled and gave a little wave back. Except for the times Mike Petrie had asked witnesses to formally identify Pickton in court, it was the first time any witness had acknowledged his presence. No family member or friend had yet come in to lend support; their designated seats remained empty.

Houston, wearing slacks and a long black jacket with a hood, was looking very pretty. Slim, with long, dark hair, she has a classic oval face with a slightly square jaw, full, wide lips and a straight nose. Her large, dark eyes had deep hollows under them. She seemed jumpy and she sniffed all the time as she spoke. She was thirty-five years old, she told Mike Petrie, and she had three children, now three, thirteen and sixteen.

Although she'd met Pickton earlier, it wasn't until she moved to Port Coquitlam in 1993 that they became close friends. He helped her pay bills and rent, he bought groceries for her, even gave her about $15,000 to $20,000 over the years. Her kids went to his place with her, rode his horses, stayed in his trailer with her. In spite of this, she said, they were just friends. They'd never had any kind of romantic relationship despite casual chats about getting married, even having kids. "Willie talked about buying me a ring," she said. "Talked about buying me a bunch of things. Never went anywhere."

Petrie hesitated. "Did you want more than a friendship?" he asked.

"Yes and no. Willie was always so stable," she said. "And I wasn't, right? And he was always so hard-working. He told me . . . being a workaholic, you don't always have time for someone else. And I guess I'm a pretty demanding person."

Houston said she had visited him in jail when he was first arrested, often three or four times a week, but that ended in late March 2002. She didn't say that a furious Pickton had cut her off because she was talking to reporters, but she did tell Petrie she had given interviews to two CBC reporters, television's Darrow MacIntyre and radio reporter Yvette Brend.

During her hours on the stand with Petrie, Houston talked about learning to slaughter and butcher animals on the farm as she worked with Pickton and Pat Casanova. She was able to describe the tools they used, including a reciprocating power saw with a long, thin blade. And she often went with Pickton to the rendering plant, where he'd dump two or three barrels of animal parts each trip. She never lifted a barrel herself, she said. "They stunk too much. I think he used the BobCat to lift them onto the back of his truck." When he got to the plant, she explained, he just shimmied the barrels to the edge of the truck's flat deck and tipped them into a huge vat the size of a swimming pool. "I don't know where it goes from there," she said.

"Willie had been going there so many years he just waved at them, went to one of the open docks, backed in, dumped the stuff and we left."

When Petrie asked Houston about women who had come to Willie's place during the years she was close to him, she said she could remember many of them, including Lisa Yelds, Dinah Taylor and Lynn Ellingsen. When Ellingsen moved in, she said, "Willie showed up with a dozen roses at my door, worried that I would be upset. He told me she was just messed up and that he wanted to help her out. He wanted to get her clean so she could go into treatment." But she also testified that he wanted to get rid of Ellingsen because she was always asking him for money, even after she moved out. "He told me that she had found his court papers from the Sandra [Ringwald] incident and was trying to . . . extort money from him. He also asked me to get rid of Lynn for him. He wanted her to be gone permanently from his life."

"And what did he ask you to do then?" Petrie asked.

Well, Willie had bought her a station wagon, and he had a plan for what he wanted in return. "He asked me to take her out partying and help her to OD [overdose] . . . he would buy the dope. He wanted her offed permanently. Because it could cost a lot for lawyers and he was worried about what people would think." Houston prattled on, sniffing all the time. Behind his glass wall, Pickton stared at her in shock, frowning, his smile gone.

It seems Lisa Yelds was another threat: "Same with Lee," she told Petrie. He wanted her killed too, Houston said. Yelds scoffed at this statement when she heard about it later; she said Houston was jealous of her long friendship with Pickton.

What about the people on the missing women list? Did she know any of them? Petrie asked. "Maybe twenty of them," Houston replied. "Maybe thirty." But the only one she thought she might have seen at the farm was Sereena Abotsway.

The day before Pickton was arrested, said Houston, they had a conversation. "He looked at me. He told me he loved me. And he told me, 'There's only one way out of this for us.'" Houston began to cry. Pickton watched her carefully, expressionless.

"If you need a drink of water, take your time," said Petrie.

"Just take your time," agreed Judge Stone.

Houston sobbed for a few seconds and then calmed down. "I asked what he meant. He said, 'There's only one way out of this for us: a rope, a truck or a train.' And we had to do it before Friday because he didn't want to go to jail."

She had thought he was joking, Houston told the court. But then she saw he was starting to cry. All she could think of was that this had something to do with Mona Wilson, the last woman to go missing; she had disappeared on November 23, 2001. Houston said she had been talking to him on the phone that day* and heard a woman screaming in the background. "I asked him if that was Mona and he said, 'Yeah.' And he told me he did everything he could to stop them from hurting her, but he couldn't. And I asked him if the police are going to find anything."

"Yes," Willie replied.

"Where?"

"In the piggery."

"I asked him what was next to Mona and he said, 'There's two or three or four, maybe five.' I asked him who. He said, 'Three that weren't on the [missing women] list.'" Houston then told Petrie she had asked Willie if the police would find anything else; all he said, she testified, was, "'At the top of the loft.' I never asked him what he meant." And she said he told her it was all her fault. However you look at this, she said he told her, "It's all because of me."

"Did you have anything to do with the deaths of any women at the Pickton property?" Petrie asked.

"No, sir."

*Later in her testimony Houston said she thought she heard the woman screaming at the end of the first week of December. She was not sure of the date.

"Had you anything to do with the disposal of any people at the Pickton property?"

"No, sir."

As the day wore on, Gina Houston's testimony became more confusing. It was as if she regretted many of the things she'd said. And after Marilyn Sandford started cross-examining her, it became even more difficult to understand her. But she did say again that she had called Pickton at his office in the trailer in early December 2001 and that two people had entered the trailer while she was talking to him. She said she heard people fighting, a woman screaming, and Pickton telling everyone to "stop it." She thought the woman was Nancy Plasman, a flag girl who hadn't been paid for several months and needed a place to stay; she had been living in the trailer. Pickton, Houston insisted, was trying to stop the fight.

Sandford spent several hours taking Houston back through her years as a prostitute, alcoholic, drug addict, drug dealer and even pimp, running a brothel on Fourth Avenue in Vancouver. She also went through her early days with Pickton—when they met, what he was like, how he treated her.

"You gained some prominence among drug-trafficking circles and became fairly well-known in those circles, correct?" asked Sandford. "You were selling dope to a lot of people."

"Yes, I was."

Houston also admitted that she often supplied women to Pat Casanova when he needed what she liked to call "feminine companionship." Casanova would tell her what he was looking for in a woman, right down to her hair colour, and Houston would try to oblige. One woman was so perfect for Casanova that she became his companion for a long time.

There was friction, though, whenever a new woman came into Pickton's life; Houston resented them and she admitted that to Sandford. True, she didn't like Lynn Ellingsen, but the one she detested and feared was Dinah Taylor, who became her chief rival for Willie's attention and money. Houston told Sandford what happened one day: "She got mad and she told Willie she didn't want him to do any favours, she didn't want me coming around, she didn't want me talking to Willie. We had a good argument about that one day and I said, 'You know what, Dinah? Just like, you know, all you girls come and go, you all rip him off and leave. And I'm still here.'"

Gina Houston's testimony was tantalizing. She knew so many of the women who'd disappeared from the Downtown Eastside, even the transsexual prostitute Kellie Little, who had rented a room from her in Coquitlam for a while. She also knew Scott Chubb well; he had rented her basement suite for a time and they'd had sex together—although she testified that he had forced her. "And the pain was too great so I finally gave in and told him to do whatever he wanted to and then leave." Chubb had lots of girls, she told Sandford. "Most of them were hookers."

But because her testimony was a disconnected, stream-of-consciousness effort to distance Pickton from any evil and to blame everything on other people, it was difficult to believe almost anything she said.

As she learned about the DNA being found on the Pickton property, Erin McGrath, Leigh Miner's sister, was sure the police would find Leigh's DNA in Dave Pickton's old house on the farm. Leigh had disappeared in January 1994, when she thought Willie Pickton might still be living in the old family farmhouse. The farmhouse would be the last building to be searched, so McGrath and her mother, Doreen Hanna, expected—eventually—to hear something. There was nothing.

McGrath finally decided it was time to visit the place where she was sure her sister had died. She took the ferry over from Nanaimo in early May 2003, when other family members were gathering at the farm site, along with a local choir, to commemorate Mother's Day. "Twenty students gathered around and started to sing. Because of the juxtaposition of goodness in a place of evil, of children who had the strength of character to come to a place where countless murders have been committed, to sing for us and to Praise the Lord, I heard the words in those songs, all of which I had heard many times before, as though I was hearing them for the first time. I cannot explain the feeling adequately but it will never leave me; the despair was replaced by the power of praising Jesus through song and I knew this was a time I will carry in my heart when I succumb to the belief evil is powerful. It is only if we let it. If we stand and face evil and praise Jesus we win, plain and simple."

Still, in spite of her strong faith, Erin could not forgive the way she and her family had been treated by the police for so many years. "My big sister, Leigh, became a heroin and crack cocaine addict dependent on prostitution to support her lifestyle. Couldn't happen in a good family? It could happen to anyone's family. It took me years to come to terms with who my sister was and find compassion in my heart instead of disdain and it took me years to find a way to love her for who she was instead of disliking her because she was not the sister I wanted her to be."

Now, she said, she was finally able to say goodbye to Leigh. But she held out little hope for discovery of her sister's remains. "If they're sifting through dirt to find our loved ones and the farm has sold dirt in the form of landfill as a business, then the human remains of our loved ones could be spread throughout the Lower Mainland," she wrote. "We'll never have our answer. We deserve an answer."

CHAPTER FORTY-NINE

THE LAST WITNESSES

Soon after the police arrested Willie Pickton the second time, on February 22, 2002, Scott Chubb received death threats, followed by a near miss when a car sped up and almost clipped him as he walked along a sidewalk near his home in Vancouver. When he told his police handlers, he was advised to get in his car and "get going." Although Tasha, the girlfriend with whom he had recently reconciled, had just bought $500 worth of groceries with money from the RCMP, the couple left the bags on the kitchen counter, took their son Clayton and drove east, away from Vancouver and Port Coquitlam. They ended up hiding in central British Columbia, broke and looking for work.

"I couldn't find a place to live," Chubb remembered. "We were three weeks in a hotel with no jobs, no family, no community support. They told us to talk to welfare officials. We had no funds, there was a three-week waiting period [for welfare] and we were evicted from the place we were staying."

Tasha was furious. What made her so angry was the thought of the police spending millions of dollars on this investigation but offering nothing to the man who had made Pickton's arrest possible. And nothing for his family. "I cried and screamed," she remembered, "and I used my son Clayton so [Nathan] Wells finally caved and gave us some money."

As soon as Scott Chubb finished his testimony in Port Coquitlam, he had hurried back to the little stucco bungalow that he and Tasha were renting in a small town in British Columbia's interior. The RCMP had helped him settle there, temporarily, as it turned out.

Chubb had found a job several kilometres from the town that suited him; no one knew him or anything about his role in the Pickton case. All he wanted was anonymity; he did not want to know his neighbours, did not want to work in a local business. He was very much afraid that Dave Pickton would track him down and have him killed by one of his biker friends.

Each time he came home, Chubb drove carefully up his street and looked around before he parked his truck some distance from the house, not close enough to look as if it belonged there. He would watch carefully before getting out of the truck, waiting, rolling himself a cigarette, looking for new vehicles coming down the street.

Tasha, a slim woman with dark blond hair, a wide grin and bright, intelligent eyes, knew that Chubb had warned Dave Pickton about his brother and had told him to get Willie off the street. She also knew that Hells Angels hung around the Pickton farm and she knew about their booze can across the street.

Chubb had good reason to worry. He'd heard that Dave Pickton had been trying to make a deal with the prosecution but that it fell through. He'd also heard that Willie was going to plead guilty in July 2002, but that hadn't happened either. Chubb continued to talk to RCMP constable Nathan Wells about his fears; he believed that the RCMP were going to take care of him. Soon Ted Van Overbeek, who had worked with Nathan Wells in debriefing Chubb, came to see them. Chubb liked him, partly because he was honest. There is no way we can guarantee your safety, Van Overbeek told him.

Eventually Chubb found steady work in a remote area an hour's drive from his home, and Tasha also found a job. They remained watchful but they were able to support themselves. Sometimes his friends told Chubb he deserved the $100,000 reward for the information he had given the police that led to Pickton's arrest, but other candidates for the money had also popped up.

At the head of the pack was Bill Hiscox, who hired a lawyer to help him. Hiscox claimed that his telephone tip to the police about the identification papers and women's clothes at the farm—information passed on to him by his childhood acquaintance Lisa Yelds—was what had led to Pickton's arrest. Chubb thought Hiscox's claims were absurd. He, Scott Chubb, was responsible for Pickton's arrest. However, if he were to receive the reward, he declared, he would give the money to the families of the missing women.

Willie Pickton was back in court on June 30, 2003, when the preliminary hearing resumed. This time the judge listened to days of testimony from "last-seen" witnesses, people who had been identified as the last people to see a victim before she disappeared. Most of these were friends and relatives or people such as landlords or street nurses who normally saw certain women at regular times. Vince McMurchy, Diane Rock's former boyfriend, was one of these; so was her friend Janice Edwards, who picked her up after Diane had been tied up and raped by several men in a building on the Pickton farm. During some of this testimony her husband, Darren Rock, would come to court and take his place in the family section, sometimes with one or two of his older children and always accompanied by Freda Ens or one of the other Victim Services workers. As the details spilled out, Rock and his children sat there quietly, stone-faced, looking at Pickton in his glass box.

Just as the preliminary hearing was drawing to a close, there was an abrupt change in the work schedule on the pig farm. The task force issued a press release on Sunday, July 20, to say they were sealing off an area just east of the Ruskin Bridge in Mission, on the south side of the Lougheed Highway. "This land is designated First Nations property and today the First Nations Band responsible for this area was served with the search warrant," the press release said.

Half of the anthropology students—fifty-two of them—who were working on the picking belts and in the bone pits learned they were needed to search a new location in the Fraser Valley, about thirty kilometres east of the farm. Buses took them, along with eight RCMP police divers and several task force officers, to Mission

Slough, where Jane Doe's skull had been found. The job was to search the site, a mixture of wetland, slough and groundcover about 1,150 feet long and 165 feet wide that ran along the side of the Lougheed Highway, between Mission and Vancouver, to the west.

It was a major operation. The task force moved in excavators, two of its large soil-sifting Grizzlies and a conveyor belt to dig up the soil and search it. They also had to bring in a few prebuilt wooden staircases to get people down the steeply sloped sides of the slough from the highway. And they had to put up a large white military tent with a kitchen to feed and shelter the workers and their equipment. Within days the searchers had cleared all the bushes and small trees in the search area, and the surface was covered with small yellow flags noting possible items of interest. The searchers were there for several weeks but eventually they gave up and moved back to the farm, admitting they had found no useful evidence. Jane Doe's skull, discovered in 1995, was all they had, in spite of a deep certainty that Willie Pickton had discarded human bones in this place.

The last witness, and one of the most colourful to appear during the last phase of the preliminary hearing, was Willie Pickton's pal, sixty-four-year-old Patricio Casanova. He was there to answer questions about his butchering work with Willie and his contact with women at the farm. Mike Petrie took him through the basic facts of his life: He had emigrated from the Philippines in 1975, had been married for forty-three years and had four grown children between the ages of thirty-five and forty-one. He'd been helping Willie Pickton kill and butcher small pigs on the farm for several years.

Listening to Casanova was not easy for anyone in the courtroom. Thanks to a bout with throat cancer and a subsequent operation, he'd lost his larynx. He had to press his thumb over a hole in his throat to deliver his answers, and it was difficult for anyone to understand him. The court reporter had difficulty transcribing his testimony, and Petrie had to proceed slowly and repeat Casanova's statements to make sure everyone understood what he was saying. It was an excruciating process. Casanova soon admitted that he had helped himself to some of the women who came to the farm. Petrie wanted to know if he had known they were prostitutes.

"Well, one day," replied Casanova, "they says they're going to give me a trick for so much. Then I understand that's what—"

"When they said they were going to give you a trick for so much," Petrie interrupted, "then you understood what they were. And do you remember the names of these people?"

"I remember one, maybe—Roxanne," said Casanova. Roxanne was the street name of Monique Wood, a prostitute who was not among the women who had disappeared.

"Roxanne, eh? Did you go through with it?"

"Yes, sir."

"And what kind of a sexual favour was it?"

"Well, it's a blow job."

"All right. Not sexual intercourse?"

"No."

"Any particular reason?"

"I cannot do it no more."

"All right. And to whom did you pay the money?"

"Straight to the girl."

As the questioning went on, Casanova said he had paid several other women for oral sex. One of them was a woman he called Angel but who was, in fact, Andrea Joesbury, brought to Pickton's trailer for him by Dinah Taylor. Dinah argued with Angel, Casanova said, about the $40 he was paying for sex; she wanted a share of the money. Did he see Andrea leave the farm that day? No, he replied, he couldn't remember seeing her leave. Another time Dinah brought out another woman for him called Jacquie, and she did leave. In fact, he liked Jacquie enough to help her pay rent on an apartment where he visited her from time to time.

Under cross-examination by Richard Brooks, Casanova said that he also gave money to Lynn Ellingsen. He'd met her when she still lived in the trailer; after she left he would often visit her, give her money and have sex with her. This relationship went on for years. When she needed money or he needed sex, he said, they could usually accommodate one another. And Casanova testified that, after Willie Pickton's arrest, Ellingsen often talked to him about the $100,000 reward the police had offered for information leading to the arrest of the person responsible for the disappearances of the missing women. And she liked to talk about writing a book about her experiences, Casanova added. She thought she could make some money from that as well.

Aside from detailing his relationships with women who came to the farm, Casanova answered questions about the way Willie Pickton butchered the pigs he bought at auction. He used knives, cleavers and saws, Casanova said; he also used a large grinder, kept in the slaughterhouse, to make up packages of ground pork. The ground meat and other cuts would go into plastic bags or packages in the freezer. The tool Pickton used to take apart animal carcasses, said Casanova, was a reciprocating saw, one often called a Sawzall after a popular brand, that he would use to slice lengthwise through the vertebrae of the pigs to cut them in half.

"Did you ever use a reciprocating saw on your pigs?" Derrill Prevett asked him.

"Later on, yes," Casanova replied. "About 2000, and about 2001 I start to try to use it myself." He said he'd bought a motorized band saw—which forensic technologist Tanya Dare, an expert on blood, semen and saliva, described in court as being five feet tall—to use at his home, but after cutting himself he stopped using it. The saw was important to the case because Dare had discovered a yellow waxy substance on it. The substance was never identified in court, but most people assumed it was human because witnesses testified that human DNA had been found on this saw. The police never assigned—at least, not publicly—an identity to the DNA.

Casanova testified that he'd gone with Pickton to deliver packages of butchered and ground pork to Pitt Meadows Meats, a small store in Pitt Meadows, the next community along the Fraser Highway past Port Coquitlam. He also told Richard Brooks under cross-examination that "once in a while" Pickton would send a pig to Pitt Meadows Meats for butchering.

"Before you became involved on Dominion Avenue with Willie Pickton and the production of these pigs, had you any training in being a butcher?"

"No, sir," said Casanova. He told Prevett that besides working with Pickton in the pig business he had another job as a janitor in a steel fabricating shop.

At the end of two long days of listening to Casanova, Judge Stone adjourned the hearing to prepare his ruling on whether or not to commit Pickton to stand trial on murder charges. No one doubted that he would; the question that remained was whether Pickton would be tried on fifteen counts or twenty-two.

No one had expected extra charges to keep appearing; no one had anticipated the logistical problems of managing so much evidence, so many witnesses and such horrifying information and photographs. With the exception of Sandra Gail Ringwald, Peter Ritchie cross-examined no witnesses, nor did he often appear in court. Most of the cross-examination was done by Marilyn Sandford, who dealt with and challenged all the DNA evidence, and Adrian Brooks, who cross-examined most of the remaining witnesses. Patrick McGowan was in court most days to assist the others; he was alert to issues that came up suddenly and was everyone's right-hand man. Richard Brooks appeared only to challenge a few key witnesses.

In a case like this one, the role of the defence lawyers is not a happy one. No one in the courtroom rooted for them. No one wanted to interview them, and the victims' families loathed them. Being married to a well-known reporter made Adrian Brooks more media-friendly than his colleagues, but even he remarked one day, as Irene handed him a coffee outside the courtroom, that he felt lonely because no one ever wanted to talk to him. He smiled as he said it, but he was making it clear that this wasn't an easy time for him either. And he was almost always the lawyer who visited Pickton in the holding cell downstairs; Peter Ritchie did not deal with him.

Brooks probably had no idea how much Mike Petrie admired the way he conducted himself in court. "I think I am more of a barrister myself," Petrie said once. "I am closer to Adrian's style. Gentlemanly, until it's time to pull out the steel fist."

Everyone liked Petrie and his colleagues, Derrill Prevett, John Ahern and Geoff Baragar. They were all open, friendly, cheerful and accessible, both to the families and to the press. For the families these men were the cuddly bears of the preliminary hearing, the people they went to for reassurance. What the families didn't get from them was information; if it was information they wanted, they'd have to sit in court and listen. The Victim Services workers were not allowed to tell them anything.

Petrie and Prevett worked well as a team. Petrie questioned most of the Crown's witnesses, taking them through their stories or their forensic information step by step. And he did it without a note. "I prepare my cases and when I read things, it's like going to the movies—I see it as a story, I see it as scenes," Petrie explained. "I see it like that, visually. And I have a good memory."

Petrie knows this sounds simplistic, but it works for him. "And when there is a problem—say a witness doesn't show up or something isn't ready—I just go to a different scene. Like any good movie you have ever watched, the director has just strung it together. You have a plan, but when you get to court, you do the final edit. I know I've got to get this person to communicate, to give the judge the information to get to the next scene. It's the same with witnesses. Each has a body of evidence they need to communicate."

But Petrie, whose ability to do a complicated trial without notes is legendary, has other techniques for remembering what he has to do. He compares himself to a door-to-door salesman. "It's a mental exercise. Take some time. You are going on a call and you need to think of everything that could happen. What about the gate? The fence? A dog? What happens if the person slams the door? I prepare for every possibility. If Willie Pickton ever did take the stand I have already decided how I will handle it. And if the scene isn't playing out in the way you expect, you have to be able to adjust."

Derrill Prevett is, in his own way, just as formidable in court. By now he was used to being the senior prosecutor in his cases, but the Pickton challenges were perfectly suited to his expertise in DNA evidence. This was a DNA case, start to finish. Except for the few remains found in freezers and buckets and on the picking belts, there was nothing left of these women except their DNA. And thanks to DNA evidence, the task force was able to identify the presence of many of the missing women on the farm and to lay charges in most of the cases. Prevett had already proved himself the most knowledgeable and experienced prosecutor in the country when it came to DNA evidence. His mastery of this material showed every time he questioned forensics experts on their findings.

John Ahern's role in the preliminary hearing was as important, but unseen. He was responsible for the arrangements to disclose the evidence to the defence team, a crucial but difficult job that involved everything from photographs to DNA results to transcripts of police interviews and wiretaps. Geoff Baragar, skilled as a questioner in court with a sense of humour that often lightened a tough session, was the team's legal expert who had strategies and precedents at his fingertips to help craft arguments. He could tell by instinct what the defence might have up its sleeve.

It was now July 21, 2003, and the hearing was almost over. It had been scheduled for two to three months and it took seven—seven months to hear some of the most gruesome evidence ever delivered before a Canadian judge. The defence team had no witnesses of their own to call; anyone who could say something good about Willie Pickton or lay the crimes at the feet of another man would be saved for the trial.

Judge Stone took a few days to think through the testimony he'd been listening to since January 13, when the hearing began. On

July 23 he came into the courtroom to read his conclusions. It was one of the rare days when the room was full. Other lawyers in the building came in. Family members were there. Dozens of journalists. Court-watchers Art Lee and Russ MacKay. Most of the sheriffs in the building, especially the ones who had driven Pickton back and forth from prison every day, handled the search gates on the way in and guarded the courtroom itself. Lou and Irene, the coffee ladies. Workers from other offices in the courthouse.

Stone began by thanking the lawyers on both sides for their work in what he called "this very difficult and emotional case." But it was also unique in Canadian criminal law, he said, because of what he called its "evidentiary scope." "Not only are there thousands of exhibits involved in this case, but the case is unique in that, while the preliminary inquiry has proceeded, new evidence has been coming forward."

Stone talked about the procedural problems for both sides as the case unfolded in court. Without cooperation from both sides it would have taken much longer and cost more in resources and money. "Without sacrificing the interests of their clients," Stone said, "both sides have conducted themselves in the highest traditions of the bar in making admissions and agreeing to procedures that would be taken as new evidence became available."

Then he reminded everyone of Willie Pickton's own statements: "He admitted to killing up to fifty women. He said he got sloppy with the last one and that is why the blood and human remains were found. He disposed of the bodies by way of a rendering plant, the inference being that the remains were sent with animal remains to be disposed of. He admitted to being a mass murderer and was going to kill fifty women and then take a break before doing any more. He had not gotten rid of the personal identification of women because he had been sloppy. He admitted killing at least two women, possibly three, in the mobile trailer home, Site V-3. He indirectly acknowledges the butchering of these victims by his reference to the rendering plant as a means of disposal of remains."

Judge Stone also cited the devastating evidence given by Sandra Gail Ringwald, Lynn Ellingsen, Andy Bellwood and Scott Chubb, and even that of Pickton's friends Gina Houston and Pat Casanova about his skill as a butcher. And the judge went through the evidence produced by the forensic teams of blood and human remains found on the farm.

Stone had no hesitation about sending Pickton to trial on fifteen counts of first-degree murder—in the deaths of Sereena Abotsway, Mona Wilson, Jacqueline McDonell, Diane Rock, Heather Bottomley, Andrea Joesbury, Brenda Ann Wolfe, Jennifer Lynn Furminger, Helen Mae Hallmark, Patricia Rose Johnson, Georgina Faith Papin, Heather Chinnock, Tanya Holyk, Sherry Irving and Inga Hall. Where it became difficult for him was dealing with the seven new counts that had come in after the preliminary hearing started.

The judge began by reminding everyone that the investigation on the farm had continued throughout the preliminary hearing. "In the middle of the preliminary inquiry," he said, "the Crown asked me to consider seven new murder counts relating to Marnie Frey, Tiffany Drew, Sarah de Vries, Cynthia Feliks, Angela Jardine, Diana Melnick and one Jane Doe, whose skull had been found near Mission, British Columbia, but who, to this date, has never been identified." Pickton's lawyers had objected to his adding these new counts to the indictment, Stone explained, and rather than get into a prolonged legal sidetrack over this, he would simply let the Crown prosecutors add the charges, something they were entitled to do.

"When this matter first appeared before me, there were two counts of murder against Mr. Pickton," the judge said. "As time passed, the number went to fifteen. If the inquiry had started one month later, he would have been appearing on twenty-two counts of first-degree murder, rather than fifteen. As I said earlier, it is the very unique circumstances of this case that have created this situation." In the meantime he would commit Pickton to stand trial on the murders of the fifteen women.

David Stone took the opportunity on this last day to remind the people in the courtroom of the other seven women waiting for justice. He named each one and offered a brief summary of the evidence found in each case to a silent, tearful courtroom.

Marnie Frey was the first. Judge Stone described the evidence as being a portion of her jawbone and teeth and the fact that DNA testing showed they had been hers. Tiffany Drew was next; the evidence included a syringe with her DNA found in Pickton's trailer. Sarah de Vries was identified as a victim by DNA found on her lipstick and other cosmetics, while Pickton's DNA was found on a broken condom in her purse. In the cases of Cynthia Feliks, Angela Jardine and Diana Melnick, "the evidence with respect to these three women is interrelated," Judge Stone said. It came down to the DNA of each woman being found in freezers, some of it—that of Cindy Feliks—from ground meat in one of them; DNA from Angela Jardine and Diana Melnick was found in the second freezer. Jane Doe was the judge's seventh name, based on DNA that matched her skull, found in Mission Slough, to a rib bone found on the Pickton property.

Judge Stone rose and left the courtroom. The guards hustled Pickton out of the box and took him downstairs to a van that would take him to his cell at the North Fraser Pretrial Centre, about two miles away. Reporters, photographers, camera operators and the court artists all fought to get close to the lawyers for their comments. After forty-five minutes, though, everyone had dispersed. The courthouse in Port Coquitlam returned to its quiet day-to-day business. Its role in this drama was over. The next stage, Pickton's trial, would take place in the Supreme Court building in New Westminster.

What very few people knew as they left Port Coquitlam that Friday afternoon was that the task force had invited family members to attend a special event the following morning—the demolition of the Pickton farmhouse. The forensic teams had been searching it for weeks now, swabbing every surface, tearing out walls, looking for evidence. Large white tents had been erected around the house for the teams' equipment, with ATCO trailers hooked up close by to hold evidence. The roof of the house had been covered in blue plastic tarpaulins large enough to touch the ground and to hide the workers inside. But now they were finished, and it was time to take the house down.

Russ MacKay was one of the people who showed up to see it fall. He watched as workers moved a massive yellow backhoe into place. Victims' family members and friends clapped and cheered when the backhoe's long arm with the claw at the end swung down, crashing through the roof and the sides of the house. Again and again it fell, knocking down beams and walls and windows and, finally, the brick chimney. A bulldozer shoved the mess towards the backhoe, which lifted it up and threw it into red dump trucks.

But the searchers weren't finished with the property. Now they needed to dig up the soil under the house and truck it to the students on the picking belts.

CHAPTER FIFTY

THE ARISTOCRACY OF VICTIMHOOD

With the preliminary hearing behind them and twenty-two murder counts ahead, Mike Petrie's team wanted to start the trial early in 2004, two years after Pickton's arrest. But Peter Ritchie dug in his heels. There is just too much new evidence coming in to think about any start date at all, he told Judge Robert Crawford of the British Columbia Supreme Court, on September 11, 2003. Maybe it could happen later in 2004, Ritchie said, but at this stage his people were overwhelmed by the evidence that was pouring in.

With a core group of eight lawyers working on the case full-time, Ritchie began adding others on a part-time basis to take over work on specific witnesses or subjects. He also hired private detectives. Their job was to check out the stories of the witnesses who'd already appeared at the preliminary hearing and to investigate witnesses expected to appear at the trial. A former judge was helping as well; so were researchers, including one who specialized in forensic evidence such as DNA. They would be ready to challenge the prosecutors' findings.

By now the Pickton case had racked up its own records. It was the biggest in Canadian history: from the size of the criminal investigation, with about five hundred investigators in all, to the size of the crime scene, which consisted of the entire farm, to the horrific statistic of the most victims of a serial killer ever. And, as people discovered on September 15, 2003, it was probably the most expensive case in the country's history. On that date British Columbia's solicitor general announced that the province had already spent between $40 million and $50 million on the case, and the ongoing investigation would cost at least another $26 million. The trial, when it happened, would probably add another $4 million to the bill. Through its legal aid system, British Columbia's government would pay about seventy percent of the total cost, while the federal government would cover the remaining thirty percent.

And that was the optimistic view. Others believed that the Pickton case could cost taxpayers more than the Air India case, which ended up at $130 million. In that case, two Canadians were tried for putting a bomb on an Air India flight from Vancouver to India; 331 people, 82 of them children, were killed. It was the biggest mass killing in Canadian history.

For the families, the news the trial was going to be delayed was tough to take, but when they learned that the attorney general's office was thinking about limiting the murder charges to the first fifteen identified by Judge Stone—and not putting Pickton on trial for the remaining seven, as he had suggested—they were beside themselves. This is how the categorization of victims into four layers, in descending importance, became official policy. The first layer in the aristocracy of victimhood was "the Fifteen," as people began to call them. Judge David Stone had committed Pickton to trial on first-degree murder charges for this group, and their status appeared to be solid.

Next were "the Seven"—dead women waiting for justice, whose remains had been found and identified and the results presented in court. Stone had ruled that the Seven should be included in the trial through direct indictment by the Crown prosecutors. If his preliminary hearing had started a month later, he'd said, they'd be included with the fifteen. Technically, however, they arrived late, so he had to leave it to the Crown to lay the charges—which was well within the law.

Third were the women whose DNA had been found on the farm, but not enough of it, or enough other evidence such as identification documents and personal belongings, to lay charges. Last and least were the families who hadn't heard anything at all about what had happened to their missing wives and mothers, daughters and sisters. For this group the big issue was the slow processing of DNA tests because of backlogs at the RCMP labs. Since the search began on the farm, tests that should have been done within thirty to sixty days were taking sixty to ninety days. The families in this last group were sure the tests, when they were finished, would show that their girls had died on the farm.

On September 21, 2003, Don Adam once again presided over a family meeting in the task force's Surrey offices, the fourth since the first gathering in October 2001. With police and prosecutors present, Adam confirmed the bad news. We can't promise you that charges will be laid in all the cases, he said. Not even in the last seven. It was going to take at least another year to process the rest of the evidence. The cases they presented in trial needed to be strong, their best cases, without any openings for defence challenges.

The families were unhappy with this news, but they told reporters later that they still had faith in Adam's team. As Lorraine Crey, Dawn Crey's sister, later told Lori Culbert of the *Vancouver Sun*, "They [the police] haven't given up. And they made that perfectly clear that they are searching for the ones that are still missing. There were many, many tears."

Yes, there were tears. During the four-hour meeting the police showed the families a videotape of a memorial service held at the last pit to be dug up on the farm. The anthropology students had finished searching the dirt from this pit on their conveyor belts and now it was time to truck it back. But the students told their bosses they needed to commemorate the victims they had been looking for during the past eighteen months. Before a bulldozer shoved the last piles of dirt back into the hole, the students stood around its edge holding a white rose for each of the sixty-one women on the missing women list, as well as a card with her name on it. One by one they named each woman and dropped a rose into the pit, followed by her card. A piper played a lament as the hole was filled in. As they watched this video in the task force offices, tears streaming down their faces, the families saw that the students and many of the police officers were weeping too.

———

A few weeks later, on November 18, 2003, the yellow crime-scene tape, barriers, trailers and tents were gone from the Pickton property, leaving behind a bleak and barren mess of mud and the rusty machinery and vehicles that had been there when the police seized it almost two years earlier. The tent across Dominion Avenue that had been a refuge for the families was also gone. Beside where it had been, the Hells Angels clubhouse was up for sale. Developers were eyeing the shabby little farmhouses and hobby farms scattered along Dominion east of the farm for new projects. The shopping centre across from the farm was growing quickly to the west and south, with more and more stores and restaurants going in each month. The houses east and north of the property, which had been barely framed in when Pickton was arrested, now formed a subdivision that was home to dozens of young families. And the curious had stopped coming by to peer through the wire fence around the farm.

Strangely, the stories of Pickton and Gary Leon Ridgway, Seattle's Green River Killer, intersected at this period. Ridgway, who also chose prostitutes and drug addicts as his victims, had just cut a deal to plead guilty on forty-two counts of murder in return for escaping the death penalty; now he would spend the rest of his life in prison. Like Pickton, Ridgway was a suspect for every missing woman in communities around Seattle, but he remained a suspect in Canada as well. "Early on in our investigation, Mr. Ridgway was identified as a potential suspect in addition to hundreds of other suspects," RCMP constable Cate Galliford told reporters on November 5, 2002. "He has not been ruled out as a suspect in the cases up here."

On December 16, seven families were overjoyed to receive some good news for a change. Crown prosecutors announced that charges would go ahead after all in the cases of Sarah de Vries, Angela Jardine, Cindy Feliks, Marnie Frey, Diana Melnick, Tiffany Drew and Jane Doe. The trial should begin in the fall of 2004 on twenty-two counts of first-degree murder. Inevitably, other families felt neglected and disheartened to learn that nothing would be going forward for them.

Early in January 2004, task force officers went to Ernie Crey's house in Chilliwack to tell him and Dawn Crey's extended family that her DNA had been positively identified at the farm and that they believed she had died there. Dawn had disappeared in 2000, and as Crey said to the *Toronto Star*'s Daniel Girard on hearing the news, "I've always thought there was a connection to the Pickton property but didn't know for sure. Now we do. There's closure in the sense that we're not sitting up at night or going through our days thinking that she might reappear. Even though we now know it's not yet over by a long shot. We have to wonder if the evidence they found is sufficient for charges and then there's the prospect of a long trial."

A few days later, on January 26, Cara Ellis's family also had a visit from the police to confirm what they already knew: they'd found her DNA on the farm. Lori Ellis, Cara's sister-in-law, was still seething about the way the police had handled Cara's case from the beginning. She explained why in a note she sent to a families' Internet message board. "I was in Vancouver August 1997 and spoke to the Vancouver police department. They had me on the phone for over one hour asking questions about Cara; where she lived, age, birth date, where she worked. I was told that the police would look for her but if she did not want to be found we may not hear. I unfortunately thought that was the case, that she did not want to be found. When I had not heard anything for a long time I spoke to the family and together we approached the Missing Women's Task Force. That was in the year 2002, October. We heard nothing from them until October 2003 when they said that the next day there would be a press conference releasing Cara's picture [and] asking for info.

"On January 26, 2004 we were visited by the R.C.M.P. telling us about Cara's DNA. I got really angry when I recently found out that Cara was also reported missing by a dear friend in April 1997 and nothing was done . . . how many women could have been saved if they only paid as much attention to the Vancouver missing women as they do to higher income people?"

Two days after Cara Ellis's family heard the news, the task force held a press conference. Besides Cara's DNA, they finally had lab results on nine sets of DNA tests; from those, six women could be identified. The first was Saskatchewan's Yvonne Marie Boen, who was last seen on March 16, 2001, and whose blood had been found both on the farm and in Surrey's infamous crack house the "House of Horrors." Another woman who had been identified was Andrea Borhaven, from Vernon, B.C., who had disappeared in 1997. Andrea's DNA and blood were found on earrings hidden under some floorboards in Pickton's trailer along with some other jewellery.

The third was British Columbia's Wendy Lynn Crawford, who had been reported missing in December 1999. The forensics experts identified her DNA from a small whittled bone found near the cistern outside the piggery. To obtain the DNA they'd had to grind the bone with liquid nitrogen, just as David Sweet had done for some of the teeth. Dawn Crey, who had disappeared in November 1999, was identified by a DNA sample so small that police feared they would not be able to lay charges. The sixth woman in this group was Kerry Koski, who had disappeared in January 1998. Investigators found her blood on two earrings hidden under the floorboards of Pickton's trailer.

Pickton had not yet been charged with murdering any of these six. And the police told reporters that the DNA of three remaining women didn't match any of the sixty-five on the missing women list. It was quite possible these three had never been reported missing. In issuing an appeal to the public for help, Sheila Sullivan, a detective with the task force, was blunt: "The description would be that of a young woman whose family or friends believe may have been addicted to drugs or was involved in the sex trade and who hasn't been heard from since before February 2002."

But by this time people in British Columbia were heartily tired of the Pickton story. Some had little sympathy for the hard times of addicted, abused, poverty-stricken women who'd survived on the money they earned as prostitutes and had died in the most horrifying circumstances anyone could imagine. A few months earlier, in July, the International Olympic Committee had chosen Vancouver to host the 2010 Winter Olympics; the inevitable reference to the Pickton case in almost every story written about the decision was embarrassing to the organizing committee. This wasn't the story they wanted the world to hear. By now the *Los Angeles Times*, *Dateline NBC*, British and German television and many other international news organizations had given the Pickton story their full attention, never missing the city's running sore, the Downtown Eastside. Drug addicts and sex-trade workers gave one interview after another; so did many of the missing women's families. "The poorest postal code in Canada" was a phrase embedded in almost every report that went out around the world, and British Columbians wanted the story to just go away.

Nobody believed it could get worse, but on March 10, 2004, it did. They should have expected it—it was the elephant in this very large room. Dr. Perry Kendall, British Columbia's senior health officer, announced that meat from the farm could have been mixed with human flesh and sold to the public. And that a mixture of human and pig meat could be sitting in people's freezers right now. His words were more careful than that, of course. What he actually said was, "As a result of information we received from the RCMP, we have reason to believe there is a strong possibility that some of the product from the Pickton farm—and how much the RCMP do not know—may still be sitting in some people's freezers in the Lower Mainland."

Police and health officials quickly offered up calming bromides. The health risk of eating this meat, according to Dr. Kendall, could be a bacterial infection, but even that was unlikely unless someone ate it raw or undercooked. "We have an obligation to mitigate what may be a small public health risk, even though the meat is two years old and frozen," he said. "It would still have the capacity to carry the infection." The good news was that only a few people might still have it in their freeze ne meat was distributed or sold to at least forty relatives, friends and associates of Pickton, but was never sold in retail stores or widely available to the public," reported the *Vancouver Sun*.

The police declared that no commercial meat processors were involved, but the *Sun* discovered that they had visited Pitt Meadows Meats, the company Pat Casanova had talked about in court. Mino Kuiper had owned Pitt Meadows Meats until October 2002, the paper reported, and he told reporters that the police had studied his records for four days looking for any reference to Pickton. They found nothing, he said, and in an interview with the *Sun*, Kuiper said "there had never been any animals bought from Pickton, period. We never dealt with him. We didn't want nothing to do with him in the first place."

When Lisa Yelds heard what Dr. Kendall and other officials had said in downplaying the danger, she rolled her eyes. "That is ridiculous!" she snapped. After all, didn't her former husband, Dave Yelds, who used to work with Willie Pickton in the slaughterhouse, sell pork to several small butchers in the Fraser Valley? Didn't Pat Casanova? Didn't Willie himself? She even remembered going with Willie in his truck to three meat stores in the Pitt Meadows–Abbotsford area when he was making deliveries, and one of them was Pitt Meadows Meats. She remembered her ex-husband taking three hundred pounds of ground meat out of the farm every month to sell to Fraser Valley stores. Dave Yelds himself had no problem talking about it to a reporter from Global television. He said he'd bought plenty of pork from Pickton. "It was also eaten at parties and given to friends," he added. "Probably gave away to hundreds of people."

Then there were all the friends and hangers-on who'd helped themselves to meat from Willie Pickton's freezers. Gina Houston had testified before Judge Stone about the meat she had taken for her family. Lisa Yelds had too, but she soon stopped; she just didn't like the look of it. Today she wonders if that's how she contracted hepatitis C, which has since become so s▓▓▓ that she is disabled by severe pain around her liver and flare-ups of jaundice.

The government had checked its records, Dr. Kendall told reporters, looking for outbreaks of food poisoning and infections that might have come from the Pickton farm, but could fine none. They had also contacted the BC Centre for Disease Control for advice; its director of communicable diseases, Dr. David Patrick, said the dangers to the public would come from infections caused by salmonella bacteria or by pig parasites such as trichinosis, which can bring on diarrhea and vomiting. He also said that the risk of getting hepatitis or HIV from human remains, even if they were infected, would be low. Still, people should look through their freezers, advised Kendall. "The bacteria would still be viable and still infectious."

If it was grim for any person to think they might have bought or eaten some of this meat, it was far worse for the families of the victims. "My heart goes out to them," said Rich Coleman, B.C.'s solicitor general. "They are going to hear about another piece of this investigation which is very difficult and very extensive."

It didn't take long for the news to hit the Downtown Eastside. Volunteers at WISH, the drop-in program for sex-trade workers at First United Church, were calling contacts at other programs for extra support. "This is going to be really hard for people to take because it's so graphic," Kate Gibson, a worker at WISH, told the Canadian Press. "It's awful for the women who ever went to the farm and women on the street. It's their friends . . . A lot of people are really upset, angry. There will be crying, sadness, everything. This is beyond belief and it just puts it right back in their face again."

Ruth Wright, the minister at First United, braced herself for many difficult days ahead with her traumatized congregation. She was upset that it had taken so long for the warning to be made public, calling it a slap in the face to an already degraded group. "For women not valued by society it somehow seems like a greater level of not being valued," she said. For women in her congregation who had been to the farm and eaten food there, this would be a nightmare. They would need support. "The only thing I know how to do is to listen and respect," Wright said. "People have to find their peace and it takes time. You can't be dismissive. You also don't want to be overly emotional yourself. They're very real fears, very real experiences."

The next few months were quiet. The administrative details for the coming trial were cranking into gear. It would be a jury trial held in the Supreme Court building on Begbie Square in New Westminster, not in the special high-security courtroom built in Vancouver's Law Courts for the Air India trial. This news was a surprise; as in the Air India case, Pickton's would be a long mega-trial, with hundreds of witnesses and international attention focused on it, a trial that would require the same level of security as Air India because of concern for Pickton's safety. He was being kept in protective custody at the North Fraser Pretrial Centre, and armed sheriffs ferried him to court when necessary, but everyone knew there was a real threat from relatives of some of the dead women, some of whom had spent time in prison for serious crimes.

The only excuse that anyone could think of for choosing the New Westminster Courthouse was that officials had decided to dial down the unpleasant publicity they knew was coming by holding the trial in a less accessible city. The Downtown Eastside community would have no problem mobilizing crowds at the Vancouver courthouse; doing that out of town would be more awkward. The New Westminster Courthouse is only two blocks from the SkyTrain station, but poor people would not be able to afford the fare, at least not on a regular basis. And the location made sense simply because it was the regional courthouse for the area, serving communities such as Port Coquitlam, Coquitlam, Pitt Meadows, Maple Ridge and Abbotsford.

Mike Petrie kept Judge Patrick Dohm updated on the progress of his case, but at the end of June 2004 he had to tell him it wasn't going to start as soon as they'd hoped. The plan had been to start the trial in the fall, but he didn't think they could start even in January

2005, he told Dohm. The main reason was the DNA testing. The police had developed a robotic system to test swabs taken at the farm and it was working well. Already 90,000 out of 100,000 DNA exhibits had been extracted. Of these, 360 samples were ready to compare to the known DNA they had on file. Petrie told Dohm the police hoped to finish the extractions within a month or two, but it was still too early to set a trial date.

As everyone waited, there was one question people asked more often than any other: "What about the brother?" Willie was just too damn dumb to do this by himself, wasn't he? He was just the disposal guy; he got rid of the bodies. It had to be Dave Pickton who was killing these girls. So went the talk in Port Coquitlam, and just about everywhere else in Canada.

Mike Petrie, John Ahern and the other prosecutors heard this question all the time; so did reporters covering the story and the sheriffs who ferried Willie back and forth for court appearances. The answer is that the task force had investigated the brother, and while Dave was a biker, crafty and brutal, with a criminal record and a history of violence against women, his convictions had been rare. They were there in the police records for them to pick through; so were all the tips and interviews that mentioned him. Any phone conversations he'd had with Willie since he'd entered the Pretrial Centre had been recorded. Dave had intimidated, even threatened, a reporter, and the police were well aware that she believed her children could be in danger. But they could not find any evidence connecting him to the murders.

What they did find, during the search of the old family farmhouse before it was demolished, was an ugly collection of restraint devices and sex toys in a chest of drawers in Dave's old bedroom. Here they found oral sex creams in various flavours as well as dozens of condoms and dildos of varying lengths. There was a rusty, blackened pair of steel animal-castration pliers. There were also thirteen three-inch Magnum 7 shotgun shells, a brass shell for a starting pistol, and two wrist-restraining devices, one of which was a wide black leather strap with a heavy steel buckle. The police also seized from Dave Pickton a pink backpack stuffed with used syringes, condoms, wipes, a crack pipe and a butcher's cleaver with a black handle.

In March 2005, more than three years after the police arrested Willie, a group of five or six RCMP members began close surveillance of Dave, taking turns watching him from six a.m. until three o'clock the following morning. RCMP constable Doug Forsyth was one of the watchers; he later said the orders came from a senior investigator but he wasn't sure if it was Don Adam or his deputy, Wayne Clary. The surveillance lasted twelve days. After it ended, Forsyth was ordered to follow Dave again, this time hoping he would lead them to another target of their investigations, someone who has never been identified. Sometimes the surveillance was as intense as it had been in March 2005; other times it was lower-key. But it had been going on for a long time—the task force would never lose interest in Dave Pickton. The evidence was just not strong enough to lay charges against him.

The other big topic that obsessed many people was the possibility that Willie Pickton hadn't acted alone, that he had killing partners. The police dismissed this one as well. They thought that a couple of the women—Dinah Taylor and Gina Houston—might well have lured women out to the farm for Willie in return for money and drugs, but there was no evidence that they had known about or taken part in the murders.

How anyone could call it good news to have someone you love declared dead, and probably murdered, is beyond understanding for most people, but most people are not related to Vancouver's missing women. When the police announced, on October 6, 2004, that they were adding another eight names to the official list, the families' reaction was a heartfelt "At last!" Unfortunately the investigators had not been able to match the DNA of three women found on the farm; to this day they remain three more Jane Does.

The message from the RCMP's Heather Street headquarters was long and detailed. The official list of missing women now stood at sixty-nine; they included the fifteen cases in which charges had already been laid and the seven that everyone expected would be laid. The police had reviewed more than 220 missing-person cases from agencies in British Columbia, the northwestern United States and across Canada. This review had included older cases that pre-dated the task force, several that had turned up during the task force's work, and another forty-four reports that had come in after the task force appealed for help nearly a year earlier.

But the good news now was that the Missing Women's Task Force had discovered eighty-eight other women who had been missing for years. "In those cases where the missing women fit the task force profile," the police said, "our investigators have undertaken further investigative steps, including checking various police and government databases, interviewing family and friends and in some cases, obtaining the women's DNA profiles." Some were alive and well and living in various locations around the world, the police said; others were now dead—"from various causes unrelated to our investigation." Their families had received some measure of closure, as the police put it. But for the rest, the officers had decided there was no connection between the remaining DNA profiles and the women who were still on missing-person lists in various jurisdictions. It's time, the officers said, for the local police who reported women missing to continue with their own investigations in their own jurisdictions.

But the review hadn't been a waste of time. They now had these eight new names on their list of women who had gone missing and who fit the task force profile. Sharon Abraham, last seen in 2000, when she was thirty-five, was the first on the list. The others included Sherry Baker, twenty-five when she went missing in 1993; Cara Ellis, also twenty-five, who disappeared in 1997; and Tammy Fairbairn, who disappeared in 1998; Gloria Fedyshyn, who disappeared in 2002; and Mary Lands, who disappeared in 1993—all three were twenty-seven. Also among the eight were Tania Petersen, who disappeared in 2003, and Sharon Ward, who disappeared in 1997, both twenty-nine years old.

With these additions to the list, the task force issued a new poster. It contained the pictures of all sixty-nine missing women arranged chronologically in the order in which they disappeared, from the earliest to the most recent. Each picture had the woman's name under it as well as the date when she was last seen. Included were pictures of the fifteen women Pickton had so far been charged with killing. As time went on, the police would update this poster again and again, removing some names, adding others and changing the information on charges.

Almost three years had passed since Pickton's arrest and everyone wanted the trial to start. It didn't happen. On December 20, 2004, a judge allowed a third delay at the request of Pickton's lawyers. Another 150,000 DNA swabs remained to be examined—they needed more time.

CHAPTER FIFTY-ONE

FROM TWENTY-SIX TO SIX

Next to "What about the brother?" the most frequently heard question in March 2005 was "Why is everything taking so long?" Any attempts to answer that went on about the numbers of DNA samples, more witness interviews or more locations to search just seemed like excuses. Even so, the Crown had disclosed more than 500,000 pages of documents, and DNA tests were still under way in forensic labs across Canada and even in the United States.

At the end of March, when Geoffrey Barrow, an experienced and respected Supreme Court judge in Kelowna, was chosen to preside over Willie's trial, it seemed like progress. Still, people wondered why a judge who had to commute 370 kilometres each way was doing this. All the attorney general's office would say by way of explanation was that he was experienced in criminal prosecutions and an excellent judge.

Barrow was in court on May 25, 2005, when Mike Petrie told him the Crown was bringing twelve new charges against Willie Pickton, for a new total of twenty-seven counts of first-degree murder. Willie wasn't there in person; he watched on closed-circuit video at the North Fraser Pretrial Centre in Port Coquitlam as Petrie read out the names: Cara Ellis, Andrea Borhaven, Kerry Koski, Wendy Crawford, Debra Lynne Jones, Marnie Frey, Tiffany Drew, Sarah de Vries, Cynthia Feliks, Angela Jardine, Diana Melnick and, last, Jane Doe, the only woman without an identity, the woman whose skull had been found in Mission Slough by the whirligig man. These names were added to the original list of fifteen put forward in July 2003 by Judge David Stone: Sereena Abotsway, Mona Wilson, Jacqueline

McDonell, Diane Rock, Heather Bottomley, Andrea Joesbury, Brenda Ann Wolfe, Jennifer Lynn Furminger, Helen Mae Hallmark, Patricia Rose Johnson, Georgina Faith Papin, Heather Chinnock, Tanya Holyk, Sherry Irving and Inga Hall.

Although the laying of twelve new counts was a dramatic courtroom event, so too was Peter Ritchie's attempt to prevent reporters coming to court. He needed to protect his client's right to a fair trial, he said, and the best way to do that would be to close the courtroom altogether to the public and the media. Perhaps realizing that was not likely to happen, he had another suggestion: Judge Barrow should order the reporters in the courtroom not to talk to anyone outside the courtroom, including their editors and producers, about what they had heard there.

Normally publication bans allow reporters to work with their editors to prepare stories for print and broadcast, but the stories are held until the ban is lifted by the court, usually after any and all appeals to the province's court of appeal and the Supreme Court of Canada are exhausted, a process that can take several years. The only other events that can effectively lift a publication ban are the death of the accused or a guilty plea. At this point, in 2005, almost everything that had been said during the 2003 preliminary hearing under Judge Stone was still under a publication ban. The same was true of almost everything that was being said now in the provincial Supreme Court under Judge Barrow. Ritchie told reporters outside the court that he trusted them, of course; his concern was "the foreign media who do not give a hoot about Canadian law." But there had been only one, very minor breach of the ban in the United States during the seven months of the sensational, heartbreaking preliminary hearing in Port Coquitlam, a hearing attended by very few journalists and almost no members of the public.

Michael Skene, who is a media lawyer and partner in the Vancouver law firm Borden Ladner Gervais, was in the courtroom that day representing the *Globe and Mail* and CTV. He was appalled by Ritchie's demands. "There is no evidence before the court that a publication ban would not be effective in preventing publication in the mainstream media," he argued. Later, outside the courtroom, Skene met with reporters. If the judge allows this, he told them, it would set a bad precedent. "It says that people who attend the court, when they leave it, aren't free to talk to other people about what they'd seen or heard."

There was another big complication to deal with before a decision could be rendered as a result of Ritchie's request. When sheriffs walked into the courtroom on June 1, 2005, to get it ready for the day's proceedings, they were amazed to hear that Associate Chief Justice Patrick Dohm, the man who had cut the deal with Peter Ritchie about his fees for defending Pickton, would be in the judge's chair. Dohm's explanation, when proceedings began, was terse: He was only here to make an announcement. Judge Barrow had scheduling conflicts and couldn't proceed with the trial. The new judge would be Justice James Williams, who had been assigned to the New Westminster court in April 2002, although he lived in Vancouver. Asked for his response when he heard the news, Michael Skene could barely restrain his skepticism. "I think everyone would have thought those sorts of issues would have been worked out before the trial started on Wednesday," he said.

Rumours about Barrow flew about: his wife was sick; it was a long commute; it would mean a year away from home. Whatever the reason, once everyone had recovered from the shock—the biggest case in the province's history and the first choice of judge gets bungled?—the general agreement was that Williams would do fine.

Williams had been on the bench for only three years, and though he'd run thirty cases, he'd never managed a large criminal trial. But he had a background that could help him understand the complications and stresses of the Pickton case. Williams had come to law from the RCMP, where he worked in commercial crime (white-collar offenders in the business community). After a decade or so with the force, he decided to go to law school at the University of

British Columbia, where his interest in criminal law led him to article under criminal defence lawyer Len Daoust in 1985. He became an associate at Daoust Smith in 1988 and was made partner in 1990.

Williams developed a specialty in criminal defence cases, often acting for police officers in trouble. One of his best-known cases was that of Staff Sergeant Hugh Stewart, an RCMP member known as "Sergeant Pepper" for pepper-spraying UBC students during the 1997 Asia-Pacific Forum in Vancouver. The RCMP Public Complaints Commission had criticized his actions, saying they could not be justified. Williams's other high-profile client was Marty McSorley, a Boston Bruins defenceman who'd been charged with assault after cracking his stick across the head of Vancouver Canucks player Donald Brashear, causing severe concussion. A Vancouver judge found McSorley guilty.

James Williams first walked into the Pickton courtroom on June 8, 2005. He was slim and fit and sported a grey moustache that matched his short grey hair. He was accompanied by a young lawyer, Christine Judd, whom he introduced as "counsel to the judge," a surprise to most people in the courtroom, who had never seen a judge with his own lawyer before. Judd had been an assistant to Justice Ian Josephson, the judge who presided over the Air India trial in 2003 and 2004. With another mega-trial under way, Williams may have felt that her experience could prove useful.

Williams rejected the defence's efforts to keep reporters out of the courtroom or, failing that, to discuss what they had heard with their colleagues. He told the legal teams that the trial would go ahead in three stages, all of which would be open to the public and the media, though with the publication ban still in effect. The first stage would deal with an application from Peter Ritchie's defence team to force the prosecutors to give them more documents. The second stage, known as the voir dire, allowed the defence to attempt to have information removed from the case—evidence, witness statements and anything else they thought could influence the jury against their client. The third and final stage would be the trial proper, to be held before a jury of twelve people.

Pretrial hearings continued for the next few months. Gina Houston made a brief appearance in court on October 14; she was there with her lawyer to fight the defence team's demands for her personal records from the provincial child welfare department. Her argument was that the disclosure of these records would injure her children. She succeeded in her request, but it was obvious that she had problems of a more serious nature. She told people she had been diagnosed with breast cancer; instead of the feisty, good-looking woman who had testified in the preliminary hearing, the court saw a grey wraith, aged and shrunken almost beyond recognition. Her cheekbones were sharp in her thin face, her eyes were sunken, with dark pockets below, and she was bent over like an old lady. By now she had become such a legend in the Pickton mythology that people stared, fascinated at first, then looked away in pity. Soon after Gina Houston's appearance, the pretrial hearings ended.*

Almost three months later, on Monday, January 30, 2006, the second stage of the trial started. This was the voir dire, a term that mystified most of the people in the Port Coquitlam–New Westminster orbit of Pickton's world and many of the families. What was a voir dire? Why couldn't the trial start right away? Hadn't it been almost three years since Pickton's arrest at his trailer, on the night of February 5, 2002? The prosecutors explained to the families that what was starting now was essentially a hearing within a trial. Voir dire, a French term that roughly translates as "to see and speak (the truth)," is held under a publication ban and no jury is present. The prosecutors present their evidence through witnesses who can be cross-examined by the defence; the defence does not have to provide any of its own witnesses—they will be saved for the jury trial. As the voir dire progresses the

---

*After battling breast cancer for eight years, Gina Houston died in a B.C. hospital on April 10, 2010.

presiding judge decides what evidence can and, more important, what can't go before the jury. The defence wanted many of the sensational witness statements removed, or at the very least "edited"—i.e., with the damaging information removed before it went before a jury. If Judge Williams decided that some evidence was inadmissible, or that the defence had a good legal argument for editing a witness statement, the information would not go forward.

The voir dire began with a good crowd of journalists, family members and members of the general public arriving early to get a good seat in Courtroom 102. This was a small courtroom, with space for only forty-five spectators, but despite predictions of a large audience, there were plenty of empty seats. Two were permanently reserved for Willie Pickton's family and friends, as they had been for the Port Coquitlam preliminary hearing, but no one ever sat in them. Two other spaces were available for watching proceedings on large monitors. One was a comfortable sitting room near Courtroom 102 with deep sofas and armchairs instead of hard courtroom seats; it was for the families, and there they had privacy. The other was a courtroom twice the size of 102 for overflow crowds; it too was never full and often wasn't needed at all. Like the good folk of Port Coquitlam, the people who lived and worked in New Westminster appeared indifferent to the country's most sensational murder trial ever.

The courthouse itself, completed in 1981, is a simple but stunning structure of stone, brick, glass and steel built into the side of a steep hill on Carnarvon Street. It sits on a rectangular stone plaza called Begbie Square, after the province's first judge, Sir Matthew Begbie, who served in the second half of the 1800s. There is a statue of Begbie in the square, and a wide flight of steps that climbs up the steep hill to Victoria Street, where the land levels out and there are condominiums and office buildings; this is where Peter Ritchie's team had rented offices. Just beyond the courthouse is one very new development built on land cleared by Dave Pickton and his motley crew.

Below the courthouse, going south down the steep hill, is the city's original red-brick Victorian courthouse complex, built in

1892, where a warren of small old offices in the basement had been turned over to Mike Petrie and his colleagues who had moved back to New Westminster from their temporary offices in the Port Coquitlam courthouse. Normally Petrie's office was on the third floor of the Begbie Square building, but his team had grown and needed secure space, so it borrowed offices in the old building. There was a small balcony at the front of the building where the lawyers sometimes gathered to smoke; below them was a steep drop down to the next street so out there they could see the Fraser River, just three blocks directly south, flowing parallel to the railroad tracks built on the river's banks. It is easy to walk down to the river from there: the next street south of Carnarvon is the city's main street, Columbia, and past that, still heading south, is a dark, narrow road called Front Street. Shops on the north side of Front face a vast yard of railroad tracks and overpasses. One of these shops is Wes Baker's gun store.

Mike Petrie's legal team had grown from four prosecutors— Petrie himself, John Ahern, Derrill Prevett and Geoff Baragar—to seven, with the addition of Satindar Sidhu, Jay Fogel and Jennifer Lopes. Sidhu was best known for successfully prosecuting a fifteen-year-old boy from Surrey for causing the death of eleven-year-old Tina Burbank. Fogel also had a difficult and high-profile case behind him; he had prosecuted Derek Post, who had raped and murdered nineteen-year-old Breann Voth in Port Coquitlam when she was on her way to work early one morning. Jennifer Lopes, an experienced Surrey prosecutor, was the last lawyer to join; among her responsibilities was putting together the case for Jane Doe.

For his part, Peter Ritchie had assembled a distinguished group of lawyers to fight for Willie Pickton. In addition to preliminary-hearing veterans Adrian Brooks, Marilyn Sandford and Patrick McGowan were newcomers David Layton and Peter Schmidt, on loan from Gibbons Fowler Nathanson, a well-known Vancouver criminal defence firm; Frida Tromans, who had practised criminal law in Vancouver and worked for the Insurance Corporation of B.C.; and Joseph Saulnier, who had completed requirements for a law degree only two years previously. But several other lawyers were working part-time on the case, eighteen in all, including Sandford's husband, Richard Brooks, and criminal defence lawyer Glen Orris, who had defended Terry Driver, known as the Abbotsford Killer, as well as Roger Warren, who was convicted of the murder of nine miners in Yellowknife. No one knew how much they were being paid. The funding agreement, put together years earlier with the help of Judge Dohm, remained one of the most talked-about topics in the city's gossipy legal community.

At first the voir dire moved ahead in much the same way as the preliminary hearing had progressed, taking the same police officers through the arrest, charging and interrogation of Willie Pickton in the RCMP's Surrey headquarters in February 2002. The major difference between the preliminary hearing and the voir dire was that nothing was withheld at this stage. Judge Stone only needed to hear enough to send Pickton to trial. Now, under Judge Williams, all the evidence would come forward and the lawyers would fight over how much would go forward to the trial. The defence team challenged evidence and questioned the Crown witnesses, working hard to get Judge Williams to throw out material damaging to their client. But few suspected what the judge's first move was going to be.

On March 2, 2006, Williams quashed count 22, the first-degree murder charge against Pickton in the case of Jane Doe, the woman whose half-skull had been found in Mission Slough in 1995 and whose bones had been found on the farm in 2002. This was a bitter blow to the prosecutors. When Mike Petrie asked Judge Williams to stop proceedings for a few days so his team could absorb the implications of his decision, the judge agreed. It was a major defence victory, "a positive step," Adrian Brooks said. "It is essential that minimum requirements of fairness be shown to every accused, and this decision is part of that fairness to be shown to Mr. Pickton." It was the fact that there had been no identification of Jane Doe that led the judge to quash the charge. Although DNA found in her skull matched DNA found in bones on the farm, although saw cuts on the skull matched saw cuts on the bones, it wasn't enough for the judge.

The prosecutors felt they had no choice but to accept Judge Williams's ruling. There were twenty-six other counts to deal with, too many battles still to fight, and too much time had gone by already. But it was a shock, and it didn't bode well for the rest of the voir dire. Witnesses rolled in and out of the courtroom throughout the spring and summer, and most of that time the seats for the public were empty.

In early August Judge Williams delivered a second body blow to the prosecution. For several days he had heard both sides argue about the number of counts. The position of Pickton's lawyers was that the judge should cut back on the number of counts. No jury, they argued, could listen to evidence on twenty-six charges. It was too much to ask of any human being; it would take far too long. In the interest of justice, the number should be reduced. The prosecutors disagreed. Vehemently. The evidence is the same in almost every case, argued Derrill Prevett, who was handling this issue for the Crown. "The nature of the evidence and the legal and factual nexus between the counts requires a single trial in the interest of justice.

"The Crown's case requires proof of several key elements, obviously," Prevett went on. "It would be necessary for the Crown to establish that each of the named victims are dead, and they're dead as a result of culpable homicide, specifically first-degree murder, and, ultimately, that the applicant murdered them." That, he said, the Crown could do. And, he said, the deaths of these women are all related. "Their remains or other personal items were found on a parcel of land at 963 Dominion Avenue in Port Coquitlam in this province. The human remains recovered by the investigators show that these remains were treated in a certain and consistent manner."

The Crown can prove these women are dead, Prevett repeated. Investigations showed they had all disappeared suddenly, yet all had family and friends and routines. "They had their own lives, regardless of their lifestyles," he said. "They were known to have certain things in their lives that were important to them. Some of them were known to regularly phone or visit loved ones, and then inexplicably stop doing so." These women abandoned residences, personal belongings and children without any explanation; they didn't pick up prescriptions; they didn't go to their doctor appointments; they didn't pick up their welfare cheques. "In short," Prevett told Judge Williams, "there was a complete end to the pattern of living without any known reason."

But the police had been able to identify the remains—even if all they could find was DNA in blood or hair or bone—of all twenty-six women named in the counts against Pickton. And they had found these remains on his property, in and around his property, within a radius of a hundred metres from his trailer. Painstakingly Prevett took Judge Williams through the evidence, showing him again and again that the counts were so similar that a jury would be able to proceed through it all quickly.

On August 9, 2006, in a stunning victory for Pickton, Judge Williams ruled that the trial would proceed on six counts only and that Pickton could be tried later on the remaining twenty. He wasn't buying the prosecution's argument that the facts of some counts would speed up the jury's ability to proceed with reasonable dispatch on others. Williams had made the decision, he said, in the "interests of justice," because the evidence in the six cases was what he called "materially different" from the evidence in the other twenty. A trial on twenty-six counts, he said, would be too much for jurors to understand and would drag the case on needlessly.

The six included Sereena Abotsway, Mona Wilson, Andrea Joesbury, Brenda Wolfe, Georgina Papin and Marnie Frey. The other twenty were Cara Ellis, Andrea Borhaven, Kerry Koski, Wendy Crawford, Debra Lynne Jones, Tiffany Drew, Sarah de Vries, Cynthia Feliks, Angela Jardine, Diana Melnick, Jacqueline McDonell, Diane Rock, Heather Bottomley, Jennifer Furminger, Helen Hallmark, Patricia Johnson, Heather Chinnock, Tanya Holyk, Sherry Irving and Inga Hall.

The voir dire chugged along through the fall with one legal argument after another. The families of the twenty women removed from the indictment clung to the government's assurances that there would be a second trial. Skeptics shook their heads.

And Dave Pickton was back in the news in October, when someone tried to shoot one of his truck drivers with a .22 calibre sawed-off rifle. Police charged Brian Betker, a fifty-four-year-old man from Maple Ridge, with using a firearm in an effort to kill George Baart. Dave Pickton told reporters that he was too busy to talk about it.

CHAPTER FIFTY-TWO

THE JURY

Who would want to sit on the Pickton trial jury? Many people shared Judge James Williams's concerns about finding a dozen sturdy souls to take on this grim responsibility. He said to one potential juror, "I think this trial might expose the juror to something that might be as bad as a horror movie, and you don't have the option of turning off the TV." As it turned out, however, many people were willing; it took only two days to find a jury from a pool of five hundred. On December 12, 2006, seven men and five women emerged. They included five retirees: a brewery worker, a racetrack security guard, an electrical engineer, a mill worker and a nurse. The rest were a condo complex manager, a building engineer, a bartender, a university student, a waitress, a community living worker and a physiotherapist. Sitting four days a week—the court wouldn't be in session on Fridays—they would be paid $20 a day for the first ten days of the trial, $60 a day from the eleventh to forty-ninth days, and $100 a day from the fiftieth day to the end of the trial. Williams told the jurors they would be starting work on January 22, 2007, four years and eleven months after Willie Pickton had been arrested and charged with the murders of Mona Wilson and Andrea Joesbury.

Four days after the jury was chosen, Mike Petrie was appointed a Queen's Counsel, catching up with his colleagues Peter Ritchie and Adrian Brooks, who had been appointed a year earlier, in December 2005, and Derrill Prevett, who'd been made Queen's Counsel in 2003. This honour, coveted in legal circles, is given by the provincial government for service to the legal profession.

——

After six months of listening to arguments, Judge Williams had decided that the jury wouldn't hear a word about Sandra Gail Ringwald's experience with Willie Pickton, not from any of the witnesses, and especially not from Ringwald herself. Williams said that her experience with Pickton didn't meet the requirements of "similar fact evidence" as it is known, partly because Ringwald was not herself one of the twenty-six counts. Some of her story went to the jury in the form of written admissions, but those admissions stopped right at the point where things took a violent turn in Willie's house. The admissions would help the Crown to a certain point because they established a specific case of Pickton's taking a Downtown Eastside working girl to the farm for a date. On the other hand, as far as the jury would learn, nothing untoward happened during or after the pair had sex. They would never hear from Ringwald, never hear that the date ended up with Pickton trying to handcuff her, never hear that after she'd been saved and taken to hospital the doctors found the handcuffs dangling from one wrist. Nor did the jury hear anything about the mutual stabbings.

The defence team won several victories in the year of voir dire arguments. After the Ringwald decision, the other two big ones came first when Williams quashed the Jane Doe murder charge, to bring the total number of counts down to twenty-six. His next move was to sever the remaining twenty-six counts into two trials, the first with six counts and the second with twenty. Pickton's trial would now go ahead with the six, with vague reassurances from the provincial attorney general's office that a second trial would go ahead . . . sometime. The families of the twenty remaining victims were among those who worried that the second trial would never happen. By taking these actions, Judge Williams made it impossible for the Crown prosecutors to bring up any information attached to the three rulings. And the fallout went beyond that. No evidence could go forward if it linked one of the six counts going to trial to any of the twenty whose counts had been severed. The prosecutors were stunned. As far as they were concerned, Williams had just gutted their case.

The trial began on January 22, 2007. At six thirty that morning it was still chilly when camera operators, bundled in quilted jackets and toques, unzipped the front doors of the white media tents set up in front of the courthouse and began turning on lights and computers and setting up chairs. Just as the sun was beginning to come up over the Fraser River below, Peter Ritchie, wearing his trademark beret and a heavy coat, walked down the long stairs from his office at the top of the block on Victoria Street, accompanied by Patrick McGowan. About eight a.m., Mike Petrie, Derrill Prevett, Geoff Baragar and Satindar Sidhu, gowned and ready to go, ambled across Carnarvon Street from their basement offices in the old courthouse. Family members, the general public and reporters without a reserved seat in the courtroom were lining up at the front door, sending runners off for coffee to help stay warm.

When the doors finally opened at eight thirty, security remained as strict as it had been for the voir dire. Armed sheriffs in bulletproof vests stood by the safety gates for everyone—except lawyers, police and security personnel—who entered the building, and the two additional checkpoints to enter the courtroom itself. The room filled up quickly, and the overflow moved into the large courtroom beside it to watch the proceedings on large monitors. Some family members came into the main courtroom and the remaining seats were quickly filled by reporters, task force members and a few members of the public. As always, the two seats reserved for the Pickton family or friends remained empty. Wherever they watched, with the exception of the family room, the onlookers were expected to remain silent, with cellphones turned off.

Pickton arrived clean-shaven, with his greasy hair trimmed into a short mullet. By now reporters had heard that he saved the little packets of Becel margarine he got every morning with his toast so he could use it to slick back his hair. He wore a new grey cotton shirt and black jeans and carried a binder with paper in it for making notes. He took his seat directly in front of the public gallery, his back to the people, separated from them by a wall of glass that extended across the room; it had a locked glass door to allow the lawyers and witnesses entry into the court itself. A second glass wall wrapped around his chair on three sides. Beyond him sat the lawyers, with Judge Williams at the front and his own lawyer, Christine Judd, at his left, down a step and to the side of the jury box. Adrian Brooks walked in; when he saw Mike Petrie, he walked over and the two shook hands.

As soon as everyone was seated, the jury filed in and Williams asked the legal teams to introduce themselves; the lawyers stood, bowed to the jury and gave their names. Petrie, Derrill Prevett, Geoff Baragar and Satindar Sidhu were there for the Crown; the defence team today included Brooks, Peter Ritchie, Marilyn Sandford and Patrick McGowan. Judge Williams offered up a short sermon to the jury members about the publication bans that remained on the preliminary hearing and the voir dire. "Use your common sense and experience," he told them. "Consider the evidence with an open mind. Please do not talk about the case with other people, do not hang around in the halls. You will have red maple leaf pins on so others will know not to approach you."

And they were off. Derrill Prevett led the way by telling the jury that Pickton had admitted to killing forty-nine women. He gave a thorough outline of the Crown's case, explaining that they were looking at the lives of six addicted women in the sex trade. "Each had people and places and things that were important to her," he said. "They were known to phone their loved ones. They stopped using their drug plans. There was a complete end to a pattern of living. The Downtown Eastside is a social community and the women were conspicuous by their absence."

He told them about the efforts made to find these women and how in February 2002 the police, armed with a search warrant, went to the seventeen-acre Pickton farm to look for illegal guns. He described the discovery of clothes, medicines and identification owned by many of the missing women and the subsequent seizure of the property, which was then searched until November 2003. Prevett also took the jury through the various buildings on the property, identifying each one and showing how each had been given a letter: Site A, Willie's trailer; Site B, the slaughterhouse; Site C, the mechanical shop; Site D, the workshop/garage; Site V-3, the motor home; and finally Site F, the old Pickton farmhouse, almost always called "Dave's house" because it was where Dave Pickton had lived for many years. Prevett explained that all the primary evidence relating to the six women at the heart of this trial was found in the trailer or the area right around it. "DNA analysis," he said, "has identified the remains of each of these women."

And very quickly he went through that evidence as it applied to each of the six. But he also addressed what he called the "elephant in the room"—the fact that there were many other counts against Pickton that were not part of this trial. Prevett's style was conversational and friendly, and the jury was riveted by his story. He went on to tell them what they might expect to hear over the next months. "It is not in dispute that the six women are dead. It is not in dispute that they died at 963 Dominion. It is not in dispute that the accused killed the named deceased." But did Pickton murder them? "That's the issue in dispute," Prevett said. "The judge will instruct you on that matter but the Crown intends to prove these murders."

He took the jury on a quick run through the evidence on each of the six murder counts, including Pickton's gabby admissions to his cellmate after his arrest. Prevett told the jury Pickton had confided that he killed forty-nine women on his farm and that he was planning to do one more to "make it an even fifty." Prevett also told the jury what they could expect to hear from key Crown witnesses such as Lynn Ellingsen, Scott Chubb and Andrew Bellwood.

Unusually for a murder case, Judge Williams allowed Peter Ritchie to make his own opening statement. The reason for this, explained Steven Skurka, a legal expert hired by the CTV television network to comment on the trial, was that the trial was going to be so long that the defence needed to be able to lay out its own road-map right at the beginning. "The jury will then be able to connect the dots from the cross-examination of the various Crown witnesses to the defence opening."

"I suggest you not be overwhelmed by the information you've heard today," Ritchie told the jurors. "The defence does not accept the Crown's case. We will be vigorously contesting the Crown's case. Mr. Pickton did not participate in the killing or kill any of these women." Yes, the human evidence is shocking, said Ritchie, but Mr. Prevett hadn't given them the full picture. "I ask you to approach [this evidence] impassionately. Some DNA evidence is not easy to understand. Be alert. You will hear about other people. Their roles are particularly significant."

After the lunch break, the first witness was Don Adam. The trial progressed from his testimony much as it had in the preliminary hearing, explaining how he had come to the case and managed the file review conducted by his new Missing Women's Joint Task Force and describing their eventual focus on Pickton. Adam proved to be a difficult man to shake; in his cross-examination Ritchie had no luck at all in punching holes in his story. Nor could he unsettle Bill Fordy, who testified about interviewing Pickton after his arrest.

The days rolled along, each bringing Crown witnesses to add their stories, their findings and other evidence. This case was now in the public record, and some members of the public made it clear they didn't like reading about the horrible details of the case as they unfolded in witness testimony day after day. This information had previously been cloaked by publication bans, but now, in the presence of a jury, the bans were lifted.* Although people had been waiting to hear about what they didn't know, some decided they didn't want to know any more, thank you. Very quickly newspapers began

---

But lifted only for testimony in this trial. The bans on publication for the preliminary hearing in 2003 and the 2005–2006 voir dire remained in place.

putting disclaimers at the beginnings of their stories, warning people they might be upset by the content. Soon the stories were off the front pages and buried deep in the paper, often in the second section.

It was the same for television and radio: *If you listen to this story it will upset you.* In his weekly online column, Tony Burman, then the CBC's news editor, said viewers were angry about all the coverage. "Do we need to know that these poor women's bodies were found terribly dismembered in buckets?" a radio listener asked him. "Where is your discretion?" Burman wrote that, now the first day of the trial was over, "the network will pull back from saturation coverage." Within a few months the Pickton trial had almost disappeared from the public consciousness. "Pickton?" people would ask. "Is that still going on?"

But the drama in the courtroom was real. On February 22, the anniversary of Pickton's arrest for murder, RCMP sergeant Tim Sleigh told the jury about finding the severed heads, hands and feet of Andrea Joesbury and Sereena Abotsway in a freezer in Pickton's workshop, and how another searcher found Brenda Wolfe's jaw where Pickton used to feed his pigs.

In March 2007 a Vancouver police officer, Constable Mike McDonald, under cross-examination by the defence, said that Dave Pickton was still under investigation because it was thought possible he could have been involved in the disappearances of the missing women and their deaths. In May Judge Williams had to stop proceedings for a break when some of the jurors became upset after looking at gruesome photographs of evidence: autopsy pictures of the remains of Sereena Abotsway, Mona Wilson and Andrea Joesbury.

And in late June Richard Brooks was back in court to dismantle as much as possible of Lynn Ellingsen's testimony about finding a dead woman hanging on a chain in Pickton's slaughterhouse. Brooks spent seven days on the attack, and Ellingsen, who began her testimony cheerful and self-confident, smartly dressed in a new outfit of slacks and a jacket, fell apart under Brooks's merciless interrogation. The fact that she was high on crack cocaine when this incident was said to have happened, he insisted, meant that she couldn't know what she had seen. Brooks was particularly unpleasant as he questioned Ellingsen about the financial help she had received from the police. Yes, they'd helped her with rent and food sometimes. Yes, they bought her an outfit for court, she acknowledged—she had nothing fit to wear. Yes, they had paid for rehab and more.

Scott Chubb and Andrew Bellwood also faced strenuous attacks from the defence, attacks that succeeded in unnerving both men. Chubb arrived in court in mid-June looking like an extra in the 1955 film of the musical *Guys and Dolls*; his bleached hair had been cut short, parted in the centre and gelled into place. He wore dark glasses and a tight-fitting suit over a dark shirt and a pale silk tie. After lengthy and unfriendly questioning from Peter Ritchie as he picked away at Chubb's criminal record, his addiction to drugs, and the money the police gave him for rent, Chubb finally had had enough. "Well, Mr. Ritchie, you can attack me, and attack my character," he said, "but I am not on trial for six counts of murder."

When it was Andrew Bellwood's turn to face hostile questions, they came from Adrian Brooks. Bellwood had shocked the courtroom earlier when he spoke about the conversation he had with Pickton about how he killed prostitutes. "He had mentioned to me, 'You know what I do with these prostitutes?'" Bellwood testified. "From there he reached underneath his mattress. He pulled out a set of handcuffs that looked like a set of police handcuffs. He pulled out a belt and he pulled out a piece of wire. The wire had looped ends on it that looked like it had been spliced. The wire was the same consistency as piano wire." He went on to say that Pickton had explained how he killed the women. He had sex with them from behind and then, before they knew what was happening, he handcuffed them, strangled them and took them to the slaughterhouse, where he gutted them and fed them to the pigs.

Brooks wasn't having any of this. He called Bellwood a liar. He pointed out Bellwood's history of theft, possession of stolen property, public mischief and fraud. You lied to probation officers and judges eight years ago, the lawyer declared, as he paged through Bellwood's old criminal records. Bellwood refused to accept Brooks's interpretation. He had never lied in court, he told Brooks. For a while Bellwood was distressed by the continuing barrage of hostile statements, but finally he'd also had enough and he went after Brooks for inaccuracies in the reports he was using. It made for a rare moment of humour. As one reporter chuckled, "Andy's got his mojo back."

Bellwood, who now lived in Alberta, where he ran a motel, said that the Edmonton police had questioned him about a number of women who had gone missing there. "I was so pissed off that I would be interrogated on the Edmonton missing women," he stated. "The only reason they questioned me," he said, "was because they knew I was a witness in the Pickton case."

Gina Houston testified in August 2007. Still dealing with cancer, grey-faced and emaciated, confined to a wheelchair and wearing dark glasses, she looked much older than her thirty-nine years. She testified that Willie Pickton had told her, shortly before his arrest, that the police would find up to six bodies on his property. And she talked about a conversation she said she'd had with Pickton two days before his arrest. He told her that Mona Wilson had been hurt while he was talking to her (Houston) on the telephone late in 2001. That was when he told Houston that he'd tried to help Mona but she "didn't make it." He also told her he hadn't called 911.

"I asked if she was still somewhere in the piggery, and he said yes," she testified. "I asked what was next to her. He told me one, two, three, four, five or six bodies." When Houston asked him where exactly he'd put the bodies, he said they were in what he called the "cock pen," which was the place in the slaughterhouse once used for cockfights. She also testified that Pickton had said the only way out for him was suicide. But Houston did her best to direct blame onto Dinah Taylor in the deaths of some of the women. She testified that when she was living at the Pickton farm, she had seen Dinah Taylor in Pickton's bedroom arguing with Sereena Abotsway.

———

By the middle of August 2007, the Crown had called ninety-eight witnesses, and they were done. It was now up to the defence to call its own witnesses—there would be thirty-one of them—to help prove that their client was innocent. Everyone was intrigued; these were the first witnesses for the defence to appear since Pickton's arrest in 2002. Who would come to stand up for Willie Pickton? Who were his friends and allies? What was the defence's strategy to save their client? It soon became clear. The strategy was, first and foremost, "the other guy did it." What other guy—or woman as the case might be, because Pickton's lawyers tried again and again to say it could have been Dinah Taylor or Gina Houston—wasn't clear, but the farm was full of people day and night. It was, in fact, a beehive of activity, there were many people who could have killed these women and it wasn't fair to blame Willie Pickton.

Bill Malone, who testified in early September, was the defence team's choice to deliver this line of argument. There was a steady stream of people coming into the farm, night and day, Malone told the court—the truck drivers who worked for Dave, friends of the family, strangers, you name it. They were all over Willie's place. Anyone could do anything there and who'd know? Malone, now sixty-three years old, was one of the worst choices the defence could have made to stand up for Willie Pickton. When Mike Petrie asked him on cross-examination about his "self-appointed job to spread disinformation about the investigation that was going on," Malone retorted that he was entitled to free speech under the Canadian Charter of Rights.

"Your free speech," said Petrie, "was essentially propaganda on behalf of the Pickton family." Malone didn't back off. "I did not feel that this investigation would be going in the right direction, and nobody else would say anything," Malone said. And yes, he'd refused to let Baltej Dhillon, a task force member, question him because Dhillon wore a turban. In Canada, blustered Malone, people should adopt Canadian ways. "You're a racist, aren't you?" Mike Petrie asked. Flushed and humiliated but still defiant, Malone didn't deny it. Petrie also forced him to admit that Pickton's trailer wasn't bustling with people and trucks, as he had claimed earlier, but isolated from the rest of the farm and at least a hundred metres away from the closest townhouse to the north.

Malone turned into a win for the Crown, but their satisfaction was short-lived. The following day, October 10, 2007, Judge Williams delivered his last, crushing blow to the prosecutors. Even though the judge had quashed Count 27, the count involving Jane Doe, evidence around her death had been presented to the jury. They knew that half her skull had been found in a slough in Mission; they knew that her heel and rib bones had been found on the farm, buried close to the slaughterhouse. They knew that her head and bones had been severed like the others found on the farm. And they knew that she'd been found in 1995 and that hers were considered the oldest remains found on the farm. She was also the only woman in the counts who had not been identified.

Judge Williams's instructions to the jury, in what he called a mid-trial instruction, were astonishing. Never before, in almost a year of trial, had he told them to forget about evidence they'd heard. And it was a lot of evidence. "You must put the Jane Doe evidence out of your mind," he said. "It must simply be ignored. I have decided that the Jane Doe evidence is not anything that you can consider in any way in determining whether the Crown has proven that Mr. Pickton is guilty of any or all of the offences on the indictment, or whether you have a reasonable doubt on any or all of those offences." To ensure they obeyed him, Williams ordered the court registrar to remove the transcripts and notes concerning Jane Doe from their binders, which she did, one by one, in the silent courtroom.

The judge realized how shocked people must be. "You must not speculate why I have done this," he said. "And you must also not for a moment think this is the fault of the Crown or the fault of the defence." Outside, later that day, Jennifer Lopes wept. On the prosecutors' team she had been responsible for the Jane Doe file, and she found the loss of this evidence unbearable. "For me, Jane Doe represented all the unknown women who disappeared and were never found, the women who were found dead and never identified, the women who never had a chance at having their cases heard," she explained through her tears. "It's as if she never existed. As if she never mattered."

Derrill Prevett may not have been crying but he was just as upset. He could not believe what had happened to their case. It wasn't just losing Jane Doe, it was losing Sandra Gail Ringwald too. And it was losing twenty counts of first-degree murder.

Over the next few weeks the defence brought in the rest of their witnesses. While few of them were as embarrassing as Bill Malone, they were not as helpful as Pickton's lawyers probably hoped they'd be. When Sandy Humeny, who managed Dave Pickton's office at the Tannery Road building, testified that Willie was slow, Petrie forced her to admit that he was smart enough to put accounts together, manage money and run his own small business.

Jon Nordby, a blood-spatter expert like the RCMP's Jack Mellis, said that in his opinion the big stain on the foam mattress in the motor home was not blood, nor did he accept that a "blood-shedding" incident had happened here. Yet this is the place where Mona Wilson died after she had been beaten with a shower hose, stabbed and dragged out onto the ground. Her blood had been found in twenty places in the vehicle. When Nordby stuck to his theory that the blood had not come from one attack, Petrie asked him how he made that decision. Nordby said he had been able to look at pictures and reports prepared by the police and given to him by Pickton's lawyers. He conceded under questioning that the photographs were of poor quality and the sample too small to support a solid opinion. He also said he'd studied only about a hundred photos of the 2,668 supplied to him.

A psychologist, Larry Krywaniuk, an expert on early childhood intelligence, was there to show yet again that Pickton was too dumb to get away with a crime this big. However, he agreed that Pickton's IQ was average and that he was capable of expressing himself in letters and in his business dealings.

Probably the most embarrassing witness for the defence was Ingrid Fehlauer, Sandy Humeny's sister. She admitted, under Mike Petrie's cross-examination, not only that she was a friend of Willie Pickton's and biased towards him, but also that she had lied when giving her evidence earlier. She had told the jury she'd never seen anything unusual in Pickton's trailer. But after Mike Petrie asked her if in fact she had seen blood in the trailer, she said yes, she had. That would have been right after the stabbing incident with Sandra Gail Ringwald in March 1997.

"On one occasion, when you cleaned [Pickton's] trailer, you saw lots of blood everywhere, isn't that correct?" Petrie asked.

"Yes," she said.

"You would agree with me that's something unusual."

"Yes," she said.

Petrie thought for a moment. "Why didn't you tell the jury about the blood this morning?" he asked.

"It was my understanding that this was not going to be mentioned when I was being cross-examined," Fehlauer answered. She was nervous and glanced at Pickton's lawyers.

At this point Judge Williams jumped in. Looking at the jury members, he asked them not to "carry a grudge" against Pickton or his lawyers. "It may be an issue that goes to [Fehlauer's] credibility that she chose to answer the question as she did," Williams said. "I think it's established by the question and answers that we just heard, that she answered the questions in a way that wasn't truthful."

Thanksgiving Day, October 11, 2007, brought one of the strangest encounters seen in Courtroom 102. It was a holiday and the courthouse was closed—closed except for a secret emergency session that had been called. It started about nine o'clock in the morning and lasted until six that afternoon. They were there because a report had come in from the police that led Judge Williams to demand that he question a member of the jury, a young woman who sat at the left end of the top row. Most of the reporters covering the case had noticed her: she rarely seemed to pay attention, didn't take notes and giggled a lot with her neighbour. Her pen had a spray of coloured strands sticking out of the top that matched the little ponytail that poked from the top of her head. Both topknots seemed to flip back and forth constantly.

The story was that a man who co-owned a bar in Metrotown—a large shopping centre in Burnaby, the city between New Westminster and Vancouver—had been charged with date rape. Two women who worked in this bar, one of whom was the other co-owner, had made the complaint. But when the police questioned the women, they found they had a second story to tell. They said that a colleague of theirs who worked in the bar was off serving on the Pickton jury, and that she often came into the bar to see her friends. She held strong opinions about the Pickton case, which she didn't hesitate to share with them. This juror had told them some time ago that she didn't think Pickton was guilty, the women told the police. The woman who was the bar's co-owner told the police she thought the juror was a psychopath; she disliked her and wanted to fire her.

Twice the police interviewed both of the women who had made the complaint. They took statements, and the female co-owner said again that the juror had told her what she thought of Pickton, that she didn't think he was guilty. Later, before Judge Williams had called her in for this unusual talking-to, the juror told the co-owner that she had changed her mind—she thought he hadn't killed the women but had helped dispose of the bodies. She remained convinced that he hadn't killed the women. A kitchen worker confirmed to the police that the juror would often talk about the case during her visits to the bar.

Judge Williams listened to all of this and brought the juror in to question her at ten a.m. "She was very cocky," remembers one person who was in the courtroom. "She didn't seem at all flustered, even when Williams asked her question after question. She completely denied it all."

The defence and the Crown argued about what to do. The

Crown wanted her thrown off the jury and the defence wanted her to stay. Judge Williams finally said that, while he was suspicious of her, he had to consider the fact that the statements from the two making the allegations were not taken under oath. So he was reluctant to throw her out.

The judge repeated his first instructions to the juror, to not discuss the case with anyone outside the jury room, and he let her stay. "She was really cocky—she denied it all," said the witness again, who had watched it all from the public gallery, taking notes.

The following day, October 12, the case resumed and the juror was in her seat, twiddling her tasselled pen as usual. On October 16 the defence finished with the last of their thirty-one witnesses. It was time for a month-long break to prepare the final arguments.

The family section of Courtroom 102 was almost empty when Adrian Brooks, not Peter Ritchie, began presenting the closing arguments for Pickton's defence on November 19. Ritchie had been ill—rumours flew through the courthouse that he'd become ill quite suddenly, maybe with a minor stroke, and had been taken to hospital—and while he was now back in the courtroom, he didn't have the stamina to fight for their client's acquittal. The families were huddled together in the private room nearby, watching the monitor. They were too anxious to sit still in court, unable to talk to each other.

Using a PowerPoint presentation for the first time since the legal stages had started back in Port Coquitlam in 2003, it took Brooks three and a half days to present his case. He stuck to his "some other guy must have done it" thesis, saying that the evidence showed that many of Pickton's closest friends were better suspects than he was. Brooks attacked the credibility of the Crown's witnesses and argued that Pickton's confession meant nothing; all he was doing was parroting what the police were saying to him. This was part of Brooks's strategy: along with the other-guy-did-it argument, he told the jury that Pickton was just too stupid to carry off these crimes. His client hadn't really understood the questions the police asked during his interrogation; they were far more sophisticated than Willie Pickton, who is a man of "limited intelligence."

And the jury shouldn't trust the evidence from the likes of Scott Chubb, Lynn Ellingsen and Andrew Bellwood. Their memories were poor, insisted Brooks, and they had a history of lying to get what they wanted. And don't forget, they received money from the police. Chubb, said Brooks, had a long history of lying. Bellwood, he said later, was a con man: "He is a leopard who has never changed his spots." Ellingsen never saw a woman hanging from a hook in the slaughterhouse, he said. Surely what she saw was a pig.

Brooks also challenged the forensic evidence, saying that Pickton would never have hidden heads in a freezer. "Why would he hide it in a freezer that other people have access to?" He also stated that the forensic evidence against Pat Casanova was far stronger than it was against Pickton. "Take into account, please," he begged the jury, "how it is stronger than the evidence against Mr. Pickton." As for the jewellery and other belongings of the murdered women that were found in Pickton's loft—well, who knows how they got there? How do we know it was Pickton who put the stuff up there? If the police hadn't been so hard on Willie, who knows who might be on trial today? Brooks took dead aim at Dinah Taylor as a real possibility; he quoted her as saying about Andrea Joesbury, "I am going to kill the bitch." He was indefatigable. "This is a case," he said in his final words to the jury, "that's fuelled with reasonable doubt."

The *Toronto Star*'s Rosie DiManno summed it up well: "Among the rogue's gallery of hookers, junkies and grifters drawn to Robert Pickton's pig farm, like moths to a flame, there lurked an assortment of at least potential killers. To hear the defence team tell it, punitive maniacs were thick on the ground, any one of whom could have slain the six drug-addled prostitutes Pickton stands accused of murdering and dismembering."

Now it was Mike Petrie's turn for closing arguments. Like Brooks, he too used a PowerPoint presentation for the first time, a surprise to all who had watched him work without notes for so many years. But before he turned to it, he spent time trying to dismantle Adrian Brooks's arguments. Witnesses hadn't testified about anyone besides Pickton, he told the jury. "You didn't hear evidence of stories like 'Pat Casanova was out butchering someone in the slaughterhouse' or 'Dinah Taylor was shooting someone' or 'Dave Pickton was taking drugs and putting it down someone's throat.' You heard evidence about that man right there."

And Pickton was smarter and more sophisticated than the feeble-minded person portrayed by the defence, he said, citing his crafty efforts to negotiate with Don Adam and to make the police feel sorry for him with all his tales of his hard life as a poor little farm boy. And when the defence tried to shunt blame onto Bellwood, Petrie said, because Bellwood had testified that Pickton told him how he killed prostitutes from behind, handcuffing and strangling them with wire, how could they explain away the fact that the police found evidence that supported his story? "Was it just a lucky guess on the part of Mr. Bellwood?" asked Petrie. "We know there are butchered remains on the property, but he wouldn't have."

As for Lynn Ellingsen, regardless of how unpleasant and humiliating her six days of cross-examination by Richard Brooks were, her story never changed, said Petrie. She was an easy target, he said: "She's got a lot of skeletons in her closet. But she didn't waver on what she saw. She said, 'I went into that barn and I saw a woman hanging there and it was Willie Pickton who was butchering her.'"

Setting aside the witnesses, Petrie talked about the "constellation of evidence" piled up in and around Willie's home, and he named a few: Sereena Abotsway's asthma inhalers in a garbage can outside his trailer; a .22 revolver with a dildo on the end, found in his laundry room, that contained Mona Wilson's DNA, as well as a pillowslip that held Andrea Joesbury's DNA; and Georgina Papin's hand bones in the piggery behind the slaughterhouse.

It was the same with Scott Chubb, said Petrie. The things he had told police, years before anyone else knew, before the police had even found the evidence, were true. Petrie used the word *confirmatory* to describe Chubb's knowledge of the syringe and windshield-wiper fluid found by searchers long after he'd described them to the police. "Is that just a lucky guess?" asked Petrie. And, he added, when the defence subjected Chubb to days of hostile questions, they had nothing to do with what Petrie called "core issues." "The purpose of that," Petrie said to the jury, "was to destroy Chubb's life so that he would become laughable to you. But that's a trick of the trade."

These witnesses—Ellingsen, Chubb and Bellwood—were not Rhodes Scholars and they did have criminal records, Petrie said. But they were also three independent people. "There was no collusion." Nor was Pickton as stupid as the defence tried to make them believe. "He was not a naive person who has been duped." He was described, said Petrie, as "'cagey as a fox,' and that is exactly what he was."

Petrie spent some time playing short sections of the videotaped conversations from February 23, 2002, between Pickton and the undercover police officer in the holding cell. "The most compelling," Petrie said, happened just before Pickton went to sleep after his long interrogation by Bill Fordy and Don Adam. The courtroom was silent as the video played. No one moved; all eyes were on the monitor. Pickton is under his blanket. He sighs several times. "So close," he murmurs, before closing his eyes. "So, so close."

"The conversation is over," Petrie told the jury. "There are those long pauses that last one, one minute and thirty-nine seconds. And then he ends by saying, 'So close.' It is welling in [his] mind that he almost did it. He almost pulled it off."

Petrie used his PowerPoint presentation to show, through coloured graphics and maps, how the evidence was stacked up around Willie Pickton's trailer and the slaughterhouse, workshop/garage, mechanical shop and motor home. If Willie Pickton is not guilty, Petrie said, he "must be the unluckiest man alive, because he has the remains of not just one, not two, but six women on his property within metres of his home.

"He's a butcher. That's an unfortunate coincidence if he's just an unlucky man. The personal effects of these women just happened to be in his house. Again, if he's an unlucky man, that's a very unfortunate coincidence." Then there is the fact that he told the police he had killed forty-nine women, Petrie said as he ended his closing arguments. "That's probably as unlucky a coincidence as you could possibly have."

CHAPTER FIFTY-THREE

GUILTY!—BUT OF WHAT?

On Tuesday, November 27, 2007, soon after Mike Petrie had finished making the case for the Crown, Judge Williams began his charge to the jury, telling them it would take about three days to go through the evidence with them. "Keep an open mind but not an empty head," he advised them. Methodically he plowed through the case as it related to each of the six counts, going over the evidence and the testimony of many of the key witnesses, including the expert who had testified about Pickton's intelligence. He told the jury to play the tapes of Pickton's interviews with the police after his arrest, as well as the conversations he'd had with the undercover officer in his cell.

"If you conclude that his words in either or both of the statements are admissions of responsibility for the murders of women," the judge said, "and you conclude that he was speaking truthfully, you can use both statements in determining whether the Crown has proven its case against Mr. Pickton." He explained that the police were allowed by law to lie to Pickton and to interview him for the eleven hours he spent talking to Bill Fordy and Don Adam—unless the jury believed that the lies and the length of the interview had "worn down or exhausted [him] in a way that impacted on the meaning or truthfulness of the statements."

Several members of the missing women's families arrived to listen to the final legal arguments. When a plan to have the families stay in a hotel in New Westminster fell through because the hotel didn't have room for everyone and the authorities wanted to keep everyone together, Victim Services switched them to a much better hotel in downtown Vancouver. Freda Ens and Norma Parr, a long-time Victim Services worker who, like Ens, had been on the Pickton case for several years, escorted these relatives to the trial. Usually they came out on the SkyTrain because the station in New Westminster was only two blocks from the courthouse. Some members stayed in the family room to watch; others preferred to sit in court.

Wayne Leng flew up from California, taking a break from his job as service manager at a large General Motors dealership. He couldn't afford the plane ticket and Victim Services did not consider him a relative, so Cara Ellis's sister-in-law, Lori-Ann Ellis, who was there with her mother, Judy Trimble, paid for his ticket. Like almost all the other family members, the Ellis family were grateful to Leng. He had set up and was running the missingpeople.net website, which kept friends and relatives informed of developments and contained an archive of past news stories; it also gave people a message board where they could post their memories, questions and comments. Leng found a cheap hotel room, but when Lynn and Rick Frey arrived and found out where he was, they invited him to share their spacious room in the Vancouver hotel. He happily slept on the floor there and they shared their meal vouchers with him as well.

To their surprise, the families began to have some fun. As Lori-Ann Ellis told the *Sun*'s Lori Culbert, "[She] and Cara's mother, Judy Trimble, have 'pyjama parties' at night with Kraft and Lynn Frey, the step-mother of Marnie Frey."

The Freys had brought their granddaughter Brittney, Marnie Frey's daughter, who had become a dark-eyed, vivacious teenager. She quickly struck up a friendship with Sarah de Vries's daughter, Jeanie. Jeanie had arrived with her grandmother Pat de Vries and her aunt, Sarah's sister Maggie de Vries. During breaks the girls would run up and down the corridors of the courthouse together, giggling, while the sheriffs looked on indulgently. Every so often the emotion of what was happening around them would hit, and then they would be seen sobbing in a relative's arms.

Lilliane and René Beaudoin came to Vancouver from Welland, Ontario; Lilliane was Diane Rock's sister. Marilyn Kraft, stepmother to Cynthia Feliks, came from Edmonton. Like the others, they stayed in the hotel in Vancouver. Barry Bottomley, whose daughter, Heather, was one of the women Pickton had been charged with killing, came almost every day, as he had during the voir dire. He never spoke to reporters, sticking close to Freda Ens and Marilynne Johnny and watching the proceedings in the family room. And the irrepressible Papin sisters, Cynthia Cardinal, Elana Papin and Bonnie Fowler, were there. They all lived in or near Edmonton and had made six trips to British Columbia to attend the trial. This time, broke and sharing a single set of meal vouchers meant for one family member, they'd come all the way by bus and were cheerful about having to share a room.

Mona Wilson's brother, Jayson Fleury, who was forty-three and a member of the O'Chiese First Nation near Rocky Mountain House, came from Edson, Alberta. This was a painful trip for him; he hadn't known he had a sister Mona until he was an adult, because she'd been in foster care since she was eight years old, but he had met her when she was an addicted teenager turning tricks in the Downtown Eastside. Nineteen-year-old Troy Boen, the son of Yvonne Boen, who was last seen in 2001, was there by himself; the other families soon adopted him as one of their own.

It was a strange time. People were emotional. Tempers flared and small slights, real or imagined, ballooned into ugly arguments, often directed at the hapless Victim Services workers. It was cold, Christmas was coming and the trial had lasted nearly a year. How much longer would everyone have to wait?

It took Judge Williams three days to instruct the jury. Armed with thick three-ring binders of evidence that included photographs of exhibits such as guns, knives, saws and freezers, photographs of the farm property and the buildings—inside and out—as well as maps, diagrams, statements and other relevant information, the jurors left the courtroom on November 30, 2007. No one knew how long this was going to take, but until they came back with a verdict, the court would remain open every day, including weekends and into the evenings, until the jurors quit to go to bed. They were sequestered in a nearby hotel so they couldn't go home and call friends or talk to anyone else about the deliberations.

What this meant to the weary, emotional families of the missing women was that they wouldn't leave the courthouse until the jury did. The reporters couldn't leave either; they had no idea when there would be a verdict. Task force members and the lawyers for both sides had offices nearby they could go to, but they spent almost as much time hanging around the courthouse as the reporters did. It was a strange out-of-body experience for almost everyone. At first no one wanted to go even to the Starbucks two blocks away in case the jury came back, so Lou Ferguson was so busy she kept running out of food. The smell of canned chicken soup drifted through the building. The jury sat through the evening, so the days were long; no one went home until ten p.m. at the earliest.

There were unpleasant complications that no one had considered. The heating system, for example, was turned off every weekend by a central control system managed, it was rumoured, out of some place like Kelowna. Victim Services staff brought in quilts and afghans to keep people warm but there was no one to restock or clean the bathrooms, so they stank. It wasn't all bad, though. Victim Services staff—carrying cellphones so they could be notified and return immediately if the jury announced it had reached a verdict—took family members for lunch every day to a restaurant a couple of blocks away called the Heritage Grill. The only problem was that only people with vouchers could come, and that left people such as Wayne Leng on their own.

On December 6 there was news. A verdict? No. In the early afternoon, word raced around the building that the jury had a question for the judge. Everyone trooped back into Courtroom 102 to find out what was happening. The jury foreman, a retired man who had a short grey beard and wore an open-necked sports shirt, told Williams that the jury didn't understand what the judge had meant when he told them, "If you find Mr. Pickton shot Miss Abotsway, you should find the Crown has proven this element. On the other hand, if you have a reasonable doubt about whether or not he shot her, you must return a verdict of not guilty on the charge of murdering her."

The foreman's question sounded simple enough: "Are we able to say yes if we infer the accused acted indirectly?" Judge Williams was shocked. At this point few in the room really understood what was going on. What did this mean? However, Williams clearly understood what had happened. He looked over at Geoff Baragar, one of the prosecutors who had returned to the courtroom.

"Crown . . . Crown!" stormed Williams. "You signed off on this!" People in the gallery were mystified, and Baragar was stunned. He didn't reply. Williams asked for a break. The sheriffs cleared the courtroom and the jurors returned to their room. Two and a half hours later, everyone was called back into Courtroom 102. Williams wasn't blaming anyone but himself now.

"I have concluded I was not sufficiently precise," Williams told the jury. "I was in error with respect to three paragraphs of your charge. I regret I misinformed you. It was inadvertent." The amended charge he now gave the jury made reference to three women: Sereena Abotsway, Mona Wilson and Andrea Joesbury. This time Williams instructed the jury that Pickton could be found guilty if he shot Abotsway or was an "active participant" in her death, and the case was the same for the other two women. All three had been shot in the head. Williams rewrote his original instructions to read: "If you find that Mr. Pickton shot Ms. Abotsway or was otherwise an active participant in her killing, you should find the Crown has proved this element. On the other hand, if you have reasonable doubt that he was an active participant in this killing, you must return a verdict of not guilty."

In other words, even if Pickton didn't act alone, they could find him guilty. Williams continued to try to clear up his instructions:

"You may find Mr. Pickton acted in concert with other persons although you may not yet know who they are. It is sufficient if you are satisfied beyond a reasonable doubt, having considered all the evidence, that he actively participated in the killings of his victims; it is not sufficient that he was merely present or took a minor role."

The jurors returned to their deliberations; the journalists and families went back to the courthouse lobby and looked for places to sit; the lawyers drifted back to their offices to think through this strange experience with the jury. What would it mean to their trial? Was it good news for the defence? Bad news? No one really understood the gravity of the mistake that had been made. And if they suspected, then who exactly had made the mistake? Judge Williams? Or the Crown prosecutor who had caught the first blast of the judge's dismay?

Some journalists used the time over the next few days to complete in-depth feature interviews with family members. Others read, gossiped and played computer games. Except for one weak spot in a corner of the main floor, there was no wireless signal for Internet access, so for most there was no email. Everyone got bored, and boredom bred trouble. A rift developed between some Native families and some non-Native ones, and it showed signs of getting ugly; the groups began to separate into different parts of the waiting room.

Then one of those clichéd Christmas miracles happened that made everyone feel ridiculous but a whole lot better. Some anonymous soul put up a Christmas tree in front of the courthouse and hung twenty-six white angels on it. Pretty corny, yes. But it suddenly sunk in that there were twenty-six women they needed to remember now, not just the six named in the trial. Early on Sunday afternoon, December 9, someone else had a bright idea. It was time to stop arguing about who had suffered more, who'd been treated worse than others, who deserved justice or rewards or better accommodation or more meal tickets. It was time for a healing ceremony.

Outside, near the Christmas tree with the twenty-six angels, it started with the Native family members, who formed into a circle and began to dance. White family members outside for a smoke or a breath of fresh air found themselves pulled in one at a time. Next to join were others from the courthouse when they strolled outside to see what was happening. As each new person was pulled into the circle and encouraged to dance—sheepishly and awkwardly at first—the other people smiled and cheered. Each newcomer was hugged by everyone in the circle. Even the cynical reporters watching from inside found themselves with lumps in their throats.

It was ten minutes after two in the afternoon when a shout came from one of the sheriffs—we have a verdict! The families outside heard the news a second or two later. Their circle blew apart and everyone ran towards the courthouse doors. The sheriffs tried to calm them down; the jury wouldn't be delivering their verdict for another hour. Everyone still had to go through the security gates and everyone still had to make sure they had their tickets to get into Courtroom 102. Task force members arrived, and so did the lawyers. Everyone pushed towards the courtroom. Some had tears rolling down their faces. Everyone looked worried, especially the legal teams.

Within a few minutes the crowd was in the large waiting room just outside the courtroom itself. There was not a ticket to spare for 102, so some people had to go into the overflow courtroom. When the doors finally opened, the reporters filed in and took their seats in the two front rows; seven of them pulled out their BlackBerrys. They would be filing short messages directly from the courtroom as they heard the news. The court artists, also in the front row, set up their drawing pads and selected coloured pencils and chalk.

The families and the general public, including some journalists who didn't have reserved seats in the front, sat in the next few rows. The two seats set aside for the Pickton family and friends remained vacant, as they had for the entire time they'd been reserved in the Port Coquitlam and New Westminster courts. The last row at the back of this tiny courtroom was for members of the task force and the general public. Don Adam, now officially retired and no longer the head of the task force but still working with them as an advisor, came in with his replacement, Ward Lymburner, as well as Bill Fordy, the RCMP member who first interviewed Pickton after his arrest. Margaret Kingsbury also joined them.

The legal teams arrived; Mike Petrie, Derrill Prevett, John Ahern, Geoff Baragar, Jay Fogel and Jennifer Lopes for the Crown, and Peter Ritchie, Adrian Brooks, Patrick McGowan, Richard Brooks and Marilyn Sandford for the defence. They waited in the well of the court while Judge Williams and Robert Pickton, wearing his usual grey sweater, took their places. As the jury filed in, people stared at them, trying to read their faces. They all looked grim. It was impossible to guess what they had decided.

Adrian Brooks and Peter Ritchie walked over to their client and stood on either side of him as he got to his feet. Judge Williams asked the foreman to deliver the verdict. The man with the grey beard stood up, his hands shaking, tears streaming down his face. A quick look at the other jurors revealed that two of the younger women were crying as well. One who wasn't was the woman with the perky ponytail. None of the jurors would look at the families or at Pickton. It was 2:53 in the afternoon.

"Not guilty," the foreman said.

"*Uh!*" exhaled Ward Lymburner in shock, collapsing forward in his seat so hard that his head almost hit his knees. Don Adam could only stare in disbelief, and Maggie Kingsbury's face was so white she looked as if she might faint. They said nothing, but several family members screamed. Charlotte Frey, Marnie's birth mother, howled in disbelief and grief and had to be led out of the courtroom. Andrea Joesbury's mother began to cry; Troy Boen wept like a small child.

The foreman continued. They had found Pickton guilty of second-degree murder. He went through the rest of the counts. Not guilty of murder in the first degree in all six cases—Sereena Abotsway, Georgina Papin, Marnie Frey, Brenda Wolfe, Mona Wilson and Andrea Joesbury—and each time he made this statement, family members cried "No!" The judge cautioned them to be quiet. Though they were shocked and mutinous and not sure they could put up with anything more, eventually they became quiet.

The jury found Pickton guilty of murder in the second degree in all six cases. Willie Pickton showed no emotion at all.

Judge Williams thanked the jurors for their hard work. "You know what an enormous responsibility it is to judge your fellow man," he said. "You have represented the people of Canada in this very important task, and on their behalf I want to offer my most sincere thank-you." Dismissed, they filed out and went home to their families. Their job was done.

Willie Pickton still did not react. There was no expression on his face. Mike Petrie told people on the way out of the courtroom that he was happy and relieved with the jury's decision, but his usually cheerful smile was missing. Peter Ritchie and his team had nothing to say; they all looked exhausted and disappointed. Elaine Allan, who had known and helped look after so many of the missing women in the Downtown Eastside, was furious. She couldn't believe the verdicts. If ever first-degree verdicts were warranted, surely to God this was the time.

After the courtroom had cleared, Don Adam and his colleagues, the prosecutors and the journalists all walked over to the media centre, a short block from the courthouse. A room had been set aside in the centre for the families to talk to reporters later, but to their fury they were not allowed in the media room for the press conference. They felt they were being treated like children. Both the families and the reporters were confused by the second-degree verdict and needed an explanation.

Stan Lowe, a spokesman for the attorney general's office, ducked the issue when he spoke to the media. "The evidence was the product of the exceptional investigation by the Missing Women's Task Force," he said, "as well as the Vancouver police and the RCMP. One of the biggest jobs was dealing with the forensic work and 1.25 million pages of documents. The working relationship between the task force and the team of prosecutors was good and the gravity of the crimes was never lost on them. Mr. Pickton murdered these women. That's what the jury has found."

That may have been true, but there was no question that a second-degree murder verdict in a case that seemed so clearly first-degree was unexpected, to say the least. But Lowe had one other thing to say, and it brought hope to many family members when he spoke to them later that day: "We still have work left on this case. Our focus will shift to the second trial. We're making preparations for a second date."

Mike Petrie also tried hard to be upbeat. "We are relieved after five years that we made it to this point. The jury vindicated our work. As for not guilty in the first degree? Well, my first thought—it was a sinking feeling. But I didn't ever think it was going to be an acquittal."

When reporter Stephen Smart asked him about the significance of a second-degree verdict, Petrie said there was very little difference between first and second degree: "It only determines the eligibility date for parole." Someone asked him why Dinah Taylor and Dave Pickton were never arrested. "The defence built straw men and scattered red herrings," Petrie said. "Arresting them was not justified based on the evidence." Another reporter asked him what he had gone through, given the grisly nature of the case. Petrie's answer was that any multiple murder was difficult, and in this case the personal lives of everyone involved were turned upside down. "It's not anything you can get away from," he said. "And you can't do this for five years and not have it bother you."

And then someone asked Petrie about the mistake that had forced the judge to correct his charge to the jury. "The judge saw the error here," he answered carefully, "and he saw that it had to be corrected. There were many twists and turns in this case; that was just one of them." Are you happy? asked another reporter. "I think it's a very good result. Mr. Pickton was convicted on six counts of murder."

The prosecutors then stepped aside to be replaced by a panoply of officers from the Vancouver Police Department and the RCMP. They stood there looking uncomfortable while two spokeswomen, one in English and one in French, delivered a carefully prepared statement crammed with statistics: ". . . 13,000 tasks . . . interviewed hundreds . . . received 1,500 statements . . . filled 688 boxes . . . 2,000,000 pieces of paper . . . 700 people worked on the task force . . ." Bill Fordy told the *Vancouver Sun*'s Lori Culbert that "it was fair to say officers on the case were disillusioned with the verdict. They think that we as a society . . . let these girls down in life and at some level let them down in death as well."

Though he had just retired, Don Adam held an informal, unauthorized press conference all on his own two days after the verdict. Reporters found out about it by word of mouth and raced to New Westminster. His message was plain: the verdict was a joke. "Full justice was not done. If there is a person here who doesn't know Pickton planned these murders, then I'm on the wrong planet," he said. "That he walked away and we legally consider him innocent of that—that wasn't right."

Adam tried to be pleasant about the judge, calling him intelligent and compassionate, but said that his three-day charge to the jury was impossible to understand. It was "legalese driven by the appeal courts," he said. "I don't think there was a person here who understood it." But the worst failure, he felt, was that the jury never heard most of the really important evidence. "I believe we let the jurors down. We took a year out of their lives and we didn't give them everything. What's going to happen when they learn everything? How are they going to feel? Haven't we betrayed them?"

Adam also told the reporters that, based on his own experience interrogating Pickton for so many hours, it wasn't possible to say he was too stupid to plan those murders. "Willie Pickton is a chameleon," he said. "Let's not be confused about his capabilities. He got every break in the world and people underestimated him. I was left sitting there looking into his eyes with a real sense of malignant evil. I had just the smallest sense he was playing with me, and [of] what it must have been like for those women when they were in his control. And it didn't make me happy."

Another issue that had become a sore point for him was all the talk from the defence lawyers about the failure to charge Dinah Taylor and Dave Pickton. It was unjustified, said Adam. There simply wasn't any evidence that they had anything to do with the murders. And he wanted everyone to know that the problem of poor, drug-addicted women in the Downtown Eastside had not gone away. "Do you think Willie Pickton just entered this picture out of the blue? I mean, we created a pool that nobody cared about, and he went to it."

The next day Courtroom 102 was full again. The families of the six murdered women finally had their chance to tell the world how the tragedy of loss had affected them. Of all the days in two court-houses, this day was the most painful. The families had about five minutes each to describe their loss and the impact it had had on them. Some could not handle reading their statements, and asked Mike Petrie to do it for them.

Bonnie Fowler and Elana Papin wanted to deliver their own statement about their much-loved sister Georgina Papin. "I can't handle it. I wish I could have done so much more," Fowler said. "I always thought of her as being tough, someone who could always take care of herself." It really hurt to hear people describe her sister as a drug addict and a prostitute, said Fowler. "I didn't know Georgina that way." Elana Papin told the court that Georgina was "a loving mother, our sister and my mother's child. There's a rage inside of me over never really knowing what happened to her. All we had were bone fragments." And then, looking at Pickton, she said, "I will never forget the damage you've done to our family."

Like some of the other relatives, Jay Draayers, Sereena Abotsway's foster brother, talked about the horror of imagining the way his sister had died and was disposed of. "Every day I try to only think of the fun-loving Sereena that I knew, but then the unthinkable reality takes over," he said.

Mona Wilson was remembered by her older sister Lisa Big John, who had given up drinking to honour her sister but still talked about living in a "dead world." "A part of me is still out there searching for her . . . I hear her scream, screaming for her life." Big John told the court she had been sober for seven years, and that "each day of sobriety is my promise to her."

Lynn Frey read Brittney's impact statement about her mother, Marnie. The teenager, who had been raised by her grandparents Rick and Lynn Frey, had already won the hearts of people who'd come to know her during the last days of the trial. Her words now made them cry. "I'm here for my real mother," Brittney wrote. "I don't have much to say, but Mr. Pickton, why did you hurt my mother and those other women? When you took her from me, it was like ripping out my heart. Marnie, if you were here, I would have so many questions to ask you. Marnie, I miss you."

Mike Petrie read the statements from other family members, a job that undid him. It was the first time anyone had seen him come apart in all the years he'd been the chief prosecutor. His voice choked up and he wept as he read Laila Cummer's note about her beloved granddaughter Andrea Joesbury: "She was a beautiful little girl who loved to dress up. The last phone call from her was that she was going to a party. She was getting dressed up in her best clothes because she had never been to a party. I heard someone telling her she looked pretty. That was the last we heard from her. She was so kind and so nice. She is forever loved."

Petrie also read a statement from Brenda Wolfe's mother, Elaine Belanger. "There is a pain in my heart that will not heal," she wrote. "If the teardrops I shed made a pathway to heaven, I would walk all the way and bring you home, hold you in my arms again, and never let you go." As he finished these words, he could hardly speak. Almost everyone in the courtroom was in tears.

When the statements were finished, Judge Williams told Willie Pickton that he was going to prison for life with no right to parole for twenty-five years. "Nothing I say can adequately express the revulsion the community feels at the killings," he said.

Once again Peter Ritchie and Adrian Brooks stood with their

client, who received the news unblinkingly. When Williams asked Pickton if there was anything he wanted to say, Pickton lurched forward half a step, but his lawyer quickly spoke up. Ritchie said that Pickton wanted to speak, but because he was facing twenty more charges in a second trial, he had accepted their advice to keep silent.

As the doors opened and people left the court for the last time, few had anything to say. The sheriffs who had managed court security for so many years, the lawyers who had fought for the women who had died, the police officers who had brought Pickton to justice, the families, the journalists—for them at that moment, there were no words left.

AFTERMATH

For a few months early in 2009, with all the players worn out by seven years of dealing with the Pickton case, things were fairly quiet. Both the Crown and the defence filed motions to appeal the verdict with the provincial Court of Appeal while Dave Picton and Linda Wright launched a lawsuit against the government, demanding compensation for the destruction of their farm by the task force. In March, Adrian Brooks left the hurly-burly of high-profile defence work for the deep peace of life as a provincial court judge in Victoria. Like Derrill Prevett, he'd been commuting from Vancouver Island to New Westminster for years and he'd had enough.

On January 7, 2009, a senior Crown prosecutor, Gregory Fitch, started the appeal process by sending a notice to the B.C. Court of Appeal that listed the Crown's problems with the verdict and, indeed, the whole trial process as it had played out in the Pickton case. Judge James Williams had erred in law on several occasions, Fitch said, beginning with his severance of the twenty-six counts to six. Williams has also erred in law in his instructions to the jury on similar-fact evidence, said Fitch, by failing to instruct the jury on Pickton's post-offence conduct—"specifically, the dismemberment and disposal of the victims' remains"—because this was "relevant to the issue of planning and deliberation." And he'd erred in law on reversing his decision to admit the Jane Doe evidence as similar-fact evidence.* The remedy

---

*Although Judge Williams quashed the Jane Doe count, he allowed the jury to hear the evidence in her case. Near the end of the trial he decided that was a mistake and he told the jury to forget everything they had been told

he sought, Fitch said in his letter to the court, was a new trial to be held on twenty-six counts of first-degree murder—"or such further or other relief as this Honourable Court deems just and appropriate."

Things heated up in the spring of 2009 when Pickton's new lawyer, Gil McKinnon, and Gregory Fitch appeared before the B.C. Court of Appeal to make their arguments. McKinnon argued that because of Judge Williams's mistakes, the jury was confused about whether or not Pickton had acted alone. "At least one or more jurors seemed to be having difficulty on whether Robert Pickton was the sole shooter of the three women," McKinnon said. He was referring to Mona Wilson, Sereena Abotsway and Andrea Joesbury.

A few days later, on April 6, Gregory Fitch responded in a cross-appeal by expanding on the charges he had made in his January notice. Judge Williams had cut off the Crown's case at the knees, he said, when he let only six counts go forward against Pickton instead of the original twenty-six. What this did was to remove powerful similar-fact evidence—that of Sandra Gail Ringwald—that would have proved that Pickton's crimes were planned and deliberate, two components required for a first-degree murder verdict. "It left the jury with a highly distorted picture of Mr. Pickton's conduct," Fitch told the court. "An efficient trial was achieved but in our submission it was achieved at the expense of a just one." He described Pickton's method of killing the women as "singular in its brutality and utterly unique."

"All of the victims fit a common and distinct profile," he added. "The Crown had an overwhelming case [that] these murders were planned and deliberate. The jury never heard that case." Still, Fitch said, if the Crown won the application they would not ask for a new trial because Pickton had already been given the maximum sentence of life in prison.

The court's response, on June 25, was tough. Two of the three judges, Chief Justice Lance Finch and Justice Richard Low, sided

---

about Jane Doe. He also instructed the court clerk to remove all the Jane Doe material from each juror's binder.

with the Crown, stating that Judge Williams should never have removed Sandra Gail Ringwald's evidence, nor should he have quashed count twenty-seven, Jane Doe, nor should he have severed the counts from twenty-seven to six. Cindy Feliks and Inga Hall, whose ground flesh was found in Pickton's freezers, should have been included. So should Wendy Crawford, whose bone was found in a cistern. As for Ringwald's evidence, the defence had argued for months at trial that the farm was such a beehive of activity Pickton couldn't have murdered anyone without people knowing about it, but the Crown was not allowed to bring in evidence of a woman who had nearly died there, with no one nearby to help her until she made it to the main road and flagged down a passing motorist.

These decisions, so bitterly denounced six months earlier on the courthouse steps by Don Adam and the families were echoed by the Court of Appeal. But the third judge, Justice Ian Donald, agreed with the defence arguments. And because it was a split decision, the appeal automatically moved to the Supreme Court of Canada. On March 25, 2010, the judges heard arguments from both sides. Gil McKinnon, again representing Pickton, went through the mistakes made by Judge Williams in his instructions to the jury when he failed to deal clearly with the issue of whether or not Pickton had acted alone. The defence position all along was that Pickton didn't act alone, if indeed he acted at all. John Gordon, in Ottawa to argue for the Crown, said their position was simple: they didn't think the judge had made a mistake in law, and if he had it was not a major mistake, certainly not one so grave as to overturn the conviction of a self-confessed serial killer.

By this time, because the Pickton farm had long been abandoned by the task force, many people believed that the police had finished with the case. Not so. The investigators were still looking for missing women and still receiving DNA results and other information. By now they had DNA matches from the farm for thirty-two of the missing women and in October 2009 they recommended that Pickton be charged with six more murders—of Sharon Abraham, who disappeared in December 2000; Stephanie Lane, who disappeared in January 1997; Yvonne Boen, who disappeared in March 2001; Jackie Murdock, who disappeared in January 1997; Dawn Crey, who disappeared in November 2000; and Nancy Clark, who disappeared in Victoria in August 1991. Although the task force knew there was almost no chance Pickton would be tried for these deaths, they sent their findings to the Crown anyway.

And the Vancouver Police Department? What of the people there who had let down the women of the Downtown Eastside so badly for more than twenty years? Deputy Chief Doug LePard conducted a lengthy investigation into the VPD's failure to take their cases seriously. He joked with one journalist that he might have to go into witness protection once it was made public. LePard criticizes the Coquitlam RCMP because it knew Pickton was a suspect yet didn't watch him carefully. But he is just as tough on several senior VPD officers, including those responsible for the Missing Persons Unit, saying that they should have listened to Kim Rossmo and paid attention to his expertise.

Still, to its credit, the Vancouver Police Department agrees with the demands of many groups that there should be a public inquiry into the botched investigation of the missing women. In an email to Maggie de Vries, LePard wrote, "I am responding on behalf of Chief Constable Jim Chu and myself in stating that the Vancouver Police Department does support a public inquiry into the missing women case. We believe a public inquiry is clearly in the public interest, and that this inquiry should be held at the earliest opportunity after the criminal matters regarding Robert Pickton are concluded."

Maggie de Vries turned to Lindsay Kines, the reporter who started the series in the *Vancouver Sun* that forced the police, finally, to pay attention to the missing women of Vancouver. Burned out by the effort of bringing their story to light, Kines had moved to a Victoria newspaper in 2003. Now, returning to it after so many years, Kines published LePard's note on November 29, 2009, in the Victoria *Times Colonist*, adding that the deputy chief had also told

Maggie de Vries that his report contained "extensive recommendations for improving policing in B.C. The ones relating to the Vancouver department have all been acted upon."

Finally, the decision made by the Supreme Court of Canada, after a wait of many months, to uphold the verdict ends the case once and for all. Pickton will not stand trial again, not for the six cases nor for the remaining counts and possible new charges. Should there have been another trial? What chance could there be for justice for the other twenty-six women whose DNA was recovered at the farm? Like the families of the six, their families will also have to learn to live with the absence of women who were murdered, an absence that is heavy enough to feel like a presence, with all the complications of their short lives. We don't know if life for women in the Downtown Eastside is any safer now. All we know is that Willie Pickton will remain in prison and will not be able to kill any more of them himself.

A second trial was always unlikely, as memories fade, money runs out, important witnesses die. Early in 2010 Pat Casanova, Pickton's trusted friend, died, and Gina Houston died on April 6, 2010, after an eight-year struggle with breast cancer. But there is one witness who could return to tell her story, the story that gripped a courtroom back in 2003.

Sandra Gail Ringwald is still alive to tell everyone what happened to her in Pickton's trailer in 1997. Today, she is a happy, healthy woman who kicked her drug habit nearly four years ago and has completely turned her life around. She works full-time in a high school cafeteria and has won new friends with her easy, frank and forthright personality. A few years ago she applied to the court to regain custody of her three children, and was successful. They have a good family life together.

ACKNOWLEDGMENTS

None of us thought at the beginning that telling this story would take eight years. It should be a relief to be done, but I part with the history of Robert Pickton and Vancouver's missing women with reluctance. It has been a fascinating, heartbreaking and all-consuming project. And I need to tell you that this is not my story at all. Hundreds of people have helped me by sharing their family's experiences, by guiding me through complicated legal and forensic processes, or by showing me the extent of the addiction, poverty, tragedy and compassion that are to be found in Vancouver's Downtown Eastside. Just a few of the people I need to thank include:

Ron MacKay, who lives in Ottawa, is a former RCMP inspector and the first Canadian criminal profiler, and he worked in British Columbia for many years. He was my consultant on this project and became my friend. Former B.C. provincial coroner Larry Campbell, now a Liberal senator but then a candidate (successful) for mayor of Vancouver, understands the Downtown Eastside better than most people; he was always generous with his time and advice. Larry introduced me to Fred Maile, a retired RCMP officer who investigated the serial killer Clifford Olson; Fred steered me to areas of research that would never have occurred to me. I was sad to learn of his death a few years ago. Ken Doern, a retired senior Vancouver Police Department officer, also died a few years after we met; he too was a great help in my first year in Vancouver. So was Doug MacKay-Dunn, another senior VPD officer, who is now a member of the district council in North Vancouver.

Journalist Trude Huebner, who grew up in Port Coquitlam, introduced me to the town and its citizens, found court records and other documents I needed, and filled in for me when I couldn't be in the courtroom. Her help was invaluable.

Another person who has always been ready to give me a hand on a moment's notice is Wayne Leng. Thanks to Wayne, who set up www.missingpeople.net nine years ago, all of us working on the story can find photographs, websites, story archives, family message boards and more. And if we can't find what we need, he responds quickly to our emails with the answer. Wayne has probably done more to unite the families than anyone else, simply because he created the communication system that keeps them connected to one another.

Lindsay Kines, the *Vancouver Sun* reporter whose stories about the missing women forced the police to start an investigation, was always available with contacts and good advice. So was Justin Beddall, now the editor of North Vancouver's *Outlook* newspaper, who worked as a reporter in Coquitlam.

Over the years I couldn't have had a better friend than Greg Joyce, a long-time editor and reporter for the Canadian Press in Vancouver. Greg, who covered the story for years, read a great deal of the manuscript in its various stages and always found the weak spots.

To this day, Liz Fox, a retired CBC journalist in Vancouver, keeps a clipping file for me. I have been fortunate in her friendship.

Bonnie Fournier, a gifted psychiatric nurse who dearly loved and cared for so many of the missing women as she rode the Health Van through the Downtown Eastside every evening, shared her experiences with me. She also explained the complicated structure of Essondale and the provincial institutions in Coquitlam that are part of this story.

Like Bonnie, Freda Ens, a Victim Services worker since the task force began its investigation, has been a friend from the start. She shared her story as an abused child from a Native family in Haida Gwaii who has raised her own gifted children, Juanita, a jewellery maker, and Bill, a chef, with all the love and care that she lacked in her own childhood. Before joining the task force, Freda ran the Native Liaison Office in the Vancouver Police Department's Main

Street headquarters, and she knew almost every one of the women who disappeared. Ruth Wright, the minister at First United Church, at the corner of Hastings and Gore, during most of my time in British Columbia, is another wise and cherished friend who taught me how much a church can do for the sick and the homeless.

During these years I learned how fortunate the people of British Columbia are in having the lawyers, police officers, sheriffs, court officers and Victim Services workers who managed all the stages of Robert Pickton's trial. Pickton's lawyers, a team put together by Peter Ritchie, Marilyn Sandford and Adrian Brooks, spent eight years fighting a case no one wanted them to win—it can't have been easy. For their part, the Crown lawyers sought justice for the victims with a skill and compassion that no one who was involved in this case will ever forget. The police officers were unavailable to journalists until the trial ended, but we were never in any doubt about their ability and commitment. Kerry McIntyre and the other sheriffs who managed the prisoner, the witnesses, the journalists and the general public to ensure security and order in the courthouses in Port Coquitlam and New Westminster were tactful, firm and compassionate and kept everyone, even Willie Pickton, safe.

I want to thank all the people who loaned me their homes, included me in their lives and took such good care of me during the many years I spent commuting back and forth between Toronto and Vancouver. These friendships will last the rest of my life. I also want to thank the kind people at the Vancouver School of Theology, who run a splendid small hotel that has been my home on many occasions.

Here in Toronto, how lucky I have been. My agent, Linda McKnight, has been with me on this adventure from the start. So has Louise Dennys, the executive publisher of Knopf Random Group Canada.

And so has Diane Martin, my publisher at Knopf Canada. In 2007 Diane edited and published my first book on this case, *The Pickton File*, which was a personal account of what it was like to work on the Pickton story as well as a guide to the case. The team of editors who worked with her to make *On the Farm* as polished and error-free as possible are not only encouraging but endlessly picky and demanding—everything a writer could ask for. They include Knopf's managing editor, Deirdre Molina, editor Michelle MacAleese, copy editor Gillian Watts and indexer Meghan Behse, as well as our proofreaders Barbara Czarnecki and John Sweet. And my thanks go also to Scott Richardson for his compelling jacket design.

Readers should know that Diane Martin has attended court with me many times since the first days in Port Coquitlam in 2003, and she has been as committed to telling this story as I am. Many of the friends I made in Vancouver have become her friends too, and none more so than our beloved Elaine Allan. Elaine has met us at more planes, driven us more places, walked us through more Downtown Eastside locations and helped us in more ways than we can ever describe. She has always been a champion of the women she looked after at WISH in the Downtown Eastside, and it was her love and respect for these women that inspired us.

Finally, as always, this book was possible only because of the constant, patient support of my family—my husband, David, and our girls, Tassie and Amy.

PHOTO CREDITS

All photos are copyright Stevie Cameron except where otherwise noted. Grateful acknowledgement is expressed to the following people and sources for permission to reprint these images.

FIRST INSERT
ii
(top) © *Toronto Star*/GetStock

iii
(top) courtesy of the Port Coquitlam Heritage & Cultural Society

viii
© Ian Lindsey / *Vancouver Sun*

ix
(top) © CP / Chuck Stoody

SECOND INSERT
ii
(bottom) © CP / Jonathan Hayward

iii
(top and bottom) © Felicity Don

v
(top left) © CP / Chuck Stoody
(top right) © CP / Richard Lam
(bottom left) © CP / *Vancouver Sun*–Peter Battistoni
(bottom right) © CP / Chuck Stoody

vi
(bottom) courtesy of Wayne Leng

vii
(bottom right) © CP / Richard Lam

Every effort has been made to contact the copyright holders; in the event of an inadvertent omission or error, please notify the publisher.

INDEX

A woman of many talents, STEVIE CAMERON is a successful author, investigative journalist, commentator, and humanitarian. Her investigative reports have been published by the *Globe and Mail* and her award-winning books have brought scandals to the public eye. they include *On the Take: Crime, Corruption and Greed in the Mulroney Years* and *The Last Amigo: Karlheinz Schreiber and the Anatomy of a Scandal*. Cameron's passion for writing, uncovering and dissecting stories of the day have earned her acclaim as one of Canada's foremost investigative journalists. She lives in Toronto.

www.steviecameron.com